REFUGEE CRISIS IN INTERNATIONAL POLICY

VOLUME V - VI

REFUGEES IN TURKEY AND BEYOND

REFUGEE CRISIS IN INTERNATIONAL POLICY

VOLUME V - VI

REFUGEES IN TURKEY AND BEYOND

Edited by

Hasret Çomak, Burak Şakir Şeker, Mehlika Özlem Ultan,
Yaprak Civelek, Çağla Arslan Bozkuş

TRANSNATIONAL PRESS LONDON

2023

MIGRATION SERIES: 32

REFUGEE CRISIS IN INTERNATIONAL POLICY

VOLUME V - VI - REFUGEES IN TURKEY AND BEYOND

Edited by Hasret Çomak, Burak Şakir Şeker, Mehlika Özlem Ultan, Yaprak Civelek, Çağla Arslan Bozkuş

First Published in 2023 by TRANSNATIONAL PRESS LONDON in the United Kingdom, 13 Stamford Place, Sale, M33 3BT, UK.
www.tplondon.com

Paperback
ISBN: 978-1-80135-018-1
978-1-80135-018-1Digital
ISBN: 978-1-80135-019-8

Cover Design: Nihal Yazgan
Cover Photo by Meric Dagli on unsplash.com

Transnational Press London Ltd. is a company registered in England and Wales No. 8771684

CONTENTS

PREFACE

Every day, in many parts of the world, people make the hardest decisions of their lives. With these decisions, they have to leave their homes behind for a better and safer life. Many people in the world, by deciding to leave where they grew up, move to another settlement. Some have to leave their country for a short period of time or for a lifetime.

In many parts of the world, there are many reasons why people try to re-establish their lives in other countries. Some leave their home country to find a job or for education. Others are forced to escape human rights violations such as inhumane treatment and torture. Millions run away from armed conflicts or violence. These people who do not feel safe; might be targeted due to their characteristics that establish their identity or faith, such as their ethnic origin, religious beliefs, gender, and political thoughts.

These journeys that have begun in pursuit of a better future might be full of danger and fear; some might fall into the trap of human traffickers or other forms of exploitation. Also, some are taken into custody by authorities as soon as they arrive in a country. Many, who settle in a country and start a new life face racism, xenophobia, and discrimination almost every day. They may feel lonely and isolated.

Many reasons make it difficult and dangerous for people to stay in their country of origin. Violence, war, hunger, and poverty are the most important ones. Sexual preferences and sexual identity also take an important place. People may also have to leave their home country because of climate change and natural disasters. It is possible to encounter many of these difficult conditions all at once.

Fleeing danger is not the only reason people leave their country. Some think of becoming a part of a qualified workforce or gaining capital in another country. Moreover, they suppose there is a higher possibility of finding a job in a foreign country. Others seek to live with their relatives and friends currently living abroad. Also, some might aim to begin and continue their education in another country. Therefore, there are many reasons why people might start out to establish a new life in another country.

It is noteworthy to mention the words 'refugee', 'asylum seeker' and 'migrant' in terms of International Law. A refugee is a person who leaves his home country due to the threat of being subjected to grave human rights violations and persecution. These people have to leave their home country and seek asylum in another country due to security threats and threats against their lives. As they have no other choice and they feel their governments cannot or will not protect them against these threats, they are forced to take this decision.

According to the provisions of the 'United Nations Convention Relating to the Status of Refugees', adopted on 28 July 1951 by the United Nations Conference of Plenipotentiaries on the Status of Refugees and Stateless Persons convened under General Assembly resolution 429 (V) of 14 December 1950 and entered into force on 22 April 1954, refugees have 'the right for international protection'.

An asylum seeker is a person who has left his home country to seek asylum in another country to be protected from persecution and grave human rights violations. However, in this case, one only has the status of asylum applicant and legally has not yet been accepted as a refugee. Seeking an asylum application is a human right. This means everyone should be permitted to enter a country to seek asylum.

Migrants, on the other hand, are those who live outside their home country and thus who are not asylum seekers or refugees. Migrants generally leave their home countries to work, have an education, or live with their family members in another country. Some feel the need to leave their home country because of poverty, political turmoil, natural disasters, or other difficult conditions.

The issue that should be emphasized here is that many people who do not fit into the 'refugee' definition might be in danger once they return to their home country. Therefore, even if they may not be escaping from persecution, no matter their legal status in the country they established themselves, migrants' human rights must be protected, and these rights must be respected.

States must protect all migrants against violence based on racism and xenophobia, exploitation, and forced labour. Migrants should not be detained without legitimate reasons or forcefully sent back to their home country.

Human rights have become both a subject and a legitimate instrument of international politics. Therefore, the human rights of refugees, asylum seekers and migrants must always be protected internationally. States must fulfill their joint responsibility to protect the rights of refugees, asylum seekers and migrants.

People are not the source of the problem. The main problem is the reasons that force families and individuals to cross borders. Those who cause these reasons have responsibilities. The attitude of authorities who are trying far-sighted and unrealistic approaches matters in the creation of this problem.

States must ensure that refugees, asylum seekers and immigrants are safe, not subject to torture, discrimination and living in poverty. States should assess the applications of asylum seekers according to international rules except for the ones

- who has committed a crime against peace, a war crime, or a crime against humanity, as defined in the international instruments drawn up to make provision in respect of such crimes;

- who has committed a serious non-political crime outside the country of refuge prior to his admission to that country as a refugee;
- who has been guilty or suspicious of acts contrary to the purposes and principles of the United Nations.

The situation of asylum seekers should not be left in a state of uncertainty for years. Unlawful detention practices should not be carried out and the necessary diligence should be taken in this regard. Also, international regulations must be made in order to protect migrants against the exploitation of employers or human traffickers and abuse.

States must take responsibility for and fulfill these responsibilities meticulously for refugees, asylum seekers and immigrants to be able to rebuild their lives safely against serious dangers. Sharing responsibility for global problems is fair in the 21st century.

Welcoming people from other countries might empower host communities by making them more diverse and more flexible in a rapidly changing world. Some of the successful, impactful, and productive people in the field of arts, politics, and technology can be refugees, asylum seekers, or migrants. There are very successful people in the international community who have been given the opportunity to start a new life in another country and become a member of a new community.

In the 21st century, leaders should produce and develop new projects to relocate people fleeing conflict and persecution in their countries by showing sufficient political will.

Furthermore, the practice of other safe approaches should be implemented to enable refugees to start a new life. Providing the necessary financial support for refugee families to come to the country and granting them a study or work visa might be considered an appropriate method to establish a new life.

States should not force anybody to return to a country where they might be subjected to human rights violations. Instead, states should ensure a safe place for refugees and asylum seekers, and migrants to live, a job, access to education, and health services.

Refugees, asylum seekers, and immigrants should be treated with dignity without being deprived of their freedom, as stated in the United Nations Universal Declaration of Human Rights. Under all the circumstances requiring detention and retention, refugees, asylum seekers, and immigrants should be informed about their current and fundamental rights. Their detention conditions should comply with international standards in terms of rights and freedoms.

Comprehensive programs should be prepared with the United Nations Member States and the United Nations High Commissioner for Refugees on the provision of social and legal assistance to refugees, asylum seekers and migrants. For this purpose, a valid and secure 'country of origin information system' should be established. This system should be targeted to be structured as an 'international joint system'.

All these developments have revealed the necessity of preparing a multidimensional, original, up-to-date, original and rich content about refugees, asylum seekers and immigrants in the international community and presenting it to science.

This six-volume book series, titled 'Refugee Crisis in International Politics' are prepared to clarify the above-mentioned issues and, enrich the content, context, and add depth to this field.

Volume V brings us detailed analyses of the circumstances and experiences of refugees in Turkey. Contributions in this volume are as follows: Talip Menekşe and Soyalp Tamçelik 'Regulations Introduced by Law on Foreigners and International Protection in Turkey'; Ayşegül Bostan 'The Asylum Policy of Republic of Turkey: Within the Context of Temporary Protection'; Derya Alimanoğlu Yemişçi 'The Evaluation of Social Policies Regarding Refugees Living in Turkey'; Talip Menekşe and Soyalp Tamçelik 'Services and Rights Provided for Refugees in Turkey'; Göknil Erbaş Doğan 'The Impact of Refugees on Turkey's Geopolitics'; İsmail Köse and Metin Aksoy 'The Role of Syrian Immigrants in the Turkish Foreign Policy'; Şebnem Akipek Öcal 'Refugees Position from the Family Law Perspective in Turkey'; Hüseyin Pusat Kıldiş 'The Progress and Challanges of Refugee Education in Turkey'; Gamze Uşar 'Refugees in Turkey and their Education in Terms of Identity'; Hatice Nur Germir 'Irregular Migration and Employment Effects of Refugees Heading to Turkey; Unregistered Employment'; Aslı Okay Toprak 'The Impact of Syrians Under Temporary Protection to the Labour Market in Turkey'; Hatice Nur Germir 'Turkey and the Employment of Refugees'; Gülşen Sari Gerşil 'Syrian Immigration and Integration Policies in Turkey'; Yüksel Kamacı Erkan 'The Extent of Syrian Refugees in Election Bulletins: 2015 and 2018 Elections in Turkey' and Levent Uzunçıbuk 'The Impact of Immigration on Urban Planning in Turkey'.

We would like to thank all the contributing and researching colleagues who supported us with their research and findings.

We would like to express our gratitude to Prof. Dr. İbrahim Sirkeci who made the publication of 'Refugee Crisis in International Politics' possible. Special thanks should be given to Transnational Press London (TPLondon) staff for their valuable guidance and technical support during this process, for preparing our books for publication, and for designing the covers.

We sincerely hope that the work will be useful and useful to the world of science.

Hasret Çomak, Burak Şakir Şeker, Mehlika Özlem Ultan, Yaprak Civelek, Çağla Arslan Bozkuş

ISTANBUL, MARCH / 2021

CHAPTER 1

REGULATIONS INTRODUCED BY LAW ON FOREIGNERS AND INTERNATIONAL PROTECTION IN TURKEY

Talip Menekşe[1] and Soyalp Tamçelik[2]

Introduction

Turkey is geopolitically an important country when it comes to migration. Having been a country bridging Europe and Asia, having borders and historical ties in the Middle East, and rich historical and cultural features of Anatolia, Turkey is a prime destination country for immigrants whether voluntarily or involuntarily. In order to effectively manage ongoing migrations, Turkey has carried out serious work and drawn new legislation, in particular, protective mechanisms have been adopted regarding foreigners seeking refuge. The new law covering all areas of international protection has been title '*Law on Foreigners and International Protection No. 6458*' *(LFIP)*. Thanks to the LFIP, the *Turkish International Protection System*, or in other words, the *Turkish Asylum System*, has gained fine regulation from beginning to end. Therefore, the Turkish International Protection System has been legally and comprehensively established together with the LFIP for those who had to leave their country, cannot receive protection, and have fled from persecution. Thus, this study will discuss the effects of LFIP on foreigners seeking international protection in Turkey. In this context, foreigners coming to Turkey as part of regular migration, for tourism, education, labour and so on are out of the scope of this chapter.

LFIP has a special place in historical development of Turkish International Protection System. Regulations made before LFIP regarding asylum seekers and refugees had some shortcomings. However, the most important of these shortcomings was that these regulations were not equivalent to laws. With the LFIP, the Turkish International Protection System has been regulated in detail in every step, from the first moment of a foreigner requesting international protection to the last. Thus, in a way, Turkey has systematized the mechanism for international protection provided for foreigners seeking asylum. Therefore, when analysing the Turkish International Protection System, it is important to examine the detailed effects of LFIP on the Turkish International Protection System. This study discusses the development of the Turkish International Protection System from past to present and the importance and role of LFIP in this historical process. In

[1] Migration Expert, General Coordinator and Founder of Decision Centers/Mobile Teams (2016 - December 2019), International Protection Department, Directorate General of Migration Management, Ministry of Interior. ORCID ID: 0000-0002-6423-9331, E-mail: talip.menekse@goc.gov.tr

[2] Prof. Dr.; Ankara Hacı Bayram Veli University, Faculty of Economics and Administrative Sciences, International Relations Department, ORCID ID: 0000-0002-2092-8557, E-mail: soyalp@hotmail.com

this process, LFIP regulations will be examined together with the period before LFIP and each phase will be dealt with separately from the point of foreigners seeking asylum. A comparative analysis will be made in particular with LFIP and Ministry of Interior/Turkish National Police legislation, which was in effect for many years before LFIP. In this way, LFIP effect on procedures of foreigners seeking international protection in Turkey can be identified more realistically.

Another feature of the study, for the point of foreigners seeking international protection from Turkey, all actions in Turkish International Protection System such as registration, interview and decision are compared with the pre-LFIP period and TNP practices and the study includes comparative analysis of each action both in practice and in legislation. With this aspect, the effects of the LFIP on the Turkish International Protection System will not be taken only in the new period, and it will reveal how the same international protection process was carried out in the past. By doing so, the operability and effectiveness of the LFIP can be evaluated in a healthier way.

In the study, domestic and foreign monographs, articles, documents, theses, project activities and legislative studies are examined and evaluated; the implementation areas and results of the LFIP and TNP period practices in the field were investigated; country studies and trainings and internships in the field of asylum are analysed. This study has taken a structuralist-functionalist perspective as a method and with the comparative analysis method of the LFIP with international protection legislation studies in the period before LFIP. As a result, a general evaluation is carried out on the subject and recommendations are put forward for the future of the Turkish International Protection System.

Historical Development of the Turkish International Protection System

In the historical process from the past to this day, the Turkish International Protection System has provided international protection to large numbers of asylum-seekers. The most recent example of this is seen in the United Nations High Commissioner for Refugees (UNHCR) data dated June 18, 2020. According to UNHCR's data on *forcibly displaced persons* dated June 18, 2020, 79.5 million people worldwide have been forcibly displaced.[3] Of these, 26 million are refugees, while 4.2 million are asylum seekers. Among the countries that host foreigners who are forcibly displaced and seek international protection, Turkey is the country hosting the most with 4 million people in the world, more than 3.6 million Syrians and more than 300 thousand other nationalities.[4] This shows how many foreigners there are in the Turkish International Protection System.

---

[3] UNHCR, **Figures at a Glance**, 2020, URL: https://www.unhcr.org/figures-at-a-glance.html, (Access 02.07.2020).

[4] UNHCR, **Refugee Data Finder**, 2020, URL https://www.unhcr.org/refugee-statistics/, (Access 01.07.2020).

Migration to Turkey and Statistics

Anatolia is a geography that has hosted many immigration movements from past to present. In the process that started with the migration from Central Asia to Anatolia, the Migration of Tribes, the migrations from the Caucasus in 1864, the exchange migrations during the First World War, II, the migration of people who fled fascist regimes in Europe during World War II, migration movements as a result of the Arab-Israeli Wars in the Middle East, the Iraq-Iran War, Bulgaria, Yugoslavia, the Gulf War and migration from Iraq after the invasion of the United States, migration due to the effects of the Arab Spring, and since 2011 migration from Syria because of the *Syrian Civil War* hold an important place in *Turkey's immigration history*.[5] Indeed, as a result of international developments caused hundreds of thousands, even millions of foreigners to come to Turkish borders and seek international protection from Turkey. From 1922 to this day, Turkey has opened its arms to more than 6.5 million people. This number does not include foreigners coming for work, tourism, or education purposes.[6]

When the recent migration history is examined, it is safe to say that approximately a million people have immigrated to Turkey from Iran, due to Iran Islamic revolution in 1979. Many people have migrated from different ethnic backgrounds such as Farsi and Kurdish, however, the majority were Turks of Azerbaijan. The Soviet Union- Afghanistan War played an important role in the formation of Afghan migration in the early 1980s. Most of the migration from Iraq occurred after the chemical attack in Halabja in the North of Iraq in 1988, and the number of migrants reached 51.542. After the Gulf War 467.489 people have fled to Turkey.[7] When the Civil War began in Syria in 2011, Turkey assumed the most responsibility and has become the country that hosts the most migrants worldwide.[8]

Turkey is the bridge between the countries on its South and East where there are conflicts and instability in Asian and Middle Eastern countries, and in its West European high prosperity countries where the standards for human rights are higher when compared to Middle Eastern countries. Due to conflicts, financial and political instability in the Middle East and neighbouring countries, challenging circumstances for controlling the Eastern border because of the mountainy area,

---

[5] İbrahim Sirkeci and Deniz Eroğlu Utku, **Türkiye'nin Kitlesel Akınlar Deneyiminin Çatışma Modeli ve 3Ka Ekseninde Değerlendirilmesi** (Evaluation of Turkey's Mass Influx Experiences of Conflict Model and 3Ds). Göç Dergisi (Migration Journal), Vol. 7, No. 2, October 2020.

[6] "Directorate General of Migration Management (DGMM)", **Göç Tarihi**, https://www.goc.gov.tr/goc-tarihi, (Access 05.07.2020).

[7] DGMM, **Türkiye ve Göç (Turkey and Migration)**, T.C. İçişleri Bakanlığı Göç İdaresi Genel Müdürlüğü Yayınları (Turkish Ministry of Interior Directorate General of Migration Management Publications). No. 4, December 2013, http://www.goc.gov.tr/files/_dokuman19.pdf, (Access 08.05.2018).

[8] BBC, (20.06.2016) **"BM: Türkiye En Çok Mülteciye Ev Sahipliği Yapan Ülke" (UN: Turkey is the Country Hosting the Most Refugee)**, http://www.bbc.com/turkce/haberler/2016/06/160620_bm_multeci, (Access 23 May 2017); Monica Pinna, Euronews, **Dünyanın En Çok Sığınmacı Ağırlayan Ülkesi Türkiye (Turkey, the Country Hosting the Most Refugees in the World)**, https://tr.euronews.com/2018/10/27/dunyanin-en-cok-siginmaci-agirlayan-ulkesi-turkiye, (Access 29.10.2018); Reliefweb, ***UNHCR Turkey Factsheet*** (August 2018), URL: https://reliefweb.int/report/turkey/unhcr-turkey-factsheet-august-2018, 2018, (Access 16.11.2018).

and the Sea of Islands (Aegean) and the Mediterranean being convenient for illegal crossings, Turkey has become the transit country for migrants wishing to cross to Europe. Especially in recent years, Turkey has become the center of attraction for both regular and irregular migration movements with the increasing economic and regional power.[9]

In order to better understand the development of the Turkish International Protection System, it is beneficial to look at the asylum statistics. To this end, statistical data affecting the Turkish Asylum System directly or indirectly are given below.

Whether individual international protection or temporary protection, all of the foreigners whose numbers are specified above, are in the Turkish Asylum System since they seek asylum in Turkey. In this respect, all foreigner is granted international protection by Turkey. Between the years of 2010-2017, a total of 363.772 foreigners applied for international protection, and as of 18.10.2018 there were 100.118 international protection applicants in Turkey. Also when the current statistics are examined on the distribution of foreign nationals who individually ask for protection in Turkey, it is seen that Iraq, Afghanistan and Iran nationals form the top three.[10] Thus it is safe to say that, the number of foreigners, whose cases regarding national and international regulations within the scope of *international refugee law* are considered by Ministry of Interior affiliated *Directorate General of Migration Management (DGMM)* on behalf of Turkey, exceed 4 million in total.[11] DGMM carries out actions and procedures of these foreigners in line with the provisions of LFIP No. 6458 in national law.

---

[9] DGMM, **"Göç Tarihi" (History of Migration)**, Second Edition: DGMM Publications, http://www.goc.gov.tr/ icerik/goc-tarihi_363_380, 2016, (Access 05.12.2016).

[10] DGMM, **2019-2023 Stratejik Plan (Strategic Planning)**, p. 70, https://www.goc.gov.tr/kurumlar/goc.gov.tr/Mali-Tablolar/STRATEJIK-PLAN-2019-2023/Stratejik-Plan-2019_2023.pdf, (Access 17.05. 2020).

[11] DGMM, **Türkiye'de 2005-2016 Yılları Arasındaki Uluslararası Koruma Başvuru Sayıları (Number of Applications for International Protection between 2005-2016)**, 2018, URL: http://www.goc.gov.tr/icerik6/uluslararasi-koruma, (Access 23.03.2018).

Figure 1. Number of International Protection Applications in Turkey between 2010-2019

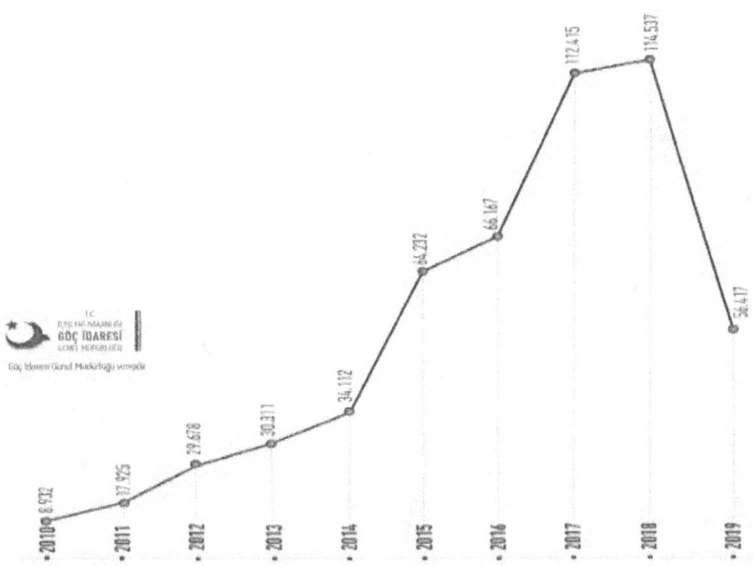

Source: DGMM, DGMM statistics-International Protection, https://www.goc.gov.tr/uluslararasi-koruma-istatistikler, (Access 26.08.2020).

Figure 2. Number of International Protection Application in Turkey in 2019 and Distribution by Nationality

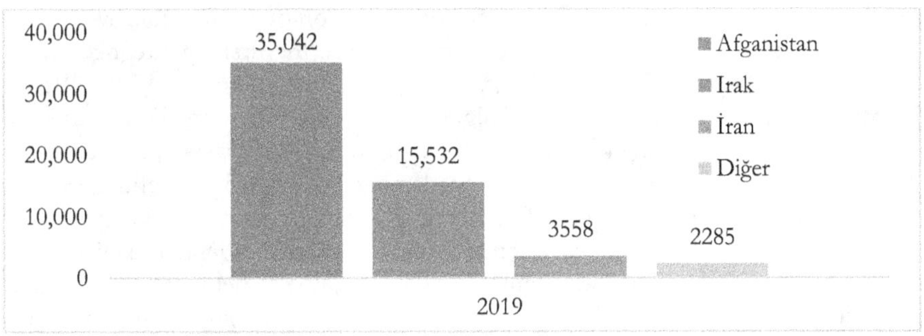

Source: DGMM, DGMM Statistics-International Protection, https://www.goc.gov.tr/uluslararasi-koruma-istatistikler, (Access 26.08.2020).

Figure 3. Syrians under Temporary Protection in Turkey per Year

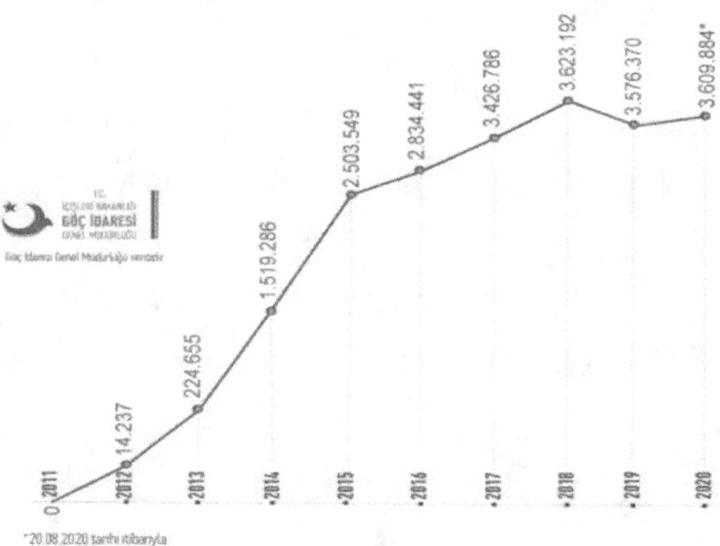

Source: DGMM, DGMM Statistics-Temporary Protection, https://www.goc.gov.tr/gecici-koruma5638, (Access 20.08.2020).

Legislation of Turkish International Protection System and International Refugee Law

Within the scope of development of Turkey's international protection legislation, for the period starting from the proclamation of the Republic in 1923 to the date of being a party to international convention, the first legal regulation on migration was *Settlement Law No. 2510*, which entered into force on 14 June 1934.[12] Mentioned Law regulates asylum and migration movements toward Turkey and the settlement of those coming to Turkey. In 2006, Law No. 2510 was replaced by Law No. 5543 of the same name. Although Settlement Law No. 5543 defines various types of migrants such as migrant, free migrant, settled migrant, individual migrant and mass migrant, it envisions a structure limited to cognate oriented regulations.[13] Settlement Law does not include regulations regarding the settlement to Turkey and acquisition of citizenship of people who are not Turkish descendants and not connected to Turkish culture. Article 4 of the same law states that people who are not connected to Turkish culture, anarchists, spies and nomad Gypsies, shall not be

[12] Turkish Official Gazette, **5543 Sayılı İskân Kanunu (Law on Settlement)**, http://www.resmigazete.gov.tr/eskiler/2006/09/20060926-1.htm, 2006, (Access 11.11.2019).

[13] Talip Menekşe, "Türk Uluslararası Koruma Sistemi'nde Karar Merkezleri" (Decision Centers in Turkish International Protection System), **Göç Araştırmaları Dergisi (Migration Research Journal)**, No. 8, Ankara, 2018, http://www.gam.gov.tr/files/8-7.pdf, (Access 01.10.2019).

allowed in as migrants if they leave the country.[14] On the other hand, mass influxes continued due to wars between countries, civil wars, instability and anarchy. Two of the main Laws regulating the legal status of foreigners, *Passport Law No. 5682* and *Law on Foreigner Residence and Travel in Turkey No. 5683* entered into force in 1950.[15] However, neither one was drafted specifically to asylum in the Turkish International Protection System. Although legislation work regarding foreigners had been carried out and some partially contributed to the Turkish International Protection System, the international protection system and related legislative work could not be formed fully and systematically for foreigners fleeing from persecution and seeking asylum. In the period of these legislative shortcomings regarding foreigners, governments' international legislative works on international refugee law and the drafting and signing of conventions specific to *refugee law* have undeniable importance for Turkey. Making preparations for drafting national legislation and at the same time being a party to international legal text on refugee law, Turkey has managed to get its legislation in line with international legislation.

Pre-LFIP Period

Although Anatolian geography has been subjected to population movements for years, Turkish International Protection System gradually began to develop after the 1950s. However, the protection of these developments by law is relatively new. TNP Foreigners carried out all actions and procedures regarding f*oreigners, Borders and Asylum Department affiliated to Ministry of Interior*[16] on behalf of Turkish Republic up until 2013 in Turkey, which is a party to *1951 Geneva Convention on the Legal Status of Refugees*[17] and *1967 Protocol on Legal Status of Refugees.*[18] However, in the TNP period, legislation regarding foreigners does not go beyond the level of regulations, circulars, directives or instructions to the governorates of 81 provinces on certain subject[19] and mainly there are two. These are, '*Regulation on Procedures and Principles Implemented for Singular Foreigners Seeking Asylum in Turkey or Requesting Residence Permit in Turkey to Seek Asylum in Another Country, and Foreigner coming to Turkish Border in*

[14] Senar Ataman, "**Türkiye'nin İltica Politikası**" (Turkey's Asylum Policy), 2010, http://www.multeci.net/tr/ h/T%C3%BCrkiye_nin_iltica_politikas%C4%B1, (Access: 17.05.2017).

[15] **Yabancıların Türkiye'de İkamet ve Seyahatleri Hakkında Kanun (Law on Foreigners' Travel and Residence in Turkey)**. Turkish Official Gazette, 24.07.1950, Official Gazette No. 5683.

[16] TNP, **İltica Göç İşlemleri (Asylum Migration Procedures)**, https://www.egm.gov.tr/Sayfalar/iltica-goc-islemleri.aspx, (Access 27.08.2018).

[17] Will be mentioned as "1951 Geneva Convention". 1951 Geneva Convention, was accepted in 1950 in UN General Assembly, signed on July 28, 1951 and entered into force on April 22, 1954. Turkey is one of the first countries to sign the Convention, August 29, 1961, and approved it with Law No. 359 and with geographical limitations clause which was a right given to the countries by the Convention. (Turkish Official Gazette, (1961). Law on the Approval of the Convention on the Legal Status of Refugees Signed in Geneva on July 28, 1951. Date of the Official Gazette: 5 September 1961, No. 10898). UNHCR, (2007). 1951 Geneva Convention on the Legal Status of Refugees, 1967 Protocol, European Convention on Human Rights, Geneva.

[18] AKA New York Protocol. From now on will be mentioned as "1967 Protocol". Source: Turkish Official Gazette, (1968). Cabinet Decree on Approval of 1967 New York Protocol, Official Gazette Date: 5 August 1968, Official Gazette No. 12968.

[19] TNP, **Yabancıyım İkametgâh ve Seyahat Haklarımla İlgili Bilgi Almak İstiyorum (I am foreigner wanting information on my rights of travel and residence).** https://www.egm.gov.tr/yabanciyim-ikametgah-ve-seyahat-haklarimla-ilgili-bilgi-almak-istiyorum, (Access 19.07.2020).

Mass Seeking Asylum, and Possible Population Movements'[20] and *'Circular No 57 on Implementation Instructions dated 22 June 2006'*.[21] Compared to previous periods, these developments in the Turkish International Protection System became more comprehensive in defining actions and procedures of international protection. Yet, since there was no legislation equivalent to a Law, it was seen in the time that these regulations were insufficient.

With *1994 Asylum/Refugee Regulation,* Turkey has made its first national regulation on refugee law regarding international protection theme. This regulation defines asylum seeker-refugee for persons coming to our borders, explains the procedure for foreigners from the first moment of application until the last decision, states rights and obligations and cooperation with other organizations and institutions are elaborated. Moreover, first procedures for foreigners who have left their country and came to our border in mass influx and seeking international protection are also specified generally.

Procedures of international protection regulated by the 1994 Asylum/Refuge Regulation are explained in detail in *Circular No. 57.* Circular No. 57, just at the beginning, underlines why this regulation is needed, meaning and importance of regulations on international refugee law, and works and studies on international protection procedures Turkey needs in the way of the European Union (EU). In addition, No. 57 Circular on asylum, asylum, refuge, refugee definition, access to asylum procedures, applying authorities, identification, registration, asylum-refuge interview, points to be considered in the interview, how to arrange residence of foreigner in Turkey during the process, the decision on the application, appeal remedies, opportunities to be provided to asylum seekers and refugees, and many other topics are elaborated in details. In this respect, it can be said that Circular No. 57 is the first detailed and comprehensive legislation study in the Turkish International Protection System.

Need for the LFIP and the Drafting Process

Essentially, the LFIP was drafted since legislation before was inadequate, criticism on the implementations had increased, and Turkish Grand National Assembly (TGNA) was adopted unanimously. During the period until the LFIP entered into force, the pre-LFIP legislation in force has been criticized in many ways.

The 1994 Asylum/Refuge Regulation, in general, filled the gap in domestic law

[20] From now on as "1994 Asylum Regulation". Turkish Official Gazette (1994). Regulation on Procedures and Principles Implemented for Singular Foreigners Seeking Asylum in Turkey or Requesting Residence Permit in Turkey to Seek Asylum in Another Country, and Foreigner coming to Turkish Border in Mass Seeking Asylum, and Possible Population Movements, Official Gazette: 30 November 1994, Official Gazette No. 6169/22127.

[21] From now on as "Circular No. 57". TNP–UNHCR, Türkiye'de İltica/Sığınma Başvuru Sahipleri İçin Temel Bilgiler El Kitabı (Basic Information Guide for Applicants of Asylum in Turkey), Ministry of Interior TNP Foreigners-Passport Border-Asylum Department-UNHCR. For Circular No. 57. See also http://www.egm.gov.tr/Documents/uygulama_talimati_2010_genelge.pdf, (Access 01.01.2015).

regarding refugee law; however, there were still areas where implementation was insufficient. Because the existing regulation in the field of asylum is not at an equivalent level with the Law, it has been criticized that the regulations for foreigners are carried out with the legislation in the form of lower regulations such as regulations, circulars or instructions. Therefore, by adoption of '*Regulation on Amendment of Regulation on Procedures and Principles Implemented for Singular Foreigners Seeking Asylum in Turkey or Requesting Residence Permit in Turkey to Seek Asylum in Another Country, and Foreigner coming to Turkish Border in Mass Seeking Asylum, and Possible Population Movements*'[22] areas such as time periods for asylum, the national legislation was attempted to get in line with the international legislation and the Circular No. 57 was announced on 22 June 2006. However, both the 1994 Asylum/Refuge Regulation and the Circular No. 57 received criticism in the national and international arena for not being equivalent to the law, it was deemed inadequate on the grounds that human rights are not protected by law, and the European Court of Human Rights (ECtHR), detected human rights violations in the decisions made by the administrative authorities in line with mentioned documents. Not just the ECtHR, also in domestic law, decisions were nullified on the grounds of implementation of the legislation, execution of legal time frames and inadequate expertise of executive authorities in the field of international protection. For example, personnel of TNP, however, tried to implement 1994 Asylum/Refuge Regulation within the bounds of circumstances, since their main job is law enforcement, where change of place and unit of assignment can happen any time, they could not get specialized in the field of international protection.

Regarding the documents of international protection where detailed analysis requiring specialization could not be carried out due to the workload of the main assignment, administrative authorities found the information shared by the UNHCR, which is accepted as having specialized information on the field, more acceptable. Also, in the EU accession process, Turkey was asked to strengthen the national legislation, to provide protection in an effective manner to persons seeking international protection, to abolish the geographical limitations in the framework of the Copenhagen Criteria, to establish institutions and staff specialized in migration so that the process is efficient and fair.[23] In light of all of these, a need for legislation arose.[24]

---

[22] Turkish Official Gazette, Türkiye'ye İltica Eden veya Başka Bir Ülkeye İltica Etmek Üzere Türkiye'den İkamet İzni Talep Eden Münferit Yabancılar ile Topluca Sığınma Amacıyla Sınırlarımıza Gelen Yabancılara ve Olabilecek Nüfus Hareketlerine Uygulanacak Usul ve Esaslar Hakkında Yönetmelikte Değişiklik Yapılmasına Dair Yönetmelik (Regulation on Amendment of Regulation on Procedures and Principles Implemented for Singular Foreigners Seeking Asylum in Turkey or Requesting Residence Permit in Turkey to Seek Asylum in Another Country, and Foreigner coming to Turkish Border in Mass Seeking Asylum, and Possible Population Movements) (27 January 2006), Official Gazette Date: 16.01.2006, Official Gazette No. 2006/9938. For Amendment see also http://www.resmigazete.gov.tr/eskiler/2006/01/20060127-2.htm, (Access 01.06.2020).

[23] Cemil Güner, **The Road-Map of Turkey About Refuge: The National Action Plan**, AÜHFD, 2007.

[24] DGMM, **Türkiye'nin Avrupa Birliğine Katılım Sürecinde İltica Alanında Yapılması Öngörülen Çalışmalara İlişkin Strateji Belgesi (Strategy Document for Proposed Actions in the Field of**

With Circular No. 57, the issues regulated in the 1994 Asylum/Refuge Regulation were tried to be made more compatible with international conventions. Considering the national and international developments, Turkey needed new legislative regulations to raise human rights standards and get national legislation more compatible with the international refugee law.[25] Also, the violation decision of ECtHR underlined the need for comprehensive legislation. These reasons are explained in detail in General Preamble of the LFIP No. 6458.[26]

In the pre-LFIP reform exercises, migration and international protection subjects in the EU process, *holds an important place* in the EU negotiations under '*Chapter 24*: *Justice, Freedom and Security*. In this respect, '*Turkish National Action Plan for the Adoption of the European Union (EU) Acquis in the Field of Asylum and Migration*'[27] drafted in the direction of '*2003 Turkish National Program on the Adoption of EU Acquis*' was approved by the Prime Ministry on 25 March 2005 and entered into force.[28] As per this plan, the main reason for drafting this Law is legal regulations in line with EU Acquis in the field of migration.[29] '*Ministry of Interior Undersecretariat Bureau of Development and Implementation of Migration and Asylum Legislation and Administrative Capacity*', or as known as '*Migration and Asylum Office*', was established in 2008 upon approval of Ministry of Interior, prepared a draft for the LFIP to fill the gaps in the legislation and give regulations on asylum a legal ground.[30] On 4 April 2013, draft LFIP was approved by TGNA and referred to Presidency. The Law approved by the President on 10 April 2013 and announced in Official Gazette numbered 28615 on 11 April 2013. Thus, legal grounds for actions on foreigners and international protection has been formed.

With the LFIP which the TGNA approved on the necessity to carry out actions and procedures of foreigner by a specialized institution, '*Directorate General of Migration Management (DGMM)*' was established under Ministry of Interior.[31] With

---

Migration in Turkey's European Union Accession Process), 2015, http://www.goc.gov.tr/icerik3/iltica-stratejibelgesi_327_344_69 6, (Access 07.03.2018).

[25] In EU accession process, EU Qualification Directive, Procedure Directive and Reception Conditions Directive stand out as main documents to which Turkish legislation needs to be aligned (Prof. Dr. Cengiz Başak, **Mülteciler, Sığınmacılar ve Yasadışı Göçmenler (Refugees, Asylum-seekers and Illegal Migrants)**, Ankara, 2011.

[26] DGMM, **LFIP General Preamble**, to see the full version of LFIP General Preamble https://www.goc.gov.tr/genel-gerekce18, (Access 01.07.2020).

[27] From now on as "*Asylum and Migration Action Plan*". DGMM, **İltica ve Göç Alanındaki Avrupa Birliği Müktesebatının Üstlenilmesine İlişkin Türkiye Ulusal Eylem Planı (National Action Plan on the Adoption of EU Acquis in the Field of Asylum and Migration)**, 2015, Source: (Turkey's Asylum and Migration National Action Plan) Türkiye'nin İltica ve Göç Ulusal Eylem Planı, No. B.05.1.EGM.0.13.03.02 (25.03.2005), http://www.goc.gov.tr/files/files/turkiye_ulusal_eylem_plani(3).pdf, (Access 09.10.2018).

[28] **İltica ve Göç Mevzuatı (Asylum and Migration Legislation)**, Başkent Matbaası, Ankara, 2005.

[29] Directorate General of Migration Management (DGMM), **Yabancılar ve Uluslararası Koruma Kanunu Genel Gerekçe (General Preamble for Law on Foreigners and International Protection)**, URL: http://www.goc.gov.tr/icerik6/genel-gerekce_327_328_330_icerik, 2015, (Access 10.09.2018).

[30] Nuray Ekşi, **Yabancılar ve Uluslararası Koruma Hukuku (Foreigners and International Protection Law)**, Beta Yayınları, İstanbul, 2014.

[31] With LFIP, DGMM a civil and specialized institution under Ministry of Interior has been established, actions and procedures regarding foreigners and asylum which was previously carried out by TNP Foreigners, Borders and Asylum Department have been taken over by DGMM, making the DGMM a decisive authority on asylum on behalf of Turkish Republic.

this a new chapter for the *Turkish Asylum System* has been opened.[32] DGMM, in a nutshell, carries out actions and procedures regarding foreigners' entry, exit and stay in Turkey. Under international protection topic, international protection law is regulated and actions and procedures regarding persons seeking international protection from Turkey are defined.

In order to regulate rules and principles on implementation of the LFIP, *Implementing Regulation of Law on Foreigners and International Protection*,[33] based on Article 121 of LFIP, was entered into force on 17 March 2016, following the announcement in the Official Gazette.[34] *LFIP Regulation* and provisions of the LFIP are elaborated.

The LFIP is the first law to regulate Turkey's migration management system including regular and irregular migration, and international protection system comprehensively. Purpose of the Law is about actions and procedures of foreigners coming to Turkey regularly or irregularly as well as international protection.[35] The Law consists of 3 parts; second part includes broad and in detail provisions for 'international protection'. Thus, providing legal basis for Turkish International Protection System, offered the most important contribution in the field of international protection.[36]

Changes and Effects Introduced by the LFIP to Turkish International Protection System – In Comparison to the Pre-LFIP Period

LFIP's entry into force with all its provisions on April 11, 2014 has been a new milestone in the Turkish International Protection System. LFIP provisions have started to apply to all foreigners forcibly displaced by the violence in their country, who cannot find state protection and seek asylum in Turkey. The LFIP is a law regulating international protection process with many details. So much so that many details in Circular No. 57, which was in effect before the LFIP, are also included in the LFIP. In this respect, the LFIP, rather than presenting a general framework in the field of international protection, is a detailed law that explains each action to be taken. Although the quality of the LFIP can be seen through the draft of the LFIP being prepared by considering the opinions of many national/international stakeholders and subsequently a law passed by the Turkish Grand National Assembly unanimously and the high standards in the field of international protection, the changes brought forward by the LFIP in practice, and their effects

---

[32] Menekşe, op.cit., (Access 01.10.2019).

[33] From now on as "LFIP Regulation". For LFIP Regulation see URL: https://www.resmigazete.gov.tr/eskiler/2016/03/20160317-11.htm, (Access 02.02.2020).

[34] Turkish Official Gazette, **Yabancılar ve Uluslararası Koruma Kanununun Uygulanmasına İlişkin Yönetmelik (Regulation on Implementation of Law on Foreigners and International Protection)**, No. 29656, 17 March 2016.

[35] LFIP Article. 1 (1) The purpose of this Law is to regulate the principles and procedures with regard to foreigners' entry into, stay in and exit from Turkey, and the scope and implementation of the protection to be provided for foreigners who seek protection from Turkey, and the establishment, duties, mandate and responsibilities of the Directorate General of Migration Management under the Ministry of Interior.

[36] Meral Açikgöz and Hakkı Onur Ariner, **Turkey's New Law on Foreigners and International Protection: An Introduction**, Turkish Migration Studies Group (TurkMiS), University of Oxford, 2014.

will become clearer by comparing them with the TNP practices in the pre-LFIP period. This comparison is made in 3 aspects. These are; the scope and terminology of international protection, the institution providing international protection and the process and procedures of determining the status of international protection. Thus, the effects of the LFIP can be understood more clearly by making a multi-dimensional comparative analysis.

Scope, Types and Terminology of International Protection

Considering the terminology and scope of international protection, there are differences between the LFIP and the 1994 Asylum/Refuge Regulation and Circular No. 57. As can be understood from the definitions, these differences also differ in terms of purpose and scope.

In the 1994 Asylum/Refuge Regulation, the purpose is specified in Article 1 and the scope in Article 2. Hence the scope of the 1994 Asylum/Refuge Regulation, has been identified as actions and procedures of individuals requesting international protection and foreigners coming in masses to Turkish borders requesting international protection from Turkey. In Circular No. 57, the main purpose is to determine rules and principles to be applied for foreigner or stateless persons who seek asylum within the scope of the 1951 Geneva Convention, 1967 Protocol and 1994 Asylum/Refuge Regulation.[37] The scope of the same Circular is stated in Article 2. As it can be understood from here, the purpose and scope drawn within the framework of individual or mass asylum requests in the 1994 Asylum/Refuge Regulation were further detailed in Circular No. 57 as people coming from Europe and from outside the European countries. Another detail is the distinction made between requesting residence permit to seek asylum from Turkey or from another country. This subject will be further detailed in the following sections, a person's requesting international protection from Turkey and requesting to stay in Turkey until he/she can go to another country are two different situation which can lead to different outcomes in terms of international protection. Finally, in Circular No. 57, foreigners or stateless persons seeking asylum/refuge are emphasized. This is an important point in terms of terminology and scope in international protection law.

In 1994 Asylum/Refuge Regulation and Circular No. 57, differences can be seen in both the purpose / scope and the use of terminology. However, in the 1994 Asylum/Refuge Regulation, the term '*international protection*' is not included in any way, while the terms asylum and refuge are used. On the other hand, in Circular No. 57, where the legislation was further detailed, the terms of asylum and refuge are used, and the term of *international protection* started to be used in 11 different places together with the preparation justification part of the Circular and the introduction part of the Circular. This situation shows that there are terms that are sometimes used interchangeably, or that the use of terms may differ depending on the importance of the subject to be expressed. All these issues are largely systematized with LFIP; although, even in LFIP, there may still be uncertainties

[37] Circular No. 57, under Practice Direction "Purpose".

about the definition or scope of some terms.[38]

The purpose of the LFIP and the scope it draws are as follows: The purpose of the LFIP is determined by Article 1 and its scope by Article 2. In both articles, individual international protection and mass international protection are emphasized and applications from within the country or at borders are included in the scope. In this respect, a similar purpose and scope is determined with the regulations before the LFIP. However, in terms of terminology, clearer definitions have been made in the LFIP rather than definitions conflicting each other or can be used interchangeably, when compared to the legislation of the TNP period.

International Protection /Asylum

International protection or in other words *asylum*, is a system formed to protect asylum seekers who are forcibly displaced. Persons who are forcibly displaced and cannot find state protection from their own country or does not want to benefit from this protection are to be protected from the violations of basic human rights and violence. This statement mentioned in many national and international texts can be realized through asylum system.

With a general definition, international protection or asylum is the process that begins when a person requests protection from another country for the protection that he / she could not receive from his / her own country and cannot receive due to persecution, and providing international protection to the asylum seeker in that process, as stated in Article 14 of the Universal Declaration of Human Rights (UDHR).[39] In fact the concept of asylum has emerged in different areas through centuries as different implementations. However, clearly playing a part in an internationally accepted text in a systematic manner had not happened until 1951 Geneva Convention.

Since there are different reasons for international protection, the names of the statuses given to the persons also differ. The name used in the legislation of a country even may change in time. Likewise, there are differences between the terminology used in TNP period before LFIP and the terminology of LFIP.

1994 Asylum/Refuge Regulation does not mention international protection, however terms such as asylum and refuge which imply international protection, are used in the content. In Circular No. 57 there is no direct definition for international protection application, however, when defining *'asylum/refuge application'* it is mentioned as *desire to benefit from international protection* for foreigners coming from or outside Europe and stateless persons.[40] In this respect, the term international protection, which is not included as a direct definition in the TNP period legislation before LFIP, was met with the terms asylum and refuge. However, it would be

[38] However, in LFIP, when using the term "*first country of asylum*" *asylum* definition has not been given.

[39] Turkish Official Gazette, Cabinet Decree on Approval of "Universal Declaration of Human Rights" Official Gazette Date: 27.05.1949, No. 7217, 1949, pp. 16199-16201.

[40] Circular No. 57 "Definitions" paragraph (c).

incomplete to say that the term asylum directly expresses international protection here. Because in the first article of the 1994 Asylum/Refuge Regulation, the expression '... *to take refuge in countries...*' is used to mean *seeking international protection.* However, even though the term asylum is included in the Circular No. 57 in the form of a *desire to benefit from international protection*, its prominent feature is that it is used for foreigners or stateless persons *coming from European countries.* In these aspects, in the legislation of the TNP period, the term asylum has sometimes been used for the term international protection, and sometimes for people who come from Europe and seek international protection.

LFIP, on the other hand, defines international protection with the types of the statuses. In LFIP's definition article international protection is mentioned as; '*refers to the statuses of refugee, conditional refugee and subsidiary protection....*'[41] Since a person who reads the Law for the first time, the terms refugee, conditional refugee and subsidiary protection would not mean anything, the definition of international protection can be understood after these statuses are understood. On that sense, only after stating the meaning of *international protection,* can the statuses of refugee, conditional refuge and subsidiary protection are explained. Because more than being a name of a status, international protection starts with the request of international protection. Another matter is the '*temporary protection*' part, which is not included in definitions however mentioned in the content. Both 1994 Asylum/Refuge Regulation and Circular No. 57 underlines individual or in mass asylum movements. Indeed, in LFIP there is a distinction between individual and mass international protection under Article 2, but the situation is not clearly explained in definitions part, instead explained later on.

It is stated that indeed the terms international protection and asylum has the same content; yet can be used in different ways. Accordingly, ambiguity in interchangeable use of these terms partially continues in the LFIP. LFIP prefers the term *international protection* yet uses *asylum* in 7 different places in the Law, in 4 of which directly implying international protection.[42] Consequently, although it is not explained in the definitions part, the term asylum used in a way similar to the meaning of *international protection.*

Asylum/Asylum Seeker

The terms *asylum* or *asylum seeker* was used to describe persons not coming from European countries and seek international from Turkey, in the TNP period. This situation is stated in paragraph 3 of Article of 1994 Asylum/Refuge Regulation. The same definition is reiterated in subparagraph (g) of Definitions Article in Circular No. 57. Interesting subject for the both is, in 1994 Asylum/Refuge Regulation 5 criteria[43] of refugee status stated in the 1951 Geneva Convention is referred,

[41] LFIP Article 3 "Definitions" subparagraph (r).

[42] See also LFIP Article 46 and 73.

[43] According to 1951 Geneva Convention, for refugee status 5 criteria of which at least 1 is required are as follows: Race, religion, nationality, affiliation to specific social group or a political view.

however the condition of European country is not clearly stated. Yet in Circular No. 57, this is clarified and stated in the provision of the Article explaining persons not coming from European countries are included in the scope of asylum seeker. LFIP does not use the term *asylum seeker* in its provisions. Instead, as it will be mentioned in the following sections of the study, prefers the term '*applicant of international protection*' for anyone requesting international protection regardless the place they come, Europe or not. LFIP preferred the term *conditional refugee* for the asylum seeker status which was granted to asylum seeker outside of Europe in the period of TNP regulation prior to LFIP.

Refugee

As defined in Article 1 A (2) of the 1951 Geneva Convention, a *refugee* is a person who cannot find protection as a result of events in his country due to at least one of the 5 criteria and who requests protection from another country due to his well-founded fear. Both the 1994 Asylum/Refuge Regulation, Circular No. 57 and LFIP have adhered to this definition.[44] However, in Circular No. 57, in terms of the form of expression, the definition of *refugee* is made for foreigners whose asylum applications are approved. In other words, the term *refugee* has been used to describe the approved status of a foreigner or stateless persons seeking asylum. However, as a geographical criterion for refugee status, the criterion of coming from a European country has been specified and maintained in both TNP period practices and in LFIP.

Conditional Refugee

Status of conditional refugee roots in geographical limitations of 1951 Geneva Convention. In the 1967 Protocol, the expressions '*as a result of the events that occurred before 1 January 1951...*' and '*...as a result of these events*', which are present in section A (2) of Article 1 of the 1951 Geneva Convention, are deemed to have been removed from the text, and the 1951 Geneva Convention 'means every person included in the definition in the Article 1. Thus with 1967 Protocol, time limitations have been removed and leave the choice to remove the geographical limitations. In paragraph 1 (B) 1 of the 1951 Geneva Convention, the expression '*events that occurred before January 1, 1951*' can be understood as either '*events that occurred in Europe*' or '*events that occurred in Europe or elsewhere*' and the states parties must make a declaration stating the scope of this statement in terms of the obligations undertaken during signature, ratification or accession to the Convention. For this reason, countries that reserve the right to geographical restrictions can grant refugee status to the person who requests international protection due to '*events that occurred in Europe*' after the status determination process, and for those who demand international protection due to events outside of Europe, they can make different status definitions. Turkey, Monaco, Congo and Madagascar are parties to the 1951 Geneva Convention with

---

[44] See LFIP Article 61, 1994 Asylum Regulation Article 3 paragraph 2, Circular on Practice Direction No. 57, Definitions Article, Paragraph (f).

geographical limitations.[45] Turkey uses the right of limitation arising from 1951 Geneva Convention and thus in its national legislation differentiate between refugee and conditional refugee.[46]

In this context, asylum seeker status defined in 1994 Asylum/Refuge Regulation and Circular No. 57 are expressions used for applicants coming from outside of European countries due to geographical restrictions. The same is valid for the LFIP. Conditional refugee definition is made in article 62 of LFIP. As it can be understood from the provision of the Article, the 5 criteria for conditional refugee status are the same as the 5 criteria for refugee status. The difference is whether geographically the country is a European country or not.[47] However, in the LFIP, conditional refugee expression is preferred instead of asylum seeker status. When compared to the terminology of the TNP period, the refugee status in TNP legislation is the equivalent of the conditional refugee status in LFIP. However, the fact that the term conditional refugee is preferred instead of the term asylum seeker in LFIP, has made it more compatible with international legislation.

Subsidiary Protection

Subsidiary protection, is the type of international protection developed for persons who do not meet the 5 criteria set for refugee or conditional refugee statuses however, there is a risk of serious harm upon returning to his/her country. The person eligible for subsidiary protection and the status of subsidiary protection are defined in article 2 of the European Union (EU) legislation, 2004 and 2004/83 EC[48] of the EU Council Directive.[49]

In the pre-LFIP period, the definition of *subsidiary protection* was not included in the 1994 Asylum/Refuge Regulation. However, since the deficiency of the term *subsidiary protection* has been felt in practice in that time and in order to improve the legislation in the EU membership process, the *subsidiary protection* status was included in the Circular No. 57. To this end, although the subsidiary protection status is not directly included in definitions, it is expressed in Article 12 of the Circular. Thus, when the Article content is analysed, it can be said that if there is a risk that the applicant would face serious harm if returned to the country of origin, subsidiary protection status should be granted.

---

[45] United Nations Treaty Collection (UNTC), (b.t.). Chapter V, *Refugees and Stateless Persons*. 26.12.2017. https://treaties.un.org/Pages/ViewDetailsII.aspx?src=IND&mtdsg_no=V-2&chapter=5&Temp=mtdsg2 & lang=en.

[46] DGMM, **Law on Foreigners and International Protection Regulation on Implementation of Law on Foreigners and International Protection, Regulation on Combatting Human Trafficking and Protection of Victims, Temporary Protection Regulation**, Publication No. 20, Second Edition: DGMM Publications, Ankara, 2017.

[47] In terms of whether a country is a European country, if a country is a member of the Council of Europe, it is accepted as a European country. In addition, the Presidency may determine whether a country outside the Council of Europe is a European country. This is clearly stated in article 3 (1)/b of the LFIP.

[48] European Union [EU] Official Gazette, Dated 29 April 2004 and numbered 2004/83 EC EU Council Directive. 2004/09/30- L 304/12, 2004.

[49] It will be mentioned as "*EU Qualification Directive*".

Subsidiary protection is regulated under Article 63 of the LFIP. This definition of *subsidiary protection* is the same as the definition in EU Qualification Directive. Thus, it can be seen that with LFIP the necessary legislative changes are made in EU harmonization process.

Temporary Protection

Although there are differences in the practices between countries, '*temporary protection*' generally refers to the status that is temporarily granted by the states as individual status determination procedures cannot be made by the states as a result of the *mass migration* of people who are forcibly displaced due to situations such as war, ethnic and sectarian conflicts. The difference here is that the individual application right, which is the most important element in refugee movements, and these individual actions and procedures are not individual but massive in temporary protection. This situation is handled in a similar way in LFIP and pre-LFIP period. As a matter of fact, even in the name of the 1994 Asylum/Refuge Regulation, the expression '*...foreigners coming to our borders for mass asylum...*' is used, and the mass expression in the temporary protection definition is expressed as '*mass movement*'. In addition, in the part starting from the third part of the 1994 Asylum/Refuge Regulation, it is stated how the asylum applications to be made in mass for the borders should be managed. In this respect, it can be stated that the 1994 Asylum/Refuge Regulation contains many details on how to manage mass asylum applications compared to Circular No. 57. In fact, in Circular No. 57, details regarding the asylum applications are not regulated, and provisions are made specific to individual asylum/refuge applications.

LFIP defines temporary protection in part 4, Article 91. On the basis of this provision Temporary Protection Regulation, drafted on 22.10.2014 and entered into force following its announcement on Official Gazette No. 29153, states that as of 28.04.2011, Citizens of the Syrian Arab Republic, stateless persons and refugees who come to or cross the borders in mass or individually due to the events that have occurred, are under temporary protection even if they have applied for international protection. In this regard, as it can be seen in the Table 3, more than 3.6 million foreigners are under temporary protection in Turkey since 2011 and has Access to rights and services offered until then.

Novelties brought forward by Temporary Protection Regulation on the basis of LFIP can be summarized as follows:[50]

- Unconditional reception of Syrians fleeing from the Syria due to Civil War with open door policy,
- Implementation of the non-refoulement principle without any

[50] For details see also DGMM, **"Geçici Koruma Yönetmeliği ve Getirdiği Yenilikler" (Temporary Protection Regulation and Novelties Brought Forward)**. https://www.goc.gov.tr/kurumlar/goc.gov.tr/gk_yon_getirdigi_yenilikler.pdf, (Access 20.08.2020).

exception,

- Meeting the basic needs of those who came.

To sum up, as per Article 1 of Temporary Protection Regulation, temporary protection status is granted to the people who fled from Civil Wars in their country and came to Turkish border in mass in search of immediate protection.[51] Foreigners who are not included in temporary protection regime and seek protection in Turkey are included in the scope of individual international protection. International protection in Article 3 of the LFIP; refers to the status of refugee, conditional refugee and subsidiary protection. However, although the temporary protection status is not directly addressed within the international protection statuses in the definitions part of LFIP, temporary protection status can be seen as a type of international protection. Even though it is the status granted to foreigners who come in mass influx, it is generally accepted that temporary protection is a complementary tool in accessing international protection. Since foreigners under temporary protection regime, like foreigners under international protection, benefit from international protection provided by a state other than their nationality. The protection provided, in this aspect, is indeed a kind of international protection.

The Other Type of Protection: Humanitarian Protection

Types of protection provided in the field of international protection are mainly refugee[52] and subsidiary protection statuses. However, the term '*humanitarian protection*' has emerged as another complementary type of protection due to the fact that protection is provided for persons outside of these two basic international protection statuses. Although the definition of *humanitarian protection* may differ from country to country, it is a type of international protection developed for people who cannot be included in refugee, conditional refugee, subsidiary protection and temporary protection, and who are still in a situation where there are risks or irreparable consequences if they are sent to their country. Humanitarian protection is not regulated in the 1994 Asylum/Refuge Regulation. Nonetheless have been regulated in Circular No. 57 under '*Residence Permits based on Humanitarian Considerations*'.[53] As it can be understood from the Article, it elaborates on *humanitarian considerations such as health, education, family integrity, family reunification etc.*

LFIP regulates *humanitarian protection* under Article 46 as humanitarian residence. LFIP deals with humanitarian consideration stated in Circular No. 57 in a more comprehensive manner, thus aiming to prevent any flaws and unrecoverable situations.

---

[51] Turkish Official Gazette, Temporary Protection Regulation No. 2014/6883, No. 29153, 22 October 2014, Article 19.

[52] The term *conditional refugee* is used by a few countries (Congo, Monaco and Madagascar) who apply geographical limitations, thus for conditional refugee, refugee status has been chosen here.

[53] See Circular No. 57, Article 12 "**İkincil Koruma ve İnsani Mülahazalara Dayalı İkamet İzinleri**" (Subsidiary Protection and Residence Permits based on Humanitarian Considerations).

The Institution Providing International Protection

Turkish International Protection System has continued to develop under the responsibility of Ministry of Interior. In this process, many national and international stakeholder has contributed to the system directly or indirectly. In order to better analyse the effects of LFIP to Turkish International Protection System, it is useful to understand the organizational structure of institutions carrying out actions on international protection. This way, operation fields of the executive institutions in the field of international protection can be seen in a clear light.

DGMM

The need for DGMM has essentially the same grounds as need for LFIP. As stated in the general preamble part of the LFIP, in order for Turkey to fulfil the obligations in the international arena in the process of EU accession and need for '*civil and specialized institution*' and the need for this institution to be the one which will implement the legislation in the international protection field, serves on a similar purpose as LFIP indeed. Previously it was mentioned that the *Migration and Asylum Office*, which was formed in 2008 with the approval of the Minister of Interior, prepared the LFIP draft in order to eliminate the deficiencies in the legislation and to give a legal basis to regulations in the field of asylum. As a result of these, LFIP was announced in the Official Gazette dated 11 April 2013 and numbered 28615 and DGMM was established.

DGMM established by LFIP, is the responsible authority for foreigners' entry into, exit from and stay in Turkey as well as scope of the protection which can be granted to the foreigners seeking protection from Turkey and rules and principles regarding their implementation.[54] For this purpose, DGMM establishes coordination between national and international stakeholders through its central HQ and provincial organizations in 81 provinces of Turkey. Abroad organization is not functional yet. Actions and procedures on international protection are carried out by units specialised in the field.

One of the most important legislative developments affecting the Turkish Asylum System in recent years is the *Statutory Decree No. 676 on Making Certain Arrangements under State of Emergency*[55] which entered into force in 2016. Changes were made in some Articles of the LFIP with the Decree No. 676. Again, in 2018, the *Presidential Decree No. 4 on Organizations of Institutions and Organizations Affiliated to the Ministries and other Institutions and Organizations*[56] changes were made regarding the

---

[54] Turkish Official Gazette, 6458 Sayılı Yabancılar ve Uluslararası Koruma Kanunu (Law on Foreigners and International Protection No. 6458), No. 28615, 11 April 2013. Article 1 and 2, 2013.

[55] Turkish Official Gazette, Olağanüstü Hâl Kapsamında Bazı Düzenlemeler Yapılması Hakkında Kanun Hükmünde Kararname (Statutory Decree on Making Certain Arrangements under State of Emergency). Decree No. KHK 676, Decree Date: 29 October 2016, Decree No. 29872, 2016.

[56] Turkish Official Gazette, Bakanlıklara Bağlı, İlgili, İlişkili Kurum ve Kuruluşlar ile Diğer Kurum ve Kuruluşların Teşkilatı Hakkında 4 Nolu Cumhurbaşkanlığı Kararnamesi (Presidential Decree No. 4 on Organizations of Institutions and Organizations Affiliated to the Ministries and other Institutions and Organizations). Date: 15 July 2018, Official Gazette No. 30479, 2018.

organizational structure and establishment of DGMM.

DGMM carries out actions and procedures related to international protection in the central organization by the International Protection Department. International Protection Department, within the central organization of the DGMM, is responsible for actions and procedures of foreigners requesting individual international protection from our country and foreigners under temporary protection as well as country of origin research.[57] Currently actions and procedures of 3.6 million Syrians under temporary protection regime and more than 300 thousand individuals with international protection are carried out by DGMM in Turkey, all of whom amount to more than 4 million foreigners under the responsibility of International Protection Department.[58] These actions are carried out by the International Protection Working Groups within the structure of Provincial Directorate of Migration Management under the Governorates of 81 provinces. From this point of view, in the introduction part of the Circular No. 57, which can be described as the preamble of the Circular No. 57, it is stated that the international protection field is a separate area of expertise, where specially trained staff should work and that this expertise knowledge should be protected and developed. Even the names of the personnel who have been trained in the field of asylum/refuge are included in the Annex 13 of the Circular No. 57.[59] With this aspect LFIP similarly claims that specialised personnel should work in the field and acknowledge that it is a field requiring expertise and aims to protect and support units established with that name directly.

As two institutions operating in the same field in the context of the successor-predecessor relationship, the aspect of DGMM that differs from the TNP is that although TNP tried to carry out activities in the field of asylum/refuge with the personnel it has trained in this field, a very large part of these personnel are in the position of law enforcement personnel. This situation creates uneasiness for those who cannot find protection in their country, who have faced various acts of violence and who seek international protection, both during the initial registration and during the interview. Although explanations were made regarding confidentiality and privacy issues during the interview, the fact that the foreigners seeking international protection know that the other person is a law enforcement officer may cause uneasiness in terms of sharing the information in the registration or the interview. In this respect, DGMM is a civilian institution both in terms of its establishment purpose and personnel. This development allowed foreigners to speak more freely during their actions and procedures.[60] The devoted desire of TNP staff to work

---

[57] DGMM, **Responsibilities of International Protection Department**. http://www.goc.gov.tr/icerik6/uluslararasi-koruma-dairesi-baskanliginin gorevleri_274_759_828_icerik, (Access 14.06.2018).

[58] DGMM **2017-2021 Strategical Plan**, DGMM Publications, Ankara, http://www.goc.gov.tr/files/files/stratejik_plan_sitede_yay%C4%B1nlanan.pdf., June 2017, (Access 03.03.2019).

[59] Circular No. 57, Annexes, Annex-13(A) and Annex-13(B).

[60] Observations made before, during and after the interviews of international protection affirm this. Even though the TNP personnel working in asylum were not in uniforms, building of the institution, foreigners' knowing that building is TNP may arise anxiety in the phases or interview or registration. The situation sometimes hindered the details of information provided during the interviews.

with regard to asylum cases can sometimes be distributed as providing support to different units within the framework of the needs of the day due to the limited number of personnel. In this case, it may cause unwanted interruptions in the work of TNP staff. In this respect, DGMM continues its activities with all its personnel only in the field of foreigners and international protection, as it is included in the name of the law. DGMM has an institutional structure that aims to be civil and specialized.

International Protection Status Determination Procedure and Actions

The international protection is a process that starts from the first moment when a foreigner leaves his country and requests international protection from another country and arrives at the border, and does not end until the final decision is made. The main thing in this process is to determine whether this protection will be provided to the applicant by the state authorities that provide international protection. Accordingly, a positive or negative status decision is made about the applicant. The changes introduced by LFIP to the Turkish International Protection System should also be addressed in terms of the international protection status determination process and procedures. Thus, the impact of the changes brought by LFIP can be analysed more accurately.

Application and Registration of International Protection

The application process for the Turkish International Protection System, starts with the applicant access to the territory of Turkey and informing Turkish authorities about desire to request for international protection. This situation was preserved in both TNP and DGMM applications.

In 1994 Asylum/Refuge Regulation under procedure to be followed for foreigner seeking asylum/ refuge it is stated that foreigner should lodge his/her application to Governorates of their residence if he/she came regularly, or he/she entered the country irregularly, should lodge their application without delay to the Governorate of their first entry province.[61] It is stated that following the lodging of application, collecting finger print and taking a photograph of the applicant is needed for application to be completed.[62] The procedures summarized about access to international protection in 1994 Asylum/Refuge Regulation are detailed in the Circular No. 57.

In Circular No. 57, under '*Access to Asylum Procedures*' between Articles 1 and 6, contains provisions on registration procedures of foreigners came to Turkey for asylum. According to this, actions are detailed such as making the applications individually, submitting the application request to the authorized units of TNP *(Foreigners-Passport and Foreigners Branch)* as soon as possible, informing the applicant about his rights and obligations within 3 days at the latest, having the examinations

[61] 1994 Asylum/Refuge Regulation Article 4 (application authorities).

[62] 1994 Asylum/Refuge Regulation Article 5 (duties of application authorities).

of those at risk of contagious diseases, informing the authorities about unaccompanied children immediately, informing about the necessity to provide information and documents for accurate identification and they will be given '*foreigner identification document*' in this process, a pre-interview will be hold in preparation for the interview and they will be given an appointment document for the interview date.[63] Thus clarified the actions. In the same part, there are areas where some changes have been made with LFIP. When these are examined briefly, in the same part of Circular No. 57; it is stated that informing the applicant would be made in a language that the applicant could understand reasonably, foreigners coming from outside European countries would be directed to register with UNHCR, the information of foreigners who knew the applicant could be used for identification, and the personnel who would make the preliminary interview should not be in uniform.

The subject of registration and access to procedures is generally regulated in the following way in LFIP: Article 65 states the steps of process to be followed for international protection application from Turkey. In article 65 of LFIP; it is stated that international protection applications must be made by the applicant himself and within a reasonable time to the Governorates, that the applicant will not be punished for irregular entry to the country, provided that the reasons are explained, applications can be made on behalf of the family, and the application will not prevent the implementation of judicial and administrative actions or measures.

Accordingly, international protection applications are made to the Governorships personally. What is meant by this is that the applicants' lodging their application to the Provincial Directorate of Migration Management, which is the provincial organization of the DGMM in 81 provinces. However, if an application is lodged at border gates or Governorate units or any institution, this application should be referred to the nearest Provincial Directorate of Migration Management as soon as possible. The individuality of international protection procedures is always at the forefront. Therefore, asylum applications must be made by the applicant him/herself. Foreigners cannot request international protection through his/her lawyers or legal representatives or through foreign representations of Republic of Turkey abroad, or by petition[64] Responsible authorities are Governorates and foreigner should lodge the application personally. Exception of this is lodging the application on behalf of the family members. If other family members seeking international protection, seek protection on the same grounds as the applicant, an adult from the family member may apply on behalf of all family members. However, in that case, it is still needed to have interviews with each family member. In the interview, it is explained that they are applicants in any case and their cases can be evaluated individually if they wish. Following this notification, if

---

[63] See Circular No. 57 Articles 1 to 6.

[64] In order to be able to claim international protection, the foreigner must reside outside his / her own country. This is one of the basic principles of international refugee law. This situation is explained in the Handbook on Procedures and Criteria for Determining Refugee Status (UNHCR Handbook), paragraphs 87 to 93. This principle is also applied in the Turkish International Protection System.

the family members consent, the applicant can also apply for international protection on behalf of the rest of the family. In this case, consent is not sought for persons under the age of 18 (children) due to their custody, while consent is sought for those who are over the age of 18. As stated in Article 89 of LFIP, after the international protection application is made to the Governorships, applicants can access many rights and services. These include the right to health, access to universal health insurance, counselling, information, the right to education and legal aid.[65]

International protection requests must be made within a reasonable time. There is no lower or upper limit for this period. It is completely evaluated on the basis of the specific case. However, it is essential for the applicant to make his international protection application to the Governorates as soon as possible. For applications not made in a short time, the applicant is required to explain the reason for this. As stated in the UNHCR Handbook, no penalty is imposed on the applicant due to the fact that the applicant was unauthorized in the country within this period if they provide reasonable grounds. Persons whose liberty is restricted can also seek international protection.[66] However, it is clear that this situation does not affect the judicial or administrative measures applied to them.

Article 66 of LFIP includes provisions regarding the application procedures of unaccompanied children. In this context, the principle of observing the best interests of the unaccompanied child in all situations is emphasized. It has been stated that the Child Protection Law No. 5395 will be applied for all procedures to be applied to children. In addition, as stated in Article 67 of LFIP, procedures of persons with special needs regarding international protection are carried out within the framework of the provision that they are given priority.

Article 69 of the LFIP specifies the procedures to be carried out during the international protection application registration. According to this; while international protection applications are registered by the Governorates, the applicant is obliged to submit documents that will confirm their declarations. During the registration and control procedures, the applicant and his belongings can be checked. Information and/or documents regarding international protection claims can be requested from the applicant. The aim of all these is to inquire the information provided by the applicant on departure from their country, coming to Turkey and the accuracy of the claims. These are to prevent the abuse of the international protection system. The statements of the applicant who cannot submit any document to support his statements are taken as basis. In order not to endanger public health, necessary health checks are carried out in coordination with the Ministry of Health.

Applicants whose registration procedures are completed are given an international protection identity document as specified in Article 76 of LFIP. The

[65] Talip Menekşe, **Uluslararası Sistemde İltica: Almanya, İngiltere ve Türkiye'nin Karşılaştırmalı Analiz (Asylum in International System: A Compared Analysis of Germany, United Kingdom and Turkey)**, Gazi University, Unpublished master's degree Thesis, Ankara, 2019.

[66] See **UNHCR Handbook** paragraph 61.

identity card is free of any charge, substitutes for residence permit and gives the applicant the right to benefit from almost all of the rights and services from the first moment.[67]

The applicant who receives the international protection identity document is included in the Turkish International Protection System. The applicant has to reside in the satellite province, which they are allowed to stay and they are notified, until the international protection status decision is finalized.[68] During this period, they must fulfil their obligations specified in article 90 of LFIP.

The provisions introduced by LFIP and LFIP Regulation[69] to the Turkish International Protection System in terms of registration procedures include many provisions before the LFIP period, moreover, are in favour of foreigners in certain areas. For example, in Circular No. 57, the language determination, which the applicant is thought to be able to understand reasonably, is left to the staff conducting the interview. However, since informing is the first step of the process, the failure or misunderstanding that may occur here may also affect the rest of the procedure, so this issue is regulated by LFIP and LFIP Regulation, as *in a language in which the foreigner can easily express himself.* Likewise, during the application, a procedure such as directing the applicant to UNHCR, like it is a mandatory stage of the application, is not specified. However, verbal information is provided in order to get the necessary consultancy service from UNHCR within the framework of UNHCR's protection mission, but there is no such direct compulsory guidance provision in the legislation. Again, in the Circular No. 57, it is stated that the information of foreigners who know the applicant can be used for identification. However, this is an Article that may conflict with the confidentiality clause expressed in article 94 of LFIP. Since, in order to obtain information about an applicant, making interviews with people who know the applicant or with people whom the applicant comes with, can be a risky process in terms of disclosure or endangering the information that should be kept confidential at every stage of the international protection process. In this aspect, applying for the statement of the applicant in the event that identification cannot be determined from the information provided by the applicant and the documents accompanying as stated in LFIP and LFIP Regulation, is more protective in terms of not experiencing possible grievances.

As a result, in the application and registration procedures for international protection, the scope and content of international protection has been expanded by making arrangements in LFIP and LFIP Regulation with an approach that covers the practices prior to LFIP, however, is more flexible in some provisions.

[67] For some types of status in terms of rights and services, a claim arises after a certain period of time, not from the moment of registration. For example, in order for the applicant to request a work permit, 6 months must have passed from the date of international protection application.

[68] These provinces are called *Satellite Provinces* and currently there are 62 in Turkey.

[69] Provisions regarding application and registration to international protection in LFIP, Articles between 65 and 71.

International Protection Interview

The international protection interview is very important for the assessment of the applicant's claim for international protection. In this way, many details on the cause of the applicant leaving the country, why the applicant came to Turkey and what can happen to the applicant in case of their return is learnt during the interview.

In Article 5 of the 1994 Asylum/Refuge Regulation, it is stated that the application authorities should carry out interviews and decision-making processes within the framework of the 1951 Geneva Convention. This situation is detailed in Circular No. 57, as to include the process from preparing the interview to the writing of the interview report.[70] Accordingly, it is stated that for asylum/refuge interviews; the interview is the mission of collecting information, the existence of the fear of persecution in the 1951 Geneva Convention is investigated, special circumstances such as the life, culture, and vulnerability of the applicant should be taken into account during the interview, the country of origin information should be searched from relevant sources before the interview, the interpreter should be informed on the purpose and method of the interview, the interview should be carried out in confidentiality and the interviewer should trust the applicant, individual interview should be made with each applicant over the age of 18, the interviewer should be in plain clothes, the interview is not a questioning process, the foreigner needs to feel physically and mentally ready for the interview, format questions should be asked firstly and then following the method of from general to specific questions, the information provided by the applicant should be associated with the 5 criteria in the 1951 Geneva Convention and at the end of the interview, the interview report should be prepared in line with all these information in the light of documents and declarations and opinion of the interviewer.[71] It is also stated that all the information collected during the interview should be specified in the interview report in a certain order. This order is essentially a line of questions starting from the applicant's leaving his/her country and coming to Turkey and requesting asylum on what grounds.[72] In this direction, the interview phase, the general framework of which was drawn in article 5 of the 1994 Asylum/Refuge Regulation, is detailed with the Circular No. 57.

In LFIP and LFIP Regulation, the part of the international protection interview is regulated with similar sensitivity. Accordingly, the international protection interview in the Turkish International Protection System is one of the most important topics in the international protection section of LFIP. Caseworkers in 81 provinces and decision-making staff in the Headquarters finalize international protection interviews on behalf of DGMM. In article 75 of LFIP, the points to be considered in the international protection interview are given in general terms. In the *general / normal / routine procedure*, an individual international protection interview

---

[70] See Circular No. 57, Articles 7. (Preparation for interviews), 8 (interview room), 9 (conducting personal interview) and 10 (preparing interview report).

[71] See Circular No. 57, Articles 7-10.

[72] Başak, op.cit., 2011.

is carried out with the applicant within 30 days after the application for international protection is lodged. However, if the applicant is included into an *accelerated evaluation* within the scope of Article 79 of LFIP, an interview must be carried out with the applicant whose application is considered as accelerated within three days from the date of application. However, the basis is the general evaluation, the accelerated evaluation is a special procedure and is valid in exceptional cases. Article 75 of LFIP regulates the details of international protection interview procedures.

In LFIP, the purpose of the international protection interview is basically defined as being able to make effective and fair decisions. It is stated that, in the interview the applicant could express himself individually or, with his consent, he could be interviewed with family members. The applicant's lawyer, on the other hand, does not directly attend the interviews, but can attend only as an observer upon the request of the applicant. The lawyer is reminded at the beginning of the interview that he should not interfere with the course of the interview. If the interviewee is a child, with the awareness of this, a psychologist, child developer or social worker or parent or legal representative may be present at the interview. Thus, during the interview, as stated in LFIP as well, the best interest of the child is aimed. Interview phase is a detailed discussion on why the applicant had to live his/her country and come to Turkey, and what he/she went through in the process, this process may not finish in one go. Interviews can take an hour, three hours, and even 6-7 hours. Furthermore, additional interviews can be taken on a different day from the day of the interviews. Matters that need clarification can be clarified in additional interviews. However, if the interview of the applicant could not be carried out for any reason, a period of not less than 10 days is set and then the interview is carried out. In the interviews, the applicant is obliged to tell the truth. The meaning of this obligation is that if the applicant obtains status through fraud, perjury or misrepresentation, this international protection status is revoked and the necessary administrative and / or judicial proceedings are initiated.[73]

The details of the international protection interview, whose general framework is drawn in Article 75 of LFIP, are determined by LFIP Regulation. In the LFIP Regulation, how to carry out an international protection interview is clearly stated under many subheading such as the general principles of the interview, preparation before the interview, the preparation of the interview room, the persons who can attend the interview, the steps to be completed before the interview, the failure to carry out the interview, the additional interview and the interview report.[74]

UNHCR, within Turkish International Protection System, is an important international stakeholder that is in constant contact and cooperation with DGMM in the field of international protection. In order to observe Turkish Asylum System, UNHCR organizes it activities such as observing registration, interview, and decision writing according to the availability of DGMM. Accordingly, UNHCR can participate in international protection interviews as an observer. This observation

---

[73] Menekşe, op.cit., Unpublished Master's Degree Thesis, 2019.

[74] Regarding how to take an interview for international protection see LFIP Regulation, Articles 81-90.

has no bearing on the decision to be made regarding the applicant's case.

One of the important recent development in Turkish International Protection System on the importance and quality of decisions is, establishing and operating Decision Centers and Mobile Teams. Decision Centers which was established by *Directive on Operating Procedures and Principles of International Protection Offices*[75] under the coordination and leadership of DGMM, was opened at first in Ankara on 28 March 2018, and then the second in İstanbul on 28 March 2019. Mobile Branch of the Decision Centers for the 81 province of Turkey is called *Mobile International Protection Decision Teams.* Mobile teams became operational under the coordination and leadership of DGMM on. 18 March 2019. In Yozgat, Denizli, Eskişehir and Aksaray interviews of the cases identified by DGMM has been carried out status determination procedures have been completed. Very small proportion of DGMM, which is responsible for more than 5 million foreigners in 81 provinces of Turkey, personnel (of decision centers and mobile units) are carrying out interviews of persons who are directed to them by DGMM planning and coordination, and write interview reports. Decision Centers has become Centers of International Protection, where only the procedures of decision and interview thus having specialised personnel on interviewing and decisions. It is planned for the future that, Decisions Centers become Processing Centers, by turning them into Regional Decision Centers where all of the procedure can be carried out from one place.[76] This shows that how important and how much contribution Decision Centers and Mobile Units, which are under DGMM coordination and established based on LFIP, make on International Protection System Case workers working at Decision Centers are responsible for accepting and implementing the Work Flow and Working Principles of Decision Centers, from the first moment on. These are some basic principles determined by DGMM on work flow of how international protection interviews and decisions will be, case management, reporting and work ethics. For example, if there is no force majeure, the interviews of the applicants who are directed to the Decision Centers by the DGMM within a certain plan and program and through an appointment system are definitely taken. The day and time of the interview are fully respected. The case of the asylum seeker to be interviewed is examined beforehand, the necessary country of origin information and other case preparations are completed before the interview. Interviews can be recorded audibly and / or visually. In this case, the asylum seeker is informed about this situation. All procedures regarding the interview are carried out within the framework of the

[75] "*Directive on Operating Procedures and Principles of International Protection Offices*" will be mentioned as "*Decision Centers Directive*". For the Directive see Source: KAYSİS Elektronik Kamu Bilgi Yönetim Sistemi (Electronic Public Information Management System), (2018). **Directive on Operating Procedures and Principles of International Protection Offices dated 25.06.2018,** https://kms.kaysis.gov.tr/Home/Goster/143205, (17.07.2018).

[76] Menekşe, op.cit., Unpublished Master's Degree Thesis, 2019. The establishment and operation of Decision Centers between approximately 2016 and December 2019, starting from the preparation process, is a process that has been directly under the coordination of DGMM. The coordination role of DGMM is also very important for this structure to become a Regional Center. Therefore, the information shared about the Decision Center and Mobile Teams mentioned in this study is valid for the Decision Centers. Our study for the Decision Centers process has a time limitation in this respect, and this limitation includes the period between 2016 and December 2019. For details see Menekşe, op.cit., 2018.

confidentiality principle specified in Article 94 of LFIP and under the required privacy conditions.[77]

Both in the pre-LFIP period and in LFIP and LFIP Regulation as stated in various provisions, the international protection interview is very important. However, to mention the fundamental differences between these statements, in Circular No. 57, the main objective of the interview is to reveal whether the events experienced by the applicant constitute the persecution in the 1951 Geneva Convention or not. Yet the main objective in LFIP and LFIP Regulation is to examine the events the applicant has encountered in terms of both cruelty and serious harm criteria, in order to make effective and fair decisions. Because persecution points to 1951 Geneva Convention, while serious harm points to the secondary protection status. In other words, while Circular No. 57 puts forward a perspective only in terms of refugee status,[78] in LFIP and LFIP Regulation, a wide area has been determined to include refugee and secondary protection statuses.

Country of Origin Information

Country of Origin Information (COI) is the subject-specific information that is needed at every stage of the international protection process and can be used at every stage, obtained from reliable, impartial, open, accurate and accessible sources. This information is used to confirm the objective consistency of the facts and documents or information shared by the applicant in the interview. Thus, the accuracy of the information and documents submitted by the applicant during the registration, interview, administrative appeal and judicial processes can be confirmed. However, this is not always possible for the international protection cases, and the use of COI can be applied carefully to the cases containing very specific or very general information or in cases where the source is not reliable. In case of a contradiction between the COI information and the information and documents submitted by the applicant, the applicant is given the chance to explain the situation again and the necessary confirmations can be provided with up-to-date COI information.

When the role COI played was examined in the pre-LFIP period, we see that

[77] Menekşe, op.cit., (Access 01.10.2019).

[78] Although subsidiary protection is mentioned in Article 12 of Circular No. 57, this determination is not an evaluation made concurrently with refugee status in the interview, and it is envisaged as a status that can be given to the applicant whose first negative decision is made after the interview. In this respect, Circular No. 57 has only targeted the determination of refugee status in the interview and put the subsidiary protection analysis in the second plan. In the LFIP, both analyses are included in the evaluation to be made after the interview. Meaning, if a person is not eligible for the status of refugee / conditional refugee, the subsidiary protection analysis is made immediately within this evaluation and the decision is made accordingly. In Article 10 of Circular No. 57, it is stated that the interview report should include evaluation in terms of cruelty or serious harm. However, the subsidiary protection status that should be given in case of serious harm is determined as a separate procedure. In other words, the international protection analysis is limited to refugee status. However, both refugee status and subsidiary protection status are evaluations before / after the same analysis but carried out together. First, the analysis for the refugee status and then the analysis for the subsidiary protection status can only be carried out, which should be evaluated together in any case, otherwise that may cause possible victimization.

COI is not directly included in the 1994 Asylum/Refuge, while in Circular No. 57 there are provisions regarding COI in 12 different places.[79] In these provisions, the areas where COI should be used in international protection processes, the importance of this, the list of TNP personnel with training of COI and the importance of interviewers' specialization on at least 1 country are emphasized. In this respect, it can be said that Circular No. 57 attached the necessary importance to COI. In terms of LFIP and LFIP Regulation, COI is defined in Article 93 of LFIP. Article 93 highlights, as in the interviews, COI information is collected in order to be able to make effective and fair decisions, and that resources of international organizations such as UNHCR can be used for this. In LFIP Regulation, there are provisions regarding COI in 10 different places.[80] Provisions where COI is mentioned, underline repeatedly that the current COI is taken into consideration in the procedures to be carried out regarding the foreigner, the international protection interview is made in line with the COI and the status determination decision is made within the framework of the COI. Article 115 of LFIP Regulation directly deals with the COI. Accordingly, in Article 115, in order to determine the accuracy of the claims of the applicant in the evaluation process of international protection applications, information regarding the countries of origin, residence and transit is collected from more than one source, and DGMM can open the information collected for this purpose and the country of origin reporting studies to the access of other institutions and organizations. Also, it is stated that DGMM can cooperate with the relevant institutions and organizations, and can assign personnel abroad for the same purpose.[81]

As it can be understood from here, many provisions underline the importance, research and use of COI. Indeed, in Circular No. 57, the idea of having every personnel, who carries out the asylum/refuge asylum procedures, responsible for a country of origin is underlined, while LFIP Regulation states this as '*The Directorate General may assign personnel in the relevant countries to collect the country of origin information*'. As can be seen from the statistics shared in the first parts of the study, international protection cases can be finalized in a much shorter time and effectively by the experts and / or case workers specialized in Syria, Iraq, Iran and Afghanistan countries.

International Protection Decision Process and Types of Decisions

The evaluation and decision process is the part where the international protection application and interview is analysed and finalized. At this part, the information and documents submitted by the applicant during the first registration, the information and documents submitted during the interview, as well as current developments, are tried to be confirmed with reliable country of origin information as a whole. While looking at the external consistency of the applicant on the one hand, on the other, his/her attitude and behaviours during the interview are also taken into

[79] See Circular No. 57, Basic Principles, Articles 7 and 11 and Annex 13.

[80] See LFIP Regulation Articles 4, 81, 83, 86, 92 and 115.

[81] DGMM COI Resource: "Kaynak Ülke Rapor Edinme (Acquisition of Country of Origin Report) (KÜRE)".

consideration and internal consistency is considered within the framework of his/her individual situation. As a result, within the framework of all these analyses, a positive or negative decision is made about the applicant. In the pre-LFIP period, in Article 6 of TNP 1994 Asylum/Refuge Regulation, it is stated that the asylum/refuge cases would be prepared by the Governorates, and the decision could be executed by the Ministry of Interior or Governorates if authorized by the Ministry. This provision is detailed in Circular No. 57. Circular No. 57 states that the decision can be made by the Ministry of Interior or relevant Governorate if authorized, and if the first decision taken by the Ministry is positive, the residence of the refugee/asylum seeker shall be allowed.[82] However, if the *first decision taken by the Ministry is negative*, the applicant may appeal to the relevant Governorate within 15 days, this objection can be made with a petition or sometimes an additional interview, and if the objection is found justified, he/she will continue his/her residence, if the objection is found unjust, he/she will be subjected to the general provisions. The decision made on the appeal is the *Final Decision*, and a solution mechanism is established under the name of subsidiary protection or residence permits based on humanitarian considerations for persons who are likely to suffer serious harm in the event of returning to their country after this decision. However, these are evaluated in the post-objection process of the international protection process.

When the international protection decision process is examined in LFIP and LFIP Regulation, it is seen that there are many relevant provisions. However, Article 78 of the LFIP, which includes the decision part directly, it is evident that a detailed description is provided regarding the decision process. Apart from Article 78 of LFIP, there are many provisions that contain or explain the decisions on international protection status. Similarly, in LFIP Regulation, there are many articles that contain or explain the decisions on international protection status. Yet here, general principles are regulated in Article 92, which is directly related the international protection decision. Apart from these the following are explained individually; the *Positive Status Decisions* regarding international protection in Articles 61-62 and 63 of the LFIP, the *Decision on Exclusion from International Protection* in Article 64, within the framework of accelerated evaluation in Article 79 requirement for having the interview within 3 days, and the decision to be made within 5 days following the interview, Article 72-73 and 74 the decisions of *Inadmissible Application*, Article 78 (4) *the decision that applicant does not need International Protection*, Article 85 the *Decision for Termination of International Protection*, Article 86 the *decision on the Cancellation of the International Protection Status.*

In LFIP and LFIP Regulation, international protection decisions are aligned with the above provisions. However, *the Decision Centers Project*, which has been implemented in line with LFIP and the sub-legislation of LFIP, has brought a new working method or decision management approach to the decision area.

While the Decision Centers process has being carried out under the

[82] See Circular No. 57 Article 12.

coordination of DGMM, the *Decision Centers Directive and Working Principles on the Operation of Decision Centers* determined the new evaluation and decision form in the Turkish Asylum System. Accordingly, Turkey not having the Decision Centers organization until 2018, *the model is a first* for Turkey in terms of *successful migration management model.* In Decision Centers System, caseworkers carry out international protection interviews for 2 international protection cases daily. Case workers carry out interviews four days a week, and remaining 1 day is the decision writing day. Personnel working in Decision Centers System is trained to specialize in Iraq, Iran and Afghanistan, and interviews are planned in this direction. In case the Decision Center caseworker who needs to make an international protection status decision on the asylum case that they have interviewed, however they have doubts or hesitations, the decision can be made by using the *'Branch Based Joint Commission Decision Method'*.[83]

This method involves the caseworkers gathering around a round table weekly or in certain periods, discussing the case that they are hesitant about with other caseworkers who are trying to specialize in their field, and reaching the best conclusion with group discussions. Considering the number of DGMM staff, since there is no opportunity to assign a separate consultant/ supervisor for each caseworker, the *Branch-Based Joint Commission Decision Method* is one of the most ideal methods for effective use of resources, increasing intra-group relations and sharing experience. This method both improves a collaborative working culture and accelerates the transfer of expertise to other caseworkers. With Decision Centers established in the framework of *Lean Method*[84] considering the conditions of Turkey and which carry out its operations under DGMM management, LFIP has being implemented more effectively. All these developments directly affect the international protection decision process in the post-LFIP period. Decision Centers' effective operations in Turkish Asylum System and complementary role of Mobile Decision Teams had an effect on UNHCR Turkey Office's stopping its activities regarding registration-interview and decision procedures outside the procedures of DGMM as of September 10, 2018.[85]

In the Turkish International Protection System, the decision given to the applicant during the decision process and which cannot be appealed is the *'final*

---

[83] This decision method was coined to Turkish International Protection System fort the first time by Talip Menekşe. *Joint Commission Decision Method on the basis of Branches Method* same as Decision Centers and Mobile Units Projects is included in the legislation and operations of DGMM as a method for decisions first used in Turkish International Protection System. For details see Soyalp Tamçelik and Talip Menekşe, "*Uluslararası Sistemde Başarılı Göç Yönetim Modelleri Kapsamında Türk İltica Sistemi'ne Özgü Yeni Bir Göç Yönetim Modeli Denemesi: Karar Merkezleri*" (Successful Migration Management Models in International System and A New Migration Management Model Specific to the Turkish Asylum System: Decision Centers), **Düzce University, II. International Migration and Refugee Congress Statement**, 2018, for the full version see... https://www.academia.edu/40752150/Uluslararas%C4%B1_Sistemde_Ba%C5%9Far%C4%B1l%C4%B1_G%C3%B6%C3%A7_Y%C3%B6netim_Modelleri_Kapsam%C4%B1nda_T%C3%BCrk_%C4%B0ltica_Sistemi_ne_%C3%96zg%C3%BC_Yeni_Bir_G%C3%B6%C3%A7_Y%C3%B6netim_Modeli_Denemesi_Karar_Merkezleri_Successful_Migration_Management_Models_In_International_System_And_A_New_Migration_Management_Model_Specific_To_The_Turkish_Asylum_System_DecisionCe, (Access 29.10.2019).

[84] Lean Method in Turkish Asylum System see... Menekşe, op.cit., (Access 01.10.2019).

[85] Menekşe, op.cit., Unpublished Master's Degree Thesis, 2019.

decision'. The final decision is included in the definitions section of Article 3 of LFIP. As per Article 80 of the LFIP, the provision states that the applicant is allowed to stay in the country until the appeal or trial process is concluded. However, for the applicant, whose request was not accepted by the administration and courts, the final decision was made, and the administrative appeal or judicial remedy is closed and the execution of the decision is required. The applicants with a positive status decision are issued an '*international protection status identity document*' within the scope of Article 83 of LFIP. Thus, the evaluation and decision procedures of the Turkish Asylum System are concluded.[86]

As can be seen, the international decision part in LFIP and LFIP Regulation is regulated in a very inclusive manner. The distinction between the first decision and the final decision in the pre-LFIP period was abolished with LFIP. Decision authority is both in DGMM and in case of authorization the Governorates.[87] In addition, in LFIP, the international protection process ends with a negative *final decision*. The final decision, defined as the decision not subjected to an objection, is the final decision on the status of the applicant. TNP practices such as providing subsidiary protection or residence based on humanitarian considerations following the first negative decision, changed with LFIP. As in LFIP and LFIP Regulation, international protection includes both refugee/conditional refugee and subsidiary protection statuses.

Administrative Appeal and Judicial Process

As clearly stated in the 1982 Constitution, judicial remedy is available against any action by the administration.[88] In this context, people seeking international protection can either object to the administration carrying out their actions and procedures to the administrations, or they can apply to the judicial remedy by going to the competent authorities in this field. In terms of country examples, the applicants are sometimes given only the right to administrative appeal against the decisions of the administration, and sometimes both *the administrative appeal* and the right to apply to the *judicial remedy*. Indeed it is possible to see the both situation in the development of the international protection law in Turkey.

In the pre-LFIP period, the decision process according to 1994 Asylum/Refuge Regulation and Circular No. 57 is explained at the start of this part. As it can be understood from here, in the pre-LFIP period, TNP implementations provided an administrative appeal regarding the decisions made by the administration during the asylum/refuge process. This appeal remedy was limited to 15 days and it is stated that the period could be shortened if necessary. As a matter of fact, in no provision of the 1994 Asylum/Refuge Regulation, the application to the court is regulated.

[86] Menekşe, ibid., 2019.

[87] With amendment made on 06.12.2019, DGMM passed its authority on decision making to the governorates. However, DGMM may continue to use this authority on condition that governorates are informed beforehand.

[88] Turkish Official Gazette, **Türkiye Cumhuriyeti Anayasası (Constitution of Turkish Republic)**. No. 2709, 07.11.1982.

However, this single grade appeal path is criticized, both in terms of harmonization of legislation in the EU accession process of Turkey, and restriction of the right of access to both judicial jurisdictions, as well as consequences that are unrecoverable. The administration's review of the action taken by the same administration and also the denial of the right to apply to a different court in the legislation has been criticized as a violation of rights in the context of international protection law.

Circular No. 57 on Implementation Instruction regulates this issue in the beginning and justification sections. In fact, while TNP was at the phase of drafting Circular No. 57, it would only be right to state that they were aware of the developments and legislative requirements in the context of national and international refugee law. As a matter of fact, this can be understood from the Preface of Circular No. 57. However, the fact that the provisions that will ensure this awareness are not directly regulated in the legislation that have put into effect, is a matter of criticism. Actually, in the Article 12 of Circular No. 57 titled '*Actions Carried Out by Governorates after the Decision of the Ministry and Legal Assistance*', it is stated that the process will be expected and the procedures will be carried out within the framework of general provisions regarding the situation of foreigners who apply to *administrative judicial remedy* against the decision. However, detail such as what is this administrative judicial remedy mentioned here, its content, form, duration etc. are not regulated in Circular No. 57.

When the issues of administrative appeal and application to judicial remedy in the international protection process are examined in terms of LFIP and LFIP Regulation, administrative appeal and application to judicial remedy are regulated in the Article 80 of LFIP and Articles 99, 100 and 101 of LFIP Regulation. According to Article 80 of LFIP, an objection can be made to the *International Protection Evaluation Commission* within ten days after the notification of the decision by the person concerned or his legal representative or lawyer, however, they can only apply judicial remedies against decisions made in accordance with Articles 68, 72 and 79 of the law. On the other hand, *International Protection Evaluation Commission* is an administrative appeal mechanism that is directly stated in LFIP under that name.[89] In addition, it is stated that the applications made to the court within the framework of Articles 72 and 79 of LFIP is concluded within fifteen days and the decision of the Court on this matter is final. In case of applicant's application to administrative appeal or judicial remedy, the provision states that the relevant person is allowed to stay in the country until the appeal or judgment process is concluded, thus preventing the wrongful deportation of the applicant as a result of possible wrong decisions at the very beginning. So unrecoverable results are prevented.

The same issue is detailed in LFIP Regulation, Article 99 and 100 under '*Appeal to the International Protection Evaluation Commission*' and '*Commission Decisions and Qualification*' regarding the procedures of appeals, and under '*Application to the*

[89] Article 71 of Statutory Decree dated 02.07.2018 and numbered 703 made amendments in LFIP, provisions regarding International Protection Evaluation Commission were abolished however, this commission continues its duty as an administrative authority for complaints under DGMM.

Administrative Court' in the Article 101 regarding application to the court. Accordingly, in addition to the matters specified in Article 80 of LFIP, the administrative appeal can be made through Provincial Directorate by forwarding the information and documents to be submitted, to the Commission; , the Commission will examine the decision of the administration in terms of procedure and merits, and appeal to the International Protection Evaluation Commission will not hinder the application to the competent administrative court or will not interfere with the time period for applying to court, however, in case it is understood that the person who applied to the Commission also applied to the administrative court then the examination being made the Commission will be suspended.

When both LFIP and LFIP Regulation's the relevant provisions are examined, it can be seen that LFIP formed a dual mechanism of appeal as to the Commission and to the Court for applicants came to Turkey seeking international protection. Thus, foreigners' right to access the judiciary system is paved and the necessary legislative regulations are completed in order to minimize possible victimization.

Other Regulations Introduced by LFIP and Its' Effects

DGMM, established upon the LFIP's entry into force in 2014, has been the main institution for both as an authority carrying out actions and procedures regarding foreigners requesting international protection from Turkey itself, and an agency for establishing coordination with relevant institutions and organizations. One of the most powerful features of the DGMM is that with LFIP many issues regarding international protection is regulated in detail under the law and protected at the law level. Until this part, this study, dealt with legislative works and implementations in pre-LFIP, TNP period in comparison, and the effects of LFIP on the basic stages of the Turkish International Protection Procedure, namely the first application/registration, interview, decision, country of origin information and administrative appeal-judicial remedy.

In this part, the effects on other international protection areas will be discussed in general. This way, the effect of the changes introduced with LFIP can be seen more clearly.

Rights and Obligations

Turkey, in the face of the mass burden of asylum seekers, pulling ahead of many international examples, has provided *access to a wide range of rights and services* to foreigners under international and temporary protection with LFIP. When the basic legislation in the pre-LFIP period is examined, it is stated that in the 1994 Asylum/Refuge Regulation, asylum/refuge applicants could be granted access to rights and services within the scope of the possibilities in the fields of religious freedom, health, communication, work and education, it is expected that the expenses will be covered by the foreigner, and if this is not possible, the general procedures will be carried out within the framework of the provisions and in accordance with the relevant legislation.[90] A similar approach is also available in Circular No. 57. Accordingly, in the Circular No. 57 states that, regarding asylum seekers and refugees; an identification document will be issued to them, they have the right to request inter-provincial referrals, health assistance and accommodation facilities are essential to be covered by themselves, the health needs of people who do not have the means will be covered by the state, people with financial difficulties can apply to Social Assistance and Solidarity Foundations, foreigners with the residence permit of at least 6 months can apply for a work permit regardless of their status, children in the age group of 06-14 have education rights within the scope of basic and compulsory primary education, and secondary education and higher education will be encouraged.[91]

As for obligations, those are regulated as such; respecting and obeying the laws of Turkey, the obligation to signature on certain days, and the obligation to present the truth in the information and documents to be submitted to the administration.

LFIP has provided a very comprehensive framework in terms of rights and services. Rights and obligations are regulated in Article 88 and 89 of LFIP. According to this; international protection status holders are exempt from the reciprocity stipulation and the rights and services provided to persons under international protection cannot be interpreted as being more than the rights and services provided to Turkish citizens. In addition, people under international protection will be provided with primary and secondary education services, people in need can have access to social assistance and services, for international protection applicants who do not have any health insurance and do not have the means to pay, for one, the state will over the costs a period of one year starting from the registration of international protection application under the provisions Social Insurance and General Health Insurance Law dated 31.05.2006 and numbered 5510, with regard to access to the labour market, the applicant or conditional refugee can apply for a work permit six months after the date of international protection application, and foreigners with a refugee or subsidiary protection status can start working dependently or independently upon acquisition of status. LFIP Regulation, coordinates the access of foreigners to rights and services, under titles such as informing and interpreting, informing about legal aid and consultancy services, travel documents, education and training, access to social assistance and services, health, work, and allowance.[92] As per these, millions of foreigners who come to Turkey in search of international protection are provided with Access to mentioned rights and services. In that sense Turkey, undertook a very important mission, both for its geographical location and providing millions of foreigners access to rights and services in the field of international protection, Furthermore, foreigners' Access to these rights and services are free to a large extent. In turn for ALL of these rights and services provided to foreigners under international protection, the main obligation stated in LFIP and LFIP Regulation, just as it was

[90] See... 1994 Asylum/Refuge Regulation Articles 18-19, 21 and 27.

[91] See... Circular No. 57 Article 19 and Annex-1 Issues to be Notified to the Applicants of Asylum/Refuge.

[92] See... LFIP Regulation Articles 102 and 109.

in the pre-LFIP TNP period, is observance of the law. And this is essentially, residing in the province they are directed, obligation to notification and obligation to tell the truth. In the event of disobeying these obligations the law states '*...restrictions may be imposed to the rights and services, except the rights to education and basic health, of foreigners who disobey written obligations and whose applications or status decisions are negative*'.

Persons with Special Needs

Persons with special needs, is the group of people whose follow up regarding their process of international protection should be prioritized, due to their situation of disadvantage. LFIP defines persons with special need, on the Definitions section.[93] There are no Article directly related to persons with special need in 1994 Asylum/Refuge Regulation or Circular No. 57. However, Circular No. 57 states that in the interview of vulnerable persons, vulnerabilities are observed.[94] Moreover, although persons with special need are not mentioned by name, it defines unaccompanied minors and Article 6 details the situation of children in the international protection procedure. It is stated that, actions of unaccompanied minors are carried out observing their vulnerabilities, unaccompanied minors in need of accommodation will be placed to the Children's Home of Social Services and Child Protection Agency (SSCPA-SHÇEK).[95] Beside these, there is no arrangement regarding persons with special need.

While people with special needs are defined in LFIP, it is stipulated that priority will be given to rights and procedures in the field of international protection and that people who have been subjected to torture, sexual assault or other serious psychological, physical or sexual violence will be provided with adequate treatment opportunities to eliminate the damage caused by such acts.[96] In addition, it was stated that these situations will be taken into consideration in the interviews to be made with the persons with special needs, health insurances will be made without seeking a time limit for general health insurances and priority will be given to their accommodation in the *Reception and Accommodation Centers*.[97] Furthermore, the definition of unaccompanied minor, included in the definition of special needs in LFIP, and it is stated that the best interests of the child should be taken into consideration in all proceedings regarding unaccompanied children, further international protection applications of unaccompanied minors cannot be evaluated in accelerated evaluation. [98] Therefore, LFIP has introduced many protective and inclusive measures in the field of international protection for those with special needs. The same issue is regulated in many places in LFIP Regulation. In line with

---

[93] LFIP Article 3(l) Definitions: Definition for person with special needs.

[94] See... Circular No. 57 Article 7 (Interview Preparation).

[95] See... Circular No. 57 Article 6 (Procedure regarding unaccompanied minors).

[96] See... LFIP Article 67 (Persons with special needs).

[97] See... LFIP Article 75 (interview), Article 89 (Access to aid and services), Article 95 (Reception and Accommodation Centers).

[98] See... LFIP Article 3(m) Definitions: (definition of unaccompanied minor), Article 66 (unaccompanied minors) and Article 79 (accelerated procedure).

this, LFIP Regulation Article 113 on persons with special needs; first whether the applicant has any special needs is identified, and if they are with special needs they will be prioritized in their procedures and cooperation with relevant public institutions and organizations, NGOs and international organizations for treatment of those in need of treatment. Same sensibility in LFIP Regulation is preserved under *rules and principles regarding notification, matters to consider during international protection registration, and matters to consider before the international protection interview.* [99] Each of these regulations can be seen as an indicator of comprehensive protection of LFIP concerning persons with special needs.

Conclusion and Recommendations

Turkey, being a dynamic country in terms of migration for centuries, has become a country with considerable experience and cumulative knowledge. Not only have the numerical statistics in the field of migration but also the legislative regulations shaping the implementation been very important in reaching this point.

With LFIP, Turkish International Protection System formed its legal basis first. Thus all legal arrangements regarding foreigners are not regulated by sub-legislations which are not equivalent to the law such as regulations and circulars, but by direct provisions of the law. Basic framework on terminology is drawn and harmonized with the international legislation. In this way, statuses, stated merely as status holder or applicant, are regulated with the clarification on who is refugee, conditional refugee, subsidiary protection status holder and under temporary protection. Since subsidiary protection is not directly regulated in the TNP period however exist in EU legislation, LFIP has regulated the status of subsidiary protection directly and coined the term to Turkish International Protection System for the first time. Standards set by 1951 Geneva Convention are incorporated into national legislation via LFIP. LFIP with its human-oriented structure, gives particular importance to individuality in international protection. In all stages of international protection process such as registration-interview-decision and administrative appeal/judicial process; accurate, impartial, up-to-date and reliable country of origin information is brought into the forefront and as a result, country of origin research unit has been established within DGMM and KÜRE (Country of Origin Report Acquisition) system is formed as a tool to be used to this end. Again, many other rights and services such as education, health, access to the labour market, consultancy, translation services, right to appeal, right to information, non-refoulement, identification procedures, right of habitation, right to travel for foreigners with international protection application/status, is regulated together and legally secured. In fact, there is not much difference between being an applicant and having a status in accessing all these rights and services. In this aspect, LFIP provides an inclusive framework for everyone in the field of international protection in ensuring access to rights and services. LFIP, prioritizes persons with special needs at every stage of the international protection. For administrative appeal and judicial

[99] See... LFIP Regulation Articles 70, 85 and 120.

process, before LFIP, the appeal was made to TNP as it was the authority, regarding a decision of TNP, while LFIP stipulates that the administrative appeals can be made to International Protection Evaluation Commission and for judicial process administrative courts are direct authorities that can be applied. Thus, a dual system for appeal has been established. By adopting an attitude open to cooperation with national and international stakeholders, LFIP states that cooperation can be established with other non-governmental organizations, especially UNHCR and the International Organization for Migration (IOM). Another gain that LFIP introduced to the Turkish International Protection System is the *Decision Centers Project* under the management of DGMM, which is implemented with sub-regulations within the framework of LFIP provisions, although it is not directly with LFIP. With these centers, it is aimed to establish *Regional Centers* with specialized units in the Turkish International Protection System, to relief the cases waiting in the pipeline in 81 provinces by the Regional Centers, while ensuring the quality and standardization in 81 provinces by extending specialization, and efficient usage of all tools, labour and time in this field. *Mobile Decision Teams*, which were established with a mission to complement the structuring of Decision Centers, aims to establish standardization in 81 provinces by volunteer and specialized teams in the field. However, in order for the Decision Centers structure to work effectively and efficiently, it is very important these centers to be coordinated and managed by DGMM until such Regional Centers are established. As a matter of fact, DGMM is an institution that established and operates Decision Centers as a central institution in the field of migration on 81 provincial Governorships and can transfer their management if necessary. However, these centers, which were established with the aim of transitioning to the process of Regional Decision Centers, should be managed by DGMM, not by the Provincial Directorate of Migration Managements under the Governorates, until they become Regional Process Centers. In other case, Provincial Directorate of Migration Management, to which the Decision Center is affiliated, since it is not hierarchically superior to the other PDMMs, may fail to satisfy when planning a regional workshop which requires planning necessary interviews, coordinating with the provinces, meeting needs of foreigners during the process, identifying the foreigners to be interviewed, planning priority order considering foreigners residing in other provinces, thus DGMM direct intervention and coordination is crucial. On the other hand, the personnel to be employed in the Decision Centers must be interested in the field, trained and keen on self-improvement. Therefore, as emphasized in the Decision Centers Directive, both the selection of personnel and the supervision of these personnel should be carried out by DGMM. Within the framework of '*specialization and preserving specialization*' which is most need in the field of international protection, it is essential to keep the personnel specialized within long period of times and benefit from their expertise. Decision Centers should be managed by DGMM, and procedures of planning international protection cases, interview and decision should be coordinated by DGMM, until such time the legislative preparations and institutional infrastructure are completed so that Decision Centers can be turned into Regional Decision Centers. Otherwise, since there are about 4 million foreigners in Turkey, whose actions and procedures regarding international protection is carried out, local needs and priorities also may differ from time to time and as a result trained personnel can be directed to work on the area of current need rather than their area of expertise. This can negatively affect specialization that requires a long time. On the other hand, if more than 3.6 million Syrians' '*temporary*' status is terminated, even a small proportionate applies for international protection, it would increase the work load across the country, however cases can be processed in much shorter periods by this *Regional Decision Centers.* As a result, effective management of *Decision Centers* established with the aim of more efficient use of resources, more specialization and making more effective and fair decisions in the status determination process, and these becoming regional process centers, will further strengthen the Turkish International Protection System in the national and international arena. In the event that these centers became Regional Decision Centers, structuring of these centers can be supra-province while carrying out processes of status determination of international protection through personnel trained in this area and its sub-specialty units formed in relative field.

LFIP was drafted in line with the needs of Turkey in the field of international protection. Therefore, although the existence of LFIP as a text is important in itself, it is important to train more case workers / decision makers who will work in the field of international protection and aim to specialize for the effective implementation of LFIP, to increase the number of country/region experts especially on Syria, Iraq, Iran and Afghanistan, to increase the rate of effective and fair decisions by using suitable decision-making tools in the status determination process such as the Branch-Based Joint Commission Decision Method, to continue with the examination of international examples of the status determination process and to evaluate good practice examples in the national/international arena and finally to analyse the court decisions regarding the international protection process and make the necessary legal arrangements in practice. For all these activities, an '*Asylum Academy*' can be formed within DGMM, this way, required specialized personnel can be trained and specialization can be achieved. Thus, while the Turkish International Protection System can take its place in the international arena to a higher level, '*Turkish Asylum School*' could gain a stronger representation power and further strengthen its position as an example in the international arena.

CHAPTER 2

TURKEY'S ASYLUM POLICY IN THE CONTEXT OF TEMPORARY PROTECTION

Ayşegül Bostan[1]

'You will feel a great tolerance in this land, where people of various cultures have lived in peace and serenity for thousands of years.'[2]

Introduction

The Syrian Crisis beginning with the protests in 2011 and turning into a civil war, has affected the world. The immigration wave of people fleeing Syria caused the most severe migrant crisis the world has ever witnessed after the 1994 refugee crisis in Rwanda. The Syrian citizens abandoning their homes in fear of death firstly took refuge in the neighbouring countries. In the succeeding period, they followed a dangerous path to reach Europe. Arriving in Turkey and Greece with boats, the refugees aimed to reach countries like Germany, Sweden, and Austria by using the humanitarian corridor through the Balkan countries. Thereby European countries faced an immense wave of refugees. Since this flight and resistance to accept refugees turned the Aegean and Mediterranean seas into a cemetery, Turkey applied an active policy in favour of welcoming Syrian refugees. Under mutual exemption of visa with Syria in 2009, Turkey followed an open-door policy.[3] In this chapter, the efforts of the Republic of Turkey for Syrian refugees as 'guests' are elaborated with an emphasis on their legal status.

Syrian refugees in Turkey

Syrians preferred the sea route to enter Europe, which caused many deaths, including the death of a baby named Aylan. This situation made the countries soften their policies toward Syrian refugees. These catastrophic events led Ankara to follow an open-door policy for Syrian refugees and hosted them since 2011.[4]

---

[1] Research Assistant, Department of International Relations, Çankırı Karatekin University, Çankırı, Turkey. E-mail: aysegul_bostan@yahoo.com and abostan@karatekin.edu.tr ORCID: 0000-0002-8731-2757.

[2] It was used by Süleyman Soylu, the Minister of the Interiorof Turkey, on the official letter of approved resident permit of the Syrian applications. Gülay Uğur Göksel, **Integration of Immigrants and the Theory of Recognition**, Cham, Palgrave Macmillan, 2018,p. 155.

[3] Suna Gülfer Ihlamur Öner, "Türkiye'nin Suriyeli Mültecilere Yönelik Politikası", **Ortadoğu Analiz**, Sayı 6, 2014, pp. 42-45.

[4] Ferhat Pirinççi, "Suriye'ye Komşu Ülkelerin Suriyeli Mültecilere Yönelik Politikaları",**TESAM Akademi Dergisi**, Cilt5, Sayı 2, 2018, p. 44.

It is noteworthy to remember that Turkey showed the same hospitality in other cases. Pomaks and Turks of Bulgaria fleeing from the intimidation policy of the communist regime reached the border between Turkey and Bulgaria in the 1980s. Turkey welcomed and integrated these people. At the same time, Turkey hosted Kurdish people and other minority groups fleeing from Iraq following the 1988 Halabja Massacre. Likewise, Bosnian, Albanian, and Turkish families took refuge in Turkey after the ethnic conflicts in Yugoslavia during the 1990s. Subsequently, they gained citizenship and integrated into Turkish society. But it is important to underline that Turkey, known for its hospitality, has faced such an immense wave of refugees for the first time when Syrian people entered through the southern border because of the Syrian crisis.[5] According to the data obtained from the Directorate General of Migration Management, the number of Syrian people who took refuge in Turkey was 14,237 in 2012. Table 1 shows figures for the period between 2012 and 2020. Accordingly, the number of Syrians under temporary protection has constantly been increasing to reach 3,635,410 in 2020.[6]

Table 1. Syrian refugees under temporary protection

Years	Syrian refugees under temporary protection
2012	14,237
2013	224,655
2014	1,519,280
2015	2,503,549
2016	2,834,441
2017	3,426,786
2018	3,623,192
2019	3,576,370
2020	3,635,410

Source: www.goc.gov.tr/gecici-koruma5638.

As seen in Figure 1, there has been an increasing momentum since 2012, and the number of Syrian citizens in Turkey has increased. Depending on the global conjuncture, this number decreased slightly in 2019. But despite the decline in the number of Syrian refugees under temporary protection in 2019, Turkey has still maintained its first place in the world in terms of hosting the largest number of refugees.[7]

[5] Kemal Kirişçi, "Syrian Refugees and Turkey's Challenges: Going Beyond Hospitality", Brooking Institute, 12 May 2014, http://www.brokings.edu/research/syrian-refugees-and-turkeys-challengesgoing-beyond-hospitality (Access: 22.07.2020).

[6] "The Up-dated of Temporary Protection (2020)", The Offical Website of Directorate General of Migration Management, http://www.goc.gov.tr/gecici-koruma5638 (Access: 1.11.2020).

[7] Ibid.

Figure 1. Syrian refugees under temporary protection by years

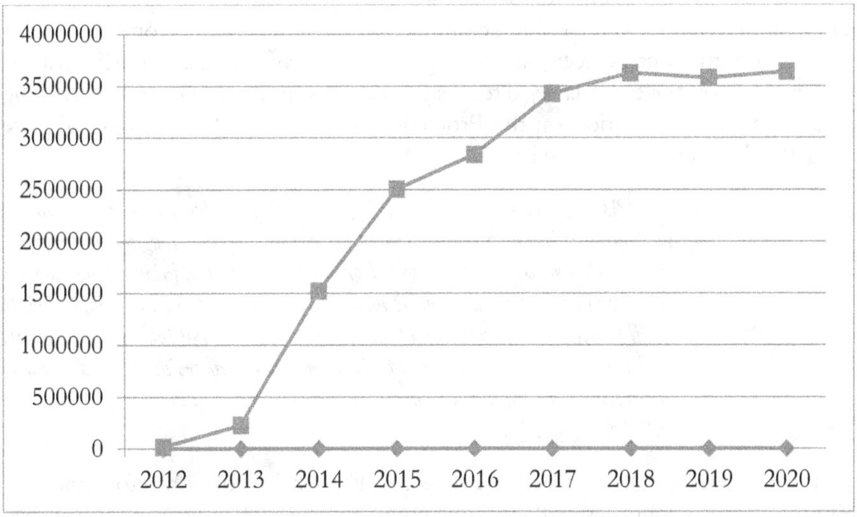

Source: www.goc.gov.tr/gecici-koruma5638.

As the initial stage of the Syrian refugee crisis, the encampment policy was mainly adopted by the Turkish authorities. Currently, temporary accommodation centres have hosted some Syrians moving to Turkey, but the vast majority of refugees have lived in cities.[8]Midyat Temporary Accommodation Centre in Mardin, Nizip Temporary Accommodation Centre in Gaziantep, Cevdetiye Temporary Accommodation Centre in Osmaniye, and Ulubey Neighbourhood of Altındağ District in Ankaraare some of these accommodation centers.[9]According to the data of 2020, Istanbul is in the first place in hosting Syrians under temporary protection with 515,083 people. Gaziantep with 451,480 people and Hatay with 435,283 people follow Istanbul. There are also temporary accommodation centres in Adana, Kilis, Kahramanmaraş, Hatay and Osmaniye provinces. The number of people in these centres is 59.376, but the number of Syrians living outside these centres is 3.576.034. [10]

From guest status to temporary protection

The legal status of the Syrian people in Turkey has made up a significant agenda for a long time. The general belief was that the Syrians who moved to Turkey under

---

[8]Ahmet İçduygu and Maissam Nimer, "The Politics of Return: Exploring the Future of Syrian Refugees in Kordan, Lebanon and Turkey", **Third World Quarterly**, Vol. 41, No.3, 2020, p. 4.

[9] Cihan Çetinkaya, Mehmet Erbaş ve Eren Özceylan, "Türkiye'deki Suriyeli Geçici Barınma Merkezlerinin Durumu ve Senaryo Analizleri",**Birey ve Toplum Sosyal Bilimler Dergisi**, Vol.6, No.2, 2016,p. 11; Meltem Demirtaş, **Suriyelilerin Türkiye'ye Göç Süreci ve İlişkiler Ağı: Ulubey Mahallesi,(**Yayınlanmamış Yüksek Lisans Tezi), Ankara, Hacettepe Üniversitesi, Sosyal Bilimler Enstitüsü,2019, p. 75 http://www.open access.hacettepe.edu.tr:8080/xmlui/bitstream/handle/11655/8810/10281703.pdf?sequence=1&isAllowe=y (Access: 1.11.2020).

[10] "The Up-dated of Temporary Protection (2020)", ibid.

the open-door policy would remain temporarily and they would return back if the war in Syria is over. Therefore, Syrians were guests in the public opinion. Turkey met their needs of shelter, food and clothing. However, regulations concerning their rights and status became necessary as long as Syrians stayed in the Turkish territory. In fact, there are the essential legal texts signed by Turkeyabout refugees. According to the Geneva Convention on the Protection of Refugees (1951)[11], one of these texts, the definition of refugee is:

> *'As a result of events occurring before 1 January 1951 and owing to wellfounded fear of being persecuted for reasons of race, religion, nationality, membership of a particular social group or political opinion, is outside the country of his nationality and is unable or, owing to such fear, is unwilling to avail himself of the protection of that country; or who, not having a nationality and being outside the country of his former habitual residence as a result of such events, is unable or, owing to such fear, is unwilling to return to it.'(Article 1/ A.2).*

For the refugees defined as above, there is the principle of non-refoulement of refugees to third countries or their home countries where their lives may be at risk. The 1951 Convention defines the term of refugee, refugee rights, and the principle of non-refoulement. Despite the 1971 Protocol aiming to eliminate geographical and historical limitation, Turkey has applied geographical limitation.[12]

According to the 1951 Convention and the 1974 Protocol ratified also by Turkey, Syrians can not gain this status because of geographical limitation while the refugees only coming from Europe can gain refugee status.[13] This situation made it crucial to make some regulations in national law for the legal status of Syrians. The first regulation is Law No. 6458 on Foreigners and International Protection (YUKK) dated 2013. Grand National Assembly of Turkey put the law into effect on 11 April 2013. According to this law, international protection covers refugees (coming from Europe), conditional refugees (coming from outside Europe), and those under secondary protection status. Syrians have temporary protection status under Article 91 of the Law on Foreigners and International Protection. A temporary protection is applied for*'foreigners who have been forced to leave their country, cannot return to the country that they have left, and have arrived at or crossed the borders of Turkey in a mass influx situation seeking immediate and temporary protection*'.[14]

Besides, this law grants Turkish authorities the right to cooperate with international organisations and access the UNHCR's international protection applications in accordance with Article 92. This law defines and formalises certain

[11] "Convention and Protocol Relating to the Status of Refugees", The Offical Website of UNHCR. https://www.unhcr.org/3b66c2aa10.html (Access: 12.11.2020).

[12] Ibid.

[13] Kemal Kirişçi, "Turkey: A Country of Transition from Emigration to Immigration", **Mediterranean Politics,**Vol.12, No.1, 2007, p. 94.

[14] "Law on Foreigners and International Protection, Directorate General of Migration Management", 11 April 2013, https://en.goc.gov.tr/kurumlar/en.goc/Ingilizce-kanun/Law-on-Foreigners-and-International-Protection.pdf (Access: 13.11.2020).

duties such as the establishment of the Directorate General of Immigration Management under the Ministry of Interior, determination of policies and strategies concerning migration, ensuring smooth communication between institutions. According to Article 95, the Directorate General's duties include establishing asylum centres and providing basic needs such as food, shelter, health, and social protection to Syrians under temporary protection.[15]The Directoral General of Migration Management works with Disaster and Emergency Management Authority (AFAD), Turkish Red Crescent, Governorship of Hatay, Ministry of Health, Ministry of Interior, Presidency of General Staff, and Ministry of Customs and Trade to meet these needs.[16]

In addition, with a more comprehensive regulation on temporary protection, the Temporary Protection Regulation came into force in 2014. According to this law, temporary protection is '*protection status granted to foreigners, who were forced to leave their countries and are unable to return to the countries they left and arrived at or crossed our borders in masses to seek urgent and temporary protection and whose international protection requests cannot be taken under individual assessment*'. Article 7 details the characteristics of refugees under temporary protection. Refugees under temporary protection will receive a temporary protection identification document after the registration process. Besides, with this law, Syrians are exempt from the administrative regulations applied for foreigners who illegally entered Turkey (Article 5/1).[17]Article 27 and Article 28 state that they can access basic health services and benefit from education, language training, and vocational courses. According to Article 28, Turkish Council of Higher Education (CoHe) will determine the conditions for Syrian students to receive a university education. Also, with Article 31, the Turkish government grants Syrians under temporary protection the right to benefit from translation services.[18]

Turkey and the European Union signed a Readmission Agreement in 2016 to cope with irregular migration and the wave of refugees and to better manage the process. In accordance with this agreement, '*one-to-one initiative*' will be applied. A Syrian who is logged into Greece illegally and does not apply for asylum will be sent to Turkey. In return, a refugee in Turkey will be accepted by the European Union. Accordingly, another aspect of this agreement is a matter of granting Turkey a visa exemption.[19]

The Law on International Labor Force dated 2016 is another law related to this subject. According to Article 11 of this law, foreigners can acquire a work permit with a Turquoise Card. Academics with a reputation, scientists, and also businessmen who can make export, investments and can provide employment in

[15] Ibid.

[16] "Temporary Protection in Turkey", The Offical Website of the Directorate General of Migration Management, https://en.goc.gov.tr/temporary-protection-in-turkey (Access: 14.11.2020).

[17] "Temporary Protection Regulation", The Offical Website of UNHCR, 22 October 2014, https://www.refworld.org/docid/56572fd74.html (Access: 14.11.2020).

[18] "Temporary Protection in Turkey", Ibid.

[19] Kim Rygiel, Feyzi Baban and Suzan Ilca, "The Syrian Refugee Cirisis: The EU-Turkey 'deal' and Temporary Protection", **Global Society Policy**, Vol: 16, No: 3, 2016, pp. 315, 316.

Turkey are able to acquire this card. However, the Turkish government underlines that Syrians under temporary protection cannot benefit from this provision.[20]

Thanks to these regulations, guest Syrians who fled from persecution in their country and arrivedat the Turkish borders with a massive influx can acquire temporary protection status. Thus, it could be said that the deficiencies in the legal status of Syrians, arising from Turkish national law, were eliminated. In addition, the rights given to them were protected and the obstacles preventing them from getting better service from the Turkish state were removed with the clarification of the place of Syrian refugees in Turkish law.

With the granting of legal status to Syrians, legal uncertainty is no longer a problem. Syrians are in close contact with Turkish society as they mostly choose to live in city centres and establish a new order for them in these regions. Although the Turkish people regarded Syrians who came in the first years of the war in Syria as guests, they now think that Syrians have settled in these lands permanently.

The survey study called Syrians Barometer, conducted by HUGO (Hacettepe University Immigration and Politics Research Center) in 2017, revealed that Turkish citizens have a '*reluctant acceptance*' towards Syrians under temporary protection status.[21] The ongoing conflict in Syria and the integration of Syrians with Turkish society may be the main causes of this perception.

---

[20] Act No. 6735 on International Labour Force (28 July 2016), International Labour Organization, http://oit.org/dyn/natlex/natlex4.detail?p_lang=en&p_isn=103259 (Access: 14.11.2020).

[21] Murat Erdoğan, **Suriyeliler Barometresi: Suriyelilerle Uyum İçinde Yaşamın Çerçevesi,** İstanbul: İstanbul Bilgi Üniversitesi Yayınları, 2018, p. 172.

CHAPTER 3

THE EVALUATION OF SOCIAL POLICIES REGARDING REFUGEES LIVING IN TURKEY

Derya Alimanoğlu Yemişci[1]

Introduction

Throughout history, migration has continued since the existence of humanity. Faced with many difficulties such as wars, political authorities and conflicts, people were forced to migrate. The concept of migration is defined as the long or short-term abandonment of the place where different people live for different reasons, and this concept includes not only the change of the place of residence, but also socio-economic and cultural changes[2]. As it can be understood from the definition, migration is not just a simple phenomenon of moving from one place to another, but it also implies the struggle of people to survive due to the mistreatment that they are exposed to[3]. During the migration process, these people, whose freedom, rights to life and security are under threat, are forced to abandon their territories and establish a new life in a place that they do not know. Refugees live under very poor conditions. Unfortunately, neither the regulations imposed by the international law nor the internal legal regulations of the countries are sufficient to create effective social policies for the welfare of these people.

The concept of migration has gained a wider dimension in terms of definition, determination of causes and effects, and classification over time. Migration is an individual and mass act of displacement or change of place of residence for economic, social and political reasons. These displacement movements, whether short-term or long-term, often occur in the form of 'internal migration' within the same social system. Sometimes they occur in the form of 'external migration' between social systems due to their specific conditions[4]. Migration can be classified as economic and non-economic migration in terms of its purpose; voluntary and involuntary migration in terms of factors that trigger migration; temporary and permanent migration in terms of its duration; transit and settled migration in terms of its final settlement; legal and illegal migration in terms of legal status, and skilled

---

[1] Doctor Faculty Member, Manisa Celal Bayar University, Faculty of Economics and Administrative Sciences Academic Member, Türkiye.

[2] Elenore Kofman, Annie Phizacklea, Parvati Raghuram, Rosemary Sales , **Gender and International Migration in Europe: Employment, Welfare and Politics**, New York. Routledge, 2000, p.1

[3] Hilal Barın, Türkiye'deki Suriyeli Kadınların Toplumsal Bağlamda Yaşadıkları Sorunlar ve Çözüm Önerileri [Syrian Women in Turkey: Social Struggles and Solution Proposals], **The Journal of Migration Studies**, Cilt 1, Sayı 2, 2015, p.12.

[4] İlhan Tekeli, Leila Erder, **İc göçler [Internal Migrations],** Ankara, Hacettepe University Publications, 1978, p.17.

migration (brain drain) and unskilled migration in terms of the characteristics of the migrants[5].

Since the second half of the 20th century, along with globalization, international migration and the problems it has caused have constituted the area of social problem to which the whole world attaches importance. The intensification of migration movements as a result of globalization and the changes in the nature of migration have included developing countries among the migration receiving-sending countries due to some economic, political and social reasons.

According to UNHCR data, there are currently 70.8 million people in the world who have been forcibly displaced due to conflict, violence and persecution. Within this number, 25.9 million people have the status of 'refugee', and nearly 4 million people live stateless, and the rest have different status[6]. The number of refugees in the world continues to increase every day. According to the calculations of the relevant institutions of the United Nations (UN) and UNHCR, 30 more people are forcibly displaced every 1 minute. Considering the refugees' countries of origin, three countries account for 53% of all refugees. Of these, 4.9 million are Syrians, 2.7 million are Afghans and 1.1 million are Somalis. Turkey has also faced the most refugee migration in the world in this process as a result of being a neighboring country to Syria and Afghanistan. Turkey hosts 3,635,410 registered Syrian refugees, as well as around 370,000 other nationals who are of UNHCR interest, according to November 2020 data. Considering these data on migration, it is possible to define migration mobility from Syria to Turkey as forced, irregular and external migration. Such an uncontrolled and mass migration has resulted from the announcement of Turkey that it would implement an 'open door policy' for Syrians and provide the basic needs such as shelter, food, hygiene of the Syrians identified by the Turkish authorities as 'guests'[7] .

This study firstly addressed the concepts of refugee, asylum seeker and migrant and tried to reveal the differences between these concepts and then discussed and evaluated the social policies on the problems experienced by the refugees living in Turkey.

Concepts of Migrant, Asylum Seeker, Refugee

The concepts of 'migrant', 'asylum-seeker' and 'refugee' are often confused with each other. The people who leave their country of residence voluntarily for various reasons, especially economic ones, and enter another country through legal means

[5] Fuat Güllüpınar, Göç Olgusunun Ekonomi-Politiği ve Uluslararası Göç Kuramları Üzerine Bir Değerlendirme [The Economy-Politics of Migration and a Review of the Theories of International Migration], **Yalova Journal of Social Sciences,** 2012, Issue: 4, pp. 67-68.

[6] UNHCR, The UN Refugee Agency, Global Appeal, 2020-2021. https://www.unhcr.org/tr/wp-content/uploads/sites/14/2020/10/Global-Appeal-2020-2021.pdf Access: 18.10.2020

[7] İbrahim Kaya, Esra Yılmaz Eren, Türkiye'deki Suriyelilerin Hukuki Durumu Arada Kalanların Hakları Ve Yükümlülükleri [The Legal Status of Syrians in Turkey: Rights and Obligations of Those Remaining in between,], İstanbul, Seta Publications 55, 2015, p.16.

and live in that country legally are called **migrant**'[8]. Migrants continue to benefit from the protection of their state of nationality, and their applications may be accepted or rejected depending on the migration policies. In this sense, these countries do not have responsibilities arising from a fundamental human right. The distinction between migrants and refugees is mainly due to the fact that migrants leave their state of nationality for economic reasons. A migrant is a person who, for reasons other than those contained in the definition of refugee, voluntarily leaves his country mostly for economic reasons in order to settle in another country within the knowledge and permission of authorities of that country[9]. Although each country has different criteria for accepting migrants, migrants do not have an international protection area as refugees have. The subject of migration covers a wide area from individuals to society, from the nation state to international organizations. Migration necessarily requires a new form of social relationship between migrants and the societies of the place to which they've migrated[10].

While the term of migrant is used as a generic term covering all foreigners in a country, it has a different meaning in Turkish law. According to Article 3/d of the Settlement Law No. 5543, migrants are 'those who are of Turkish ancestry and linked to Turkish culture and, who come to Turkey alone or collectively for the purpose of settling and recognized under this Law'. According to paragraph (c) of Article 12 of the Turkish Citizenship Law No.5901, the people who are recognized as migrants can be granted Turkish citizenship by the proposal of the Ministry of Interior and the decision of the Council of Ministers, provided that there is no obstacle in terms of national security and public order[11].

According to United Nations Glossary on Migration, an asylum seeker is defined as 'someone whose asylum request or application has not yet been finally decided on by the potential asylum country'[12]. An asylum seeker is defined as a person who meets the legal requirements of being a refugee, that is, who can prove that the reason for fleeing from his country and seeking asylum in another country is to have been exposed to persecution or the justified fear that he will be persecuted, but whose refugee status is not officially recognized[13]. The Universal Declaration of

---

[8] Taşkın Deniz, (2014). Uluslar Arası Göç Sorunu Perspektifinde Türkiye [Turkey from the Perspective of International Migration Problem],**Tsa Journal**, Cilt, 18, Sayı 1, 2014, p.176.

[9] William Peterson, Population, Macmillan; 3rd Edition 1975. Murat Urk, Göç Olgusu Bağlamında Mülteciler, Sığınmacılar ve İnsan Hakları [A Case of Immigration in the Context of Refugees Asylum Seeker and Human Rights], (Unpublished Postgraduate Thesis), İstanbul, Maltepe University, 2010, p.18

[10] Yusuf Adıgüzel, **Göç Sosyolojisi [Sociology of Immigration]**, Ankara, Noel Akademik Publishing, 2016, p. 23.

[11] Gülşen Sarı Gerşil, The Migration and Social Exclusion Dimension in Turkey and in The World, **New Trends and Issues Proceedings on Humanities and Social Sciences**, Volume 4, Issue 10, 2017, pp.238-239; .İbrahim Kaya, Esra Yılmaz Eren, **Türkiye'deki Suriyelilerin Hukuki Durumu Arada Kalanların Hakları Ve Yükümlülükleri [The Legal Status of Syrians in Turkey: Rights and Obligations of Those Remaining in between,]**, İstanbul, Seta Publications 55, 2015, p.17.

[12] United Nations Glossary on Migration, https://multeci.net/2010/08/terimler-sozlugu/

[13] Sema Buz, Zorunlu Çıkış, Zorlu Çıkış: Mültecilik [Forced Exit, Challenging Exit: Refuging], Ankara, SGDD Publications, 2004, p.8.

Human Rights[14] also included the concept of asylum.

It has been provided for the Asylum seekers to enjoy certain fundamental rights, especially the principle of 'non-refoulement', and minimum standards must be met to let them live as a human being. The status of asylum seeker is a temporary status, and after the status of refugee is recognized, it is considered that the status of refugee is valid from the very beginning. In this aspect, it can be said that status of refugee –in the legal sense– is a retroactive concept. Almost because people are refugees, this status is recognized by states, otherwise people are not refugees because the states recognize them.[15] The concept of refugee was mentioned in the 1951 Geneva Convention Relating to the Status of Refugees[16] and its 1967 Protocol signed in New York. According to the Convention and Protocol, a refugee is 'owing to well-founded fear of being persecuted for reasons of (1)race, (2) religion, (3) nationality, (4) membership of a particular social group or (5) political opinion, is outside the country of his nationality and is unable or, owing to such fear, is unwilling to avail himself of the protection of that country; or who, not having a nationality and being outside the country of his former habitual residence as a result of such events, is unable or, owing to such fear, is unwilling to return to it'. In order for a foreigner to be granted the refugee status, there must a state of danger related to these five factors, and he must fear that he will be persecuted, and this fear of persecution must be justified and he must be located outside his country. UNHCR (United Nations High Commissioner for Refugees) uses the distinction between 'refugees' and 'displaced persons' in its activities[17]. UNHCR avoided the confusion of concepts by defining 'displaced persons' as those not being granted the refugee status but seeking the right to asylum; and 'internally displaced persons' as those being displaced within a country due to various pressures[18].

Although the concepts of refugee and asylum seeker are often used to mean the same thing, being an asylum seeker with the right to asylum is de facto and short-term refuging that does not provide for availing himself of the laws of the asylum country as refugees do, rather than being granted a legal status[19].

The legal differences between the concepts of refugee and asylum seeker are expressed, according to the Convention Relating to the Status of Refugees and its 1967 Protocol, by defining refugee as 'a person entitled to benefit from the protection of the United Nations High Commissioner for Refugees', and defining

---

[14] According to Article 14 of the Declaration, everyone has the right to seek and to enjoy, in other countries, asylum from persecution"

[15] Kaya, Eren, po.cit. p.18.

[16] The Geneva Convention was adopted at the Conference convened by the United Nations General Assembly's Resolution No. 429 (V) of 14 December 1950, and signed in Geneva on 28 July 1951, and entered into force on 22 April 1954 in accordance with Article 43 thereof.

[17] Senem Ermumcu, Sığınmacıların ve Mültecilerin Sosyal Güvenlik Hakkı [Right to Social Security of Refugees and Asylum Seekers], **Journal of Labour Relations**, Cilt 4, Sayı 2, 2013, p. 65.

[18] Yücel Acer, İbrahim Kaya, and Mahir Gümüş, Küresel ve Bölgesel Perspektiften Türkiye'nin İltica Stratejisi [The Asylum Strategy of Turkey from a Global and Regional Perspective], Ankara: USAK Publications, 2010, p.16.

[19] Canan Ender Eroğlu, Ruken Taşkıran, (2002) Sığınma Hakkı ve Mültecilerin Durumu [Right to Asylum and the Situation of Refugees], **Union of Turkish Bar Associations Review**, Sayı 1, 2002, 109..

asylum seeker as 'a person willing to be recognized as as a refugee in a country within the framework of relevant national or international documents and awating the result of his application regarding the refugee status'[20]. Consequently, being a refugee with the right of sanctuary means gaining a legal status, while being an asylum seeker with the right to asylum means a de facto and short-term refuging rather than a legal status[21].

Issues Relating to Refugees

Refugees, who are forced to leave their place of residence and their homeland by being exposed to pressure and persecution due to their race, religion, ethnic and cultural differences or other economic social structures, and who try to seek refuge in safer regions or countries, cannot have complete peace and security, because of the places that they've left, in the places and countries where they seek refuge. These people are considered as unwanted in the places from which they've fled, and as a burden, a problem, a community that disturbs the order, unwanted people, sometimes spies, sometimes terrorists, and sometimes a full exploitation material in the places where they try to seek asylum[22]. Apart from being deprived of many rights from security to shelter and from health to education, refugees are subjected to persecution and ill-treatment in an undeserved way[23]. Discrimination and hatred towards refugees and migrants in the migration-receiving country may cause conflicts between local people and refugees in the long run[24].

In addition to losing, in the asylum country, their social support mechanisms, their lack of knowledge regarding the social structures, e.g. language and culture, and legal system of the country to which they've migrated also makes their living conditions even more difficult[25]. Especially for refugees, language is important not only as a means of communication, but also as an instrument that increases their capacity to find jobs and allow them to defend themselves[26]. Refugees in need of protection go on long journeys that are full of uncertainties, sometimes seeking better living conditions and sometimes a fair protection system. In our current world, millions of people without official refugee status are struggling to survive under inhumane conditions within their own countries, in the intermediate regions or in the countries where they take refuge. Those who have become refugees, orphans, widows and all victims are left alone with a difficult struggle for life under the conditions open to all kinds of abuse. If refugees are not supported, they may be exploited by groups such as organ mafia, missionary organizations and human traffickers, and they may become drug addicts and in this context, they may be

[20] Uğur Özgöker, Gözde Doğan, Uluslararası Göç ve Mülteci Krizi [International Migration and Refugee Crisis], İstanbul, Der Publications, 2019, pp.17-18.

[21] Ermumcu, po.cit, p.65.

[22] Urk, po.cit, pp. 22.

[23] Urk, po.cit, pp.22-23

[24] Özgöker, Doğan, po.cit, p.82.

[25] Urk, po.cit, pp.22-23

[26] Nurgül Çelik, Türkiye"deki Suriyeli Kadınların Mültecilillik Deneyimi [Syrian Women's Experience on Being Refugee in Turkey] (Unpublished Postgraduate Thesis), İstanbul, İstanbul University, 2019, 110.

included in criminal networks[27].

In addition to shelter, food and clothing, the psychosocial assistance and language learning requirements of all asylum seekers and refugees cause these people to face health problems such as anxiety, depression, sleep disorders, and attention deficit over time[28]. Refugees that take refuge in Turkey are faced with difficulties such as economic, social, health, educational, and psychological problems, while they generally experience psychosocial problems, e.g. not being accepted by the local people (ostracisation), fear of the local people to share the limited facilities with asylum seekers,language problems, financial problems, high expectations of asylum seekers, domestic violence, unemployment, and the problem of food, clothing and shelter, as well as anxiety, sleep disorders and mistrust[29].

According to the legislation in Turkey, it is essential that refugees and asylum seekers meet their basic needs, such as shelter, food and health, themselves in the cities to which they are sent to live. This situation further limits the participation of refugees and asylum seekers in the labor market, which is limited to them for many reasons, especially language, and their humane living[30]. The right to work is the most fundamental right for refugees, the majority of whom are poor and do not have any income, to continue their daily lives. As a result of its nationality-based refugee policy, Turkey is based on its internal law rather than the principles of the Geneva Convention on the right to work, subjecting refugees to work permits. The study by Nizam (2017) found that refugees tend to work informally because the process of obtaining a work permit is not known to many refugees, and obtaining a permit is a difficult process[31].

Due to the fact that Turkey ranks first in refugee status for those who come from Syria, the literature mainly includes studies that highlight the problems experienced by Syrian refugees. The research by Erdoğan (2019) on Syrian refugees living in Turkey explained the problems experienced by refugees in five main categories. The first category, 'economic problems and financial difficulties' include working under severe conditions, especially with lower wages compared to other Turkish citizens, while the second category contains the problems arising from 'not knowing the language and being unfamiliar with the system'. Since they do not speak Turkish, they have problems in communicating, benefiting from public services, especially health, and finding a job. Because they do not know the legal and political

---

[27] Urk, po.cit, pp.22-23

[28] Yolanda C. Padilla, Immigrant Policy: Issues for Social Work Practice, **Social Work Journal of the National Association of Social Workers**, Cilt. 6, Sayı 42, 1997, pp.601-603.

[29] Mahmut Kaya, Ebru H. Orhan Demirağ, Türkiye'deki Suriyeli Kadın Sığınmacıların İş Piyasasındaki Çalışma Koşullarına Sosyolojik Bir Bakış: Şanlıurfa Örneği [A Sociological Perspective on Working Conditions of Syrian Female Refugees in Turkey: Şanlıurfa Case], **2nd Middle East Conferences: The Problem of Migration in the Context of Conflicts in the Middle East** April 28-29, 2016-Kilis, Turkey, p.164.

[30] Urk, po.cit, p.23

[31] Özlem Kahya Nizam, Türkiye'de Dezavantajlılığın Mülteci Halleri: Haklardan uzak "Hakk"a Bırakılmış Yaşamlar [The Refugee Appearance of Disadvantageousness in Turkey: Deserted Lives to "The God" without Rights], **Society and Democracy Journal**, Volume 11, Issue 24, 2017, p.193.

system, they also experience difficulties in their rights[32]. The other problems experienced by refugees in the third category are related to 'insecurity of their statutes and uncertainty of the future' in Turkey. Especially Syrians, who are under 'temporary protection', have expressed their concern about whether they have a future in Turkey due this status which limits what they can do in Turkey (travel, work life, financial transactions and business start-up, etc.) It is stated that in this uncertain and limiting situation, the state can change its practices and regulations frequently, and in an environment where there are no institutions representing or guiding Syrians, these problems further increase. The fourth category includes spread of incidents of 'discrimination and hatred' throughout the country. With the discriminatory hate speeches spreading particularly on social media, Syrians are increasingly exposed to discrimination in their daily lives on the streets and buses and in schools, i..e in all areas of life. Finally, the category of 'other problems' include passports, continuity of education and problems related to education[33]. When refugees go to Turkey and other countries, they have problems with educational levels. For this reason, refugees are required to participate in various educational programs so that they can more easily adapt to the environment[34].

According to results of the study on Syrian Immigrants Problems conducted by Mersin University Regional Monitoring and Application Research Center (2014), one of the main problems regarding Syrian women and child migrants was identified as unaccompanied women and children. It was found that women whose husbands died and children whose parents died were one of the most important problems. Especially as a result of the placement of unaccompanied children in dormitories, the language problem and the adaptation problems they experienced with Turkish children were noted[35].

Child labor, which has become one of the major problems of the whole world, constitutes the problem experienced by refugee children, who are the greatest victims of the war in Syria. Children share their families' struggle for life since they are deprived of the right to education. These children are forced to work in jobs that are considered dangerous even for adults. The addition of heavy workload to the civil war conditions in Syria has negative physical and psychological effects on children. Syrian migrants and Syrian children are now part of the informal economy and condemned to the hardest conditions of this area[36].

---

[32] Likewise, similar findings were revealed by the study on the living conditions of Syrians in Turkey conducted by AFAD (Disaster and Emergency Management Presidency) in 2017. For details, see Disaster and Emergency Management Presidency (AFAD), Field Survey on Demographic View, Living Conditions and Future Expectations of Syrians in Turkey 2017, Ankara, 2017, pp. 110-122

[33] Murat Erdoğan, Suriyeliler Barometresi 2019 Suriyelilerle Uyum İçinde Yaşamın Çerçevesi [Syrians Barometer: 2019 Framework for Living in Harmony with Syrians], Ankara, Orion Publishing House, pp.143-145.

[34] Özgöker, Doğan, po.cit, p.33.

[35] Mersin University Regional Monitoring and Application Research Center, Suriyeli Göçmenlerin Sorunları Çalıştayı Sonuç Raporu [The Final Report of Syrian Immigrants Problems Workshop], Mersin, 2014, p. 56.

[36] Teoman Akpınar, Türkiye'deki Suriyeli Mülteci Çocukların ve Kadınların Sosyal Politika Bağlamında

Refugees and Social Policies on Refugees in Turkey

Considering the waves of collective migrations to Turkey, it can be said that they are in the form of mass migrations. We see that these migration waves are mostly migrations of Turkish and Muslim origin from neighboring countries. Besides, some migrations are regular through international agreements, and some are infrequent and irregular based on political events, and some are in the form of collective asylum requests. There are also waves of transit migrations in Turkey.

While Turkey was originally open to migrants of Turkish ancestry, the migrations to the country have diversified especially since the early 1990s. However, what is really important at this point that Turkey has become a migration-receiving country particularly since 1990s, although it was a migration-sending country since 1960s. Due to its position as a 'transit country' for migration from Asia, Africa and the Middle East to Europe, Turkey has become the target of regular and irregular migration movements[37].

There are four main factors that determine irregular migrations to Turkey. Firstly, the increasing political uncertainties and conflicts in neighboring countries have increased the desire of the people of these countries to go to places that are safer, free from persecution and have better living conditions. Secondly, the geographical structure of Turkey, located between East - West and North - South, makes the country attractive for transit migrants who want to transit to the developed Western and Northern countries. Thirdly, the migrants aiming to reach Europe have turned to the neighbouring countries of Europe as Turkey due to strict controls and increased immigration controls imposed by Europe on borders. The fourth factor is that Turkey is attractive to migrants who want to work because it offers better economic conditions than neighboring countries[38].

Yaşadıkları Sorunlar [The Problems of Syrian Refugee Children and Women in Turkey in the Context of Social Policy], **Balkan and Near Eastern Journal of Social Sciences,** Cilt 3, Sayı 3, 2017, p.23.

[37] Barın, po.cit, p.15.

[38] Deniz, po.cit, p.184-185.

Figure 1. Top International displacement situations by host country end-2019.

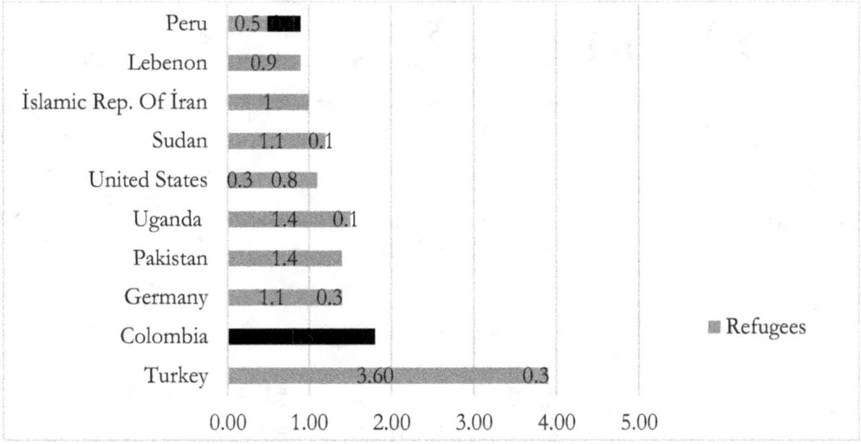

Peru 0.5
Lebenon 0.9
İslamic Rep. Of İran 1
Sudan 1.1 0.1
United States 0.3 0.8
Uganda 1.4 0.1
Pakistan 1.4
Germany 1.1 0.3
Colombia
Turkey 3.60 0.3
0.00 1.00 2.00 3.00 4.00 5.00
Refugees

Source: UNHCR, Global Trends Forced Displacement in 2019.

Turkey welcomed the highest number of people displaced across borders, 3,9 million, most of whom were Syrian refugees (92/%). Colombia followed, lodging nearly 1,8 million displaced Venezuelans, Germany opened its borders to the third largest number, almost 1.5 million, with Syrian refugees and asylum-requestors building up the largest group (42/%). Pakistan and Uganda hosted the 4th and 5th largest number, with about 1.4 million each. During crises and displacement, children adolescents and youth face with the risk of exploitation and abuse, especially while they are unattended or separated from their parents. UASC accommodated around 25,000 new asylum applications. Moreover, 153,300 unattended and separated children were recorded through the refugee population at the end of 2019. But, both figures are remarkable underestimates contingent upon the limited number of countries submitting data.

Figure 2. Migration Movements

Smugglers	Migrant	Victims	Trafficking	(Caught)	Migrant	Irregular		Permits	Residence	Entries	Illegal		(Exit)	Border Gates	Border Gates	Border Gates	(Entry)	
					600	94.		100	168.	400	51.							**2000**
					400	92.		254	161.	300	57.							**2001**
					800	82.		670	157.	200	44.							**2002**
					200	56.		203	152.	348	30.							**2003**
					200	61.		500	155.	745	34.							**2004**
			256		428	57.		964	178.	920	19.	616	672.	19.	20.	20.	275.	**2005**
			246		983	51.		058	200.	876	18.	100	373.	18.	18.	18.	916.	**2006**
			148		290	64.		208	225.	120	30.	034	926.	21.	22.	22.	249.	**2007**
			120		737	65.		926	174.	080	31.	601	096.	25.	25.	25.	002.	**2008**
			102		345	34.		326	163.			309	799.	25.	25.	25.	529.	**2009**
711	1.		58		667	32.		301	182.			422	448	26.	26.	26.	623.	**2010**
292	1.		82		415	44.		288	234.			647	976.	28.	29.	29.	093.	**2011**
484	1.		55		510	47.		548	321.			892	573.	29.	29.	29.	704.	**2012**
469	1.		21		890	39.		692	313.			760	639.	32.	32.	32.	865.	**2013**
506	1.		50		647	58.		804	379.			393	780.	34.	35.	35.	115.	**2014**
471	4.		108		485	146.		895	422.			711	285.	34.	34.	34.	633.	**2015**
314	3.		181		466	174.		217	461.			273	718.	24.	24.	24.	686.	**2016**
641	4.		303		752	175.		151	593.			516	003.	32.	32.	32.	058.	**2017**
278	6.		134		003	268.		470	856.			104	315.	39.	39.	39.	468.	**2018**
996	8.		215		662	454.	030	101	1.			083	579.	44.	44.	44.	527.	**2019**
356	1.		46		459	47.	934	107	1.									**2020**

Deportees		International	Protection	Temporary	Protection	
		5.	700			
		5.	200			
		3.	794			
		3.	966			
		3.	908			
30.	789	3.	914			
68.	343	4.	548			
123.	035	7.	690			
173.	943	12.	981			
197.	943					
221.	526	8.	932			
248.	415	17.	925			
269.	415	29.	678	14.	237	
294.	572	30.	311	224.	655	
		34.	112	1.	519.	286
		64.	232	2.	503.	549
		66.	167	2.	834.	441
		112.	415	3.	426.	786
		114.	537	3.	623.	192
95.	000	56.	417	3.	576.	370
				3.	583.	584

Source: Anadolu Agency, 2019; Directorate General of Migration Management, 2015; Directorate General of Migration Management, 2016; Directorate General of Migration Management, 2020; Ahmet İçduygu, Yener Şişman citing from Deniz Yükseler 2010, Bora Balun, Transit Göç ve Türkiye [Transit Migration and Turkey], Anadolu University Journal of Economics and Administrative Sciences, Volume 21, Issue 2, p.75. (The data for 2020 covers the period from January 01 to April 15).

Comparing the past and present experiences on the external migration and/or foreigner entry-exit numbers, it is seen that there is a steadily growing interest in Turkey. According to Figure 1, Turkey granted temporary protection status to Syrian citizens, which began with 14,237 people in 2012 and reached 3,580,263 by April 2020. Similarly, considering the recent mean of the migrants applying for international protection, it is understood that an average of 63,483 people make international protection applications annually. Similar developments are also observed in the number of irregular migrants caught and migrant smugglers.

As a result of the migrations, Turkey has adopted a number of legal regulations on international migration in order to determine the status of foreigners and to regulate their rights and obligations. The procedures to be applied to refugees and migrants are addressed by some articles of the Settlement Law No.2150, which was first enacted on 14.06.1934, and Passport Law No.5682 of 15.07.1950, and the Law No.5683 on Residence and Travel of Foreigners in Turkey enacted on 15.07.1950[39]. Depending on the international agreements signed by Turkey, the current legal status of Syrian asylum seekers who do not have a refugee status causes them to have various problems benefiting from the opportunities of settlement, business establishment, work, education and health opportunities etc. Turkey established its

[39] Adem Çiçeksöğüt, "Uluslararası Göç Hukuku Perspektifinde Yerinden Edilmiş Suriyeliler'in Türkiye'deki Statüsü"[The Status of Displaced Syrians in Turkey in the Perspective of International Migration Law], **Kırklareli University Journal of Economics and Administrative Sciences**, Sayı 6, Cilt 2, 2017, p.3.

legislation for refugees by signing the 1951 Geneva Convention Relating to the Status of Refugees. However, Turkey, which made reservations with 'time' and 'geographical limitation' in this Convention, maintained the geographical limitation exactly and removed the time limitation with the 1967 Protocol. Thus, refugee status is granted only to people from Europe in Turkey. Those from outside Europe can take temporary refuge in Turkey and are assigned 'asylum seeker' status[40]. This means that Turkey does not grant refugee status to asylum seekers from outside European countries, and defines the persons, meeting the qualifications of refugee status according to the provisions of the Convention, as 'conditional refugees'[41], and provides international protection until they are resettled in a third country[42]. This situation implies that refugees live in Turkey in a disadvantaged position in which they are deprived of both refugee and civil rights, and at this point, the duration of their stay in Turkey becomes problematic in terms of their daily life and future prospects. In fact, the emphasis on 'guest' identity under various statuses by avoiding granting the refugee status marks the uncertainty of the life and future of refugees in Turkey[43].

One of the most important developments in this period was opening, in 1960, of the United Nations Refugee Agency, with representation in Turkey, of the United Nations High Commissioner for Refugees (UNHCR), which was established in 1950 in line with the rights and obligations set out in the 1951 Geneva Convention, in order to coordinate and carry out international activities for solving refugee problems and protecting refugees. With the increasing importance of Turkey in terms of asylum, the main tasks undertaken by UNHCR are to support the efforts to strengthen the asylum system in Turkey, to oversee compliance of the asylum system in Turkey with international agreements, to make recommendations to the Turkish government on the situation of refugees from outside Europe and provide permanent solutions for them, and to help refugees meet their basic needs during their stay in Turkey[44]. The United Nations High Commissioner for Refugees provides support to refugees in the field of education, livelihood, camp, capacity (expertise) building, protection of rights, security, provision of basic needs and resettlement in a third country[45].

In order for Turkey to build an asylum system in accordance with international

---

[40] Saniye Dedeoğlu, Çisel Ekiz Gökmen, Göç ve Sosyal Dışlanma Türkiye'de Yabancı Göçmen Kadınlar [Migration and Social Exclusion: Foreign Women Migrants in Turkey], Ankara, Efil Publishing House, 2011, p.60.

[41] https://www.goc.gov.tr/kurumlar/goc.gov.tr/YillikGocRaporlari/2016_yiik_goc_raporu_haziran.pdf

[42] Kaya, Eren, po.cit, p. 23. Reyhan Atasü Topçuoğlu, Türkiye'de Göçmen Çocukların Profili, Sosyal Politika ve Sosyal Hizmet Önerileri Hızlı Değerlendirme Araştırması [Profiling Migrant Children in Turkey, Social Policy and Social Work Suggestions: A Rapid Assessment Research], 2012, pp. 19-20.

[43] Nizam, po.cit. pp.190-191.

[44] Saime Özçürümez, Şirin Türkay, "Türkiye'de İltica Politikası, Aktörleri ve Çalışmaları: Bir Epistemik Topluluk Oluşurken" [Asylum Policy, Actors and Studies in Turkey: Creating an Epistemic Community], **İltica, Uluslararası Göç ve Vatansızlık: Kuram, Gözlem ve Politika [Asylum, International Migration and Statelessness: Theory, Observation and Politics]**, the United Nations High Commissioner for Refugees Publications, 2011, p. 29.

[45] UNHCR (2017), http://www.unhcr.org/tr/turkiyedeki-multeciler-ve-siginmacilar, Erişim:.25.04.2020

standards with respect to refugees, the first asylum law, the Law on Foreigners and International Protection, entered into force on 11 April 2014. This law also regulates how foreigners will be protected upon request for protection, apart from their entry into Turkey, stay and exit from Turkey, in order to establish the basic foundations of Turkey's national asylum system. Upon satisfaction of the necessay conditions, the Directorate General of Migration Management[46] was established as an institution responsible for all transactions related to foreigners in Turkey[47].

Social policy practices are carried out within the scope of education, health, right to work and social assistance for refugees living in Turkey. Freedom of education and training is guaranteed for everyone under Article 42 of the Constitution of the Republic of Turkey. The regulations on the freedom of education and training are addressed in the Law on Foreigners and International Protection (LFIP), the Basic Law of National Education and the Law on Social Services and Child Protection Agency and Child Protection Laws. According to LFIP Art.89/1, the applicant or the person who has international protection status and his/her family members benefit from primary and secondary education services. Through the educational services provided to Syrian citizens under temporary protection in Turkey, the Ministry of National Education of Turkey aims to ensure that Syrian children are not a lost generation and can build a good future for themselves. It also supports these people to adapt to society.

One of the most important problems of refugees is that they do not speak Turkish. While those of Turkmen origin do not experience this problem, a great majority of them have difficulty communicating due to the language problem. They can't carry out formal transactions, and they don't know what to do when they have health problems, and they can't master the rules about working life[48]. For this reason, in addition to formal education, non-formal educational activities are performed to develop language learning and personal and professional skills in an environment where Syrian adults feel safe and secure for themselves and their families. In this context, 'Immigration and Emergency Education Department' was established within the General Directorate of Lifelong Learning.

In public education centers[49], which play a key role in the process of social adaptation and integration of refugees, the right to participate in courses has been provided in order to allow young and adult people to gain professional skills especially in the field of Turkish language learning[50]. As a result of the agreement signed between the Turkish Ministry of National Education and the EU Delegation

[46] The Temporary Protection Regulation, which sets out the rights, obligations and procedures related to persons granted temporary protection, was adopted on 22 October 2014 in Turkey.

[47] Ali Nazım Sözer, Türk Sosyal Hukuk (Yoksulluk/Yoksunluk Mevzuatı) [Turkish Social Law; Poverty/Deprivation Legislation] , Beta Publishing House, İstanbul, 2020.

[48] Ahmet Koyuncu, **Kentin Yeni Misafirleri [New Guests of the City]**, Konya, Çizgi Publishing House, p.24.

[49] Sözer, po.cit. p.345.

[50] Tuba Duman, Toplumsal Uyum İçin Eğitimin Önemi: Türkiye'deki Suriyeliler Örneği [Significance of Education towards Social Cohesion: The Case of Syrian Refugees in Turkey], **Selçuk University Journal of Faulty of Letters**, 2019; Issue 41, 347-348.

to Turkey under the framework of the EU Facility for Refugees in Turkey (FRIT), the 'Project on Promoting Integration of Syrian Kids into the Turkish Education System' (PIKTES project) was launched on 03.10.2016. For the entegration of the Syrian Kids into the Turkish Education System, the Project covers the Turkish and Arabic language education, catch-up and back-up trainings for the students with lost year and adaptation problems, counseling and guidance activities, training on Turkish language examination system, awareness-raising activities, training of administrative staff and other staff and trainers as well as more economic-based activities including transportation service, stationery assistance and provision of cleaning and security staff for schools[51]. Regarding universities, students can enroll in universities and continue their education with the opportunities provided by the Higher Education Council (YÖK).

The right to work is the most fundamental right for refugees, the majority of whom are poor and do not have any income, to continue their daily lives. Since the right to work is considered as a universal human right, international agreements include regulations on the right to work. The issues related to the right to work are addressed in the 1951 Geneva Convention, especially the Universal Declaration of Human Rights[52]. According to the Convention, refugees have the right to work either under paid-employment or self-employment. As a result of its nationality-based refugee policy, Turkey is based on its internal law rather than the principles of the Geneva Convention on the right to work, subjecting refugees to work permits[53]. A person with refugee or secondary protection status is given the opportunity to work from the moment he/she's granted such status. He/she can be employed (as worker) or self-employed (on his/her own behalf/account). Applicants or conditional refugees can apply for a work permit six months after their application for international protection[54].

Regarding access to the labor market, the LFIP allows conditional refugees to apply for a work permit six months after the date of application for international protection, and the refugee or the person with subsidiary protection status can be employed or self-employed from the date when he/she is granted the status. In addition, according to the Temporary Protection Regulation No. 6883, Syrian refugees have the right to work as registered. Despite all these policies, refugees are employed at very low wages without a work permit. Syrians who do not have a residence permit work in daily jobs and as seasonal workers in croplands. Syrians who do not know that they have the right to work are unaware of their rights and

---

[51] Duman, ibid., p.353.

[52] In accordance with Article 6 and 23 of the Universal Declaration of Human Rights, everyone has the right to work and to free choice of employment without discrimination.

[53] Kahya, po,cit, p. 913.

[54] Foreigners cannot work in all jobs and professions and are subject to the restrictive provisions contained in the legislation on this issue. In addition, for those not subject to restrictions, when deemed necessary, restrictions can be imposed for some sectors (agriculture, industry or service sectors), some occupations and areas (civil and geographical) for a certain period of time. Law No. 6458 on Foreigners and International Protection of 4.4.2013, Article 89.

agree low wages to make a living[55].

Another important right of refugees in their daily lives is the right to health. According to the legal regulation, if non-European refugees cannot afford their health expenses through their own means or through UNHCR and they do not have any social security, their health expenses are covered by the state within the scope of legislation and possibilities[56]. In addition, the people with special needs (people exposed to torture, sexual assault or other serious psychological, physical or sexual violence) are provided with opportunities of **adequate treatment** to remedy the ailments they've been exposed to.[57]

In-kind and in-cash support can be provided by the Directorate General of Migration Management when applicants of international protection and persons with international protection status want to repatriate voluntarily. The Directorate General can cooperate with public institutions and organizations, non-governmental organizations and international organizations for repatriation.[58]

Some services are provided to international protection status beneficiaries and their family members. Those in need can have access to **social assistance and services**. For example, unaccompanied minors applying for international protection are placed in institutions by the Ministry of Family, Labor and Social Services, after asking their opinions.

Results

Forced migration movements are not a new phenomenon all over the world, and there have been very significant number of mass migration flows in every period of history. Turkey currently faces many problems as a country providing protection to the most refugees in the world. While granting some rights to migrants, Turkey did not discriminate between qualified or unskilled ones, and it accepted, all those, without any distinction, e.g. children, young people, women and the elderly, who fled war, violence, difficult conditions and took refuge. In Turkey's refugee policies, the inclusion of refugees in different categories and definitions causes different practices, especially in terms of status and rights. Refugees who have taken refuge in Turkey have been able to live in camps since their arrival. Besides, Turkey has attached importance to social policies that would allow refugees to benefit from health and education, the right to work, and social assistance opportunities. However, the measures taken are insufficient to enable these groups to have the humane living conditions. The reason why the policies of Turkey to solve the problems of refugees are insufficient is that they focus on short-term and temporary solutions because they consider the refugees as temporary guests.

[55] Koyuncu, po.cit. p.32.
[56] Law No.5510 on Social Insurance and General Health Insurance of 31/5/2006
[57] Sözer, po.cit. p.346.
[58] Law No.6458 Article 87

Turkey mostly meets the need for education of the Syrians, along with all their needs, admitted into the camps, but there are some problems with the access to education of Syrian children living outside the camps. In addition, refugees have been granted work permits, but many are still employed informally, working at very low wages and under heavy conditions. With the (LFIP) having emerged within the framework of legal legislation, the Directorate General of Migration Management undertakes important tasks to implement the changing migration and migrant policies of Turkey. However, it will be appropriate to concentrate on the projects in cooperation with NGOs and other public institutions in order to make such practices more effective.

CHAPTER 4

SERVICES AND RIGHTS PROVIDED FOR REFUGEES IN TURKEY

Talip Menekşe[1] and Soyalp Tamçelik[2]

Introduction

History is filled with the struggle for life of the migrating. People who have to leave their place of birth and life due to various reasons often struggle to survive in a new country where they do not know their language, culture and many features. Access to rights and services is of great importance for people who have to leave their country and seek international protection by claiming asylum in another country. In the process that begins with the request for asylum, in the country where the foreigner is seeking international protection, foreign has the fundamental rights specified in international regulations, but also has given chance to access to other rights and services within the framework of the country's own national legislation. The right to asylum is at the fore of these rights. The general framework of international refugee law was established with the 1951 Geneva Convention[3] on the Legal Status of Refugees and the 1967 Protocol[4] on the Legal Status of Refugees. In this context, within the scope of the rights of the applicant in need of international protection arising from international regulations; *the right not to be sent to a place where there is a risk of torture, ill-treatment, inhuman and degrading treatment (non-refulman), the right to residence, freedom of thought, belief and religion, the right to access judiciary and appeal, the right to education, the right to access health services, the right to work has rights such as the right to benefit from social benefits, the right to request information and the right to privacy*. In addition to the basic rights set forth in international refugee law, Turkey presents many opportunities for foreign access to rights and services that provide international protection in a nationally.

In terms of access to rights and services Turkey is an important country. Turkey, a country that throughout history has been hosting many foreigners in the territory and is the country where most asylum seekers live in the world today.[5] Turkey has become a party to many other international regulations on human rights together with the 1951 Geneva Convention and 1967 Protocol. Although Turkey has offer

[1] Migration Expert, Decision Centers/Mobile Decision Teams Founder and General Coordinator (2016 - December 2019), Department of International Protection, Directorate General of Migration Management, Ministry of Interior. ORCID ID: 0000-0002-6423-9331, E-mail: talip-menekse@hotmail.com

[2] Prof. Dr.; Ankara Hacı Bayram Veli University, Faculty of Economics and Administrative Sciences, International Relations Department, ORCID ID: 0000-0002-2092-8557, E-mail: soyalp@hotmail.com

[3] It will then be mentioned as the "*1951Geneva Convention*".

[4] Also known as the New York Protocol. In the study, The Protocol will then be called the "*1967Protocol*".

[5] UNHCR, **Trends at a Glance**, https://www.unhcr.org/tr/ilk-bakista-rakamlar-2, (Access 02.07.2020).

is a constant immigration country in its geography presents a fairly inclusive attitude regarding rights and services. As a matter of fact, due to the Syrian Civil War that started in 2011 people who are forced displaced from Syria and seeking international protection from Turkey these are more than 3.6 million Syrians and with foreigners from other nationalities, Turkey provide access to many rights and services to these foreigners within the scope of international protection.[6] Thus, in this study, the rights and services provided to foreigners in Turkey within the scope of international protection will be discussed.[7] Fundamental definitions of refugee law will be made within the framework of the development of international refugee law. Thus, the place of the international definitions in the *Turkish International Protection System* will be determined more clearly. Then first of all rights and freedoms guaranteed in the international area with the 1951 Geneva Convention will be examined, will be evaluated after the rights and freedoms provided for refugees in Turkey's national legislation.[8] In doing this, the differences between individual international protection and temporary protection status processes will be considered. Thus, providing rights and offered services within both status types will be more clearly defined. In this study, while the rights and services in *Turkish International Protection Law* will be handled in an integrated structure, the differences between the statuses in Turkish International Protection Law will be presented comparatively.

In the study, literature review was conducted by examining domestic and foreign monographs, articles, documents, thesis, project activities and legislation studies. In the study, national and international refugee law was examined with a structuralist-functionalist perspective and descriptive method. Within the framework of all these studies and analyzes, the study was concluded by making a general evaluation.

Historical Background and Basic Concepts

While investigating the rights and obligations of refugees, the historical development of international refugee law should be examined first. The issue of why the definition of refugee is needed in the international area will contribute to better understanding of rights and obligations. Based on analogy to be drawn here, in the framework of basic terms and definitions relating to international protection in the context of national law for Turkey, it will provide a clear framework

---

[6] Talip Menekşe, **Uluslararası Sistemde İltica: Almanya, İngiltere ve Türkiye'nin Karşılaştırmalı Analizi (Asylum in International System: Germany, England And Turkey Comparative Analysis)**, Gazi University, Unpublished master's degree Thesis, 2019, pp. 61-63.

[7] Within the scope of this study, the term of *international protection* will be used for foreigners whose work and transactions are carried out under *Temporary Protection Status*. This situation will be expressed in the following parts broader. Because, due to the *mass influx* of persons under temporary protection, *individual status determination procedures* cannot be made. So, with foreigners taken under temporary protection as an individual requiring international protection to foreigners, Turkey as a country that provides protection outside their own country. Therefore, even if it is specified as *temporary protection*, temporary protection is considered within *international protection* in the *Turkish International Protection Legislation*.

[8] In this study, in the expression regarding rights and services which provided for *refugees* in the *Turkish National Legislation*, the term of "*refugee*" will be used an *umbrella term* that includes *individual international protection* and *temporary protection*.

describing the rights and obligations of foreigners.

Development of Refugee Law and Refugee Definition in International Regulations

The history of the term asylum actually goes back many years ago. The words '*asylon/asylia*' and '*refuge*' mean '*personal immunity, free from violence*' in the ancient Greek meaning of asylum originating in Latin.[9] These terms started to be used in the meaning of '*generally safe or secure place*' after the 1640s. In 1685, the term asylum began to be used for people seeking international protection for religious or political reasons in England, and the definition of '*refugee*' was made for the first time with the *Foreigners Act of 1905*. Accordingly, a person who wants to enter the country for religious or political reasons is defined as a refugee if there is a possibility of persecution in case of returning to his/her country.[10] Although the right to asylum is a very old right, its regulation in the international arena is considered quite new. In Article 14 of the 1948 Universal Declaration of Human Rights (UDHR), every person can apply to asylum in other countries because of persecution and in this situation, countries should treat these persons as a refugee.[11] Thus, the *right to asylum* was accepted in the United Nations General Assembly (UNSC) on December 10, 1948 and gained universal character by being regulated in the UDHR.

The development process of international refugee law can also be considered quite new. Because 2 applications are important in the development of refugee law in the modern sense. The first of these is the acceptance of '*non-extradition of political criminals*' as an inter-state practice in XIX century. Another is *mass escapes* that started at the beginning of the XX. century. Because throughout history, people have always migrated to another place for safety. The responsibility of the international community to find a solution for these immigrants extends to the League of Nations. The League of Nations defined refugees by categorizing them according to their country of origin. These are: Russian refugees in 1921, Armenians in 1924, Syriac, Assyrian-Chaldean and Turkish refugees in 1928.

The regulations on refugees are basically started to emerge after World War II. Millions of people were forcibly displaced after the devastation of the World War II. *International Refugee Organization* was established between 1947-1950 to deal with the refugee problem in Europe after the Second World War II.[12] After 1950, it was agreed to establish the United Nations High Commissioner for Refugees (UNHCR) with a 3-year mission in order to meet the needs of refugees.[13] Under the leadership of the United Nations (UN) as the first universal binding refugee protection tool,

---

[9] Işıl Özkan, **Göç, İltica ve Sığınma Hukuku**, Ankara, Seçkin Yayınları, 2013, pp. 40-41.

[10] Alyssa Girvan, **The History of British Immigration Policy (1905-2016) Timeline Resource**, Refugee History, 2018.

[11] Turkish Official Gazette, **Cabinet Decision on the Adoption of the Universal Declaration of Human Rights**, Date of Official Gazette: 27.05.1949. Official Gazette No. 7217, pp. 16199-16201.

[12] Guy Goodwin-Gill and Jane McAdam, **The Refugee in International Law**, Oxford, 2007, p. 424.

[13] United Nations High Commissioner for Refugees (UNHCR), **Statue of The Office of The United Nations High Commissioner for Refugees, Geneva**, 2010.

the international community has started to make arrangements in this area. The first of these regulations and the contract that forms the basis of international refugee law is the 1951 Geneva Convention.

The 1951 Geneva Convention has defined *refugee law* in general terms. In the convention, which deals with the rights of the refugee, the obligations of the refugees to the state from which they seek asylum has also regulated. The 1951 Geneva Convention has basically made the definition of '*refugee*'. According to the convention, the refugee was defined as; Refugee; is a person who has a well-founded fear due to his race, religion, nationality, determined social group or political views, and who cannot or does not want to receive protection from his/her own country and who seeks international protection in another country.[14] However, this brought about a point of discussion. Because in the 1951 Geneva Convention there is no definition was made for *asylum seeker* or *international protection applicant/ status holder* or any other international protection status. Therefore, when the phrase refugee in the 1951 Geneva Convention is evaluated as a status only, asylum seekers who are in need of international protection but have not yet received a status and those who are outside the refugee status but fall within the scope of other statuses in need of protection are excluded from the refugee law. According to the view that gains weight in the international area due to this, the definition of *refugee* in 1951 Geneva Convention expresses an international protection covering both *asylum seekers* and *refugees*. Refugee law includes the period of asylum valid until the time a person gains refugee status. In this respect, the refugee law has contributed to the preparation of international regulations not only for refugees but also for asylum seekers and other foreigners and stateless persons in need of international protection. This situation has also provided the development of *international protection law*.[15]

International Protection and Types of International Protection in the Turkish International Protection System

International protection or *asylum* with a general definition; It is the process that starts with the person requesting protection from another country for the protection that he/she could not get from his/her own country due to being under persecution, as discussed in Article 14 of UDHR. Due to the different reasons for *international protection*, there are different names in the statuses recognised to these persons. There are generally two types of *international protection*. These are refugee and subsidiary protection statuses. However, it can occur in different statuses due to applications that may differ between countries. Accordingly, other protection types can be gathered under *conditional refugee, temporary protection* and *humanitarian protection*.

The scope and types of international protection in the Turkish International Protection System are basically determined by the Law on Foreigners and

[14] United Nations High Commissioner for Refugees (UNHCR), 1951 Geneva Convention on the Legal Status of Refugees, 1967 Protocol, European Human Rights Convention, Geneva, 2007.
[15] Menekşe, op. cit, 2019. p. 7.

International Protection (LFIP) numbered 6458, which entered into force after being published in the Official Gazette dated 11 April 2013 and numbered 28615. Thus, the legal basis was formed for procedures foreigners and international protection issues in Turkey.[16] In the LFIP, the term international protection is defined in Article 3 titled '*Definitions*'. According to LFIP *International protection statu refers to the status of refugee, conditional refugee and subsidiary protection.* In the definition made in this form, the term international protection is expressed by defining the types of status expressed rather than the meaning contained in the term *international protection.* Based on this, when a grammatical interpretation is made, *temporary protection* falls outside the field of *international protection.* However, in the Turkish Asylum System, temporary protection is a term within the international protection area. Foreigners under *temporary protection* status are included in the scope of international protection in accordance with the spirit of refugee law, even if they are not directly included in the sharp definitions regarding *international protection* in LFIP.

Refugee

The *refugee* definition in the Turkish International Protection System is the same as the refugee definition in the 1951 Geneva Convention. LFIP is defined in Article 61 as a refugee: As stated in the 1951 Geneva Convention, it is a person from a European country who left his/her country as a result of well-founded fear due to *five reasons* (race, religion, nationality, determined social group or political views) and who could be persecuted in case of returning to his/her country.[17] Accordingly, the person eligible for refugee status is specified in *five criteria* and defined as foreigners/stateless persons from European countries who have at least one or more of the above-mentioned reasons.

Conditional Refugee

In the Turkish International Protection System, the same expressions are used in the definition of refugee and *conditional refugee*, except for a few points. Namely, in the conditional refugee definition in Article 62 of the LFIP is almost the same as the refugee definition in Article 61 of the LFIP. For conditional refugee status, at least one of the five criteria and a well-founded fear are sought. However, the crucial point of departure in the conditional refugee definition is the criteria for coming from a country other than Europe. Another distinction is that conditional refugee status is granted until resettlement in a third country.[18] As it can be understood from here, while determining the status in the Turkish International Protection System, the same reasons are sought in the definition of *refugee* and *conditional refugee.*[19] However, the main difference between the two statuses is whether they come from

---

[16] *The Directorate General of Migration Management (DGMM)* was established as a civilian institution with LFIP as the institution that will carry out the work and transactions related to foreigners and international protection.

[17] See… Turkish Official Gazette, (2013). 6458 Sayılı Yabancılar ve Uluslararası Koruma Kanunu (Law on Foreigners and International Protection No 6458), No. 28615, 11 April 2013, Article 61.

[18] See… LFIP Article 62.

[19] These reasons are stated in the refugee definition and stated as five criteria; It is race, religion, nationality, membership of a particular social group and political opinion.

a European country or not. While the refugee status determination is made for a person coming from European countries who is seeking international protection and has at least one of the five criteria, a conditional refugee status determination is made for an *international protection* applicant who is in the same condition as this person because of comes from a non-European country.[20] However, there are no big differences in terms of the rights provided and the services provided, both for *refugees* and *conditional refugees.*

Subsidiary Protection

Subsidiary protection is a type of *international protection* developed for people who fall outside the five criteria for refugee status, but who are at risk of serious harm. The person eligible for *subsidiary protection* and the status of subsidiary protection are defined in Article 2 of the European Union (EU) legislation, 2004 and 2004/83 EC of the EU Council Directive.[21] *The subsidiary protection status* in the Turkish International Protection System is regulated in LFIP Article 63, similar to the definition in the EU Qualifications Directive. Accordingly, in the provision regarding *subsidiary protection* stated that; Secondary protection status has been arranged for a person who is not included in the scope of refugee or conditional refugee status, but who will / may be subjected to death penalty, torture, inhuman treatment or degrading punishment or indiscriminate acts of violence in the country or international arena if sent to his/her country.[22]

The Relationship between Temporary Protection Status and Refugee Status in the Turkish International Protection System

Although there are differences in the definition or interpretation of the countries, *temporary protection* is a type of international protection that is massively requested from another country in order to find emergency and temporary protection. In fact, the basis of temporary protection is to demand international protection from another country. However, the main distinction point here is that this request for international protection is not made individually, but collectively/massively. As a matter of fact, individuals can always request *international protection* individually due to the events they experience. However, apart from individual reasons, especially civil war, international war, rebellion, indiscriminate violence, etc. In cases, there may be mostly mass migrations. For the state, which will meet thousands, maybe hundreds of thousands of foreigners at its border in a short time and provide international protection, this situation makes it very difficult to make individual refugee status determination procedures for each foreigner. Due to this, *temporary protection status* is applied for these *international protection* requests made collectively. Thus, both these people are provided with

---

[20] The reason for this, while being party of 1951 Geneva Convention, Turkey reserved the "*geographical limitation*" right.

[21] It will be mentioned as "*EU Qualification Directive*". See... European Union [EU] Official Gazette (2004). Dated 29 April 2004 and numbered 2004/83 EC EU Council Directive. 2004/09/30- L 304/12.

[22] See… LFIP Article 63.

international protection and their urgent and basic needs are met.

Temporary protection is regulated in Article 91 in LFIP. Accordingly, temporary protection is arranged for people who have to leave their country, seek emergency and temporary protection, and come to our borders on masse.[23] In other words, in the context of LFIP, although temporary protection is not counted by name among the types of international protection, persons under *temporary protection* are persons under international protection, just like the applicants who request individual international protection. Even if there are differences in the transactions of applicants who individually request international protection and those who come in masse and demand international protection, this situation should not be interpreted as a *temporary protection* status is type of a outside of international protection or international protection is not provided for those under *temporary protection.*

Rights and Freedoms of Refugees

In the historical process, refugees are people who have always had to migrate from their countries and lack of effective state protection. They have tried to find state protection, which they could not find in their country, by taking refuge in another state. This situation has made it necessary to determine the fundamental rights of refugees in the international arena and to provide these rights to them by the state parties. The rights and freedoms of refugees in the international area are fundamentally determined by the 1951 Geneva Convention. Other international human rights documents regarding fundamental human rights also play a complementary role in the 1951 Geneva Convention. In the Turkish National Legislation, the rights and freedoms of foreigners within the scope of international protection are regulated with LFIP and the sub-regulation of the LFIP.

Rights and Freedoms Secured by the 1951 Geneva Convention

1951 Geneva Convention, in general manner, determines the rights of refugees for the state parties. However, first and foremost of the exercise of these rights is to comply with the order of state party.[24] As a matter of fact, it was stated in the 1951 Geneva Convention that the term of *refugee* is an umbrella term that includes asylum seekers and refugees. Therefore, some of the rights regulated in the 1951 Geneva Convention are rights that must be provided regardless of the status of the person, and some of them may vary according to the status of the applicant. Apart from this, the way of foreigner's presence is in the country may also create differences in the context of the rights granted to him/her.

Many rights are mentioned in 1951 Geneva Convention that must be provided to refugees by the state parties. Prior to the implementation of these rights, a protective provision was made for refugees called as '*non-refoulement principle*' and '*the principle of non-punishment*'. These principles are designed to protect the refugees who

[23] See… LFIP Article 91.

[24] See... 1951 Geneva Convention Article 2.

do not/cannot enter into the state party lawfully due to the importance of the situation they are in, and to not send them to the place where they can be persecuted again. Because, refugees, who have to leave their country due to the persecution they have or may experience, can enter into the territory of the state party by coming directly and without permission. It was stated that if the refugees in this situation provide acceptable reasons for such illegal entry or presence by applying to the competent authority without delay, they shall not be subjected to criminal action for breaching the terms.[25] *The principle of non-punishment* expresses this and prevents the refugees from being punished or directly deported due to illegal entry into or presence in the territory of the State party. *Non-refoulement principle* interdicts that the refugee shall be returned to a place where his/her life or freedom would be threatened on account of his/her race, religion, nationality, membership of a particular social group or political opinion.[26] This situation is one of the most basic norms of refugee law.

In addition to these basic principles, many other rights are also regulated. The main point about the rights stated in the 1951 Geneva Convention for refugees is the general treatment standard. In other words, state parties shall accord to refugees the same treatment as is accorded to *aliens generally*.[27] This situation partially guarantees the protection provided for refugees.[28] Within the framework of this basic understanding, the rights that must be provided by the state parties have specified. Article 3 of Geneva Convention includes that the provisions of this Convention are applied to refugees without discrimination as to race, religion or country of origin by state parties. Following the prohibition of discrimination, freedom of religion is regulated in Article 4. State parties commit to accord to refugees within their territories treatment at least as favourable as that accorded to their nationals with respect to freedom to practise their religion with this article. When the 1951 Geneva Convention is examined, in the provisions regulating the rights of refugees, the issues of '*being treated as a citizen of the state party*' or '*the implementation of treatment applied to at least the citizen of the state party*' were expressed many times. This situation is accepted as a protective approach that guarantees the protection offered by the 1951 Geneva Convention to refugees. In the 1951 Geneva Convention, it is also stated that the 1951 Geneva Convention will not violate other rights and interests which if the state party wants to provide rights outside of the contract.[29] Thus, all kinds of services and rights to be provided by the state party for refugees are put under protection. These are all expression of the 1951 Geneva Convention's protective mission for the rights of refugees. It is also regulated that after a period of three years' residence, all refugees shall enjoy exemption from legislative reciprocity in the territory of the state party.[30] In the 1951 Geneva Convention it was stated that refugees should not be granted less rights than other

[25] See... 1951 Geneva Convention Article 31.
[26] See... 1951 Geneva Convention Article 33.
[27] See... 1951 Geneva Convention Article 7.
[28] Özkan, op.cit., p. 315.
[29] See... 1951 Geneva Convention Article 5.
[30] See... 1951 Geneva Convention Article 7.

foreigners in acquiring movable and immovable property.[31] It was stated that the refugees would benefit from the same protection provided by the state party to their citizens regarding intellectual, industrial property rights, literary, artistic and scientific studies.[32] Similarly, the right of every refugee to apply to the courts, legal aid and security interest, the right to work in a paid profession, the right to pay according to the working hour, the right to open a business and establish a company in agriculture, industry, trade, social assistance, housing, basic education, place of residence It was stated that they have rights in the titles of choosing, identity and travel document, and when providing the these rights for refugees, the state party should make arrangements in a way that is not less than the right provided to its citizens.[33] On the other hand, it was stated that in the matters of taxes, duties and fees that could be demanded from them in return for the services offered to refugees, this should be applied at a rate not higher than that applied by the state party to its own citizens.[34] Thus, in the 1951 Geneva Convention, it has been stated many times that the states parties should treat to the refugees as their own citizens regarding both providing rights/services and duties to be imposed on the refugees. Article 34 of the 1951 Geneva Convention calls upon the states parties to facilitate the absorption and naturalization of refugees. Therefore, the expression of '*being treated like a citizen*' expressed within each right in the context of rights for refugees has been emphasized once again as the final naturalization of the refugee with this article.

Rights and Freedoms of Refugees in Turkish International Protection System

In Turkish International Protection System, the rights and freedoms of refugees are basically regulated by the law No. 6458 LFIP. Many rights mentioned in 1951 Geneva Convention, are put under protection in also LFIP by regulating similarly. In the context of refugees, foreigners who are under international protection and temporary protection, gain many rights and access opportunities to the service regardless of differences status from the first moment they entry into Turkey and after applying for international protection. This reveals importance of rights and services provided by Turkey to refugees as a country hosts the most refugees in the World in the international arena. In the study, foreigners who demand individual international protection and foreigners under temporary protection will be examined together in terms of access to each right and service.

The rights and obligations are regulated in the third section of LFIP. The 88th Article of LFIP includes that international protection beneficiaries are exempted from reciprocity principle.[35] It is also stipulated that the rights and services provided to persons under international protection cannot be interpreted in a way that

[31] See... 1951 Geneva Convention Article 13.
[32] See... 1951 Geneva Convention Article 14.
[33] See... 1951 Geneva Convention Article 16, 17, 18, 20, 21, 22, 23, 24, 26, 27 and 28.
[34] See... 1951 Geneva Convention Article 29.
[35] See...LFIP Article 88 (1).

exceeds the rights and opportunities provided to Turkish citizens.[36] After these general principles, in the 89th Article entitled '*Access to assistance and services*', basically, the right of education, access to social assistance and services, right to health and access to the labour market for the people under international protection are regulated. Furthermore, in the second part of LFIP and international protection section, other rights and services that are not listed in Article 89, are detailed. Some of these rights are *confidentiality, registration, documentation, translation, information and consultation services etc.*

Right to Information

Right to information is very important for both foreigners and the state providing protection and must be granted from the first moment. Because, language, culture, lifestyle, etc. of that country is generally different for foreigners who seek protection from another country by leaving their country due to persecution. If this difference cannot be overcome by appropriate instruments, it may cause difficulties for both asylum seekers and the state providing international protection. Also, the easier it is for newly arrived migrants to access the information they may need, the more migrants' ability to navigate will improve and their integration into the society in which they live will be equally easier.[37] In the light of all these, information and access to information is a right that should be provided first within the scope of international protection.

Right to information is ensured in LFIP as: Regarding the matter of being informed, it was stated that in LFIP, during the registration the applicant will be informed about the international protection application, the evaluation process, his/her rights and obligations in this process and the right to appeal.[38] The same issue has been stated in Article 102 (1) of Implementation Regulation on LFIP. In the Temporary Protection Regulation, it is stated that foreigners within the scope of the Regulation will be informed in a language they can understand about the processes, rights, obligations and other issues related to temporary protection. It was also stated that information brochures and documents could be prepared in case of need.[39] Although there are many provisions related to inform in LFIP and Implementation Regulation on LFIP; there is an obligation to provide information on many subjects in fact. For example, the applicant, his/her lawyer or legal representative should be informed about the outcome of any decision and decision

[36] See…LFIP Article 88 (2).

[37] Peter Waxman, "Service Provision and the Needs of Newly Arrived Refugees in Sydney, Australia: A Descriptive Analysis", **The International Migration Review**, No. 32, 1998, pp. 761-777.

[38] See… LFIP Article 70 (1).

[39] Turkish Official Gazette, **Temporary Protection Regulation No. 2014/6883, No. 29153**, 22 October 2014. Article 19. For details see, DGMM, UNHCR and Ministry of Health, **"*Türkiye'de Geçici Koruma Kapsamında Bulunan Yabancıların Sağlık Hizmetine Erişimine İlişkin Bilgilendirme Broşürü*"** (Information Leaflet on Access to Health Services in Turkey for Foreigners Who Are Under Temporary Protection). Also see, DGMM, CFCU and ICMPD, **"*Geçici Koruma Kapsamında İzlenecek Kayıt Süreci, Hak ve Hizmetler ile Yükümlülüklere İlişkin Bilgilendirme Broşürü*" (*Information Leaflet on the Registration Process, Rights and Services and Obligations to be Followed Under Temporary Protection*).**

taken under international protection. Similarly, where a decision related to status determination cannot be reached within six months the applicant must be informed.[40] The applicant, whose interview is recorded visually or audibly is informed about this issue.[41] Applicants who do not fulfill their obligations are informed that the rights they enjoy may be restricted.[42] These are all examples of how important the right to information can be in the international protection process.

DGMM has established a *Foreigners Communication Center (YİMER)* in order to enable them to obtain information both in the field of international protection and in other areas that may be of interest or need. DGMM provides support for people who call them in Turkish, English, Arabic, Pashto, Persian, Russian and German languages 7 days 24 hours with its free line ALO 157. Foreigners can get information about migration issues (international protection, temporary protection, visa, residence permit, etc.) via the YIMER 157 line, as well as people who are subject to human trafficking and migrant smuggling can submit their notices and assistance requests.[43] With these aspects, YIMER 157 won the gold medal in the Best Emergency Services Award category.[44]

Registration, Documentation and Right of Residence in Turkey

It must examined of situation of foreigners who demand individual international protection among the people who have to leave their country and seek asylum from Turkey first. Under normal circumstances regarding the entry and exit rules in the LFIP, entry to Turkey and exit from Turkey can be passports or passports contain the provision can be made with the document.[45] Similarly, it was stated that document checks can be done during entry and exit to the country, too.[46] However, it is also assured that presence of these provisions cannot be construed and implemented to prevent the international protection claim.[47] Because, as stated in the 1951 Geneva Convention, regular migration is often not possible in refugee mobility. Therefore, in the second section of international protection part of LFIP, each situation in the international protection process is arranged separately and in detail.

It was stated in Article 65 of LFPI that, international protection applications must be lodged with the governorates within the country or law enforcement units at the border gates in person. In the same Article, also as stated in 1951 Geneva

[40] See… LFIP Article 78 (1).
[41] See… LFIP Article 75 (6).
[42] See… LFIP Article 90 (2).
[43] DGMM (2020), https://www.goc.gov.tr/yimer-157-pestuca-dilinde-hizmet--vermeye-basladi, (Access 25.02.2020).
[44] DGMM (2020), YİMER 157, En İyi Acil Servis Hizmetleri Ödülü Kategorisinde Altın Madalya Kazandı (YIMER 157 won the gold medal in the Best Emergency Services Award category), https://www.goc.gov.tr/yimer-157-en-iyi-acil-servis-hizmetleri-odulu-kategorisinde-altin-madalya-kazandi, (Access 30.10.2020).
[45] See… LFIP Article 5.
[46] See… LFIP Article 6.
[47] See… LFIP Article 8.

Convention, is mentioned about provision that from foreign who entering, accomodating and departing for Turkey in irregular ways, provided a description of the reasons for using the irregular path is specified will not be given punishment for those to these foreign who seek international protection.[48] The registration issue is detailed in Article 69 and Article 76 of LFIP. According to these articles; international protection applications are recorded by the Governorships (Provincial Directorate of Migration Management). After the registration process, the '*International Protection Applicant Identity Document*' is issued to the applicant and accompanying family members.[49] This identity document substitutes a residence permit and is not subjected to any fee. Foreigners who demand individual international protection from Turkey, are admitted to country and registrated in this way, and they obtain the right to residence in the country with their international protection applicant identity documents issued. There is one more provision about right to residence of foreigners under international protection in the LFIP like that: Foreigners at the time of exercising their rights in administrative appeals and judicial processes, these processes are allowed up to the outcome in Turkey.[50] Accordingly, applicants whose applications are evaluated negatively by the administration and who exercise their right to appeal against this decision are allowed to reside in the country in order to prevent possible aggrievement until the appeal and judicial process is concluded.

From the perspective of foreigners who demand international protection in mass, in other words, who are under temporary protection, the issues of admission to the country, registration, documentation and residence in the country are regulated between Article 17 and Article 25 of the Temporary Protection Regulation.[51] It is stated that various checks can be made during registration and documentation procedures, as in foreigners who request individual international protection. According to these articles *Temporary Protection Identity Document* is issued free of charge for a certain validity period or indefinitely, grant the right stay in Turkey, but does not substitute a residence permit. In addition to these, it is also stated in the same regulation that those who are under temporary protection can make subscription contracts with their own identity documents.[52]

Right to Education

The 42nd Article of Constitution of the Republic of Turkey includes '*No one may be deprived of the right of learning and education*' provision and assures to access the right

---

[48] See… LFIP Article 65.

[49] Within the scope of the Law on Population Services Law No. 5490 and dated 04.25.2006, for each of foreigners who seeking international protection from Turkey, *foreign identification number* is assigned that starts with 99 and consists of 11 digits. Access to rights and services is through this identification number. Source: Bursa Valiliği, İl Göç İdaresi Müdürlüğü (2017), **Soru ve Cevaplarla Suriyeliler ve Göç** (Bursa Governorship, Provincial Directorate of Migration Management (2017), **Syrians and Migration with Questions and Answers**), p. 21.

[50] See... LFIP Article 80.

[51] Turkish Official Gazette, **Temporary Protection Regulation No. 2014/6883**, No. 29153, 22 October 2014.

[52] See… Temporary Protection Regulation, Article 26.

to education for everyone who lives in Turkey legally even if he/she is Turkish or not Turkish.[53] In national legislation, right to education is regulated in Article 89 of the LFIP like that: persons and their family members who are under international protection benefit from primary and secondary education services.[54] Right to education is also regulated in Article 105 of *Implementing Regulation on the Law on Foreigners and International Protection*.[55] According to Article 105; applicants and international protection status holders can benefit from education services by presenting their documents showing their status. In addition to this; enrolment proceedings in the primary and secondary education institutions and other matters shall be conducted within the framework of Ministry of National Education (MoNE) legislation.[56] The same Article continuous like that: It was stated that people who benefit from education services within the scope of international protection do not need to obtain a student residence permit.[57] It means that foreigners in the scope of international protection can benefit from education services without being required to obtain a separate student residence permit. They also can benefit from the free educations on language and vocational competency provided by Public Education Centres.

In the 28th Article of Regulation on Temporary Protection regulates education services for temporary protection status holders. According to this Article: Courses in personal development or other fields (vocational, artistic, technical) can be organized depending on the demand, and the procedures regarding the education of foreigners at the university are determined by the Presidency of Council of Higher Education. The equivalence procedures of the education received in different curricula are also carried out by Presidency of Council of Higher Education and MoNE. After 2011, the education of children under temporary protection was initially carried out in Temporary Education Centers.[58] Then, with the Circular on Education and Training Services for Foreigners[59] dated 23.09.2014 published by the MoNE and the Circular numbered 2019/15[60] published on 6.09.2019, the access to education of school-age children under temporary protection and the improvement of Turkish language knowledge were regulated. Within the framework of these studies, 684,253 Syrian children under temporary protection were enrolled in Temporary Education Centers. According to data of

---

[53] Turkish Official Gazette, **Türkiye Cumhuriyeti Anayasası** (Constitution of Turkish Republic), No. 2709, 07 November 1982. Article 42.

[54] See… LFIP Article 89.

[55] From now on as "LFIP Regulation". Turkish Official Gazette, **Yabancılar ve Uluslararası Koruma Kanununun Uygulanmasına İlişkin Yönetmelik** (Regulation on Implementation of Law on Foreigners and International Protection), No. 29656, 17 March 2016, Article 105. For LFIP Regulation see https://www.resmigazete.gov.tr/eskiler/2016/03/20160317-11.htm, (Access 02.02.2020).

[56] See… LFIP Regulation Article 105.

[57] See… LFIP Regulation Article 105.

[58] Türkiye Büyük Millet Meclisi İnsan Haklarını İnceleme Komisyonu Mülteci Hakları Alt Komisyonu, **Göç ve Uyum Raporu** (Grand National Assembly of Turkey Human Rights Investigation Commission for Refugee Rights Sub-Commission on Migration and Integration Report), March 2018, https://www.tbmm.gov.tr/komisyon/insanhaklari/docs/2018/goc_ve_uyum_raporu.pdf, s. 86.

[59] See… http://mevzuat.meb.gov.tr/dosyalar/1715.pdf, (Access 17.07.2020).

[60] See… http://mevzuat.meb.gov.tr/dosyalar/1715.pdf, (Access 20.07.2020).

The Council of Higher Education related to education of foreigners who are under temporary protection, in the 2018-2019 academic year a total of 154.446 foreigner students from 179 different countries study in higher education institutions in Turkey. 18% of this figure is 27,034 Syrian students. The number of Syrian students correspond to %4 of the total number of students enrolled in educational institutions in Turkey. As of October 2019, the number of Syrian students are stated as 33,554 by The Council of Higher Education official.[61] With the protocol signed between DGMM and MoNE, it is provided that Syrians under temporary protection can benefit from courses in Public Education Centers free of charge. In this context, 599,475 Syrian trainees attended general and vocational courses organized in public education centers.[62]

Within the scope of access to education services, *Conditional Education Aid (CCTE)* has been implemented since 2003 in order to increase the schooling rate of children under both individual international protection and temporary protection and to ensure them regular attendance at school. The National CCTE Programme is implemented by Ministry of Family, Labor and Social Services. CCTE was expanded as including refugee children are under temporary protection/international protection and at school age in Turkey by the cooperation of Ministry of Family, Labor and Social Services, MoNE, Turkish Red Crescent and UNICEF in 2017. In this context, the beneficiary families, whose children attended their education regularly (at least 80 percent) in the previous school months, were provided with cash assistance every two months through the Red Crescent Card. The program also includes students who missed school for 3 years or more, but resumed their education with the *Accelerated Education Program*, which started in 2018. Thus, children who are away from school life, but continue their re-education, who are under both temporary protection and individual international protection status, can benefit from this program.[63]

In the *Turkish International Protection System*, the right to education is operated similarly for both of foreigners under international and temporary protection and Turkish citizens. Thus, none of refugees are prevented to access to right to education. In addition, in Article 90 (2) of the LFIP, the right to education has been regulated as non-derogable rights and protected.

Right to Health

Right to health is one of fundamental rights in the context of provided rights to the refugees by Turkey. The opportunity of healthcare access is provided to applicants by the competent authority as soon as international protection

[61] YÖK, "Yüksek Öğretim Bilgi Yönetim Sistemi" (YÖK, "Higher Education Information Management System"), https://istatistik.yok.gov.tr/, (Access 09.11.2020).
[62] MEB, Göç ve Acil Durum Eğitim Daire Başkanlığı, "Ocak 2020 Bülten" (MoNE, Department of Migration and Emergency Education, "January 2020 Bulletin), https://hbogm.meb.gov.tr/mebiysdosyalar/202001/27110237OCAK2020internetBulteniSunu.pdf.
[63] UNICEF, **ŞEY Programı (CCTE Programme)**, https://www.unicef.org/turkey/media/10476/file, (Access Nisan 2020).

registration is completed. In LFIP Article 89, the right to health is regulated as '*Those who do not have any health insurance and have do not the ability to pay are subject to the provisions of the e Social Security and Universal Medical Insurance Law o 5510 of 31.05.2006 for a period of one year from the international protection registration. A one-year time limit is not sought for those with special needs and those whose insurance registration is deemed appropriate by the Ministry....*' Before the law change dated 06.12.2019, the maximum period for universal health insurance registration was not stipulated. However, with the law amendment dated 06.12.2019, general health insurance registration was limited to 1 year from the date of application. However, not seeking a time limit for opening general health insurance records for people with special needs and those deemed appropriate by the Ministry has prevented possible victimization. In the continuation of the same article, it was stated that people who have health insurance or who have the ability to pay, will be notified to the Social Security Institution within 10 days and the treatment and medicine costs shall be collected from these people. The same applies to people who are understood to seek international protection just to receive health care.[64] Thus, it is provisioned that the expenses incurred so far can be recourse to those who come for the sole purpose of health needs or who use public resources despite having the ability to pay. Similar provisions are preserved in Article 107 of the LFIP Regulation on the right to health.

The health services provided to Syrians under temporary protection in Turkey are presented under three main headings. These are: 1) 112 Emergency Health Services, 2) Primary and Preventive Health Services, 3) Second and Third Level Health Services.[65] In this direction, the provision of health services starts at the border, people who reach the border are given the health care they need after general health screening, injured and urgent patients are referred to hospitals, relevant vaccines are applied to those who are in the risk group for infectious and epidemic diseases, and necessary measures are taken.[66]

Regarding the access of those under temporary protection to health services, Article 27 of the Temporary Protection Regulation regulates health services. Accordingly, health services are basically carried out under the coordination of the Ministry of Health. The cost of healthcare service provided is paid by DGMM, under the control of the Ministry of Health, in a way that does not exceed the cost specified in the health implementation communiqué determined by the Social Security Institution for general health insurance holders. In the same article, it is stated that measures will be taken against the risk of communicable diseases, information will be provided on reproductive health, and necessary measures will be taken regarding vaccines for children. The one-year period specified for benefiting from universal health insurance within the scope of individual

---

[64] See... LFIP Article 89.

[65] DGMM, **Geçici Korunan Suriyelilere Sunulan Sağlık Hizmetleri Ağustos 2018 Raporu (Health Services Provided to Temporary Protected Syrians August 2018 Report).**

[66] TBMM İnsan Hakları İnceleme Komisyonu, "**Göç ve Uyum Raporu**" (TBMM Human Rights Investigation Committee, "Migration and Integration Report"), Ankara, March 2018, p. 257, https://www.tbmm.gov.tr/komisyon/insanhaklari/docs/2018/gocveuyumraporu.pdf, (Access 17.07.2020).

international protection is not specified for persons under temporary protection. However, it has been stated that those under temporary protection cannot apply to private health institutions directly, except in emergency and compulsory situations. In addition, foreigners under temporary protection are required to apply to the health institutions in the city where they are registered in order to benefit from health services with their valid identity documents. If they benefit from any health service other than the province they are registered in, they may be required to pay the service fee.[67] While foreigners under temporary protection are exempt from the contribution fee in services received from primary health care institutions, in accordance with the amendment made on December 12, 2019, with the provision '*A contribution fee can be obtained from the primary and emergency health services and the treatments and medicines within this scope over the amount or rate determined by the Ministry' It has been arranged that participation share can be obtained*'.[68] As it is about education, the basic health right is expressed as a right that cannot be restricted in LFIP Article 90.

Right to Benefit from Social Assistance and Services

The Right to Benefit from Social Assistance and Services is regulated in LFIP. In LFIP, it is stated that people under international protection who are determined to be in need can benefit from social assistance and services.[69] This provision is detailed in the LFIP Regulation. Accordingly, in the LFIP Regulation, 'neediness' criterion has been introduced in accessing social assistance and services. Accordingly, in the determination of needy ownership to be made by the Governorships, accommodation facilities, income status, number of family members, movable and immovable properties, whether there is aid received and where these aids are obtained, health insurance, disease status and other issues that may be determined by the administration are taken into consideration.[70]

Within the framework of these criteria, the people in need are determined by the commissions established within the governorships and the necessary support is provided for them to receive social assistance and services or they are directed to the necessary units.[71] Social assistance and service support to be provided to those

---

[67] F. Deniz Mardin, "Right to Health and Access to Health Services for Syrian Refugees in Turkey", p. 5, https://mirekoc.ku.edu.tr/wp-content/uploads/2016/11/PBRight-to-Health.pdf.

[68] Turkey in primary, secondary and tertiary health institutions are grouped as follows: Primary health care is done outpatient and home health agencies are the treatment of patients. These include Family Health Center, Community Health Center, Tuberculosis Health Dispensaries. Secondary healthcare institutions are outpatient or inpatient healthcare institutions that provide diagnosis, treatment and rehabilitation services. These include state hospitals, oral and dental health centers affiliated to the Ministry of Health, and private hospitals. Tertiary healthcare institutions are healthcare institutions that contain high technology and / or can provide education and research services for diseases that require advanced examination and special treatment. These include oncology hospitals and mental health and illness hospitals. (T.C. Sağlık Bakanlığı, Sağlık Hizmetleri Genel Müdürlüğü, **Sağlık Hizmeti Sunucularının Basamaklandırılması**, Genelge 2019/10 - T.R. Ministry of Health, General Directorate of Health Services, **Staging of Health Service Providers**, Circular 2019/10).

[69] See… LFIP Article 89 (2).

[70] See… LFIP Regulation Article 106.

[71] These referrals can be directed to national public institutions/organizations, as well as to non-governmental

in need are made in accordance with the procedure determined by the Ministry of Interior (DGMM) and the Ministry of Family, Labor and Social Services. Furthermore, in LFIP, an additional emphasis is made for people with special needs. As stated in Article 67 of LFIP, transactions are carried out within the framework of the provision that priority is given to persons with special needs in their transactions under international protection. However, the person with special needs mentioned here is not the person who is determined to need support economically, but has a special need defined in the 'Definitions' Article in LFIP.[72] Identified persons with special needs are directed to the relevant institutions and organizations in order to receive the necessary physical, legal and economic support, and for this purpose, the DGMM provides the necessary information and consultancy services. For this purpose, 'Protection Desks' were established by DGMM in 2017 within the Governorates. Protection Desks, which carried out transactions for foreigners under Temporary Protection between 2017-2019, have also been providing social-legal-economic and etc. services to persons under international protection since 2019. To this purpose Protection Desks has been started to giving information/guidance and support activities in the fields. People identified as having special needs at the Protection Desks are subsequently directed to national guidance mechanisms. As of 2020, Protection Desks are actively determining special needs in 50 provinces.

Regarding social assistance and services for persons under temporary protection, Article 30 of the Temporary Protection Regulation has been regulated. Accordingly, it has been stated that the follow-up and control of the works and procedures to be carried out for the persons identified as needy, the psychosocial support to be provided to these persons and the assistance to be provided to these persons by international non-governmental organizations shall be carried out in accordance with the procedures and principles determined by the Ministry of Family, Labor and Social Services. As a matter of fact, as mentioned on the right to education, the CCTE National Program and Social Cohesion Aid (ESSN) provided to persons included in the scope of Temporary Protection are programs followed and partnered by the Ministry of Family, Labor and Social Services. After the determination of needy needs, ESSN and CCTE aids made to the beneficiaries with the Red Crescent Card stand out under the heading of access to social assistance and services in terms of providing cash support to individuals.[73] However, although the financial support is intended for the refugees to economically relieve a little bit, planning and implementing them within the framework of international cooperation for a sustainable and permanent solution may yield more effective results.

organizations or international organizations. For example, referrals can be made to UNHCR for their support within the framework of UNHCR's Protection Mission. Or it may be assistance provided by UNHCR. For example: Information, guidance, financial aid, etc. are some of them. See UNHCR Turkey, (2017), "***Compendium of Counselling for Asylum-Seekers and Refugees in Turkey***" p. 23.

[72] See… LFIP Article 3 (1) (Person with special need definition).

[73] "Kızılay Kart (Red Crescent Card)", http://kizilaykart-suy.org/TR/faq0.html, (Access June 2020).

Right to Access the Labor Market

The right to access the labor market is essential for refugees to maintain their lives. In this way, they both have the opportunity to provide added value for the country they are in and feel the power to stand on their own feet. This, plays an important role in lessen the effect of negative experiences which are stem from they have had in the past and difficult situations that required them to leave their country.

In the Turkish International Protection System, there is a basic provision regarding the right of refugees to access to labor market in Article 89 of LFIP. Accordingly, just as it is about education and health, the basic regulations regarding access to the labor market are managed by the specialist public institution that makes direct arrangements in the field. This institution is Ministry of Family, Labor and Social Services. However, in areas where the right to work of foreigners who are under international protection and international protection issues intersect, DGMM and the Ministry of Family, Labor and Social Services make arrangements together. Thus, both institutions have the opportunity to express their opinions in terms of their own subjects and to put them into practice.

The following provisions are regulated in LFIP regarding access to the labor market: Foreigners under international protection (applicants and conditional refugees) can apply for a work permit 6 months after the international protection application date. Status holders other than conditional refugees can work from the date they receive their status, and their identity documents replace work permits. However, if required by economic conditions, restrictions can be made in the areas of business sectors.[74] But if the status holder who married with Turkish citizen or having Turkish children or living in Turkey for 3 years, where restrictions will not apply to these people.[75] In the context of people under international protection, refugees and subsidiary protection status holders have more advantageous than applicants and conditional refugees to access the labor market due to their status. However, according to Article 89 (5) of LFIP, a person who is under international protection that would be determined to be in need may be provided with an allowance with the assent of the Ministry of Treasury and Finance, regardless of status. Regarding the right to access the labor market, the same provisions in LFIP are preserved in the 108th Article of Implementing Regulation on LFIP. The most basic regulations applied by the Ministry of Family, Labor and Social Services regarding the access of people under international protection to the labor market are International Labor Law dated 28.07.2016 and numbered 6745 and the Regulation on the Employment of International Protection Applicant and International Protection Status Holders published in the Official Gazette No. 29595 dated 26.04.2016. In the International Labor Force Law, it is stated that, within the framework of LFIP, international protection applicants, conditional refugees or

---

[74] See… LFIP Article 89 (4).

[75] DGMM and ICMPD (2019), **"Yabancıların Türkiye'de İş ve Yaşam Rehberi" (Work and Life Book of Foreigners in Turkey).**

temporary protection status holders can be exceptionally granted work permits.[76] Furthermore, according to the International Labor Law, '*it is obligatory to obtain a preliminary permit in evaluating the work permit applications of foreigners who will work in health and education services that require professional competence*'.[77] Accordingly, MoNE in the field of education and the Ministry of Health in the field of health are the Ministries authorized to issue pre-authorization. There is a provision directly regulated in Article 17 of the International Labor Law for persons under international protection. Accordingly, it has been stated that for work permit application, they are needed 6 months which starting from international protection registration, opinions of the Ministry of Internal Affairs (DGMM) will be taken and work permit will not provide a absolute right of stay in Turkey to foreigners. In addition, as stated in the LFIP, it is stated that the working areas can be limited in terms of province, duration, sector, line of business, job and occupation and by considering the international labor policy. In addition, it is stated that the work permit/work permit exemption certificate will be cancelled after the notification to be made by the Ministry of Interior (DGMM) about the foreigners who have been decided from the decisions specified in the LFIP about the international protection these decisions are withdraw the international protection application, the application is deemed withdrawn, the status is terminated or the status is cancelled decisions. Thus, it has been regulated that foreigners under international protection can benefit from work permit while they are in the international protection process, and work permit will be terminated accordingly in cases such as the cancellation or termination of the international protection process.[78] This provision is important in order not to abuse the international protection process. Regarding the access of persons under international protection to the labor market, there are more detailed provisions of the provisions of the International Labor Law in the International Protection Work Permit Regulation. Accordingly, it has been stated that an international identity document is mandatory for obtaining a work permit, and that the work permit will also be terminated in the absence of an identity document or if the DGMM cancels the identity document or deportation decision is taken. Also, it has been stated that will be request opinion from the DGMM for foreigners who want to work outside the province where they are registered in and if this opinion is negative, the work permit will be terminated and the work permit fee can be taken from foreigners who are deemed appropriate to be granted a work permit. In addition, in the same Regulation, it is stated that international protection applicants or conditional refugees cannot be paid less than the minimum wage and it is aimed not to abuse the labor of foreigners and these rights are protected. Moreover, foreigners who will work in seasonal agriculture or animal husbandry are included in the work permit exemption these are international protection applicants and conditional refugees.[79] Thus, the process of obtaining work permits for applicants

[76] 28.07.2016 tarihli ve 6745 sayılı Uluslararası İşgücü Kanunu (International Labor Law dated 28.07.2016 and numbered 6745), Article 16, https://www.mevzuat.gov.tr/MevzuatMetin/1.5.6735.pdf, (Access 06.08.2020).
[77] See… **Uluslararası İşgücü Kanunu** (International Labor Law), Article 8.
[78] See… **Uluslararası İşgücü Kanunu** (International Labor Law), Article 17.
[79] See… **Uluslararası Koruma Başvuru Sahibi ve Uluslararası Koruma Statü Sahibi kişilerin**

who will work in seasonal agriculture or animal husbandry and foreigners with conditional refugee status has both included in the scope of exemption, and foreigners has allowed to carry out their procedures in their province. Thus, the process has been facilitated for these people.

In the Temporary Protection Regulation, it is stated that the procedures and principles regarding the access of foreigners under temporary protection to work service will be determined by the President upon the proposal of the Ministry of Family, Labor and Social Services, taking the opinion of the Ministry of Interior. Also it is stated that a work permit can be requested with a temporary protection identity document and the duration of the work permit cannot be longer than the duration of the identity document, the work permit granted under temporary protection will not replace one of the types of residence permit listed in the LFIP and the work permit obtained accordingly will be cancelled if the temporary protection status is terminated.[80] In fact, as in individual international protection, the work permit obtained by the foreigner based on the identity document of the foreigner within the scope of temporary protection ends when this document is cancelled or expired. *The International Labor Law* on the access of foreigners under temporary protection to work service and the *Regulation on Work Permits of Foreigners with Temporary Protection* numbered 29594, which was published in the Official Gazette on 15.01.2016, are the basic regulations. It is stated In the Regulation on Work Permits of Foreigners under Temporary Protection that, persons under temporary protection cannot work without a work permit, can apply for a work permit six months after the date of temporary protection registration, temporary protected persons who will work in seasonal agriculture or animal husbandry within the scope of work permit exemption, workplaces where they can apply, where the total number of employees is less than 10, where at most one foreigner under temporary protection can be allowed to work, for those who will work in areas where they need a preliminary permit, such as foreigners under individual international protection, they must obtain preliminary permission from the relevant institutions and to temporary protected persons working with a work permit cannot be paid below the minimum wage.[81] All of this information in particular in the framework of the Syrians under temporary protection status, as of 2018, there are 34 563 Syrians in Turkey's legal work permit.[82] For eight years, Syrians in Turkey has established more than 10,000 companies which consist of percent 60 are Syrian

---

Çalışmasına Dair Yönetmelik (Regulation on the Work of International Protection Applicants and International Protection Status Persons), https://www.resmigazete.gov.tr/eskiler/2016/04/20160426-1.htm, (Access 26.06.2020).

[80] See... **Temporary Protection Regulation**, Article 29.

[81] See… **Geçici Koruma Sağlanan Yabancıların Çalışma İzinlerine Dair Yönetmelik (Regulation on Work Permits of Foreigners Under Temporary Protection)**. https://www.mevzuat.gov.tr/Mevzuat Metin/3.5.2 0168375.pdf, (Access 30.06.2020).

[82] Aile, Çalışma ve Sosyal Hizmetler Bakanlığı, **"Suriyelilerin Çalışma İzni"** (Ministry of Family, Labor and Social Services, "Work Permit of Syrians"), 2018, https://ailevecalisma.gov.tr/media/31746/yabanciizin 2018.pdf.

and where an average works 7 persons.[83]

Other Rights and Services

In the Turkish International Protection Legislation, there are many rights provided for foreigners seeking asylum, whether within the scope of individual international protection or under temporary protection. Among these, *the right to appeal, legal aid, the right of privacy (confidentiality), to seek consultancy and to benefit from translation services are other rights* that will be discussed in this study.

The Right of Privacy (Confidentiality)

The right of privacy is very important in the context of refugee law. From the first moment that foreigners seek international protection, every transaction, all information shared by the applicant and the document they provide are extremely important for their life. In fact if the applicant is not given the necessary confidence in confidentiality and privacy issues, the necessary information cannot be obtained from the applicant in the international protection record or international protection interviews. The privacy policy is not only used for information purposes. This is a responsibility in itself for government officials. As a matter of fact, under the title of '*Personal Data*' in the LFIP this provision has been arranged: Personal data of foreigners are received, stored and protected by DGMM in accordance with the relevant legislation.[84]

The right of privacy is very important in the Turkish International Protection System and this issue is directly regulated in the LFIP. In the LFIP, the subject of confidentiality was arranged as in the following statements and it is protected under the heading of 'Privacy Policy and Access to Personal File; Confidentiality is essential in all information and documents of foreigners under international protection, and these information/documents can only be examined by the foreigner's lawyer or legal representative in accordance with the legislation or a copy may be requested.[85] In this context, confidentiality in their information and documents is essential for anyone under international protection, whether an applicant or a status holder. Information and documents of persons under international protection cannot be shared with third persons and institutions/organizations, including their own country authorities. However, the information about the applicant can be shared with their lawyer or legal representative within certain limits, as stated in the LFIP.

Legal Aid and Consultancy Services

The subject of legal aid and consultancy services is another right and service

[83] TEPAV, "Türkiye'de Suriyeli Girişimciliği ve Mülteci İşletmeleri: Türkiye Tecrübesinden Nasıl Faydalanılabilir?" (Entrepreneurship and Business Syrian Refugees in Turkey: How to take advantage of the experience) (2019) https://www.tepav.org.tr/tr/haberler/s/10024.

[84] See… LFIP, Article 99.

[85] See… LFIP, Article 94.

directly regulated by the LFIP. According to this, Foreigners under international protection can be represented by a lawyer, provided that their fees are paid by them. However, those who cannot afford this fee are provided with legal service in accordance with the legal aid provisions of Law No. 1136. In addition, these can benefit from the consultancy services provided by non-governmental organizations.[86] The same issue is regulated in Article 103 of the LFIP Regulation. Another issue regarding legal aid and consultancy services is the condition of reciprocity. Regarding this, in accordance with Articles 7 and 16 of the 1951 Geneva Convention and Article 88 of the LFIP foreigners under international protection are exempt from the reciprocity requirement. In the Temporary Protection Regulation, the subject of legal aid and consultancy services is regulated as: '*Foreigners within the scope of this Regulation can be represented by a lawyer during administrative transactions provided that their fees are paid by them. The provisions of the Attorneys' Act No. 1136, dated 19.03.1969, regarding legal aid are reserved.*'[87] Legal aid and consultancy services are regulated similarly for foreigners under temporary protection and foreigners under individual international protection. It has been regulated similarly that there is the opportunity for both groups to be represented by a lawyer, the fee must be borne by the person concerned, and those who cannot afford the fee can apply for legal aid within the framework of the Attorneys' Act and finally are exempted from reciprocity conditions.

Administrative Appeal and The Right of Judicial Appeal

As clearly stated in the 1982 Constitution, there is a judicial remedy against any act of the administration.[88] In this context, people seeking international protection can either object to the administration against the work and transactions carried out in relation to them, or they can apply to the judicial remedy by going to the competent authorities in this field. In terms of country examples, the applicants are sometimes given only the right of administrative objection against the decisions of the administration, and sometimes both the administrative objection and the right to apply to the judicial remedy. Indeed, during the development of international protection law it is possible to see both cases in Turkey. In the Turkish International Protection System, foreigners can use the right of administrative objection or appeal to judicial remedies, depending on the nature of the transaction, for all kinds of transactions established against them. Therefore, they can apply to both simultaneously. However, in this case, the administrative appeal assessment is suspended as a judicial remedy is applied and the court process continues.

If we examine the issues of administrative objection and application to judicial remedy in the international protection process in terms of LFIP and LFIP Regulation, Administrative objection and application to judicial remedy are regulated in LFIP Article 80 and LFIP Regulation Article 99-100 and 101. Accordingly, the following provisions are regulated in the LFIP: It has been stated

---

[86] See… LFIP, Article 81.

[87] See… **Geçici koruma Yönetmeliği (Temporary Protection Regulation),** Article 53.

[88] See… **Türkiye Cumhuriyeti Anayasası (Constitution of Turkish Republic),** Article 125.

that, with the exception of the decisions made within the framework of Articles 68, 72 and 79, there is an administrative objection against international protection decisions, and that the International Protection Assessment Commission can be apply within 10 days. Within the scope of Articles 68, 72 and 79, only the judicial remedy can be applied. In this process, the foreigner himself/herself, his/her lawyer or legal representative is informed about the process. Furthermore, foreigners who apply for a judicial or administrative appeal have the right to stay in Turkey until the conclusion of the judicial process.[89] In addition, the International Protection Assessment Commission is an administrative objection mechanism which takes part directly and in name in the LFIP.[90]

As a result, there are administrative means required to apply the International Protection Assessment Commission as well as a dual recourse to a competent court of appeal and judicial review the scope of international protection for foreigners in Turkey. This situation is important in terms of providing a double-level appeal right for foreigners and preventing possible victimization.

Right of Using Interpreting Services

Foreigners under international protection are mostly stranger to the language, culture and lifestyle of the country they seek protection from. At the very beginning, the language barrier poses the biggest difficulty in the businesses and transactions to be carried out by foreigners. If the language barrier is not overcome, the process will be blocked and each job or process will be incomplete. For example, in the international protection interview, in an interview with someone who has little knowledge of the language of the country of asylum, if there is no interpreter who knows the language of the applicant, every question asked by the interviewer and every answer given by the applicant will contain incomplete or incorrect information. In the procedure progressed in this way, it is also possible to encounter irreparable results. Precisely at this point, the provision, there is a provision that translation support can be provided to the applicant in the international protection process if requested.[91] In the LFIP is used regarding the interpreting service the same issue is regulated in more detail in the LFIP Regulation. According to this; In the event that it is understood that communication cannot be established at the desired level without an interpreter in the application, registration, interview and other processes deemed necessary by the administration, translation services will be provided free of charge, and if the applicant submits written documents that are not in Turkish to support the request, copies of these documents will be requested by authorized persons; however, if the applicant cannot obtain translations of these documents, the administration can benefit from the opportunities of public institutions and organizations and international organizations, including

[89] See… LFIP, Article 80.

[90] Article 71 of Statutory Decree dated 02.07.2018 and numbered 703 made amendments in LFIP, provisions regarding International Protection Assessment Commission were abolished however, this commission continues its duty as an administrative authority for complaints under DGMM.

[91] See… LFIP, Article 70 (2).

cooperation with non-governmental organizations, and the translation services provided at every stage of international protection procedures are provided by DGMM or DGMM provincial directorates, by their own personnel or by service procurement. It has been stated that it can be provided and cooperate with the administration, public institutions and organizations, non-governmental organizations and international organizations regarding translation services.[92] In this context, foreigners under international protection can benefit from the interpreting service. Thus, the language barrier in transactions to be carried out against foreigners is overcome. If there are situations where communication cannot be made properly despite the provision of interpreting service, this situation is recorded with a report and the same issue is re-evaluated at a more convenient time and with the support of a more competent interpreter. As a matter of fact, international protection interviews are very important in this sense. In cases where mutual communication during the interview is not smooth, this situation is determined with a report and the interview is postponed to take place on another date. Before the interview planned to be held, necessary measures are taken to eliminate the issues that caused the failure to communicate in the first interview.[93] This shows how important the access to interpreting service is for both the applicant and the staff in charge. In terms of foreigners under temporary protection, it is stated in Article 26 of the Temporary Protection Regulation that the interpreting service is a service that can be offered to those under temporary protection. In the 31st Article, it is stated that interpreting services will be provided free of charge in the works and transactions within the scope of the Regulation, when the desired level of communication cannot be established with the foreigner without an interpreter. Thus, in the Turkish International Protection System, interpreting service is included as a service offered at every stage, both within the scope of individual international protection and temporary protection.

Obligations of Refugees in Turkish National Legislation

As stated in the 1951 Geneva Convention, every refugee has obligations to comply with the laws of that country and to comply with the measures taken for public order.[94] Within the framework of this basic provision, the states parties also set certain obligations for refugees in their national legislation. In terms of Turkey, the Turkish National Legislation on refugees, there are certain obligations considered as exhaustive. These obligations are generally: The obligation to comply with the national legislation, the obligation to report, the obligation to tell the truth, the obligation to cooperate, the obligation to demonstrate, the obligation to sign, the obligation to repay, the obligation to comply with the invitation and the obligation to stay in the specified city of residence or the residence itself.

In the Turkish National Legislation, the obligation of foreigners to comply with the national legislation is the most basic obligation. Obligations to tell the truth and

---

[92] See… LFIP Regulation, Article 102.
[93] See… LFIP Regulation, Article 86.
[94] See… 1951 Geneva Convention Article 2.

cooperate with the authorities during the implementation of national legislation are also an integral part of the obligation to comply with national legislation. Regarding the right to be informed, there is a situation where foreigners are be informed about the procedures to be followed regarding international protection applications during the first registration, their rights and obligations during the evaluation process of the application, how they will fulfil their obligations and the possible consequences that may arise in case they do not comply with these obligations or cooperate with the authorities, objection procedures and periods. In addition, among the obligations determined for persons under international protection; residence obligation and notification obligation in LFIP Article 71, obligation to comply with the invitation in Article 96 of the LFIP and other obligations in Article 86 of the LFIP are regulated. However, there are other provisions that refer to obligations in the section on international protection.[95]

In Article 71 of the LFIP, it is stated that the applicant may be imposed with administrative obligations such as the obligation to reside in the reception and accommodation centre designated to him/her, in a certain place or in a certain province in the desired form and time. A signature obligation may be imposed for foreigners within the scope of the notification obligation. In this context, foreigners may be obliged to sign at regular intervals in the province/place shown to them in order to reside. In addition, the applicant is obliged to register in the address registration system and to inform the governorship of their residence address.[96] Also, foreigners under international protection have the obligation to prove their claims. This is particularly evident at the stage of international protection registration and interview. As a matter of fact, the foreigner is expected to prove their claim with their statements and supporting documents regarding the events he declared to have lived in his country. Regarding the burden of proof, it is stated in the LFIP that the foreigner must submit the information and documents to the authorities that will support their claims, and their statements will be taken as basis for those who do not have supporting documents.[97] In this case, the statement submitted is expected to be accurate and consistent. In the LFIP, the following obligations are specified directly under the heading of '*Obligations*': Persons under international protection are obliged to report their marital status, address and identity information within 20 days, and their current employment status, income, movable and immovables within 30 days. Those who benefit from unfair rights and services have a repayment obligation. In this process, there is an obligation to comply with the obligations imposed by DGMM. While all these obligations are specified in the same article, it is also stated that the use of two rights will not be restricted. These are: access to basic health and education right.[98]

Foreigners, foreign applicants and persons with international protection status

---

[95] See… LFIP Article 68, 69, 77 and 82.

[96] UNHCR Turkey, (2017), **"Compendium of Counselling for Asylum-Seekers and Refugees in Turkey"**, p. 23.

[97] See… LFIP, Article 69 (3).

[98] See… LFIP, Article 90.

face with the hesitation regarding their entering or remaining in Turkey may be invited to DGMM or to Provincial Directorate to obtain information. Within the scope of the obligation to comply with the invitation, foreigners have the obligation to comply with this invitation and to tell the truth.[99] Another liability within the scope of obligations is the obligation to pay the price of these services by those who benefit from rights and services unfairly. Thus, it is aimed to prevent the abuse of the system.

Regarding the obligations of persons under temporary protection, obligations in the field of individual international protection have been preserved in the field of temporary protection. In the Temporary Protection Regulation, it is stated that foreigners who come to our country for temporary protection are obliged to comply with the laws and administrative requirements, otherwise the necessary judicial procedures and administrative sanctions will be fulfilled according to the general provisions.[100] Following this basic provision, provisions regarding the obligation to comply with the invitation and the restrictions that may be imposed on those who do not comply with the obligations are regulated.

It is possible to state that the basic obligations in the Turkish International Protection Legislation for foreigners who are under the scope of individual international protection and under temporary protection are the obligation to comply with the law, to tell the truth and to cooperate with the authorities. As there will not be an unfair acquisition for foreigners who have already fulfilled these basic obligations, there will be no need to mention the obligation to pay back, the obligation to comply with the invitation due to cooperation with the authorities, and the obligation to sign or notify because the laws will be complied with. This will create a healthy process for both foreigners and the state within the scope of effective management of migration.

Conclusion and Recommendations

Refugees are people who leave their country and seek international protection from another country due to the persecution they face or may face. In a foreign country, they try to continue their lives often without knowing the language, culture and lifestyle of that country, with the effect of the events they have experienced beforehand and the feeling of being an outsider in the country of asylum. The rights and services to be provided for a refugee in such a situation are very important. Regarding this, the 1951 Geneva Convention for refugees specifies the fundamental rights that states parties should provide to refugees. Not only the 1951 Geneva Convention, but also the regulations on fundamental human rights in the international arena are mostly binding on states, whether they are a party or not, and therefore it is accepted that basic human rights should be provided to everyone. In this framework, refugees have direct rights arising from international regulations. As a matter of fact, the right of life, the prohibition of torture, the prohibition of

[99] See… LFIP, Article 97.

[100] See… Temporary Protection Regulation, Article 33 (1).

slavery, freedom of religion, and the prohibition of non-refoulement are some of them. In addition, states have the authority to determine the rights to be regulated and the services to be provided for refugees in their own national legislation. In this context, Turkey has determined the services and the rights that it provides to 4 million people located under international protection with the LFIP, The LFIP Regulation and the basis Temporary Protection Regulation. In addition to these, there are also legislations prepared by the MoNE in the field of education, the Ministry of Health in the field of health, or the Ministry of Family, Labor and Social Services, either individually or together with DGMM, depending on the subject of the relevant right. All these regulations deal with the rights and services to be provided to persons under individual international protection and temporary protection in Turkey.

Regarding the rights and the services provided to foreigners under international protection; many rights and service issues are protected in the LFIP and other relevant legislation like the 1951 Geneva Convention such as the right to be informed, the right of education, the right of health, the right to access the labour market, access to social assistance and services, legal aid and counselling, interpreting, the right of privacy, registration-documentation and residence rights, the right of objection. It has been accepted that whichever public institution falls under the jurisdiction of the relevant right or service in the provision of rights and the services to be provided the relevant Ministry/public institution regulates this area directly or together with the relevant institutions.

Indeed DGMM is not only the major coordinating body for all foreigners seeking international protection from Turkey but also has repeatedly stated in both LFIP and LFIP Regulation and Temporary Protection Regulation that regarding the right of education; MoNE and Higher Education Council, with regard to the right of health; the Ministry of Health, regarding the right to work; The Ministry of Family, Labour and Social Services are the authorized public institutions that should regulate this area. The regulation of the rights and the services to be provided for the refugees by the institutions specialized in this field and the coordination between the institutions has been an effective method in minimizing the possible victimization that may be experienced. The international protection application made by the refugees provides them with some rights and also brings along some obligations. As a matter of fact, it is also stated in the 1951 Geneva Convention that the states parties may impose some obligations on refugees. The most important of these obligations is the refugee's obligation to comply with the laws of the country of asylum. In this framework, some obligations have been determined for foreigners included in the Turkish International Protection System. Some of these obligations are the obligation to comply with the national legislation, the obligation to report, the obligation to tell the truth, the obligation to cooperate with the authorities, the obligation to prove their claims, the obligation to sign, the obligation to pay back, the obligation to comply with the invitation and the obligation to stay in the city of residence or residence determined for the foreigner. A foreigner is expected to fulfil these obligations, whether they are under individual international protection or under temporary protection. For foreigners who do not fulfil their obligations, restrictions may be imposed in terms of rights and services other than basic education and health. The rights of education and health have been protected in the Turkish National Legislation as one of the rights protected under all circumstances. In addition, although it is not directly specified under the heading of 'rights and services', many other related rights such as compliance with the principle of non-refoulement, protection of the right of life, and the sanctity of the right of asylum are also protected under various headings in the LFIP. Thus, it is aimed to operate an effective protection system for refugees in the Turkish National Legislation. In line with this goal, the topics of inter-institutional coordination, efficient management of resources, prevention of abuse of the international protection system and minimization of possible victimization are prominent. For this purpose, a detailed analysis of the fundamental rights that should be provided to foreigners under international protection to whom, when, how, in which way and to what extent these rights should be provided, ensuring equality in opportunity for everyone in the same position in accessing rights and services, and preventing recurrent benefits and preventing duplicate benefits, establishing effective detection and prevention mechanisms in cases where the international protection system is used solely to benefit from certain rights in order to protect the dignity of the asylum institution will benefit the international protection process. Thus, foreigners in need will be able to access the rights and services they need, and the risk of abuse of the asylum system will be minimized

CHAPTER 5

THE IMPACT OF REFUGEES ON TURKEY'S GEOPOLITICS

Göknil Erbaş Doğan[1]

Introduction

Geopolitics stand out as a distinctive area of research that focuses on the reflection of the geographical location of countries on their politics. As a generally accepted argument, the geographical advantages or disadvantages presented by the location of a country have a strong impact on its politics. In addition to that state actors in the age of globalization are not limited by the geographical and other conditions they find themselves in. States have to find ways to devise various policies to cope with the dynamism related to social, economic and environmental conditions. Migration is one such condition that substantially affect the countries. If a country finds itself faced with intense migration, it will have to alter its policies in a radical fashion.

This study benefits from the discourse analysis approach presented by the critical geopolitics and seeks to investigate the utilization of migration policies by Turkey as a geopolitical instrument.

Turkey was introduced to mass migration waves as an effect of the Syrian crisis which started in 2011 and grew increasingly violent as time progressed. The migration wave from Syria has transformed Turkey's rhetoric on migration. Located on the migration route to Europe, Turkey was considered to be a 'transit country' for a long time. Today, Turkey retains that transit character yet also hosts approximately 4 million refugee and shelter seekers. Among the refugees in Turkey, there are approximately 3.6 million Syrians and approximately 330,000 registered refugees[2] from other countries. The changing conditions have naturally altered Turkey's approach and policies on migration. Turkey has also utilized the phenomenon in its geopolitical discourse.

Turkey has reviewed its migration policies in this period and has felt its impacts in two dimensions. The first is Turkey's position as a destination country and the second is about its approach to migrants and the related change in its geopolitical discourse and policies. In both dimensions, the management of the process stand out with its significant character in close relation to the security dimension of the issue.

In this context, the migration wave that Turkey has been dealing with for the

[1] Asst. Prof., Mersin University, Türkiye.

[2] https://www.unhcr.org/tr/unhcr-turkiye-istatistikleri (Access 01.11.2020).

last nine years, brought about new approach and new policies. These elements have altered Turkey's position in its immediate region, a transformation which is also reflected in the discourse. This chapter handles the effects of the migration phenomenon on Turkey's policies during this period in which Turkey is initiated as a destination country. Then, the Turkish rhetoric in this critical process will be examined in order to underline Turkey's changing approach to geopolitics. The article argues in conclusion that the discourse adopted by Turkey toward especially the Syrian refugees is a consequence of the country's shifting geopolitical understanding.

Transformation from Country of Transit to Destination Country

The phenomenon of migration and migrants stand out as one of the issues that affect the societal dimension of the security of countries and retains and important place in political and economic debates in the context of globalization. The causes that impact people's decisions to translocate rest on a wide spectrum ranging from seeking economic opportunities and religious freedom to fleeing oppression. In addition to that, war, terrorism and natural disasters are also factors that cause mass migration. Turkey has experienced such a phenomenon since 2011 for the reason that it is in proximity to a civil conflict in its neighboring country. Formerly both a source country and a country of transit in terms of migration, Turkey has started to acquire a new role. In 2015, Ahmet Davutoğlu, then-Prime Minister of Turkey wrote an article in the Guardian[3] where he underlines this point:

- 'Turkey, traditionally a transit country for irregular migration, is now also a top destination. The Turkish people have made huge sacrifices in hosting more than 2 million Syrians and Iraqis. By so doing, we have damped the mass influx to the EU and effectively become a buffer between chaos and Europe. Meanwhile, EU member states account for ridiculously low shares in the global resettlement rates.'

Transit migration is generally accepted as a sub-category of irregular migration and has no universally-accepted definition. A transit country is one of the temporary stops in the migrants' route to their destination. Turkey has long deemed itself as the bridge between the east and the west, which has actually meant a transit route for migrants. When international migration increased in intensity during the last few decades, Turkey had to formulate a coordinated response to the worsening problem and started participating in international efforts aimed at tackling the crisis. In 2004, Turkey has joined the International Organization for Migration (IOM), which was founded in 1951 in order to ensure humane management of migration and to promote international cooperation. In addition to that, Turkey signed the United

---

[3] Ahmet Davutoğlu, "Turkey cannot deal with the refugee crisis alone. EU nations need to help", **The Guardian**, 9 September 2015, https://www.theguardian.com/commentisfree/2015/sep/09/turkey-refugee-crisis-christian-fortress-europe (Access 21.10.2020).

Nations Convention against Transnational Organized Crime and its supplements, the Protocol to Prevent, Suppress and Punish Trafficking in Persons, Especially Women and Children; the Protocol against the Smuggling of Migrants by Land, Sea and Air in December 2000. In line with its increasing international commitments, Turkey has assumed the term presidency of the Global Forum on Migration and Development, an international non-binding forum that aims the address some of the root causes of migration.

Regarding refugees, Turkey signed the 1951 UN Refugee Convention. The convention is about the legal status of refugees which was also a significant crisis after the Second World War. In addition, the geographic scope of the convention was limited to the countries affected by the war. The convention's supplement protocol in 1967 has eliminated the geographical limitations. Turkey signed the 1951 Convention with a 'geographical restriction' by using its right of choice for place which has been stipulated in Article 1 of the Convention.[4] Accordingly, Turkey grants the legal status of 'refugee' only to people coming from the European countries. This preference was also stipulated on the Law No. 6458 on Foreigners and International Protection adopted by the Turkish Parliament in April 2013. The Law sets out the main pillars of Turkey's national asylum system and established the Directorate General of Migration Management (DGMM) as the main entity in charge of policy-making and proceedings for all foreigners in Turkey. Turkey also adopted Temporary Protection Regulation on 22 October 2014, which sets out the rights and obligations along with procedures for those who are granted temporary protection in Turkey.

The civil conflict in Syria drove thousands of Syrians to Turkey from 2011 onwards. In the beginning, Turkey adopted an open-door policy yet has not granted official asylum status to the Syrians fleeing the regime. Therefore, the Syrians in Turkey are not officially categorized as refugees; rather they are 'Syrian guests under temporary protection'. In September 2015, the tragedy of migrants and refugees came to the forefront of the international public opinion when the lifeless body of a 3-year-old Syrian child, Aylan Kurdi, washed up on the Aegean coast of Turkey. The tragic photos of the child triggered talks between Turkey and the European Union aimed at addressing the irregular migration through the Turkish territories and into Europe. The phenomenon of irregular migration into Europe was nothing new yet the governments of the European countries had been increasingly worried about the rising issues related to the influx of people into Europe. The most important reason for the readiness of the European government to tackle the irregular migration was probably the rise of the far-right political parties, which feed on the discomfort and xenophobia within the societies.

According to the figures of the UN Refugee Agency, the number of migrants arriving by sea into Greece was 856,723 in 2015. It is a sharp increase from the

[4] "Conditional refugee", https://en.goc.gov.tr/conditional-refugee (Access 01.09.2020).

41,038 in 2014.[5] The situation constituted a dire emergency not only for Greece but also for the other European countries. The capacity of Greece for absorbing the refugee influx remained ineffective while refugees intended to move further into the north and west Europe. At this critical juncture, Turkey sought to emphasize the fact that it hosted a large number of refugees and to underline the need to develop an international response to the phenomenon. The then-Turkish Prime Minister Ahmet Davutoğlu wrote in his article for the Guardian that the root causes of the irregular migration must be addressed, which would involve finding solution to the crises in 'Iraq, Syria and elsewhere'[6]. While a long-term solution would require crisis resolution to such crises, the immediate situation had to be addressed in some way and Turkey opted for emphasizing its undertakings and asking for burden-sharing from Europe.

In this context, several high-level meetings between Turkey and the EU took place. On 15th September 2015, the EU leaders have agreed on the 'EU-Turkey Joint Action Plan on Migration'[7] for addressing the current crisis. The plan involved a three-pronged approach: (1) addressing the root causes of the problem, (2) supporting the Syrians under temporary protection in Turkey and (3) cooperation to prevent irregular migration to Europe. In addition to that three Turkey-EU summits (29th November 2015, 7th and 18th March 2016) were held in five months. The summits had various agenda items besides migration. Yet the reason for holding three summits in five months was definitely the migration crisis. In the second summit held on March 7th, Turkey presented a proposal to the EU side, which involved a temporary and extraordinary measure. Turkey's proposal was accepted in the third summit on March 17-18. According to the March 18 Agreement[8], all new irregular migrants crossing from Turkey to Greece will be returned to Turkey an in exchange for every returned Syrian, one Syrian from Turkey will be resettled in the EU. This one-in/one-out formula was actually the Turkish proposal presented on March 7. In addition to that, the EU committed to provide additional funding to help Turkey deal with the crisis. In this context, an additional 3 billion Euros would be made available until the end of 2018. The agreement also included commitment on speeding up visa-free travel to the EU for Turkish citizens. Looking retrospectively, the efforts and cooperation proved valuable in bringing down the irregular migration numbers. The sea arrivals were down to 173,450 in 2016 and 29,718 in 2017, according to the UNHCR data[9].

At this point, the irregular migration issue in the EU-Turkey relations focused on the prevention of migrants to Europe. The EU seeks to address the effects of

---

[5] UNHCR Operational Portal, https://data2.unhcr.org/en/situations/mediterranean/location/5179 (Access 11.10.2020).

[6] Davutoğlu, op.cit.

[7] "EU-Turkey joint action plan", https://ec.europa.eu/commission/presscorner/detail/de/MEMO_15_5860 (Access 04.09.2020).

[8] "Migrant crisis: EU and Turkey plan one-in, one-out deal", https://www.bbc.com/news/world-europe-35749837 (Access 03.10.2020).

[9] UNHCR Operational Portal, https://data2.unhcr.org/en/situations/mediterranean/location/5179 (Access 24.10.2020).

unresolved conflicts, organized crime, drug trafficking, irregular migration and international terrorism in order to prevent their entry to Europe.[10] Therefore, its approach to international migration proved to be exclusionary. It also provided Turkey with a certain degree of leverage against the EU. In February 2020, Turkey accused the EU of failing to act on its commitments of the March 18 agreement and declared that it would no longer stop refugees from crossing to Europe.[11] Turkey's decision was also triggered by the recent events around the Syrian opposition stronghold in Idlib. A new refugee wave headed towards the Turkish border as the Syrian regime and its backers launched assaults in Idlib countryside. Therefore, Turkey sought to convey the messages that it cannot absorb new refugee waves, it is displeased with the EU side about the March 18 refugee deal. More importantly, Turkey wanted to attract the attention of the international community to the developments in Idlib, which it hoped to produce additional pressure on the Assad regime and its allies to cease their attacks.

Forming A New Narrative For Turkey

The classical understanding of geopolitics considers that human communities as 'population' form one of the main elements of geopolitics. In the era that we live in, human communities mean much more than population. The most striking example for that is the phenomenon of migration. Migration routes, destination countries or the causes for migration are political in character. The political character involves attaching meaning to geography. In current times, geopolitics implies a specific meaning attached to geography.[12] Turkey reshapes the imagination of its geography through the rhetoric and policies of decision makers on migration. Turkey suffered from mass migration waves for the last nine years primarily due to its geographical location since it shares an approximately 1,000 kms long border with Syria ridden by civil conflict. In this context, its approach toward migrants has a humane character. It sought to respond to the challenge the migration waves in a humanitarian manner. Turkey's approach stands in accordance with its humanitarian rhetoric in foreign policy.

In the beginning of the 21st century, Turkey's foreign policy rhetoric adopted a vision of Turkey that is capable of contributing to an international order as the heir to the historical experience and values of the Ottoman Empire. This new vision was presented as the story of Turkey. The statement[13] of İbrahim Kalın, Spokesperson of the Turkish Presidency, 'The stories of others were narrated to us for one hundred and fifty years, in the name of modernization. It is time for us to write our own story' stands out as the summary of the narrative of Turkey, which is for a long

---

[10] Gareth Winrow, "Geopolitics and Energy Security in the Wider Black Sea Region," **Southeast European and Black Sea Studies**, Vol. 7, No. 2, June 2007, p.220.

[11] "Turkey: Irregular migrants heading to European border", https://www.aa.com.tr/en/turkey/turkey-irregular-migrants-heading-to-european-border/1748127 (Access 03.10.2020).

[12] For the literature on critical geopolitics, See Simon Dalby ve Gearóid Ó'Tuathail (2002), "Introduction: Rethinking Geopolitics: Towards A Critical Geopolitics", Dalby, Simon ve Gearóid Ó'Tuathail (Der.), **Rethinking Geopolitics**, London: Routledge, pp.13-27.

[13] Twitter, https://twitter.com/ikalin1/status/1288743764794605568 (Access 30 Temmuz 2020).

time in the making. Detailed as 'Turkey's narrative, one of the most important global narratives from East to the West' in one of Kalın's articles[14], the new narrative rested on the claim that there is a need for a new geographic imagination. The onset of this new approach is related to Ahmet Davutoğlu who served until June 2016 as Senior Advisor to Prime Minister, Minister of Foreign Affairs and Prime Minister. During this period, the Turkish political elite considered Turkey as a country that seeks to 'make its peace with its history and geography'. Accordingly, this new approach involved a rhetorical construct which shaped the understanding of geopolitics through various ideological and political processes. Therefore, Turkey's rhetoric towards migrants and migration helped acquire a specific position for itself.

The new narrative of Turkey, which was in the making, has involved two elements toward migration. The first is Turkey's preference for compassionate and humanitarian policies toward migration unlike the Western countries. The second is Turkey's encompassing and inclusive geopolitical outlook.

Compassionate and Humanitarian Policies

Turkey has recently set a vision for its foreign policy which is compassionate, in favor of equity and humanitarian and it has implemented this vision in its actual policies. According to Turkey's Ministry of Foreign Affairs, Turkey views 'all problems in its foreign policy agenda in a responsible, human-focused, compassionate and principled manner'[15]. The compassionate character of this approach is observed with regard to the migration of Syrians. The open-door policy and temporary protection status for Syrians along these nine years are the most indicative of this vision. Ibrahim Kalın's article[16] sets a summary of the policy toward Syrian migration in this period:

> *'In a world bleeding from the wounds of human greed, ignorance and injustice, every act of justice is immediately owned by countless people around the world. Turkey has been able to capture the imagination of Arabs and other Muslim nations since its multifaceted policies are seen as serving justice, not just for the Turks and the Turkish national interest but for everyone yearning for justice in the region.'*

Turkey's perspective on migration focused not only on the legal and formal aspects of the phenomenon but also emphasizes humanitarian values related to justice and compassion. Turkish government officials have for a long time emphasized Turkey's capacity for solving humanitarian crisis, which stems from its moral values. In addition to that Turkey's Ottoman/Islamic heritage brings about a

---

[14] İbrahim Kalın, Türk Dış Politikası ve Kamu Diplomasisi, in Usul, Ali Resul (ed.), "Yükselen Değer Türkiye", **MÜSİAD Araştırma Raporu**, 2010, https://www.musiad.org.tr/icerik/yayin-40/pr-237 (Access 21.10.2020).

[15] Speech by Foreign Minister Mevlüt Çavuşoğlu in the Turkish Parliament Session on Budget Talks, 2020. http://www.mfa.gov.tr/site_media/html/2020-yilina-girerken-girisimci-ve-insani-dis-politikamiz.pdf (Access 21.10.2020).

[16] İbrahim Kalın, "Debating Turkey in the Middle East: The Dawn of a New GeoPolitical Imagination?" **Insight Turkey**, Vol.11, No.1, 2009, p.87.

responsibility for Turkey to acquire moral leadership in the Islamic civilization according to this perspective.[17] Moral leadership in the Islamic world with its expansive and diverse character does not necessarily and immediately imply a political character yet its rhetorical value is derived from the potential for influence that it provides to Turkey. It also differs from an Islamist political project seeking to unify the entire Muslim wols as a single political unit.[18]

There is also an element related to religion adopted in the Turkish rhetoric on Syrians. The Hijrah in the Islamic history, which narrates the migration of Prophet Muhammad and his followers from Mecca to Medinah, retains an important place in the mindset of the Turkish policymakers. According to the Islamic history, Prophet Muhammad and his followers, the Muhajir (the immigrants), moved to Medinah and there they received aid from the locals, who are called the Ansar (the helpers). Symbolizing the flight of Prophet Muhammad from the oppression of the Meccan polytheists, the narrative of hijrah is associated with solidarity in the mindset of Muslim people.

The Turkish politicians utilized this rhetorical element mainly towards the domestic audience and as a way to address the Muslim communities all around the world. The rising number of the Syrians in Turkey has been viewed as a potential for social tensions within the Turkish society. Turkey provided temporary shelters with high living standards yet only a tiny fraction of Syrians stays in these camps. Syrians mostly live close to city centers, where they can find employment. The Turkish cities near the Syrian border as well as big cities such as Istanbul were almost flooded by Syrians. The city center of Kilis along the Syrian border houses more Syrians than Turkish citizens. Also, there are approximately one million Syrians in Gaziantep.

Encompassing and Inclusive Geopolitical Outlook

Turkey's rhetoric on Syrian migration has been maintained over the course of the past nine years. It is coupled with Turkey's changing foreign policy vision and to some extent stood out as its practical extension.

In his speech at the Council on Foreign Relations[19] in 2014, when he was in the US for attending the 69th session of the UN General Assembly, President Erdoğan defined Turkey as 'the country standing at the center of this region and knows, understands and analyzes it the best'. His approach depicts an image of Turkey that claims the Ottoman heritage, forms heartfelt bonds in the wider region and thus stands out as the most influential regional state. Erdogan stated that Turkey can no

---

[17] Murat Yeşiltaş, "The Transformation of the Geopolitical Vision in Turkish Foreign Policy", **Turkish Studies,** 2013, Vol.14, No.4, p.678.

[18] Cenk Saraçoğlu, Özhan Demrikol, "Nationalism and Foreign Policy Discourse in Turkey Under the AKP Rule: Geography, History and National Identity", **British Journal of Middle Eastern Studies**, 2015, Vol.42, No.3, p.311.

[19] For the full-text of the speech: (23.09.2014) https://www.tccb.gov.tr/haberler/410/1367/turkiye-merkezinde-bulundugu-cografyayi-en-iyi-taniyan-anlayan-ve-analiz-edebilen-ulkedir.html (Access 11.09.2020).

longer remain aloof from the regions that share such heartfelt bonds.[20] Such statements signal intent about addressing a wider region and situating itself at its center. In the same speech, Erdoğan mentions the Balkans, Middle East, North Africa, the Caucasus, Africa, South Asia and Central Asia as the regions that Turkey cannot ignore. Therefore, Turkey undertakes a rhetorical responsibility to its related communities in these regions.

The Syrian crisis and the following migration waves have created an environment which supports Turkey's wide and encompassing geopolitical vision. The open-door policy toward the Syrians was both an effort to act up to the responsibilities stemming from the Ottoman heritage and a requirement to fulfill the claim of a compassionate and humanitarian vision for international order, in which Turkey seeks a central place. President Erdoğan remarked in his speech at the G-20 summit in 2015[21] that Turkey considers the open-door policy a humanitarian duty toward the migrants regardless of their belief and origins. Therefore, the Ottoman heritage and historical values seems to have formed a starting point for Turkey to define a new place for itself. Turkey approached the developments in the last decade that took place in its immediate region from such a starting point. Yet, as the dynamism and optimism of the Arab Spring faded and the cruel reality of the Syrian crisis challenged the regional actors, Turkey continued its ongoing approach toward the Syrians. It has also started to promote a global perspective with regard to the responses for the migrant crisis. It has continued to provide shelter for Syrians both in its own and Syrian territories while at the same time asking global actors for more burden-sharing. In President Erdoğan's words in the Global Refugee Forum in December 2019[22], 'It is evident that the refugee issue cannot be tackled by the efforts of just a few countries like ours which properly host these people. Finding a sustainable solution to this problem, which hurts the consciences, is contingent upon steps to be taken globally.' This approach implies a reformulation of the Turkish rhetoric stemming its own historical and cultural values and moving towards a universal and global character.

Conclusion

In geopolitical sense, Turkey had been situating itself between east and west facing westwards until the first decade of the 21st century, when it starting altering its vision in a different manner. Afterwards, it started to depict and maintain a self-image which consisted of elements as (1) undertaking its Ottoman heritage, (2) attaching importance to the Islamic values and (3) little to zero problems with neighbors. This self-image or narrative developed in parallel to a new geopolitical

[20] For the full-text of the speech in the Turkish Military Academy: (28.03.2016) https://www.tccb.gov.tr/haberler/410/41293/gonul-bagimizin-oldugu-cografyalarin-hicbirine-kayitsiz-kalma-hakkina-sahip-degiliz.html (Access 03.09.2020).

[21] For the full-text of the speech: (16.11.2015) https://www.tccb.gov.tr/haberler/410/35997/g-20-ulkeleri-terorizmle-mucadele-konusunda-guclu-bir-durus-ortaya-koydu.html (Access 04.09.2020).

[22] For the full-text of the speech: (17.12.2019) https://www.tccb.gov.tr/konusmalar/353/113993/kuresel-multeci-forumu-nda-yaptiklari-konusma (Access 04.09.2020).

rhetoric. Turkey has defined such a narrative and has undertaken a role accordingly. The rhetoric of change that Turkey's narrative underlines has been tested against the concrete circumstances of the Syrian migration since 2011.

In this period, the migration waves exacerbated by the Syrian crisis proved to be an opportunity for Turkey to play the role that its narrative outlined. The open-door policy toward the Syrians fleeing the regime violence reinforced Turkey's image as a country that is sensitive and caring about the problems of the region. Throughout the passing years, the number of refugees in Turkey and the high standards of the camps shaped Turkey's rhetoric accordingly. Therefore, Turkey's enterprising and humanitarian foreign policy vision and its image of a country that welcomes and hosts refugees mutually interact with Turkey's way of identifying itself and attaching meaning to its geography.

In conclusion, the period that starts with the Syrian crisis provided Turkey with an occasion and necessity to develop rhetoric for a wider geography and fulfill it with humanitarian values. Migration is one of the factors that transformed Turkey's geopolitical understanding from 'a bridge between east and west' to a country with a central location sharing common values, history and culture with a wider geography.

CHAPTER 6

THE ROLE OF SYRIAN IMMIGRANTS IN THE TURKISH FOREIGN POLICY

İsmail Köse[1] and Metin Aksoy[2]

Introduction: Basic Parameters of Turkish Foreign Policy

Turkish Foreign Policy (TFP) at the very beginning akin small powers during the first decades of Ottoman period based on playing conflicts among stronger powers. For instance during its foundation at the beginning of the 14th century Ottoman Begs played Byzantine, Mongols and, other powers in the vicinity against each other to survive. Similar to European counterparts almost all Ottoman Begs built alliances with other small or big powers to terminate their enemies. In that era, same has been done by small or middle sized European princedoms. This universal policy experienced by Turks in Central Asia during their never ending fights against China and has been transferred to Anatolia.

When at the mid of 15th century Ottomans reached to the peak of their power, could bend any single or common enemies in lands and seas Turkish foreign policy evolved onto level of *'attack and victory'* so the long lasting balance of powers policy has been put aside. The first grave defeat Ottomans faced with at the gates of Vienna in 1683 was the restoration point of the foreign policy to its first days. Ottomans could not adapt new reforms, age of rationality, modern state structure of era, the worse the huge state structure could not adapt technological developments no more capable of defeating its enemies. Rise of Tsarist Russia at the North was another emerging vital danger for the existence of Ottomans. Therefore, especially after mid-18th century Ottoman Turks once upon a time put in use the playing balance of powers policy. That kind of changes were always easier in theory whereas there are numerous difficulties for practice. It is what Türkiye faced with during its foreign policy in the late dates of Ottomans and during the modern Republic.

The history of Ottomans after Vienna was mostly serial defeats and drawbacks that broke off Empire's valuable lands. New conditions forced Ottomans for new alliances and the basics of modern Turkish Foreign Policy (TFP) have been reconstituted during that period. Therefore traditional balance and status quo based TFP took its way after Vienna and has been put in use almost without any major change by the Republic of Türkiye. The Founder of Turkish Republic Mustafa

[1] Assoc. Prof., Gümüşhane University, Türkiye.
[2] Assoc. Prof., Gümüşhane University, Türkiye.

Kemal Atatürk's essential desire was to construct a developed nation state

The first era of Turkish Republic's foreign policy is called as 'The Türkiye of Ataturk' the TFP has been conducted under the directives of Atatürk by Foreign Minister Tevfik Rüştü Aras. Together with anti-revisionism and balance of powers approach, main objectives of TFP were to seek recognition, enjoy full benefits of peace and modernize the country.[3] By the way, there are some critical spots TFP changed its traditional way. For instance, revisionist policies put in use such as Montreux in 1936, annexation of Hatay in 1939, intervention to Cyprus in 1974, proactive policies during the last two decades in Syria, Iraq, and Libya also could be seen as axial dislocation from traditional TFP. Whereas some radical revisionist movements, foreign policy makers of Türkiye, generally consider the capabilities and disabilities of the country while they have been conducting the foreign policy of the country.

Abilities of a country strictly related with its economic might, militaristic power and development level. As a matter of fact, mostly favored state power classification bases on economic, militaristic and structural capacity. According to this categorization states could be divided into three categories such as: (1) Hegemonic powers (2) Middle sized powers (3) Small sized powers. Hegemonic powers are countries capable to implement critical policies and conduct selfish operations such as: US, Russia, China and the EU. Those powers are very hardly could be bent while they have been conducting their policies. Sure enough, hegemonic powers do not bear the power of The King of Pantheon Zeus' Son Hercules but they have enough might to perform number of policies as major players in international relations could do.

Small sized powers such as Arab dictatorships or poor African states are the countries which have not completed its nation building process yet. They need external assistance to survive and generally their domestic relations are intervened by external powers. Those countries cannot conduct unpermitted operations and they must very careful during implementation of their foreign policy. Middle sized powers such as Türkiye, Indonesia, Iran, and India are mostly developing countries, can conduct some critical operations but when they breach hegemonic world order their interests could be punished by hegemons through use of force but generally economic and political sanctions are the hard sticks used by hegemons for such punishments. For instance, Türkiye's second Cyprus intervention in August 1974 have not been approved by the hegemons and Türkiye still bears serious difficulties due its unapproved operation. One of the lessons TFP makers learned after Cyprus intervention not to break traditional un-revisionist balance policy and not to act against hegemonic interests. Whereas post-Cold War era changed a lot in the world politics soon after Cold War balance policy and lessons of past were still in the memories of TFP bureaucracy. Nevertheless a decade after the end of Cold War

---

[3] Ayla Göl, "A Short Summary of Turkish Foreign Policy: 1923-1939", **Ankara Üniversitesi SBF Dergisi**, 48 (01), pp. 57-58.

Turkish foreign policy come across with some radical changes.

Changes on Traditional TFP

Justice and Development Party (JDP) came power at the end of 2002 declared that it would put in use some radical changes. In convenience of that new concept after the year of 2010 traditional well-balanced policy making of TFP has been put aside. JDP seeking a convenient opportunity to intervene Arab relations used Syrian crisis as a ladder to conduct its newly shaped so called pro-active policies. Thus the first major change came with Syrian crisis ignoring traditional policy making the ruling party tried to help Ikhvan Movement (Muslim Brotherhood) to seize power in Syria and Egypt. It was actually clear that such a proactive policy for a middle sized power at the very beginning could not be successful. Soon after flames of civil war in Syria started to threaten Türkiye's own security and an unpredictable immigration influx took its way towards Türkiye.

There were two options on the table: (1) to let immigrants march to Europe and (2) to prevent passage and be immigrant a container country of Europe. The Government due several reasons no need to explain here preferred to choose the second option. As a natural result of this decision the country became a haven of Syrian immigrants. According to official figures the number of irregular immigrants in Türkiye is over 4 million including Afghans, Iranians, Iraqis, Palestinians etc. According to official figures 89% of those immigrants are Syrians. Unofficial numbers are much higher than these figures and the country keeps almost 5% immigrant of its population. How this crisis could be managed and the process for re-admission of immigrants still are unsolved problems. Field researches show that even after the war more than half of Syrian and other nation immigrants reject to back their native countries. This was not a crisis Türkiye could face with alone. The burden needed to be shared by developed European countries. The process threaten the EU's common foreign policy and internal integrity.

When Syrian irregular immigrants marched up in Balkans and thousands of them walked in European streets all humanistic criteria and founding ideals of the EU were put aside. Member countries selfishly started to seek unreasonable and unimplementable solutions to take themselves out of immigrant crisis. None of the members including the biggest economy Germany could have produced reasonable and sustainable solution addressing immigration crisis. Thus a container country vitally needed to sacrifice itself and solve the crisis instead of Europe. The compromise between Ankara and EU members has been occurred at this point. Turkish Government accepted to home Syrian and other nation immigrants in Türkiye, in return the EU promised lifting visa for Turkish citizens. Sure enough, the EU did not keep this promise due some setbacks in TFP, Ankara started to use Syrian immigrants as a foreign policy tool to force the EU from its vulnerable soft belly. The aim of this study is to bring out how and at what level TFP has been using Syrian immigrant card against the EU.

How Syrian Immigrants Effect Turkish Foreign Policy Making

Since its seizure of power it has been argued that secular state structure of Türkiye, under the governance of *'pro-Islamist'* JDP has been facing with some severe grave setbacks. Arguments on freedom of talk, neutral judgement, transparency, basic democratic rights and most importantly protection of European standards for human rights are the hot topics during the last decades. As it has been promised more democratic, modernized, free, and predictable country, at the very beginning of its long-lasting rule JDP had been supporting EU reforms trying to put in force Copenhagen reforms to enlarge freedom of speech and achieve betterments in human rights.[4] In that days JDP lacked support of Nationalist Movement Party (NMP) whose voters mostly are secular Turkish nationalist conservatives. Another obstacle standing before JDP's pro-Islamist policies was Turkish Army which until the unsuccessful coup attempt in 2016 the Army was the protector of modernity and secularism constructed by the founder of Turkish Republic Mustafa Kemal Atatürk.

The democratic reforms issue still on the table in Türkiye needs serious engagement. Another hot spot of last decades is foreign policy making. When it came to power one of the agenda of JDP was to produce good relations to coreligionist Arab brothers. Syria and Egypt were the first hot areas of newly conducted TFP. Ahmet Davutoğlu, close associate of JDP and chief foreign policy advisor since 2003 has been influential in major foreign policy changes including Syria.[5] Immigration crisis has come out due that misled policies.

During those days despite Türkiye being an immigration passage route and target for underdeveloped neighboring countries the country in its long history never faced with such a mass movement, such an unmanageable immigration influx. Soon after 2011, Syrian Crisis broke out Foreign Minister Ahmet Davutoğlu said that *'we will perform afternoon prayer in Damascus Mosque'*, implying the rhetoric he has been representing will be in rule in Damascus overthrowing almost 60 years lasting Baas dictatorship. Despite his refusal of this rhetoric when conditions changed, his statements in that days proves the fact that he was very willing to produce such ultrarealistic metaphors.[6] One of the direct or indirect grave consequences of Davutoglu's ultrarealistic vision and axis dislocation of TFP has been immigration crisis. Syrian immigrants when civil war started left the country to find access in more safe and livable areas leaving their homelands entered Türkiye. Open door policy for all was the slogan of that days. After 2015, noticing impossibility of implementing Davutoğlu's imaginary vision TFP radically has been reset.[7] But it

---

[4] See Erol Kalkan, The Europeanisation of National Politics and Change in Foreign Policy: Transformation of Turkish Foreign Policy in the EU Accession Process, unpublished dissertation thesis, University of Kent, Brussels School of International Studies, Brussels: 2014. pp. 157-182.

[5] Bülent Aras, "The Davutoğlu Era in Turkish Foreign Policy", **Insight Türkiye,** Vol. 11 (3). p. 130.

[6] https://www.birgun.net/haber/davutoglu-emevi-camii-nde-namaz-meselesinde-topu-erdogan-a-atti-297902 (Accessed 07.12.2020).

[7] See Fuat Keyman, "A New Turkish Foreign Policy: Towards Proactive 'Moral Realism'", **Insight Türkiye,** Vol. 19 (1). pp. 56.

was not easy to restore all misconducts of the past.

The migration movement of societies from the lands where they are living toward safer and more comfortable areas is a coetaneous fact with humanity. Immigration almost aged with humankind. Since the emergence of homo-sapiens, humankind being in active motivation to move safer, more fertile and warmer, livable areas. Social contracts and first state organizations are more or less natural results of immigration processes and the motivation forced people to form societies. Even though this fact immigrants never have been welcomed by hosting societies. When its foundation criteria considered it could be expected that EU's migrant policy would be different. As it is seen the EU took reverse course to manage the crisis.

Turkish Foreign Policy vs EU and Irregular Immigrant Crisis

Immigrants generally belong to underdeveloped, poorer, uneducated classes of societies. In addition due their negative effects on demography and economy mass movements and migrants are the chestnuts on fire nobody want to touch. When Syrian crisis broke out and thousands of people passing from Türkiye started to flee and ask shelter in Europe, including newly accepted Balkan Countries regardless level of their development almost all European countries could not produce common or single sustainable policy to manage the crisis. It was the most severe crisis Türkiye and European Countries faced with after WWII.

To manage the crisis and cope with the problem there were three options before EU: (1) to force Bessar Esad's Baas regime to democratize the country and respect minority rights (2) considering development level, economic ability and geographic size to allocate national quotes and share migrants accordingly among EU members and handle the case in humanitarian perspective (3) to contain immigrants in a safe country which they will not shake up European integrity and well-being. It was Türkiye, the most convenient country to contain Syrian immigrants and save Europe. Türkiye, a long-lasting candidate for full membership, the EU never willing to grant; during Cold War, was the southeast wing country of NATO, protected Mediterranean from any possible Soviet attack right now one more time would be asked for a new sacrifice.

The question whether Türkiye would accept to shelter almost 3.6 million Syrians for an unknown period or not. As it has been underlined before there is no need to say that unofficial numbers are much higher. In the world, since WWII, no developed country come across with huge immigration numbers as Türkiye faced with during the last decade. As it is very-well known and mentioned above countries are reluctant and egoist to receive irregular unqualified immigrants. In this context Türkiye has been trying to produce sustainable policies for immigrants.[8]

---

[8] See Murat Erdoğan, Syrian **Refugees In Turkey, Konrad Adenaur Stiftung, September 2019.** https://www.kas.de/documents/283907/7339115/T%C3%BCrkiye%27deki+Suriyeliler.pdf/acaf9d37-7035-f37c-4982-c4b18f9b9c8e?version=1.0&t=1571303334464 (Accessed 08.12. 2020).

When the crisis broke out the rhetoric of ruling party was to produce good relations with Arab coreligionists and that was time for a litmus test. The number of Syrian immigrants at Türkiye in October 2015 was 2.2 million and the number of Syrian immigrants in all European countries at the same date was about 250 thousand.[9] In that days the EU used vise liberalization and economic assistance programs as soft havoc policy. The hard stick was provisional turning blind-eye to domestic so-called antidemocratic policies and inconformity with Copenhagen criteria. Foreign Minister Davutoğlu, volunteer to handle the job instead of the EU, signed Readmission Agreement in 2016 under above mentioned conditions.[10] Actually the EU never planned to grant promised visa liberalization and the number of official Syrian migrants in 2020 is more than 3.6 million. In addition according to UNCHR figures, Türkiye hosts 370 thousands different country originated irregular immigrants.[11]

The text of Readmission Agreement never guaranteed visa liberalization and high numbered mass movements always bear the risk of social and economic problems. It is not surprising that Türkiye in near future will face with such risks and unmanageable problems. No need to say that readmission agreement was unacceptable for traditional TFP. The Agreement would come into force in 2017, and one year before again with his imaginary discourse Davutoğlu presented it as a victory upon his return after signing ceremony saying that the visa liberalization would start in June 2016.[12] Sure enough those ultrarealistic statements never come to true.

EU's reluctance and inability to manage immigration crisis had shown TFP makers the possibility to play carrot and stick policy over migrants. As it will be remembered at the beginning it was the EU decided to conduct carrot and stick policy in return Türkiye did the same. Therefore, instead of Davutoğlu's never implemented infamous Readmission Agreement, an unsigned consensus has been reached between Ankara and Brussels. Accordingly: (1) Türkiye would home Syrian irregular immigrants and prevent illegal passages being a migrant container country of Europe would not allow passages to Greece in sea and land where EU's borders lined (2) In return Brussels would allocate credit and financial support to Türkiye and would not use hard discourse and strict criticism against domestic human right abuses. In addition a blind eye would be turned to all kind of internal policies

---

[9] **Hürriyet,** Mülteci Tablosu Böyle Süremez [The Rise of Immigration Figures Unmanageable]", 6 Ekim 2015. p. 1.

[10] See İsmail Köse, "Avrupa Birliği'nin Mülteci Açmazı ve Türkiye-Avrupa Birliği Geri Kabul Anlaşması [European Union's Immigrant Dilemma and Türkiye -EU Readmission Agreement]", **Electronic Journal of Political Science Studies,** January 2016, Vol. 7(1). pp. 1-26.

[11] Türkiye'deki Mülteciler ve Sığınmacılar [Immigrants and Refugees in Türkiye], https://www.unhcr.org/tr/turkiyedeki-multeciler-ve-siginmacilar (accessed December 8, 2020); Mehmet Kızmaz, "Arafta Süren Hayatlar [Lives in Limbo]", **Cumhuriyet,** 08 December 2020. pp. 1, 12.

[12] Lenka Petkova, "EU's Readmission Agreement and Visa Liberalization Talks with Türkiye:Backing up Türkiye's Protracted way to the EU", **Gobal Political Trends Center,** August 2012. p. 8; Davtuoğlu: Vize Muaffiyeti [2016] Haziran Ayında Başlayacak [Davutoğlu: Vize Exemption [For Turkish Citizens] Will Start in [2016] June], https://www.hurriyet.com.tr/gundem/basbakan-davutoglu-avrupa-ile-vize-muafiyeti-haziran -ayinda-baslayacak-40065589 (accessed 08.12.2020).

contradictory to EU criteria (3) The limbo status of Türkiye, at the front of EU's gate would be protected whilst neither side willing for full membership.

Facing one of the most unmanageable crises since the Treaty of Rome (1957) Brussels was volunteer to accept new compromise as a gift. As it has been very well evaluated in EU Headquarters the new policy would save EU's sustainability which has been shaken up by immigrants, would save EU Countries' stability and most importantly would protect EU's cultural, demographic unity. When compared with the price to be paid the earnings of the EU much more beyond its concessions. The crisis had been solved at the borders of the EU and the honor, integrity and unity of the EU saved by Türkiye.

EU's policy to use Türkiye as immigration home and container for irregular migrants show that the EU never planned to grant full-membership to Ankara in foreseeable future. When come across with the price and refusal of visa liberalization Ankara tried to rise its voice against the EU and using migrant crisis as a stick and threatened Brussels that it would no more shelter Syrians.[13] All those hard discourse bore no result. The first time Ankara stopped using hard discourse and declared that Türkiye no more will prevent Syrian passages to Europe came four years after signing of Readmission Agreement.

At the beginning of 2020, in February 27, Syrian Baath Regime bombed Turkish base in Syrian city Idlib killed 34 Turkish soldiers. Public tension rose up spontaneously, blaming both immigrants not to fight for the sake of their mother country and the government. Unexpectedly the migrant card put in use declaring that after now open door policy would be conducted for immigrants who wants to leave Türkiye. The new policy meant that all irregular immigrants who would like to go Europe free to pass Turkish borders. But due wide spread of COVID-19 pandemic, migrants' reluctance to leave Türkiye and some other reasons the card could not be played as it has been expected at the beginning.[14] The EU, soon after this declaration and opening of borders blamed Türkiye to use Syrian immigrants as a foreign policy tool. That argument theoretically could be correct whereas when their selfish, international convention preaching illicit policies addressing migrants and migration crisis considered European Countries did not have any moral, legal and legitimate argument to put forward last complaints.

The EU Migration Policy

The migratory movements of people between Türkiye and the EU should not be conceived simply as persons' replacement from one point to another. Factors such as the socio-political conditions of the source country, security and stability

---

[13] Erdoğan Alnımıza Enayi Yazmıyor [Erdogan: There is no Sign of Fool on Our Forehead], https://www.bbc.com/turkce/haberler/2016/02/160211_erdogan_omer_celik_multeciler_aciklama (Accessed 08.12.2020).

[14] Mültecileri Gönüllü Olarak Avrupa'ya Taşırız [We Transfer Immigrants Voluntarily to Europe], https://www.sozcu.com.tr/2020/gundem/multecileri-gonullu-olarak-avrupaya-tasiriz-5651942/ (Accessed 08.12.2020).

issues of the region where that country located as well as sociological dynamics play a significant role behind these migratory movements. As it has been underlined previous pages either the main motive of the movement is economy or security, migrants venture on their voyages bearing all the prospective dangers with the desire of reaching to the fruits of the target country. The notions such as security, welfare and stability constitute the prominent themes of their story of migration.

Data shared by Ministry of Internal Affairs of Türkiye display that Türkiye has been a transit country for the migrants mainly from the Middle Eastern countries, Syria, Pakistan, and Afghanistan, Iran so on whose target is the EU countries and that their current number within Türkiye's borders is 5,074,908.[15] The reality that Türkiye, as a transit country for the migratory movements, has common borders with the EU creates security concerns along these borders. For this reason, certain measures among whom the most prominent one is the EU migration policy has been adopted to eliminate these security concerns bringing new regulations for the entry of persons to the EU.

The EU migration policy can be separated three periods with different time lengths: The first period between 1957-1990; the second period between 1990-1999; the third period from 1999 to the present. The characteristic feature of the first period was that the migration policy was arranged in coordination by the founding members of the European Economic Community (EEC) since its foundation in 1957. In time, goals, means, methods and rules in relation to the migratory movements targeting Europe had substantially changed. The founding agreement of EEC had been regulating the free movement of workers in the Community. The freedom of movement aimed to standardise working conditions and wages in the Community, avoiding different national policies among the member states. The obstacles before free movement of workers were abolished in compliance with the policy developed at the beginning of the EEC integration process of which target was to create a common market among the member countries. To stimulate the European integration that ground to a halt in the 1970s and to create a common 'European Citizenship', the unemployed persons were also granted the free movement. With this, all citizens would be able to benefit from the privileges of the European integration.

The freedom of movement was the most heated subject which came into the table at each of the European Community (EC) enlargement phases. In the 1960s, there were concerns that the poor citizens of Italy would dominate the European labour market. The same concerns, this time that Commonwealth citizens would immigrate to the Community without control, emerged in the 1970s when the United Kingdom joined the Community. When Greece, Portugal and Spain joined the Community in the 1980s, their nationals were exempted from freedom of movement for a temporary period to offset the fears of the members regarding repercussions of free movement. Nonetheless, the anxiously anticipated migratory

---

[15] https://www.ntv.com.tr/turkiye/bakan-soylu-turkiyedeki-yabanci-sayisini acikladi,DxY63bOgc0qlHsp _Eb5f0w (Accessed 04.12.2020).

mass flows had never taken place.[16]

The Community members, for the first time, adopted the policy of shaping their immigration policies with third countries outside the Community in the 1970s.[17] The EC Council of Ministers declared the first action plan about migrant workers and their families in 1974.[18] In 1976, TREVI (Terrorism, Radicalism, Extremism and International Violence) was inaugurated as an ad-hoc forum. It was temporarily assigned to find ways of cooperation in these topics alongside the subjects regarding Community law.[19] The EC assigned the European Commission to take over the coordination between the member countries and third countries in 1976. The Commission determined the principles of the Community's migration policy in 1985 for the first time. In the following year, the Single European Act (SEA) which foresaw the creation of a single market until 1992 was signed.

The SEA aimed to lift the barriers before the free movement of capital, people, goods and services within the Community borders, and to enhance the harmony of members paving the way for the creation of a competition area in the Community.[20] Moreover, it included legal measures for immigrants from third countries, such as determining limits for their entry to and presence in the EC countries. In 1985, Benelux countries, Germany and France signed the visa agreement committing to harmonise their national visa policies and to lift the internal borders. The irregular immigration from third countries to the member countries was to be prevented by subjecting the immigrants to common control acquis. By this way, the external border controls would be implemented collectively while lifting the borders between the member countries.[21]

In the context of the target set out with TREVI to increase the external border controls, The Palma Document was prepared in 1989 by a coordination group assigned by the European Community Council. It constituted the first the EC document aimed at coordination in subjects such as the judiciary matters, immigration and asylum-seeking.[22] The Community Charter on the Fundamental

---

[16] **Sachverständigenrat für Zuwanderung und İntegration, Migration und İntegration –Erfahrungen nutzen, Neues wagen**, Bundesamt für Migration und Flüchtlinge. Nürnberg, 2004, s. 298-299

[17] Barış Özdal, Avrupa Birliği'nin Göç Politikası ve İstihdam Stratejisi Bağlamında Türkiye'nin Üyelik Süreci, **Uluslararası Göç ve Nüfus Hareketleri Bağlamında Türkiye** Barış Özdal (Ed.), Bursa, Dora, 2018, 233-267.

[18] Katharina Stöcker, **Migration in der Europäischen Union: Versuch einer Kohärenten Politik**, Hamburg, Diplomica Verlag, 2014, s. 25.

[19] Simon McMahon, "Handbook of the International Political Economy of Migration", **Regional integration and migration in the European Union**, Leila Simona Talani, Simon McMahon, (Ed.) Northampton, Edward Elgar Publishing, 2015. s. 292.

[20] **The Single European Act, the official journal of the European Communities**, No L 69/1, 29.06.87. https://eur-lex.europa.eu/resource.html?uri=cellar:a519205f-924a-4978-96a2-b9af8a598b85.0004.02/DOC_1&format=PDF (Accessed 01.12.2020).

[21] The Schengen area and cooperation, https://eur-lex.europa.eu/legal-content/EN/TXT/?uri=LEGISSUM %3Al33020 (Accessed 01.12.2020).

[22] "Palma Document", Free Movement of Persons. A Report to the European Council by the Coordinators Group, **Council of the European Community**, 1989 Madrid. https://www.ab.gov.tr/files/ardb/evt/1_avrupa_birligi/1_4_zirveler_1985_sonrasi/1989_madrid_zirvesi_baskanlik_avrupa_topluluklari_en.pdf (Accessed 01.12.2020).

Social Rights of Workers, in which the legally residing migrant workers' rights set out, was adopted by eleven member states in December 1989. With this Charter, it was aimed to eliminate differences in wage, in working and living conditions that would occur between the native and migrant workers. However, this aim did not become a supranational policy of the Community; instead, it was implemented by intergovernmental cooperation of the members.

The Dublin Convention signed in 1990 was a turning point as it assigned the countries of the first arrival to examine once for all the asylum-seeking applications. By this way, misuse of the asylum-seeking application would be prevented by standardising the rules in the refugee assessment process across the Community. This Convention later was to be revised with the Dublin II in 2003 and Dublin III regulations in 2013. However, especially Italy, Hungary and Greece, as the first arrival points of immigrants crossing the Mediterranean, were negatively affected by the Convention as they were held responsible for examining the asylum-seeking applications of these immigrants. Conversely, the countries in the north had the right to return the immigrants who 'illegally entered' into their soils. Upon the deadlock in the examination processes due to numerous applications, the European Court of Human Rights (ECHR) issued a decision regarding the return and readmission procedures of the asylum-seekers in the Community. According to this decision, immigrants who crossed to another country would not be returned to the countries of first entry for asylum application.[23]

The European Community became the European Union (EU) with the Maastricht Treaty, which was signed in 1992 and came into force in 1993. This agreement also authorised the EU institutions for standardising the visa policies of the member countries and for the creation of a single type of visa for the Union. In the subjects regarding refugees and migration policies, the agreement envisaged intergovernmental cooperation between the members. Visa policies of the members for third countries and determining the conditions for granting visas to individuals were kept outside the Union's jurisdiction. In these respects, the Maastricht Treaty proposed a hybrid model with combined authorisation of intergovernmental institutions and the Union's institutions in policy-making processes.[24]

By signing the Treaty of Amsterdam in 1997, the EU leaders had taken crucial steps towards the creation of community laws. The underlying factors behind this initiative were to avoid the Europeanisation of the cross-border issues which surged from the beginning of the 1990s by coordination of the member countries to securitise the unstable borders and to help the member states which underwent the pressure of migratory movements. Furthermore, some governments' desire to push the integration process forward in domestic matters and judicial policies are

---

[23] http://www.spiegel.de/politik/ausland/fluechtlinge-so-funktioniert-die-dublin-verordnung-a-1029803.html (Accessed 01.12.2020).

[24] Steffen Agenendt, Regelung und Vermittlung: Die Rolle internationaler Migrationen, Dietrich Thränhardt, Uwe Hunger (Ed.) **Migration im Spannungsfeld von Globalisierung und Nationalstaat**, Wisbaden, Westdeutsche Verlag, 2003, s.188.

interpreted other important factors behind this initiative.[25] With the incorporation of new Title IV which covered the subjects regarding refugees, visa regulations, and freedom of movement to the treaty, it was aimed to create an area of freedom, security and justice. Consequently, internal borders were to be lifted within the Union's soil in 5 years.[26]

However, the means, measures to be taken and the way to realise this aim were not clearly expressed. To avoid this uncertainty, the Vienna Action Plan was inaugurated in 1998 whose first target was to clarify the ambiguity in the notions. In this plan, it was concluded that the area of freedom meant providing a legal guarantee for free movement of persons and their fundamental rights and combating 'all forms of discrimination'. The fight against 'illegal immigration' was adopted as a primary target. The Tampere Council (1999) supplemented the Treaty of Amsterdam by concretising the steps needed to be taken in areas of justice and internal affairs. Specifically, it was concluded to strengthen the member states' cooperation in the control of the external borders and to develop 'common policies on asylum and immigration' of the Union.[27] The European Border and Coast Guard Agency (FRONTEX) was founded in Warsaw, the capital city of Poland, in 2005 to protect the EU's external borders.[28]

This agency, in general, is missioned to prevent unlawful entries into the EU. In 2006, directive for data storage came into force. In this way, data of individuals are stored and provided institutions with upon demand. Nonetheless, an important law was issued determining the extend of time and purpose regarding the use of the individuals' data in one hand and ensuring the security in the other. With the EU Internal Security Strategy in Action adopted in 2010, the EU aimed to work together 'to be more effective in fighting and preventing serious and organised crime, terrorism and cybercrime, in strengthening the management of our external borders and in building resilience to natural and man-made disasters'.[29] However, when it comes to the refugee crisis, it was evident that the EU were not able to adopt an approach by common consent.[30]

Refugee Crisis and EU

Mass refugee flows towards European borders started in 2015 summer as a result of security issues. The migratory pressure shaped the dynamics of a new era

---

[25] http://www.europarl.europa.eu/topics/treaty/pdf/amst-de.pdf (Accessed 01.12.2020).

[26] Daniela Jahn, Andreas Maurer, Verena Oetzmann, Andrea Riesch, **Asyl- und Migrationspolitik der EU Ein Kräftespiel zwischen Freiheit, Recht und Sicherheit**, Diskussionspapier der FG 1, 2006/ 09, Juli 2006 SWP Berlin, s.7.

[27] Schlussfolgerungen des Vorsıtzes, **Tampere Europäıscher Rat**,15. Und 16. Oktober 1999.

[28] Europäische Agentur für die operative Zusammenarbeit an den Außengrenzen – Frontex, Verordnung (EU) Nr. 1168/2011, http://eur-lex.europa.eu/legal-content/DE/TXT/?uri=URISERV%3Al33216 (Accessed 01.12.2020).

[29] Strategie für die innere Sicherheit der Europäischen Union Auf dem Weg zu einem europäischen Sicherheitsmodell, Luxemburg: **Amt für Veröff entlichungen der** Europäischen Union, Brüssel, 2010. s.1-36 https://www.consilium.europa.eu/media/30736/qc3010313dec.pdf (Accessed 01.12.2020).

[30] Ekrem Yaşar Akçay, Avrupa Birliği'nin Göç Politikası: Göçün İnsani Olmayan Güvenlikleştirilmesi, Gökhan Teletar, Umut Gedikli (Ed). **Uluslararası Göç ve Güvenlik**, Ankara, Nobel, 2019, 181-202

in which the developed acquis and the officials' abilities fell short. Human rights have been violated within the EU's borders, and there has been no solidarity with the refugees.[31] The EU, unable to produce a unified solution in the face of the crisis, seemed to have hit the wall.[32] The EU's way of approaching this humanitarian crisis as an economic matter in the readmission agreement it concluded with Türkiye is not also compatible with human rights and human dignity that the EU defends.[33]

Refugees have appeared as convulsive dynamic disrupting the effectiveness of all the EU Council conclusions, the EU Commission's decisions and the treaties, and they may cause a domino effect in other areas. It can be argued that the reasons behind these developments are the EU's failure to show the necessary unity to implement the decisions drafted in the Dublin Treaty in 1990 and coastal countries' loneliness in their response to the humanitarian crisis of the refugees.[34]

Another reason for the EU's failure in managing this humanitarian crisis is that a sustainable refugee regime has never been accomplished due to the lack of enthusiasm of the member countries. It is a matter of the fact that there has been no consensus between the eastern/poorer and western/wealthier EU member states on the composition of 'the EU values'. As a result of this, the member states have prioritised their interests even in the most vital subjects that the EU should handle collectively. As an example, a treaty which proposed to take the necessary legal steps for distribution of the refugees to the member states was rejected by the qualified majority.[35] As the EU members could not reach a commonly agreed solution, signing the readmission agreement with Türkiye appeared to be imperative.

Readmission Agreements

By Readmission Agreements, the parties undertake the responsibility of readmitting their citizens who do not obtain authorisation for residing in the other party countries as well as the third-country nationals who crossed their soils to reach the other countries. The object persons of these agreements are who travel without necessary official documents such as a valid passport and a visa, and who enter the party countries from the ways other than officially recognised border crossing points. The persons who previously met the requirements for entry but no longer have authorisation for residing due to reasons such as visa duration ending are also subjected to readmission procedures. The Readmission Agreements are the means encouraging to employ measures against irregular migration and ensuring the return

---

[31] J. Lehmann: Flucht in die Krise – Ein Rückblick auf die EU- Flüchtlingskrise, **Aus Politik und Zeitgeschichte**, Nr. 52/2015, 21.12.2015, s. 7-11. https://www.bpb.de/apuz/217302/ein-rueckblick-auf-die-eu-fluechtlingskrise-2015 (Accessed 01.12.2020).

[32] J. Fischer: Zeit für Antworten, Süddeutsche Zeitung vom 8.5.2016. s.7

[33] See Kose, Passim.

[34] Metin Aksoy, Faruk Taşkın (2017), Avrupa Birliği'nin Göç Politikası ve Mülteci Sorunu, Osman Köse (Ed). **Uluslararası Göç**, Uğur Ofset, Samsun, 1719-1724. https://www.sondakika.com/haber/haber-milli-savunma-baklanligi-idlib-de-sehit-olan-34-12968677/

[35] **Beschluss des Rates der Europäischen Union vom** 22.9.2015. https://eur-lex.europa.eu/legal-content/DE/TXT/PDF/?uri=CELEX:32015D1601&from=SK (Accessed 01.12.2020).

of the irregular migrants to their countries.

As a deterrent force, these agreements are crucial cooperation tools for governments in easing the expelling of irregular migrants, and they regulate the returning of irregular migrants to the country of origin or the transit country. The vital part of the Readmission Agreement within the framework of the fight against irregular migration is the inclusion of the third-country nationals in the agreements. By including the third-country nationals in the Readmission Agreements, parties undertake the responsibility of bearing the consequences of the problems stemming from their soils. That is to say that the states should undertake the responsibility of the irregular migrants who use their soils as a transit route and should avoid the activities which may harm the neighbour states.

Inclusion of the third-country nationals to the extent of readmission has been easing the EU's burden in returning the irregular migrants. Thus, the Readmission Agreements which include both transit countries and the countries of origin are a useful tool as it enables the EU to exceed the deadlock in returning the irregular migrants found in its soil. Türkiye has signed Readmission Agreements with source, transit and target countries affected by irregular migration guaranteeing readmission of irregular migrants by Türkiye and their return to the source and transit countries. The initiatives made in this context led to the signing of Readmission Agreements with 16 countries and the EU since 2001.

The Türkiye – EU Readmission Agreement aims to return the persons who 'do not or no longer, fulfil the conditions in force for entry to, presence in, or residence on, the territory of Türkiye or of one of the Member States_msocom_3'[36] based on the reciprocity principle. The Readmission Agreement came into force after being published in Official Newspaper with Prime Minister Decree numbered 2014/6 on 16 April 2014.[37] The point which should be paid attention is the role cast to Türkiye in stopping the intense refugee flows to the EU in exchange for the granting of 'visa exemption'.[38] This role naturally requires Türkiye to deal with the hardship of hosting the refugees whose numbers are increasing day after day. Therefore, this agreement does not have the potential to solve the problem permanently. As both the EU and Türkiye prioritise their profits, interpreting this agreement as the parties' initiatives towards their domestic affairs to reduce public pressure seems highly plausible[39].

With the guide of the decisions reached at the meeting of the EU heads of state or government with Türkiye on 18 March 2016, the returns of the irregular migrants

[36] **Lex Access to European Union law**. https://eur-lex.europa.eu/legal-content/EN/ALL/?uri=CELEX%3A22014A0507%2801%29 (Accessed 01.12.2020).

[37] https://www.resmigazete.gov.tr/eskiler/2014/04/20140416-10.htm (Accessed 01.12.2020).

[38] Kamuran Rençber, Türkiye Cumhuriyeti Devleti ile Avrupa Birliği Arasında Akdedilen Geri Kabul Antlaşması'nın Yaratabileceği Sonuçların Analizi, Barış Özdal (Ed.), **Uluslararası Göç ve Nüfus Hareketleri Bağlamında Türkiye**, Bursa, Dora, 2018, s.310

[39] Kutluhan Bozkurt, Geri Kabul ve Vize Serbestisi Anlaşması, **Türkiye Barolar Birliği Dergisi**, Cilt: 29, Sayı: 125, Temmuz 2016, s.398 http://tbbdergisi.barobirlik.org.tr/m2016-125-1594 (Accessed 02.12.2020).

entered to Greece through Türkiye from 20 March 2016 onward started under the coordination of Directorate General of Migration Management (DGMM) on 04 April 2016. Only the persons whose asylum applications rejected or who do not qualify for international protection among those arriving Greek islands would be returned. Within the framework of the EU- Türkiye Statement, for each Syrian immigrant readmitted by Türkiye, a Syrian immigrant who is under temporary protection in Türkiye has been resettled in the member states.[40]

The agreement has been a dissuasive tool for human smugglers as a result of ensuring the control of irregular migration in the Aegean Sea. Consequently, the number of unlawful entries to Türkiye in the hope for reaching the EU soil has also decreased significantly. These results show that the agreement has proved to be a necessary temporary measure in bringing an end to the humanitarian plight and in rebuilding the public order.[41] In that point Türkiye being a container country of irregular immigrants use this burden in its foreign policy to achieve some of its aims.

Conclusion

The EU developing its relations towards Türkiye under the context of historical pre-judges and religious differences never volunteer to grant Türkiye full membership. Actually, Turks during the history have contributed development of European History, during Cold War as it is very well-known Türkiye was the southeastern gate of European security. Ignoring this fact the EU has been trying to implement all selfish policies to drive irregular immigration crisis out of its borders passing from River of Maritsa and Aegean. The EU countries know that mass numbered irregular migrants including instability cause a lot of problems in the future.

An unstable Türkiye is an essential challenge to the security and stability of Europe. Most probably European policy-makers are very well aware about this fact. But they mostly steered by historical past and religious bigotry prefer to overestimate the role and status of Türkiye. It is thought that, keeping Türkiye in front of the door and making it an irregular immigrant container would solve all problems. Nevertheless it is not possible to keep Türkiye before door or to prolong the engagement which never turns into marriage forever also is not a sustainable policy. For instance if Türkiye was an unstable country, about 5 million Syrian, Afghan, Iraqi, Iranian migrants would go to Europe. As it is very well experienced despite its supra national strong structure the EU has not have the capacity to cope with such mass immigration crisis.

EU's immigration policies has some radical changes during its history. The EU, until the end of Cold War put in use a migration policy steered in accordance with

---

[40] Nuray Ekşi, 18 Mart 2016 Tarihli AB-Türkiye Zirvesi Bildirisinin Hukuki Niteliği. Contemporary Research in Economics and Social Sciences 1 (2017), s.51-53. https://dergipark.org.tr/tr/pub/conress/issue/35705/398384 (Accessed 06.12.2020).

[41] https://www.goc.gov.tr/kurumlar/goc.gov.tr/YillikGocRaporlari/2016_yiik_goc_raporu_haziran.pdf (Accessed 06.12.2020).

its needs. After the Cold War due comprehensive enlargements and that partly liberal policy has been changed. The rise of illicit acts such as organized crimes, drug trafficking, international terrorism and illegal migration forced the EU to tighten internal cooperation on security issues. Because of its ultra-national structure and member states' differing interests and priorities the implementation of this new policy was not easy. Meanwhile EU faced with unmanageable immigration crisis especially after the broke out of Syrian civil war.

Because the EU could not produce any sustainable, long-lasting solution addressing the crisis, member countries instead of cooperation preferred to handle their national interests. The deadlock as a catalyzer paved the way emergence of long-lasting internal disagreements. If the flow restart to address Europe inevitably all problems reemerge.

The migration process is related with both EU's security and expectations of migrants for a wealthier and better life conditions. Past events during last decade prove the fact that the EU neither volunteer nor capable to manage the irregular mass migration flow or to put in use sustainable integration policies. So and so one directive or decision after a short period has been changed with a new one and this blind process never ends. This deadlock prevent development of any kind of solution method alternatives. Concrete strategies addressing solutions should be put in use immediately. Leaving the crisis to Türkiye and acting as nothing happened is not sustainable both for the EU and for Türkiye.

The mostly sustainable solution for Türkiye and the EU is to remove reasons of immigration process. Surely this is not a way as easy to implement. But, the unnamed compromise between the EU and Türkiye is not sustainable. In near future the crisis will force the borders of the EU and before this date major building measures should be put in force. Türkiye, could use Syrian migrants as a foreign policy tool because the EU turns blind eyes to realities and ignore the fact of human movement.

CHAPTER 7

REFUGEES POSITION FROM THE FAMILY LAW PERSPECTIVE IN TURKEY

Şebnem Akipek Öcal[1]

Introduction and the Problem

There are many people in the World who are forcibly or with several different reasons displaced, and they are staying in different countries as refugees. Turkey currently hosts a large number of refugees Worldwide[2]. Especially the number of Syrian refugees in Turkey is very high and the total number is more than 4 million.

Turkey is a member state to the 1951 Refugee Convention and also the 1967 Protocol. Till 2013 there was no direct legislation related with asylum and refugees in Turkey. In 2013 the Law on Foreigners and International Protection was enacted by the Turkish Grand National assembly and it entered into force on 11 April 2014.

The Law sets out the main pillars of Turkey's national asylum system and establishes a Directorate. The General Directorate of Migration Management is the main state entity in charge of policymaking and proceedings for all foreigners in Turkey. Therefore, it should be stated that this Law is not only to regulate the situation refugees in Turkey, but all foreigners.

Turkey also adopted Temporary Protection Regulation on 22 October 2014, which sets out the rights and obligations along with procedures for those who are granted temporary protection in Turkey. 'Temporary protection' may be defined as a protection status granted to foreigners, who were forced to leave their country, who cannot return to the country they left, arrived at, or crossed our borders in masses or individually during a period of mass influx[3], to seek emergency and temporary protection and who international protection request cannot be taken under individual assessment.

[1] Prof. Dr., TED University, Türkiye.

[2] According to UNHCR, since 2014, Turkey has been the country hosting the largest number of refugees under UNHCR's mandate in the world – with the vast majority being nationals of the Syrian Arab Republic. In 2019, the number of Syrians with temporary protection status remained stable at nearly 3.6 million. Over 98% of Syrians lived in urban, peri-urban and rural areas, with less than 2% residing in seven remaining temporary accommodation centers. In 2020 Turkey sill continues to host the largest number of refugees worldwide. There are 4.1 million refugees and 3.7 million of them are Syrians: https://reporting.unhcr.org/turkey (03.12.2020).

[3] Significant number of arrivals of persons over a short period of time from the same country is named as "mass influx". For detailed information see: http://www.mhd.org.tr/images/yayinlar (05.12.2020). As an example, to this situation Syrian nationals can be given. Syrian nationals are admitted to Turkey as a part of the temporary protection regime and they will not be sent back to their country against their will.

The refugees to be legally recognised must register with the authorities. For the registered refugees there are many national and international legal rights and Turkish law brings protection for the refugees from many different aspects.

Directorate General of Migration Management is the responsible authority for the refugees in Turkey. The registration of the refugees is also conducted by the mentioned Directorate. After registration the refugees have access to many rights in Turkey, like access to health, access to education, access to the labour market and access to social assistance.

As stated above there are more than 4 million refugees living in Turkey. Their access to social rights and their ability to work are important concepts. However, there is another concept may be even more important than the others, but which is not dealt mostly and that is they live as a foreign national in Turkey and they have many problems related with family law issues. They get married, they want to be divorced, they have children, custody can be a problem etc. Which law shall be applied to them and to those issues? This question should be answered by care because it can have delicate results.

Foreign nationals in a foreign country are subject to private international law, the conflict of law rules and the choice of law rules. Private international law mainly governs civil and commercial law transactions and disputes that contain foreign element[4]. The Turkish International Private and Procedural Law (TIPPL) is enacted on 27 November 2007 and it entered into force on 12 December 2007. The refugees shall also be subject to the mentioned Law.

In TIPPL marriage and divorce are regulated by different provisions. According to article 13/1, 'The legal capacity to marry and the conditions thereof shall be governed by the respective national laws of the parties at the time of the marriage.'. Second paragraph of the mentioned article regulates the form of marriage as 'The form of marriage shall be governed by the law of the state where the marriage is solemnized'. Article 14 regulates divorce and separation, and it states: 'The grounds and provisions for divorce and separation shall be governed by the common national law of the spouses. If the spouses have different nationalities, the law of the place of their common habitual residence, in case of absence of such residence, Turkish law shall govern.' The maintenance of the divorced spouses is also governed with the provisions of this clause. According to article 19, the habitual residence law of the creditor shall govern the alimony.

Apart from the form of marriage and alimony according to TIPPL, the national law of the foreigner is applicable. Despite this fact, there is another provision regulated by TIPPL, that should also be taken into consideration and that is article 5. This provision brings the concept of public order. According to article 5: *If the*

[4] Private international law is also defined as the law governing the legal relations between individuals the elements of which of which affects the law of more than one state: Kosters, J, "Public Policy in Private International Law", The Yale Law Journal, Vol. 29, No. 7 (May 1920), p. 745.

provision of the foreign law to be applied in a certain case is openly contrary to the public order of Turkey, the said provision shall not be applied. Where it is deemed necessary, Turkish law shall be applied.'

The concept of public order dates to the middle ages. Public order rules are the rules that concern the basic political, social, economic, and legal structure and the basic interest of the society. They are the legal rules that have been accepted due to special conditions and that are deemed to be of substantial interest of that country at a certain time.

Public order is designed to keep out domestic public interests, and it functions in both choice of law and the law of foreign judgments. The concept of public order allows courts to rely on national public considerations and reject the applicable foreign law if its content is sufficiently contradictory[5]. In comparison to the common law systems, the civil law systems are making more extensive use of the public policy exception, where in matters of public concern, such as family law matters, so that the *lex fori* shall be the only applicable law.

Since Turkey is a civil law country, concept of public order is important, and it may restrict the application of foreign legal rules and therefore the forum is applied. Family law in that sense is an important area of law, especially due to compulsory legal rules and moral concepts regarded as of public order concern in Turkish Law.

Therefore, first the main aspects of Turkish law shall be explained, then their applicability to the refugees shall be discussed.

General Aspects of Turkish Family Law

Evaluation of Turkish Law

Turkey is a continental law (civil law) country. As is known Turkish Republic was founded in 1923. After the foundation of the new Republic, it was impossible to continue with the legal system that was applicable in the Ottoman Empire. Because in the Ottoman Empire there was the reign of the Sultan and for the private law issues mainly the religious rules were effective. For that reason, Turkey has chosen to make reception. Legal reform was regarded as a very important tool in the modernization of the young Republic. The main method of legal reform was codification. Since the most important daily legal relations are the relations regarding the law of persons, family, property, succession, and the law of obligations, first there was the need to fill the legal gap in these areas.

It was decided to adopt the Codes of Switzerland. So, in 1926 Civil Code and the Code of Obligations had been enacted. The Civil Code was effective till 1 January 2002, and the Code of Obligations was effective till 1 July 2012. Then they have been replaced by the new Civil Code and new Code of Obligations

[5] Fassberg, Celia Wasserstein, "The Public in Private International Law", https://law.huji.ac.il/sites/default/files/law/files/fassberg_-_international_law.pdf (08.12.2020).

consecutively, but the new versions of these codes are also following nearly the same modernisation pattern of the Swiss laws, therefore they are also no different than the existing Swiss originals mainly. The family law is Turkey is regulated by the Civil Code. During the amendment process it was the mostly changed part of the Civil Code and it was codified with a new perspective of equality within the family.

Family Law

Together with this effort of reception, Turkey was able to adopt modern, secular laws mostly depending on equality especially within the family. In general, it could easily be stated that Turkish laws are no different than the main European laws. Therefore, there is no specific or different legal rule for women regarding the matters of family in general. Together with these amendments it could easily be mentioned that there is complete equality between man and woman regarding the family law.

As mentioned, family law is regulated with the Turkish Civil Code, family law is the second book of the Civil Code[6]. Turkish Constitution also brings some provisions that regulate the family in a general way. According to these provisions' family is regarded as the basic unit of the society and the State has a duty to protect the family. Actually, the approach of the Constitution towards the family clearly identifies its nature as a concept of public order. Secondly article 10 of the Constitution regulates the equality principle. On 07.05.2004 a new paragraph is added to this provision: '*Women and men have equal rights. State has a duty to provide this equality in reality*'.

Compared to the Civil Code of 1926, the new Civil Code of 2002 has especially significant changes towards gender equality within the family. Individual freedom and gender equality in family law were the main concern of the lawmaker.

Marriage

According to Turkish Civil Code, only 'engagement' and 'marriage' are the sole legally accepted unions. Engagement is not a registered relationship, whereas marriage is a registered relationship. Since these are *numerus clausus,* the parties do not have any discretion to freely create new types of legal unions which have not been set forth in the Civil Code or apply the consequences of marriage to other civil unions by analogy. Accordingly, civil unions and registered partnerships are not accepted under Turkish Law. Therefore, marriage is the only legally accepted registered civil union.

In order to get married first of all a person should have the capacity to marry. This means that a person to marry should first have discretion. Secondly should be of a required age. The normal age of majority is the conclusion of 18 years of age, but the marriage age is 17. A person of 17 could get married with the permission of

[6] For more information on family law see: Sağlam, İpek, Turkish Family Law, Oniki Levha Publishing, İstanbul 2019.

the parents.

Monogamy is an essential principle of marriage. Marriage between close relatives is prohibited[7]. Adoption is also a bar to marriage. Mental illness is also a bar to marriage. Married women whose marriage has been dissolved cannot marry for 300 days. This is named as a period of gestation, but it is a relative impediment.

Only civil marriages performed by authorized marriage officers are allowed in Turkey[8]. The procedures of a wedding ceremony are regulated by the Turkish Civil Code between articles 140-142. According to these provisions there is a strict requirement of form which is the oral form, and the parties (man and woman) who wish to marry should express their will in front of an official authorized to certify the wedding.

As required in any legal transaction the declaration of the intentions of the parties is the essential element. In a wedding the presence of the official and the completion of the official formalities are added to that. But very lately there has been an addition to the official by bringing 'müftü' as an authorized person. Therefore, in our legal system non-presence of the authorized official has the same effect with the non-declaration of the intention of the parties.

It is argued that presence of the authorized official is only a 'requirement of formality'. This is not correct from the legal point of view. The presence of the official person is a prerequisite for the validity of a marriage contract, together with the declaration of intentions. As stated above, the requirement of form in a marriage contract is the oral declaration of intentions. If one does not observe the oral form, the marriage shall be null and void; but if there are no intentions declared orally or no official is present, then there will be no marriage at all. Also, there is a need of two witnesses and after they all have to sign the marriage registry, but these requirements are only regarded as requirements of proof.

Divorce and Marital Agreements

Marriage may be terminated by the death of one of the spouses or by the declaration of a judge. The judge may either declare the marriage void or decide to grant a divorce. There are two main types of grounds for divorce: special grounds and general grounds. Adultery, attempt on life, grave assaults and insults, crime and dishonorable life, desertion and mental illness are categorized under the special grounds. Breakdown of marriage, in other words incompatibility is regarded as the

[7] Under Turkish Law close kinship is a bar to marriage. Marriage between lower and upper lineage, between aunts and uncles and their nephews and nieces, marriage between the parents and children of the ex-spouse is forbidden.

[8] In Turkey, the marriage ceremony is performed publicly, and religious marriages are not recognised. After the official marriage ceremony is performed, the marriage officer provides a marriage certificate to the newly wedded couple. If the spouses want to have religious ceremony as well, they have to present this marriage certificate. Without presenting the marriage certificate they will not be able to hold a religious ceremony. It should clearly be noted that according to article 143 of the Civil Code the validity of marriage does not depend on religious ceremony: https://uk.practicallaw.thomsonreuters.com/6-616-4228?transitionType=Default&contextData=(sc.Default)&firstPage=true (19.11.2020)

general ground. Moreover, the parties may have an uncontested divorce (agreed divorce) before Turkish Family Courts.

According to Turkish jurisdiction, marriage and many matters related to this, such as marital agreements, are causally related to the public order. Marital agreements can only be made for the purposes and methods as outlined in the Turkish Civil Code. Under the Turkish Civil Code, marital agreements are limited to the election of the matrimonial property regime. For this reason, spouses cannot make marital agreements covering other issues.

Child Maintenance and Custody

According to the Turkish Civil Code, article 327, regardless of custody arrangements, parents have the responsibility of meeting costs of expenditure of children's education and care in accordance with their financial situations. Parents are able to request this care maintenance from each other. But, for children born outside of marriage, in order to demand participation from the other parent in terms of costs, paternity should be established between the father and the child through recognition of the child or a paternity suit.

Notwithstanding custody and the state of their marriage, both the mother and the father have the right to request to have contact with their child, the right to custody also provides the right to represent the child as their parent, and the right to the administration and use of the child's assets. But, this right, related to the assets of child is limited by Turkish Law; parents can use the assets for primarily for the care, education and then for the needs of family as far as is reasonable. According to the Turkish Civil Code, for divorced couples, custody is as a rule only given to one parent.

As known, custody rights are absolute rights that are strictly personal and therefore, it is not possible to waive from and transfer such rights. Custody rights do not only consist of rights and powers; but also consist of duties. It should be used for the benefit of the child. According to article 348 TCC, these rights could be abrogated if they are used without regarding the benefits of the child by biological or adoptive parents.

The scope of custody rights is regulated under article 339. Accordingly, their scope consists of supervision, (general, professional, religious) education of the child, protection needs, management of the assets, protection of the personality and representation. Apart from these, custody also gives the right to determine the name and the domicile of the child.

Applicable Family Law Provisions to the Refugees

The refugees are as a rule subject to their respective national laws in most matters related with family law according to the Turkish International Private and Procedural Law. However, TIPPL in some matters regulate the usage of the law of the forum. The most important example to that is the celebration of the form of the marriage. According to TIPPL, *the form of marriage shall be governed by the law of the state where the marriage is solemnized.* Therefore, if refugees want to get married in Turkey, for the marriage ceremony Turkish law shall be applied. Since civil and official marriage is the form and this rule is a binding rule, religious marriages shall not be accepted under Turkish law. In other words, religious and customary marriages are not allowed in Turkey and if they are celebrated, they shall not be binding and valid[9].

Another important point is the concern of public order. Though the principle is the application of the respective national laws, the public order criteria may prohibit the national law and the law of the forum is applied. In Turkish Law especially the subjects regarding the capacity to marry, form of divorce, grounds for divorce, custody and maintenance of children are considered as a concern of public order and *lex fori* is the applicable law, meaning Turkish Law shall be applied.

Refugees wishing to marry in Turkey shall have the legal capacity of marriage under Turkish Civil Code. Persons lacking the capacity to marry, like not completing 17 years of age, shall not be allowed to marry. Also, even if in their respective countries it is allowed, monogamy is an essential principle of marriage and polygamy is forbidden.

It should be noted that the above-mentioned rules are applicable to the marriages celebrated in Turkey. If the marriage is celebrated in the respective countries of the refugees, the civil status they have acquired in their country of origin shall be valid and it shall be recognised in Turkey according to Turkish Law.

When the refugees seek for divorce in Turkey, it is important to mention that only the courts may grant a divorce decision according to Turkish Law. Therefore, other forms of divorce are not valid in Turkey. A person who is seeking for divorce should file a case and submit a divorce petition to the competent court[10]. In divorce cases mostly it is advised to be supported by an attorney at law, if the refugee seeking for divorce is unable to pay the attorney fees, like the Turkish nationals, he/she can also apply to the local bar association for legal aid. All the divorce procedures will be subject to Turkish law, including the grounds for divorce.

In Turkish law agreed (consensual) divorce is possible under certain conditions. To apply for agreed divorce, the marriage must have lasted for at least one year. Spouses must file the divorce case together or if one spouse files the case, the other spouse must accept the divorce. The spouses should have prepared a protocol covering all the results of divorce. The judge is obliged to hear the spouses in person and consider the protocol signed by the parties in order to pronounce the divorce.

---

[9] http://www.mhd.org.tr/images/yayinlar (05.12.2020).

[10] The Code of Civil Procedure determines which court has jurisdiction to hear family law proceedings. However, since family law requires various levels of expertise and knowledge, separate family courts were established in the year 2003 by the Code of the Foundation, Competence and Procedures of Family Court: for detailed information see: Arslan, Aziz Serkan, "The Family Courts and Trial Procedures in Turkish Law", http://www.acarindex.com/dosyalar/makale/acarindex-1423908135.pdf (26.11.2020).

Custody of the child shall also be subject to Turkish Law, and at this point not only the Civil Code provisions but also the international conventions to which Turkey is a party are also applicable. Therefore, regarding the custody the most important thing is to protect the high interest of the child. This rule is clearly expressed in the United Nations Convention on the Rights of the Child.

According to Turkish Law only a judge may decide on the custody of the child after divorce. It is possible to award sole custody to one of the parents or joint custody, but the main criterion is the high benefit of the child.

Problems Faced by the Refugees and the Result

Turkey is a country hosting the largest number of refugees in the world[11]. Most of the refugees in Turkey are coming from Syria and they are Syrian nationals. Though the principle is the application of their respective national laws in matters regarding the family law, either due to the compulsory provisions of Turkish Law or public order, mostly Turkish Law provisions are applied. Even though, this situation is legally correct, the refugees may suffer from some important problems because of this.

The most important problem at this point is, many refugees and especially women refugees[12] are ignorant of their rights in Turkey. In most Arab countries including Syria, issues of marriage, divorce and custody are subject to religious rules. Islamic Law is applied and according to Islamic Law rules, there are more rights granted to the men compared to the women. For example, a husband can divorce his wife without her knowledge or consent. That means a unilateral declaration of intention of divorce by the husband shall be valid for divorce. In Islamic Law marriage and divorce are performed with a cleric, and many clerics acknowledge verbal divorce without formal confirmation[13]. This kind of divorce is not valid in Turkey, but if the refugee is ignorant about that, he/she may assume that, by the declaration of the husband they are divorced, tough they are not. The same applies in marriage as well, when a religious ceremony is performed the man and woman may believe that they are marries, whereas their ceremony is not regarded as a valid official marriage. Therefore, they will not be subject to the rights of marriage and the children born shall not have any kinship to the father, unless the father recognises the child, or a paternity suit is filed. When the man leaves the woman and the children, he shall be under a burden of no obligation, whereas the left behind woman and children shall struggle to survive. In this situation since the woman and children do not have any valid legal right, filing a suit shall also not be fruitful.

---

[11] https://reporting.unhcr.org/turkey (03.12.2020).

[12] Most of the women refugees are in a marginal and secondary position, some of them are illiterate and even if some can read and write, they do not know Turkish. They live in communities and do not have a chance to interact other people apart from their own nationals. Therefore, thy lack the chance to learn about their rights and position in Turkey and Turkish Law.

[13] https://daraj.com/en/57861/(10.12.2020).

The children born in an illegal marriage are also not registered in Turkey and therefore, they shall not enjoy many of the rights that are granted to the refugees.

In Syria, though the marriage age is 17, the clergyman may decide and enable underage marriages as well and the incidence of underage marriages is quite common, whereas these marriages cannot be celebrated in Turkey. For that reason, the families let their daughters to get 'married' only with a religious celebration, which does not have legal validity in Tukey. The same applies to the polygamous marriages.

Another problem faced by the refugees is obtaining the official documents from their countries, like marriage certificate or divorce certificate.

Asa result, due to ignorance the dilemma between their national law and Turkish Law is creating different and difficult issues for refugees and most of them result with either loss of a right or non-recognition of a legal status. The only way to overcome this problem is 'education'. Their rights under Turkish Law should be explained and the related information should be given to the refugees.

CHAPTER 8

THE PROGRESS AND CHALLANGES OF REFUGEE EDUCATION IN TURKEY

Hüseyin Pusat Kıldiş[1]

Introduction

The global number of refugees has continuously trended upward in recent years. According to the United Nations High Commissioner for Refugees (UNHCR), the most recent number of refugees is about 26 million.[2] Although refugee status was assumed to be a short-term event in the past, the cases of Afghanistan, Iraq and Syria have changed this understanding. Nowadays, the status has become 'the norm rather than the exception'.[3] The case of Syria is particularly important since the Syrian conflict has created more refugees than any other current conflict.[4]

The uprising in Syria for human rights turned into a civil war in 2011, and the war has evolved into one of the worst humanitarian crises of our time. The war has created such devastation that it will reverberate throughout the region for years. In the conflict that continues, hundreds of thousands of people have been either wounded or killed in the violence. Many more people staying in Syria have difficulties in accessing basic services such as electricity, health care, education, water, and sanitation.[5] Moreover, the political actors in the Syrian conflict are still unable to agree on how to end the war.

Although the impact of the war goes beyond the region, it has especially affected the neighbors of Syria. The war, now almost in its tenth year, has displaced millions of people. Thus, many countries, especially countries neighboring Syria, have had to host an unprecedented number of people. As a result of the war, more than 6.6 million Syrians fled from their own country. In addition, 6.7 million have lost their homes and are trapped in the country.[6] Realizing that the war will not end soon, the

[1] Ph.D. Candidate, International Relations, Ankara Yildirim Beyazit University, Social Sciences Institute, Türkiye. E-mail: hpk12333@gmail.com

[2] "Figures at a Glance", https://www.unhcr.org/en-us/figures-at-a-glance.html (Access 20.10.2020).

[3] Ahmet İçduygu and Doğuş Şimşek, "Syrian Refugees in Turkey: Towards Integration Policies", **Turkish Policy Quarterly**, Vol. 15, No. 3, Fall 2016, p. 60.

[4] "Global Trends: Forced Displacement in 2019", p. 3, https://www.unhcr.org/5ee200e37.pdf (Access 21.10.2020).

[5] "Water and Sanitation Services in Syria Severely Disrupted by Conflict, Says UNICEF", https://www.unicefusa.org/press/releases/water-and-sanitation-services-syria-severely-disrupted-conflict-says-unicef/8206 (Access 20.10.2020).

[6] "Syria Refugee Crisis Explained", https://www.unrefugees.org/news/syria-refugee-crisis-explained/#:~:text=More%20than%206.6%20million%20Syrians,remain%20trapped%20inside%20the%20country (Access 14.10.2020).

integration of refugees into host countries has become a priority for the affected states. In other words, Syrian refugees require economic, social, and political responsibility if the host countries are determined to find a long-term solution for this crisis.

The migration crisis is mostly associated with Europe. However, ninety percent of the refugees are located in only three neighboring countries of Syria: Turkey, Jordan, and Lebanon.[7] In fact, Turkey has become 'the world's largest recipient of refugees' after the influx of people from Syria. Turkey has emerged as a regional hub for these waves of immigration by maintaining an 'open-door' policy towards the refugees since the outbreak of the war.[8]

Even though these refugees are able to escape from Syria, they still have to cope with various challenges. One of these challenges is the need for a proper education. In addition, education is one of the determining factors in the integration of refugees. For example, education is essential for refugees to learn about the culture, language and rules of the host country. Education is also a good opportunity for refugees to interact with the community. Moreover, considering that half of the Syrian refugees in Turkey are children (1.7 million) education is particularly important for these refugees. [9]

Education is essential to support refugee children. For instance, it can be used to motivate these children, reduce the impact of their trauma, give them a sense of stability, and convince them that they have a future in the host country. It can also provide the necessary physical and emotional support for refugee children. In fact, lack of schooling and poor education are some of the important reasons why Syrians move to Europe instead of staying in the neighboring countries of Syria.[10]

The paper uses both quantitative and qualitative data. Quantitative data is used in the first part of the study. In this first part, the legal framework of refugee education through the international, national agreements and regulations is explained. This part also explores how Turkey responds to the issues of refugee education by creating some new laws and regulations over the years since the beginning of the Syrian war. Most of the data were obtained from publications of international organizations such as UNHCR, the United Nations Educational,

---

[7] Nergis Canefe, "Migration as a Necessity: Contextualising the European Response to the Syrian Exodus", **Refugee Watch**, No. 48, 2017, p. 5.

[8] Kemal Kirişçi and Elizabeth Ferris, "Not Likely to Go Home: Syrian Refugees and the Challenges to Turkey and the International Community", Turkey Project Policy Paper, **Center on the United States and Europe at Brookings**, No. 7, September 2015, p. 2, https://www.brookings.edu/wp-content/uploads/2016/06/Turkey-Policy-Paper-web.pdf (Access: 19.10.2020).

[9] "Humanitarian Action for Children (HAC)", https://www.unicef.org/turkey/en/humanitarian-action-children-hac (Access 16.10.2020).

[10] Melissa Fleming, "Six Reasons why Syrians are Fleeing to Europe in Increasing Numbers", **The Guardian**, https://www.theguardian.com/global-development-professionals-network/2015/oct/25/six-reasons-why-syrians-are-fleeing-to-europe-in-increasing-numbers (Access 15.10.2020); Bülent Aras and Salih Yasun, "The Educational Opportunities and Challenges of Syrian Refugee Students in Turkey: Temporary Education Centers and Beyond", **The Istanbul Policy Center-Sabancı University-Stiftung Mercator Initiative**, July 2016, p. 2.

Scientific and Cultural Organization (UNESCO), and the Asylum Information Database (AIDA) starting from 2011 to October 2020. Moreover, the United Nations sources, databases and documents, are used in order to explain the legal framework of refugee education around the World, with an emphasis on Turkey. Acquiring such data and verifying its reliability requires cross-checking many sources. Thus, the publications of various ministries, particularly the Ministry of Interior and the Ministry of National Education as well as the Council of Higher Education that supervises the higher education system in Turkey, and non-governmental organizations are used.

In the second part of the research, mainly qualitative data is used to analyze the main challenges in refugee education in Turkey such as the language barrier, cultural and economic problems. Although official documents are beneficial to explain some of these challenges such as the financial problems of Syrian refugees, these documents mostly do not cover personal experiences, like the experiences of teachers. These experiences are crucial to understand and analyze the challenges in refugee education since teachers can 'observe a large number of refugee children and their parents particularly in locations where refugee population are concentrated'.[11] Thus, further research is required. Academic articles, mostly based on case studies, are used to reflect the personal experiences in this part of the research in addition to official reports.

This study aims to explore the progress of refugee education, especially for Syrian refugee students, in Turkey since the beginning of the war. Furthermore, it describes and analyzes the challenges faced by the teachers in the education of Syrian refugee children. It also has suggestions to these problems. The results and findings of this research can be used to improve education conditions and tackle the challenges in refugee education and to meet refugee education needs in Turkey to improve education conditions.

This study addresses the following questions: What are the legal steps taken by Turkey for the education of refugees since the outbreak of the war? What is the current educational status of Syrian refugee children in Turkey? What are the educational challenges faced by these children? How can these problems in the field of refugee education be addressed?

Legal Framework of Refugee Education

The Protection of the Right to Education by International Law

International law protects the universal right to education for every person including refugee children. These children are entitled to receive quality education in the host country. The right to education is stated in the Universal Declaration of Human Rights (1948), the European Convention on Human Rights (1950), the Convention Relating to the Status of Refugees (1951), the International Covenant

[11] B. Dilara Şeker and İbrahim Sirkeci, "Challenges for Refugee Children at School in Eastern Turkey", **Economics and Sociology**, Vol. 8, No. 4, 2015, p. 123.

on Economic, Social, and Cultural Rights (1966), and the Convention on the Rights of the Child (1989).[12]

The universal right to education begins with the 1948 Universal Declaration of Human Rights. Article 26 of the Declaration asserts as follows:

'Everyone has the right to education. Education shall be free, at least in the elementary and fundamental stages. Elementary education shall be compulsory. Technical and professional education shall be made generally available and higher education shall be equally accessible to all on the basis of merit.'[13]

The European Convention on Human Rights states the right to education in Protocol 1, Article 2 as the following:

'No person shall be denied a right to an education. In the exercise of any functions which it assumes in relation to education and to teaching, the State shall respect the right of parents to ensure such education and teaching is in conformity with their own religious and philosophical convictions.'[14]

The 1951 Convention is particularly important to refugees since it defines 'who is a refugee, the rights of refugees and the legal obligations of States ratifying the Convention'. The Convention states that refugees should be treated as citizens with respect to primary and other educational levels. Moreover, they should be encouraged by the host country to receive other educational levels.[15]

The International Covenant on Civil and Political Rights (1966) and the Convention on the Rights of the Child (1989) made also contributions to refugee education since they 'promised children intellectual rights that help guarantee an education' to help them to make their own decisions based on their socio-economic circumstances.[16]

Unfortunately, despite these international agreements, it is difficult to argue that refugee children receive the appropriate education they need due to the limited access and low quality of education. Nowadays, more than half of the 7.1 million refugee children, 3.7 million children, are out of school. In addition, the number of refugees who can use their right to education is still much less than non-refugees. At primary level, access to education for refugees is 63 percent compared to a global level of 91 percent. At secondary level, only 24 percent of refugees can attend school compared to 84 percent worldwide. Lastly, at higher level, the figures are 3 percent

---

[12] Jootaek Lee, "The Human Right to Education: Definition, Research and Annotated Bibliography", **Emory International Law Review**, Vol. 34, No. 3, 2020, p. 763.

[13] "Universal Declaration of Human Rights", https://www.ohchr.org/EN/UDHR/Documents/UDHR_Translations/eng.pdf (Access 16.10.2020).

[14] "Guide on Article 2 of Protocol No. 1 to the European Convention on Human Rights: Right to Education", p. 5, https://www.echr.coe.int/documents/guide_art_2_protocol_1_eng.pdf (Access 21.10.2020).

[15] Rolla Moumné and Leticia Sakai, "Protecting the Right to Education for Refugees", **UNESCO**, Working Paper, Second Edition, p. 16, https://unesdoc.unesco.org/ark:/48223/pf0000251076 (Access 21.10.2020).

[16] Joel Spring, The Universal Right to Education: Justification, Definition, and Guidelines, Mahwah, New Jersey, Routledge, 2000, pp. 51-52.

for refugees compared to 37 percent globally.[17]

The ongoing COVID-19 pandemic has badly affected refugee education worldwide. According to Filippo Grandi, UN High Commissioner, 'half of the world's refugee children were already out of school', and the number has increased because of the lockdowns. Even though, refugee children were more likely to be out of school compared to non-refugee children before the pandemic, this situation got worse now. The situation of refugee girls is worse than that of boys. Although they already had less access to education compared to boys before the pandemic, UNHCR data reveals that half of these girls in secondary school will not return to school even if it opens within a short time.[18]

According to Fons Coomans, UNESCO Chair in Human Rights and Peace at the Department of International and European Law at Maastricht University, one of the main problems to fulfill the right to education for refugees is accountability. He explains the situation as follows:

'International accountability mechanisms exist either through State reporting or dialogue within the UN system or at UNESCO level but in terms of what States have been actually doing there is again a gap. The main reasons for this are, that in many cases and countries, education or educational rights are not seen as human rights. Particularly in European and North American settings people don't realize that they are enjoying their right to education as a human right. For that reason, States do not feel the need to justify what they have done or have failed to do in terms of human rights and education'.[19]

Nowadays, UNHCR is trying to create a global framework for refugee education. Accordingly, the first Global Refugee Forum took place in Geneva in December 2019. The purpose of this Framework is to 'create the conditions for global support for the education of refugees and host communities'.[20] Moreover, this framework is part of a bigger refugee education strategy, namely 'Refugee Education 2030: A Strategy for Refugee Inclusion' aims to prove the conditions for all 'refugee, asylum seeker, returnee and stateless children'.[21]

The Right to Education of Refugees in Turkey

Although it is considered that the beginning of the migration crisis is 2015, the first wave of migration from Syria to Turkey took place in April 2011. In fact, the first refugee camp was established within two months after the first wave, years

---

[17] "Access to Education for Refugees", p. 1, https://www.unhcr.org/5df9f1767.pdf (Access 24.10.2020); Tuba Bircan and Ulas Sunata, "Educational Assessment of Syrian Refugees in Turkey", **Migration Letters**, Vol. 12, No, 3, 2015, p. 228.

[18] "UNHCR Report: Coronavirus a Dire Threat to Refugee Education – Half of the World's Refugee Children out of School", https://www.unhcr.org/news/press/2020/9/5f4cc3064/unhcr-report-coronavirus-dire-threat-refugee-education-half-worlds-refugee.html (Access 18.10.2020).

[19] "Fulfilling the Right to Education for Refugees and Undocumented Migrants", https://en.unesco.org/news/fulfilling-right-education-refugees-and-undocumented-migrants (Access 19.10.2020).

[20] "Global Framework for Refugee Education", p. 4, https://www.unhcr.org/5dd50ce47.pdf (Access 16.10.2020).

[21] "Refugee Education: 2030", p. 9, https://www.unhcr.org/5d651da88d7.pdf (Access 15.10.2020).

before the European migration crisis.[22] Turkey welcomed all these refugees by adopting an open-door policy and therefore, it took on a great responsibility regarding the refugees.

However, as the civil war continues, the waves of migration continued to increase over the years. According to the Turkish government, as of November 11, 2020, the number of Syrian refugees in the country is 3.632.442. This number is significant, since it is more than the number of Syrian refugees in all other countries combined. This figure corresponds to 65 percent of the displaced Syrians worldwide.[23]

Turkey is a party to the 1951 Refugee Convention and 1967 Protocol, yet it maintains a geographical limitation to the Convention. According to this limitation, Turkey offers refugee status only for those fleeing from 'events occurring in Europe'. Thus, Syrians in Turkey are not refugees and partially because of this, they were referred to as 'guests' at the beginning of the conflict by both media and politicians.[24] However, this term has no place in international law.

Another reason for the guest rhetoric was the expectation in Turkey that there would be a short war in Syria at the start of it, as it was stated by Ahmet Davutoğlu, the former Turkish prime minister. Accordingly, the war would end in a few weeks, in a few months at most.[25] However, when it was revealed that Syrians in Turkey will not leave the country as long as the war continues in Syria, legal steps such as laws and regulations as being part of the process of refugee integration have been taken by the country over the years. UNHCR describes the reforms in the Turkish national asylum system to reach international standards as the following:

'In April 2013, Turkey's first ever asylum law, the Law on Foreigners and International Protection, was endorsed by the Parliament and entered into force on 11 April 2014. The Law sets out the main pillars of Turkey's national asylum system and established the Directorate General of Migration Management (DGMM) as the main entity in charge of policy-making and proceedings for all foreigners in Turkey. Turkey also adopted Temporary Protection Regulation on 22 October 2014, which sets out the rights and obligations along with procedures for those who are granted temporary protection in Turkey. [26]

Temporary protection is based on the principle of non-refoulement, that is 'no Contracting State shall expel or return ('refouler') a refugee in any manner

---

22 "Syria Refugee Crisis Explained", https://www.unrefugees.org/news/syria-refugee-crisis-explained/ (Access 14.10.2020); Laçin Idil Öztığ, "The Syrian Conflict and Turkey's Humanitarian Response", **Turkish Policy**, Vol. 15, No. 3, Fall 2016, p. 140.

23 "Syrian Regional Refugee Response", http://data2.unhcr.org/en/situations/syria (Access 15.10.2020).

24 "Protecting Refugees", https://www.hrw.org/reports/2000/turkey2/Turk009-10.htm#:~:text=Turkey%20retains%20a%20geographic%20limitation,can%20be%20given%20refugee%20status (Access: 18.10.2020); Burcu Toğral Koca, "Syrian Refugees in Turkey: from "Guests" to "Enemies"?", **New Perspectives on Turkey**, Vol. 54, May 2016, p. 63.

25 "Davutoğlu Esad'a Ömür Biçti", https://www.ntv.com.tr/turkiye/davutoglu-esada-omur-bicti, Nsez_e7zmEO7uz5O9Pv6hw (Access 19.10.2020).

26 "Refugees and Asylum Seekers in Turkey", https://www.unhcr.org/tr/en/refugees-and-asylum-seekers-in-turkey (Access 19.10.2020).

whatsoever to the frontiers of territories where his [or her] life or freedom would be threatened'. This principle is present in international law and can be found in many international agreements such as the 1951 Convention and the 1967 Protocol.[27] The Directorate General of Migration Management, operating under the Ministry of Interior, explains this status as the following:

'Temporary protection may be provided for foreigners who have been forced to leave their country, cannot return to the country that they have left, and have arrived at or crossed the borders of Turkey in a mass influx situation seeking immediate and temporary protection.'[28]

The Ministry of National Education is responsible for the execution of educational services of refugees in Turkey.[29] All children including refugees and asylum seekers have the right to education at primary and secondary levels as long as they obtain their foreign ID number. Public schools are free of charge. Those who have not received the foreign ID number or been registered can be temporarily enrolled as a 'guest student'. These students can attend classes, yet they cannot receive any type of certificate or diploma in return. Moreover, there are programs such as Turkish language courses provided by the Public Education Centers for the refugees and asylum seekers in the country. They are also free of charge.[30] For those who want to use a foreign school certificate, they must have their documents validated by the Provincial Education Directorate.[31]

As the number of people coming from Syria to Turkey has increased, the number of Syrian students has also risen over the years. At the start of the 2019/20 academic year, the number of Syrian students enrolled in formal education was 684.253 representing only 63 percent of school-aged Syrian children in the country.[32] This situation also applies to Syrian refugee students enrolled in higher education. The number of these students has increased from 14.747 during the 2016-2017 academic year to 33.000 in the 2019-2020 academic year.[33]

Graphic 1.1 The numbers of Syrian children enrolled in higher education in Turkey

[27] "Advisory Opinion on the Extraterritorial Application of Non-Refoulement Obligations under the 1951 Convention relating to the Status of Refugees and its 1967 Protocol", p. 2, https://www.unhcr.org/4d9486929.pdf (Access: 16.10.2020).

[28] "Temporary Protection in Turkey", https://en.goc.gov.tr/temporary-protection-in-turkey#:~:text=%E2%80%9CTemporary%20protection%20may%20be%20provided,seeking%20immediate%20and%20temporary%20protection.%E2%80%9D (Access 18.10.2020).

[29] "Turkey 2019 Operational Highlights", p. 7, https://reliefweb.int/sites/reliefweb.int/files/resources/74411.pdf (Access 16.10.2020).

[30] "Access to Education: Turkey", https://www.asylumineurope.org/reports/country/turkey/access-education-1#_ftn28 (Access: 16.10.2020)"; Bircan and Sunata, op.cit, p. 228.

[31] "Syrian Refugees in Turkey: Frequently Asked Questions", p. 5, https://www.unhcr.org/tr/wp-content/uploads/sites/14/2017/02/frequently_asked_questions.pdf (Access 24.10.2020).

[32] "Turkey 2019 Operational Highlights", p. 7, https://reliefweb.int/sites/reliefweb.int/files/resources/74411.pdf (Access: 16.10.2020).

[33] "Access to Education: Turkey", https://www.asylumineurope.org/reports/country/turkey/access-education-1#_ftn28 (Access: 16.10.2020).

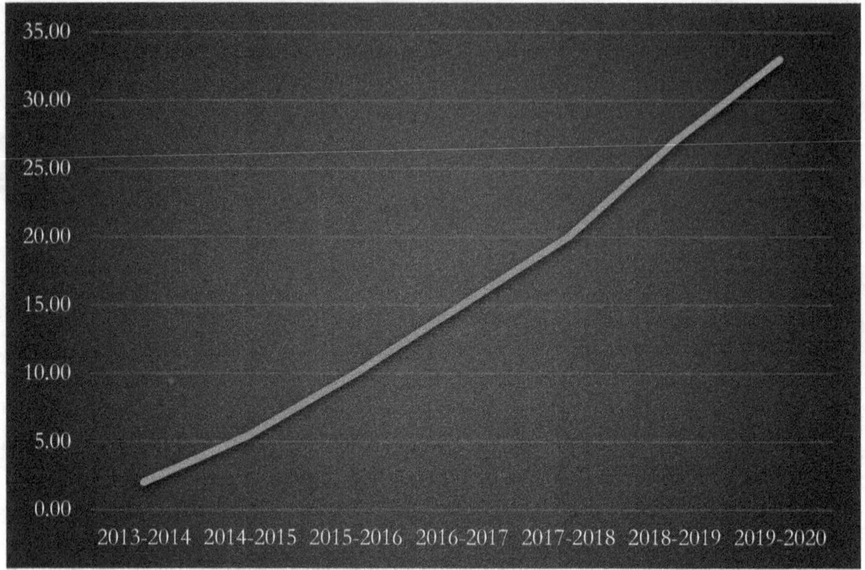

This graphic is designed by the author based on the statistics of the Council of Higher Education (CoHE) collected from the statistics section of the website of CoHE.[34]

Various arrangements of accessing education have emerged for Syrian refugee children inside and outside of the refugee camps since 2011. In refugee camps, Syrian children have access to pre-school, elementary and high school education.[35] One of the initiatives is the Temporary Education Centers introduced on 23 September 2014. These centers provide 'primary and/or secondary level education to Syrian child refugees in Turkey'. They can continue their functions both inside and outside the camps. Most of the teachers at these centers are Syrians and lessons are conducted in Arabic. Moreover, the curriculum of the centers is the modified version of the Syrian curriculum developed by the Syrian transitional government.[36]

These centers first started in the 25 refugee camps located in the Turkey-Syria border, as well as in large refugee communities. The centers are mostly funded by non-governmental organizations and lessons are usually given by volunteer Syrian teachers. Only a few of them had professional qualifications. However, Syrians moved to big cities for education over time because of the general concern among them regarding the validity of their diplomas and lack of teachers both in terms of number and quality.[37] As of September 2020, over 98 percent of the refugees live

---

[34] "Öğrenci Sayıları Raporu", https://istatistik.yok.gov.tr/ (Access: 17.10.2020).

[35] Bircan and Sunata, op.cit, p. 228.

[36] Emine Gümüş, et al., "Current Conditions and Issues at Temporary Education Centres (TECs) for Syrian child refugees in Turkey", **Multicultural Education Review**, Vol. 12, No. 2, 2020, p. 3.

[37] Melissa Hauber-Özer, "Schooling Gaps for Syrian Refugees in Turkey", **Forced Migration Review**, No. 60, March 2019, p. 50.

within the host community. [38]

The centers were first run by the DİYANET (Turkish Presidency of Religious Affairs), and later some non-governmental organizations and Syrian charities were also included in the education process. In September 2016, Turkey adopted a new policy to abolish these schools and now requires Syrian children to enroll in Turkish public schools. Thus, the importance of these centers has steadily decreased ever since.[39]

Another program for the Syrian refugees in Turkey is the Early Childhood Education program, which is defined by UNICEF as the following:

'The Early Childhood Education (ECE) home-based program, implemented in partnership between UNICEF, GAP Administration and Development Foundation of Turkey (DFT) and with the financial support of European Union and Norway, targets Syrian refugee children in ten provinces of Southeast Turkey, areas with the highest numbers of refugees.'[40]

The purpose of these home-based programs is to prepare Syrian refugee children for the first grade in Turkish schools. In order to achieve that, these programs help them to increase 'their language and motor skills, while supporting mothers in conducting school readiness activities for their children to help them prepare for grade school'.[41]

There are also programs for Syrian refugee children in Turkey to recover them from the trauma of war and violence by encouraging their resilience and coping mechanisms. For instance, the Psychosocial Support Programme for Syrian Children is such a program started in May 2013 and based on the cooperation agreement between the Türk Kızılay (Turkish Red Crescent) and UNICEF. According to Türk Kızılay, the aim of this program is 'to increase the adaptation and social harmonization of school-aged Syrians by enhancing their resilience in the host community'.[42]

UNHCR assists Turkey in refugee education. The organization works with the Ministry of National Education to help children learn Turkish. It also works closely with the Higher Education Council and the Presidency for Turks Abroad and Related Communities to integrate refugees into higher education. Moreover, UNHCR provides scholarships to Syrian refugee children in Turkey.[43]

---

[38] "UNHCR Turkey-Fact Sheet September 2020", p. 1, https://data2.unhcr.org/en/documents/details/79121 (Access 16.10.2020).

[39] Iman Sarmini et al., "Integrating Syrian Refugee Children in Turkey: The Role of Turkish Language Skills (A case study in Gaziantep)", **International Journal of Educational Research Open**, 2020, p. 2.

[40] "Education Starts at Home", https://www.unicef.org/turkey/en/stories/education-starts-home (Access 21.10.2020).

[41] Ibid.

[42] "Syria Crisis Humanitarian Relief Operation", p. 16, https://www.kizilay.org.tr/Upload/Dokuman/Dosya/august-2020-syria-crisis-humanitarian-relief-operation-02-10-2020-38659163.pdf (Access 23.10.2020).

[43] "Education", https://www.unhcr.org/tr/en/education (Access 20.10.2020).

The Challenges of Refugee Education in Turkey

The Language Barrier

A lack of Turkish language skills is a significant problem for the integration of Syrian refugees, especially for the students. In fact, in a number of studies conducted over recent years, the language barrier has emerged as either the primary problem or at least a major challenge in refugee education in the country.[44] For instance, a study reveals that the lack of language proficiency is the main reason why the Syrian students in Kırıkhan, a district of Hatay Province, do not attend Turkish schools.[45] Another study shows that the lack of language skills prevents Syrian refugee students from socializing with others.[46] Moreover, the communication between teachers and Syrian students' parents is also problematic because of the language barrier.[47] The language barrier is not only limited to education. It is also a significant handicap to access public services such as healthcare and social services.[48]

In order to overcome the language barrier, some teachers use technology such as the internet while conducting their courses. In fact, a case study based on the experiences of Syrian refugee students reveals that these students can better understand their lessons when teachers use a smart board and visual equipment.[49] The importance of technology in education is increasing especially nowadays since distance education is becoming more and more widespread related to the current pandemic.

The language barrier is especially a problem in schools implementing the Turkish curriculum. In these schools, Syrian students first need to learn how to read and write in Turkish. They need to learn the language either in schools or language centers since they cannot improve their language skills at home with their parents. While some teachers try to help Syrian students to overcome their language problems, teaching Turkish students the Turkish curriculum at the same time can lead to curriculum delays. Moreover, some refugee families do not allow their children to learn Turkish due to fear that they would lose their culture.[50]

Although the Ministry of National Education launched free Turkish language

---

[44] See. Pelin Taşkın and Özge Erdemli, "Education for Syrian Refugees: Problems Faced by Teachers in Turkey", **Eurasian Journal of Educational Research**, No. 75, 2018, pp. 155-177; Iman Sarmini op.cit, pp. 1-8; Hasan Aydın and Yeliz Kaya, "The Educational Needs of and Barriers Faced by Syrian Refugee Students in Turkey: a Qualitative Case Study", **Intercultural Education**, Vol. 28, No. 5, 2017, pp. 6-7.

[45] Stephanie Dorman, **Educational Needs Assessment for Urban Syrian Refugees in Turkey**, İstanbul, YUVA Association, September 2014, p. 5.

[46] Şeker and Sirkeci, op.cit, p. 127.

[47] Iman Sarmini op.cit, pp. 2-3.

[48] "Language Barrier, High Numbers a Challenge for Refugee Care", https://www.dailysabah.com/turkey/2019/03/29/language-barrier-high-numbers-a-challenge-for-refugee-care#:~:text=The%20report%20says%20Turkey%20allowed,same%20conditions%20as%20Turkish%20citizens.&text=Refugees%20can%20access%20health%2C%20social,%2C%22%20according%20to%20the%20report (Access:22.10.2020).

[49] Mehmet Nuri Gömleksiz and Sibel Aslan, "Refugee Students Views about the Problems They Face at Schools in Turkey", **Education Reform Journal**, Vol. 3, No. 1, 2018, pp. 49-54.

[50] Taşkın and Erdemli, op.cit, pp. 162-163.

and vocational courses, the language barrier has been still a problem for Syrian refugee students. The reason is that some of them have to work instead of attending lectures to deal with financial problems. It should be emphasized that institutional support of language learning is important not only for refugee education but also for ensuring that refugees meet the skills and knowledge needs of the labor economy and market.[51]

Financial Problems

According to UNICEF's 2019 annual report, despite Turkey's progress in refugee education, the number of Syrian refugee students who remained out of school was about 400.000. Moreover, in addition to 1.7 million Syrian refugee children, there are about 130.000 registered asylum-seekers and refugees under the age of 18 from other countries. Although Turkey strives to meet the needs of these refugees, the fact that the number of refugees is high and they live in unideal conditions, especially in financial circumstances, they decide to move to richer countries. [52]

One of the biggest obstructions to Syrian children's schooling is the fact that many Syrians under 18 need to work to help their families financially. The situation may be even worse for refugee girls as some families do not allow them to go to school due to cultural inclinations. Another major problem for refugee girls being able to attend school is that some families want to marry their daughters early for financial reasons such as minimizing expenses and receiving marriage payments.[53]

The inability of some Syrian refugee students to participate in socio-cultural activities such as going to a park or cinema organized by schools due to financial difficulties is another factor that prevents them from adapting to the host country. In fact, some Syrian students cannot even spend time with their friends outside of school for the same reason. Not being able to attend these activities also negatively affects these students' classroom performance.[54]

The ongoing Covid-19 pandemic has also had a negative impact on the financial difficulties of refugees. Many refugees lost their jobs due to regular curfews. The pandemic also pushes the refugees to accept jobs that are not preferred by other workers since they are dangerous and/or laborious.[55]

---

[51] F. Melis Cin and Necmettin Doğan, "Navigating University Spaces as Refugees: Syrian Students' Pathways of Access to and through Higher Education in Turkey", **International Journal of Inclusive Education**, 2020, p. 2.

[52] "Turkey-Unicef - Country Programme of Cooperation 2016-2020: Annual Report 2019-Executive Summary", pp. 5-6, https://www.unicef.org/turkey/media/10456/file/UNICEF%20Annual%20Report%20-%202019.pdf (Access 20.10.2020).

[53] Selçuk Beşir Demir and Volkan Özgül, "Syrian Refugees Minors in Turkey. Why and How are They Discriminated Against and Ostracized?", **Child Indicators Research**, Vol. 12, No. 6, 2019, p. 1990.

[54] Aras and Yasun, op.cit, p. 10.

[55] Kemal Kirişçi and M. Murat Erdoğan, "Turkey and COVID-19: Don't Forget Refugees", **Brookings**, https://www.brookings.edu/blog/order-from-chaos/2020/04/20/turkey-and-covid-19-dont-forget-refugees/ (Access 22.10.2020).

Cultural Problems

The main cultural problem is called the 'cultural clash' or 'cultural shocks' which refer to refugee children finding themselves in a new environment. These children find it difficult to adapt to a new environment dominated by a new language, culture, and lifestyle.[56] Their bad experiences from the civil war are also another factor preventing them from socializing. Many of these children still try to understand why they are now in a new country.[57] The fact that many refugee families still try to go to Europe even after moving to Turkey increases the feeling of instability.

Another cultural problem stems from the difference between religious practices. Although Turkey is a Muslim-majority country, it is also a secular country. This is a fundamental principle in the education system. For example, Syrian refugee students pray during class while Turkish students do not. This situation prevents conducting the classes during prayer times. [58]

Also, the link between religion and culture is strong so the difference between the religious practices has an impact on daily life. For instance, in a study conducted with nine teachers of Syrian refugee students, female teachers were able to communicate better with female students since male students did not want to engage with female teachers. That study also shows that wearing a headscarf has also a positive impact on the communication between female teachers and refugee students.[59]

Discrimination is also a significant problem. The refugee crisis has an economic, social, and psychological impact on Turkish society. Thus, various disturbances arose among Turkish people. For instance, Turkey has so far spent $40 billion dollars on refugees. There are also some provinces such as Kilis, where the population of Syrian refugees is more than the local population. Therefore, a majority of the citizens perceive Syrian refugees as an 'economic burden, a security threat, and a danger to the ethnic makeup of the country'.[60]

One of the reasons for the discrimination towards Syrian refugee children is related to their socio-economic status. Since many of these children cannot afford to buy clean and proper clothes, they face discrimination from other students and sometimes even adults. Another way of discrimination is by giving nicknames. Even if there are Syrian students who can afford proper clothes, they still get nicknames such as 'Suri', a short version of saying Syrian in Turkish. The lack of language skills is another reason why other students discriminate against them, such as by imitating

---

[56] Sevda Akar and M. Mustafa Erdoğdu, "Syrian Refugees in Turkey and Integration Problem Ahead", **Journal of International Migration and Integration,** Vol. 20, No. 3, 2019, p. 935.
[57] Şeker and Sirkeci, op.cit, p. 127.
[58] Taşkınlı and Erdemli, op.cit, p. 163.
[59] Ibid, pp. 162-163.
[60] Laura Pitel and Michael Peel, "Turkey Eyes more EU aid as Funding Pays Off for Syrian Refugees", **Foreign Policy,** https://amp.ft.com/content/7abb5212-1c2b-11ea-97df-cc63de1d73f4 (Access: 21.10.2020); Gönül Tol, "Erdoğan's Achilles Heel", **The Cairo Review of Global Affairs,** https://www.the cairoreview.com/essays/erdogans-achilles-heel/ (Access: 21.10.2020).

their accent.[61]

Since a lot of Syrian students experience these types of discrimination, they tend to make friends and group together with other Syrian students. However, this situation negatively affects their adaptation to the host country and language development process. Therefore, they are becoming more and more alienated from Turkish society.[62] As one of the leaders of the education centers states, 'students live at the heart of Istanbul, yet remain distanced to the Turkish culture'.[63]

Conclusion

Turkey has made important reforms in refugee education since 2011. For example, Turkey's first-ever asylum law and its temporary protection regulation entered into force in 2014. However, the findings of this study demonstrate that there are still unmet educational needs for Syrian refugee students. The understanding of multiculturalism in education is essential to meet these needs. Since the problems in refugee education are divided into 3 categories, namely language, financial, and cultural, the suggestions to these problems are listed in the same way. Furthermore, these problems should not be considered independently from each other. For instance, the cultural clash is related to the lack of Turkish language skills. Hence, the solution to one problem will follow the others.

In this study, it is revealed that the lack of Turkish language proficiency in refugee students prevents them from socializing with Turkish students and demonstrating good academic performance and socializing. Furthermore, it also negatively affects their adaptation to Turkish culture. These students need to master the Turkish language first, before attending school. Therefore, the Turkish government as well as international and non-governmental organizations should give more emphasis to language training. Without this priority, many refugees will continue to go to public school without knowing proper Turkish. Therefore, they will not be able to be a part of Turkish society since they cannot socialize with others.

The language problem has a multifaceted nature, such as economic and cultural aspects. For instance, if there were more attractive wages, the availability of teachers in language centers would significantly increase. Another way to address this problem is to give free Turkish lessons by qualified teachers in public schools. In addition, it should be explained to refugee families that learning a new language will not affect their existing culture negatively.

Syrian refugee students should socialize with other students in order to learn Turkish. Providing school lunch in primary schools can increase socializing opportunities between Turkish and Syrian students. Moreover, such a plan can reduce the financial problems of Syrians, stated as one of the reasons for dropping

[61] Demir and Özgül op.cit, p. 2003.

[62] Ibid, p. 2005.

[63] Aras and Yasun, op.cit, p. 10.

out of schools.[64] In addition, culture-based taboos must be overcome in refugee education. For example, dogmatic ideas, such as not sending girls to school but instead forcing them to marry early and using young boys in labor markets as a financial source must end by either making provisions or penalties.[65] Furthermore, some of the assistance in refugee education can be oriented towards improving the process of the students' socialization. This would contribute positively to their adaptation.

Financial problems in refugee education are related to other problems faced by Syrian refugee students. The major problems in refugee education, namely culture and language, are difficult to address without good policies and practices and also adequate investments. Increasing investment in refugee education is, of course, the first suggestion that comes to mind, but instead of doing this which would be difficult during the pandemic period, it may be more effective to increase the coordination between the municipalities and non-governmental organizations in both refugee education and aid programs.[66] Another suggestion to overcome this problem is to make sure that the financial assistance transferred to refugee education is used efficiently.

Unlike the language barrier and financial problems, cultural problems in refugee education such as discrimination among students are hard to detect. This problem can only be noticed with the close observation of teachers. The main challenge regarding cultural problems is the lack of high-quality and experienced teachers to deal with the psychological trauma of Syrian refugee students. These teachers should not only teach math and science to the refugee students, but also pedagogically support them. They should also be aware of the 'socio-cultural, economic and educational background of refugee students'. These issues are very serious and can affect the student's social skills and their ability to learn.[67] However, the difficulty of finding and training such qualified teachers cannot be denied. Moreover, it takes a long time to train such well-equipped teachers. Nevertheless, cultural problems in refugee education could be properly addressed with well trained teachers. To achieve this goal, more investment should be made to improve the quality of the teaching and learning processes.

In conclusion, although Turkey has made many reforms in refugee education, there are still special needs to be addressed regarding Syrian refugee students. Given that education is crucial for the adaptation of young refugees into host countries, meeting these needs is beneficial for both Syrian refugees and Turkish society. If Turkey cannot properly address and overcome the challenges in refugee education, consequently the refugee children will become a lost generation with serious implications for the security and the stability of the country. The best way to avoid such a threat is undoubtedly through the adoption of a comprehensive policy and

---

[64] Ibid.

[65] Bircan and Sunata, op.cit, p. 236.

[66] Aras and Yasun, op.cit, p. 11.

[67] Khalid Arar, et al., "These Students Need Love and Affection: Experience of a Female School Leader With the Challenges of Syrian Refugee Education", **Leading & Managing**, Vol. 24, No. 2, 2018, p. 31.

effective commitment by Turkey's authorities and their international partners towards refugee education.

CHAPTER 9

REFUGEES IN TURKEY AND THEIR EDUCATION IN TERMS OF IDENTITY

Gamze Uşar[1]

Introduction

Turkey has had vast experience on admitting refugees and migrants since the times of the Ottoman Empire. The problem with the refugees was and still is to be based on the nationality and sometimes religious standards. Since the beginning of its foundation, Turkey has had to work with the problems of refugees in their territory and also with their own citizens. The concept of refugee was not only used to describe the incoming people, but also outgoing of their own citizens to other countries -mostly European-, as was the case in the 1960s. In the 1960-1970s, Turkish citizens went to Europe as labour workers.

The problems of the refugees can be considered both fort he refugees and the state that accepts them. In this manner, we can talk about the importance of mutual care and responsibility in a mutual way, especially while concerning about the rights and the obligations for the individual; just like in citizenship concept. As it has been studied on lately, the term for citizenship may also be utilized in a global manner. Global citizenship notion has come up especially after the Second World War, with the changing international atmosphere, focuses on not just national identity, but also comes up with tolerance and respect to the 'others'. National identity and citizenship are fictionalised to include who is similar to you and exclude the others/strangers; and now we have been experiencing the problems or the people who go beyond the borders, both in real terms and tralatitiously.

Considering the official statistics of the refugee population, there are 26.3 million refugees and 4.2 million asylum seekers worldwide by mid-2020. Turkey hosts the largest number of refugees, with 3.6 million people. According to the UNHCR Report, 3.7 million refugee children are out of school.[2] Not only the problems that were listed above about the education of the refugee children and youth, but also the circumstances brought on by the Covid-19 pandemic makes the support for education even more strenuous. The education of the refugees, especially higher eduction, should be handled differently from the education that the regular youth undergo. Normally, we take granted the education opportunities

[1] Ph.D., Istanbul Unviversity, Türkiye. E-mail: gamzeusar@gmail.com

[2] The UN Refugee Agency, https://www.unhcr.org/refugee-statistics/#:~:text=Some%20102%2C600 %20refugees%20returned%20to,with%20or%20without%20UNHCR's%20assistance).&text=Data%20on %20some%204.2%20million,estimated%20to%20be%20significantly%20higher(Access 09.12.2020).

that are offered to us as an inalienable right to build up our knowledge, expand our horizons, and discover our passions. The education for the refugees, however,plays significant additional roles, for which recovering from their trumas and engaging back in normal life as soon as possible can be given as examples. As receiving education may be a life-changing opportunity, United Nations in particularputs in a great deal of effort into appealing to the children and the young generation in order to have them interested in schools and universities. UNHCR even supports a platform providing verified information on higher education programs available to refugees worldwide. This platform contains the eligible degree program for refugees, scholarships and the current information about the opportunities.[3]

Refugees in Turkey and the legal system

The refugees who have been accepted to Turkey can be basically classified in three groups. One of these groups is the one that is mostly preferred, the one who is of Turkish descent and culture. The ones who are not of Turkish descent or culture are known and defined as 'visitors' and they are supposed to stay in Turkey temporarily. While there is no formal legal definition of an international migrant, most experts agree that an international migrant is someone who changes his or her country of usual residence irrespective of the reason for migration or legal status. Generally, a distinction is made between short-term or temporary migration, covering movements with a duration between three and twelve months, and long-term or permanent migration, referring to a change of country of residence for a duration of one year or more.[4]

The legal regulations for the refugees were firstly established in 1934, the Law on Settlement (Law 2510), which was adopted in June 14, 1934.[5]This law regulates the admission and settlement policy for refugees and mostly focuses on the homogeneity of the society. It can clearly be seen in the law that the refugees were classified to three groups, mostly according to their language and ethnicity. First of them were the Turkish native speakers with Turkish origin;the second were the ones who had Turkish cultural origin but can not speak Turkish, and the last ones were the non-Turkish speakers with a different background other than Turkish. In an effort not to harm the pure Turkish nationality, the settlement for the three groups were organised differently.[6]

The Convention Relating to the Status of Refugees, also known as the 1951 Refugee Convention or the Geneva Convention of 28 July 1951, is a United Nations multilateral treaty that defines who a refugee is, and sets out the rights of individuals who are granted asylum and the responsibilities of nations that grant asylum.[7] Turkey accepted the 1951 Convention in 1961 with a geographical limitation. After

---

[3] The UNHCR, https://www.unhcr.org/news/press/2020/10/5f7709524/unhcr-launches-new-portal-verified-higher-education-opportunities-refugees.html, (Access 29.11.2020)

[4] https://refugeesmigrants.un.org/definitions (Access 20.11.2020)

[5] https://www.resmigazete.gov.tr/arsiv/2733.pdf (Access 21.11.2020)

[6] https://www.resmigazete.gov.tr/arsiv/2733.pdf (Access 29.10.2020)

[7] https://www.unhcr.org/1951-refugee-convention.html (Access 12.10.2020)

the Convention, Turkey also became a part of 1967 New York Protocol,which concerned the Status of Refugees. [8] Geographical limitation, the most important issue that Turkey is criticised for, as it only allowed to accept refugees exclusively from European borders. Therefore, there was no need to build a legal privilege for these asylum-seekers, who came from non-European countries.[9]

One of the main elements of the immigrant / refugee procedure is that Turkey did not have any formal regulations regarding the refugees until the acceptance of the Geneva Convention on Refugees in 1951. As mentioned above, the only legal procedure was the Law 2510- Law of Settlement, which only allows to regulate the refugees' status only if they were of Turkish descent and culture.

1994 Asylum Regulation was the third major legal document regarding the admission of the refugees. The purpose of the 1994 Regulation was to '*determine the principles and procedures and to designate the bodies competent in respect of, aliens who individually seek refuge or seek residence in our country in order to seek refuge in other countries or as a group arrive at our borders for the purposes of refuge or asylum, or possible population movements, under the 1951 Geneva Convention relating to the Status of Refugees and the Protocol of 31 January 1967 relating to the Status of Refugees.*' [10]

Comparing the refugee politics, the Ottoman Empire had a more welcoming politics for refugees as the empire hadcitizens who were speakers of various languages and of different ethnicities. After the establishment of the Republic, Turkeyformed a different policy, as it had to protect its unity at first. The Turkish language and the Turkish ethnicity were the two major elements to be focused on in order to preserve the status quo.Accepting refugees from the same religious background could be seen as the first priority.[11] We can see the effects of this policy in the coming years, especially in 1980s.

As Turkey is located in an unstable region, it has to face the fact of the legal system should be updated in accordance with the new era and its newly emerged conditions. That's why, we can analyze the legal system before and after the year 2005. In 2005, The EU National Action Plan in the field of Asylum and Migration was accepted. Hence, the bureaucratic steps were regulated with regards to the refugee system. It also helped the Turkish legal system to co-operate in line with the international standards. The main purpose of outlining standards for international asylum and immigration was to offer better living conditions for the refugees, especially in terms of righs and integration opportunities. This comes to a point where the nation state mostly prefers the 'wanted' or 'unwanted' migrants to their

---

[8] Juliette Tolay,"The Legal Framework of Asylum Policy in Turkey: Towards More Protection?",**Turkey: Beyond The Fortress Paradıgm At The Southeastern Borders Of The EU, ed.by.Nurcan Özgür Baklacıoğlu and Yeşim Özer,** Edwin Edgar Melen Press 2013, p. 83.

[9] Kemal Kirişçi, "Asylum, Immigration , Irregular Migration and Internally Displacement in Turkey: Institutions and Policies", European University Institute, 2004, p.11.

[10] https://www.refworld.org/docid/49746cc62.html , Online, 30.11.2020

[11] Kirişçi,"Asylum, Immigration , Irregular Migration and Internally Displacement in Turkey: Institutions and Policies p. 3.

territory.[12] Accepting or not accepting these immigrants also can be examined together with the issue of citizenship.

Starting in 2005, the legal regulations have been established with regards to the admission process of the refugees. The every-day activities and problems show the main problematic area, which is the registeration to the system (The Asylum and Migration Bureu was established in 2008). It's also important to work together with the UNHCR, which was established in Turkey in 1960, in order to lead and coordinate the international response to protect refugees and find solutions to refugees' problems. They both need to ensure that every individual can exercise their right to seek asylum and stay safely as a refugee in another country, with options for voluntary return home, local integration, and resettlement in a third country.

Refugees in Turkey and the concept of citizenship

The young republic of Turkey focused on the education to create an '*eligible citizen'* (Makbul Vatandaş). This policy might have been reasonable for the sake of unity, especially if the boders of the citizenship can be viewed in parallel with the boders of the territory of the state. It can also be criticised as it highlights the gap between different etnicities that speak different languages. Turkish language was and,in most cases, still is the most important element to construct a national identity. This also means how to differentiate between whom to include and exclude. [13]

Turkish Republic, as well as the Ottoman Empire, has faced the problems of admitting refugees for a long period of time. The difference between 'refugee' and 'immigrant'manifests itself here. According to the UN, Refugees are persons who are outside their country of origin for reasons of feared persecution, conflict, generalized violence, or other circumstances that have seriously disturbed public order and, as a result, require international protection. The definition of refugee can be found in the 1951 Convention and regional refugee instruments, besides the UNHCR's Statute.

As is known, the citizenship process can be handled from legal, social, and political perspectives. Every person is born a citizen of her or his own country. There is no exception to this principle. The rights and obligations come along with the citizenship that is granted with birth.

When citizenship rights are mentioned, two of the leading discussion topics regarding the refugees are rights and obligations of them. Of course, it should be noted that this principle is based on the legal assessment of nation-state citizenship. In classical nation-state citizenship, rights and duties are the same for all citizens of that state. However, in the post-nation-state model; that is, in the post-national

[12] Tolay, "The Legal Framework of Asylum Policy in Turkey: Towards More Protection?," p. 80

[13] Kemal Kirişçi, "Disaggregating Turkish Citizenship and Immigration Practices", Middle Eastern Studies, Vol.36, No.3, July 2000, p.2.

process, we can see the diversity of citizenship identity. We can includenot only the citizens of a given country, but also individuals who are considered guests, who come to work, those seen as refugees or asylum seekers, and those with partial citizenship rights. Nuhoğlu states that individuals in some refugee groups are more privileged compared to other groups that are not considered citizens, namely those who have legal residence permits, political refugees, dual citizens or citizens of any EU member country.[14]

The creation of the nation state is longer and more powerful compared to that of international organizations. Accordingly, economic, political, and even religious oppositions have the potential to reduce the probability of finding a common point to almost zero. Especially, the economic crisis experienced in recent years and the immigration issues that emerged afterwards have enabled the nationalist tendencies to increase and sometimes to become radical in some countries of Europe. Although this situation does not threaten the international arena that has been shaped since The World War II, where there is a higher number of nation states and political organizations, the idea that its acceleration should be prevented is generally agreed upon.

The concept of citizenship has been resurrected and sharpened with the age of the nation state. We have already explained that the essence of citizenship is a bond of land and blood. Here, we can look at the difference between the state that intends to neutralize the population that comes with immigration, and the states that are immigrant friendly. Is national identity, which is the main element of an individual's identity, measured by the place of birth or by the place where s/he lived for years? How does a person determine her/his belonging? Are blood ties or residency sufficient for citizenship ties? The answers to these questions cannot be given easily. Ethnic identity, which comes with questions of citizenship, is actually a component taken into account during the rise of racism. However, it can be said that ethnic purity is actually just a dream.[15] It is almost nonexistent that a citizen of any country has a one hundred percent pure racial base. This situation is related to the permeability of the borders, especially cultural diversity. So to judge, humiliate, or glorify anyone according to their race is just as unreasonable as labelling them with a title that he himself did not earn.

Globalization, in its simplest terms, can be applied to concepts belonging to both individuals and societies since it is a process that 'eliminates borders.' Education is one of the most important points that guide the existence of both the nation state and the individual. Education has been one of the ideological apparati used by the power, especially in the processes where the ideology of nationalism created nations and thus nation states. Along with modernization, the penetration of communication tools into the life of the individual has helped in the process of

---

[14] Yasemin Nuhoğlu Soysal, "Limits of Citizenship: Migrants and Postnational Membership in Europe", The University of Chicago Press, Chicago and London, 1994, p.141.

[15] Lawrence M. Friedman, **Yatay Toplum**, (The Horizontal Society), Türkiye İş Bankası Kültür Yayınları, İstanbul, 2003, p.128.

creating an '*eligible citizen*' in terms of power.[16]The fact that the education process goes on a parallel level along with these communication tools has helped the individual to become a beneficial citizen to the state.

The importance of educational policies can manifest itself in many areas ranging from official historiography to the implementation of an ideological curriculum. If we look at the example of Turkey, especially the establishment of the Republic during the Ottoman Empire and the early phases of the republic, the state started focusing on the use of education as a tool to create the '*eligible citizen*'. One of the points to be taken into consideration here is the creation process of the nation-state. In this respect, we can consider education as the most important ideological device that stands out. Education has the potential to shape an individual's entire life and personality, after basic education from the family[17]

If we talk about the massive migration movements of Turkey since the establishment of the Republic, we can start with the population exchange between Greece and Turkey in the 1920s. Both those who spoke Turkish and those who did not, nearly 400.000 migrants have moved to Turkey. Also, we can count the Bulgarian Muslims, who had moved from Bulgaria to Turkey as well. The polulation can be counted as nearly 200.000. After the Second World War, especially in 1950-51, many people from Bulgaria arrived to Turkey, mostly because of the communist regime in Bulgaria.[18]The newly-established Republic of Turkey was reluctant to accept more immigrants from Greece because of the homogeneity of the population in the Western borders. The immgirant population besides the Balkans may be limited comparatively.

The other significant period was the Second World War, which allowed Turkey to accept the Jewish refugees from Europe. This movement was different compared to the previous ones as it turned Turkey into a transit country, just as from Europe to Palestine. In that case, these people were neither viewed as refugees nor citizens.

The immigration policy shows an alteration on accepting the refugees, their legal status and the admission to citizenship. Not only the geographical limitation on the Geneva Convention, but also the issue of preserving the homogeneity of the Turkish citizenship help develop the legal status of the refugees. If we take an overall look at the legal process, only thoseof Turkish descent and Turkish as their native language were the ones who could be accepted as eligible. This policy also shows the importance of the Sunnibackground. The inclusion and the exclusion of citizenship was mostly based on language, but religious issues mattered even to a higher extent. [19]Despite the fact that some immigrants did not speak the language,

---

[16] Füsun Üstel, **Makbul Vatandaşın Peşinde II. Meşrutiyet'ten Bugüne Vatandaşlık Eğitimi**, (In pursuit of the ideal citizen: Civic education from constitutional monarchy to today), İletişim Yayınları, İstanbul, 2004, p.11.

[17] Üstel, Makbul Vatandaşın Peşinde II. Meşrutiyet'ten Bugüne Vatandaşlık Eğitimi, p.13.

[18] Kirişçi, "Asylum, Immigration, Irregular Migration and Internally Displacement in Turkey: Institutions and Policies", p. 7-9

[19] Kirişçi, "Disaggregating Turkish Citizenship and Immigration Practices", p. 14

because they were of Sunni background, many of them were deemed eligible candidates for citizenship. With the Law no.2510 (İskân Kanunu), the state of having Turkish origins differentiates people as visitors or refugess. The visitors who are not of Turkish origin or culture can only be classified as visitors.[20]

The citizenship process can be tackled as the most important issue concerning the homogeinty of the population, especially in a young republic. Governments have lots of strategies they employ to maintain their sovereignty, but citizenship can be regarded as the most important one. Therefore, the concept and the boundaries of the citizenship notion should be calculated carefully, as it also shows the difference between refugees and immigrants, who should be included and who should not. It's also about the trust, both in the citizens of Turkey and in the government itself. That's why the emigration from the Balkans are always welcomed compared to other areas. The sovereignty and the security of the state is also closely linked with the notion of citizenship[21]and that's why, similar to each and every state, Turkey also prefers to restrict the population who is allowed to cross its borders.

When The Geneva Convention (with the geographical limitation) is utilized with the Law of Settlement, we can easily see the difference on the definition. As mentioned above, the individuals who are of Turkish culture or origin can be accepted as migrants, while the others can be accepted only as refugees.

Refugees in Turkey and their education

The important area asylum seekers that we will focus on is education. Apart from other legal boundaries, education may not be viewed as the primary problem compared to health or residence permit. However, regardless of the label s/he has been assigned, be it a citizen, refugee, or immigrant, every individual has the right to education. Besides legal obstacles or opportunities, individuals (young people), who should get education, should be divided into groups according to their age and cycles. We can simply divide these groups into three as children, youth, and adults. Another problematic issue with the refugee problem can be seen as the boundaries and the rights of citizenship. As mentioned above, the construction of the 'citizen' goes hand in hand with the curriculum offered to the students, which is a tool for the state to build a national identity. It also emphasizes the homogeneity of the society, with the strict definition of the 'other'. As national identity can be used as a way to determine whom to include or exclude from the society, refugees and righs of the refugees should also be regarded as a humanitarian problem, not only a legal issue.

In Turkey, every child between the ages 6-14 must get compulsory education regardless of their legal status. Higher education is not compulsory, but every individual must have their national identification number or foreigner's

[20] Tolay, "The Legal Framework of Asylum Policy in Turkey: Towards More Protection?", p.83

[21] Julie Matthews&Ravinder Sidhu, "Desperately Seeking The Global Subject: International Education, Citizenship And Cosmopolitanism", Globalisation, Societies and Education, Volume 3, 2005 - Issue 1, p.52.

identification number in order to attend school / university.[22] This obligation brings us to the problem that every individual should pay a fee to get this identification number. As education may be viewed as one of the most important items, the right to get educated is protected by the international law and regulations. Besides this, we can talk about the obstacles that hinder the individual's partaking in the education system: Bureaucratic or economic obstacles, the language barrier, the perception that their stay in Turkey is temporary, the difficulty of Turkish language as it is offered in the curriculum.[23] In this direction, long-term, permanent, and sustainable policies are aimed at instead of short-term measures. The most urgent issues can be listed as the language, curriculum, and the problem of adaptation.

While creating the identity of the individual in the process of becoming a citizen, starting from the family, the values / country, and so on, the role of education is worth examining sinceoutside of the family, the education offered by the state is the first step of the process where the outline of an ideal citizen is instilled in each and every individual.

The most common problem for the education of refugees can be seen as the adaptation. Unlike the international students, the education, higher education in particular, of the refugees may not be seen as the first important issue. As they're mostly seen as visitors or guests, they are being separated from international students who stay in Turkey at least 4 years for their education.

Many of the children and young refugees are also trying to deal with the trumatic experiences and adaptation problems, which stems from the difficulty of the situation itself as well as the unpredictibality of the future. Not only the primary schools, but also the universities play a significant role on the adaptation process of the refugee children. First of all, having the right to education can be tackled from a human rights perspective.[24] As refugees escape from their countries for fear of persecution because of their race, religion, ethnicity, or political stance, the protection that is granted by another country should involve the right to education as well as the basic human rights. [25]

The importance of education, especially for refugee children and youth, can be seen in the fact that it acts as a means to bring together the local people and the refugees themselves. Education is not limited to the curriculum helping an individual with her/his personal development since the education process, especially in the presence of equal standards, helps with the inclusion and the acceptance of the refugees by the society. The acceptance by the host society helps

---

[22] Tolay, "The Legal Framework of Asylum Policy in Turkey: Towards More Protection?", p. 116

[23] Kristen Biehl, "Migration 'Securitization' and its Everyday Implications: An Examination of Turkish Asylum Policy and Practice", RSCAS Research Reports, 2009/1, p.1

[24] The Universal Declaration of Human Rights states the education as one of the fundamental rights for everyone. For further details, check on the website : https://en.unesco.org/news/what-you-need-know-about-right-education

[25] Rebecca Leela Thomas, "The Right to Quality Education for Refugee Children Through Social Inclusion", J. Hum. Rights Soc. Work (2016) 1:193–201, p.193, file:///Users/gamzeusar/Downloads/Thomas2016_Article_TheRightToQualityEducationForR%20(1).pdf , (Access 28.11.2020).

the refugee children and youth to connect with the local community as well as forming a new identity.[26] This new identity may be different from the national identity, which is a natural outcome of formal education. As the identity of refugee children and youth mostly consists of traumas, education equips them with the skill to cope with the difficulty of adapting to a new environment, and psychological, social, and economical difficulties.

The main problems connected with the refugees can be counted as the adaptation, difference for language and curriculum and economic/ bureaucratic obstacles. The curriculum and language problem are the most critical of them.[27] While the curricula of primary and high school students are included in a standard, the differences between departments, especially the equivalence problem in higher education, make it difficult to follow the curriculum. The requirement to have an identity card or passport number to enroll in higher education is one of the most bureaucratic and economic obstacles. Although solutions such as special student status and additional quotas are produced for refugees who are not legally considered citizens but who are envisaged to benefit from the right to education, it should not be overlooked that the important thing should be a sustainable and wide-ranging policy.[28]

Conclusion

Turkey, and the Ottoman Empire before in history, has a government structure that guests immigration and refugees, since her establishment. Turkey had not had any legal regulation in international standarts until the Geneva Convention, which was accepted with the geographical limitation. Turkey's opting for this caution to the convention also gave us a hint with regards to the refugee policy of Turkey as it approached the refugees of Turkish origin with a milder attitude, compared to its predecessor, the Ottoman Empire.

The Law of Settlement (İskan Kanunu) may be the leading legal document about the admission and settlement of the refugees in Turkey. It was enacted in June 16, 1934 and enabled the ones with the Turkish origin and culture to settle in Turkey as migrants or muhajirs. The second important legal document is the Geneva Convention, whihc was accepted in August 29, 1961 with the rule number 359. With the alteration in 1967, the supplementary protocol disassembled the time limitation while keeping the geographical one. The legal regulations about the admission process of refugees in Turkey has received wider attention since 2005. With the National Action Plan for Asylum and Immigration which was regulated in 2005, the legal and bureaucratic regulations has progressed promptly and in

[26] Rebecca Leela Thomas, "The Right to Quality Education for Refugee Children Through Social Inclusion", p.195.

[27] Zeynep Özde Ateşok, Karşılaştırmalı PerspektiftenUluslararası Mülteci RejimiBağlamında Mülteci Eğitimi Ve Türkiye Örneği, (Unpublished PhD Thesis),Istanbul, Istanbul University, 2018.

[28] YÖK, 03.09.2013, "Bakanlar Kurulu Kararı'nın 4'üncü Maddesi. Sayı: 57802651/1008", (Access 15.11.2020) www.yok.gov.tr. YÖK, 9.10.2013, "Suriye ve Mısır Ülkelerinden Yurdumuzda Bulunan Yükseköğretim Kurumlarına Yatay Geçiş Kararı", (Access 15.11.2020) www.yok.gov.tr

coordination with the European Union Acquis. Meanwhile,this brought about the opportunity to put theory into practice.. With taking the steps towards a well-founded refugee policy, it became clear that the regulations should be sustainable and extensive, an example of which was accepting Open Door Policy, after the Syrian Civil War.

Organizing the living conditions as well as the law regulations shows how important to implement the bureaucratic, social and economic arrangements to the case of the refugees. Education is most probably the significant issue in this respect as it could be the primary tool to integrate the refugees with the local population.As mentioned before, the role of higher education is in a way downplayed and regarded as arbitrary or secondary, probably on account of not being compulsory. Nonetheless, having access to higher education is crucial for refugees considering that it helps form a sense of belonging and contributes quite positively to the adaptation process.

As we perceive education as a process which begins at family and continues through primary school, we can clearly see the relation between the consciousness of citizenship and national identity, which also can be easily molded and manipulated. With the official curriculum,which is also a part of the public sphere as is education itself, the individuals to the age of 18, are obliged by the state to attend the school. Therefore, this situation brings us the problem of the education of the refugees, whom should get an education in their own native language. Not only they have economic and social problem or obstacles that take priority over education, they also experience adaptation problems that are aggravated due to a language barrier. If we talk about the refugees aged 18 and older, who have the right to study in higher education, we can see deeper and large scaled problems like the diploma/ transcript accreditation problems, the bureaucratic obstacles to register to the higher education unit (YÖK) system and the similar ones before: language and adaptation problems.

With the legal documents which were accepted and put into practice by Higher Education Unit (YÖK) and Ministry of National Education (MEB), the objective has been to regulate the system for the refugees, mostly Syrian students. Despite the fact that most of these regulations have been planned to secure the educational right of the refugees, the adaptation problems remain the same to this day. Apart from these, it is obvious that the issue od education is not something that can be handled via legal documents or accreditation alone. It's essential to ensure they get enough tolerance and convenience, as well as economic and bureaucratic support. These policies may only be sustainable if they're accepted, both on a social and a legal basis, as permanent residents in Turkey. It is essential to manage education as a beneficial tool to integrate the refugees into the society, as it was used to bind the population together as eligible citizens and have them adopt the national identity. For this reason, setting up the regulations both socially and legally may be helpful to resolve the possible inequalities as social and legal regulations always go hand in hand.

CHAPTER 10

IRREGULAR MIGRATION AND EMPLOYMENT EFFECTS OF REFUGEES HEADING TO TURKEY: UNREGISTERED EMPLOYMENT

Hatice Nur Germir[1]

The Civil War, which started in the spring of 2011 in Syria, displaced millions of Syrians from their homes. According to United Nations (UN) figures, approximately 5 million Syrian refugees have hadto flee to neighboring countries. Until 2014, which spread out around the region of southeastern. Turkey, and especially built by the government of Turkey and the controlled refugee. Starting from 2014, refugees are located in cities where the camps, especially other regions in Turkey, hoping to get official work permits eventually another European country to asylum have done[2].

Turkey offers, hosting the world's largest refugee population of more than 4 million, with a population of more than 3.6 million Syrians fleeing the war, which continues to devastate their country, as well as people from other countries in the Far East and Africa, especially Afghan, Iran, Iraq, registered refugees to education and health facilities laudable efforts to ensure access to basic rights and services including in the country. Despite all these efforts, many refugees may find themselves faced with difficult and often unstable conditions. After years of displacement, refugee families have difficulty meeting their basic needs due to the cost of living and the inability to reach a regular income in order to survive as they deplete their available resources[3].

Clarifying the Refugee Concept

The definition of the words 'refugee', 'asylum seeker' and 'immigrant', which are used to describe people on the move, leaving their countries and crossing borders, needs to be clarified. Even though the concepts of 'immigrant' and 'refugee' are mostly use dinterchangeably, it would be appropriate to analyze theseterms that contain important legal differences. **Refugees** are the people who have to leave their country because they are at risk ofsevere human rights violations and persecution in their own country. Refugees feel that the security threat and the

---

[1] Assistant Professor Dr., Manisa Celal Bayar University, Faculty of Applied Sciences, Türkiye.

[2] Evren Ceritoğlu, H.Burcu Gurcihan Yunculer, Huzeyfe Torun and Semih Tumen, The Impact of Syrian Refugees on Natives' Labour Market Outcomes in Turkey: Evidence from Aquasi-Experimental Design, **IZA Journal of Labour Policy**, Vol.6, No.5, 2017, p.1-28, DOI10.1186/s40173-017-0082-4.

[3] Eren Aygün, "The Emergency Social Safety Net (ESSN): Offering a Lifeline to Vulnerable Refugees in Turkey", **European Commission**, European Civil Protection and Humanitarian Aid Operations, https://ec.europa.eu/echo/essn_en (Access 04.10.2020)

dangers to their lives leave them no choice but to leave their country and seek refuge in another country, because their own government cannot or will not protect them from these dangers, and refugees have the right to international protection. **Asylum seekers** are those who have left their country, who have taken refuge in another country to be protected from persecution and serious human rights violations, but who have not yet been legally recognized as refugees and are waiting for the result of their asylum application. It follows that it is a human right to seek asylum and that everyone should be allowed to enter another country to seek asylum. While there is no internationally accepted legal definition of the word **migrant**, Amnesty International, as well as many other human rights agencies and organizations, accept migrants as people who live outside of their home country but are not asylum seekers or refugees. There are different reasons for immigrants to be abroad, such as working, learning, or living with family members outside. Poverty can be the subject of political turmoil, gang violence, natural disasters, or other difficult individuals leaving their countries[4].

Literature Review

Research into the consequences of migration's impact on the local labor market has long been a topic of interest to researchers. There are textbook models that suggest the migration lead stoan outward shift in labor supply speeds of the labor market. This is expected to ultimately lead to a decline in the wage balance and employment rates[5].

It has been criticized by Borjas et al. (1996) on the basis of the idea that immigrant flows to a particular region could potentially have several secondary effects, such as capital flows, outward movements of local workforce, and changes in intercity trade patterns.This criticism reports that immigrants have a greater influence on local markets, perhaps more than initial research suggests, and that migration has greater effects on labor market outcomes[6].

Using data showing changes in the number of immigrants across regions and over time, the impact of immigration on wages and employment in the US local labor market was analyzed by Altonji and Card (1991) and Goldin (1994). Pischke and Velling (1997) conducted a similar study using German data and consistently found that migrants have adverse effects on the labor market. In this context, they added that the consequences of migrants' effects on the domestic labor market can also occur only during the activity[7],[8].

---

[4] https://www.amnesty.org.tr/content/refugee rights (Access 11.09.2020)

[5] Ceritoğlu et al., op.cit., p.2

[6] George J. Borjas, Lawrence F. Katz, TheEvolution of the Mexican-Born Workforce in the United States. In:Borjas, G.J.(ed), Mexican Immigration to the United States, 2007, **National Bureau of Economic Research**, Cambridge.

[7] Rachel M. Friedberg, YouCan'tTake it WithYou? Immigrant Assimilation and The Portability of Human Capital, **JLaborEcon**, Vol. 18, No. 18, 2000, p. 221–251

[8] YoramWeiss, Robert M. Sauer, Menachem Gotlibovski, Immigration, Search and Loss of Skill, **JLaborEcon**, Vol. 21, No. 21, 2003, p. 557–591.

Using long-term census data reflecting the co-evolution of immigrant and indigenous populations, it can be characterized as a common feature of different studies that have been carried out using non-experimental data from developed countries, most of which are of US origin, to conclude that immigration is often a voluntary act and therefore the use of appropriate techniques to address selection bias. is required. Although it is based on instrumental variable methods used in studies in the literature, there is no limit to relying on the research to estimate the impact of migration on the local labor market. With some exceptions, quasi-experimental evidence does not outweigh the consequences of significant immigration, with some exceptions in studies that exploit an involuntary influx of a mass immigrant population due to civil war and other political factors to predict the causal effect of attention without relying on the classical selection-correction methods underlying refugees' emigration[9].

Ceritoğlu et al in their research, which forms an important part of Syrian refugees heavy inflows to Turkey of refugees in Turkey has started since the year 2012, in this context, putting a symmetrical window this date, assuming the initial examination January 1, 2012 2010-2011 pre-migration, 2012-2013 migration after the period is defined as, the Syrian refugees in Turkey's southeast to abandon the country's northern and western parts of the right have gone if they are refugees, a large portion above the average that the city close to the Turkey-Syria border, Turkey's Disaster and Emergency Management Presidency (DEMP), published by official of the refugee population ratio in the Southeast of Turkey using the figures from the cities that 2% over the 'study area' was created, only negligible amounts of Syrian refugees in hosting the remaining cities in the neighboring region, cultural aspects, socio-demographic characteristics and economic development flat, It has been formed as 'control zones' similar to 'examination area' in the meaning of good, and when all kinds of data belonging to refugees are taken into consideration, it is the element that reveals the difference in the strategy, based on the comparison of the data regarding the post-migration period in comparison with the control area, that the effect on the results has been determined; they reported that the flow of Syrian refugees negatively affected the probability of finding a job for local people, while wage results were not statistically significantly affected.In addition, Ceritoğlu et al.'s studies focus on four labor market outcomes: (i) not in the labor force, (ii) formal employment, (iii) unregistered employment, and (iv) unemployment, which are differentiated according to the ratio of local workers aged 15-64 to the population; As a result of refugee arrivals, the rate of informal employment decreased by around 2.2 percentage points relative to the population, approximately 50% of this decrease in informal employment went out of the labor market, 32% were unemployed, 18% went to a formal job For men, the decline in the ratio of informal employment to the population is 1.9 percentage points, that most of the men who lost their informal jobs are unemployed, for women the decrease is realized at a much higher level of 2.6 percentage points, that women who lost their

[9] Jean-Francois Maystadt, Philip Verwimp, Winners and Losers among a Refugee-Hosting Population. **Econ Dev. Cultural Change**, Vol. 62, No. 62, 2014, p. 769–809.

informal jobs almost notes that all of them exit the labor market.These findings suggest that local market workers who lost their informal jobs are being replaced by unregistered Syrian refugees. This substitution made it extremely difficult to find new jobs among women in the local market, resulting in a situation that resulted in them leaving the labor market. Men, on the other hand, preferred to remain in the labor force, which caused an increase in the unemployment rate. To summarize, while unemployment has increased, labor force participation, informal employment and employment rates have decreased for domestic workers.Women, younger workers and less educated workers, who are disadvantaged groups, have been worst affected.It can also be stated that there is a small but unexpected increase in formal employment among men, due to the increasing presence of organizations providing health, education, nutrition, security, childcare and other services to Syrian refugees in the region. The prevalence of unregistered employment in Turkey's labor market, entry of Syrian refugees has reached the conclusion that the negative effects on the domestic labor market improves results[10].

View of Refugees inTurkey

More than 65 million people who have had to leave their countries and migrate to other countries, especially in conflict, violence or human rights violations, are in a state of migration mobility around the world. Turkey most refugees in the world by hosting more than 4 million refugees located in the hosting country. United Nations High Commissioner for Refugees, according to data declared by more than 4 million people in Turkey Syrians, 169 thousand Afghan citizens, 143 thousand Iraqi nationals, 35 thousand Iranian citizens, 4 thousand 800 Somali nationals, over 4 million refugees have to be another 10 thousand. Turkey busiest refugee group stood out as Syrians, Syrians mostly of Istanbul, Ankara, Hatay, Gaziantep, Mersin, Adana and Kilis in their housing, civil war due to the country that leaves the 5.6 million Syrians 4 million is back in Turkey of that bar in the EU remains, after Turkey is the country which hosts the most refugees in the world, Pakistan (1.4 million refugees), Uganda (1.4 million refugees), Lebanon (998 thousand refugees), Iran (979 thousand refugees).

Officials from the International Refugee Office visited Gaziantep, Istanbul and Ankara provinces in July 2019 to investigate the access of refugees to the labor market. The employment of refugees, which is a priority issue for humanitarian assistants and donors, becomes a political theme for the population of the host country. As of 2019, the ninth year of the Syrian crisis is happening. The record increase in unemployment, as well as the decline experienced in Turkey constitutes a critical turning point in the economy on behalf of the refugee population, including employment climate primarily Syrians living in Turkey.

It is reported that Turkish authorities carried out widespread identity checks in Syrian districts, metro and bus stations in July 2019 and extended the duration of those who did not register until August 20, and then until October 31, 2019.

[10] Ceritoğlu et al., op.cit.p.3

Istanbul is the preferred province in the first place as it offers more job opportunities than many other cities. International Refugee Office meeting his Syrian some circles in the xenophobic actions of the increasingly common come and they expressed that they feel uncomfortable about the hostile exhibited an attitude also, although it runs many Syrians in Turkey, exploited by unregistered labor in this case the majority of employers stated that they applied as a run in the labor market. Turkey a work permit system for access to a large population of Syrian refugees rather been put into practice in 2016. However, permits are often stated by employers who are reluctant to cover the costs and who are faced with administrative barriers to recruiting a refugee or who have no knowledge of how the process works, demanding the unregistered employment of refugees, and the majority of refugees work in low-wage jobs, particularly in small textile workshops and the construction sector. It is stated that they remain in the state. According to the International Refugee Office, there are many Syrian refugees with highly skilled qualifications, but these individuals are also forced to work in the informal market due to barriers to entering their traditional professions, while non-Syrian refugees have to work under stricter conditions because they are entering a different work permit system, and He argues that their access to the formal labor market has been made more difficult. Since the change in the registration system for non-Syrian refugees in 2018, it has been reported that many Afghan refugees are not registered with the Turkish authorities at all, making them unable to obtain work permits[11].

Table 1. Distribution of Syrian Refugees by Provinces[12]

Provinces	Registered	Population	Comparison Percentage with Provincial Population
Kilis	116.135	136.319	85.19
Hatay	444.576	1.575.226	28.22
Şanlıurfa	453.083	1.985.753	22.82
Gaziantep	422.850	2.005.515	21.08
Mersin	206.142	1.793.931	11.49
Mardin	89.999	809.719	11.11
Adana	232.315	2.216.475	10.48

When the 2018 data of the population of Turkey's total population of 80 million 810 thousand 525 individuals consisting of 3 million 622 thousand 366 Syrian refugees who are registered number of countries are taken into account at the moment which corresponds to 4:48% of the total. On October 21, 2020, the city with the highest number of Syrians was Istanbul[13] with 512 thousand 578 people, but as shown in Table 2 prepared according to the data obtained as a result of the ratio of registered Syrian refugees to the population living in the province. It is noteworthy that they reside in the provinces of Kilis, Hatay, Şanlıurfa, Gaziantep,

[11] IzzaLeghtas, InsecureFutureDeportationsandLack of Legal WorkForRefugees in Turkey, **Field Report, September 2019**, (Access 10.10.2020)

[12] Yaman, op.cit.

[13] Number of Syrians in Turkey, October 2020, https://multeciler.org.tr/turkiyedeki-suriyeli-sayisi/ (Access 16.11.2020)

Mersin, Mardin and Adana.

In Turkey for the first time April 29, 2011 Syrian refugees / asylum seekers have logged in. In this context, the political authority from anyone 'Temporary Protection Regime' unrest in the country is under until sheltering in Turkey, food, and have made the distribution of tasks to be done and work to ensure their basic needs, and certainly the biggest effort in this regard Disaster and Emergency Management Presidency (DEMP) and It was carried out by the Red Crescent. According to data from 2018, more than 4 million refugees are living in Turkey. About 250 thousand of these refugees, who remained with their own efforts, continue their lives in temporary accommodation centers established by DEMP. It is not possible to express this number precisely because of the people who use illegal ways, first seek asylum and then flee from the shelter centers. Overall shows that Turkey has no barriers and citizens in its territory without discrimination the same way as people interested in the focus of policies behind[14].

According to occupational groups, the Syrians who live in refugee camps and constitute the largest part of the refugee groups; It can be seen from Table 2 that 68.40% of the males and 90.30% of the females in the camp do not have a profession or any qualified qualifications. It is noteworthy that 39% of the Syrian male population outside the camps and 61.10% of the female population do not have any qualifications.

Following the defection occurred towards Turkey, especially in the eastern part, experienced the largest increase in labor supply in major cities as a result of workers' wages has declined dramatically. The main reason for this situation, which negatively affects the competition of the domestic labor force and leads to a small amount of unemployment, especially because they demand low wages or no wages, is due to the fact that incoming refugees demand only enough wages to provide their daily living. It reveals that company owners or employers employ uninsured workers with the idea that they can increase their profits because it is a factor that lowers the costs too much, or they also resort to tax evasion by showing the state as if there are less number of workers in that workplace.Although there are refugees who have been given a work permit, company owners who know that those who do not have a work permit will hardly demand any wages, take advantage of this situation. Nevertheless, these workers were allowed to work as a result of a regulation published on January 15, 2016, in order to keep everything transparent and recorded.

The number of registered Syrian refugees in Turkey under temporary protection over the previous month registering an increase of 2 thousand 549 people as of October 21, 2020, reaching a total of 3 million 624 thousand 517 people. 1 million 694 thousand 242 people, who make up 46.7% of these people, consist of children and young people between the ages of 0-18. When this number is added to the number of women it is reached 2 million 558 thousand 139 people, which

[14] Yaman, op.cit.

corresponds to the total of Syrian refugees in Turkey, 70.5% of the population. According to a statement issued by Ministry of Family, Labor and Social Services on March 31, 2019, the number of Syrian granted a work permit in Turkey was reported to be 31 thousand 185 people (Figure 1).[15]

Table 2. Professional Groups of Syrians in Refugee Camps (2018)[16]

Occupational Group	Inside the Camp		Out of Camp	
	Men %	Women%	Men%	Women%
Engineer	0.60	0.20	1.10	0.70
GovernmentOfficial	9.00	7.30	1.00	0.50
Hand Mader	8.20	0.50	41.80	34.10
No Job	68.40	90.30	39.00	61.10
Office Worker	0.50	0.30	3.30	1.10
Driver	2.40	0.00	1.20	0.00
Army Staff	2.10	0.00	0.30	0.00
HealthcareProfessional	0.30	0.20	0.50	0.60
Agriculture / livestock	2.40	0.00	1.60	0.70
Artificer	6.20	1.20	10.20	1.20
Total	100	100	100	100

Figure 1. Number of Syrian Refugees Given Work Permits (2018)

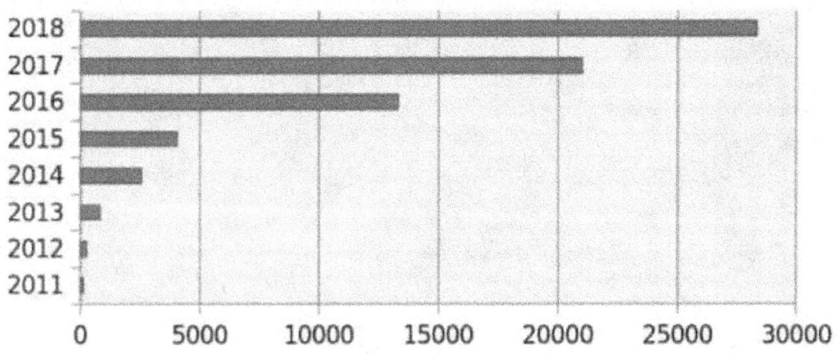

Unregistered Employment in Turkey

The word employment, which means 'use in a job, in a job', includes employees subject to or affiliated to an employer, daily workers (daily casual) and unpaid family workers. Entire working life with the concept of employment in many studies including the household labor force survey and further research in the context of other surveys conducted in Turkey is trying to express.There are employers as well as self-employed workers in the working life, that is, in the labor market. In this context, the word employment is tried to explain all persons involved in working life. Unregistered employment, on the other hand, refers to the whole of employment forms that work in informal economic activities on their behalf or on

[15] https://multeciler.org.tr/turkiyedeki-suriyeli-sayisi/ (Access 13.11.2020)

[16] Yaman, ibid

a paid basis, and whose activities are not reflected in public records and statistics and cannot be included in statistical calculations, as well as in formal and informal sectors. Failure to fulfill legal obligations such as tax and social security premiums against the state as a result of the employees not notified at all or missing the relevant institutions and organizations is defined as unregistered employment[17].

Figure 2. Unregistered Employment Rates by Years[18]

Years	Agriculture	Non-Agric.	Industry	Services	Construction	Total
2010	85,47	29,06	32,68	27,11	-	43,25
2011	83,85	27,76	31,5	25,71	-	42,05
2012	83,61	24,51	27,89	22,73	-	39,02
2013	83,28	22,4	25,23	20,9	-	36,75
2014	82,27	22,32	20,26	21,09	36,61	34,97
2015	81,16	21,23	19,13	20,05	35,58	33,57
2016	82,09	21,72	20,2	20,35	35,76	33,49
2017	83,33	22,1	20,03	20,95	35,8	33,97
2018	82,73	22,28	20,29	21,46	34,39	33,42
2019	86,62	22,96	20,03	22,55	37,74	34,52

Figure 2 shows the development of the 2010-2019 year between unregistered employment in Turkey; It is noteworthy that the rate of unregistered employment, which was 43.25% in 2010, is generally in a decreasing trend over the years, reflecting the level of 34.52% in 2019, and that the most important informal employment data in the overall total is experienced in the agricultural sector. Although unregistered employment data has a decreasing trend throughout the country in the period of 2010-2019, it is observed that the agricultural sector has increased and the construction sector, where unskilled personnel are employed intensively, has attracted attention especially since 2014 and followed a course above the overall unregistered figures of the country. Figure 3 shows the regions where

[17] Ahmet Oğuz Sarıca, **Kayıt Dışı İstihdam ve Mücadele Yöntemleri, (Planlama Uzmanlığı Tezi), Ankara,** T.C. Başbakanlık Devlet Planlama Teşkilatı Müsteşarlığı Yıllık Programlar ve Konjonktür Değerlendirme Genel Müdürlüğü, 2006, p. 16-17.

[18] TÜİK Hane Halkı İşgücü İstatistikleri, http://www.sgk.gov.tr/wps/portal/sgk/tr/calisan/kayitdisi_istihdam/kayitdisi_istihdam_oranlari (Access 01.11.2020)

unregistered employment shows ratio is above the national average.

Figure 3. Unregistered Employment Rates by Regions (%)[19]

Regions	2009	2010	2011	2012	2013	2014	2015	2016	2017	2018	2019
Şanlıurfa, Diyarbakır	67,92	63,59	60,69	63,27	61,6	67,67	65,05	62,77	62,04	60,11	58,06
Hatay, Kahramanmaraş, Osmaniye	57,57	61,28	58,61	53,69	48,94	40,95	36,72	42,18	42,14	45,80	45,14
Mardin, Batman, Şırnak, Siirt	63,82	61,08	57,26	51,47	49,06	54,67	51,47	41,21	40,46	39,45	42,36
Gaziantep, Adıyaman, Kilis	59,32	57,82	53,18	49,13	44,27	38,45	35,09	33,99	38,71	40,76	40,61
Adana, Mersin	53,9	52,77	53,42	47,52	43,97	45,71	43,31	41,74	39,96	38,99	39,71

Result

Anywhere around the world, the host communities and refugee populations have differences in lifestyle, religion, language and culture. Refugees cause some economic and social challenges in the country of immigration. Many migrants and refugees are unskilled or do not have any recognised professions, so they accept to work for lower wages or just enough to earn a living. This may cause various issues such as unregistered goods or services appear to be produced with less labour, avoiding taxes and social security premiums by business owners, and employing uninsured workers. On the other hand, the high number of people who can work for a lower wages instead of the minimum wage causes a decrease in the wages of the workers in the resident labor markets and even job losses.

[19] http://www.sgk.gov.tr/wps/portal/sgk/tr/calisan/kayitdisi_istihdam/kayitdisi_istihdam_oranlari (Access 02.11.2020)

CHAPTER 11

THE IMPACT OF SYRIANS UNDER TEMPORARY PROTECTION TO THE LABOUR MARKET IN TURKEY

Asli Okay Toprak[1]

Introduction

Due to its geographical location, Turkey is an important transit country for irregular migrants to reach European countries. Along with the Syrian crisis, there has been a noticeable increase in the number of Syrians among the irregular migrants[2].Turkey has accepted Syrians fleeing their country due to the civil war in Syria since April 2011, fulfilling the requirements of international law and conscience by providing 'temporary protection' within the framework of its 'open door policy'. This is a policy that is compatible with the principles of international law, especially the Universal Declaration of Human Rights and the Geneva Agreement of 1951[3]. Turkey has fully implemented its open-door policy for Syrians fleeing the conflict with all its elements and has provided temporary protection to these people as a result of its legal arrangements[4]. Temporary protection is a kind of protection which is developed for immediate solutions in the event of a mass influx. It is a practical and complementary solution that is implemented in the framework of *non-refoulement* of States without loss of time with individual status determination procedures, to persons arriving at the borders. In the framework of international and customary law, Turkey provides temporary protection to Syrian nationals within the following three factors: Clean acceptance to Turkey within the open border policy, Implementation of the *non-refoulement* principle without exceptions, meeting basic needs of newly-arrived Syrians in Turkey[5]. Given the general situation in Turkey, Syrians who have been granted temporary protection can legally remain in Turkey until their temporary protection is terminated with an identity document obtained as a result of their biometric registration. Social and legal actions can be carried out with the foreign identification number they receive. In accordance with the Temporary Protection Regulation adopted in 2014, the provision of education, access to the labor market, social assistance and services, as well as translation and similar services to these foreigners is regulated in detail[6].

---

[1] PhD, Assistant Professor, Kırklareli University Faculty of Economics and Administrative Sciences, Department of Economics, Türkiye.

[2] Yusuf Furkan Şen, Gözde Özkorul," Türkiye-Avrupa Birliği ilişkilerinde yeni bir eşik: Sığınmacı krizi bağlamında bir değerlendirme", **Göç Araştırmaları Dergisi**, Cilt2, Sayı:2, Temmuz-Aralık 2016, s.104.

[3] **Türkiye'deki Suriyeliler: Toplumsal Kabul ve Uyum Araştırması,** Hacettepe Üniversitesi Göçve Siyaset Araştırmaları Merkezi, Ankara, 2014, s.11.

[4] Şen, Özkorul, op.cit, s.102.

[5] https://en.goc.gov.tr/temporary-protection27(Access 09.11.2020).

[6] Şen, Özkorul, op.cit, s.102.

Due to the internal chaos and war environment in Syria, it is expected that their stay will increase further. So Syrian immigration can be considered mandatory, chained and mass. Because it is mandatory, because it contains all the layers in the region, its chaining is due to the fact that it gains continuity under the influence of networks in places where it goes. It is important because it shows the chain effect and consequences of migration in concentrating Syrian migration to specific regions[7].

The wave of forced migration that began with the Syrian Civil War is considered the largest migration movement of the Twenty-First Century. Turkey, which is home to close to four million Syrians under temporary protection, is the host country most exposed to the effects of forced migration. There is no doubt that the human losses of forced migration are unfortunately quite high. However, asylum seekers who have been forced to leave their homeland also face various deprivation in the country from which they came. At this point, it is of great importance for their adaption to working life in order to achieve better living conditions. For this reason, the study of the Turkish labor market, which is facing a high increase in labor supply with the arrival of Syrians, is of great importance. Before addressing the impact of Syrians on the job market, it would be useful to consider the concept of migration and theories that explain the migration movement with economic factors. There are many approaches that address the issue of immigration from different angles.

The concept of migration and economy-based migration approaches

Migration, which is considered a sociologically important movement, can be caused by inequality in the geographical distribution of Labor and capital, as well as by many other reasons, such as the desire for adventure, the need for security and also social, political, economic, ecological or individual reasons[8]. So, migration is a process of change that needs to be studied both in terms of time and space and purpose[9]. While internal migration is defined as the movement of people from one area of a country to another for the purpose or with the effect of establishing a new residence. This migration may be temporary or permanent. Internal migrants move but remain within their country of origin. International migration is defined asthe movement of persons who leave their country of origin, or the country of habitual residence, to establish themselves either permanently or temporarily in another country. An international frontier is therefore crossed[10].

According to the definition of Everett S. Lee, Migration is defined broadly as a

---

[7]Ahmet Yaman, "SuriyeliSosyal Sermayenin inşası ve yeniden üretim sürecinin sivil toplum ve ekonomik hayat alanlarında incelenmesi", **Göç Araştırmaları Dergisi**, Cilt2, Sayı:3, Ocak-Haziran 2016,ss.105-106.

[8] Erdem Selman Develi, "21. Yüzyılda Göç Olgusu:Uluslararası Göç Teorilerinin Ekonomi Politiği", **Süleyman Demirel Üniversitesi İktisadi ve İdari Bilimler Fakültesi Dergisi**, Cilt 22, Göç Özel Sayısı, 2017, s.1344.

[9] Canan Emek İnan, "Türkiye'de Göç Politikaları: İskân Kanunları Üzerinden Bir İnceleme", **Göç Araştırmaları Dergisi**, Cilt 2, Sayı3, 2016, s.15.

[10] **International Migration Law: Glossary on Migration**, International Organization for Migration, Switzerland, 2004, s.32-33.

permanent or semi-permanent change of residence. No restriction is placed upon the distance of the move or upon the voluntary or involuntary nature of the act, and no distinction is made between external and internal migration. Thus, a movefrom one apartment to another is counted as just as much an act of migration as a move from Bombay, India, to Iowa, though, of course, the initiation and consequences of such moves are vastly different. However, not all kinds of spatial mobility are included. For example, the continual movements of nomads and migratory workers, for whom there is no long-term residence, and temporary moves like those to the mountains for the summer are not included in his definition[11].

Michael J. Green wood classifies the migration literature in two broad areas of research, one dealing with the determinants and one dealing with the consequences of migration and some studies treat both the determinants and consequences within the same framework. But Greenwood emphasizes that the vast majority of migration research concerns the determinants of migration. The 'determinants' of migration are the factors that affect migration, including characteristics both of places and of persons and their families. The term refers to the qualitative and quantitative importance of each factor. Place characteristics are specific to a given area, such as employment and wage opportunities, the presence of family and friends, and location-specific amenities. Personal and family characteristics help shape individual and family responses to opportunities that may exist at different locations. The 'consequences' of migration refer both to the performance of migrants in their new locations relative to a benchmark, such as their presumed performance in their former place of residence had they not moved, and to the impacts that migrants have on others in sending and receiving areas[12].

Numerous old theories about immigration have focused on push-and-pull factors. Push factors refer to the dynamics within the source country that force people to migrate, such as war, famine, political pressure or population pressures. Conversely, pull factorsare the characteristics of countries that attract immigrants; for example, a thriving labor market, better living conditions, and low population density can attract immigrants in other regions. Push-and-pull migration theories have been criticized for providing exceedingly simple explanations for a complex and multifaceted process. Proponents of the system approach to immigration emphasize that one thing cannot be enough to explain the migration process. Each specific migration movement is a product of macro-and micro-level processes. Macro-level factors refer to issues of the upper dimension, such as the political structure in the region, laws and regulations governing internal and external migration, or changes in the international economy. On the other hand, micro-level factors are interested in the resources, knowledge and styles of understanding that immigrant communities themselves have[13]. Jessica Hagen-Zanker summarizes the

[11] Everett S. Lee, "A Theory of Migration", **Demography**, Vol.3, No.1., 1966, p. 49.

[12] Michael J. Greenwood, "Internal Migration In Developed Countries", **Handbook of Population and Family Economics**. Edited by Manfred M. Fischer, Peter Nijkamp, Berlin Heidelberg, Springer-Verlag, 1997, s.648.

[13] Anthony Giddens, **Sosyoloji**, İstanbul, Kırmızı Yayınları, Eylül 2012, s. 570.

factors that affect the migration decision in three categories. Macro-level factors are included labor demand, migration laws, world economic development. Micro-level factors are individual & household characteristics, structural tensions, risks, values, income differences. And Meso level factors are relative deprivation, migration institutions and networks[14].

Anthony Giddens describes migration models with four different significant migration movements observed since 1945affected by World War II. The first is the *classic migration model*, which applies to countries that develop as 'migrant nations' such as Canada, the USA and Australia. In this model, immigration is largely encouraged, although restrictions and quotas limit annual migrant intake. Citizenship is offered to new arrivals as a promise/blessing. *The colonial migration model* is followed by countries such as France and the United Kingdom, which prefer immigrants from colonies to those from other countries. Countries such as Germany, Switzerland and Belgium follow the third way, *the guest worker model*; in such an order, immigrants are usually admitted to the country to meet the demands of the labor market. Finally, *the model of illegal immigration* is becoming increasingly common as a large number of industrialized countries tighten their immigration laws. Immigrants who have the opportunity to enter the country illegally can often live outside the borders of official society[15].

Neo-classical macroeconomic theory perspective

According to Neo-classical economic theory, migrations lie in the resulting geographical difference in supply and demand for Labor. Countries with a surplus of Labor have a low wage market, while countries with a limited labor market compared to capital have a high wage level. Because of this openness due to the wage gap, low-wage workers are migrating to high-wage countries. As a result of this demographic movement, the labor market is shrinking in labor-rich countries, so wages are rising, while wages are falling in capital-rich countries, thus creating a balance. As a result, the macro theory of the neo-classical economic approach suggests that differences in wages and employment conditions between countries are the main cause of migration[16].The assumption of the theory is that in the long term, the international equilibrium charge will be reached, and therefore, migration flows will end[17].

The economic literature of migration focus on labor reallocation in response to market needs. The framework for most analyses is the classical competitive model of factor mobility. Migration of labor occurs in direct response to the average wage

---

[14] Jessica Hagen-Zanker, "Why do people migrate? A review of the theoretical Literature", **MPRA Working Paper no.28197**, January 2008, s.19.

[15] Giddens, op.cit,s. 569.

[16] Fuat Güllüpınar, "Göç Olgusunun Ekonomi Politiği ve Uluslararası Göç Kuramları Üzerine Bir Değerlendirme", **Yalova Sosyal Bilimler Dergisi**, Sayı 4, 2012, s. 57-58.

[17] Rudi Robinson, "Beyond The State-Bounded Immigrant Incorporation Regime: Transnational Migrant Communities: Their Potential Contribution to Canada's Leadership Role and Influence in A Globalized World". **The North-South Institute**, Ottawa, 2005, s.5.

differential between areas. As the wage differential increases, the volume of migration increases. The model entails assumptions of full employment and perfect competition. Perfect competition assumes that persons maximize their interests, knowledge of employment opportunities is perfect, workers are many in number and homogeneous in skills and choices, and there are no barriers, either social or economic that prevents mobility[18].

Neo-classical microeconomic theory perspective

In contrast to the macroeconomic equilibrium model, the microeconomic perspective emphasizes individual choice. According to the microeconomic model, individuals are rational actors; they will choose to migrate to countries where they can be most productive, given their human capital attributes[19]. Douglas S. Massey and others indicate migration as a decision process of individuals who decide to migrate because of a cost-benefit calculation that leads them to expect a positive net return. International migration is conceptualized as a form of investment in human capital. People choose to move to where they can be most productive with the skills they have. But before they can capture the higher wages associated with greater labor productivity they must undertake certain rates like costs of traveling, the costs of maintenance while moving and looking for work, the effort for learning a new language and culture, the effort for adapting to a new labor market, and the psychological cost of cutting old ties[20].

Actors take rational actions to perform social action that best suits them. Factors such as the presence of life-threatening in their position, low socioeconomic level, and ethnic exclusivity can make individuals act to migrate from their current position, which they think is rational for them.If actors cannot achieve a social position that meets their expectations in the geographical area in which they migrate, they use their current position as a transit zone and move to another geographical region[21]. Neo-classical models do not consider historical and sociological facts in some sense when examining the decision stage of individuals who make free choices[22].

The new economics theory perspective

Neo-classical economic models, based on only the immigrant herself/himself as an economic unit. In the analysis, it is believed that individuals make decisions on immigration within the framework of their own special interests, without being subjected to external influence. Neo-classical economic models analyze the international migration process without taking into account the family connection

---

[18] P. Neal Ritchey, "Explanations of Migration", **Annual Review of Sociology**, Vol. 2, 1976, p. 364.

[19] Robinson, op.cit, p.6.

[20] Douglas S. Massey and others, "Theories of International Migration: A Review and Appraisal", **Population and Development Review**, Vol. 19, No. 3, September 1993,p. 434.

[21] Şeyda Nur Koca, "Suriyeli Sığınmacıların Türk Emek Piyasasına Katılım Süreçlerinin Toplumsal Boyutları", **Göç Araştırmaları Dergisi**, Cilt5, Sayı2, Temmuz-Aralık 2019, s.319.

[22] Melih Görgün, "Ekonomi Temelli Göç Yaklaşımları Perspektifinde Göçmenlerin Karar Alma Süreçleri", **Süleyman Demirel Üniversitesi İktisadi ve İdari Bilimler Fakültesi Dergisi**, Cilt 23, Sayı 3, 2018, s.1158.

and cultural affiliation of the migrant individual's homeland[23].According to a new economic theory developed by Oded Stark in the 1990s, households in underdeveloped countries can more effectively direct the family's productive sources of income. Individuals of households adopt different strategies in the economic crises. Some find jobs in the local economy, some work in another part of the same country, and some find the opportunity to work abroad. According to the basic claim of this model, immigration decisions are not made by individual actors alone. the joint decision of the group of connected people is taken not only to maximize expected income; it is also taken to minimize risks. Therefore, in cases of rapid change, the family decides to send one or more members to another country or region to work in order to reduce their income and chances of survival. As a result, transfers sent by immigrants in underdeveloped countries allow families and households to get consumption or new investment opportunities. In this sense, international migration is a portfolio investment decision[24]. Mobility between borders does not stop with the elimination of wage differences. In addition to the labor market, the absence of other markets in the countries sending workers and the lack of effective work leads to the continuation of migration. Governments can control the migration process not only by policies that will affect labormarkets but also by influencing insurance, capital and future markets. Unemployment insurance, in particular, has significant effects on global mobility[25].

Dual labor market theory perspective

Neoclassical human capital theory and the new economics of migration are both micro-level decision models that lead to divergent conclusions about the nature of international migration. Standing distinctly apart from these models, dual labor market theory sets its sights away from decisions made by individuals and argues that international migration stems from the intrinsic labor demands of modern industrial societies. In developed countries, the labor market has a professional structure divided into two parts, and the international migration movement is based on labor demands made through states or firms. International migration is caused by a permanent demand for immigrant labor that is innate to the economic structure of developed nations. Immigration is not caused by push factors in sending countries (low wages or high unemployment), but by pull factors in receiving countries (an inescapable need for foreigner workers)[26]. Because the demand for migrant workers stems from employment practices rather than the structural needs of the economy and wage proposals, international wage differences are neither sufficient nor necessary conditions for migration.[27].

The division of Labor into primary and secondary sectors is typically articulated by the ethnic division in the 'host' country. Employers who can't find domestic

---

[23] Güllüpınar, op.cit, s. 61-62.
[24] Ibid., p. 62-63.
[25] Massey and others, op.cit, p. 434.
[26] Ibid., p.440-441.
[27] Ibid., p.444.

workers are turning to immigrants who are willing to accept low-status jobs. Immigrants can only be motivated by wages, which are higher than what they earn in their home country. When domestic workers avoid working in low-status jobs, it leads mainly to immigrants working in certain jobs. So, it leads to a further decline in the status of these jobs. The fundamental point of dual labor market theory, according to Piore (1979), is that migration is driven by demand for low-level labor, which Indigenous workers do not accept[28].According to this theory, it is impossible to prevent migration in these conditions, as developed industrialized societies and economies will constantly need flexible and cheap labor. Low-level wages in countries that accept immigrants do not rise with a decrease in the number of migrant workers. The factor that keeps wages low is social and institutional mechanisms. So Piore states that immigrants are an integral part of today's post-industrial society. divided labor market theory does not deny that people who want to emigrate make decisions that are rational, that prioritize their own interests. On the contrary, he also acknowledges that in many cases, the earnings and savings that the migrant worker can provide significant support to the family left behind[29].

The situation of Syrians under temporary protection in Turkey

There are 3.638.288 Syrians under temporary protection in Turkey. 63.518 of them are in temporary shelter centers[30]. As can be seen in figure 1, it is seen that the reflections of the civil war in Syria began in 2011. In 2012, the mass migration flow to Turkey was 14,237. Looking back at 2013, there were 224,655 Syrian under temporary protection. Compared to 2012, the number of asylum seekers increased significantly in 2013. By 2014, this had increased to 1,519,286 and by 2015 to 2,503,549. After 2016, the size of the increase was relatively lower. But the flow of migration continues to have its effect. In 2017, the number of Syrian under temporary protection in Turkey was 3,426,786, while in 2020 it reached 3,638,288. It can be said that the increasing migration flow numerically is caused by the chain migration movement. The increased migration mobility of Syrians is due to the positive perception of the living conditions of leading migrants. Actors in the migration movement also made individuals affected by the negative conditions in Syria an attractive factor in participating in the migration movement[31].

Figure 2 includes the 10 cities where Syrian under temporary protection are most likely to reside. With 548 thousand 483 people, Istanbul is the most populated city of Syrian under temporary protection. Then, the border cities of Sanliurfa, Hatay and Gaziantep have an average of 434 thousand 860 Syrian under temporary protection. In Istanbul, where most Syrians under temporary protection are located, when compared to the provincial population, it can be said that Syrian under temporary protection make up about 4 percent of the population. 53,8% of Syrian

[28] **Uginar Proje Raporu**, Marmara Üniversitesi Çalışma Ekonomisi ve Endüstri İlişkileri Bölümü, İstanbul, 2004, ss.9-10.

[29] Güllüpınar, op.cit, s.66-67.

[30] https://en.goc.gov.tr/temporary-protection27 (Access 08.11.2020)

[31] Koca, op.cit, s.326.

nationals in Turkey are male and 46,2% female. The rate of Syrian nationals under the age of 10 is 29%. While the proportion of the Turkish population between the ages of 15-24 is 15.6%, the Syrian nationals rate for the same age group is 20.9%. The average age of the population of Turkey 32, 4 and the Syrian population's average age is 22.7. The ratio of registered Syrians under temporary protection to the Turkish population is 4.3% across the country. The number of Syrians granted Turkish citizenship is 110 thousand. 48% of these people are adults and 52 % are children. Only1, 8% of Syrian national sare living in camps[32].

Figure 1. Distribution of Syrians in the Scope of Temporary Protection by Year

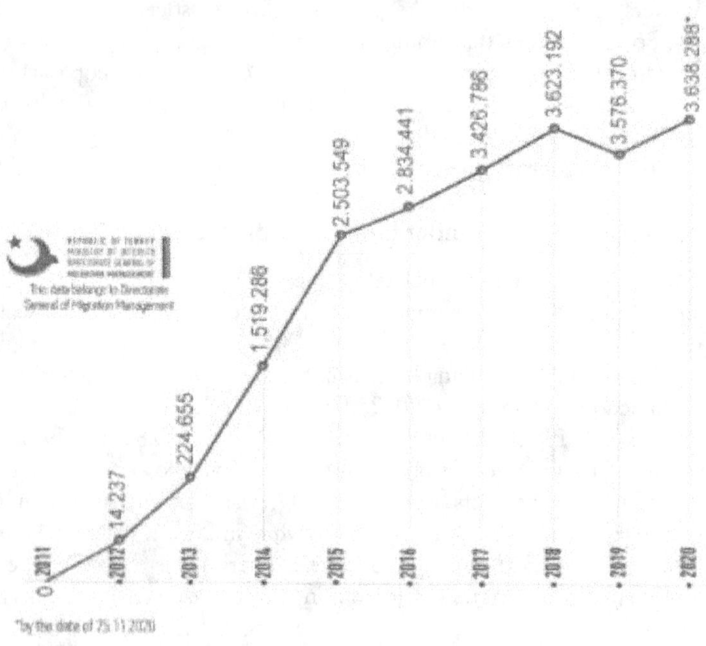

Source: https://en.goc.gov.tr/temporary-protection27

The level of education of Syrian under temporary protection is quite low. As the age group shrinks, there is an increase in participation in formal education. According to the relevant population ages over 15 years of age, they received basic education mostly in Syria. The reason for this is that those who come to Turkey come from a rural and highly traditional region of northern Syria, and as a policy of the Syrian regime for decades, their access to education has been limited.

32 Attitudes Toward Syrians in Turkey, İNGEV TAM, March 2020, p.4-5.

Figure 2. Distribution of Syrians under Temporary Protection by 10 top provinces

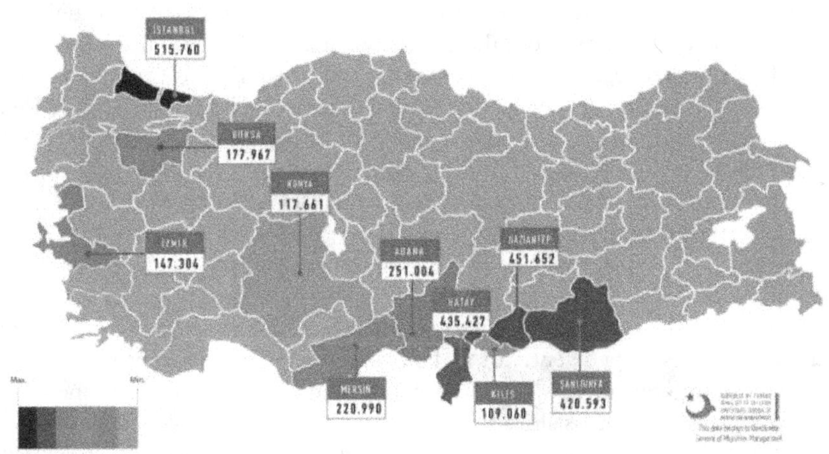

Source: https://en.goc.gov.tr/temporary-protection27

Table 1. Number of Work Permits Issued to Syrians by Year

2011	2012	2013	2014	2015	2016	2017	2018	2019
118	220	794	2541	4019	13290	20,966	34,573	63,789

Source: https://ailevecalisma.gov.tr/en-US (Access 05.11.2020)

In Table 1, the numbers of Syrians receiving work permits in the years between 2011-2019 are given. Although the number of Syrians receiving work permits has increased over the years, the number remains very low, given the number of Syrians under temporary protection. Although the number of Syrians receiving work permits has increased over the years, the number of those receiving work permits remains very low compared to the number of Syrians under temporary protection.

Labor force and employment size of Syrians under temporary protection in Turkey

The mass migration of Syrians in Turkey creates a significant degree of unease in the local population about the job market like in the other countries. Apart from the discomfort experienced in society, from the point of view of many businessmen, the employment of people who are desperate and ready to work very cheaply provides an advantage[33].Syrians are employed as cheap labor by illegal means in industry, agriculture and small-scale enterprises. This has led to the widespread opinion among the local population that Syrians are taking away job opportunities.

[33] Hacettepe Üniversitesi Göç ve Siyaset Araştırmaları Merkezi op.cit,s.16.

Even if local workers lose their jobs for different reasons, there is a perception that this happens because of asylum seekers. But on the other hand, owners of firms operating in the border provinces claim that local people do not want to work as workers in the agricultural sector or factories, and a large amount of labor force is needed in this area. Therefore, Syrians do not take away the job opportunities of the local people, but rather close the gap in jobs that require unskilled labor. Firms in border provinces want Syrians to enter the labor market. But Company owners believe that this should be brought into a legal framework. Because of the problems that will arise in the event of accidents at work, the growing reaction among the local population that their jobs are being taken away, the risk of a social explosion that this will create concerns businessmen. In addition, unfair competition between companies that employ and do not employ unregistered workers and the risk of deterioration of the labor market in the long term also cause concern. One of the most important problems created by the illegal employment of Syrians is that they work on low wages, and this is likely to have a long-term impact on the labor markets. It seems that the entry of asylum seekers into the labor market has both positive and negative effects[34]. The growth of the informal economy one of the negative effects but there is already a widespread problem of the informal economy in Turkey. Informality is an important component of social culture and working life. Despite the high unemployment figures and underemployment in the labor market in Turkey, there is a demand for migrant workers. The growth of irregular migration makes illegal activities more profitable, displaces unskilled local labor, worsens working conditions by weakening collective bargaining, leads to tension in society and leads to the growth of informal sectors of the economy[35].

In their study, in which they discussed the labor markets of the five cities that received the most Syrian immigrants, Lordoğlu and Aslan noted that they do not have a homogeneous appearance, contrary to the general opinion about Syrian immigrants. But the current temporary protection status leads Syrian migrants to become a source of cheap labor, mostly in construction and agriculture. The study also noted that the proportion of Syrian immigrants who set up commercial companies and have work permits is low. Employees and customers of companies owned by Syrian refugees are mostly Syrian immigrants. Self-employed Syrian migrants are mostly employed as small tradesmen[36]. It is now seen that mostly Syrians work in jobs previously done by the local poor. This means that some professions are 'closed' by some ethnic groups. Therefore, it is envisaged that some non-legal ethnic monopolies will be formed within a short period of time[37].

When we examine the impact of Syrian migrants on the labor market within the framework of gender, in the reports of many non-governmental organizations, it is stated that the working rate of Syrian women is quite low, even almost the vast

[34] Suriyeli sığınmacıların Türkiye'ye etkileri rapor no:195, ORSAM&TESEV, 2015, ss.17-18.

[35] Gülay Toksöz, Şerife Türcan Özşuca,"Enformel Sektörde İstihdamın ve İş gücünün Özellikleri", **İktisat, Ev Eksenli Çalışma Özel Sayısı,** Sayı430, Ekim 2002, s.21.

[36] Kuvvet Lordoğlu, Mustafa Aslan, "En fazla Suriyeli göçmen alan beş kentin emek piyasalarında değişimi:2011-2014", **Çalışma ve Toplum**, 2016/2, s.806-807.

[37] Ortadoğu'dan Göçün Türkiye Üzerindeki Etkileri Raporu, Akdeniz Üniversitesi, Antalya, 2018, ss.52-54

majority of them are not working. Employees work mainly in workshops in the textile sector; where agriculture and animal husbandry are developed, they work seasonally in the agricultural sector. Employment of Syrian women is also low on grounds such as language and security. Syrian women who do not have enough qualifications for a permanent job are trying to ensure the continuation of their lives by trying to find day-to-day jobs with low wages without job security[38]. The women who find a chance to work generally work as cleaning up or looking after a child, ill or an old person, farming, tourism and servicing sectors yet as their work goes unrecorded with low wages and in a context of bad working conditions[39].

Working at low wages mainly as informal labor also affects the social status of Syrians and their place in society. Social and class change with the inclusion of immigrants as a sub cultural group brought about by migration mobility, the group with a low economic structure that was at the bottom of the previous labor market climbs the social ladder. So, this situation presents the economic dimension in the view of stratification. As a result of migration, social differentiation between immigrants and natives takes place in the lower position of immigrants in the stratified order, which is based on the political and economic dimensions. It can be seen that immigrants, who are considered by society to have the same level of the class position as subculture groups, differ greatly from natives in many areas such as income groups, settlement Regions, Types of social interaction, forms of consumption, leisure activities, thought and attitude structures[40]. Immigrants are mostly low-status and disadvantaged in the society in which they are newly included. Due to this situation, they face social exclusion, discrimination and poverty, they become alienated from the society in which they live[41].

Syrians are also experiencing financial adjustment problems. In order for Syrians to open an account in a bank, a temporary protection ID alone is not enough, but a residence certificate is also required. Outside of legislation, banks are known to take different approaches in practice. Obtaining a credit card or using a loan can only be possible for high depositors with the permission of general directorates. Financial exclusion is therefore directly related to banking practices. However, financial inclusion is important for promoting regularity. As expected, financial compliance increases as education levels rise[42].

The most concrete indicator of the outlook of Syrians in the labor force based on the informal economy is that work permits remain at a fairly low level despite the working-age Syrian population[43]. According to the Regulation on Work Permits of Foreigners under Temporary Protection issued in January 2016, the conditions that enable Syrians to work in the Turkish labor market should have a temporary

[38] Hilal Barın, "Türkiye'deki Suriyeli kadınların toplumsal bağlamda yaşadıkları sorunlar ve çözüm önerileri", **Göç Araştırmaları Dergisi**, Cilt1, Sayı2, Temmuz-Aralık 2015, s.45.
[39] The Report on Syrian Woman Refugees Living Out of The Camps, MAZLUMDER, May 2014, s.41.
[40] Koca, op.cit,s.319.
[41] Ibid,s.320.
[42] Suriyeli Mülteci Hayatlar Monitörü Özet Değerlendirme,INGEV, Mayıs 2017, ss.2-4.
[43] İNGEV TAM, op.cit, ss.4-5.

protection ID card and a valid identification number. Those who apply to work should have been under temporary protection for at least 6 months prior to the date when the application is submitted. Foreigners under Temporary Protection can work only in the province where they are registered. Applications are to be made by employers. If the applicant will start a business and work independently, then he/she should apply himself/herself. The number of foreigners under temporary protection to be employed in businesses cannot surpass 10% of the number of Turkish citizen employees. As to work in agriculture, he/she should apply for work permit exemption at the Provincial Directorate of Labor in the province where he/she is registered. Foreigners who would liketo work in the health or education sectors also should approach the relevant ministry before applying for a work permit. The application procedure is simple and quick but long waiting periods are prevalent to prevent fraud and abuse. Despite the legislative changes that facilitate access to formal job opportunities, the informal market is still more attractive for both Syrians and employers[44].

If the vast majority of Syrians were rural and lower-income segment investors and traders, especially from Aleppo, have also settled in Turkey. In this respect, Mersin stands out. Syrians belonging to the upper-income group prefer Mersin because of its ancient commercial connections and the trade opportunities offered by the port. In addition, the trade opportunities offered by the port also attract rich Syrians to Mersin. Another province that stands out in this regard is Gaziantep. The number of Syrian companies registered with Gaziantep Chamber of Commerce increased significantly after 2011[45].

By now, it is clear that the refugee problem will not only have short-term impacts, but itwill also impose several long-term results on the hosting countries. These results cover a large horizon of topics including economic, social, and political outcomes[46].

Conclusion

In March 2011, with the crisis in Syria, a mass flow of migrants to Turkey began.It is not yet possible to predict what the long-term effects and consequences of Syrians under temporary protection will be on the Turkish labor market. As a result of the nine-year war, it can be said that there are certain effects observed in working life in Turkey, which has hosted close to four million Syrians.Visible socio-economic effects have occurred in many job markets in areas with a large Syrian population, especially in the provinces bordering Syria. The fact that Syrian migrants are willing to work for low wages, especially in the informal economy, deepens the problem of the informal economy that already exists. The Syrian population, which

[44] Ahmet İçduygu, Eleni Diker, "Labor Market Integration of Syrian Refugees in Turkey: From Refugees to Settlers", **Göç Araştırmaları Dergisi**, Cilt3, Sayı1, Ocak-Haziran 2017, ss.20-22.

[45] ORSAM&TESEV, op.cit, s.18.

[46] Evren Ceritoğlu vd., "The Impact of Syrian Refugees on Natives" Labor Market Outcomes in Turkey: Evidence from a Quasi-Experimental Design", **Central Bank of the Republic of Turkey Working Paper No: 17/05**, February 2017, p.26.

is willing to pay lower wages, has resulted in the displacement of domestic labor and Syrian immigrants in certain business areas and sectors which are mostly on construction and textile. On the other hand, the division of labor into primary and secondary sectors occurs as immigrants accept low-status jobs that domestic workers reject.

Especially in the eastern part of Turkey the jobs that domestic workers avoid lead mainly to immigrants working in certain jobs. This trend results in firms closing the labor gap in these jobs with Syrian migrants. The fact that Syrian migrants' consent for lower wages and bureaucracy obligation associated with temporary protection statutes increases the number of informal workforces, which are already at a high rate. this can also be observed in the fact that the number of work permits is quite low compared to the number of Syrians of working age. In other words, the supply shock with the arrival of Syrian migrants can be said to have had a negative impact due to regulatory deficiencies.

Apart from paid Syrians, self-employed Syrian migrants mostly operate as small retailers. However, both the employees and customers of the businesses are Syrian immigrants, such as the owner of the firm. This is one of the factors that show that Syrian immigrants live in isolation from Turkish society. They spend the majority of their time with immigrants like themselves, and mainly with other Syrians. Although they did not experience a break from their own culture, it is seen that they could not integrate with Turkish society. Therefore, refugees prefer to move to places where they have more relatives and friends and live together. The language barrier has a significant effect on the isolation from society. Language problems are quite common in age groups other than school-age children. No doubt, this is a significant obstacle to entering business life.

Among Syrian migrants who work in the informal sector mostly, the most disadvantaged groups are women and children. Women and children are lopsidedly affected when it comes to labor exploitation. Women who work for very low wages in daily work live in ghettos in poverty. In the same way, children who are employed to provide income to the family, face more permanent poverty by staying away from their educational life. At this point, we should note that international agencies leave Turkey alone about the needs and deprivation of Syrians. While existing public resources are an increasing financial burden for Turkey, the lack of international aid funds is a remarkable point. At the moment, it is clear that the common sense of the international community is needed for those affected by the migration crisis. Because aid funds are insufficient, Syrian migrants who cannot find work in the provinces where they are registered and can benefit from public services are trying to make a living by migrating to major cities and working on informal day labor. Because their income is not sufficient, families get together, rent single apartments and live in crowded environments.

The course of the Syrian Civil War and the worsening living conditions in the region are increasingly denting the hopes of Syrian migrants to return to their country. Therefore, the harmony and adaptation of Syrian migrants with Turkish society is important in both social and economic terms for eliminating the negative impact on the labor market. At this point, there is no doubt that the temporary protection status also needs to be reconsidered. Because informality dominates the general outlook of the Syrian migrant workforce. Although the Syrian labor force does not exhibit a homogeneous structure, contrary to popular belief, the relatively higher unemployment rates of highly skilled Syrians indicate that Syrian immigrants mostly work in low-skilled jobs.

CHAPTER 12

TURKEY AND THE EMPLOYMENT OF REFUGEES

Hatice Nur Germir[1]

Introduction

According to the International Migration 2019 Report prepared by the Population Sub-Division of the United Nations Economic and Social Affairs Department; It has noted that with international immigrants having a small share of the world's total population, their share rose from 2.9 in 1990 to 3.5 percent in 2019.In 2019, it was calculated that international migrants accounted for 12.0 percent of the more developed total population, 1.9 percent of the total underdeveloped population, and 14.0 percent of the total high-income population. This figure was significantly lower in middle-income and low-income groups, where international migrants accounted for 1.4 percent and 1.7 percent of the total population. However, over the 1990 and 2019 pages, it was found that the number of international migrants in terms of the total population share increased more developed and high-income, and low-income decreased with little change[2].

According to the Global Trends report of the United Nations High Commissioner for Refugees (UNHCR), the number of people forced to migrate reached 65.6 million at the end of 2016, representing the highest number of displaced persons ever. 22.2 million people have become refugees. The main reason for the huge increase in the number of refugees is the Syrian civil war. 8 million Syrians have been internally displaced, and 5.1 million have left the country to become refugees. Three million Syrians are refugees in Turkey that Turkey's goal of worldwide has become the largest refugee hosting countries. 47 percent of Syrian refugees are in Turkey as of April 2016. Turkey, the start of the civil war have followed since open-door policy. Since then, many studies have analyzed and reported the political and social impact of Syrian refugees[3].

Between 1990 and 2019, the number of international migrants increased in 169 countries or regions, while a decrease was recorded in 60 countries or regions. Between 1990 and 2019, the United States ranks first with 27.4 million international immigrants, followed by Arabia with 8.1 million international immigrants, and the United Arab Emirates third with 7.3 million. The countries with the highest increase in the international immigrant population are Germany with 7.2 million and the

---

[1] Assistant Professor Dr., Manisa Celal Bayar University, Faculty of Applied Sciences, Türkiye.

[2] International Migration by the United Nations, UN, New York, 2019, p. 5.

[3] Oguz Esen and Ayla Oğuş Binatlı, "The Impact of Syrian Refugees on the Turkish Economy: Regional Labour Market Effects", **Social Sciences**, Vol. 6, No. 129, 2017, pp: 1.

United Kingdom of Great Britain and Northern Ireland with a population of 5.9 million, respectively. In contrast, the world stock of international migrants declined by about 3 million people in Pakistan between 1990 and 2019[4].

Between 2000-2020, there was an annual average of 317 thousand net migrations in North Africa and West Asia. About half of the countries in the region are net senders and the others are net recipients. Most recipient countries from the United Arab Emirates (263 thousand), Saudi Arabia (211 thousand) and Qatar (97 thousand) and the recent introduction of refugees living in Turkey (155 thousand), respectively. Among the top sending countries were the Syrian Arab Republic (377 thousand), Sudan (116 thousand), Morocco (92 thousand) and Egypt (41 thousand), which experienced a large number of forced migrants and refugees[5].

Refugees pose major difficulties for the potential host, in particular moral, political and economic difficulties. More than 60 million people have been reported who have been forced to migrate from their homelands for many reasons, including conflicts around the world. The war in Syria has led to a greater number of people and, more than any other conflict in the past two decades, 7.6 million people have been displaced within the country and some 4.6 million as refugees. Many Syrian refugees have sought refuge in Turkey, which has made him the biggest country that is home to refugees worldwide[6].

Afghan refugees in Turkey, Iraq, Iran and the Far East and several African countries, including primarily occurs because of Syrian refugees Syrian refugees who studies investigating analysis, rather than in our article are included.

Labor Market Effects and Economic Benefits of Refugees

It tries to explain that in economic theory, migration should lower the wages of rival workers and increase the wages of complementary workers. For example; The inflow of workers born abroad means that all working people will face stricter competition for workers, which will reduce economic opportunities. Likewise, it is possible to pay low wages for unskilled jobs such as painting the house and mowing the lawn, as well as high earnings for high-skill owners, which may also lead to specialization in producing goods and services that are more suitable for their skills.Because of the policy significance associated with determining the impact of migration on employment opportunities for domestic workers, a large literature has been developed over the past two decades attempting to measure this impact. The starting point for most of this literature is that immigrants in the United States are clustered in a small number of geographic regions. Many studies make use of this geographic cluster to describe the empirical exercise for measuring the labor market impact of migration. The typical study defines a metropolitan area (or state) as the labor market that immigrants penetrate. The study then proceeds in the form of

---

[4] UN, op.cit, p. 9.
[5] UN, ibid, p. 24
[6] Ximena VaneaasDel Carpio and Mathis Christopfer Wagner, The Impact of Syrian Refugees on the Turkish Labor Market, **World BankPolicy ResearchPaper, No.**7402, Washington: The World Bank, 2015, pp: 2.

calculating an inter-city correlation that measures the relationship between the local wage in a region and the relative number of immigrants in that region. A negative correlation that shows that local wages are lower in immigrant markets indicates that immigrants worsen employment opportunities for competing domestic workers. There is a large distribution in the findings in this literature. However, predicted inter-city correlations tend to cluster around zero, which helps create traditional wisdom that immigrants have little effect on labor market opportunities for domestic workers, perhaps because immigrants do jobs that locals don't want to do. However, recent research raises two questions about the validity of interpreting near-zero inter-city correlations as evidence that migration has no impact on the labor market. First, immigrants may not be randomly distributed in labor markets. If immigrants tend to cluster in cities with emerging economies (and higher salaries), there will be a built-in positive correlation between migration and wages. This positive correlation will weaken, and perhaps even reverse, whatever the negative impact of migration on wages in local labor markets. Second, locals can react to the wage effect of immigration by moving their labor or capital to other cities. For example, cities in Southern California, which are flooded with low-skilled immigrants, appear to be paying lower wages to refugee workers at companies owned by indigenous companies. Employers who hire workers will want to move to these cities. The flow of jobs to areas where immigrants flock reduces the negative impact of migration on the wages of rival workers in these regions. Similarly, workers living in Michigan were perhaps considering moving to California before immigrants entered that state. These workers learn that immigration has reduced their potential wages in California and may decide to stay or move elsewhere instead. What's more, some Californians may leave the state in search of better opportunities. The flows of capital and labor tend to equalize economic conditions between cities. As a result, intercity comparisons of local wage rates will not be very revealing: capital flows and local migration differentiate the impact of migration on the national economy. Ultimately, all working people, regardless of where they live, will face worse conditions because there is an excess of labor supply. As local labor markets are adapting to migration, a number of recent studies have highlighted that the labor market impact of migration can only be measured at the national level[7].

Literature Review

It is stated in textbook models that migration increases the labor supply and will lead to a decrease in employment figures and wages. However, there is a large literature that has little or no impact on employment or wages. The literature on the labor market effects of forced migration is small compared to the relevant literature in the context of 'voluntary' migration[8].

---

[7] George J. Borjas and Lawrence F. Katz, "The Evolution of the Mexican-Born Workforce in the United States", Mexican Immigration to the United States, **National Bureau of Economic Research**, George J. Borjas (Ed.), Chicago, University of Chicago Press, 2007, pp.44-46.

[8] Esen and Binatlı, op.cit., pp.2.

Akgündüz et al. (2015) prices for the Syrian refugee crisis in Southeast Turkey, employment rates and their impact on internal migration, examines differences-differences using fixed effects models. They reported that they realized that the influx of refugees led to increases in food and housing prices, reduced internal migration to affected areas, but had no impact on employment. Their explanation for the lack of employment effects is based on the slowing of internal migration as a counterbalancing factor. Their analysis includes only two years of investigation, 2012 and 2013, in regions and provinces where most of the refugees are still in refugee camps and where the number of Syrian refugees is still relatively low compared to current figures. Therefore, it is not surprising that in the early years they did not have a significant impact on labor markets, but their demands or the demands of workers and visitors in refugee camps exert an upward pressure on prices and deter other internal migrants from them[9].

Del Carpio and Wagner (2015) argue that the arrival of refugees is a supply shock in the informal sector and a demand shock in the formal sector. Immigrants can have an impact on the informal sector in reducing wages. The impact on the registered sector is reported uncertain. Whether the demand shock is positive or negative depends on whether the decrease in formal labor demand as a result of substitution between informal labor and formal labor dominates the expansion of production due to low production costs. They also noticed that the average wage fell in the informal sector, but they were unable to detect any significant impact of refugees on average wages in the formal sector[10].

Bahçekapılı and Çetin (2015) provide a descriptive analysis of the impact of Syrians on unemployment rates, foreign trade and internal migration by calculating the differences in average rates in the years before and after the arrival of Syrian refugees. Using 2010-2012 data for the previous period and 2013 and 2014 data for the next period, they report that Syrian refugees increased unemployment and lowered prices in the regions most affected by the crisis. While its analysis is illustrative, it does not control other effects that may be responsible for differences in rates before and during the Syrian refugee crisis[11].

Views of Refugees in the Turkish Labor Market

Syrian refugees not only with labor supply decisions, their entrepreneurial skills have also become an economic actors in Turkey. The number of new companies established by Syrian refugees increased from only 157 in 2012 to 1599 in 2015. The share of Syrian companies in total foreign partnerships reached 26 percent in 2015. Syrian refugees have an impact on regional labor markets[12].

---

[9] Yusuf Emre Akgündüz, Marcel van den Berg, and Wolter HJ Hassink, **"The Impact of Refugee Crises on Host Labor Markets: The Case of the Syrian Refugee Crisis"**, Disscussion Paper, no.8841; Bonn: IZA, 2015.

[10] Del Carpio and Wagner, op.cit.

[11] Cengiz Bahçekapılı ve Buket Çetin, The Impacts of Forced Migration on Regional Economies: The Case of Syrian Refugees in Turkey, **International Business Research,** 2015, Vol. 8, No. 8, pp: 1–15.

[12] Esen and Binatlı, op.cit., pp.1.

Many of the ten bilateral migration corridors that saw the greatest increase in the period 2010-2019 consisted of refugee movements reflecting crises, conflicts or instability in Myanmar, South Sudan, the Syrian Arab Republic and Venezuela. While the United States was the target of two of the ten bilateral immigration corridors with the largest increase, India was recorded as the starting point for three of the twelve-sided migration corridors during this period[13].

Figure 1. Ten bilateral migration corridors with the highest annual average increase in the number of international migrants, 1990-2017 (million)[14]

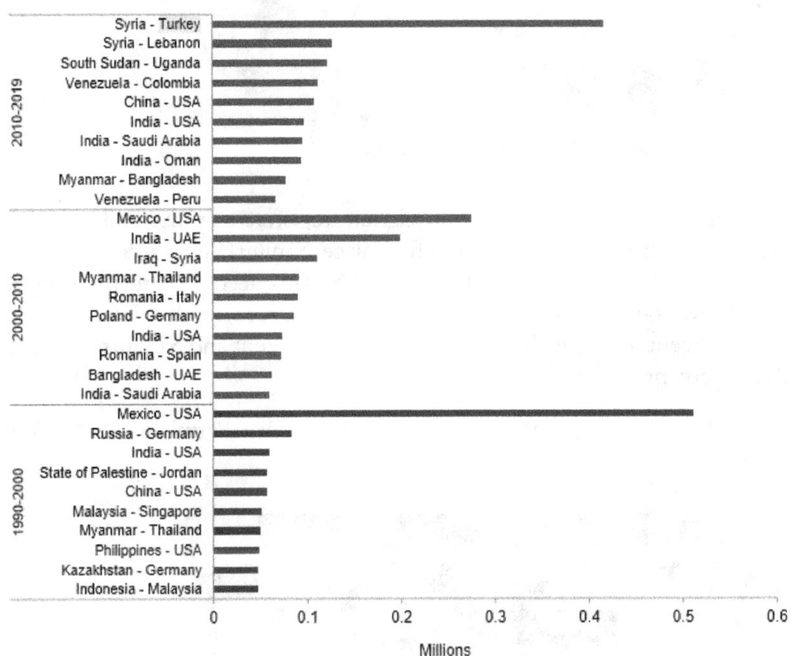

The Syrian civil war resulted in mass migration from Syria to neighboring countries. The majority of the refugees have come from Syria in Turkey and have often initially placed in refugee camps in southeastern Turkey. The intensification of the conflict in Syria and in the number of Syrian refugees in Turkey has increased with the extension and as Syrian population residing in neighboring provinces and have begun to make significant impact on the local economy. In 2016, Syrian refugees were allowed to obtain work permits, causing them to become more geographically dispersed[15].

[13] UN, op.cit, pp: 12.

[14]https://www.un.org/en/development/desa/population/migration/publications/migrationreport/docs/InternationalMigration2019_Report.pdf (Access 20.10.2020)

[15] Esen ve Binatlı, op.cit.

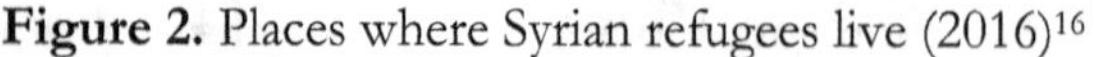

Figure 2. Places where Syrian refugees live (2016)[16]

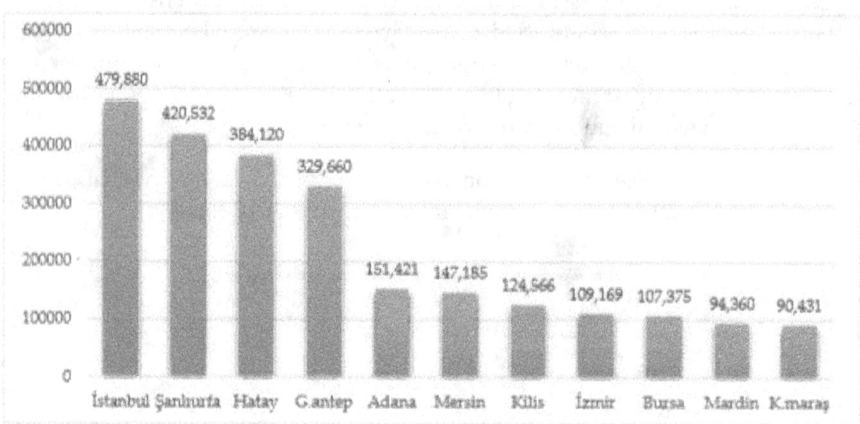

When the distribution of Syrian foreigners registered by the end of 2016 by provinces is analyzed; İstanbul is in the first place, Şanlıurfa is in second and Hatay is in third place. When the rates of registered Syrians according to the provincial population are examined; It is understood from the records that Kilis is the first with 93.50 percent, Hatay is the second with 24.38 percent and Şanlıurfa is the third with 21.90 percent (Figure 2)[17]

Figure 3. Foreigners Found with Family Residence Permit in 2016 (Top 10 Countries)[18]

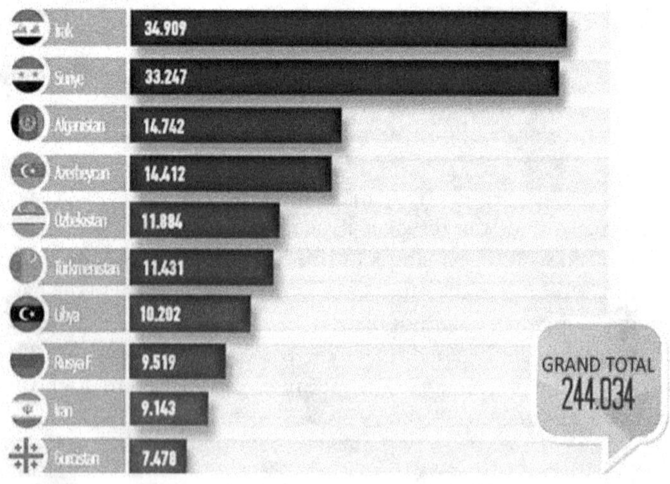

[16] Turkey Migration Report 2016, **T.R. Ministry of Interior Directorate General of Migration Management Publications**, Publication No: 40, 2017, https://www.goc.gov.tr/kurumlar/goc.gov.tr/YillikGocRaporlari/2016_yiik_goc_raporu_haziran.pdf (Access 15.10.2020)

[17] https://www.goc.gov.tr/kurumlar/goc.gov.tr/YillikGocRaporlari/2016_yiik_goc_raporu_haziran.pdf

[18] https://www.goc.gov.tr/kurumlar/goc.gov.tr/YillikGocRaporlari/2016_yiik_goc_raporu_haziran.pdf

According to the data of the Directorate General of Migration Management the family residence permit issued in Turkey in 2016: 63 thousand 546 foreign, Azerbaijani citizens first with 7 thousand 377 people, the Russian Federation citizens second 6b of 563 people, Syrian citizens are located 4 ranked third with a thousand 813 people (Figure 3).

The number of Syrians registered under temporary protection increased by 2 thousand 549 in Turkey compared to the previous month as of October 21, 2020. reaching a total of 3 million 624 thousand 517 people. 1 million 694 thousand 242 people, 46.7 percent, are children between the ages of 0-18. 2 million 558 thousand 139 people constituting 70.5 percent of the total number of refugees in Turkey[19].

Figure 4. Distribution of Registered Refugees (2018)[20]

(Kayıt altındaki sığınmacıların dağılımı 2018)

Age	Men	Women	Total
0-4	304.035	284.075	588.110
5-9	246.826	231.657	478.483
10-14	192.839	176.746	369.585
15-18	161.659	128.064	290.523
19-24	320.911	255.552	546.463
25-29	197.609	141.586	339.195
30-34	162.790	121.041	283.831
35-39	113.701	90.067	203.768
40-44	76.134	68.231	145.365
45-49	57.424	53.934	111.358
50-54	46.469	44.736	81.205
55-59	31.112	31.209	62.321
60-64	22.374	23.164	45.538
65-69	14.511	14.655	29.166
70-74	8.043	8.924	16.967
75-79	4.531	5.505	10.036
80-84	2.551	3.319	5.870
85-89	1.315	1.684	2.999
90+	687	896	1.583
Total	1.965.521	1.656.845	3.622.366

According to the age range table published by the Immigration Administration; Syrian men make up 53.8 percent of the total number of Syrians. The proportion of Syrian women is 46.2 percent. The number of Syrians under the age of 10 is 1 million 45 thousand 622, and their proportion in the total is calculated as 28.8 percent. According to the table, the number of Syrian men is 276,177 more than the number of Syrian women. The biggest difference between the number of men and women occurs between the ages of 19-24 with 73 thousand 891 people. As the age increases, this difference decreases; It is observed that the number of women is

---

[19] Number of Syrians in Turkey in October 2020, https://multeciler.org.tr/turkiyedeki-suriyeli-sayisi/ (Access 21.10.2020)

[20] Şule Yaman, **The Effects of Syrian Refugees on the Economy 2020**, https://www.yatirimkredi.com /suriyeli-multecİler-ekonomiye-etkileri.html (Access 19.10.2020)

higher than men in the age range above 55[21].

In all kinds of work permit applications made by the Ministry of Labor and Social Security from within the country and abroad, the relevant employer and the foreigner for whom work permit has been requested in the application for an independent work permit or indefinite work permit; it was stated that a work permit application would not be possible if the applicant does not have a REM account and electronic signature, making it necessary to have a registered electronic mail (REP) address suitable for electronic notification. In order to obtain a work permit, the Job and Vocational Counseling desk at the refugee association also shares information about the conditions for obtaining a work permit. Work permit applications are made free of charge at the Refugee Association's Job and Vocational Counseling desk through the automation system of the Ministry of Labor and Social Security. Work permit applications are made by companies that want to employ a foreign employee at their workplace. The application evaluation period is normally reported as 30 days[22].

Documents Required for Work Permit and Documents are as follows;

Documents required if a work permit is obtained on behalf of a private company;

1- Temporary protection card or residence permit card

2- Residence document

3- E-Government password (can be obtained from PTT)

4- E-signature

5- REM Address

6- Tax plate

7- 1 passport photo

If you are getting a Work Permit on Behalf of the Company, the required documents;

1- Temporary protection card or residence permit card

2- E-Government password (can be obtained from PTT)

3- E-signature

4- REM Address

---

[21] https://multeciler.org.tr/turkiyedeki-suriyeli-sayisi/

[22] https://multeciler.org.tr/yabancilar-icin-calisma-izni-kep-adresi-ve-e-imza/ (Access 21.10.2020)

5- Certificate of Activity

6- Income Statement

7- SGK Registration Number

8- Company Registry Gazette

9- 1 passport photo

Business and working license

In order to apply for a license to the Municipality for your company, you must have the following documents with you:

1- Temporary Protection ID Card

2- Work Permit Certificate

3- Lease Contract

4- Tax Board

5- Fire Extinguisher Bill

Figure 5. Number of Syrian Refugees with Work Permits (2018)[23]

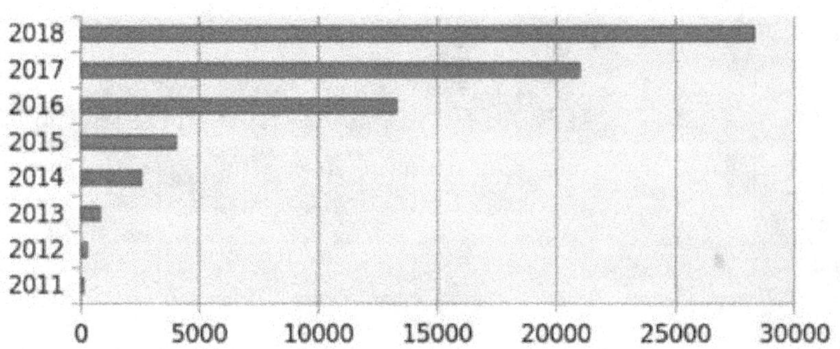

Family, the Ministry of Labor and Social Services according to a statement made on 31 March 2019 the number of Syrian granted a work permit in Turkey was reported to be 31 thousand 185 people[24].

As of October 21, 2020, the number of Syrians staying in temporary accommodation centers was announced as 59,427 people. This number was reported as 59 thousand 785 persons last month (August 2020), 143 thousand 558 persons at the beginning of 2019 and 228 thousand 251 persons at the beginning of

[23] Yaman, op.cit

[24] https://multeciler.org.tr/turkiyedeki-suriyeli-sayisi/ (Access 01.11.2020)

2018. Only 1.6% of Syrians live in camps[25].

The International Labor Organization (ILO) defines a migrant worker as 'an international migrant individual of working age and older, working or unemployed in his current country of residence'. This term is a subset of international immigrants. The ILO (2018) estimates that 6 out of 10 international migrants are migrant workers in 2017. It is noted that only 4 out of every 10 migrant workers are women, approximately 68 percent of migrant workers live in high-income countries, and those between the ages of 25-64, who are referred to as Prime age adults, dominate the composition of migrant workers by 87 percent[26].

Legal or illegal ways of asylum seekers over $ 3 billion in Turkey are estimated to bring in capital. As of the end of 2018, it has been learned that they hold 1.2 million Turkish liras in their bank deposits. 6b 790 pieces Syrian-owned company in Turkey can be understood from these figures are normally covered establishment. In addition, Turkey Union of Chambers and Commodity Exchanges (TOBB), worth 750 million Turkish lira in Turkey in the last 4 years, according to data to be recorded as capital companies by Syrian citizens are[27].

Figure 6. The Amount of Capital Invested by Refugees in Companies (million TL)[28]

Years	Incorporated Company	Limited Company	Total
2015	4,5	70,3	74,8
2016	14,9	181,4	196,4
2017	7,06	226,4	233,5
2018	9,9	236,9	246,8

It was reported that 72 companies were established by Syrian refugees in 2012. Both the government's optimistic approach should result in refugees' confidence in Turkey, this figure was realized as 764 thousand in 2018. When Graph.5 is examined, it is clearly possible to see that especially since 2014, the increasing amount of capital has increased[29].

[25] https://multeciler.org.tr/turkiyedeki-suriyeli-sayisi/(Access 06.11.2020)
[26] International Migration Report 2019, **United Nations**, https://www.un.org/en/development/desa/population/migration/publications/migrationreport/docs/InternationalMigration2019_Report.pdf (Access 15.09.2020)
[27] Yaman, op.cit
[28] Yaman, ibid
[29] Yaman, ibid.

Figure 7. Number of Companies Established by Syrian Refugees and Their Capital Totals (million TL)[30]

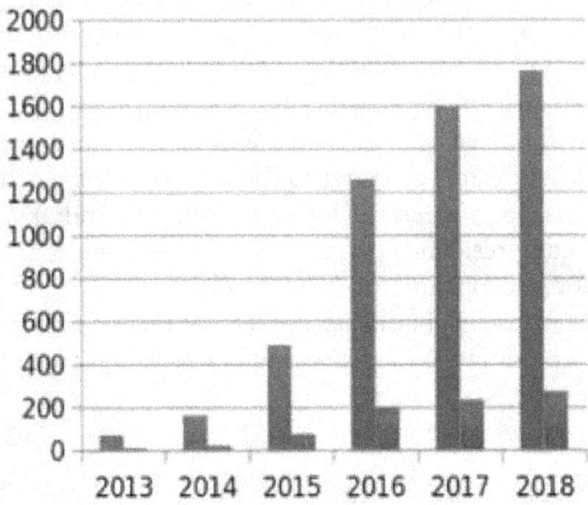

number of companies   total capital of Syrians (million TL)

According to the statement made by the Ministry of Commerce as of February 26, 2019, the number of companies with at least one Syrian partner was reported as 15 thousand 159[31].

Syrian small or large scale companies established in Turkey of refugees Posts 4b was recorded as 500. Since the refugee crisis that started in 2011, Syrian refugees have brought a figure of over 666 million TL to the Turkish economy, and with this figure, they took the first place among foreign investments[32].

Employment of Refugees in Turkey

Mainly related to the work of foreigners in Turkey published in the Official Gazette dated 08.13.2016 is regulated by the International Labor Law No. 6735 came into force. The law aims to pave the way for our country to benefit from the internationally qualified workforce at the highest level. However, since the provisions of the existing regulations that are not contrary to this Law will be implemented until the implementation of the Law comes into effect in the fourth paragraph of the Provisional Article 1 of the aforementioned Law, the current practice continues in some subjects. Currently, legislation on work permits for foreigners is scattered. Apart from the Law on Work Permits for Foreigners numbered 4817, there are regulations on work permits for foreigners in other legislations such as the Free Zones Law No.3218 and the Higher Education Law No.2547. However, most of the works and transactions related to work permits granted to foreigners are carried out within the framework of Law No. 4817.Work

[30] Yaman, ibid

[31] https://multeciler.org.tr/turkiyedeki-suriyeli-sayisi/ (Access 28.10.2020)

[32] Yaman, ibid.

permit valid in Article 27 of the Law on Foreigners and International Protection (LFIP) No.6458 and Work Permit Exemption Certificate issued pursuant to Article 10 of the Law on Work Permits of Foreigners dated 27/2/2003 and numbered 4817 shall be deemed valid instead of residence permit and the Law of foreigners will be allowed within the scope of Article 7 will not be allowed to enter Turkey must not be covered by foreigners is regulated to be searched. Law No.6458, Article 27, which regulates that the foreigners who have been granted a Work Permit or Work Permit Exemption Confirmation Certificate, according to the Law on Fees dated 02/7/1964 and numbered 492, has been amended by Law No.6735, and It is reported that the practice of collecting residence permit fees from foreigners has been terminated. In Turkey, Labor and operating permit except Social Security, Ministry of Culture and Tourism Ministry, Higher Education Department, Ministry of Economy of Free Zones in order to arrange the work permit to the Directorate General of General Directorate of 6458 No. foreigners and opinion on the frame 7 and Article 15 of the International Protection Act[33].

Regarding the right of refugees to work, there are provisions both in international conventions and in the Turkish Legal System. The right to work of refugees who have a foreign status in their country of refuge should also be provided to foreigners (refugees, conditional refugees, subsidiary protection holders) legally residing in the country within the scope of international protection. In essence, the working rights of refugees are regulated in 1951 Geneva Convention, article 17-19; In the 24th article of the same Convention, the regulations regarding the social security rights of the refugees are also mentioned. In Article 89/4 of the Law on Foreigners and International Protection, there is a clear provision regarding the access of persons who have applied for international protection and who have this status to the labor market; Based on the authority granted by this provision, the 'Regulation on the Work of International Protection Applicants and Persons with International Protection Status' prepared on the work of international protection applicants and persons with international protection status has been published in the Official Gazette on 26.04.2016 and entered into force. Shortly after the regulation came into force, the International Labor Law was adopted. The International Labor Law has not repealed Article 89 of the Law on Foreigners and International Protection. In this context, regarding applicants for international protection and persons with international protection status of studies in Turkey Foreigners and International Protection Law and International Business Law is applied together. Regarding the right to work, the classification of the persons concerned by the Law on Foreigners and International Protection and the regulations in the International Labor Law is considered as a reflection of the acceptance of the 1951 Geneva Convention with geographical limitation[34].

Located on a work permit in Turkey in the year 2016 56.591 foreigners, citizens

---

[33] https://www.goc.gov.tr/kurumlar/goc.gov.tr/YillikGocRaporlari/2016_yiik_goc_raporu_haziran.pdf; (Access 13.10.2020)

[34] Hatice Hilal TİRİTOĞLU ERSOY, "Labor and Social Security Rights of Refugees in Turkey," **Yildirim Beyazit Law Journal**, Vol. 4, No. 2, 2019, pp: 453-454.

of Georgia in the first person by 8014, Syrian citizens are second with 7,053 people, citizens of the People's Republic of China is in third place with 3,756 people. (Figure 8)[35].

Figure 8. Foreigners Found with Work Permit (Top 10 Countries) (2016)

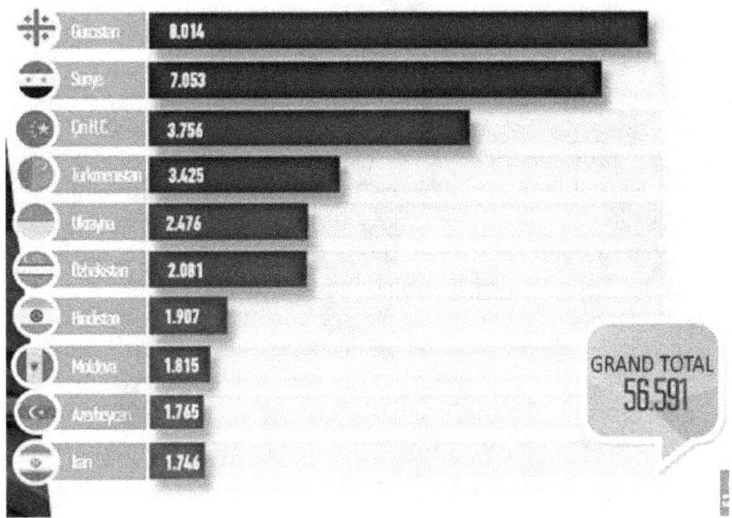

As of 2020, over 4 million refugees for the seventh consecutive time the world's highest number of refugees in host countries that Turkey is in the position of refugees coming from Syria in the majority of close to 3.6 million, 400 thousand Afghans, Iranians and Iraqis are home to refugees in his country. In the ten years since the beginning of the Syrian conflict, a quarter of the 25.9 million refugees in the world has been calculated as Syrian.Recognizing the need to devise long-term approaches that enhance the resilience of refugees, the Turkish government has designed strong protection frameworks that provide access to education, healthcare, social services and the labor market. Starting from 2016, refugees can obtain work permits through their employers. The International Labor Office (ILO) places decent work, including the promotion of international labor standards, at the center of its interventions. The only tripartite UN agency, the ILO collaborates closely with government, employers 'and workers' organizations to support refugees access to economic opportunities central to restoring hope, dignity and human security; This also means that refugees in Turkey as well as manage the increasing pressures on the labor market and support for communities to host governments and social partners to promote access to decent work.Refugees and Regional Stability Plan, which is coordinated under the Turkey section is part of the wider efforts of the international community. As an active member of the Livelihoods working group, the ILO, together with other UN agencies and NGOs, supports the government to

[35] https://www.goc.gov.tr/kurumlar/goc.gov.tr/YillikGocRaporlari/2016_yiik_goc_raporu_haziran.pdf (Access 01.11.2020)

strengthen the resilience and self-confidence of refugees. Regional Refugee and Resiliency Plan of Turkey country section of 2020-2021, many Syrian refugees can access the gradual business opportunities, but the employees of refugees only doing it as a picture of 3 percent and 71 percent of households revealed that not have access to skilled and reliable work. This is further emphasized by rising unemployment rates, especially among youth. The ILO is guided by the Global Compact for Refugees (GCR). Global solidarity and represents a milestone in the ILO moved to refugee protection, the JCC supports the practical implementation in Turkey. In this regard, the ILO, the JCC is to contribute to the achievement of two main objectives: the host countries and refugees to ease pressure on Turkey to increase its self-sufficiency. The government of Turkey as a co-organizer of the Global and Regional Refugee Refugee Forum showed a strong presence and Durability Plan has been depicted as one of the best apps that show innovative ways of disrupting the refugee crisis.The ILO's approach is also consistent with its commitment to 'leave no one behind' in the 2030 Agenda for Sustainable Development, and the ILO supports the implementation of Goal 8 on inclusive, sustainable economic growth, full and productive employment and decent work for all. refugees in Turkey, and accessing the labor market is still faced with difficulties when they start work. The difficulties in accessing the labor market can be summarized as follows;

*low employability (due to low education and technical skills),

*Limited language skills,

*restricted access to information and services (mainly due to language barriers).

Although refugees have been able to obtain work permits through their employers since 2016, very few of them have so far obtained work permits, only a few of the Syrian refugees are working officially. From 2.16 million Syrians in Turkey in working age is estimated that 1 million of participating in the labor market, most of them are employed as low-skilled and low-paid jobs in the informal[36].

2017 Turkey Statistical Institute (TSI), according to data from the ILO, the Syrian refugees, the largest refugee sector in Turkey in the Turkish labor market participation has been summarized as seen in Figure 13. Accordingly, 930 thousand of 2 million Syrians of working age were included in the labor market as part of the labor force. 130 thousand of the 813 thousand employed people are self-employed. This data represents 2.8 per cent of people working in Turkey. The employment rate of Syrians is reported to be around 40 percent. It is estimated that more than 97 percent of Syrian workers are unregistered[37].

---

[36] The ILO's support to refugees and host communities in Turkey, https://www.ilo.org/ankara/projects/wcms_379375/lang--en/index.htm (Access 18.10.2020)

[37] Syrian Refugees in Turkey Labor Market, https://www.ilo.org/ankara/publications/WCMS_738602/lang--en/index.htm (Access 19.10.2020)

Figure 9. SyriansLabour Force in Turkey

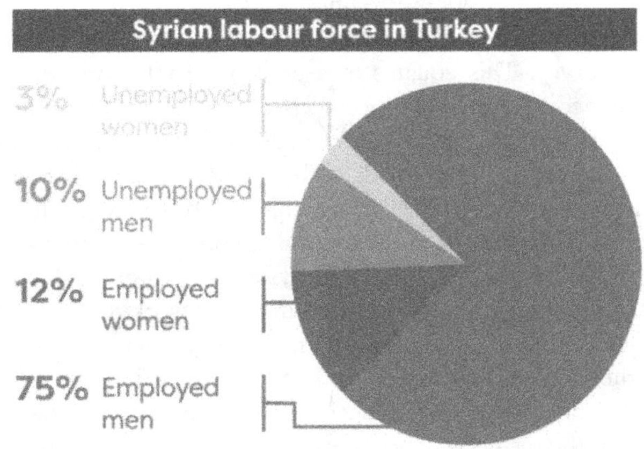

Turkish Red Crescent and World Food Program, Livelihoods developed the survey to provide additional evidence to inform the design of the transition to more sustainable livelihood opportunities from basic needs assistance for refugees in Turkey. The survey sample is taken from The Emergency Social Safety Net (ESSN) application pool and aims to assess the potential for refugee integration into Turkish labor markets as well as identify key constraints. Surveys, 19 in ESSN beneficiaries and Turkey was carried out from the applicant as appropriate yl. Provinces are divided into three geographic regions: Western Turkey, Central Anatolia and southern Turkey.

Map 1. Overview of grouping of provinces into three regions, West, Central and South[38]

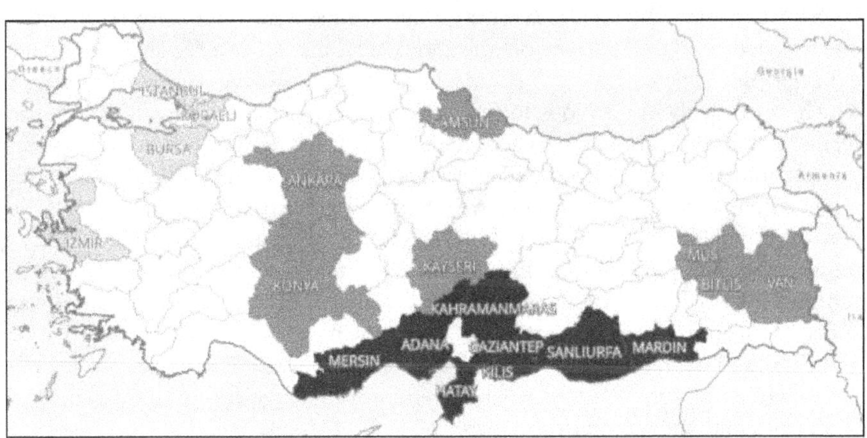

[38] Refugees in Turkey, Livelihoods Survey Findings, **Turkish Red Crescent and World Food Programme,** Ankara, 2019

In order to have representative data at the provincial level, 284 survey sample sizes were determined in each province and a total of 5,332 surveys were conducted[39]. This questionnaire represents the ESSN applicants in the 19 provinces included in the survey. This equates to a total of 413,025 households, including about 2.4 million people. Data collection took place between June-November 2018. The results show that 84 percent of refugee households have at least one employee. Only 3 percent of the refugees work with a work permit. This shows that the majority of them work informally with limited job security. Those with work permits tend to be concentrated in the Central region of the country and 17 percent of refugees in Konya are reported to work with a work permit. Before coming to Turkey, most of the refugees have reported that they work regularly; 30 percent of them are self-employed. 17 per cent of the refugees before arriving in Turkey reported that they were unemployed in the country of origin. In this case, among the respondents shows almost identical results with the unemployment rate in Turkey. However, the results of labor market conditions in their own countries and refugees and their participation in the labor market in Turkey registered work, conditions of employment, in terms of types of work and wages shows that are very different.20 percent of refugees in Turkey, according to the survey results when working in unskilled service, her textiles (19 percent), construction (12 percent) and handicrafts (10 percent) followed. Sectors with the least employment of refugees are shoe-making (6 percent), commercial services, and mechanic jobs (both 5 percent). These national percentages vary by provinces. Almost half of the refugees in Istanbul and almost a quarter of those working in agriculture in Mersin work in the textile sector.The data show that unemployment is relatively high among refugees without formal education, as well as among refugees with higher education levels. One-fifth of the 18 percent of refugees classified as educated (ie graduating from university or high school) are reported as unemployed.

Similarly, one-fifth of those without any formal education were registered as unemployed. For this reason, organizations working on refugee livelihoods may consider providing support for educated refugees to achieve degree accreditation, which can help them find jobs in their specialty.Participants were asked about the regularity of their work in the survey. Regular work was defined as a contractual and predetermined working hours. The results showed that more than half of the refugees (54 percent) were working irregularly; This figure is 80 percent for unskilled service providers. Regularity of work is highest in the textile industry; 79 percent of refugees working in textiles work regularly. As noted, only 3 percent of working refugees have a formal work permit, which provides job security, minimum wage and social security. largely informal and unreliable nature of refugee work in Turkey, hampers the integration of refugees in host communities. Therefore, policies that encourage employers to provide work permits for refugees can increase the self-sufficiency and integration of refugees[40].

---

[39] 95 percent confidence level, 5.8 percent margin of error and 50 percent assumed prevalence

[40] http://www.igamder.org/wp-content/uploads/2017/01/Challenges-and-oppurtunities-of-refugee-integration-in-turkey-full-report.pdf (Access 19.10.2020)

Irregularly working refugees reported earning an average of 1,058 TL per month, while regular workers reported earning an average of 1,312 TL per month. The textile industry generated the highest revenue among sectors (1,332 TL); This is logical because it is also the sector with the highest rate of refugees in regular jobs. The lowest income was 768 TL and 756 TL, respectively, with unskilled services and agriculture.Among the unemployed, 55 percent of men and 39 percent of women are looking for a job. The vast majority of job seekers explained that this was due to disability (among men) and childcare responsibilities (among women). These factors should be carefully considered during program design and development of targeting strategies. When asked about training courses, only 1 out of 10 people reported having attended a training before. The trainee profile is mostly made up of unemployed women, suggesting that others at home may be busy at work. Most of the trainings attended were provided by the Government and mostly Turkish courses were established. In general, Turkish language skills remain low. Four out of five refugees are beginners, and only 3 percent are advanced. The data show that language skills affect employability. While 50 percent of refugees who speak Turkish at the beginner level are employed full-time, this rate has increased to 60 percent for asylum seekers who speak Turkish at intermediate and advanced level. In terms of monthly income, refugees with advanced knowledge of Turkish earned on average 70 TL more than refugees with intermediate Turkish knowledge (1,280 TL and 1,211 TL, respectively). Participants who are Turkish at beginner level earned an average monthly income of 1.015 TL.

When asked what kind of support refugees need to find a job, 60 percent mentioned Turkish language training and almost 50 percent mentioned vocational training or social skills training such as interview skills and CV writing. The extensive findings of the livelihoods survey show that successful policy and program interventions need to be evidence-based and well targeted. The majority of refugees in Turkey comes from the less educated and less skilled past, but there are also large regional differences. Livelihood programs should first understand the regional and contextual factors that determine job opportunities and align interventions accordingly. These interventions should then target the right people, taking into account previous work experience, expertise and education levels. Therefore, it is important that the international community and the Turkish Government cooperate to share knowledge and design interventions. This cooperation will work towards the common goal of encouraging refugees to be more confident, ensuring maximum use of limited resources[41].

Findings

Syrian refugees in Turkey, mainly Turkey's impact on regional labor markets are complex, multifaceted and evolving exhibit a structure. Their demand for goods and services or the increased demand for goods and services necessary for their maintenance is likely to affect both the formal and informal labor.market. As they

[41] Refugees In Turkey: Livelihoods Survey Findings, op.cit.

are expected to do so in the medium term, their final access to the formal labor market will likely have an impact as the numbers increase. If a sufficiently large number of refugees can be integrated into the formal labor market, this will create additional demand.

The Syrian population, which makes up the majority of the refugees, is now more geographically dispersed, yet a large proportion still live near the border. These areas are unquestionably more affected across borders than the Syrian refugees they host. Given these limitations, the findings in this article show that Syrian refugees negatively affect unemployment and employment in the informal sector. The impact of Syrian refugees on formal employment needs to be explored further.

CHAPTER 13

SYRIAN IMMIGRATION AND INTEGRATION POLICIES IN TURKEY

Gülşen Sarı Gerşil[1]

Introduction

Although immigration is a phenomenon as old as human history, it results from different reasons. The phenomenon of immigration, which emerges both voluntarily and for compelling reasons, has positive and negative consequences for both the receiving and sending countries. While immigration based on compelling reasons such as especially wars causes people to leave their geography and move to other countries, it also brings along significant problems with its sociological and psychological dimensions. The whole world witnessed massive population movements and refugee crisis as a result of the civil war that occurred in Syria in 2011.

Syrians, who had to leave their country and their homes for compelling reasons, faced with some economic, social, political and security problems in the countries they went to since the war continued for a long time. Turkey has been mostly exposed to mass migration because of being neighbor to Syria and implementing open door policies. According to the data of September 2019, 3 million 643 thousand 870 Syrian refugees are living in Turkey. As of August 2019, the Syrians corresponded to 4.44% of Turkey's population of 82 million. Istanbul is numerically followed by Gaziantep with 445 thousand Syrians (21.4% of the population), Hatay with 432 thousand Syrians (26.8% of the population) and Şanlıurfa with 429 thousand Syrians (21.1% of the population). The ratio to population in these provinces is extraordinarily high. Kilis is the province with the highest number Syrians compared to its population on a provincial basis. The population of Ankara is 142 thousand, and the number of Syrians is 116 thousand. In other words, the number of Syrians corresponds to 81.6% of the population. In Turkey, the number of provinces with more than 100 thousand Syrians is 10[2]. In general, the arrival of very high numbers of Syrians in cities that already have many structural problems, impoverishment in these cities, and the problems in public services have further increased. While 177,376 of this immigrant population live in refuge centers, 3 million 408 thousand 362 of them are distributed to different provinces. Turkey accepts Syrian migrants under Temporary Protection and provides humanitarian aid such as shelter, food, health, and education in order to meet their basic needs within

[1] Dr. Lecturer, Manisa Celal Bayar University, Türkiye.

[2] Erdoğan M. Murat, (Eylül 2019), Türkiye'deki Suriyeli Mülteciler [Syrian Refugees in Turkey], TAGU – Türk-Alman Üniversitesi, Göç Ve Uyum Araştırmaları Merkezi, s.7

the framework of its possibilities. However, it had to turn to more permanent and effective solutions as the process took a long time. When it is considered that the Syrian Foreigners Under Temporary Protection are permanent in Turkey, it is quite important to ensure their social integration quickly for the solution of the problems.

In this study, the conceptual dimensions, causes and types of immigration were examined by literature review. Immigration was analyzed and compared with the statistical data in Turkey and in the world. Furthermore, the legal dimensions of immigration were examined by including its national and international legal regulations. Based on all these data, the practices and policies regarding the social integration of Syrian Foreigners under Temporary Protection in Turkey were discussed with different dimensions.

Phenomenon of Immigration

Nowadays, migration mobility has been experiencing its fastest period after the Second World War. According to the data of the United Nations, nearly 300 million immigrants, in other words 3% of the world population, live outside their countries of birth. More than 60 million of the immigrants are living away from their families and homes with the status of asylum seeker, refugee or another protection status. When the numbers, results and process are considered, it would be a very correct assessment to call our age as 'the Age of Immigration'[3]

The phenomenon of immigration, which is a social problem, requires the citizens of the country migrated to live together with the immigrants. The phenomenon of immigration leads to economic, social and cultural differences for both sides. In this regard, conflict is inevitable. It is important to minimize the effects of this conflict and to ensure social integration in a short time.

Asylum-seeker refers to the person whose 'refugee status' has been examined and therefore provided with temporary protection. Asylum-seeker is an individual who seeks international protection on an individual or group basis. Asylum-seeker is *a person whose protection request has not yet been finally decided by the authorities of the relevant country.* Therefore, each asylum-seeker may not be ultimately considered as a refugee, however, each refugee is initially an asylum-seeker[4]

Population movements, that cause displacement of people within the state or cause them to cross a state border, regardless of their duration, structure and reason, are broadly defined as immigration. Those who carry out this population movement also include refugees, displaced people, and finally, economic immigrants[5]. In other words, migration in the most general sense is defined as 'all displacements that occur

[3] Türkiye Büyük Millet Meclisi (TBMM), (Mart 2018), İnsan Haklarını İnceleme Komisyonu Mülteci Hakları Alt Komisyonu Göç Ve Uyum Raporu [Committee on Human Rights Inquiry Refugee Rights Sub-Commission Immigration and Integration Report], 26. Dönem 3. Yasama Yılı, p. 242

[4] Reçber, S. (2014). Hayatın yok yerindekiler: mülteciler ve sığınmacılar [People with no place in life: refugees and asylum seekers]. Sosyal İnsan Hakları Sempozyumu VI. Petrol İş Yayını 119, İstanbul: p.251

[5] ILO, Göç Sözlüğü, 2009, p.22

within a period sufficient to cause a significant distance and effect' [6]. On the other hand, immigration that occurs as a result of settling in a new place without returning is defined in the narrow sense or as traditional immigration [7].

Refugee is 'the person who considers that he/she is oppressed due to his/her religion, race, political thought, social position and ethnic identity in his/her own country, does not count on his/her state and therefore leaves his/her country with the thought that he/she is not treated impartially, and who has requested asylum in another country and is accepted by that country'. In other words, 'people who have no life security in their countries and have to leave their countries and take refuge in another country due to racial, ethnic, religious, political, sexual discrimination or war or conflict in their regions are named as refugees in daily use' [8].

Asylum-seeker; being an asylum-seeker with the right of asylum refers to an actual and short-term housing situation, rather than gaining a legal status. As it was mentioned previously, asylum-seeker refers to the person whose 'refugee status' has been examined and therefore provided with temporary protection [9]. Syrian immigrants admitted by Turkey with the names such as *temporary guest* and *temporary protection* since 2011 are in '***refugee status***' according to the 1951 Geneva Convention, to which Turkey is a party. In this context, the fact that Syrian immigrants are not in the refugee status limits their rights and makes their living conditions unfavorable [10].

Causes of Immigration

Another criterion used in classifying the phenomenon of immigration is to classify immigration in terms of the way of immigration. In terms of the way of immigration, it can be stated that there are individual, mass and chain types of migration[11]. In ***individual migration,*** individuals act as rational actors and have more precise information about the causes and consequences of their immigration [12]. The individual immigrates based on his/her own experience and economic knowledge with his/her own personal decision [13]. Likewise, as it is indicated in the

---

[6] YILMAZ, A., (2014), **"Uluslararası Göç: Çeşitleri, Nedenleri ve Etkileri [International Migration: Types, Causes and Effects]"**, *Turkish Studies - International Periodical For The Languages, Literature and History of Turkish or Turkic,* Cilt 9/2, KıÇ 2014, pp 1685-1704.

[7] BAKLACIOĞLU, N.Ö., (2010), Dış Politika ve Göç (alt başlık, Yugoslavya'dan Türkiye'ye Göçlerde Arnavutlar [1920-1990]) [Foreign Policy and Immigration (subtitle, Albanians in Immigrations from Yugoslavia to Turkey [1920-1990])], Derin Yayınları, İstanbul, p.7.

[8] BMMYK, (1997). Sığınma İkilemi, Dünya Mültecilerinin Durumu [Asylum Dilemma, The Situation of the World's Refugees], BMMYK, p.183.

[9] ibid, Reçber, p.251

[10] BMMYK, (1997). Sığınma İkilemi, Dünya Mültecilerinin Durumu [Asylum Dilemma, The Situation of the World's Refugees], BMMYK, p.183.

[11] KAYGALAK, S., (2009), Kentin Mültecileri, Neo-liberalizm Koşullarında Zorunlu Göç ve Kentleşme [Refugees of the City, Forced Migration and Urbanization Under Neo-liberalism Conditions], Dipnot Yayınları, Ankara 2009, p.12.

[12] Ibid.

[13] AĞIR, O., M. SEZİK, (2015), "Suriye'den Türkiye'ye Yaşanan Göç Dalgasından Kaynaklanan Güvenlik Sorunları [Security Problems Caused by the Immigration Wave from Syria to Turkey]", *Birey ve Toplum,* 2015, 5 (9), ss.95-123.

Immigration Dictionary, such migrations are usually self-financed or take place with the support of individuals, organizations or states, in contrast to mass migrations in which individuals migrate individually or with their families[14].

Mass migration develops with the emergence of social, economic or political reasons, and in a sense, it can be used synonymously with the concept of ***forced migration***[15]. In other words, this kind of migration usually occurs as a result of traumatic events that deeply affect the social memory. Syrian immigration can be shown as an example of this kind of migration in this sense[16].

Labor migration is a kind of migration that occurs when individuals leave their homeland and go to another foreign country for employment, in other words for working[17]. While it is similar to labor migration, ***brain drain*** is a kind of migration that summarizes the depletion of the resources of talent in the source country (sending country) as a result of the immigration of educated and talented individuals from their homelands to another country[18]. According to these definitions, both brain drain and labor migration are the derivatives of external migration. In addition to them, they are the terms that are called ***brain gain*** or '***reverse brain drain***' and used to describe the migration of skilled and educated individuals to the destination country[19] Many states have enacted immigration laws on their citizens who have immigrated for employment purposes and adopted immigration laws to guarantee their rights and create better opportunities[20].

There is no precise and universal definition of irregular migration. From the perspective of the destination country, irregular migration means entering, staying or working in the country without the legal permits and documents required during immigration to the country. From the perspective of the sending country, irregular migration occurs when a person crosses the international boundary without a valid and legal passport or fails to carry out the necessary administrative transactions while leaving the country. In recent years, there has been a tendency to use the concept of ***irregular migration***, which is also known as '***illegal immigration***,' synonymously with ***migrant smuggling*** and ***human trafficking***[21].

In the definition of irregular migration, distinctions should first be made between 'destination country', 'transit country' and 'country of origin'. As the name implies, destination country is the country desired to be reached, and entry to this country may be through legal means as well as illegal means. Even though the country is entered through legal means, an irregular migration is caused by staying in the country by not leaving the country at the end of the period allowed by the

---

[14] ILO, Göç Sözlüğü [Immigration Dictionary], 2009, p.5.

[15] ibid, Kaygalak, p.13.

[16]ibid, Ağır and Sezik, p.98.

[17] ILO, Göç Sözlüğü [Immigration Dictionary], 2009, p.8.

[18] Uluslararası Göç Örgütü(IOM) (2009); Göç Terimleri Sözlüğü [Glossary of Immigration Terms], No.18, p.5 http://www.goc.gov.tr/files/files/goc_terimleri_sozlugu(1).pdf Access, 21.10.2020)

[19] ibid, IOM, p.5.

[20] ILO, Göç Sözlüğü [Immigration Dictionary], 2009, p.5

[21] ibid, IOM, p.15.

laws. The country left for the occurrence of irregular migration is the country of origin. People who enter the destination country or the transit country by following or not following legal procedures while leaving the country of origin can stay in the transit country for a while or leave this country after a certain time and arrive in the destination country[22].

Irregular migration, which was 57,478 in 2005 in Turkey, has increased by 454,662 as of 2019(Chart 1).

Chart 1. Number of Irregular Migrants between 2005-2019 in Turkey

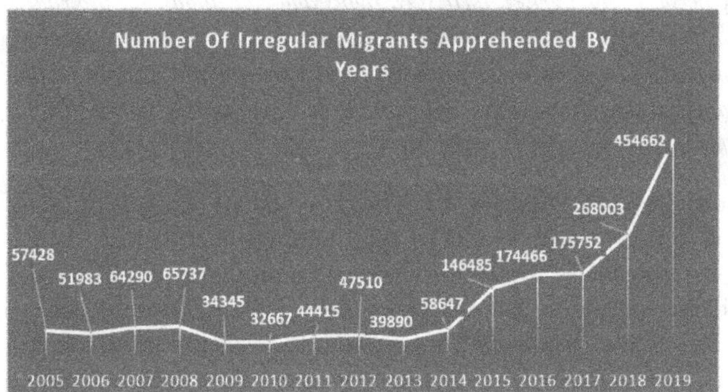

Source: GİGM: https://www.goc.gov.tr/duzensiz-goc-istatistikler (E.T: 05.10.2020)

National and International Legal Regulations of Immigration

There are many international regulations on immigration. Some of them are the UN Convention on the Protection of the Rights of All Migrant Workers and Members of Their Families, the Universal Declaration of Human Rights, the Convention Relating to the Status of Refugees, and the Convention Relating to the Status of Stateless Persons. Nevertheless, the most important regulation for migrant workers at the European level is included in the Revised European Social Charter. Article 19 of the relevant charter introduces a regulation on the right of migrant workers and their families to protection and assistance. In article 11 of the ILO's 1949 and 1975 Conventions no. 97 and no. 143, 'a migrant worker is defined as a person who migrates from one country to another or is accepted into a country as a migrant worker with the intention of being employed by someone else rather than on his behalf'. In our country, the work permit for foreigners was regulated by the International Labor Law No. 6735, which entered into force on 13.08.2016, and clause 7 of article 27 of this law, and the Law No. 4817 on Work Permits of Foreigners were repealed. In Law No. 6735, as in the abolished Law No. 4817, the work permits for foreigners wishing to work in Turkey are divided into four groups as 'temporary work permit', 'indefinite work permit', 'independent work permit', 'exceptional work permit'.

[22] ILO, Göç Sözlüğü [Immigration Dictionary], 2009, p.63

It is observed that the Foreigners and International Protection Law (FIPL) is evaluated within the scope of '**temporary protection**' regarding ***mass migration movements***. '**Temporary protection**' status, which is still valid for Syrians due to the mass migration movements in the region, is of great importance. The regulation on temporary protection has been made in the law as follows:

Temporary protection:*(1) Temporary protection can be provided to foreigners who have been forced to flee their countries, cannot go back to that country, have come in mass influx to or crossed our borders to receive emergency and temporary protection.*

(2) Acceptance of these persons into Turkey, their stay, rights and obligations, the procedures to be followed upon their departure from Turkey, precautions in cases of mass movement, coordination among national and international institutions and organisations, specifying duties and powers of institutions and organisations that will serve in the headquarters and rural areas will be regulated by cabinet directives. (FIPL -Md. 91)

Temporary Protection Regulation [23]**:** The content of the 'Temporary Protection' regulation defined by Article 91 of the FIPL has been regulated by a regulation. The Regulation obliges foreigners to have 'biometric' register in order to eliminate the problems experienced and to be experienced in registration, and to this end, both fingerprints and registration in the address registration system are obligatory. Foreigners are entitled to access basic services and other social assistance only if they are present in the provinces in which they are registered. According to the regulation, the procedures and principles regarding the work of temporary protected persons are determined by the President, upon the proposal of the Ministry of Family, Labor and Social Services, in consultation with the Ministry of Interior. These foreigners can only work in sectors, business lines and geographical areas determined by the President and apply to the Ministry of Family, Labor and Social Services to obtain this permission[24].

In the regulation, the 'refoulement ban' is clearly expressed with an interpretation in favor of refugees (Art.6). According to the regulation, no one within the scope of the regulation shall be returned to a place where he or she may be subjected to torture, inhuman or degrading punishment or treatment or, where his/her life or freedom would be threatened on account of his/her race, religion, nationality, membership of a particular social group or political views. Article 11 of the same Regulation regulates the termination of temporary protection. Accordingly, the Ministry of Interior may present a recommendation to the Council of Ministers to terminate temporary protection. Temporary protection is terminated by the decision of the Council of Ministers. Along with the termination decision, the Council of Ministers (2); a) can decide to stop the temporary protection completely and return those under temporary protection to their countries, b) can decide to grant the status of temporary protected persons collectively or to evaluate

---

[23] http://www.resmigazete.gov.tr/eskiler/2014/10/20141022-15-1.pdf (Access, 12.11.2020)

[24] Temporary Protection Regulation was arranged in detail in the study "Regarding the Syrians in Turkey: Social Acceptance and Harmony".

the applications of those who apply for international protection individually, and c) can decide to allow temporary protected persons to stay in Turkey under the conditions specified under the Law.'

Figure 1. International Protection Regulation According to Turkish Law Foreigners and International (Protection Law (6458 / 4.4.2013) and Temporary Protection)

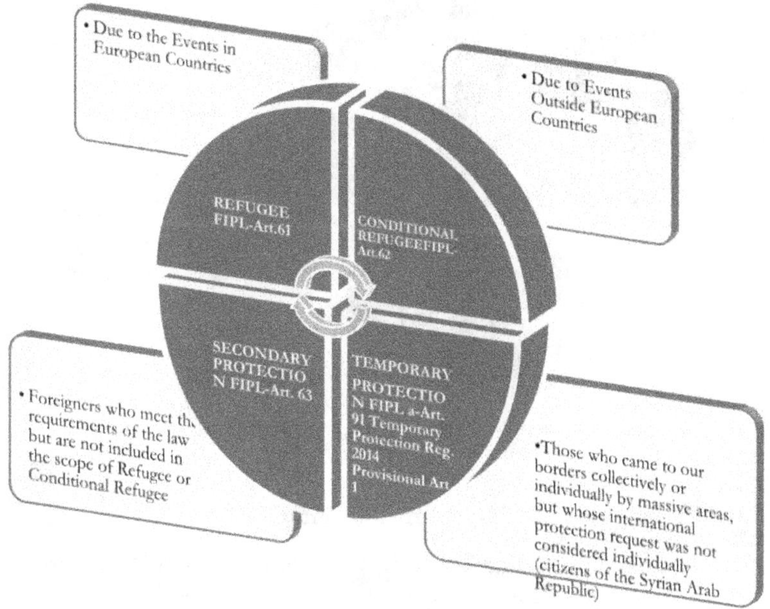

Chart 2 above on the countries where Syrian refugees, who had to leave their country after April 2011, in other words, in the last nine years, are located clearly reveals the magnitude of the responsibilities undertaken by Turkey. The number of Syrians who are still forced to leave their country is calculated as 6 million 650 thousand[25]. As of December 31, 2019, the number of Syrians in Turkey was 3,576,370, which is 54.1% of the total of those who had to flee abroad. Turkey is followed by Lebanon (919,578) by 15.8%, Jordan (654,266) by 10.4%, Iraq (Northern) (246,592) by 3.8% and Egypt (126,027) by 1.9%. Approximately 15% of Syrian refugees live in countries such as the European Union, other European countries, Canada, and the USA. In Europe, Germany hosts 532,100 Syrians, followed by Sweden with 109,300 Syrians, Austria with 49,200 Syrians, Netherlands with 32,100 Syrians, Greece with 23,900 Syrians, Denmark with 19,700 Syrians, Bulgaria with 17,200 Syrians, Switzerland with 16,600 Syrians, France with 15,800 Syrians, Armenia with 14,700 Syrians, Norway with 13,900

[25] https://data2.unhcr.org/en/situations/syria (Access, 16.11.2020)

Syrians and Spain with 13,800 Syrians [26].

Chart 2. Countries Where Syrian Refugees Are Located (6.6 Million / December 31, 2019)

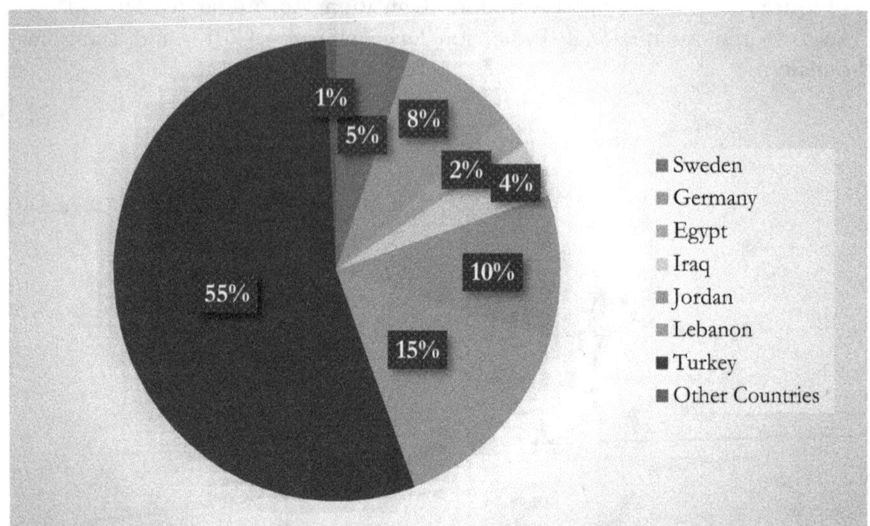

Source: UNHCR-Global Trends: Forced Displacement in 2018 https://www.unhcr.org/5d08d7ee7.pdf (Access, 12.11.2020)

Social Integration of Syrian Immigrants

The phenomenon of immigration, which is a social problem, requires the citizens of the country migrated to live together with the immigrants. It is inevitable to experience some conflicts due to economic, social and cultural differences. It is necessary to minimize the negative effects of these conflicts and to realize the adaptation process in a short time.

Immigration, which is an event closely related to the whole structure of society such as social, cultural, economic, and political structures, leads to the displacement of labor, which brings along many problems in terms of both business and social security law. The number of work permits received by foreigners coming to our country constitutes a very small rate compared to the total number of illegal migrant workers in our country. Since migrant workers usually find employment opportunities in informal jobs with harsh working conditions that are not preferred by the domestic labor, some general protective provisions are included in international regulations.

The phenomenon of immigration, which is a social problem, requires the citizens of the country migrated to live together with the immigrants. The phenomenon of immigration leads to economic, social and cultural differences for

[26] **https://www.uikpanorama.com/blog/2020/04/29/onuncu-yilinda-turkiyedeki-suriyeliler/** (Access, 18.11.2020)

both sides. In this regard, conflict is inevitable. It is important to minimize the effects of this conflict and to ensure social integration in a short time.

Syrian Children born in Turkey

According to the official data of the Ministry of Health, 82,850, 111,325, 140 thousand Syrian babies were born in 2016, 2017 and 2018, respectively, in Turkey. With a simple projection, it can be predicted that the number of newborns in 2019 would be at least 170 thousand. In other words, the number of Syrian babies to be born each day in 2019 seems to be 465 on average per day[27]. In this context, it can be easily said that the number of Syrian babies born in Turkey has still exceeded 450 thousand. 'De-facto statelessness' ('haymatlos') is an important problem of Syrian babies born in Turkey since the Syrian State and Turkey do not automatically grant citizenship.

Education of Syrians in Turkey

Chart 3. Number of Syrian Students Provided with Access to Primary and Secondary Education in Turkey by Years

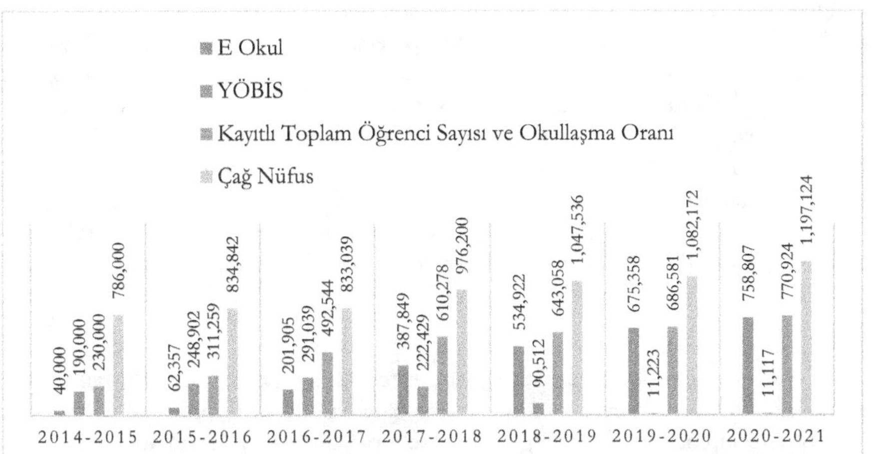

Source: MEB:https://hbogm.meb.gov.tr/meb_iys_dosyalar/2021_01/27122650_ocak_2021.pdf (Access, 08.02.2021)

Limited data available on the general educational background of the Syrian population, which corresponds to 4.42's% of Turkey's population, indicate that the Syrians have an educational level well below the average in Turkey and that approximately half of them are illiterate or have never gone to school. This is because immigrants to Turkey came from a rural and highly traditional region in northern Syria and have had a limited access to education as a policy of the Syrian regime for decades. The ratio of illiterate Syrians, which is observed to be 33.3% in

[27] https://www.haberturk.com/son-dakika-bakan-soylu-dan-onemli-aciklamalar-2514831 (Access, 22.10.2020)

Turkey, is 13% in Jordan, 14% in Lebanon and 10% in Iraq[28]. The second important factor is that the around 700 thousand Syrians who left Turkey between 2014-2016 had relatively higher education levels.

According to the September 2020 data of the Directorate General of Migration Management, efforts to gradually register the Syrian school-age population, which is 1,197,124, to official schools affiliated to the Ministry of National Education are going on. In official (except Temporary Education Centers) schools affiliated to the Ministry of National Education, a total of 770,924 students Syrians under temporary protection, who came to our country through mass migration, receive education with a Turkish curriculum. In 211 temporary education centers in our country, 11,117 students, all of whom are Syrians, receive education based on intensive Turkish education[29]. For the immigrant students, the most encountered problems are adaptation, behavioural disorders and unsuccessfulness[30].

Syrian university students in Turkey

Among the Syrians in Turkey, some of them discontinued their education in Syria and came to Turkey, and some of them passed the Foreign Student Exams and language exams after receiving primary and secondary education in Turkey, and the number of Syrian students entering universities is constantly increasing. The number of Syrian university students studying in around 100 state and 50 foundation (private) universities in Turkey increased to 14,747 in the 2016-2017 academic year, 20.701 in the 2017-2018 academic year, and 27,606 in the 2018-2019 academic year. Syrians continue their education by being exempt from all fees from state universities. The ratio of those who receive scholarships among Syrian university students seems to be around 15%. The presence of university students is extremely important for Syrian youth to continue their education and careers and play an active role in their adaptation processes[31].

There are several important reasons why Syrian children stay away from school at compulsory school age, which can be listed as the perception of 'transience', financial difficulties, especially boys having to work, capacity problem of schools, transportation costs, not sending girls to schools, and assimilation anxiety. In this regard, it is extremely important that the European Union (EU) and United Nations (UN) institutions contribute to conditional school support. This support is paid as

---

[28] United Nations Development Programme (UNDP), the International Labor Organization (ILO) and the World Food Programme (WFP) (2017) Jobs Make the Difference Expanding Economic Opportunities for Syrian Refugees and Host Communities Egypt - Iraq - Jordan - Lebanon - Syria – Turkey, p.83.

[29]EB:https://hbogm.meb.gov.tr/meb_iys_dosyalar/2019_06/26115239_14_HAziran___2019_YNTERNET_SUNUUU_.pdf (Access, 10.11.2020)

[30] Perihan Şara Hürsoy, Derya Alimanoğlu Yemişçi, "A Study On The Vıews Of Prımary School Teachers About Refugee Chıldren", **New Horızons In Educatıonal Scıences – II**, Lambert Academic Publishing, 2018, pp. 27-44

[31] M.Murat Erdoğan ve diğerleri (2019) "Elite Dialogue": Suriyeli Akademisyenler ve Lisansüstü Öğrenciler Aracılığı ile Türkiye'de Bulunan Suriyeli Sığınmacılar ile Diyalog [Dialogue with Syrian Refugees in Turkey through Syrian Academicians and Postgraduate Students], AB HOPES-MADAD, Türk Alman Üniverisitesi Göç ve Uyum Araştırmaları Merkezi-TAGU. https://docplayer.biz.tr/166937778-Turkiye-deki-suriyeli-multeciler.html (Access, 13.11.2020)

40 TL for girls attending elementary school, 35 TL for boys attending elementary school, 60 TL for girls attending secondary school, and 50 TL for boys attending secondary school. However, it should not be forgotten that the implementation of active 'provisional support' programs with higher amounts without going below these numbers is vital, by considering the regional differences.

Chart 4. Syrian Students in the Turkish Higher Education System 2011-2019

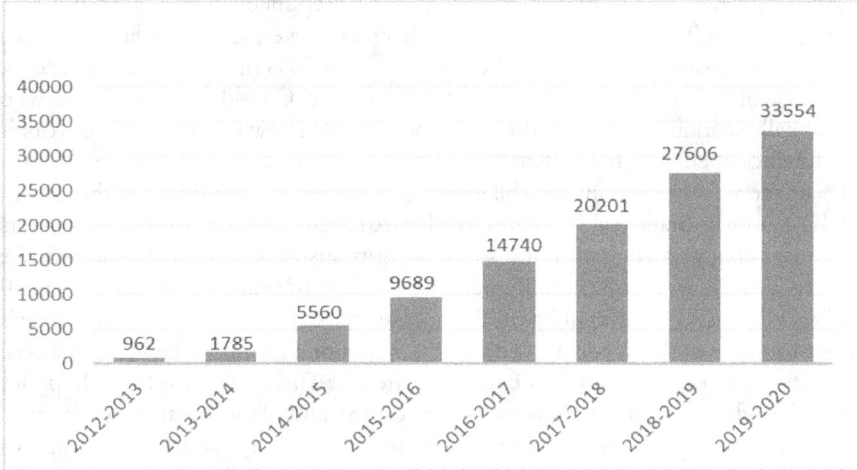

2012-2013	2013-2014	2014-2015	2015-2016	2016-2017	2017-2018	2018-2019	2019-2020
962	1785	5560	9689	14740	20201	27606	33554

Source: YÖK: https://istatistik.yok.gov.tr/ Annual issues published by YÖK (Council of Higher Education) were tabulated by M. Murat Erdoğan.

Labor Markets and the Employment of Syrians

Working area is one of the most sensitive issues of all mass human movements. The local community is concerned that the immigrants-refugees-asylum seekers, who have arrived later and will most likely work as 'cheap workers', will take their jobs. In Turkey that received more than 5% of its population in a few years, the issue of employment has naturally come to the fore. In the TİSK report which was prepared in 2015 and included the relevant views of the Turkish Business World[32], it was observed that not only laborers who felt uncomfortable with the risk of losing their jobs due to cheap labor supply, but also corporate employers who drew attention to the negative consequences of the informal economy were anxious. Corporate companies drew attention to the difficulties of competing with cheap labor and informality.

The fact that the Syrians were involved in economic activities by living in the areas outside of the camps and in city centers since 2013 automatically initiated the process. When the number of Syrians who started to work in the informal area reached 400 thousand, the Turkish state needed to make arrangements in this regard, and Temporary Protected Syrians living in Turkey were granted with the

[32] https://www.tisk.org.tr/yayin/26_genel-kurul-raporu-2016.pdf (Access, 25.11.2020)

right to work as of January 15, 2016. According to this regulation, *Syrians who have been registered in Turkey for at least 6 months can have the right to work at a workplace at the rate of 1/10, at the request of their employers, provided that they work for at least the minimum wage.* However, this regulation, which was extremely important for the economic activities and adaptation of Syrians in Turkey and allowed Syrians to work officially, was not very effective on the registration of Syrians working informally. According to the statement made by the Ministry of Family, Labor and Social Services on March 31, 2019, the number of the Syrian Arab Republic citizens granted with a work permit in Turkey was 31 thousand 185[33]. However, studies indicate that the number of Syrians working in Turkey is more than 30% of their total population, in other words, at least 1.2 million Syrians are working. Considering the Syrians who are actually working in Turkey, these numbers clearly show that the right to work is not functional enough for Syrians under temporary protection and that more than 95% of the working Syrians are still working informally[34]. According to the data of TUIK (Turkish Statistical Institute) in May 2019, the ratio of informal ' workers 'without being affiliated with any social security institution' is 34.4% among the citizens actively working in the Republic of Turkey. In other words, more than 10 million citizens of the Republic of Turkey are still working informally in Turkey's 'labor force' over the age of 15, which is 32.3 million in total[35]. Many international institutions, especially the World Bank, indicate that Turkey pursued the right policy since they do not force Syrians to stay in camps and allow them to work (even though informally), which both contributes to the economy and makes it easier for refugees to live with dignity, and that it can also be called as 'developmentalist refugee policy'[36], which can be considered as an important reason for the high level of social acceptance towards Syrians in Turkey, which is 'fragile' but still remains at a very high level [37].

Syrian entrepreneurs certainly have made significant contributions to the economic cohesion of the Syrians in Turkey. Syrians can establish their own businesses in Turkey in accordance with the Turkish Code of Commerce. In the businesses that are formally registered in Turkey, the owner of the business can officially apply for work permits. The number of businesses established by Syrians in Turkey has a tendency to increase significantly, although some of them consist of self-financing micro-level businesses. Most foreign companies established in Turkey in 2017 and 2018 belonged to the Syrians. According to the statement of the Ministry of Trade, it was indicated that the number of companies with at least

---

[33] https://www.kas.de/documents/283907/7339115/T%C3%BCrkiye%27deki+Suriyeliler.pdf/acaf9d37-7035-f37c-4982-c4b18f9b9c8e?version=1.0&t=1571303334464 (Access, 02.10.2020)

[34] Turkish Red Crescent and World Food Programme (2019). Refugees In Turkey: Livelihoods Survey Findings. Ankara, Turkey

[35] Türkiye İstatistik Kurumu-TUIK: http://tuik.gov.tr/HbGetirHTML.do?id=30683 (Access, 07.10.2020).

[36] Dünya Bankası: World Bank Report: Turkey's Response to the Syrian Refugee Crisis and the Road Ahead, December 2015

[37] M.Murat Erdoğan (2018) Suriyeliler Barometresi: Suriyelilerle Uyum İçinde Yaşamın Çerçevesi [Syrians Barometer: a Framework for Achieving Social Cohesion with Syrians], İstanbul Bilgi Üniversitesi Yayınları", İstanbul.

one partner of Syrian origin was 15.159 as of February 26, 2019 [38]. This figure is estimated to be even higher along with the companies established informally. Syrians can establish their own businesses in Turkey in accordance with the Turkish Code of Commerce. In the businesses that are formally registered in Turkey, the owner of the business can officially apply for work permits. The number of businesses established by Syrians in Turkey has a tendency to increase significantly, although some of them consist of self-financing micro-level businesses. Most foreign companies established in Turkey in 2017 and 2018 belonged to the Syrians. According to the statement of the Ministry of Trade, it was indicated that the number of companies with at least one partner of Syrian origin was 15.159 as of February 26, 2019[39]. This figure is estimated to be even higher along with the companies established informally. The leading companies established are wholesale trade, real estate and construction sectors. According to information provided by the UNHCR, Syrians' entrepreneurial capital in Turkey reached 400 million dollars at the end of 2018[40].

Conclusion

While the issue of Syrian refugees in Turkey has entered its tenth year, 3.6 million Syrians under temporary protection, 117 thousand Syrians with residence permit, and approximately 100 thousand Syrians in the category of 'irregular migrants' are living in the country today. Furthermore, 117 thousand Syrian refugees were granted citizenship as of the end of 2019. Thus, a total of 4 million Syrians are living in Turkey, regardless of their status. While 60 thousand of them are living in camps, the remaining 99% are together with the Turkish society as 'urban refugees'. It should be said that this process, which was carried out unexpectedly and reluctantly, has been overcome despite the problems. Syrians are living outside of camps as urban refugees, by spreading in almost all parts of Turkey. Turkey has not made any settlement plan for the Syrians. Especially when the capacity in the camps was filled since the end of 2013, Syrians were allowed to settle wherever they wanted. As it was expected, Syrians are scattered in places where they have relatives to support them and where they can work.

In Turkey, the presence of Syrians in the country is evolving from being a guest to permanence. While the nine years passed, the damage caused by the chronic conflict environment in Syria, deepening of the hate atmosphere in the country, the survival of the regime, and inability to make any prediction for the future are the ('driving') factors that strengthen the permanence, the establishment of life in Turkey and other returns encourage Syrians for a new life. After this stage, neither the establishment of safe zones nor the collapse of the regime will provide

[38] CNN-TÜRK:https://www.cnnturk.com/ekonomi/bakan-pekcan-15-bin-159-suriyeli-sirket-var (Access, 16.11.2020)

[39] In the study conducted by TEPAV, it is reported that more than 15 thousand companies established by Syrians have provided employment for at least 44 thousand Syrians. 100 See.: http://www.hurriyet.com.tr/ekonomi/patron-da-calisan-da-suriyeli-41322721 Access, 16.09.2020)

[40] UNHCR- Update: Durable Solutions for Syrian Refugees: https://data2.unhcr.org/en/documents/download/70892 (Access: 02.10.2020)

comprehensive voluntary repatriation of Syrians in Turkey. Repatriation can now be considered as an exception. Moreover, it is observed that the hope of Syrians in Turkey crossing to Europe has decreased.

General education level is important in the process of social adaptation, especially for getting the support of families for the education of children. The issue of the education of Syrian children in Turkey is of great importance both in terms of minimizing the lost generations, a dignified life, and future plans for living together in peace. It is observed that the MoNE made significant moves for Syrian students in 2016. The first important step of the MoNE was signing 300 Million € agreement for education spending under the EU Facility for Refugees in Turkey with the EU Delegation on 3 March 2016. However, the most important step was taken in August 2016 and the MoNE determined the 'road map' on Syrian children's access to education, and also established the 'Immigration and Emergency Education Department' within the General Directorate of Lifelong Learning by strengthening its institutional capacity[41]. The issue in the road map was based on the understanding of being more 'permanent' than 'temporary', and the integration of Syrian children into the Turkish education system has been determined as the main objective. Undoubtedly, it is a great success that 771 thousand of more than 1 million Syrian school-age children in Turkey have been provided with access to education. The education is a field the contribution of which is late even if investments are made quickly. In other words, the need for qualified educators is as high as new schools and classrooms.

According to the data of the United Nations High Commissioner for Refugees (UNHCR), the number of those who returned from Turkey to Syria and stayed there in the four years between 2014 and 2018 was 55.000. Turkey should face this reality and develop its cohesion policies for a peaceful common life. It is extremely important to accept this reality and to reflect it in state policies. Although Turkey has developed projects to solve current problems in cooperation with the international partner, it is still not possible to talk about a comprehensive strategic determination and planning. However, it is another challenge for Turkey to make efforts to develop cohesion policies for over millions of 'refugees', the future of whom is not known, not for the 'immigrants'. It is a fact that cohesion policies encourage permanence, and the states all over the world avoid cohesion policies in case of such uncertainty or unwillingness. Worries such as Germany's implementation of cohesion policies to the Turks who came in 1961 in the mid-1980s are also experienced in Turkey. However, this situation causes Turkey to lose time and resources and increase its risks. The economic, social, political and security risks of 3.6 million refugees in Turkey are an important problem for Turkey.

Turkey should face the reality, take strategic decisions, consider Syrians as people who will live here, not as 'guests', and produce permanent and effective policies. The state needs to develop a proper communication strategy that includes

---

[41] http://www.meb.gov.tr/suriyeli-cocuklarin-egitimi-icin-yol-haritasi-belirlendi/haber/11750/tr (Access, 03.11.2020).

transparency in a way that will enable Turkish society to accept Syrian refugees. It is necessary to take measure so that Turkey would not be considered as a 'cheap buffer zone' by the EU and this perception can be changed. It should also be underlined that Turkey's relations with the EU should be developed on a more comprehensive and realistic ground, going beyond just partial financial burden sharing and developing strategic cooperation.

CHAPTER 14

THE EXTENT OF SYRIAN REFUGEES IN ELECTION BULLETINS: 2015 AND 2018 ELECTIONS IN TURKEY

Yüksel Kamacı Erkan[1]

Introduction

The Syrian Arab Republic is a Middle Eastern state which has experienced quite turbulent periods in this knife-edged region. Since the independence from the Ottoman Empire, Syria had different political systems and different official contexts. Today on the paper, as a republic from capital city Damascus with its President Bashar al-Assad, it has actually been a devastated country for more than a decade. Although Syria consists of different ethnic and religious communities in addition to a long diplomatic history, these qualities failed to compose an intertwined and harmonious community. Instead, they were transformed into the dynamics which have provoked the tensions around the homeland.

One of the crucial turning points for Syria like many other regional states was the Arab Spring, in other words, Arab Winter in fact. Since 2010 the effects have spread rapidly such as spill over effects. At first some idealistic arguments (democracy, human rights, etc.) paved the way for activist people to change their nations' future. But in the process of time, international developments differed from the start undeniably. The ideas at the beginning remained romantic or utopic rhetoric when we look at the past with current perspective. Moreover, there is no consensus concerning Arab Spring process whether it was a conspiracy of hegemonic powers in appropriate with their strategic interests or it was a grassroots movement and civil disobedience simultaneously. Eventually in 2011 a chain of mass movements, uprisings, anti-government protests, demonstrations of rebel groups continued in Syria and unfortunately the violent unrest and conflicts resulted in a civil war.

In terms of Republic of Turkey, these two states are neighbours along with a remarkable border that Turkey and Syria have 911 km territorial border. This appearance made the existing situations harder during the Arab Spring and afterwards, especially regarding Turkey's red lines such as terrorist organizations. Turkey did not ignore the international events and reacted with a vital decision about its neighbour. While thousands of Syrians were abandoning their homeland, Turkey constructed the first refugee camp for them in May 2011. From then onwards several attempts such as Geneva process and Astana platform were held

[1] Assist. Prof. Dr.; Maltepe University, Faculty of Business and Management Sciences, Department of Political Science and International Relations, Türkiye. ORCID ID: 0000-0002-2741-2764.

by plenty of states including Turkey to end the civil war, but Syria is still a ruin.

What does refugee mean? The United Nations Refugee Agency describes that *'a refugee is someone who has been forced to flee his or her country because of persecution, war or violence.'*[2] Refugee issue is also a political, security, humanitarian, social, and economic matter, particularly after the Arab Spring. Furthermore, it turned into an internal problem for Turkey in company with the aforementioned angles. *'The ongoing civil war has resulted in more than 5.5 million registered Syrian refugees - dispersed in Egypt, Iraq, Jordan, Lebanon, and Turkey - as of November 2020.'*[3] According to Refugees Association in Turkey, November 2020 data mirrored there are 3.635.410 Syrians in the country. 0-4 ages are 503.300 and 5-9 ages are 542.322.[4] These official figures show more than 1 million Syrian children were born after the civil war. A recent study[5] on Syrian refugees pointed out that most of them do not have hope regarding own country and subsequently they identify a vision of their future in Turkey. On the contrary, Turkish citizens recognize: 'We are not culturally same anymore.' Actually this change is beyond culture, it comprises various fields and the level of change continues to rise year by year.

This article includes some specific goals to make a contribution for migration literature. First of all, the last two general elections in Turkey and election bulletins are very important to relate the pieces of the puzzle. I will present the bulletins of two currently major parties in the Republic of Turkey. Thus, we will be able to scrutinize those parties' future plans as official policies on Syrian refugee issue. For this goal, a systematic methodology will be used that with the help of content analysis method, I will list the whole articles concerning Syria and Syrians in Justice and Development Party (JDP) and Republican People's Party's (RPP) bulletins for 2015 and 2018 elections. Hence there will be 4 bulletins. By doing so, as an academic, I aim to reflect the readers a comparative analysis regarding not only parties, but also time factor.

2015 General (Parliamentary) Election in Turkey

2015 is a significant year for Turkey. In February, Turkey and the United States signed an agreement for Syrian moderate opponents. Moreover, Turkey attacked under the name of 'Şah-Fırat' operation in the same month. On 7th June 2015, the general parliamentary election was held. As a result, JDP won the election with 40,87 % of votes and RPP obtained 24,95 % votes[6] as the second. Therefore, JDP lost the majority for the first time since 2002 general election. On 9th July, in other words 32 days after the election, President Recep Tayyip Erdoğan gave Ahmet

[2] https://www.unrefugees.org/refugee-facts/what-is-a-refugee/ (Access 20.11.2020)

[3] https://www.cia.gov/library/publications/the-world-factbook/geos/sy.html (Access 28.11.2020).

[4] https://multeciler.org.tr/turkiyedeki-suriyeli-sayisi/ (Access 01.12.2020)

[5] https://www.hurriyet.com.tr/gundem/en-kapsamli-suriyeli-arastirmasi-turkiyede-mutlular-kalicilar-41672136 (Access 29.11.2020)

[6] https://www.ysk.gov.tr/doc/dosyalar/docs/Milletvekili/7Haziran2015/KesinSecimSonuclari/ResmiGazete/D.pdf (Access 1.12.2020)

Davutoğlu the mission to form a government. After the failure, on 25th August, President made a decision for a re-election. On 1st November, re-election results addressed the victory of JDP again with more votes than the previous one. While JDP's votes were 49,4 %, RPP got 25,4 % of votes[7] and the 64th Turkish government was established by Ahmet Davutoğlu. Now I will give a place to election bulletins of first two parties.

Justice and Development Party's 2015 Election Bulletin

Throughout this topic, I will use Syria related materials in JDP's election bulletin based on its official website[8] and translate them into English with their page numbers.

'We provide humanitarian aid without discrimination of race, religion, or language. Particularly Syria and Iraq, we are opening our gates, hearts, and tables to our brothers and sisters who have humanitarian tragedy. We provide more coordination in public space through these initiatives and we coordinate with non-governmental organizations.' (p.318)

'Syrian children learnt the language of knowledge with us, not the language of war.' (p.318)

'In addition to deepening humanitarian destruction day by day, the controversy which have continued for 4 years in Syria, exists at a primary position of our agenda in terms of regional security and stability threats.' (p.332)

'As a humanitarian and conscientious responsibility, JDP governments will continue to take sides with our Syrian brothers and sisters (who ran away from the tyranny of the regime and took refuge in our country) during their difficult days and continue to provide necessary aid to relieve them.' (p.332)

'We provide temporary protection to Syrians who took refuge in our country by running away from war and pressure, in the frame of international law. Since April 2011, we have applied open door policy for Syrians. Syrians in our country benefit from the all basic aid and health services. In fact, while the whole international community must take responsibility on refugee issue, our country could not face expected support from economically developed states and international institutions.' (p.336)

'In the geography that our country has a central position, we improved a lot of regional initiatives in the frame of the view composing a zone of peace, stability and welfare. [...] We led the establishment of Syrian People's Friends Group in 2012 to encourage the efforts towards the solution of the conflicts, in tune with Syrian people's legitimate demands.' (p. 340-341)

Republican People's Party's 2015 Election Bulletin

Throughout this topic, I will use Syria related materials in RPP's election bulletin

[7] https://www.bbc.com/news/world-europe-34694420 (Access 1.12.2020)

[8] https://www.akparti.org.tr/media/318795/7-haziran-2015-edited.pdf (Access 20.11.2020)

based on its official website[9] and translate them into English with their page numbers.

'We will remove the mines on Syrian border and distribute them to poor villagers for agricultural purposes.' (p.34)

'We will avoid the unfair competition of Syrians who live in our country with a special statute by working without legal responsibilities or taxes.' (p.58)

'JDP came to power in a positive international atmosphere that our relations with the neighbors had been straightened and powerful actors, especially European Union (EU) and the United States had supported Turkey. Convergence policy with Greece had been formed, Adana Protocol with Syria and Eurasia Protocol with Russia had been signed. Prominent EU members and the United States had tried to abolish the obstacles against accession period to EU. Today Turkey's relations with the neighbors got worse. The relations with EU and the United States reached almost the breaking point. JDP dragged Turkey to a valueless and dangerous loneliness in the region and the world.' (p.171)

'We will support all international initiatives regarding permanent peace and stability in Syria and attempts of United Nations' (UN) Syria Delegate.' (p.182)

'We, as a political party which can negotiate with the fronts of the civil war, will continue to endeavor to bring peace and security to Syria, remembering the friendship of Syrian people.' (p.182)

'We will not be a side of ongoing war in Syria. We will help to create the conditions which are determined by Syrian people, without external interventions to the future of Syria.' (p.182)

'We will vitalize the economic relations between Turkey and Syria again on legal basis.' (p.182)

'We will develop our region and cities by re-constructing them through affirmative economic relations with Syria.' (p.182)

'We will block all assistances towards terrorists in Iraq and Syria, primarily ISIS and will take a certain position against terrorism.' (p.183)

'We will erase the security threats towards our country from terrorist organizations efficient in Iraq and Syria. We will clean terrorist elements in our lands.' (p.183)

'We will prevent Turkish airports and borders from the transformation into a springboard of the terrorists on the way to Iraq and Syria. We will efficiently struggle with domestic components, who mediate passing, in legal ways.' (p.183)

'We will properly welcome the brothers and sisters who took refuge in our country due to the war in Syria, with humanitarian conditions.' (p.183)

---

[9] https://chp.azureedge.net/41d1fed67c144d45b4b3d5f770e3e243.pdf (Access 20.11.2020)

'We will put international institutions in action as soon as possible to cope with the problems derived from the migration wave coming from Syria.' (p.183)

'We will actively support the initiatives carrying on to re-provide necessary peace environment to go back to Syria.' (p.183)

2018 General (Parliamentary) Election in Turkey

Turkey experienced crucial processes in 2018. On 20th January, Afrin Operation was activated towards Syria. On 24th June, presidency and parliamentary elections were held. The new system began with the presidency of Recep Tayyip Erdoğan. Thus 66th Turkish government was established at the same time. According to Supreme Election Council in Turkey, JDP won the parliamentary elections via 42,56 % of votes and after that RPP achieved 22,65 % of votes as the second one. In terms of presidential election results, Recep Tayyip Erdoğan had the majority of the votes as 52,59 % compared to other candidates.[10] Now I will give a place to election bulletins of first two parties.

Justice and Development Party's 2018 Election Bulletin

Throughout this topic, I will use Syria related materials in JDP's election bulletin based on its official website[11] and translate them into English with their page numbers.

'Through Fırat Kalkanı Operation, we erased ISIS from our borders and we blocked terrorist corridor that PYD/YPG wanted to form in north Syria.' (p.45)

'We started Zeytindalı Operation against PKK-PYD/YPG and ISIS terrorist organizations on 20th January 2018 and successfully finalized and cleaned Afrin from terrorist organizations.' (p.45)

'We provided 62 % of Syrian children who are still in our country, to get educated. In the meantime, we will provide all students to go to school.' (p.61)

'We will complete inventory of foundational cultural existence in 10 states of the Ottoman geography (Syria, [...]).' (p.72)

'Our country was exposed to a remarkable migration wave together with the civil war exploded in Syria. During this process which is described as the utmost migration wave in the recent history of the world, Turkey demonstrated humanitarian aid reflex applying open gate policy and became the state which received the most refugees in the world.' (p.134)

'Since the first flows in 2011, we have constructed 26 temporary refugee centers in 10 cities close to Syrian border. We have placed 216.000 Syrians into these centers.' (p.134)

---

[10] https://www.ysk.gov.tr/tr/cumhurbaskani-secim-arsivi/2647 (Access 2.12.2020)

[11] https://www.akparti.org.tr/media/318779/24-haziran-2018-cumhurbaskanligi-secimleri-ve-genel-secimler-secim-beyannamesi-sayfalar.pdf (Access 2.12.2020)

'While total number of Syrian refugees who stay on temporary refugee centers in our country are 277.710, there are total 230.315 Syrian refugees in other states' refugee centers. We present services to 7 % of the refugees (whom we admitted temporary protection status) in temporary refugee centers composed of tents and containers in 10 cities.' (p.134-135)

'Approximately 3,6 million Syrians were registered by 2017 within the scope of temporary protection status. During the ongoing war in Syria, on the one hand we realized our humanitarian mission, while on the other we took serious steps for secure return of the noteworthy proportion.' (p.135)

'We spent 31 billion dollars for our Syrian brothers and sisters.' (p.135)

'We allowed the right for work permit to make Syrian refugees under temporary protection, diminish economic and social dependency and live without deprivation.' (p.135)

'We make refugee brothers and sisters benefit from education opportunities. We educate total 612.000 Syrian refugee students (384.000 in our schools, 227.000 in our temporary centers).' (p.135)

'We certified 18.691 voluntary Syrian instructors with formation education to make them support educational services in temporary education centers.' (p.135)

'We launched Turkish courses, regarding Turkish language education as mass education. We taught language education to 171.000 Syrians between 2015-2017 in these courses.' (p.135)

'We constructed 116.000 square meter sports hall, 51.000 square meter playground in temporary refugee centers to support mental and physical development of Syrian children and youth. We founded more than 1000 multifunctional tent, rest, and internet halls.' (p.136)

'We ensured psychological-social support services to erase the marks of pain, trauma, and war of Syrian brothers and sisters.' (p.136)

'We will provide a secure database system in migration area. We will continue updating studies of more than 3,5 million Syrians' (who are under temporary protection) data. The applications in our country for international protection will be finalized by our decision maker centers with meticulous attention.' (p.137-138)

'We carried our humanitarian aid initiatives out of Turkey as well. We reinforce more than 50 countries in the world. Under the coordination of Disaster and Emergency Management Presidency, we practiced more than 500 internal and external humanitarian and emergency aid activities in the last period. From Syria to [...], we took humanitarian aid to many states.' (p.276)

'Syrian children learnt the language of knowledge with us, not language of war.' (p.276)

'Together with cleaning of North Syria from terrorist elements by Fırat Kalkanı Operation, migration occurred from Syria's several points and from our country to this secure place and the population of this place is over 1 million.' (p.276)

'We successfully maintain our struggle against Syria based terror trouble. We cleaned 4000 km area on Turkey-Syria border from ISIS and PKK/PYD/YPG components. The goal of our efforts at this stage was to create necessary conditions to realize security and stability in this region permanent and not to be a threat towards Turkey again.' (p.291)

'It is essential to protect close collaboration with the United States. The main elements of our cooperation are stopping the support of the United States to PYD/YPG in Syria, the material support to our struggle against PKK, and taking substantial steps for extraditing FETÖ.' (p.295)

'We will sustain close coordination with Russia about regional issues, especially Syria problem.' (p.296)

'Without causing more pain or destruction in 8th year of Syrian controversy, we will retain our efforts to finalize an ultimate political solution based on legitimate demands of Syrian people. Today Turkey proved that it is among effective and efficient actors on Syria problem via 12 observation plots which were formed to decrease the tensions in the field, counter-terrorism troops, and active contribution.' (p.297)

'We will endeavor for a new Syria goal which comes together with millions of people had to flee his or her country, which reaches democratic and legitimate administration with peace and stability that preserves its territorial and political unity. Our wish will be to launch a new era of our relations based on historical, cultural, and humane linkages with Syrian people and to re-constitute our neighborhood relation and cooperation with new Syria.' (p.297)

'In addition to bilateral relations, we will continue close diplomatic relation with Iran during the peace process in the Middle East, especially Syria.' (p.298)

'We provide temporary protection in the frame of international law to Syrians who took refuge in our country running away from war and pressure.' Since April 2011, we have applied open door policy for Syrians.' (p.301)

'Today we host approximately 3.6 million Syrian guests in our country. We established 20 temporary refugee centers in our 10 cities. We present services 7/24 hours to our Syrian guests on education, health, security, religious services, etc. in temporary refugee centers. Actually while the whole international community must take responsibilities on refugees, our country could not face the expected support from economically developed states and international institutions.' (p.301-302)

'While we have been perpetuating our historical and conscientious responsibility and humanitarian view for ages towards needy indigent persons, we sustain to accompany with our Syrian brothers and sisters.' (p.302)

'We provide temporary protection to Syrians which took refuge in our country in tune with international law. We make them benefit from basic services including education, health, access to business market. We keep Syrian refugee issue on agenda in the international realm. We highlight international community must do their share in the frame of sharing burden and responsibilities.' (p.302)

'Turkish language education towards Syrians is still proceeding.' (p.304)

'We will implement special scholarship and education programs to raise qualified human source who can be assigned in the process of re-construction towards crisis regions like Syria, Yemen, Afghanistan.' (p.307)

'By reminding the world is bigger than 5, as in Syria, […] on peace and security issues, we will continue to be follower for bureaucratic reform concerning UN Secretary and UN Charter. Our aim is democratization of global system and transformation of UN into a global peace assurance.' (p.309)

Republican People's Party's 2018 Election Bulletin

Throughout this topic, I will use Syria related materials in RPP's election bulletin based on its official website[12] and translate them into English with their page numbers.

'Single man diplomacy caused loss of reputation of our country as the member in the eyes of all those institutions. Turkey have problems with almost all neighbors. Our country was involved in a status of crisis-produced-state, far away from solution-produced-state in the region. Palace diplomacy which approached the Arab Spring as opportunist and expansionist, caused a tremendous Syrian refugee migration due to following adventurous policies. Syrian refugee crisis became a serious matter due to not only humanitarian tragedies, but also economic cost imposed to our country.' (p.27)

'Territorial integrity of Iraq and Syria […] are our major objectives.' (p.119)

'We will end utilizing Syrian refugees for the relations with Europe as a leverage ignoring human rights.' (p.121)

'Derived from region-centered foreign policy approach, we will form the Organization of Peace and Cooperation in the Middle East that Iran, Iraq, Syria and Turkey will be founder members.' (p.124)

'We will support all international peace initiatives (towards welfare of our friends Syrian people and territorial integrity of Syria) and the practices of UN Syria Delegate.' (p.125)

'We will support a political solution as Syrian people's own decision, after the stability in Syria and after disarmament of non-governmental actors.' (p.125)

'After the peaceful solution in Syria, we will ensure a secure return incrementally, if Syrians under temporary protection in our country wish, without aggrieving them.' (p.125)

'We will take a certain position against terror in Syria. We will purify our lands from terrorist elements extinguishing security threats which were created by terrorist organizations towards our country.' (p.125)

---

[12] http://secim2018.chp.org.tr/files/CHP-SecimBildirgesi-2018-icerik.pdf?v=3 (Access 2.12.2020)

'We will take care of assistances towards Syrians under temporary protection to be transparent and controllable. We will provide the supervision of assistances by Turkish legal system and independent institutions.' (p.126)

'We will hamper unregistered working of Syrians, especially children with unacceptable conditions.' (p.126)

'We will ensure successfully completion of Turkish Armed Forces' mission in Syria as soon as possible, supporting necessary diplomatic steps.' (p.126)

'We will inhibit unfair competition of Syrians by working without taxes and legal responsibilities.' (p.195)

'Organization of Peace and Cooperation in the Middle East: With the purpose of improvement peace, fraternity, and trade in the Middle East, an organization for regional cooperation will be established that Turkey, Iraq, Iran, and Syria will be founder members.' (p.229)

Conclusion

During this article, I attempted to reflect the election bulletins of first two political parties (based on election results). By doing so, we are able to face their official goals, programs, future vision, promises, and critics. In terms of Syria and Syrian refugees, I looked for the answer whether Justice and Development Party and Republican People's Party concern about Syria issue or not. This purpose directed me to search their statements between two important elections of Turkey. The years 2015 and 2018 were crucial for Turkey on the one hand, they had separations inside, especially systematic separation on the other. Hence throughout this study, we can see not only time factor from the Arab Spring and civil war in Syria to 2018, but also political, ideological, perspective differences of those parties. Thus there are two main pillars to take into consideration.

One key point about the consequences of this article is that JDP was always in power between 2015-2018, while RPP was the main opponent party. Therefore, their discourses have been under the impacts of their position in the state. Similarly, when we look at the related articles, JDP mostly mentioned their achievements on Syria issue and their similar vision regarding the future promises. On the contrary, RPP as the opponent side, frequently explained the critics on Syria issue towards JPP governments. Furthermore, these two parties' future visions are different as well. RPP's rhetoric seem focused on a secure return of Syrian refugees actually. In addition, the number of JDP's Syria related articles in 2015 was 6, while RPP gave place 14 articles in the same year. However, in contrast, 32 articles included Syria issue in JDP's 2018 bulletin, while RPP wrote 13 articles in this respect. To conclude, this study indicated objective results concerning the relationship between Syrian issue and Turkish political parties' perspectives, without speculation. The future will show us whether the scenarios will be justified or not. Probably the most affirmative consequence might be a mutual solution for both Turkey and Syrian refugees.

CHAPTER 15

THE IMPACT OF IMMIGRATION ON URBAN PLANNING IN TURKEY

Levent Uzunçıbuk[1]

Introduction

The rapidly increasing population in the world brings the problem of migration to the forefront together with urbanization, industrialization, war, violence, conflict, exile, exchange, political prosecution, economy, disaster and environmental problems. In addition, cities are seen as places where the people they host are secured, live their lives and contribute to production. In this context, one of the purposes of urban planning is to make the living spaces of the residents livable and to increase their living standards. On the other hand, it shows that the transformation processes of the countries that started in their own urban areas are also affected by the migration movements in the urban dimension. The fact that these two situations, in other words, the country, that is, cities are located in the intersection cluster of space and migration movements, made it necessary to examine the dimension of migration movement affecting urbanization.

Today, it is seen that world cities are frequently exposed to immigration movements where people have to change their environment due to the negativities created by the changing conditions of the day. While some of these migration movements manifest themselves within the territory of the country they live in, some of them manifest themselves in the form of rapid and unplanned urbanization in the territories outside the country. The formation of places that cause an increase in urban violence and crime around the world, as well as the widespread fear of these incidents regarding life safety, prevents economic investments in countries from being made and stopping. Examples of these features are urban gang conflicts that are common in Africa, Latin America and the Caribbean. Again, all of the terrorist attacks in New York, Madrid, London, Istanbul and Ankara, as well as the recent violence in the suburbs of Paris and throughout the city, showed that cities in developed and developing countries are also vulnerable. However, many people, including nearly one billion people living in cities around the world and currently living in slums, lack job security and at least two million people are forced to evacuate and migrate each year for various reasons. Their lives are affected by poor housing conditions, particularly vulnerable women and children who have to be forced to evacuate and migrate for their safety. The fact that such migration evictions are made in the name of urban development without considering

[1] Dr. Lecturer, T.R. İstanbul AREL University, Faculty of Economics and Administrative Sciences, Political Science and Public Administration lecturer, Türkiye. E-mail: luzuncibuk@arel.edu.tr.

alternative accommodation conditions and with little thought about the consequences, shows that these people will increase social exclusion and potential urban criminals. For example, the situation of refugees from Syria and other countries coming or brought to our big cities such as Istanbul, Ankara, Izmir, Adana. On the other hand, there is a very tight link between natural events and human safety and security in settlements. It is observed that the vulnerability of cities has increased due to climate change and earthquakes that accelerate extreme air currents and the rise of average sea levels, while at the same time urban slums face floods, landslides, industrial pollution and other dangers. For these reasons, it should be kept in mind that urban planning and governance play a key role in making our cities safe and secure for future generations.

The fact that the environment in which a person lives with other people changes according to the changing conditions of the day, wants to secure his future and live in safer places forces him to migrate. In this context, Europe, Asia and Africa to take place in the north, west and south of the Black Sea, is surrounded by the Aegean and Mediterranean Turkey have brought to the center of international migration path. Our country, which has been the scene of internal and external migration movements for years, received more than five million immigrants from the Balkans, Caucasus and Crimea between 1821 and 1922, especially in the last years of the Ottoman Empire.[2] On the other hand, 'UN High Commissioner for Refugees (UNHCR)' stated in the 2019 Global Trends Report that those who left their homes or homes, in other words, refugees were 79 million 500 people, corresponding to 1% of the world population. At the same time, although an average of 1 million 500 thousand people returned to their place of origin in the 1990s, it has been observed that the refugees who have returned in the last ten years are under 400 thousand.[3] Turkey Statistical Institute (TSI), 'Address Based Population Registration System 2019 Results' 83 million 154 thousand 997 persons of the population according to, while the proportion of people living in the provinces and districts stated that 92.8%.[4] Internal and external migrations affect the social structure in our country as well as urbanization, in other words, urban planning.

Definitions and concepts are required in order to be able to think, to synthesize or analyze by providing the connection between objects, events and abstract positions, to speak the same language and to create a unity of meaning.[5] Therefore, it is beneficial to explain the basic definitions and concepts in order to better understand the relationship between urban planning and the impact of migration.

---

[2] Yusuf Adıgüzel, **Göç Sosyolojisi**, Ankara, Nobel Akademik Yayıncılık Eğitim Danışmanlık Tic. Ltd. Şti. Ankara, 2020, p.iii.

[3] https://www.dw.com/tr/d%C3%BCnyan%C4%B1n-y%C3%BCzde-1i-yerinden-edildi/a-53855540 (Access 13.11.2020).

[4] https://www.aa.com.tr/tr/turkiye/turkiyenin-nufusu-83-milyon-154-bin-997-kisiye-ulasti/1723520 (Access 13.11.2020).

[5] Mehmet Ali Kılıçbay, **Şehirler ve Kentler**, Ankara, İmge Kitabevi, 2000, p. 13.

Definition and Concepts

After explaining the definitions and concepts related to urban planning and migration separately, it will be easier to establish the interaction relationship between them.

City Concept

Human beings live on a space (space), a piece of land. This piece of space where they live, in other words, the settlement unit is called 'city' or 'village'. Some groups of people live in areas that share the common characteristics of cities and villages. For this reason, there are different opinions about what a city and a village are and how they are defined. Certain criteria are used in the definitions of city and village, which we cannot always clearly distinguish from each other. One of these criteria is the administrative limit criterion. Accordingly, a city is a place within the boundaries of a certain administrative organization unit. The village is defined as the areas outside these boundaries. Generally, the population within the municipality boundaries is referred to as the 'urban population'. Sometimes, in addition to this population within the borders of the municipality, other local government units are also counted within the city.

Turkey Statistical Institute (TÜİK) in the broadcast, to be seen as provincial and district population of the urban population in our country can be said that the criterion adopted in the administrative boundaries of towns and villages organization distinction. For example, according to TÜİK's 2018 Address-Based Population Registration Statistics, Konya's Yalıhöyük district with a population of 1,785 has the right to be counted as cities as the city of Istanbul with a population of 15,067,724, where 18.4% of the country's population lives.

Another criterion used in the definition of the city is the population criterion. Accordingly, while settlements that exceed a certain population level are called cities, others are called villages. For example, Article 1 of the Village Law No. 442, published in the Official Gazette dated 07.04.1924 and numbered 68, refers to 'dormitories (villages) with a population less than two thousand and those with a population between two thousand and twenty thousand (towns) and those with a population of more than twenty thousand (cities). Even if the population is less than two thousand, the townships, townships and provincial centers with municipal organizations are regarded as towns. And it is subject to the Municipality Law. ' as in the phrase. On the other hand, using only the population criterion in the distinction between cities and villages may result in not counting the settlements that have acquired an urban character as urban, although they remain below the population level that determines the criteria.

In order to eliminate this negativity, mixed criteria, which are added to the population criterion, which is the basis for the distinction between city and village, are used in many countries.

Another criterion used in the definitions is observed to be based on economic criteria. The city is seen as an economic mechanism that emerges to meet the constantly changing needs of the society during the production, distribution and consumption of goods and services. Apart from this general definition, the fact that a settlement can be called a 'city' generally seems to depend on the population working in non-agricultural sectors. In other words, settlements have to be named as cities or villages according to the population ratios in and out of agriculture.

The criterion used in the definition of another city is the social scientific criterion. According to them, the city is 'a group of people and structures that have come together in a manner that can be regarded as widely according to the place and time and has some distinctive features'. For example, the city descriptions made by Queen and Carpenter, one of the American sociologists, are like this. Similarly, in sociologist Louis Wirth, the city is 'relatively large, densely populated, and the space is a permanent settlement, formed by individuals who are not socially similar.' he defined. Characteristics such as a certain population density, density, division of labor, specialization and non-homogeneity are seen as common features of the city definitions made by sociologists.

Today, it is seen that the defined urban and village distinction is insufficient. In other words, the city and the village may have some mixed features. The village, which is a small settlement, is always a town and a candidate to become a city later on. Given this situation, it is likely that a community is not counted as either a village or a city, but rather as more rural or more urban than another. It is not correct to attribute the distinction between urban and village life to a single feature. It is the result of a number of properties with tightly coupled functional links. If a distinction is to be made between cities and villages, all interrelationships and functional connections must be taken into account.

The boundaries of the village and the start and end of the city boundaries are of great importance in urban planning. Especially geographers, sociologists and urban planners seem to take into account a 'rural-urban continum' since they cannot make a clear social and physical distinction between village and city. However, another concept used in the cascade of settlements is the 'metropolis (metropole)', which is generally accepted to be not smaller than 250 thousand inhabitants and varies according to countries and is also called a big city or main city. Large cities, which cannot be confined within their own borders, form a 'whole' with the surrounding settlements, large and small. On the other hand, the settlements that do not have a physical union with the city center, but which are in its close sphere of influence, integrate with their economic and social aspects and form the 'metropolitan region', in other words, the 'metropolitan region'. We can give New York, Paris, London, Tokyo and Istanbul to metropolitan areas. Urbanized residential areas, which are formed by the combination of large city regions that provide a suitable environment for urban planning, are called 'many large urban regions (megalopolis). It is a vast geographical region that is formed end-to-end by more than one densely industrialized large city region, which is generally a continuous and continuous city. A classic example of this is the hundreds of kilometers long urbanized region stretching from Washington to Boston on the north-east coast of the United States.

In another example, it is the geographical region on the strip of Tokyo, Nagoya and Osaka, which constitutes the east coast of the Japanese islands. On the other hand, a final concept is that the geographical region that is formed by the transformation of the whole earth into an uninterrupted urban area in the future with the continuation of today's urbanization movements with today's speed is called Ecumenopolis. It is predicted that there will be open and green areas in the form of small islands among the cities with a population of 100-150 million in the mentioned settlement area and the building masses in these areas.[6]

After the criterion explanations above, 'the city is in constant social development, where the needs of the society such as settlement, accommodation, going and going, working, resting, entertainment are met, few people are engaged in agricultural activities, looking at the villages, which is more dense in terms of population and consists of small neighborhood units settlement unit'.[7]

Urban Planning

Until today, urban planning has been defined in various ways. One of these definitions is by the famous urban scientist Thomas Adams; It is a definition made as 'a science, an art and a field of occupation that deals with the problems of giving a direction to the shaping of the physical needs of cities, taking into account social and economic needs'. Another definition was made by Harvey S. Perloff and expressed as 'the name given to planning actions that concern all urbanized areas covered by large metropolitan regions, smaller urban communities, and the core of a large city'. Another definition was made by JT Howard and 'evaluates urban planning as giving direction to the change of urban areas and with this characteristic, it is more advanced in the physical arrangement and shaping of urban planning action, buildings, roads, parks, public institutions and other elements of the physical existence of the city. He also stated that some of the outgoing social and economic goals were directed to the realization. However, in another definition, S.F. Chapin and expressed as 'prudence' used to achieve predetermined goals for urban planning, the growth and development of urban areas.

On the other hand, a new concept of 'Environmental Planning' has emerged in recent years, which has a broad scope to include the concepts of urban planning and regional planning.

It seems that the word 'urbanism', which is settled and used today in our country, includes a wide range of urban, regional and rural planning types, and therefore keeping this discipline at the forefront in terms of not reducing the discipline to a mere planning action seems to eliminate the confusion to a bit.[8] In this context, urban planning, regional, environmental plan and national development plan, the city's planning not only in terms of land use, but also in terms of economic, social and demographic aspects, is defined as the field of science and

---

[6] Ruşen Keleş, **Kentleşme Politikası**, Ankara, İmge Kitabevi, 2002, pp. 105-109.
[7] Ruşen Keleş, **Kentbilim Terimleri Sözlüğü**, Ankara, İmge Kitabevi, 1998, p. 75.
[8] Ruşen Keleş, **Kentleşme Politikası**, pp. 109-112.

application that acquires this business.[9] Urbanization, on the other hand, is the process of population accumulation, which results in the increase in the number of cities and the growth of cities in parallel with operationalization and economic development, increasing organization and specialization in the society, and urban-specific changes in inter-human relations.[10]

The Concept of Governance

It is said that today's interest in the concept of governance emerged with the use of the term governance in reference to the changes in the state towards the end of the 20th century and these changes started with the neoliberal public reforms in the 1980s. Literally, governance means 'a state, organization, etc. It is defined as 'the style or activity to govern and to govern' as well as to govern and control. The concept of governance, which is expressed to be derived from the Greek verb 'to manage (kubernao)', finds different focus and application areas depending on the context. Therefore, different disciplines examine the governance discourse in the literature by drawing attention to different meanings, methods and processes. For example, while political scientists use governance as a synonym for government, in the international relations literature it is perceived as global governance beyond nation-states. On the other hand, governance is defined as the internal powers, qualities and functions of the government as a state in the comparative political literature. However, it is stated that with the multi-layered structures of the European Union emerging at transnational, regional, national, local and different levels, new forms of governance are widespread and managed.[11]

Along with this, governance is also expressed as a process formed by actors who are related to each other and whose interests conflict, that matches different structures. At the same time, governance is also defined as a process of directing and controlling the actors in the society as stakeholders, in other words, a phenomenon that occurs as a result of the actions of different actors and the interaction of different economic, political and social factors.[12] In this context, it is necessary to consider a wide range of actors, starting from individuals, including private entrepreneurs, non-governmental organizations, foundations, non-profit organizations, cooperatives, local governments, central government organizations.[13]

Migration

It has been observed that migration, which is generally perceived as a population movement, is the cause and result of many structural changes at the individual and

---

[9] Ruşen Keleş, **Kentbilim Terimleri Sözlüğü**, pp. 82-83.

[10] Ruşen Keleş, op.cit, p. 80.

[11] Ebru Tekin Bilbil, **Yönetişim ve Yönetimsellik Kentsel Mekan ve Ortam**, Ankara, Siyasal Kitabevi, 2019, pp. 21-22.

[12] Sami Sezai Ural, Aigerim Shilibekova, **Uluslararası Güvenlik ve Yönetişim**, Uluslararası Güvenlik Yeni Politikalar, Stratejiler ve Yaklaşımlar, İstanbul, Beta Basım A.Ş. 2016, p. 11.

[13] BM İnsan Yerleşimleri Konferansı Habitat II, **Türkiye Ulusal Rapor ve Eylem Planı**, İstanbul Habitat II Kent Zirvesi, 1996, p. 80.

social level. Despite its different characteristics over time, migration has always been a dynamic factor affecting the social and urban structure. At the basis of the phenomenon of migration is the act of relocation. In this context, when the definitions of migration are examined, it will be seen that the common element is the displacement, although there are some differences. One definition of migration is the permanent or semi-permanent displacement, another definition is the displacement of people over a geography. It has been observed that the demographic descriptions made in the form of migration, population movement from one place to another place are insufficient. Migration, which is seen as a displacement movement, is known to interact with the individual and society living in the destination, together with the relationship of cause and effect. In this respect, it should not be forgotten that the migration movement is not only a movement of relocation, but also affects and changes the structure of society and lifestyle over time. A general definition of migration is made as a geographical, social and cultural displacement movement from one place to another for economic, political, ecological and individual reasons, aiming for short, medium or long term return or permanent settlement.[14] On the other hand, individuals' leaving their home country to settle permanently or to live for a certain period of time and go to another country temporarily or permanently is defined as 'international migration'. At the same time, being in another country (transit country) in transit to leave one country and go to another country is called 'transit migration', and the migrants who will transit are called 'transit migrants'. On the other hand, immigration is classified as 'regular immigration' and 'irregular immigration' according to its legal status. Individuals or communities entering, staying and leaving a country other than the country of their legal citizenship are considered as 'regular immigration', illegal entry, stay and exit of individuals or communities in a country other than their country of citizenship is defined as 'immigration'.

In other words, when foreigners entering Turkey via legal means, stay and exit from Turkey orderly migration, however, the entry of Turkey to the roads of illegal foreigners, stay and exit to and unauthorized operation is also called irregular migration and covers international protection.[15]

Immigrant

In general, an immigrant is the name given to an individual, family or social cluster who goes from one country to another to settle.[16] However, it is stated that the term immigrant covers all situations in which a person takes the decision to emigrate with his own free will and for personal comfort. In this context, the term migrant has been accepted as valid for the individual and his family who travel to another country or region in order to improve their financial and social conditions and improve their expectations with their family. On the other hand, the United Nations defines the immigrant as an individual residing in a foreign country for

[14] Mahmut Gürsoy, **Göç ve Kentleşme Bağlamında Suç**, Ankara, Gece Akademi, 2019, pp. 19-22.

[15] Yusuf Adıgüzel, op.cit, pp. 3-4.

[16] Ruşen Keleş, Kentbilim Terimleri Sözlüğü, p. 59.

more than one year, regardless of their reasons, volunteering, migration routes, regular or irregularity.[17] However, although the terms immigrant and refugee are often used in the same sense, there is an important legal difference between these two terms. The different use of these two terms, and their confusion with another discourse may cause problems for refugees and asylum seekers, as well as misunderstandings about migration movements.[18] Therefore, it will be useful to explain the concepts of refugee and asylum seeker.

Refugee and Asylum Seeker

Defined and protected by international law, a refugee is defined as a person or persons who are outside their country of origin and, as a result, seek 'international protection' in cases of persecution, conflict, attack or other seriously disturbing social peace. Because their situation is often very dangerous and irresistible, they have been forced out of their countries to seek security in countries in the vicinity. Hence, these people become 'refugees' with the support of the countries, United Nations High Commissioner for Refugees (UNHCR) and related organizations. It is a known fact that these people, who had to take shelter in another place because it is very dangerous for them to return to their homeland, may face potentially fatal consequences if their asylum requests are not accepted from the country of destination.[19] However, in the 1951 Geneva Convention Relating to the Status of Refugees, a refugee who is outside the country of which he is a citizen and cannot benefit from the protection of this country because he is justly afraid of being persecuted due to his race, religion, nationality, membership of a certain social group or political opinion, or the said fear It is defined as a foreigner who does not want to take advantage of it because of such events, or a person who is outside of the country where he previously lived as a result of such events, cannot return there or does not want to return because of the fear. At the same time, if a refugee leaves the host country and moves to another country, he continues to be a refugee and cannot become an immigrant.

However, an asylum seeker is defined as a person waiting to be accepted as a refugee in a country within the framework of relevant national or international documents and waiting for the result of their application regarding their refugee status. In case their application is not accepted by the relevant country, they can be deported like any foreigner.[20]

Related Legislation and Organizations With Migration in Turkey

Our country, which has been faced with serious immigration movements from the beginning of the 1900s to the present, wanted to control and manage this

---

[17] Yusuf Adıgüzel, op.cit, pp. 4-5.
[18] BMMYK, https://www.unhcr.org/cy/wp-content/uploads/sites/41/2018/02/UNHCR_Refugee_or_Migrant_TR.pdf (Access 16.11.2020).
[19] BMMYK, https://www.unhcr.org/cy/wp-content/uploads/sites/41/2018/02/UNHCR_Refugee_or_Migrant_TR.pdf (Access 16.11.2020).
[20] Yusuf Adıgüzel, op.cit, p. 5-6.

movement of relocation with settlement policies. In the legal arrangements made in the early periods of the Republic, immigration was not free, controlled and compulsory and the use of the settlement institution to restore order shows the importance of urban planning. Starting from the first years of the Republic, the settlement laws that have been applied until today, the Settlement Law numbered 885 published in the Official Gazette dated 01.07.1926 and numbered 409, the Settlement Law numbered 2510 published in the Official Gazette dated April 21, 1934 and numbered 2733 and We can list the Settlement Law No. 5543. In our country, immigrants, the first legislation regarding refugees and asylum seekers, asylum and immigration for Turkey to regulate the movement of iskânlar countries coming to our country in 1934 and 2510 'Housing Law' is counted. The purpose of the Settlement Law No. 5543, which entered into force in 2006; It is to regulate the settlement activities of immigrants, nomads, those whose places have been expropriated, the conditions and measures to be taken regarding the arrangement of physical settlement in villages, the rights and obligations of the settled.

It is seen that in the settlement laws applied in our country, there are predominantly provisions regarding the settlement order, and there are no provisions regarding international protection / asylum. 1990s business and operations related to the foreigners outside the scope of the mid to far applied settled law, transactions relating to international protection in other words, when 7/24/1950 day and 7564 numbered published in the Official Gazette No. 5682 'Passport Act' 5683 'Foreigners in Turkey The Law on Residence and Travels'. However, Turkey, in 1961, the Geneva Convention Relating to the Status of Refugees of 1951, and became a party to the Protocol on the Status of Refugees in 1968. In this context, entering Turkey by foreigners, the establishment of rules and procedures and the Interior Ministry Immigration Administration General Directorate for Turkey in the residence and the output from Turkey who demand protection from Turkey within the scope of the protection granted to foreigners and implementation, duties, powers and responsibilities Law No. 6458 on Foreigners and International Protection was published in the Official Gazette No. 28615 on 11.04.2013 and entered into force one year later.[21] Also in 2016, entered Turkey by foreigners, indicating residence and the principles and procedures regarding the principles edit the purpose of the implementation of the 6458 numbered Law and principles for the output from Turkey within the scope of the protection granted to foreigners who demand protection from Turkey and implementation in Turkey, 'Foreign and The Regulation on the Implementation of International Protection Law' was issued. However, we can briefly list the legal regulations implemented in our country within the scope of combating irregular immigration and in order to comply with the 'European Union (EU)' acquis;

- '1994 Asylum Regulation',

- 'Regulations on Border Management in the Context of Integrated Border

[21] İbid., p. 16.

Management',

- 'Asylum-Migration Action Plan on Asylum and Migration Task Force and Turkey's Action Plan'

- 'Turkey's Asylum and Migration Legislation and Administrative Capacity Development and Implementation Bureau',

- It is a 'Readmission Agreement'.[22] On the other hand, it is observed that the operations regarding foreigners carried out by the security forces, military and police, are carried out by the Directorate General of Migration Management, which is a civilian authority established by Law No. 6458.[23]

Reasons for Migration and Migration Movements in Turkey

Considering migration movements in Turkey, sometimes migration, which sometimes migrate, sometimes as a transit country, it is observed that there is a continuum of internal and external migration. In our country, especially the migration movements that took place since the 19th century are evaluated in the period of three important migration waves in proportion to the deep traces they left in the social development process. These;

a) 'The arrival of immigrants in the last years of the Ottoman Empire and the Early Republic period',

b) 'Worker migration to Europe in 1960's and 1970's' second wave of immigration,

c) 'New immigrants such as refugees, transit migrants, luggage traders, women houseworkers, European retirees, highly skilled people who came to big cities, especially from Istanbul, from neighboring geographies after 1990' can be counted as the third migration wave.

However, it is possible to qualify the mass migration movement, which started in 2011 and resulted very slowly in our country with its political, economic and social aspects, as a fourth wave of immigration.[24] On the other hand, we see that the historical periods of migration movements in our country are evaluated in four categories. These are also:

a) Balkanization migrations; Mass migration movements from the geographies where the Ottoman lost land to Anatolia between 1860-1867

b) Urbanization period; It is the period that started from 1945 with the end of the Second World War and continued until the 1980s, covering migrations from

---

[22] Aygül Kılınç, **Hukuksal ve Kurumsal Altyapısıyla Türkiye'de Göç Yönetimi,** https://www.researchgate.net/publication/331687773_HUKUKSAL_VE_KURUMSAL_ALTYAPISIYLA_TURKIYE'DE_GOC_YONETIMI (Access 16.11.2020).

[23] Yusuf Adıgüzel, op.cit, p. 17.

[24] Aygül Kılınç, op.cit,

rural to urban.

c) Urban migrations; It is the process that has dominated since 1975 with the urbanization reaching a certain level.

d) Life routes; It was thought that the change in the relationship between people and space is insufficient to define with the concept of migration.

It is stated that today's people change places in their lives, and it has been developed to explain that they can plan some of these routes.[25]

On the other hand, the basic starting point of migration movements is the desire of people to seek the better, the more reliable. Generally, natural disasters, economic reasons, wars, fear of persecution, etc. Events are considered among the reasons for migration. It is seen that the work of countries to regulate and prevent or control migration movements that take place at national and international levels is a matter of their own and requires international cooperation, coordination and solidarity.[26] In this context, Turkey also start acting on the basic factors of population growth of internal migration, the development of agricultural techniques, fragmented agricultural land, erosion, land expropriation studies, development projects, the development of the manufacturing sector, the development of transportation, we can cite as terrorism and earthquakes. In this context, although there are differences between regions and periods, we can say that the factors that trigger the urbanization process and urban planning are generally the driving force of the countryside and the attractive power of the cities as a tool that facilitates migration movements.[27]

Especially in the urbanization process between 1950s and 1980s in our country, the changes caused by rapid population growth and mechanization in agriculture affected the countryside and it is seen that migration to the cities occurred as a result of the deterioration of the living standards of a large mass. These migration movements have created new problems in urban space and the accommodation needs of those who migrated at the beginning of these emerged. Since the housing in the cities could not be met with economic and bureaucratic measures, a growing housing deficit emerged. In urban planning, it is not foreseen that immigration movements can affect the cities negatively, and as a result of the measures that could not be taken in time, political, economic and social inadequacies and the housing deficit were tried to be eliminated, and as a result, it is seen that unplanned housing, destruction of green areas and land speculation in and around cities.[28] The importance of the public administration, which has gained experience in immigration, to have an action plan against any possible migration movements and

---

[25] Yusuf Adıgüzel, op.cit, pp. 38-39.

[26] Mustafa Kara, Canan Öykü Dönmez Kara, Türkiye'de Göç Yönetişimi: Kurumsal Yapı ve İşbirliği, pp. 2-3.

[27] Ahmet Koyuncu, **Kentleşme ve Göç**, İstanbul, Hikmetevi Yayınları, 2015, pp. 50-51.

[28] Sevinç Bahar Yenigül, **Göçün Kent Mekanı Üzerine Etkileri**, G.Ü Fen Bilimleri Dergisi, Cilt. 18, Sayı. 2, 2005, pp. 273-274

to articulate or integrate it with urban planning has shown the negative effects of immigrants from Syria, especially in our big cities.

The Effects of Migrant on Urbanizatıon and Urban Planning

Today, the most important effect of mass migration movements in settlements is the unplanned growth of cities, as in the past. The demand for residence, especially as a result of intense migration, brings up the problem of insufficient housing in cities. The gradual increase of the population also increases the demand for housing, which creates speculation on land, causing an increase in housing prices and rents, and many migrants with economic insufficiencies go out of the city or to places with lower standards. In general, migrants who go to regions where urban services are not available, build unauthorized and low-standard residences (shanty houses) in order to continue their lives, and as a result, affect the uncontrolled spread of the city and social and spatial separation in the city. These cosmopolitan and dynamic places attract new immigrants in the city and have an effect on the concentration of poverty in these regions by forming immigrant neighborhoods of the city.

The housing problem has also constituted one of the important residences addressed by politics. Increasing the weight of the immigrant population with slums in the big cities such as Ankara, Istanbul and Izmir, starting from the 1970s, caused these settlements to be seen as a vote store. The efforts of these groups to articulate the city and to improve the quality of life in the areas they live in have been secretly or explicitly supported by different political parties as an important electoral investment. For example, the fact that parties such as the Republican People's Party in the 1970s, the Motherland Party in the 1980s, and the Welfare / Virtue Party in the 1990s came to the city administrations as the parties that emphasized the issues of legitimizing slums and bringing them together with urban services, among other factors. When the aforementioned reasons combined the encouraging and protective attitudes of politicians in the parliament and local governments towards the phenomenon of slums, which they adopted as an election investment, the number of slums increased rapidly.[29] Rapid slums have negatively affected urban planning. In this context, while migration brings about a spatial change, it also causes significant changes in the social, cultural, political and economic lives of people. These changes are observed not only in the places where the migration movement ends but also where it started.[30]

Fleeing Syria from internal conflict on 29 April 2011, starting with a group of 252 people mass forced migration results for Turkey 3,646,889 person to be registered as of 03/14/2019, from foreign policy issues rather than into the agenda as an internal matter came and became the subject of public policies. The sudden population growth caused by this mass migration movement has affected multiple policy areas such as education, health, access to labor force, housing problem,

[29] Sevinç Bahar Yenigül, op.cit., pp. 283-286.
[30] Ayşegül Kılınç, op.cit.

housing and security. This was the first refugee groups adopted by the beginning Turkey, 'Disaster and Emergency Management Presidency (AFAD)' has been inserted into a guest house created by the case of a rapid increase in the number by AFAD 'Temporary Accommodation Centers (TAC)' camps have been established with other discourse. The number of TACs, which reached 8 in the first year, has spread to 10 over time, reaching 26. The increase in the number of people placed in camps has strained the capacities of the camps. As of 2015, it was stated that 35 thousand people were accommodated in camps with 25 thousand people and many people had to live outside the camps due to insufficient capacity. It is observed that 96% of Syrians who migrated due to crowded camps and other reasons live outside the camps. In the camps, many social services such as education, healthcare, dishwashing and laundry are provided. However, Syrians, who try to continue their lives outside the camps by dispersing to provinces in our country, seem to stay in unhealthy rental houses, rooms, parks and shops.

In the report published by AFAD in 2013, it was stated that Syrians outside the camps live under crowded conditions, 74% of these people live in houses and apartments, but the rest are in ruined buildings, public buildings, tent temporary shelter / plastic protection or street and open, they lived in areas. Again, according to the results given in AFAD's report in 2017, it can be concluded that the rates have increased adversely. According to this, 62.40% of Syrians outside the camps live in houses and flats, 31.50% live in ruined buildings, others live in makeshift shelters, tents and open spaces.[31] For example, as of 14/03/2019, the number of Syrian refugees who registered 3,646,889 people, added 4.45% to the population of Turkey and our population became 82,003,889. In this context, the distribution of registered Syrian migrants according to some provinces is given in Table-1.

However, the Syrian mass migration movement in which our country is living has brought the necessity of rational management due to the urban, social, economic and similar severe social consequences, especially the security risk that it will create in the public sphere. On the one hand, the effort of our country, which is following the EU membership process, to harmonize the legislation with the EU legislation; On the other hand, this almost unprecedented mass migration pressure caused by the Syrian Crisis has confronted our country with the reality of seriously reconsidering all aspects of migration management and producing an effective and functional migration policy.[32]

[31] Nagihan Önder, **Türkiye'de Geçici Koruma Altındaki Suriyelilere Yönelik Sağlık Politikalarının Analizi,** Göç Araştırmaları Dergisi, Cilt. 5, Sayı. 1, Ocak-Haziran 2019, pp. 125-126.
[32] Aygül Kılınç, op.cit.

Table 1. Distribution of Syrians Under Temporary Protection by Some Provinces[33]

PROVINCE ORDER NO	PROVINCES	REGISTERED SYRIAN	PROVINCIAL POPULATION	POPULATION RATE ADDED TO THE PROVINCIAL POPULATION
1	İstanbul	559.731	15.067.724	3.71%
2	Şanlıurfa	451.501	2.035.809	22,18%
3	Hatay	439.450	1.609.856	27,30%
4	Gaziantep	428.748	2.028.563	21,14%
5	Adana	237.830	2.220.125	10,71%
6	Mersin	205.748	1.814.468	11,34%
7	Bursa	170.016	2.994.521	5,68%
8	İzmir	143.642	4.320.519	3,32%
9	Kilis	117.523	142.821	82,25%
10	Konya	106.485	2.205.609	4,83%
11	Ankara	90.652	5.503.985	1,65%

General Evaluation and Conclusion

The most important factors affecting the demand for housing in urban planning in our country have been rapid population growth and accelerated urbanization and migration movements especially since the 1950s. With the increase in the population, the need for shelter, which is among the physiological needs of the person, has also increased. Migration from the village to the city is one of the most important effects that cause this increase. We can list the reasons for this migration phenomenon as the repulsion of the countryside, the attractiveness of the city and the structural changes in the family structure in the rural areas.[34]

Today, the Directorate General of Migration Management is a public institution that coordinates migration activities in our country, monitors practices and directs migration policies. It is observed that the number of immigrants from Syria is increasing gradually with the informal and continuing arrivals. It should be borne in mind that the majority of the migrants in question are not likely to return, even if the conflicts in Syria end. In this context, if Syrian migrants are settled in cities to form a ghetto; It should not be forgotten that it may cause segregation in the society, prevent their adaptation and cause violent reactions and disrupt the social, cultural and urban fabric. For this reason, priority should be given to the regions close to the Syrian border in the resettlement of Syrian migrants, and attention should be paid to geographical, security, economic and cultural factors in their settlement or resettlement. On the other hand, in the resettlement of Syrian migrants, the provinces that constitute the first ten provinces where they live the most and the provinces with the highest ratio to the population of the province; Provinces such as Hatay, Şanlıurfa, Gaziantep, Kilis can be considered at the first stage. Syrian families in resettlement or settlement; urban and rural construction should be taken into account when considering the 92.5% of Turkey's population lived in cities and district centers to rural areas emphasis should be placed on them as possible. It is considered appropriate to settle the very small groups of Syrian immigrants, who

[33] Nagihan Önder, op.cit, compiled from p. 127.
[34] Sevinç Bahar Yenigül, op.cit, p. 236.

CHAPTER 16

DIGITAL SOCIAL MEDIA NETWORKS AS AN INTERCULTURAL COMMUNICATION AREA FORIMMIGRANTS AND LOCALS

Füsun Alver[1]

Introduction

Human migrationresults from the desire to escape adverse conditions, such as ecological and economichardships, slavery, wide-spread looting, wars, and political persecution, or to access better living conditions and opportunities. Over the course of more recent history, economic and political instabilities in developing countries and the control of land, raw materials and labor by developed countries have forced large masses of people to migrate. The global migrations observed in the early periods of the 21st centuryhave had a circular and dynamic development trend. In thereciprocal relationship thatexists between immigrants and the country receiving them, the driving forces of the global economy and technological developments have resulted in social and cultural transformations for immigrants,and political, economic and cultural issueshave emerged as topics for discussion in the countries receiving migrants. Immigration, which has been a topic of interest for politics, societies, and scientific fields,has been examined from the perspectives ofsociology[2],political science[3]and communications[4]. Sincethe 1960s, there has been a rise in the number of peopleimmigrating to European countries for economic reasons and asylum. Various studies[5]have been conducted onhowimmigrants are represented and reflected as foreigners in traditional media and on their intercultural communication[6]. Beginning in the early 2000s, thanks to the development of digital social media networks, immigrants began to have access to various communication and intercultural platforms where they could freely express themselves and counteract the negative and limiting manner in which they were being portrayed as in traditional media.As a result, research examining

[1] Prof. Dr. Istanbul Commerce University. Director of Institute for Communication Science and Internet, Türkiye. E-mail: falver@ticaret.edu.tr

[2] Petra Aigner, Migrations Soziologie Eine Einführung, Wiesbaden, Springer VS, 2017; Klaus J. Bade, Migration – Flucht - Integration. Kritische Politikbegleitung von der Gastarbeiterfragebiszur Flüchtlingskrise, Karlsruhe, LoeperVerlag, 2017.

[3] Hans-Joachim Lauth, Marianne Kneuer, GertPickel, **Handbuch Vergleichende Politik Wissenschaft**, Wiesbaden, Springer VS, 2016.

[4]FüsunAlver, **BasındaYabancıTasarımı ve Düşmanlığı**, İstanbul, Der Yayınları,2003.

[5] Siegfried Jaeger, Jürgen Link, **Die Vierte Gewalt. Rassismus und Medien**., Duisburg, DISS,1993.

[6] Hans Jürgen Heringer, **Interkulturelle Kommunikation. Grundlagen und Kozepte,**Tübingen, Basel, A.Francke Verlag,2010.

immigrants' relationships in digital social media networks, their interactions with locals, and the use of these networks as anti-immigrant instruments have become more important than ever[7].

In this study, the position of the self and foreigner is addressedwithin the context of the relationship between near and distant,as presented in Simmel's[8] Perspective of Migration Sociology, along with an analysis of the relationship between the self and foreigner, as presented in Schaeffer's[9] modelto examine how thesedynamicsarereflected in the relationships built in the new inter-cultural meeting and communication platforms on digital social media networks. The study specifically examines the instrumentalization of digital social networks in terms of democratizing the structure of communication and enabling immigrants to express themselves in response to anti-migrant organizations and protests. The study's primary objectivesare to identify the principles governing the use of new communication forms by immigrants, to determine the opportunities and limitations offered by digital social media networks as intercultural communication platforms, and to examine the potential of instrumentalizing these platforms for organizing xenophobic movements. This study used an argumentative research approach to achieve these objectives.

The following research questions were developed to guide the study: How do the new communication forms affect immigrants' social and communication practices and their self-expression processes? What opportunities and limitations do digital social media networks have for immigrants to meet and communicate with the local residents?

History of migrations and their dynamics

Human migration, a phenomenon that has occurred since the dawn ofhumanity,refers to the movement of people from one location to another owing to ecological, economic, social, political, and cultural reasons. Migrations can occur within countries or across countries. Throughout history, wars, economic and political instability, geographical discoveries, slave trading, and capitalism have all played significant roles in migrations. Thefailure to define the boundaries distinguishing theconcept of immigrant, refugee and asylum-seeker in migration processeshas resulted in confusionin the use of these terms.

---

[7] Uwe Hunger, Kathrin Kissau, **Internet und Migration. Theoretische Zugänge und empirische Befunde,** Wiesbaden, VS Verlagfür Sozialwissenschaften, 2009; Nico Dietrich, Paul Kanis, "Intergruppenkontakt auf sozialen Netzwerkplattformen. Die Rolle von sozialerIdentität und Bedrohungsdarstellung auf die Einstellunggegenüber Muslimen", **Muslime, Flüchtlinge und Pegida Sozial psychologische und kommunikationswissenschaftliche Studien in Zeitenglobaler Bedrohungen,** Wolfgang Frindte, Nico Dietrich (Ed.), Wiesbaden, Springer VS, 2017a, pp.159-180.

[8] Georg Simmel, Soziologie. Untersuchungenüber die Formen der Vergesellschaftung, Leipzig, Verlag von Duncker&Humblot, 1908.

[9] OrtfriedSchaefter, "Modi des Fremderlebens", **Das Fremde. Erfahrungsmöglichkeitenzwischen Faszination und Bedrohung**, OrtfriedSchaefter (Ed.), Opladen, WestdeutscherVerlag, 1991. pp.11-42.

Therefore, it is important to identify the differences between these concepts.[10] Although the boundariesframing the concept of migration are inexact, in general, migration can be simply defined as the movement from a country of residence to another country, regardless of the reason for the migration or the legal status of the migrant. Refugees, as a category of immigrants,refer tothose who leave their countries owing to justifiable fear of persecutionon account ofrace, religion, nationality, membership in a certain social group, and political views and tothose who do not wish to benefit from the protection of their home countries due to these fears. This category of immigrants also includes those who flee their countries because of threats to their lives, safety and freedom as a result ofwidespread violence, external attacks, internal conflicts, widespread violations of human rights, or other circumstances that seriouslydisrupt public order. Asylum-seekersrefer to those seeking international protectionwho have not yet been formally grantedrefugee status. While not every asylum-seeker is recognized as a refugee, every refugee is an asylum-seeker when applying for asylum. Immigrants, refugees, and asylum-seekers are all part of the migration process but have different legal statuses. In this study, the concept of foreigner coversimmigrants, refugees, and asylum-seekers. After determining the statuses of those involved in the migration process, this study addresses the new dynamics of migration resulting from globalization andexamines the types of migration and the reasons behind them.

Main reasons for migration and types of migrations

Immigration from Europe to North America picked up pace in the 17th century. African slave trading by Europeans extended to South America and regions around the Indian Ocean up to the 19th century. The types of immigration that took place before the 19th century included forced migration (slavery), work migration, exile and asylum-seekingmigrations, and voluntary migrations[11]: An example of forced migrations would be the African slaves who were brought to North America for work by European or American slave traders; an example of work migrationswould be the movement of both educated and non-educated workers, withuneducated migrants being employed in fields requiring no expertise and educated migrants working in international or multi-national companies and institutions; an example of exile and asylum-seeking migrationswould be people or groups whose lives arein danger or under threat due to political reasons or who leave their countriesand migrate to another country through either legal or illegal ways owing to poor living conditions; and finally, an example of voluntary migrations would bethe overseas migrations of European groups to,first, the English colonies, and later, to America. Travelling

[10] Richard Perruchoud, Jillyanne Redpath, **Göç Terimleri Sözlüğü**, IOM, Uluslararası Göç Hukuku Serisi No. 31, Ankara, 2013, p. 36, 37, 65, 74.

[11] Hein Retter, "Das Phaenomen Der Migration: GeschichtlicheUrsachen, sozio-politische Motivationen", **L'Europamulticul-turale. Das Multikulturelle Europa. Akten der 24. Internationalen Tagungdeutsch-italienischer Studien,** Akademie Deutsch-Italienischer Studienunter der Leitung von Roberto Cotteri (Ed.), Meran, 1998, pp. 89-121.

to and settling in favorite places also falls under voluntary migration.

Starting in the 19th century, western and northern countries started to become the centers of attraction for migration movements. The most significant migrations of the 20th century can be grouped as mass migrations in the 1918-1939 / 40 period and post-1945 migrations[12].The migrations that took place between 1918-1939 / 40 were a direct result of the new borders drawn up after WW1 and of post-war policies. The 1918-23 periodwitnessed migrationsinvolvingthose who were exileddue to the newly established nation states, the migration of workers and their families, the migration of refugees due to political and humanitarian reasons, forced migrations, and the migration of foreign workers due to the rise to power of the National Socialist Party in Germany. The post-1945 migrations included exiles who migrated as a direct result of WW2 and the new post-war order, migrations prompted by economic hardships and ethnic tracking, migrations inspired by the liberation of colonies in Africa and South and Southeast Asia, post-colonial migration from old colonies to western Europe, migrations related to labor and family reunification, migrations of economically eliteformer Europeans, migrations of war victims and asylum seekers from countries in Africa, Asia, and South America,and migrations due to the economic problems in the wake of the dissolution of the Eastern Bloc and the wars in the Balkans. Since the beginning of the 21st century, the civil wars and wars between countries that erupted in the Middle East and Africahave accelerated and complicatedmigration processes.

To help unravel the complexity of migration trends, it is important to determine the factors driving migrations to neighboring countries, between continents,and across national borders. In examining these factors[13], it was found thatone of the main forces driving migration was the unequal economic development levels between countries. While global capitalism creates new manufacturing plants and markets throughout the world, it also wipes out traditional fields of work, destroys rural areas,fracturesemployment opportunities, and breaks up social circles. Imbalanced global trade results in migration from rural areas in developing countries. Poverty and hunger, as symptoms of economic inequality, also trigger migrations. In more recent history, the reasons for migrations are many and include the fall of nation-states, wars and civil wars, political and social conflicts, fallout from extraction of raw materialsfrom under-developed and developing countries, power struggles between opposing groups, religious conflicts, tensions in supranational alliances as a result of geopolitical strategies, fall of totalitarian regimes, foreign

[12] Rainer Münz, “Europa und die großenWanderungen des 20. Jahrhunderts”, **Furcht und Faszination. Facetten der Fremdheit,** Herfried Münkler, Bernd Ladwig (Ed.), Berlin, Akademie Verlag, 1997, p. 260 ff.

[13] Edith Broszinsky-Schwabe, **Interkulturelle Kommunikation. Missverständnisse und Verständigung**, Wiesbaden, Springer VS, 2017. pp.5-6; Ludger Pries, “Soziologie der Migration”, **Handbuch Spezielle Soziologien,** Georg Kneer, Markus Schroer (Ed.), Wiesbaden, VS Verlagfür Sozialwissenschaften, 2010, p. 476.

interventions, and political persecution. In addition to these factors, natural disasters, climatic changes due to global warming, ecological issues, such as lack of water resources, and epidemics have been responsible for mass migrations. Finally, migrations have also been spurred by the desire for individuals to access the living conditions and lifestyles promoted by countries with a higher level of welfare through traditional and new communication and media technologies. Related to thisfactor driving migration is the greater mobility offered by the new and faster modes of transportation.

There are three different international migration types that can be identified.[14] In the first migration type, immigrants permanently settle in the country to which they migrate and continue to communicate with their countries of origin; however, they integrate with the settled society and over time completely assimilate. The second migration type is non-permanent and short-term migration for economic purposes. The labor migration to western and northern countries after 1960 fall within this scope. The third migration type can be qualified asinternational diaspora migration. Diaspora migration is primarily related to religion and/or determined through strong relationships of loyalty and organizational dependence. By its very nature, this type of migration cannot be qualified as labor migration,as changes in location often result from escape, exile, conviction, or assignments. Apart from these migration types, a new international migration type, designated 'beyond migration'has emerged. Beyond migration is characterized by situations in which change is not a singular process but normal among the different habitats in different countries,as the daily living space of the beyond migration involves different local areas that extend beyond national borders. The causes and courses of migrations have a complex trend of development, to which can be added the new dynamics of migrationsintroduced by globalization.

New dynamics of migrations within the globalization process

Tendencies towards globalization stretch back to the geographical discoveries of the 15th century, becoming clearer after WW2, and being fully realizedat the start of the 1990s. The globalization process has been analyzed in correlation with modern capitalism[15] and postmodern society[16]and has been characterized by geographic expansion, increase of international trade, expansion of the global network topology of financial markets, rise in the power of transnational companies, continuous advancesin information and communication technologies, and video streaming of global cultural industries[17]. Globalization

---

[14] Naomi Carmon, **Immigration and Integration in Post Industrial Societies,** Houndmills, Basingstoke, MacMillan, 1996; Cohen Robin, **Global Diasporas: An Introduction**, London, UCL Press (University College London), 1997; Ludger Pries, op.cit, pp. 479-481.

[15] Anthony Giddens, **Modernliğin Sonuçları,** İstanbul, Ayrıntı Yayınları, 2016.

[16] Perry Anderson, **Postmodernitenin Kökenleri**, çev. Elçin Gen, İstanbul, İletişim Yayınları, 2011.

[17] Ulrich Beck, Was ist Globalisierung? Irrtümer des Globismus – Antworten auf Globalisierung, Frankfurt am Main, SuhrkampVerlag, 2007, p.29.

has also prompted a new understanding of reality, particularly in terms of time and space and the way in which people construct meaning and act, and it has also increased interactions between cultures[18]. This process has brought about new and complex rules for states, societies, institutions, and people and has re-shaped their values and perspectives.

Globalization has followed a dynamic course and has various dimensions of impact, affecting everything from the economy, politics, and culture to ecology and social communication through modern communication technologies,[19]the latter of which has served as the primary instruments of globalization. The impacts of these dimensions permeate the borders of nation-states through the exchange of commodities, services, capital and labor. Although China has disrupted the balance of power, the western-based globalization process has reproducedeconomic inequalities between the center and peripheral countries and between developed and underdeveloped countries,where'the dynamics of development are almost entirelyoriented towards the center countries, while the rest of the world remains as a passive receiver of the dominant trends'.[20]Financial control mechanisms, such as high industry technology, planning, and development capacity, are limited to developed countries, andthrough production, distribution, control and financial mechanisms, organizational forms are changingand business processes are being restructured. These processes make western and northern countries the center of attraction for migration. The speed and ubiquity of the transportation and digital communication technologies network spread across the world have added a different dimension to the migration dynamics of the 21st century. The quantitative increase and relative qualitative improvement in transportation and communication options for those who want to or have to immigrate have further complicated international migration processes.

Local people and migrants in the dialectic of the self / foreigners

The voluntary or compulsory encountersimmigrants have with local residentsand their communication or lack thereof with them point to a painful process. Whenimmigrants are not recognized or knownby local residents and areperceived as potential threats, political actors who cannot manage global dynamics well or formulatesuccessful solutions to issues tend to use immigrants as scapegoats for these problems by making xenophobic comments.Within this

---

[18] Friedrich Krotz, "Konnektivität der Medien: Konzepte, Bedingungen und Konsequenzen", **Konnektivität, Netzwerk und Fluss Konzeptegegenwärtiger Medien-, Kommunikationsund Kulturtheorie**, Andreas Hepp, Friedrich Krotz, Shaun Moores, Carsten Winter (Ed.), Wiesbaden, VS VerlagfürSozialwissenschaften, 2006, p.30.

[19] Gerhard Preyer, **Soziologische Theorie der Gegenwartsgesellschaft**, Vol. I, Mitgliedschafts theoretische Untersuchungen, Wiesbaden, Springer VS, 2018, p.309.

[20] Wolfgang Gabbert, "Das Eigene und das Fremdeim »globalen Dorf« – Perspektiveneinerkritischen Soziologie der Globalisierung", **Postkoloniale Soziologie Empirische Befunde, theoretische Anschlüsse, politische Intervention**, Julia Reuter, Paula-Irene Villa (Ed.), Bielefeld, transcript Verlag, 2010, p.159.

framework, Simmel's[21] Perspective of Migration Sociology,in terms of the position of residents and the dynamics of the close/distant relationship, and Schaeffer's[22]modelon the relationship between self and foreigner can be appliedto demonstratehow foreigners are transformed into enemy figures.

The self and foreigners in the relationship between the close and distant

Simmel[23] determines the relationships between the self and foreigners based on the degree of closeness and distance. The self is formed on the border with the foreigner, meaning the self is determined according to how itperceivesthe foreigner,a process that reflects the relationship between the self and the other. Both categories are in a relationship of mutuallimitation, as defined by the personal borders. Self-framingis only possible by defining a person, topic or situation, otherwise, the relationship with another person or situationwouldbe regarded as foreign and perceived as different from the self.

In focusing on the relationships between the self and the foreigner, Simmellooks at the impact of foreigners on social life, where he[24]believes that the concept of foreigner includes the concept of a passenger who travels from one place to another, as well as the concept of a person who travels to a place and stays there. A foreigner is actually not a traveler who comes and goes;rather, a foreigner is a potential traveler who cannot understand the difference between going and coming, despite the absence of migration and residence in a different place. Foreigners are a part of a group but separate from the recognized, and consigned to being on the outside andopposite. Foreigners do not occupy a place in physical and psychological terms and will not occupy one so long as they are considered foreigners. Foreigners act within a limited space to which they do not belong but to which they nevertheless add certain qualities. The relationship between people is determined by the close and far distances. Distance in the scope of relationshipsmeans that the close is actually far, while the far is actually close.

Simmel[25]argues that foreigners are actually recognized in terms of national, social, professional and general human equality. The idea of theforeigners' distance arises when the common aspects of foreigners exceed the concept of local and self and are seen as being associated withthe others' personal aspects. Foreigners, despite their inorganic limbs, are necessary for the holistic life of a group and function as organic members of that group. Simmel focuses on the objectivity of foreigners arising from their distance, which is based on the idea that the far and close can be considered together. Foreigners remain objective

---

21 Simmel, op.cit.

22 Schaefter,op.cit.

23 Simmel, op.cit.

24 Simmel, op.cit,p.685 ff.

25 Simmel, op.cit,p.687.

vis-à-vis the localresidents, as they are not a part of the group and not affected by unilateral orientations. In other words, foreigners are outside the objective and subjective behaviors. The foreigners' objectivity arises from the fact that they are not committed to the dominant rules and norms of the local society and that they can interpret actions and events without any prejudices.

The objectivity of the foreigners who do not belong to the local groups provides them freedom, but because they are not known and trusted, they are perceived as threatening. The freedom and unreliability of foreigners are seen as a threat to the stability of the local established order, a perception inspired by the idea that foreigners have the potential of creating disorder and promoting uprisings.

Relationships between the self and foreigner

Relationships with foreigners are a reflection of the self. Simmel[26] believes thatforeigners have afunction within the relationship that local people have with the self. The self and the foreigner have a dynamic relationship, one that is varied, flexible, and historical, based on social and cultural definitions, and shaped by cultural definitions and changes.

The relationships between the self and the foreigner are analyzed from the perspective of the foreigner as the load-bearing and adaptation ground of the self, as the opposite picture of the self, as the provider of the dynamic change experienced by the self, and as the complementary subject of the self[27]: The relationship between the self and the foreigner as the load-bearing and adaptation ground of the self reflects the relationship between a system and environment within an ordered schema, where foreignness is lived as the experience of 'overcoming the threshold', not as an experience ofcomplete opposition. The border in between is understood as the area of 'traveling and moving'; the different parts of the order that cannot unite come togetherand dissipate. As the opposite picture of the self, relationships with foreigners negate the authenticity of the foreigners as a result of mutual disagreement. What is experienced here is not the secret relationship between form and essence, but rather the sense of attraction, and threat directs the attention to a solid and precisely defined line of demarcation that preserves authenticity. Foreigners are considered to be limited so long as they do not belong to the self and as such, distort and threaten the integration of their order as foreign subjects. Limits fulfill a certain function of opposition, which can strengthen self-identity as an opposing picture. Rather than principled oppositions, temporal problems of the mutual connection between the foreigner and the self gain importance in the relationships with the foreigners in terms of them as providers of dynamic change regarding the self. Foreigners have the function of serving as the area of movement for external

[26] Simmel, op.cit.

[27] Schaefter, op.cit, p.15 ff.

actors within a dynamic order that promotes development, provides stimuli, enables structural learning, and causes unpredictable developments. The attractiveness of foreigners in this relationship reflects the need for information and change in the relationship with the self and isa transference of curiosity and information. These characteristics largely depend on the development and status of the relevant system. The relationship with the foreigner as the complementary subject of the self is not left within a foreign property, as the 'otherness' of the foreigners is adopted by the self. Foreignness has a significant function in establishing the identity forthe underlying order of society. Based on the formation of the relationship with the foreigners, the internal and external structures are not considered as separate areas; instead, they are believed to be the places where the configuration process takes place. However, the self and foreigner determine themselves mutually and relatively.

The self and foreigner come together, whether voluntarily or by compulsory circumstances, ina complex network ofrelationships, and develop different ties. Tendencies and innovations that are redefined in the foreigner and the self emerge within the relationships between the two. The relationships with foreigners may be based on limitation or rejection, oron acceptance and adoption. The boundary in relations between the self and foreigners is not always clear, as it is permeable and dynamic and changes over time.

Transformation of the foreign figure into the enemy image

The meeting of different cultures is facilitated throughforced migrations, economic activities, scientific, cultural and artistic activities, and touristic trips. The scope of these meetingsare extended through traditional and digital media. The involvement of signs sent consciously or unconsciously in the intercultural communication between local residents and immigrants, and the perception and interpretation of these signs by the recipients canlead toprejudices, categorizing, and limitations and thereby, the eruption of conflicts.The categorization ofimmigrants with different origins as those from foreign countries refers to'asylum-seekers and non-citizen workers who are distinguished by their political, legal and social positions'.[28]Encounters between immigrants from foreign countries and local residents take place in different areas of daily life, such as working environments, shopsand entertainment venues, and can lead to mutual understanding and acceptance or to hostile attitudes and behaviors.

By focusing on historical and cultural differences and falselysuggesting that foreigners are more likely to commit crime, rather than emphasizing common human aspects, the prejudices of local residents are reinforced and result in negative perceptions and actions. 'Foreigners can be considered as the carriers of the fearsome and unreliable; the reliable self disappears in the presence of the foreigner, and the foreigner and the self are present in the constellation as

[28] Ulrich Bielefeld, Inlaendischer Auslaender: zumgesellschaflicher Bewusstseintürkischer Jugendlicher in der Bundesrepublik,Frankfurt am Main, Campus Verlag, 1988, p.10.

opposites. This constellation is frequently updated through cultural identity in right-wing populist discourse, and foreigners are designated as the fearsome uninvited guests threatening the culture of self within the cultural limitations.'[29] The thoughts and discourse driving the idea that the foreigners threaten their own culture and identity and cause unemployment by stealing the limited employment opportunities from the local residents are directed and reproduced by political actors. As foreigners are held responsible for the negative conditions and used as the scapegoats by political actors, mutual recognition and acceptance between the local people and foreigners becomes challenging.

Opportunities and limitations brought by digital social media networks for immigrants and local people

The digitalization phenomenonthat affects almost all areas of life in the 21st century, transforms the social areas and is considered a revolution indicates data collection, network formation, automation of processes and working models, artificial intelligence and robotic interaction, which exceeds the digital modification of devices and means of transportation. As a complement to the digitalization phenomenon,advanced information technologies, such as computers, smart phones, internet applications and databases,have radically transformed communication areas and processes. The popularization of communication and media technologies haspaved the way for the emergence of new communication forms and opportunities of self-expression for immigrants who have left their countries voluntarily or by force and has changed the dynamics of intercultural interaction and the structures ofintercommunication. At the same time, digital social media networks have also created a platform for anti-migrant organizations and protests.

Immigrant platforms within digital social media networks and new forms of communication

Digital social media networks offer different areas and opportunities forimmigrants to share their knowledge and experience and to express themselves. Results from a study[30] examining the internet sites and usage preferencesof immigrants in Germany, the European country receiving the highest number of immigrants,showed that immigrants tended to favor ethnic sites, informational sites, transnational-dual ethnicity sites, public and easily-accessible sites, multi-lingual sites, alternative sites and multi-cultural sites on the internet. The immigrants preference for ethnic sites suggests that immigrants carve out their own ethnic areas on the internet by drawing a bilateral border between the websites of their home countries and the countries they migrated to

---

[29] David Kergel, Kulturen des Digitalen. Postmoderne Medienbildung, subversive Diversität und neoliberale Subjektivierung, Wiesbaden, Springer VS, 2018, p.27.

[30] Kathrin Kissau, "Ethnische Sphärenim Internet", **Ethnowissen. Soziologische Beiträgezuethnischer Differenzierung und Migration,** Marion Müller, Darius Zifonun (Ed.), Wiesbaden, VS Verlagfür Sozialwissenschaften, 2010, pp.349-367.

in their communication processes with other users. Ethnic differentiation and migration within this ethnic area created by immigrants for immigrants are both subject and boundary features. In the field of information presented by the internet, there is strict adherence to the ethnic information base, cultural transference, and the conveyance of information, thoughts, emotions and experiences, all of which serve to define the common knowledge of the ethnic group.[31] The informational sites help immigrants to realize their narrative through cultural codes. 'The potential of establishing a network offers the possibility ofpreserving the narrativesby establishing relationships, sharing experiences and collaborating. Multimedia creates new opportunities for audio narrations in the form of musical pieces and podcasts, while images and video do the same for visual expressions.'[32] Sharing the knowledge, thoughts and experiences, and cultural products generated in the homeland creates the feeling of belonging to a group and builds a sense of trust among the immigrants.

Another area of the internet reported to be favored by immigrants was transnational-dual ethnicity sites, which are environments where information on the home countries and Germany is shared, allowing the borders of ethnicities and national identities to be crossed.[33] These sites have the function of forming and representing transnational and hybrid identities. The internet in generaloffers immigrants the freedom of 'crossing the borders between the public andprivate areas'.[34] Digital social media networks provide immigrants the opportunity to express themselves using new social and communicational applications. Social networking sites enabling digital communication that is based on Web 2.0 technologies, such as blogs, forums, and multimedia platforms, provide individuals, groups, and organizations the opportunity to create public or partially public profiles in a closed virtual space andto interactwith other profiles by using visual material and various other communication options available in networks.[35] The multilingual spaces created on the internet by immigrants engaging in social practices allows them to interact with immigrants from their own culture and local residents of the host country. 'Within these multi-lingual areas, immigrants tend to use the language of the host country, a partial mix of their own language and the language of the host country, or English. While this use of languages defines the borders of the user group on the relevant platform and in other areas, it is nota border unable to be surmounted by local residents'.[36] These multi-lingual areaspromote mutual recognition and trust andcan serve as

[31] Kissau,op.cit,pp. 359-363.

[32] Christina Schachtner, "Das erzählteSelbst: Narrative Subjektkonstruktionenim Zeichenmedialen und gesellschaftlichkulturellen Wandels", **Das vergessene Subjekt Subjekt Konstitutionen in mediatisierten Alltagswelten**, Peter Gentzel, Friedrich Krotz, Jeffrey Wimmer, Rainer Winter (Ed.), Wiesbaden, Springer VS, 2019, p.176.

[33] Kissau,op.cit,p.362.

[34] Kissau,op.cit,p.362

[35] Danah M. Boyd, Nicole. B. Ellison, "Social Network Sites: Definition, Geschichte und Wissenschaft", **Jounal of Computer-Mediated Communication**, Vol.13, No. 1, 1. 2007, p. 211 ff.

[36] Kissau,op.cit,p.362

a platform for peaceful encounters.

In addition to social media sites like Facebook, YouTube, Instagram, Twitter, Pinterest and TikTok, where the borders between the producers and consumers are transparent, online meeting forums and messaging programs serve as an alternative to traditional media, providing immigrants the opportunity to create written, visual and audio content personally or as a group and to share knowledge, information, thoughts and emotions. Traditional media's limited and insufficient reporting of background information about immigrantsand the negative portrayal of foreigners as scapegoats take place within the framework of financial, political and cultural discussions. 'Alternative platforms, like the internet,provide ethnic groups the opportunity to counteract the limitations of traditional media bysupplying a space to exchange information and ideas and to determine their own informational destiny. Immigrants can share alternative views and information with a wide audience on the internet.'[37] Moreover, these alternative platforms allow immigrants the opportunity tocomment on, interpret and evaluate their own and other's problems and to share suggestions for solutions. In the multi-cultural areas of the internet reported to befavored by immigrants, 'communication partners from the same ethnic backgroundwere shown to be preferred, but the fact that the immigrants also communicated with users who had no history of immigration in Germany indicates that these platforms are open to intercultural dialogs and do not function as a separate virtual space specifically carved out for immigrants alone.'[38]Multi-cultural sites in digital social media networks enable immigrants to not only meet with other immigrants from other cultures but also to interact with the local residentsand as such, has the potential of influencing the processes of recognition and acceptance.

The transnational, global communication and virtual reproduction of social interactions between immigrants and local residents within the same geographical bordersthat digital social media networks provide have changed the environment of meeting between the self and foreigners. Reflections of the relationship model between the foreigner and the self can be found in those areas open to dialogue between immigrants from different countries and between immigrants and local residents.[39] Open, free dialogue within digital social media networksis capable of prompting dynamic change, insofar as it discloses gaps, deficiencies and errors in thinking and helps to form the ground of adaptation between the local residents and foreigners, enabling the experiences of the self to take on deeper meaning. In addition, on these platforms, thedifferences regarding the relationships with the foreigners as the complementary subjects of the self are mutually accepted and defined. On the other hand, relationships with the foreigners as the opposition of the self are nurturedon the digital social media

---

[37] Kissau,op.cit,p.363

[38] Kissau,op.cit,p.363.

[39] Schaefter,op.cit,p.15 ff.

sites used by xenophobic local residents who support anti-migration movements and on those sites usedbyimmigrants with nationalist and religious orientations.

Anti-immigrant organizations in digital social media networks

The rising number of immigrants residing in European countries has led to intense discussions in digital social media networks as well as in political and social circles. These networks host xenophobic and anti-immigrant sites that include xenophobic, racist, hate-filled discourse and violent content. Xenophobic and anti-immigrant websites postprovocative and engagingmaterial and utilize propaganda strategies to reach large audiences. 'In the 1990s, extreme right-wing websites generally had only written content, but today visual and audio content has been added to these sites to capture the attention of young people. The content isstylishly designed andincludes animations, music, games and interactive texts.'[40] Xenophobic platforms also promote the activities of anti-migration organizations and protests. For instance, Patriotic Europeans Against the Islamisation of the Occident (PEGIDA), which started operating in the eastern parts of Germany in 2014 and quickly gained supporters in other European countries, has organized its extreme rightist populist movements through digital social media networks.[41]

The PEGIDA movement does not oppose the admission to Germany of war refugees or those prosecuted for political or religious reasons but expresses zero tolerancefor criminal refugees, and the group considers the protection of western culture and language to be the focal point of their objectives. PEGIDA has strongly criticized the immigration and asylum policies of Germany and the European Union, has organized street protests, and has instrumentalized digital social media networks to get their message heard. The group believes that religious and proxy wars have been gradually brought to the peaceful German land and started toencourage peopleto take to the streets to protest against this threat. They first shared their message on a private Facebook group before branching out to other digital social media networks.' Today, in addition to Facebook, the group activelyuses Twitter and YouTube to share its ideas, make comments and demands, build networks, and organize and mobilize protests.'[42] The movement, which uses social media to produce its own reality and create new identity designs,' put out a call through social media thatresulted in 25,000

[40] Stefan Glaser, "Rassismusim Internet – Anlasszur Auseinandersetzung?! Zurmedienpädagogischen Projektarbeit von jugendschutz.net", **Rechte Netzwerke — eine Gefahr**, Stephan Braun, Daniel Hoersch (Ed.), Wiesbaden, VS Verlag, 2004, p. 221.

[41] https://www.pegida.de (Access 16.11.2020); https://www.facebook.com/pegidaevdresden (Access 16.11.2020).

[42] Nico Dietrich, Enrico Gersin, Alan Herweg, "Analysemöglichkeiten der Online-Kommunikation auf Social Network Sites am Beispiel PEGIDA und Facebook", **Muslime, Flüchtlinge und Pegida Sozial psychologische und kommunikation swissenschaftliche Studien in Zeitenglobaler Bedrohungen**, Wolfgang Frindte, Nico Dietrich, Nico (Ed.), Wiesbaden, Springer VS, 2017b, p. 236.

protesters taking tothe streets on February 2015'.[43] The relationships with the foreigners as the opposite of the self[44] are reflected in digital platforms.[45] The identities of the self and foreigners designed in the xenophobic and anti-migration sites of digital social media networks portray foreigners as subjects opposed to the positive design of the self, and they are considered as external actors or disintegrated elements;in other words, they are socially, culturally and politically limited, insofar as they distort or even threaten the order of the self.

As can be seen with the PEGIDA movement, information with negative content can be created and disseminated in digital social media networks and hence lead to transforming the images of foreigners into objects of xenophobia and the activation of anti-immigrant political protests

Conclusion

Cultures throughout human history have interactedfor economic purposes, wars, and political and ecological reasons,and through all these interactions, cultures haveremained,despite the oppositions, contradictions and conflicts. Immigration plays a key role in intercultural interactions and conflicts. The inability to solve the complex issues of poverty and unemployment in developing countries,the wealth gaps in developed countries, and the challenges of establishing social equality and securing political rights and freedoms are all among the main reasons drivingimmigration. The economic, political, and social problems experienced in connection with immigration to western and northern countries and the highlighted and seemingly insurmountable differences between the concepts of the self and the foreigner result in marginalization and discrimination. Foreigners experience discrimination on account of the concerns of local residents having to share and possibly losing economic and social opportunities. The manipulation of these concerns by anti-migration groups and political actors and theinclusion of these concerns in political discourse canserve to provokexenophobic acts.

Digitalization, which has globally transformed personal and social areas and has had deep and complex effects on society, hasraised the encounters and communication between immigrants and local residents to another level. Fast transportation technology and digital social media networks enable encounters and communication on a global scale. Digital social media networks present a virtual meeting platform for local residents and immigrants, who have limited interaction in real social areas despite living in the same country, to interact, a phenomenon which suggests that the close is actually far and the far is actually

[43] Hans Vorländer, Maik Herold, Steven Schäller, PEGIDA: Entwicklung, Zusammensetzung und Deutungeiner Empörungsbewegung, Wiesbaden, Springer VS, 2016, p.8.
[44] Schaefter, op.cit, p.15 ff.
[45] https://www.pegida.de (Access 16.11.2020); https://www.facebook.com/pegidaevdresden (Access 16.11.2020).

close, as argued by Simmel[46]. Digitalization has changed and re-organized communication. Society, the world, and reality are all being re-designed, with new social structures, hybrid identities, spatial designs, and communication platforms emerging. The relationship models between the self and foreigners[47] are being reproduced from real social areas to digital social networks.

In digital social media networks,communication takes placeindependent of time and space, allowing immigrantsto express themselves freely,to share cultural signs, words and different visual materials,and to learn the perspectives of local residentsThe encountersthat occur on different platforms enable immigrants and local residents to gain knowledge about cultural values, traditions and behavioral patterns and to engage in peaceful intercultural exchanges and learn from one another. The widespread use of digital social media networks has resulted in a new relationship dialectic, where the conditions in the virtual environment are more equal between the local residents and immigrants.Yet, these networks also provide a platform for xenophobic and anti-immigrant organizations and protests.

Anti-migrant movements and xenophobia are connected to limiting or stopping immigration; yet thiswill remain an impossible dream unless the root causes of immigration areremoved. The conditions of international cooperation should be re-assessed to find solutions to the problems created bythe accelerating pace of immigration. In combatingthe hostile attitudes and behaviors against immigrants, it would be beneficial to develop intercultural communication models that are aimed at ensuring mutual recognition and understanding between local residents and immigrants and building their digital media literacy.

---

[46] Simmel, op.cit.

[47] Schaefter,op.cit,p.15 ff.

CHAPTER 17

REFLECTIONS OF REFUGEE CRISIS IN MEDIA

Hüseyin Çelik[1]

Introduction

The development of modernism and the capitalist structure took place in parallel. The bourgeoisie class that would process them was formed as a result of the capitalist countries obtaining the raw materials from the countries they colonized. The bourgeoisie needed labor and the working class emerged as a result. The capitalist structure has provided both modernization and wealth in Western countries. Ultimately, a wealthy western world and on the other hand, a structure consisting of other underdeveloped or middle developed countries emerged. While the West increases its capital, the remaining countries do this with production and export, and the remaining countries turn into imports and consumers. In the neoliberal environment, 'the free movement of capital, goods and services', 'ensuring an environment of perfect competition' constitutes a structure suitable for the discourse of capitalist ideology. In this structure, all political, social, military and economic formations are established in accordance with this dominant ideology. Therefore, the paradigm, as Wallerstein said, is formed in the West and dictated to the East.[2]

Today, the West is structured to produce information and industrial products. It will consume the rest of the world by producing information. In order to work for this system. The Eastern world should not become as competent, educated and capable of producing information like the West. In the education system in the West, individuals are already raised as people who will exploit the East. There is no longer a need for systems that will help the rulers or rulers, but systems that are less educated-ideologically refined to those governed, and if possible, which that will ensure that the economies that conflict within themselves always remain in crisis. Thus, the information produced by the West is sent to the East for processing and output as a product.

The unidirectional flow that occurred in this way increased human movements in the world and other underdeveloped human peoples aimed to migrate to the western countries. With this fact, it has turned into a vital shape and mechanism. People try to migrate by revealing their life and all their wealth, and some of them are successful. The factors that enable people to migrate are war, hunger, poverty and culture. Western culture is successful in influencing and

[1] Professor, Nisantasi University, Istanbul, Türkiye.

[2] Wallerstein, I, **World-Systems Analyses**, London: Duke Universiyt Press, 2004, pp. 26-28.

persuading people. Hollywood movies, television series, internet news, ornate images of the west can easily enter people's minds and prepare people to migrate. Although the West does not attempt to immigrate people, the Western magic displayed easily affects people and becomes a driving force for them to migrate. Today, because of war, hunger and poverty, people have turned their hopes to the west. And they want to step into the western countries in every way.

As a result of the Arab Spring that occurred at the beginning of the 21st century and the problems in Afghanistan, people chose to migrate en masse. Today, the number of Syrians who have migrated to Turkey is between three and five millions. Turkey is a bridge opened to people migrating to western countries. Although the refugees have made agreements with the European Union (EU) to Turkey, EU countries have to fulfill the terms of this agreement. Syrian Arabs in almost every city in camps in Turkey, Afghan refugees from Afghanistan and lives of millions of refugees from North Africa. Refugee issues were bothering the public in Turkey. Because in the country where unemployment is an important problem, there are millions of refugees who are willing to work illegally and for low wages. Greece does not let incoming refugees into their cities and shelters them in camps. However, wherever possible to meet refugees in Turkey. Refugees in Turkey has begun to be understood to be permanent. Refugees buy houses and start a business here. The refugee crisis become an important problem in Turkey, located in the media as well as public and it is continually being discussed and debated. In this section, how to get the refugee crisis in Turkey and in the media was focused on how to configure the news of refugees. The main idea of this section, further deepening refugee crisis in Turkey and the media's handling of this crisis is that focused specifically on the case. In this section, how to get the refugee crisis in Turkey and in the media is focused on how to configure the news of refugees. The main idea of this section is to focus on the refugee crisis in Turkey and how mass media depicts this refugee crisis. The news in this section were determined by the random sampling method in newspapers and televisions, and the view of the media on this crisis was evaluated with discourse analysis. Discourse analysis was used with the rhetoric approach in the media in order to dicuss the refugee crisis in Turkey.

Critical discourse analysis is an interdisciplinary field that includes many fields such as linguistics, semiotics, rhetoric, social-linguistics and discourse studies. Basically, it emphasizes the dominant discourses. The most meaningful of these analyzes are those who place the discourse they examine in a macro-social and even international context, not leaving an individual critical position. The examples of leading critical discourse analysts include van Beaugrande, Dijk, Fairclough (Foucaultist), Titscher, and so on. The topics they deal with range from racism to social inequality and health reform. Critical discourse analysis can focus on 'the role of discord in (re)production and opposition to sovereignty'.[3]

[3] Erdoğan, İrfan, **Pozitivist Metodoloji ve Ötesi**, Ankara, Erk, 2012, p. 129.

According to Dijk, there is a relationship between power and discourse, power is established through discourse, and it continues to operate indirectly through people's minds.[4] Dijk states that mass media play an important role in formulating beliefs, forming certain patterns, pointing out a single idea by excluding alternative thoughts, and adopting certain ideas about things that people do not encounter in their daily life practices. For this reason, the determination of news value criteria, selection of news sources, titles and spots, and the semantic structure of the words used in them are the focus of critical analysis.

Dijk[5] states that immigrants do not find a place in the mainstream media, they are not accepted as news sources, they are mentioned with a pity on them, or they are coded as 'inadequate' or 'backward' by being associated with crime, violence and aggression.

Dijk[6] wrote the following in his article *'Interdisciplinary Analysis of News as Discourse'*: 'One of the major conditions of such local coherence of texts is that their propositions refer to facts that are related, for instance, by relations of time, condition, cause, and consequence.' Thus, the concepts and the previously known begin to reveal the meaning. Another important point is implications. Words, clauses, and other textual expressions may imply concepts or propositions which may be inferred on the basis of background knowledge.[7] There are various types of implication: entailments, presuppo- sitions, and weaker forms, such as suggestion and association. In our example as well as generally in discourse about minorities and refugees, especially in right-wing news reports about minorities, the use of the word illegal.[8] News reports follow a hierarchical schema, consisting of such conventional categories as Headline, Lead (together forming the Summary), Main Events, Context, History (together forming the Background category), Verbal Reactions, and Comments.[9] The subject of the news is explained in sections and the sections that are given priority are the most important parts. As such, the text points out important parts about itself. The choice of words is very important at this stage. According to Dijk:

- 'Style is the textual result of choices between alternative ways of saying more or less the same thing by using different words or a 116 News as discourse different syntactic structure. Such stylistic choices also have clear social and ideological implications, because they often signal the opinions of the reporter about news

[4] Dijk, T. A. V., "Söylem ve İdeoloji: Çok Alanlı Bir Yaklaşım," **Söylem ve İdeoloji: Mitoloji**, Din, İdeoloji. B. Çoban, Z. Özarslan (der). N. Ateş (çev). İstanbul, Su, 2015, pp. 361-367.

[5] Dijk, T.A.V. Dijk, T. A. V. "Söylemin Yapıları ve İktidarın Yapıları," **Medya İktidar İdeoloji**, M. Küçük (çev) Ankara: Ark, 2009, p. 268.

[6] Dijk, T.A.V., "Bir Söylem Olarak Haberin Disiplinler Arası Çözümlenmesi," **Medya Metinlerini Çözümlemek,** G. Şendur Atabek (der). Ankara: Siyasal, 1999, p. 112.

[7] İbid. p. 114.

[8] İbid, p. 115.

[9] İbid. pp. 114-115.

> actors and news events as well as properties of the social and communicative situation (their use in a tabloid) and the group memberships of the speakers, for instance that a specific journalist is white, male, or middle-class. Thus, the use of mob and rentamob, instead of crowd and demon- strators, may be interpreted as signaling the ideological position of the reporter about left-wing demonstrators, while at the same time discrediting them for the readers.[10]'

Dijk states that there are mental processes that have meaning and minds give meanings to texts. Confronted with a news, the mind is not only limited to it, but also uploads its previous encounters to the last text it saw.[11]

If a news contains 'prejudice', it is because the person or institution that prepares it has an ideological perspective. For this reason, critical analysis actually reveals these mental assumptions. Dijk explains this situation as follows in his example:

- 'For instance, in discourse about minorities, both in the press and in everyday conversations, prejudiced language users usually not only express negative opinions about minorities, as represented in their models of ethnic events; in addition, they will add disclaimers such as, I have nothing against Blacks (Turks, refugees), but . . . These disclaimers are designed to avoid a bad impression (He is a racist); they save face for the speaker.[12]

'The biases in the texts' that Dijk[13] mentions while explaining the critical discourse analysis are related to the approaches of individuals or institutions. For this reason, the political and economic structure of the media institution as the medium through which the news is put into circulation affects the semantic structure of the news.

Literature Reviews

Sensational events in the media have always been available for broadcating. Earthquake, flood, drought, Pandemic, war news have been widely covered in the media as breaking news and have been covered for days, months or even years. The winds blowing in North Africa and the Middle East countries as a result of the Arab Spring caused regime changes and various civil wars. It is seen that migration movements occur as a result of these problems. Today, an important issue of asylum seekers and adventure go of these refugees in Turkey to Europe are frequently processed as seen in the Turkish media and will

---

[10] İbid. p. 116

[11] İbid. p. 117.

[12] İbid. p. 118.

[13] İbid. p. 118.

continue to be processed. It is particularly noteworthy that the Middle East is a refugee-producing geography. As a result of refugees using Turkey as a transit country they had entered their life and death struggle, and often took part in the Turkish media as negative.[14] Syrians in refugee of newspapers are located in the following way: Syrian refugees cause economic difficulties for tradesmen, they form the majority in some cities in Turkey, they are disease carriers, Turkish citizen is done, they were children, they constitute a nuisance as refugees in Turkey, it was written with the increasing number of Syrians child brides.[15] In contrast, Turkey's large showing their generosity and look to the Syrian camp has been dominated by immigrants residing in the press discourse.According to Yilmaz, during the time they are exposed to all kinds of refugees to be hosted in Turkey socio-economic, psychological, rather than to taking responsibility and work on improving the physical and sexual violence; A discourse criminalizing, blaming and judging refugees was adopted, and the asylum seekers were marginalized and recorded as unwanted guests.[16]

On social media, the sharing of exclusionary and uniform discourses about refugees and the formation of masses around these discourses started to be worrying for the safety of refugees[17]. Afterwards, it is seen that the refugees started to marginalize and they concentrated on certain neighborhoods in cities with the instinct of protection.

It is seen in television news bulletins that the government focuses on protecting refugees and succeeding in its refugee policy.[18] It is seen that the news about the refugee problem in the news on Turkish television channels has a negative content. It is considered that the drama and judicial incident related to these news, the structure established on crime and the channels have a similar attitude in the normalization of this problem, separation from the social context and individualization.[19] In the news, it is seen that refugees are a burden on the economy, they are shown as masses of victims, they are represented as fear and hate, they are established as a courthouse case, and these news appear after the tabloid news, and that human fugitives are responsible for the deaths of refugees.[20]

In another research about the press, it was written that the press was extremely politicized, for example, the articles in *Hürriyet* newspaper had

[14] Kolukırık, Suat, "Mülteci ve Sığınmacı Olgusunun Medyadaki Görünümü: Medya Politiği Üzerine Bir Değerlendirme" **Gaziantep Üniversitesi Sosyal Bilimler Dergisi,** 2009, Cilt. 8, Sayı. 1, p. 8, http://sbe.gantep.edu.trp (Access 04.11.2020).

[15] Yılmaz, Tebessüm, "Türkiye'nin 'Misafirleri' Medyada "Suriyelilerin" Temsili". **Sosyal ve Beşerî Bilimler Dergisi**, 2020, Cilt. 4, Sayı. 1, pp. 8-19.

[16] İbid., p. 21.

[17] Oyman, Nihat, "Küresel ve Yerel Medyada Mülteci Olgusu", **Eğitime Bakış/Eğitim-Öğretim ve Bilim Araştırma Dergisi,** 2016, Sayı. 36, p. 8.

[18] Boztepe, Veli, "Televizyon Haberlerinde Suriyeli Mültecilerin Temsili, **İlef dergisi,** 2017, Cilt. 4, Sayı. 1, 2017, p. 117

[19] İbid. p. 117.

[20] İbid. p. 117.

exclusionary tones and that the political position of *Sabah* newspaper close to the government was effective in the refugee-friendly discourse. It is stated that frequently mentioned in the columns, emphasis such as forced guests or not going back to their countries draw attention.[21] Another study in Syrian refugees to the existence of discrimination rational grounds in Turkey, serving to build emotional reasons and the emotional that rationalization at the intersection of these two has been pointed out that becomes a problem in four main discursive plane: The presence of the first Syrian refugees are perceived as a threat. Second, the existence of Syrians is objectified by the emphasis on the number of refugees and money spent, not human rights. Thirdly, a discursive plane emerges that emotionalizes the reactions to the excessive visibility of Syrian refugees in cities, and is that not a word is mentioned in the news about their social and political reasons by suggesting conscientious solutions. Fourth, the news is dealt with heavy examples, it is mentioned with negative words such as fugitive, terrorist, coward, dirty, traitor, thief, free rider and ignorant, and the discourse is reproduced in this way.[22]

Likewise, in the research conducted by Göker and Keskin, it is stated that a negative content is produced in press news and this content is linked to political officials.[23] Newspapers with the highest circulation in Turkey on research conducted in the seven-year period, which serve to detect the news of Syrian refugees as a threat or a problem, and it was claimed that the return of Syrian refugees stereotype field. It has been revealed that the themes of the news are mostly economic problems, crime, security threat and war. It is stated that Syrian refugees are treated as a society in the news and represented as economic burden, threat, disturbing, criminal and invader.[24]

In a research conducted in the field of social media, it was pointed out that the frequency of positive and supportive social representations regarding Syrian refugees is less than negative representations, and that there are extreme racist discourses about refugees in the society.[25] Entries for the political perceived importance of the refugees in Syria appears to reflect the view that is used to examine when ruling party in Turkey, the refugees of social media participants that they are to emphasize the relationship between the AKP and the refugees' political interests.[26] In a research on social media, the problems that Syrian

---

[21] Çağlar, İ. ve Y. Özkır, "Suriyeli Mültecilerin Türkiye Basınında Temsili", Ortadoğu Yıllığı, 2014, p. 499.

[22] Doğanay, Ü ve Çoban Keneş, H., "Yazılı Basında Suriyeli 'Mülteciler': Ayrımcı Söylemlerin Rasyonel ve Duygusal Gerekçelerinin İnşası", Mülkiye Dergisi, 2016, Cilt. 40, Sayı. 1, pp. 117-118, https://dergipark.org.tr/en/pub/mulkiye/issue/37412/432816, (Access 05.11.2020).

[23] Göker, G. ve S. Keskin, "Haber medyası ve mülteciler: Suriyeli mültecilerin Türk yazılı basınındaki temsili", İletişim Kuram ve Araştırma Dergisi, Sayı. 41, 2015, p. 254.

[24] Kolaman, Sefer, N. Demir ve S. Bolat, "Türkiye'deki Suriyeli Mültecilerin Bir Tehdit Unsuru Olarak Yazılı Basında İnşası", **Uluslararası Hakemli İletişim ve Edebiyat Araştırmaları Dergisi**, Sayı. 15, 2017, pp. 58-59.

[25] Özdemir, F. ve Öner-Özkan, B., "Türkiye'de sosyal medya kullanıcılarının Suriyeli mültecilere ilişkin sosyal temsilleri" **Nesne**, Cilt. 4, Sayı. 8, 2016, 227-244, p. 240.

[26] İbid., p. 240.

refugees are subjected to a categorical marginalization and false claims are made about the refugees who want to be marked with all kinds of malice, and new enemies are invented as a tactic suitable for a post-truth politics, and the people are invented by considering the facts points out that they demand that hate feelings look through their glasses.[27]

In order to influence the attitude of the masses in the refugee crisis, the media has been used to the maximum and it is aimed to shape their thoughts.[28] With propaganda, which is a one-way communication effort, conditional conditioning has been created in humans and the depressed masses have been made pessimistic about their future. People have tried to escape from the country and escape. The most basic instinct of man, the struggle to survive, is clearly seen and experienced in this war in Syria.[29]

Findings

This section is written, the rising epidemic coronavirus crisis in the last months of 2020, caused the refugee problem to be thrown into the background. It is seen that there is little amount of news on this problem in newspapers and on television. The news on the refugee problem on the internet are at the bottom and in short.

In the newspapers, it is seen that countries that 'accept' and 'not' a refugee are differentiated. In the process of accepting Syrian refugees it is continuously compared with the European countries Turkey, Turkey 'humanitarian' Syrian refugees as 'guests' have size made, whereas European countries have rejected them in an unscrupulous manner. Syrian refugees as 'guests' have size made, whereas European countries have rejected them in an unscrupulous manner. Syrian refugees are put forward as the reason, not as the victim of war and their becoming an international crisis after becoming refugees.

Hürriyet newspaper, in the news published on its website on November 17, 2020, stated that the situation of the refugee camps in the Greek Islands of the Deputy Minister of Foreign Affairs was a humanitarian disaster and more than 7000 asylum seekers and immigrants were pushed by Greece in 2020. Here, the term being pushed means that the refugees were forced and sent to cause their death.

In the news published on the CNN Türk website on July 6, 2020, it was written that the member responsible for the affairs of the EU Commission stated that the allegations that the European Union has thrown back the refugees by

[27] Taş, O. ve T. Taş, "Post-Hakikat Çağında Sosyal Medyada Yalan Haber ve Suriyeli Mülteciler Sorunu", **Galatasaray Üniversitesi İletişim Dergisi**, Sayı. 29, 2018, p. 203.
[28] Çelik, Hüseyin, "Suriye ve Propaganda" **Uluslararası Politikada Suriye Krizi**, Ed.: H. Çomak, C. Sancaktar ve Z. Yıldırım, İstanbul, Beta, 2016, p. 316.
[29] İbid., p. 316.

Greece should be investigated. On this site, 'refugees were rescued, Turkey most refugees carrying the country, refugee boat sank, rescued many people, Greek security forces opened fire on irregular migrants, Youth and Sports Ministry Director as sports facilities are built for youngsters rhetoric supporting policies on immigrants from Turkey it seems to take place.

In the newspapers, it is seen that countries that 'accept' and 'not' a refugee are differentiated. In the process of accepting Syrian refugees it is continuously compared with the European countries Turkey, Turkey 'humanitarian' Syrian refugees as 'guests' have size made, whereas European countries have rejected them in an unscrupulous manner.

In these news articles in mainstream newspapers, they feel sorry for the Syrian refugees or see them as a threat to disrupt economic and social peace; it is built in a way that awaits the continuation of the guest-host opposition hierarchy. This section is written, the rising epidemic coronavirus crisis in the last months of 2020, caused the refugee problem to be thrown into the background. It is seen that there is little amount of news on this problem in newspapers and on television. The news on the refugee problem on the internet are at the bottom and in short.

In the newspapers, it is seen that countries that 'accept' and 'not' a refugee are differentiated. In the process of accepting Syrian refugees it is continuously compared with the European countries Turkey, Turkey 'humanitarian' Syrian refugees as 'guests' have size made, whereas European countries have rejected them in an unscrupulous manner. While creating a 'positive' meaning about Syrian refugees, the whole meaning depicting a passive, needy and poor group is seen. *The Sabah* newspaper, which supports the government, has published publications supporting the work of the government and non-governmental organizations that express the refugee problem. There are news such as 'Syrian refugees photo exhibition, opposition responsibility and Syrians, Syrians support program'. This newspaper criticized the policies of Greece and the European Union and stated that these countries committed crimes against humanity against refugees. In Turkey's opposition *Cumhuriyet* newspaper charged that the refugees can not take anymore, migrants are expressed frustration and anger that turned to the European prospects. Syrian brought to Turkey as the government is seen that the writings that criticized the Syrian policy.

It is seen that *Milliyet* newspaper concentrates on the problems in refugee camps in Greece and the attitude of the European Union on this issue. Refugee incidents in France and Greece were mentioned in the news published in *Akşam* newspaper. As it referred praised Turkey's refugee policy and immigration and refugee that good governance is seen by Turkey as exemplified by the focus on. Sözcü, the opposition to the government newspaper, the government's refugee policy is wrong, that at least 5 million refugees in Turkey, and it seems that it did not create these problems for publications.

According to mainstream newspapers, Syrian refugees are a multi-layered threat. The primary threat is economy. A lot of money is spent for Syrian refugees and it is estimated that more will be spent.

Another aspect of Syrian refugees being seen as a threat is also a matter of security. With regard to security, two meanings are produced as social and cultural security and security against actual attacks. The meaning of the texts such as the future of terrorist organizations along with the Syrian refugees, the sale of women and children in the camps, and the conflict with the police working to ensure the security of the camps, which are frequently seen in the news texts collected under the heading of refugee camps, are formed in the form of actual attack. In the news texts, it describes a group that is not similar to 'we', and gives a description of a subclass from 'we' in various ways, especially begging and having more than 'we' children. The difference in the political stance of *Cumhuriyet*, *Sözcü* and *Sabah* newspapers is also very indistinct regarding Syrian refugees. The meaning formed by the words used by *Sabah* newspaper in events other than the statements of politicians and the texts prepared systematically enough to form the phrase 'where, how many people, how much money was spent' is common in all three newspapers.

In news portals, which set out to create alternative news content, similar to the perception of 'a group that is constantly and rapidly increasing from 'us' about the birth rates of the Syrian refugees in the mainstream media, 'Syrians' birth rates exceeded Turks!' 'Refugee children are born every day in tent cities', 'six years in Turkey 276 thousand 158 Syrians baby was born' as possible to see under the headings.

Defining Syrian refugees seems to be a big problem for the mainstream media. The words 'Syrian emigrant', 'Syrian refugee', 'illegal immigrant', 'illegal migrant', 'illegal asylum seeker', 'Syrian' are not used consistently in the texts within the institution or even in the same news text.

It can be observed that being a guest in the news texts coincides with the positioning of 'pity', 'showing sublime volunteering' and 'knowing the limits'. In addition, the word 'hospitality' is problematic in terms of observing the law of refugees. Refugee signifies a framework in national and international law. Hospitality, on the other hand, has no legal status and the human rights of refugees cannot be met with this concept. *Cumhuriyet* Newspaper, which are often used in word and seen the morning newspaper 'guest' and 'host' words leads to a serious loss on the status of refugees in Turkey

In the news that is thought to draw a positive frame, mercy is declared as strong and weak, while declaring the poor, pointing out the help, and positioning them as passive. The definitions of 'us' and 'other' in the news about Syrian refugees also vary according to the event and the subject. 'Turkey and the European countries', 'Turkish-Syrian' opposition which is positioned as lasts through benchmarking. Refugee camps, Syrian refugees on issues such as

European countries, we are working to pass to Turkey, while they have been in the European countries. Excess of the steps taken by Turkey regarding Syrian refugees is compared with the lack of initiative of European countries.

Conclusion

Immigration movements caused by war, poverty and other reasons cause refugee crises. Especially people who want to immigrate to the USA and the EU to their countries believe that their hopes will come true by immigrating to these regions. As Turkey is a transit country between western and eastern Arab spring, especially with the result of internal turmoil in the Middle East, it has become an area of intense migration. Especially Syrian immigrants settled in Turkey, some of which they look for new ways to migrate to the EU countries and have tried. Refugee problem has become one of Turkey's main issues. The problem continues in the 2020s. Due to the multifaceted dimension of this issue, it has been frequently featured in the Turkish media. It is seen that refugees are a subject in the internet as well as in newspapers and on television. This problem has become a political problem rather than a human being, and the EU countries have been positioned in the media as countries that do not accept immigrants. It is seen that the refugees staying in the camps in the Aegean Sea Islands are in a difficult situation and the news that Greece forces the refugees back and causes their deaths are frequently covered in the media.

Mainstream newspapers depict refugees as an economic and social threat. Turkey's sacrifice refugees, expressed his kindness and humanity. It is mentioned that refugees in Turkey through a variety of statements made in the media about the positive and negative meanings that are loaded while the EU countries. Especially Syrian migrants are seen as a security threat, and terrorists who are mixed with migrants are mentioned in newspapers. It constitutes a news narrative consisting of us and the other through implications in the news texts. The guest rhetoric implies that they are here temporarily. A confusion in the status is caused by creating host versus guest opposition. To sum up, it can be stated that Turkey allusions negative rhetoric in the media created the refugee crisis arises where as a threat.

CHAPTER 18

MEDIA AND LANGUAGE STUDIES: COMPARATIVE ANALYSIS OF SYRIAN CIVIL WAR'S MEDIA COVERAGE

Discourse On 'Democracy and Arab Spring Concept'

In The Years of 2011-2015: BBC and Regional Reports

Beyza Dut[1] and Nilüfer Pembecioğlu[2]

Introduction

The language of the news on television and the internet, the publications that are relevant to the whole world, are generally published in English. These publications are naturally provided through English syntax. The increasingly more abstracting attitude and universalization of the concepts in the Modern Era seem to be the mere evidence of modernity. The minute details of experiences do not include all of the factors structuring these experiences due to the global interdependence of all events. Thus, the genuine experiences of the Middle East increasingly conditioned by the international, social and political factors through certain political terminology that is mainly used by the international media.

21st century's philosophy essentially needs to place the 'language studies' with modern questionings. Through globalization, knowledge of reality depends upon the trusted resources in use. For Continental Philosophers *language philosophy* is involved with the historical, political and social events of the *nations*. It is believed that creating certain logical approaches for thinking and creating reality as well as practices depend upon the language philosophy.

Linguists such as Saussure, Meillet and Vendryes have considered language as the primary 'social *event*'. As Meillet states, '*all events in the language is organized by certain social agreements*'. According to Saussure; Language is a social system and the word is an individual action.[3]

Language studies cannot show us '*whether the language or the nation has the priority*'. According to Humboldt, the languages cannot contain the words having the same meaning, because the *nations speak different languages that taking its roots from different entities which are having different conditionals* requiring certain

[1] Istanbul University, Turkey. ORCID: 0000-0003-1715-6768 E-mail: hilaldut@gmail.com
[2] Prof. Dr./ Istanbul University, Türkiye. ORCID: 0000-0001-7510-6529
E-mail: niluferpembecioglu@gmail.com

[3] Berke Vardar, Dilbilim Yazıları, Istanbul, Multilingual, 2001, pp.28-29

agreements/settlements.[4] However, the same agreement on the same words might not be possible for two different languages.

Social interaction in one community is somewhat easy. But international interaction among the communities specifically, through print media which means through different languages require more attention. There seems to be some strict rules to become a part of the global media. According to WAN 2004[5] report, almost all countries are losing audience even in the most developed countries while the developing countries are increasing their share. Thus, the criteria of being 'global' changes in the 21st century. For example, 392 million daily newspapers are scattered throughout the world reaching to a billion of readers all over the world. Yet, being global for a newspaper requires the print media to reach at least to three continents, printed in English and reach a circulation of at least 50.000 overall in those continents.

Whereas the top of the newspapers of the world are mainly from USA and UK, it's becoming somewhat imperative to gain the global perspective within the dynamics of the English language in a world of thinking and creating global reports. Regarding the communication technology, USA seems to be the center of the North. Yet, in Europe, Germany, UK, France are among the 'producer' countries in terms of news, agenda and dissemination. Having these dynamics, the countries in Latin America, Africa, Asia and Middle East are positioned to be the 'consumers'. That's why these USA and UK newspapers, circulating more than the others, function as a mediator in between cultures, politics and societies. In other words, these newspapers are creating the pioneer international reports in English and most of the global news are delivered through them throughout the world.

This study is inspired from socio-linguistics as a starting point that is mainly studying the linguistics perspectives and language differences of the cultures in the world. As known in general, sociolinguistics not only concerned with the relationship between language and society, but also about how language use interacts with the society or how it is affected by social factors such as gender roles, ethnicity, age or social class.

According to a FP (Foreign Policy) article which is based on the book written by Christian Reus-Smit '*On Cultural Diversity: International Theory in a World of Difference*'; the researchers on international norms explored that, domestic-level structures and processes affect compliance of nations. Concentrating the '*domestic legitimacy of international norms*' on media coverage of others' case make out that there is insufficient attention on measuring the '*legitimacy or salience of international norms in the domestic arena*'.[6]

---

[4] Bedia Akarsu, Dil-Kültür Bağlantısı, İstanbul, İnkılap, 1998, p.26

[5] World Association of Newspapers 2004.

[6] Christian Reus-Smit, On cultural diversity: International theory in a world of difference. Cambridge University Press, 2018.

Even if the media studies have focused on *'journalistic roles'* of foreign news framing events for 'local readers' to render them suitable for national audiences, yet there has been less attention to similar roles played by *'other social actors'* like regional or local news that are bringing in *'new models'* about existing realities.

This study aims to question the international media from the perspective of their/our news dichotomy. Whereas different nations/state's foreign policy interests converge with each other, the meanings of 'their' news based on 'shared assumptions' are constructed by news organizations in different nations/states depending on their choice of professional or national narrative.

Introduction to Language and International Media

The language studies took its central position throughout the intellectual field throughout the 17th century with thinkers like Hobbes and Locke. In the 20th century, however, no matter which problem involves within its area of interest, the language studies began to engage almost every mind. Since the 20th century, intellectual activities seem to be not independent of language-related problems. The major philosophers such as Heidegger, Wittgenstein, Davidson and Derrida of this century also concentrated on language theories.

Ferdinand de Saussure is the first linguist to discuss the distinction between "langue" and "parole," which is the separation of language and word, and to theoretically analyze this problem.[7] Throughout the time, the concept of 'usage' has gained importance at the point where language has focused on the act of 'wording' in other words Speech Acts in Austin's terms. 'Usage' is the point of meeting and merging of the word in language. Some researchers advocated to call 'discourse' for the functional side of the 'word' and embarked the idea of adoption of this concept (discourse) as a medium term. They gave priority to 'discourse' in terms of both being an action and an abstraction.[8] The function and meaning of the media or the old word *'press'* is questionable and differs through nations; as we see in the following examples:

The word Press in English, La Presse in French, Die Presse in German, La Stampa in Italian, are mostly all covered as 'printing' in Turkish. The 'press' means art of printing. It covers not only the print material but also the dissemination of it through the 15th century. All the related concepts such as the invention of the printing press, the development of it, the spreading of ideas to a large extent, all are considered as the industry or business of printing. In the United States, the term 'Mass Communication' is used instead of the word 'Press' and 'Mass Media of Communication' refers to the tools of mass media. In Belgium, the term 'Technique de diffusion' is used instead of the word 'press'. This term includes only the material part of the means of communication. The word 'journalisme' in French, just means the 'journalism' in English, yet it is far from involving the whole content of the press.

[7] Vardar, Dilbilim Yazıları, p.33

[8] Vardar, Dilbilim Yazıları, p.35

In this respect, we see the usage of the word 'information' in the French language in the sense of 'press and publication'. It is argued that it is appropriate to the term of 'press and publication' because it represents the quality to cover the freedom of the press and the instruments of the press, but it is faced with the objection that it does not include the interpretation and judgement which is the expression as 'opinion'.[9]

The fixed terminology of the international media makes it impossible to understand the local or regional problems. Today's international media contains problems with certain news being downgraded into a certain pattern and most importantly, familiarized, standardized as much as possible. In order to solve this problem, we need to handle the international news reports on different regions a bit more suspiciously. To reach out the first-hand experience and information regarding the events the international media reports should be written down by educated, trained reporters who are used to the techniques, language, knowledge, equipment of the related area. It would be better if they could be using a more sensitive language, having the right information from the original people of the land, concentrating on human stories, instead of making quick decisions or having prejudices.

The level of linguistic and cultural imperialism cannot be adequately accounted for this situation. The historical roots of globalization lie in colonial period, and its main effect has been to create a general and standardized way of thinking. It includes the flow of ideas, cultural products from developed nations, general concepts regarding life styles. Mainly, the US produces almost all of the media content and it is consumed by the others, for example, Africa, Middle East, Europe, etc. The television stations heavily rely on the news imported from American and European contents.

Introduction to Syrian Civil War and Media Reports

Media discourse plays an important role regarding how conflicts are perceived. Unlike the domestic news, in foreign news the media outlets, are often the only source of information for ongoing events. In foreign conflicts the case is even worse. The international media coverage participates in creating what is understood as the 'reality' of the conflict through choosing which aspects of the conflict are covered, which topics are highlighted and which actors are interviewed.

Regarding the international media coverage of the *'Syrian Civil War'*; the news highly reported in collocation with the *'Arab Spring'* and *'Democracy'* concept. Through reporting the current events to the readers and viewers; the international media sets the foundation for '*imagining the future*' based on their own past experiences like comparing the '*Arab Spring*' to '*Berlin Wall*' which has been reported through many news and articles. By doing so they tend to create a vision

[9] M. Nuri İnuğur, Basın ve Yayın Tarihi, Der Yayınları, İstanbul, 2005, p.23

of how the situation looks like now and how can it look evolve in future, later.

Throughout the research, handling the topic of *'Democracy'* which is said to be the core of the *'Arab Spring'* Saussure's approach is adopted. Democracy as a *'concept'* is analyzed in both linguistic roots and philosophical critics considering the changes of methods from ancient Greek applications to modern democracy applications started in the Enlightenment era. Saussure stated that: '*language as a system of signs can be studied as a complete system at any given point through diachronic analysis which is described as; the change in the meaning of words over time*'.[10] Diachronic approach can also be classified as *historical linguistics,* it is thus the study of language in terms of how it visibly changes in use, by paying attention to affinity between language and historical transmutations. Synchronic approach analyses mean to study the similarities and differences of languages at a given point of time by focusing on their structural features and characteristics. *'A person cannot deal with something from both synchronic and diachronic perspectives at the same time nevertheless both perspectives are necessary'* Saussure added. He makes this distinction as a part of an argument for studying linguistics from a synchronic as well as a diachronic perspective. Some scholars also do not see the two approaches apart from each other. They assert that it is a mistake to think of descriptive and historical linguistics as two separate compartments.

The German philosopher Koselleck states: '*each synchronization 'eo ipsa (spontaneously) is also the diacrole*'. All temporal dimension is always nested inside from past to future and the current time are added manually or conversely, to define the future as one of the moments in the history of leaked copies cannot be held for future crossing points is contrary to the whole experience.[11]

Saussure explains the difference between these two perspectives, starting argument by imagining a plant. If we cut the body of the plant longitudinally, we can see the fibers that 'form the plant' but if we cut transversely (cross-sectional cut) we see fibers are in a certain relationship which is non-looking longitudinally.[12] Thus, a perspective that is synchronous or diachronic affects what they see. The differences between synchronic and diachronic analysis are shown in Table 1.

[10] Ferdinand De Saussure, Charles Bally, Albert Sechehaye, Albert Riedlinger, Cours de linguistique générale, Payot, 1916.

[11] Reinhert Koselleck, Kavramlar Tarihi, Politik ve Sosyal Dilin Semantiği ve Pragmatiği Üzerine Araştırmalar, Çev: Atilla Dirim, İletişim, 2009.

[12] Arthur Asa Berger, Cultural Criticism: A Primer of Key Concepts, SAGE Publication, 1995.

Table 1. A Comparison of Synchronic and Diachronic Analysis[13]

SYNCHRONIC	**DIACHRONIC**
Synchronisation	Subsequence
Constant	Evolutianary
In A System	In A Time
Connections	Connections
Sequential / Paradigmatic	Syntagmatic
LEVI STRAUSS	**PROPP**

According to the table taken from Berger's[14] Syntagmatic Analysis, a text is examined as a sequence of events that forms some kind of narrative Vladimir Propp, a Russian folklorist, who wrote a pioneering book in 1928 titled Morphology of the Folktale was following a method like undertaking a comparison of the themes for the sake of comparison by separating the component parts then making comparison of the tales according to their components. Propp refers to the essential or basic narrative unit in his study as a *'function'* which is understood as an act of a character, defined from the point of view of its significance *for the course of the action* (diachronic). Claude Levi-Strauss[15] in the 1950s, analyzed cultural phenomena and he produced more *linguistically-focused* writings where he applied *Saussure's distinction* between *langue and parole* in his search for the fundamental mental structures of the human mind, arguing that the structures that form the '*deep grammar*' of society originate in the *mind* and operate in us *unconsciously*.

In summary, the structuralism approach is applied for the comparison of languages of international media and regional media regarding the coverage Syrian Civil War; through the course of synchronic and diachronic analysis to go into deep analysis of democracy concept in both linguistic and philosophical applications throughout history.

The Aim of the Study

This study is concentrating on the international media representations through the language and concepts created during the 2011-2015 Syrian Civil War Reportings. The aim of the study is to apply a kind of 'comparative and contrastive analysis' on English and Arabic languages regarding the concepts limited with the words of 'Democracy, Freedom, Justice, Right, Arab Spring, International War'. In doing so, it explores the relationship between the news production process and the reception process of the audience from the point of view of differences regarding the native language perspective.

Consequently, this study aims to concentrate on analyzing the news reporting throughout the first era of the Syrian Civil War. That means the data is dwelling

[13] Arthur Asa Berger, (2004) Techniques of Interpretation, 2004 (Çevrimiçi https://uk.sagepub.com/sites/default/files/upm-binaries/5171_Berger_Final_Pages_Chapter_1.pdf (Erişim 8.1.2021)

[14] Berger, op.cit.

[15] Claude Lévi-Strauss, Social structure, Anthropology Today, 1953, pp.24-53.

more on the 'wording' of the news rather than the coverage itself. Yet, throughout the words, the study aims to reach to a certain 'discourse' level to include similar or substitute words.

Media linguistics is the linguistic study of media speech. It studies the function of language in the media sphere, or the modern mass communication presented by print, audio-visual and networked media.[16] Media linguistics investigate the relationship between language use and public discourse conveyed through the media. In general, it focuses on the function of the language throughout the way the news is prepared that is called the news production process. Yet, this study mainly aims to figure out the structure of the product – that is called to be the 'news itself'. In other words, the study concentrates more on the wording of the news and the way they were made to mean and cover the concepts.

Media linguistics focuses on the use of language in journalistic products; current media linguistics tendencies expand this focus in different directions. As Luginbühl mentioned, these tendencies are summarized as; the expansion on non-linguistic or paralinguistic signs (multimodality), the expansion of a cultural dimension (culturally) and the expansion on the whole communicative process (including the production and reception).[17]

The main concern of this study basically is not only questioning the media language but also questioning the process of a 'creating concepts' in international media. In other words, this study aims to concentrate on analyzing the 'process' rather than the 'product'. Throughout the research, the process of production and reception have to be taken into account as well. The study is not only concentrating on *English speaking* or *Arabic speaking* communities but also on the concepts and dynamics of the 'Western way of conceptualizations' which is rooted from Ancient Greek to Renaissance era up to the date.

The dynamics of journalism work through the society, changing the tendencies and daily habits of the people. In order to maintain this specific aim, the new media also creates new ways such as new wording and creative use of language by various hashtags, short catchy words and memorable references covering the subject in various ways. Even if it seems to be enriching the subject or making it worldwide, visible and transparent in all facades, like abbreviations, hashtags and other ways acting to direct the attention of the people to a certain think-tank defined before. Thus, this kind of wording created in certain languages and delivered as an international portray of situation, actually prevents the reality or truth to be discovered by receivers.

Since the target of the study is not a linguistic one, but more some research

[16] https://en.wikipedia.org/wiki/Media_linguistics (Erişim 15.05.2019)

[17] Marc Luginbühl, Media linguistics: On mediality and culturality. 10PLUS1 Living Linguistics, 1, 1925, pp.9-26.

focusing on the wording choices of international media. The short term objective of the study dwells on the language choice and representation of democracy. However, the long term objective extends to the linguistic studies in international media beyond discourse analysis.

This involves analyzing the roots of language differences as well as the cultural aspects and experiences which are settled in applications of reporting visions of international media. Whereas the 'language philosophy' is used throughout many other social studies, media wording seems to be a neglected field of study.

Methodology

The study is based on The Media Monitoring approach on Syria in Global Media; it includes collecting data regarding the global media coverage of Syrian Civil War between 2011-2015 and the analysis of the data. The selected global media tools are limited to BBC results and regional media. Additionally, the regional and / or local media is focused to compare the discourse of the news in English and Arabic Language, seeking an answer to the question of '*What is really going on in Syria?*'.

Generally, the global media reports include the home country's geopolitical position and its policy on Syria. According to Felm-1859 reports 2015 is the year that the coverage on the refugee topic increased from 7% to 23% only after the refugee crisis started reaching Europe in August 2015 and decreased again to 11%. The physical proximity of the refugee issue to increase the European media's interest in the topic. In the same year, '*Terrorism and Conflict*' news had the greatest share of media coverage; during the period of analysis comprising 46-48% of all coverage on Syria. There are also examples of ISIS receiving greater media attention at the expense of humanitarian aid and refugees as well as the suffering of civilians.

Thus, this research is mainly based on the concepts like '*Arab Spring*' and '*Democracy*' that are observed to be used in concordance with Syrian Civil War on international media coverage throughout 2011-2015.

The two 'forms' in the table above; 'Democracy' as background of 'Arab Spring' discourse mostly turned to be the words like 'right', 'freedom', 'justice' in Regional Media that seems to be the real demands of Syrian people. These words were observed on the banners and videos of songs or in the early posts of the rebellions commenting through the social media.

As pointed out in Table 1, the wordings of the International media changes throughout the time (2011-2015). The essence of the subject named as the '*Syrian Uprisings*' changed to be the '*Syrian Civil War*' and later to the '*International War*'. Diachronically between 2011-2015 the 'Arab Spring' concept used for Syria turned to be named as '*Terrorism*' and '*Immigration*'.

Table 2. The 'Meaning' of Syrian Civil War in the concept of the 'Form, Essence, Word and Language'

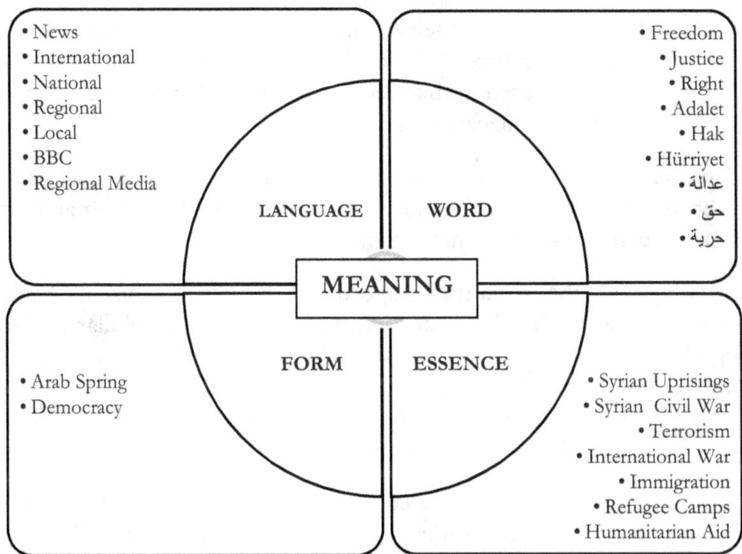

Table 2 brings forth the 'Meaning' of Syrian Civil War in the the concept of the 'Form, Essence, Word and Language' format to see how they are related to each other and how they differ. The study concentrates on Language and Media, in case of Syrian Civil War using the tools of BBC vs. Regional Media; pursuing the meaning of the Syrian Civil War media coverage differing through International Media (BBC) and Regional Media. The aspect of the use of main 'language' (English) and the 'form' (Arab Spring and Democracy) created through the global media; is not compatible with the 'essence' of the case. The time limitations force the data to be collected through the ranges of 2011 and 2015. This is due to the change of the Syrian Uprising to the Syrian Civil War and finally to Terrorism headings. Whereas the naming of the event was changing, the slip of the main discourse changes from the concept of democracy to comparative concepts such as justice, freedom, right.

The particularly selected 16 reports from BBC and Regional Arab media are analyzed regarding these concepts used for explaining the 'Syrian Civil War', 'Democracy' and 'Arab Spring'. The use of words like 'justice', 'freedom' and 'right' in the regional reports will be analyzed through the corpus they occur in. Comparing and contrasting the data the findings of the study would be evaluated through the 12T's approach.

This study will be focusing on one of those elements that; ethnicity in global media, as the global language, English dominates all the expressions to cover different regional events. In other words, this study is an attempt to contribute to our understanding of the 'Global Media Conceptualizations' through the particular era of the past events regarding 'Western World of Thoughts/Disciplines'. As people develop an understanding on focusing these given structures of forms, they lose their chances of producing original thoughts and cannot think out of the box. The theory of Saussure's synchronic and diachronic approach will be used in this study to handle and evaluate the Syrian case throughout the global media analysis.

The study will be grounded on the synchronic and diachronic analysis of Saussure who is known to be the founder of contemporary linguistics and the pioneer of the structural linguistic movement.

Concentrating on the diachronic approach the issue aims to make comparisons of specific media texts including certain vocabulary, thus considering the change of vocabulary as a part of cultural change through historical approach. Concentrating on the synchronic approach, the study aims to analyze the news wording differences of local and international media regarding the first era of Syrian uprisings' media coverage.

Reaching to a corpus of the repeated concepts such as '*Arab Spring*' and '*democracy*' in local and global media, the data is analyzed regarding the comparative discourse analysis methodology questioning the concepts like '*freedom*', '*justice*' and '*rights*' which are seem as the dominant use in Arabic language. Finally, all results are analyzed according to the analytical methodology of conceptualization with the 12T's approach, namely through the following headlines: theme, topic, text, task, transfers, transitions, thinking, tailoring, taking risks, technology and transmedia.

Literature Review

'A noble man cannot be indebted for his culture to a narrow circle;

the world and his native land must act on him.'

Goethe

Literature Review On Language Philosophy

As the main tool of the thought, the language was always in the core of the philosophy studies from the very beginning. The study of the language appeared to be a phenomenon throughout the second half of the nineteenth century. After Kant's influence, traditional metaphysics was no longer the main subject of philosophy. Thus, the use of disciplined words and concepts, which are dominant in the natural sciences turned to be the main tools used in social sciences.

Kant's approach, having its origins from empiric philosophy and positivism, has addressed the language itself *as a problem* rather than addressing the '*problems expressed by language*'. As the main subject of philosophy, language has been studied in three different branches: *language philosophy, analytical philosophy and linguistics.*

To begin with language philosophy, it is important to understand that the 'mother tongue' of any individual is intimately associated with individual's culture.[18]

Likewise, every spoken language limits the experience; the experiences in a certain culture could only be expressed in their way (language). As John Stuart Mill says in the Use and Abuse of Political Terms: '*Humanity has many ideas, but few words to say. The number of words is limited; the thoughts that can be expressed by these words are ideas, thoughts, objects and realities are potentially unlimited, this is because they have a long-term stability.*'[19]

Ferdinand de Saussure was a Swiss linguistic credited with founding the field of structural linguistics, a radical new theory of language is a structured system. He is often referred to as *the father of modern linguistics* an honor divided between him and Noam Chomsky depending on who you ask. His most influential work '*Course in General Linguistics*' was published posthumously in 1916.[20] The key ideas of structuralism are classified; as *Signifier and Signified*, *Parole* and *Langue*, *Synchrony-Diachrony* and *Paradigm and Syntagm*. Saussure's 'sign' consists of the signifier and signified; The *signifier* is the sounds of the letters that are used to denote what we're talking about, *signified* is the actual concept of the thing that is the idea in our minds when you hear or read the signifier. The actual real thing in the world is called the: *referent*; note the difference between the thought of a cat and an actual real cat; the sign is a two sided psychological entity as one can't exist without the other it just couldn't be a *sign*. However, there is an arbitrary and conventional relationship between a *signifier* and *its signified*; since there is no natural reason why we call a cat '*a cat*' that's why the different languages have different words for the same thing. The convention of language refers to the idea that a speech community needs to adhere to the same connections between a signifier and signified. For example, English speakers all share a very similar concept of cat when they hear that word.[21]

Saussure also distinguished; *the use of language* 'Parole' (what the individual speaks) and *the system of language;* 'Langue' (what is shared by the community). Langue, being the system of language, such as *syntax* or *phonology* is an *abstract* system; parole on the other hand is the use of that language based on an *individualistic matter* like people have their own language quirks. Saussure also distinguished language studies as Synchrony and Diachrony. Synchrony refers to a complete language system at just one point in time; as a snapshot of language.

---

[18] Ravi Pieris, Speech and Society: A sociological approach to language. *American Sociological Review, 16(4),* 1951, pp.499-505.

[19] Koselleck, op.cit, pp.xx

[20] Ferdinand De Saussure, Course In General Linguistics. Literary Theory: An Anthology, 2, 2004, pp.59-71.

[21] Saussure, op.cit.

Diachrony on the other hand is how that language develops over time; this is also known as *historical linguistics*. We may have noticed changes in language over our life time with different words appearing disappearing or slight pronunciation changes; that's diachrony.

Up to the structuralist approach, the study of languages was based on belief systems and politics; he did freeing language of social, cultural, political, historical associations practically this led structural relation alone independently and linguistic objects meaning is understood through its contrast with other linguistic objects in the system. Language is therefore a static system of these interconnected linguistic objects (units).

Language, Culture and Thought

Once the language philosophers have revealed the general principle of an idea, they begin to wonder about how certain characteristics of a certain language are related to the characteristics of a particular society. It is also something that changes or develops the thoughts at the same time.[22] It can be said that Humboldt was the first to examine the language in culture. Humboldt placed the language in history by linking it to the development of human culture and saw language as a historical process that has evolved with every step of human development. The words in many languages are never really synonymous, even if they show the same concepts.[23] Wilhelm von Humboldt, the pioneer in both general linguistics and language philosophy, is the one who made the first step towards classifying languages and classifying the language to certain basic types. Humboldt's view of philosophy on language is based on the assumption that; *each language is bearer of a language-specific worldview.* According to Bedia Akarsu, an advanced culture can only be achieved in an advanced language. The indicator of the identity of a person is the language of that nation, as it is the indicator of the identity of man, the language s/he speaks and writes. The problem of language-culture connection is gaining more importance in nowadays when the problem of identity is discussed as well.[24]

French Philosopher Etienne de Condillac wrote '*All the signs confirm that a language expresses the character of those people speaking that language*'. Condillac's young colleague German Johans Gottfired Herder had the same idea: '*Every language reflects the understanding and character of those who speak it.*'[25]

According to the *Whole Language Approach*[26] that connects the thought and the interpretation process to a pre-linguistic process, language is a tool only carrying

[22] Atakan Altınörs, 50 Soruda Dil Felsefesi, Bilim ve Gelecek Kitaplığı, İstanbul, 2012

[23] Akarsu, op.cit. pp.26-30.

[24] Akarsu, op.cit. p.30

[25] Guy Deutscher, Dilin Aynasından Kelimeler Dünyamızı Nasıl Renklendirir, Çev: Cemal Yardımcı, Metis Bilim, İstanbul, 2013.

[26] Stephen Krashen, Language acquisition and language education: Extensions and applications. Prentice Hall International, 1989.

thoughts and thus enables communication. It presents the '*free thought*' created by the individual as a means of communication and conveys these meaningful expressions to other language users. According to this second view, the language creates a partial determinism by offering limited options to a thought to be expressed, but it does not harm freedom in the formation of thought.[27]

Often it is said that the language of public reflects its culture/s, soul and the mentality, the way of thinking. For instance, the grammar of some languages do not have *adequate* logical expressions to clarify complex ideas. In some languages, the structure does not allow individuals to be productive, yet, the previously mentioned approaches to classify the languages as primitive and modern seem to be failed about two or three decades ago. According to Deutscher, all languages are sufficient enough to express even the most complex ideas, even in the most primitive tribes. Some languages do not have a future tense; this means the speakers of those languages have not included the time of future in their world view. So it is difficult for them to utterly understand the future tense and future perspective even if they are taught. For example, the Babylonians were having difficulties to understand crime and punishment, because their language covered these two concepts with one word.[28]

Akarsu refers to Humboldt's point of view as follows: '*One can get into the worldview of a foreign language completely because one is always under the pressure of the worldview of his/her own language. The world view of the language dominates people, providing them a certain direction in life.*'[29]

Locke insists on this: if the languages are compared, it is seen that there are no exact words matching with each other. To him, a word can be understood as a whole in its entirety with its all meanings. In each era each independent writer adds his/her own style, making use of his own individuality in his language. Thus, it is inevitable to keep the language as it is on one hand, but also it is changing, developing with each contribution.

According to Wittgenstein; speaking a language is part of an activity or a life form.[30] With the concepts of 'language games' and 'life forms' raised in philosophical questionings; the language develops a '*contextual*' and '*pragmatic*' approach that emphasizes that meaning should be sought in the context in which the sentence is used. To him, the context provides the meaning of the form.

These ideas, occurring through the second period of Wittgenstein, providing the basis for the 'pragmatic approach' of philosophers such as Austin, Searle and Grice. They gave importance to the idea that the philosophy of language could be considered as the second language to discuss the philosophy of daily language.

---

[27] Yasin Ceylan, Anlam Kavramı Üzerine Yeni Denemeler, Dil Kültür İlişkisi, Legal Devlet ve Hukuk Kuramı Kitaplığı, ODTÜ Felsefe, 2010, p.259

[28] Deutscher, Dilin Aynasından Kelimeler Dünyamızı Nasıl Renklendirir

[29] Akarsu, op.cit. pp.26-30.

[30] Ludwig Wittgenstein, Diarios secretos (Vol. 68). Anaya-Spain, 1998, p.23

To them, the speech is a social practice defined by some rules.

According to the Sapir-Whorf hypothesis, whom were inspired by Humboldt, *every society's or culture's language varies from the lifestyles of each public.* Sapir believes that the real world is built on the habits of society. '*The worlds of different societies are separated/ differs, otherwise they would be just the same objects that are labeled with different names (in other languages).*'[31] Their hypothesis includes a thought that suggests significant continuity between studies in the field of social anthropology. Hall, suggesting that each culture is a different classification style of the world,[32] with this hypothesis, puts forward that these classification schemes will be reflected in the linguistic and semantic structures of different societies.[33]

Franz Boas, the teacher of Sapir, has a general understanding of the relationship between language and culture. When the vocabulary of people from different cultures are examined, it has been observed that the word is the basic element of culture and it reflects the importance of the objects and activities surrounding that society. In every culture, vocabulary reflects the relationship between human and natural environment as the witness of their life style.'[34]

Benjamin Whorf, one of the students of Sapir underlines the more radical approach called 'cultural relativism'. To him, the language is not merely an instrument that allows reflection of our ideals but even more importantly it determines the form of mind that guides the individual's mental activities.

Edgar Morin, dwelling on the relationship between language and culture in the context of philosophical anthropology (human philosophy), says: '*Language is not merely a means of communication, but rather a complex organization of the society in general.*' According to Morin, it would be reasonable to say that not man creates the language, language creates the man.[35]

According to Michael Tomasello, people start out behind other animals in life. People have a string of scattered genetic instructions, so they can't survive on their own when they're born and even they've been around for years. As the great anthropologist Clifford Geertz put it, '*Man is an incomplete animal. The most distinctive form of human from other animals is before he become active his ability to learn much more than certain things he must learn.*' In his book named 'Social Animal' David Brooks is arguing that: '*people are successful when they have the ability to produce advanced cultures. A single human mind cannot cope with a variety of stimulants that flock to the front. We can survive in the world just because we're buried in the cultural pier. We absorb the ethnic*

---

[31] Altınörs, 50 Soruda Dil Felsefesi, p.38

[32] Stuart Hall, Culture, Community, Nation, Cultural studies, 7(3), 1993, pp.349-363.

[33] Hülya Yengin, Medyanın dili: iletişime kuramsal bir yaklaşım, popüler kültür türlerinin çözümlenmesi, Der Yayınları, 1996.

[34] Franz Boaz, 1858). 1942. Antropologia cultural/Franz Boas; tradução, Celso Castro, 1858, s. 178'den aktaran, Altınörs, 50 Soruda Dil Felsefesi, p.36

[35] Benjamin Lee Whorf, Linguistique et anthropologie (p. 220). Paris: Denoël, 1969, s. 125'den aktaran Altınörs, 50 Soruda Dil Felsefesi, p.38

cultures, institutional cultures and regional cultures that shape our thoughts to a great extent.'[36]

However, culture is a collection of habits, customs, practices, beliefs, arguments and tensions that regulate and direct human life. It contains narratives, special days, symbols and works of art that convey implicit and often unnoticeable messages about how to feel, how to react, and how to find meaning. A cultural structure like 'language' can change the way people look at the world. To Brooks, culture dissolves some patterns to our brains and destroys others. Douglas Hofstadter states that language is '*comforting but full of abstract patterns, impossible to define*' as abomination, fair play, foolishness, dreams, frigidity, moodiness, you and me.[37]

Name and Meaning (Naming and Meaning Relation)

The problem of 'meaning' is the root of language philosophy and the question of '*what is meaning in philosophy*' is searching on what makes the expression meaningful. This question leads to the language studies to the very first moment that linguistic expressions are identified. According to Foucault to reveal the roots of the language, it is necessary to point out the primitive moment of naming.[38]

According to mythological view, the meaning of each *object* is hidden in its *name.* Anyone who knows how to dominate the names, gains the ruler position over *objects.* Naming refers to the ability of intellectual thinking of a man in relationship with abstract or concrete facts. Since the creation of holy books; the ability of thinking and naming is seen as equal.[39] Nominalism studies began to emerge in the 19th century in scholastic philosophy and constitute one of the most fundamental qualities of modern Western thought. The main idea of nominalism, is that; the *concepts* are obtained by an *abstraction* that does not meet an *object.* For example, there is no object to refer the '*justice*' concept.[40]

As Bertrand Russell puts it humorously, there is no single English concept that can meet the original meaning of the French word '*esprit*'. For possible translations in a dictionary you will find a long list of different uses in English like these:

- wit (avoir de l'esprit) = to have wit- 'nüktedan olmak'
- mood (je n'ai pas l'esprit a rire) =I'm no mood for laughing- 'hiç gülecek halim yok'
- mind (avoir l'esprit vif) =to have a quick mind. 'keskin zeka sahibi olmak'

---

[36] David Brooks, Sosyal Hayvan, Çev: Orhan Düz, Say, 2011, p.204
[37] Brooks, op.cit. p.205
[38] Michel Faucault, Kelimeler ve Şeyler İnsan Bilimlerinin Bir Arkeolojisi, Çev: Mehmet Ali Kılıçbay, Ankara, 2017, p.164
[39] Mustafa Aydın, Güncel Kültürde Temel Kavramlar, Açılım, 2011, p.318
[40] Aydın, op.cit. p.317.

- spirit (esprit d'equipe) = team spirit – 'takım ruhu'

Accordingly, the concepts such as '*mind*', '*intellect*' or '*esprit*' cannot be as elemental as '*rose*' or '*bird*' concepts, otherwise they were supposed to be perfectly identical in different languages.[41]

Heraclitus' view is again represented in Socrates and Plato. According to Socrates, the word is indicative even if it does not contain it. In the Kratylos dialogue, Plato examines the question of the correctness of names and the view that language is the key to the essence of objects. A word is so linked to the object that it suggests the object and represents it in thought.[42] To Heraclitus, *every word limits its object* and this limitation leads to misunderstanding. If an object or an entity is reduced to the '*word*', its content gets limited by focusing on just a single aspect. This may cause to lose the perspective of a larger existence of that object or an entity in its living stream which could not fixated. To Heraclitus, the language is not limited by the object or entity; because the wording is constituted with fluid dynamics.[43] In modern cultures, the nominalism in every field of thinking is so naturalized, that encourage people to think limited and biased. Even though this problem doesn't seem to be recognized adequately in daily lives, yet it is causing the perception of the different values in international communities left unnoticed.

Science of Translation

Translation is a very old practice as being the oldest profession in the world, so the tradition of thinking about translation goes back to the Cicero. Throughout the 1970's scientifically, translation studies were defined as an independent science by adopting an empirical, descriptive and interdisciplinary study method and formed the fields of philology and linguistics. In 1972, James S. Holmes, with his pioneering paper '*The name and Nature of Translation Studies*' strengthened the name of this new scientific field and opened it up for discussion. Translation was often seen as a '*natural phenomenon*' and therefore was not taken into consideration from the perspective of conceptualizing the theoretical ideas. In the last two decades, the concepts like '*ideology, power relations and ethics*' have gained importance in the translation studies which have benefited from the other disciplines. As much as the concerns existing in the scientific and cultural studies translations throughout the nations but also the vocational, instructional or techno-computing fields that are included into the translation studies' concerns.[44]

The case that makes translation difficult appears when both languages are studied on the basis of *words*, exceptionally from the authentic reality of the

[41] Guy Deutscher, Dilin Aynasından Kelimeler Dünyamızı Nasıl Renklendirir, Çev: Cemal Yardımcı, Metis Bilim, İstanbul, 2013, p.21

[42] Akarsu, op.cit. pp.26-30

[43] Aydın, op.cit. p.101, 318.

[44] Mehmet Rıfat, XX. Yüzyılda dilbilim ve göstergebilim kuramları: 2. Temel Metinler, YKY, 1998, p.199

situation. Each language meets a special arrangement of data which is consisted of the '*human experiences*'. Thus, the translated words, are not always equivalent to the previously experienced realities.

In the aspect of the relation between language and culture; the last three centuries' scientific and social discoveries and innovations has become an issue of translation throughout the world. The terms and values that are formed in Western Social Sciences (from 18th century's Enlightenment era till modern age) are included into the arguments that scholars did not seem to have clarity for a long time. Translation scholars started to contribute into the field from the perspective of cultural and social approaches. As a result, translation studies are described as '*writing*' or '*rewriting*' by Bassnet and Bush,[45] '*representation*' by Gutt,[46] '*indirect speech*' by Hermans,[47] '*reparation*' by Bandia.[48] Tymoczko[49] also formalized the dynamics of the translation as '*representation*', '*transmission*' and '*transculturation*'[50]

The translation of a single word to another language (i.e. *bango in Italian*) may not sound as a direct transition to another word (*bain in French*). Each time, you have to go through the process of portioning each language's specific reality. This also explains the fact that learning a language has two meanings*: to learn the connection between structure and words* and *the non-linguistic reality*; like learning the culture and civilization of the language. In other words, each language divides itself into a non-linguistic experiences. For instance, the situation that is named as '*to run out*' (*dışarı koşmak*) in England is named as '*sortir en courant*' in French which means '*getting out by running*' (*koşarak çıkmak*). Another example can be shown by noticing the semantic approach towards the word '*cin*' in Arabic, which is known as '*genie*' in English, comes from the root 'cenne' الجنة in Arabic means '*to cover someone's senses*'. This root of word constituted another words like; cinnet: '*the hidden craziness between desire and mind*', mecnun: '*the one who falls in love madly for unfindable*', cenin: '*the baby hidden in venter*', cennet: '*the place hiding people by its trees*', cenan: '*the heart hidden in breast*'.[51]

However, in Turkish the more practical approach on the word '*cin*' seem to be ignoring the semantic roots; like embodying it in a way who has spiritual and physical image and practically serving by getting off from the lamb. In an interview of Arslan Kaynardag on Nermi Uygur's Philosophy, Language and Culture, Uygur mentions; the misrepresentations, false education policies with textbooks, institutions and cowardly practices cause how much damage on heads

[45] Suzan Bassnett & Peter Bush, (Editörler)The translator as writer. Bloomsbury Publishing, 2008

[46] Ernst August Gutt, Translation and relevance University of London, 1989

[47] Theo Hermans, Literary translation. Multilingual Matters Ltd. 2007 (a)

[48] Theo Hermans, Translation, irritation and resonance. Benjamins Translation Library, 2007 (b), pp.74, 57.

[49] Maria Tymoczko, Why translators should want to internationalize translation studies. The Translator, 15(2), 2009, 401-421.

[50] Marais Kobus, Translation Theory and Development Studies: A Complexity Theory Approach, Language Arts & Disciplines, 2014, p.78

[51] https://www.beyan.org/node/909 (Erişim 15.05.2019)

and hearts. In his book that was first published in 1962, named '*The Power of Language*' Nermi Uygur refers to the multi-meaning of language, philosophy of language, the linkage of mother tongue and dilemmas of meaning in language and translation.[52]

According to Akşit Göktürk: '*Each language is intertwined with indicators of any culture's conventions, customs, behaviors, value measures, shortly, the terms of tangible human life.*'[53] Göktürk, distinguishes the translation of scientific and artistic texts from the texts that are including daily issues of life, which are assumed to be written with direct meaning. Because, artistic and scientific texts are formed by a subjective language by more concerned on the originality, and less concerned to preserve the communication patterns, words or idioms of the mother language.

In summary, the semantic and practical part of the translations must be distinguished carefully. The views of translation scholars that mentioned above constituted the infrastructure to the '*translation of concepts*' as well.

Translation and Conceptualization

'Every dictionary expresses a civilization.'

Antoine Meillet

According to Humboldt; language examinations are not responding to the question of which one comes first: *language or nation*?[54] Since, the historical experiences of nations differ through their existences that are conditional to different situations; the '*conceptualization*' of thoughts and experiences differ as well. The climax problem of philosophy is the problem of '*translation of concepts*'. Any philosophic thesis in a certain language can only be advanced at the conceptual level, since the philosophy studies hold declaration of '*its own language*'. The process of analyzing and adopting the other language's thoughts and ideas is leading into the deep analysis on '*conceptualization in languages*'. The definition of conceptualization according to Oxford Dictionary: '*the action of the process on forming an idea*'.[55] Starting from this point, it can be said that; it takes an analysis on *action*, *movement*, *experience* and also *time*, to find out accurately what kind of observations and analysis are necessarily *done* by a subject with the intention of *creating a definitive concept* after the certain *experiences.*

However, the methodological task of defining '*translation*' across languages forms an apparent '*aporia*'. Since there is no guarantee that the new terms that are formed and considered as '*translated*' are actual translations of original concepts. One solution to form an accurate translation of concepts, is to practice

[52] Nermi Uygur, Dilin gücü: denemeler, 1962 Kitap.https://docplayer.biz.tr/15372439-Nermi-uygur-la-felsefe-dil-ve-kultur-konusunda-bir-soylesi.html (Erişim 14.05.2019)
[53] Akşit Göktürk, Çeviri: Dilleri Dili, YKY, İstanbul, 1998, p.94
[54] Akarsu, op.cit, pp.26-30
[55] https://en.oxforddictionaries.com/definition/conceptualization Accesed in 15.05.2019

a set of criteria, and a *research filter* on what the scholars imposed on the *prior multilingual data.* Considering the variability on dynamics and historicity of nations' experiences, unfortunately, the translation studies is not currently in a position to supply measures of comparison or a degree of certainty about the *distribution of concepts* across languages and cultures.[56]

In fact, the concepts should be traced across cultural boundaries according to the classes of equivalency which were held as more or less fixed position. The medieval Christian tradition tended to conceptualize '*translation*' in terms of an idealized hierarchy of languages *Hebrew, Greek, Arabic* at the top, as the language of science and authorized Biblical translation (*Latin)* on the next grade, then the vernaculars and finally the patois.[57] Tyulenev[58] described translation as 'smuggling'. According to him, the original *metaphors* that are commonly used in the development of a study and to conceptualize new theories could not be translated into other words.[59]

> *The Western Thought Discipline era starts with the 'Renaissance' which directly come up with the concept of 'Enlightenment' that has constructed the world's cultural, political and social vocabulary within the criteria of breaking the Western Middle Age experiences. However, it is well known fact that 'The Enlightenment in France' differs from 'The Enlightenment in England'. Besides that, the contemporary French philosophy is developed in France and conflicts with the sum of the discourse of today's accepted ideas; does that mean the French philosophy is not formed in accurate history or not at the stage of an advanced process?*[60]

Considering the critics on the '*Enlightenment*' concept; the '*Enlightenment*' is established within the concept of '*Progressing*' in Old European languages. The concept of *Progressing* was becoming rapidly functionless and dead according to the general acceptance when the critics started to occur. Despite of his sincere respect on Enlightenment, Hegel was mentioning about its *contentlessness* (contextlessness) and Leo was also referring it as an '*Enlightenment Junk*' and his various critics of ideology quickly turned into a familiar and old slogan just like once 'ideology' itself turned in the same position throughout its history.[61]

For good measure, Koselleck exemplified the German concept '*Bildung*' which determines the perception of the 18th century's studies with 200 years of usage experiences. 'The Bildung owner' (der Gebildete) in the community has

---

[56] Pym, Anthony, (1993) Epistemological problems in translation and its teaching, Caminade, pp.14

[57] Pym, A. (2007). On the historical epistemologies of Bible translating. A history of Bible translation, 1, 195-215. cited in Imre, Atilla, (2012). The Never-Ending Story of Bible and Qur'an Translations. Studia Universitatis Petru Maior. Philologia, (13), 293-302.

[58] Tyulenev, S. (2010). Translation in intersystemic interaction: A case study of eighteenth-century Russia. TTR: Traduction, terminologie, rédaction, 23(1), 165-189.

[59] Kobus, op.cit.

[60] Koselleck, op.cit.

[61] Koselleck, op.cit. p.334.

either the aspect of training or thinking of something. In order to explain what Bildung is in neighboring families, it is necessary to analyze the word with its complex explanations. For example, the similar concept '*selsbildung*' means self-improvement in English and French. But just as the other similar concepts like '*ecole*' in French and '*school*' in English points different kind of learning and teaching processes, the meaning of '*Bildung*' is not just '*self-education*'. The original meaning of the concept 'Bildung' in German is *to transform the external means of education into an assertion of autonomy that would transform to the world.* As a result, Bildung gains its historical profile only when it's been viewed under political or social functions. Bildung could not be gained or protected without social functions.[62]

According to Guy Debord; '*Ideological facts never a simple chimaera, but rather a deformed consciousness of realities*'.[63] Behind the abstraction of today's language; the elevated slogan like '*power of abstraction*' is tied to the rule of today's politics. One conclusion of this finding is the lack of resistance to any kind of ideology. Since now each concept can be viewed from another perspective; everything can be questioned through the '*criticism of ideology*'. In other words, the modern vocabulary which is loaded with the political advocacy and historical ideology must be analyzed with its 'a *priori*' position.

Linguistic Relativity

According to the Port-Royal logic, it is possible to create a '*universal language*' which is consisted of the same principles, regardless of the differences of nations. According to this romantic approach, language has an organic structure. Schlegel is the first to introduce the concept of an *organic form (Allgemenie)* into language studies. Like nature and freedom, nature and art is united in their organic ideals. Thus, the gap between the unconscious nature of universe and the conscious creation of the soul is desired. The concept of *organic form* was born to seek expressions of the *general structure of the language* behind the diversity of individual's languages.[64]

Parmenides was the first one who pointed to the importance of language as the essence of human. According to Parmenides, a man must give a name to everything. Empiricists, and rationalists always examine the language in terms of *knowledge*, their language understanding is based on *knowledge theories.* Rationalists claim that there are significant ways in which our *concepts and knowledge* are gained independently of sense experience. Empiricists claim that sense experience is the ultimate source of all our *concepts and knowledge.*[65] Herder was also interested in language in terms of knowledge. The sense of the person's inner state, feelings, joy, sorrow was expressed through direction of the language. For him, the

---

[62] Koselleck, op. cit.
[63] Guy Debord, Gösteri Toplumu, Çev: Ayşen Ekmekçi & Okşan Taşkent, Ayrıntı, İstanbul, 2017
[64] Akarsu, op. cit. pp. 26-30.
[65] https://plato.stanford.edu/entries/rationalism-empiricism/ Erişim 15.05.2019

richness of language is admired for its various influences, and language was considered as a miracle. There are two main ideas to explain this amazing phenomenon: on one hand, *the language was considered as a God's gift to man.* On the other hand, *language is considered as something discovered by man.* Herder argued that the language is born from the inner nature of man, but according to him, language also occurred by thinking, which is a main power of the senses and the human soul. Without senses, there is no thinking, without thinking there is no language. However, Humboldt ties the language directly to human nature. According to him, without language there is no human. This anthropological view, which is ungrounded by Herder, is improved as language cannot be thought of as a ready-made (fertiggegebene), but it is a necessity of a man's nature.[66]

Contrary to the perspective of the philosophers of the enlightenment era, Humboldt suggests that the structure of language determines the minds. According to Humboldt, *the differences of the language structures stem from the diversity of the mental structures of the nations.*[67] Humboldt argues that the languages differ according to how nations see and perceive the world. On the other hand, drawing attention to the fact that the language shouldn't be seen as a complete product, Humboldt, argues that language is not an *opus* (ergon) but an *activity* (energia). However, Humboldt perceives the language not only means of thought, but also something that turns out the thoughts at the same time.[68] Thus, Humboldt dealt the question of how a variety of languages exist, although there is one certain '*logic*'. Logic will be discussed in the next chapter that as a core issue in the comparison of Arabic and Greek conceptualizations from the aspect of Logic and Syntax.

Comparison of Arabic and Greek Conceptualizations

Although all languages have the same unlimited potential; some languages, words, phrases and contexts, have different characteristics depending on the cultural and historical experiences and richness'. Greek language has a great privilege in terms of the conceptualizing and forming ideas and philosophy which were presented to the entire world. Almost without knowing Greek philosophers, it is impossible to enter the world of thought.

The ideas and views that are underlying the Western Tradition of Thought were first expressed in ancient Greece. The Greeks developed several literary genres, such as epic and drama; which were written in Greek. In addition to its use in the cultural context, the first and most important texts of Christianity were also written in Greek. In fact, this was the main reason of bringing higher status

[66] Johann Gottfried von Herder, The Origin of Language, and the Possibility of Transcultural Narratives, 2009, (Çevrimiçi) https://www.tandfonline.com/doi/abs/10.1080/14708470408668858 erişim 26.04.2019

[67] Alexander Von Humboldt, Political Essay on the Island of Cuba: A Critical Edition. University of Chicago Press, 2011, p.136

[68] Humboldt, op.cit.

to Greek.[69] Herewith, our understanding of the world was partly invented by the Greeks; their designs and templates are still alive in the language of thought. As many Greek words entered/transferred to other languages, *the elements of their original culture and sociality also transferred*, and these elements are also often transformed like the ancient concept '*democracy*'.[70]

The *Greek alphabet* is very similar to the *Latin alphabet* which is in use of English. In fact, many letters in the Latin alphabet are derived from a variety of Greek alphabet. The works written in Greek, proceeded as a cultural accumulation, contained many elements that had also become a part of the modern Western thought tradition. Those words and concepts still existing, in English and other European languages. There are also many other borrowed words from other languages, but the ones borrowed from Greek are special. Many of them contributing to build our existence in the modern world by providing categories (categoria) by which we group the phenomena of reality (phainomena).

Some languages are linked to religion somehow; for instance, from the very beginning *Hebrew* has become *language of Judaism* and still is. Some Hebrew texts are considered as sacred/holy for both Christians and Muslims. Sanskrit is very important for Hinduism as well; the Pali and Sanskrit are the prominent languages for Buddhists. Greek and Latin still have a special place for Christianity. All these languages were still written and spoken in the religious context even long after they lost their originality.

A new written language can only emerge if community find themselves in need of it. The creators of written languages are not politicians; this work is actually for authors and educators. Political decisions are usually positioned at a later stage. Yet, in the Arabic case; it is not even possible to think about such reforms in just the linguistic context; because without political unity, homogeneity of language is unlikely possible. During the spread of Islam, numerous Arabs migrated to the capital cities and Arabic quickly became the language of many towns and cities. Despite all these conquests, the Arabic language did not dominate in the same way as Greek. The main differences occur in *the process of spreading the language.*[71]

According to Schimmel, Arabic was not necessarily only able to spread through religion to the people, but also being adopted as their second '*mother language*'. The main reason to that policy is as well known, to prevent the change on original texts of holy Quran through translations. Secondly; unlike Jesus, Muhammad, *the founder of Islam*, was also a *political leader*. His understanding of religion was more concerned on previously bringing *open answers* to the world of hereafter; so that Islamic lectures and preaches can be kept focused on towards

---

[69] Tore Janson, Dillerin tarihi. Boğaziçi Üniversitesi Yayınevi, 2016, pp.108, 109

[70] Janson, op.cit. p.117.

[71] Janson, op.cit.

of dealing with the *daily life circumstances*. Thus, Arabic soon became a living room far beyond the religious scene, where all kinds of written information were transmitted into it many aspects of daily life, from administrative discourse to even military mission. It is important to address that some aspects of the political career of the *Prophet Mohammad* have brought a *specific terminology to* Muslims life. This explains why the influence of Arabic language is not only involved in *spiritual aspect* but also in *practical* and *grounded* aspects as well.[72]

The old Arabic, *which is still in use for formal written language*, has undergone just a minimal change since the 7th century. Whereas Islam was the core reason of this process, Arabs traveled from the coast of Syria to Palestine, Egypt and Africa then passing through the Atlantic Ocean and held the power on the big part of Spain. Within this almost explosive progress in politics and culture, Arabic language gained naturally the most prestigious position; within the increase in education and philosophy after the newly established empire '*Andalusia*'. In the course of time, up to the 21st century the Arabic language was carefully being preserved in its original form, by the means of holy Quran.[73]

The comparison of Greek and Arabic language might be searched in also the similarity of the *content* that they present. The Arabic language, which is directly related to the *spread of Islam*, has come with its *own political, philosophical and practical terminology* in many field, just as the discovery of Greek productions which are considered as *'high culture language'* did the same coverage in the Western world throughout the Renaissance era till today. The similarities and differences of Greek and Arabic thought were also analyzed by many Islam philosophers.

The Philosophy in Arabic Language

The great traditional system of thought that is defined as 'Islamic Renaissance' in the 9th and 10th centuries were represented by Farabi, İbn Sina and Ibn Rushd whom generally embraced the works of Aristotle. While Plato was perceived as a danger through his views on religion on the contrary Aristotle's physics and metaphysics played a helpful role in explaining the Islamic revelation.[74]

However, the type of thought that is known as the *'felasife'* in Islamic civilization was not including just an Aristotelian logic which is called as '*Mashshai'*. In fact, to prove that Islamic thought cannot be reduced to *Mashshayan thought*; there were two types of approaches in the historical course of Islam philosophy:

1. *Philosophy of problems*; that the problems were handled and processed one by

[72] Annemarie Schimmel, ve Muhammed O'nun Elçisidir, Çev: Ekrem Demirli, Kabalcı 2011, p.103

[73] Janson, op.cit.

[74] Shlomo Pines, Moses Maimonides, "The Philosophic Sources of the Guide of Perplexed" ix. 1963, s. 193-199'den aktaran Adnan Küçükalı, İbn Sina'nın Selbî Yorumlama Metodu. Journal of Graduate School of Social Sciences, 13(1), 2009.

one;

2. *Philosophy of systems;* that were represented with Farabi, İbn-i Sina and İbn-Rushd whom are the three important representatives of the *Mashshia tradition.* Following this tradition, they also brought their own theoretical expressions into the world of thought.[75]

One of the distinctive approaches brought by Islam philosophers to the world of thought is the specifics of the Arabic alphabet. According to the '*Letterists' (Hurüfi's),* who formed the idea based on the strings that are addressing various symbolic values and meanings in Arabic letters; '*the name is the essence of the object or entity*' and '*names*' were thought to be contained in the letters of the word. The mystic Al Buni, is one of the most known proponents of this view. According to Buni, the *whole universe is seen as the product of the action of the Arabic letters.* In other words, the whole process of the universe is seen in Arabic letters. Hence, the science of '*letters*' (*ilm al hurüf)* and the science of 'words' (*ilm as simiya)* and the science of the 'universe' (*ilm al alam)* are not distinguished and identified with each other.[76]

As the follower of '*ta'wil*' tradition which is questioning the '*the root of the meaning*' Ibn Rushd was questioning these two forms: apparent (zahir) and superstition (batil). Apparent (zahir) is implying the meaning of the text through *what is said in a certain historical environment* but has the ability of existence in every time and place. Supersitition (batil) is assuming the *temporal and spatial absence of meaning* and trying to explore the unspoken *by transcending the boundaries of the past and present.*[77]

According to Ibn-Rushd; it would be wrong to suggest that any text (*religious, literary, legal, etc.*) is understandable to everyone. The obvious meanings that almost every text implies, are also including the covered aspects. To understand the other aspects of the texts that are confined, one needs a new accumulation of knowledge. Therefore, it is clear that everyone cannot have the same understanding from any text.[78]

As a summary, whereas Islam thinkers considered '*logic*' as a generalized Greek grammar mixed with thought they did not accept the criticism that '*syntax*' *(nahiv)* was only consisted of grammar. It's been emphasized that there is a certain connection between etymology, syntax and meaning.

The Baghdad Debate (Syntax vs. Logic Debate)

Syntax (Nahiv) and Logic (Mantiq) debate named by some Western

---

[75] Alparslan Açıkgenç, İslam Bağlamında Bilimden Sistem Felsefesine, İnan Yayınları, 2006, p.53

[76] Georges Ifrah, İslam Dünyasında Hint Rakamları, Rakamların Evrensel Tarihi, VII, Çev: Kurtuluş Dinçer, Tübitak Popüler Bilim Kitapları, Ankara, 2005, p.93

[77] Ocak, Hasan, İbn Rüşd Felsefesinde Yorumbilim (Te'vil), Ek Kitap, 2014, p.42

[78] Hasan, op.cit. p.65.

researchers as '*Baghdad Debate*' which had taken place, in the Bagdad's world of thought, in the first half of the 10th century. The Bagdad Debate is a kind of reflection of the conflict between the traditional sciences and new branches of science. Abu Sa'id al-Sirafi and Abu Bishr Metta took the two opponent sides of this debate.[79]

The science of Nahiv (النحو) generally takes into account the structure of language. It analyzes the parts of this structure as noun and verb. Nahiv is a branch of linguistics which deals with the formation characteristics of the sentence and the functions of the words in the sentence and the arrangement of the words within the sentence. In the West, this is known as 'syntax'.[80] The word 'logic', which comes from the Greek word 'Logike' [Logos] corresponds to the 'Mantiq' منطق [#nṭḳ msd.(root)] in Arabic which means 'speaking' or 'the art of speech'.[81]

The distinctions of the discussion between the grammarian *'nahivist'* (Sirafi) and logician (Metta), lie behind the categories of Aristo, which are derived from lexical forms and the contrastive functionality of Arabic and Greek language. According to the defenders of Aristotelian logic, syntax is a science that sets the rules for *wording* in language; logic is a science that sets rules about *thoughts* and *concepts* in language.[82]

Against the categories of Aristotle, Arabic *syntax* is functioning by activating those phrases like the name of time, space, device and it's been remarked that; without the usage of vowel point' (hareke') in Arabic some letters are impossible to pronounce. In this way, it's been intentioned to demonstrate that '*vowel point' (hareke)* in Arabic is equal to implementing '*logic*', so the syntax is also considered as associated with logic. The distinctive point is, unlike the Greek and Aryan language families, in Arabic '*syntax*' is only for declaration and not for making any judgement whether in the verb clause or noun clause.[83] However, according to *nahivists*; words and word sequences are the equivalents of the combinations of meanings that are produced directly in the mind. Finally, Sirafi asserted that the Arabic language is the founder of its own logic.[84]

The other side of to the debate, is a well-known interpreter/translator from Nesturi Christians, Metta b. Yunus who advocated the Greek '*logic*'. Metta claims that there is a '*transnational language*' which is provided the science of 'logic'. This transnational language is transparent and its structure/mathematics does not

---

[79] David Samuel Margoliouth, The Discussion between Abu Bishr Matta and Abu Sa'id al-Sirafi on the Merits of Logic and Grammar, The Journal of the Royal Asiatic Society of Great Britain and Ireland, 1905, pp. 79-129

[80] https://fasiharapca.com/nahiv-nedir-nahiv-tanimlari/302763 Erişim 15.05.2019

[81] https://www.etimolojiturkce.com/kelime/mantık Erişim 15.05.2019

[82] Fatma Dore, Farabi'nin Dil ve Anlam Kuramı, Marmara Üniversitesi Sosyal Bilimler Enstitüsü, İstanbul, 2011

[83] Mahdi, Muhsin, (1990) Farabi, Beyrut: Dâru'l-Maşrık, 1990

[84] Dore, op.cit.

contain any contradictions. According to Metta, translation from one language to another is possible, and it is not the language that is translated; it is the '*unchanging and transferable meaning*' that is carried through the translation. According to Sirafi, the translation is arbitrary, *its meaning changes*, and *the meaning becomes distorted, increases or decreases*. Therefore, the translation includes the rules of *consensual language* that are only become complete in their own society, and the principles of these rules of consensus cannot be fully confirmed.

Metta whom completely assuming the language as *non-functional* was being criticized for dramatizing *logical approach* to specify each mental activity. Nonetheless, Sirafi was not completely against of the Greek logic, he just refused to make '*logic*' look like the only way to think right; without considering the natural mental ability which is existing in all human being. Farabi, also focused on Islamic thought while analyzing the negative crisis rising against the *Aristotelian logic* which is entering into the Islamic world by the means of translations. According to Farabi to follow *Aristotelian logic* means '*to explain the laws of Aristotelian thought*' and to teach them through exemplification in the environment that they are created. By doing so, it is not the main target to keep the original words in Greek but to carry the senses. In this regard, many theologians and linguists agreed at the point that the translations of Greek thought are not compatible with Islamic thought. According to these criticisms, to reveal the correct meaning of an expression was only possible by making it Arabic (Arabicization).[85]

Democracy Philosophy

The use of the word 'democracy' has great and important connotations, from ancient Greece where the first applications are located, for the first time almost twenty-six hundred years ago, up to today. As a word 'democracy' in Greek, is composed of the *demos (public)* and *kratie (superiority, management)* and transferred into English as a '*public administration*'. Aristotle regarded democracy as the corrupted and degenerated state of the '*ideal regime of Athens*' named '*polited*'. Besides recognizing all the positive qualities of democracy, Aristotle also emphasized the other aspects of democracy like; a *low-income* and *domination of sub-class* in the administration whom are *imposing own preferences* on the large masses.[86]

Democracy is not a *universal value* which is assumed to be a link into the needs of humanity consisting of *justice, rightness, freedom* etc.; but a *global value* linked to internal, external economic and politic processes. However, it includes specific techniques to establish relative equality between individuals, groups and organizational structures. In fact, despite all the idealizations, it also means '*limiting something for the welfare of something else*'. As a concept and implementation, democracy is still important today. Democracy is the political regime of many contemporary states and at the same time the official ideology of many of them.

---

[85] Dore, op.cit.

[86] Jürgen Habermas, "Öteki" Olmak "Öteki" yle Yaşamak Siyaset Kuramı Yazıları, YKY, İstanbul,2002

However, democracy was not a concept that thinkers have viewed positively in all historical/social contexts. There were critics as well as those who defend it. A lot of criticism has been made on ancient democracy embodied in Athens. Some of them were made by political thinkers and authors of the period and some of them from later writers. As of the 5th century BC. various writers began to criticize the basic principles of democracy. These criticisms were more or less concentrated around the issues related to *corruption (political and legal abuse)* and *poverty.*

Elder Oligarch, with the pen name Xenophon, underlined that the majority is in management for their own benefit, and even the application of the judiciary through the '*Comrades' Court*' leads to unfair decisions. Elder Oligarch also stated that in the democratic regimes, excessively high taxes were received from capital owners.[87]

So therewithal, the historical and social adventure and philosophical foundations of democracy in Great Britain, France and America must be addressed as well. As being the three greatest residences of democracy these three geographies were also advanced both in the *class conflict* and in the *evolution of political ideas.*

Among the thinkers contributing to democracy in France; Montesquieu (1689-1755) Rousseau (1712-1778) and Sieyes (1748-1836) are_noteworthy to be mentioned. The French Revolution, which had been prepared within these thinkers, had been a great opportunity for changes on social and political life on the world-embracing scale. Yet, in the *pluralistic, social and political* structure of international societies of today's world, the form of *legitimacy* which is laid out on the basis of the *strategic-oriented purposes, national based relations* and *politics* is now inadequate and invalid. According to Habermas, *as one of the great critics*, democracy is struggling to keep acceptance and existence in *multi-cultural societies.*[88] *Guenon* interpreted democracy as a kind of *aristocracy*, although it was introduced as a comprehensive way of participation. Considering the most concrete expression of democracy Raymand Aron's statement of democracy through the *principles of democratic environments* (such as the *multiplicity* and *division of elite* and the ability to *compete freely* and the powerless change of power between them) it is clearly seen that they are the principles of aristocracy. Noam Chomsky also stated that democracy is primarily a problem of *public relations* and the industrial organizations greatly benefit from this, because the *priority* is not on the axis of people. Of course, in such a democracy, the elites would miss to examine of the democratic structure, and public do not seem easily play an *active role* in the country.[89] According to Sartori; the concept of democracy is scientifically reduced to *empirical level* and the concept itself has gained a new reality. This process is described in his book '*The Return To Democracy Theory*', in a sense, as an

---

87 Aydın, op.cit.

88 Habermas, op.cit.

89 Aydın, op.cit. p.102.

attempt to establish a logical connection between the *ideals of democracy* and *social realities.* Moreover, this attempt does not involve *abandoning democratic ideals* at the expense of purely social reality as data but reducing it to *practicality.* The essence of his theory is not based on the reduction of democratic ideals into purely social reality, but the attempt of construction of the *methodical and moral forms* to establish *a link between reality and ideal*, as Sartori himself sees the triumph of the *ideal* against extreme *reality.*[90] The *modern era* of democracy is, in most parts of the world, a result of the *European Enlightenment.* During the late 1700s, several countries were formulating new ideas for a government system that would not be dependent on monarchs. This radical proposal was severely criticized, but in 1776 it formed the basis for the *American Declaration of Independence*, which would eventually lead to the establishment of the world's first *modern democracy.* Similar experiments occurred in France shortly thereafter, though owing to historical circumstances the French would take several decades to finally abolish their monarchy for good (and even then the country continued to be ruled by highly centralized authorities such as Napoleon Bonaparte and Napoleon III).[91] Sartori emphasized that the concept of democracy is a *phenomenon* associated with *Western civilization.* According to him, democracy is a discourse that has not belonged to a single author for centuries; but has been shaped by the contributions of many philosophers. Yet, the fact that democracy is identified with a great civilization and historicity is already an important problem for democracy. This is because as democracy becomes more of a *symbol of civilization*, it becomes increasingly comprehensive and more complex and ambiguous. Moreover, the fact that everyone is using democracy for legitimacy turns democracy into a *pointless set of values.*[92]

By examining democracy on a semantic level, Sartori develops a hypothesis that each country's *historical* and *linguistic culture* has an impact on the understanding of the *democratic structure* in that country. According to this hypothesis, the phenomenon of democracy, called the administration of the people, can be systematized in different ways in every country, especially because of the *etymological differences* of the nations. For example, in Italy, Germany and France belong to *Continental European Enlightenment* tradition, the concept that people suggests is more focused on organic singularity. Unlike continental Europe, in the Anglo-Saxon culture where the culture of *individualism* developed in the term 'public' refers to *plural entity* which is composed of different individuals.

How can the *universal* and *normative* criteria of democracy be determined from the fact that there are so many different cultural acceptances within Western civilization? By focusing on this question, Sartori excludes the ambiguity of the public administration concept and attempts to reformulate democracy in the

---

[90] Giovanni Sartori, Demokrasi Kuramı, Siyasi İlimler, Türk Derneği No:23, Çev. Deniz Baykal, Ajans-Türk Matbaacılık Sanayi, Ankara, 1962

[91] https://philosophyterms.com/democracy/ Erişim 15.05.2019

[92] Sartori, op.cit.

sense of the *administration of the people.*[93]

In summary, the problems emerge regarding the use of *democracy concept* when the accumulation of *value systems* that are built and accepted by different societies are ignored. Nonetheless, democracy has always set up, *obvious or hidden,* its own values and limitations, which are limiting the regional specifics, wherever it is brought into, without paying attention to the original social problems of the transferred society.[94]

In the light of these critics, the comparative analysis of 'democracy' considering the semantic approach in Arabic's 'ta'wil' tradition has two components: Apparent (Zahir); relative equality between individuals, groups and organizational structures and superstition (Batil); as if including the aspects like «justice» «right» «freedom».

Democracy as Background of Arab Spring Discourse

Following the withdrawal of Great Britain from the Middle East after the Second World War, the US occupied the region, and launched a series of studies on Democracy, human rights, the role of women in social life, and so on. In addition, the United States has supported projects and studies in similar fields. The transformation process that started in the Middle East has turned into a character that changes the regime of countries with the effects of internal and external actors. This feature of the region is more or less reflected in all of the regional actors. One of the most important changes experienced in the historical process in the region is the change period which started with the Arab Spring at the end of 2010.[95]

Throughout time, the 'democracy' implementation in the Middle East has always been the subject of many discussions and researches as well as being the subject of policy. Tessler stated that: '*Through the past decade scholars analyzing the Middle East and North Africa (MENA) have focused on the factors impeding the democratization process therein, or more precisely, the factors which have added to the resilience of authoritarianism'.*[96]

Quintan Wiktorowicz stated in his article 'The Limits of Democracy in the Middle East: The Case of Jordan' published in 1999: 'Despite the persistence of authoritarianism in the Middle East, (recently) there has been movement toward democracy in the region.' In addition, he asserted that: 'The multi-party politics (ta'addudiyya) and elections –the symbols and institutional face of democracy- are frequently accompanied by political repression and manipulation which

[93] Sartori, op.cit.
[94] Aydın, op.cit.
[95] Zafer Akbaş, Ortadoğu'da Değişim Süreci ve Türk Dış Politikası, Journal of Academic Approaches, Spring 2012, Vol:3, Issue:1, 2012, pp.53-55.
[96] Mark Tessler, Islam and democracy in the Middle East: The impact of religious orientations on attitudes toward democracy in four Arab countries. Comparative Politics, 2002, pp.337-354.

sabotage the underlying principles'.[97] The circumstances regarding democracy he mentioned is validly existing in the Middle East, after a decade and even after the blooming 'Arab Spring' events.

In this regard; the explanatory and guiding definitions of '*democracy*', shouldn't be confused, because the '*democratic ideal*' does not define '*democratic reality*' and vice versa isn't true just as the *'Arab Spring concept*' where reality and ideal are intertwined within the concept of '*democracy*' and '*Arab Spring*'.

The indicative news reports, which evaluate the communicative functions as texts that include '*dialectic concepts*' aim to introduce the subject and region and influence the public opinion and movements. However, these concepts are distracting the perception of reality, by ignoring the fact that *the image of democracy in everyone's mind is different.*

Questioning of *Democracy in the Middle East* has been mostly focused on the governance and administrative aspects and also its conflicts with the conceptions and practices of Islam. But there was never enough examination of the regional facts without the spotlight of any concepts and a fortiori analysis on the features of domestic politics and regional social/economic problems. In order to do that properly, paying attention to the varying regional differences play a significant role.

The realities of the Middle East did not live up to the optimistic hopes of the first year of the Arab Spring. A continued relatively democratic but certainly not unproblematic development in Tunisia was contrasted by a chaotic situation in Egypt. In July the 2013 the Egyptian army leader General Abdul Fatah al-Sissi, after massive protests against the Muslim Brotherhood, removed the democratically elected President Mursi and consequently suspended the Egyptian constitution.[98]

In a British Broadcasting Corporation BBC article entitled 'Tunisians embrace democratic life' Allan Little wrote that: 'patronizing the dynamics of 'democratic life' towards the end states Tunisia has a strong, educated, self-confident middle class that, it is now clear, has a very developed understanding of the dynamics of 'democratic life.'[99] In fact, the situation in Tunisia was in changefulness as follows; before the Arab Spring events; the leader Zeyn Abdin bin Ali was against Islam, however El habib Burkiba who was the so called 'father of liberalism' was against the use of 'hijab'. This disparity can directly point the fact that; the meanings of freedom, democracy or liberalism may differ upon the

---

[97] Quintan Wiktorowicz, The limits of democracy in the Middle East: the case of Jordan. The Middle East Journal, 1999, pp.606-620.

[98] Peter Seeberg & Musa Shteiwi, European Narratives on the 'Arab Spring'–from Democracy to Security. Center for Contemporary Middle East Studies, University of Southern Denmark, Working Paper, 2014.

[99] Alan Little, Alan, Tunusians Embrace Democratic Life, BBC, Africa, 27 Oct 2011, (Çevrimiçi) https://www.bbc.com/news/world-africa-15462198 Erişim 15.05.2019

political tendencies of leaders.

The other exemplary case is when EU did not officially put a name in the coup that toppled Morsi in Egypt. This fact can be interpreted both as an expression of the traditional cautious European approach towards the Middle East; but also can be seen as a sign that '*Morsi did not act as the EU would have wanted*'.

As a result, these analysis' on the region; demonstrating that the Western ideal of '*liberal democracy*' limits the possibilities and potential of regional participation and contribution into the international order, which Badiou (2011), described as '*the chance of unknown possibilities*'.[100]

Arab Spring as a Background of the Syrian Civil War

The Arab Spring movements that started in 2010 and 2011 across North Africa and the Middle East sparked a new debate on the *future of democracy* in the region. Yet in the years since, the region has seen a return to civil war and proxy warfare, most violently in Syria.101

The Arab world was built by the Western powers after the First World War within the structure which is based on artificial foundations. This new structure in the Arab world consists of a series of phenomena ranging from geographical boundaries, ethnic elements, public and fragile political and administrative structures, social divisions and ultimately to economic fragilities that are broken down from their own history. However, within these interventions; the changes in international politics that occurred at the end of the Cold War era remained ineffective in the Middle East. In other words, the Middle East has been diverted from its path with artificial interventions after the First World War. The concept of the *Arab Spring* gained the meaning for the region as continuation of its natural course.[102]

What constituted the social basis of the Arab Spring; especially the unemployment amongst the youths and discontentment, affected the degree of the social anger and reaction to the regimes. There were political, economic, social and political factors that were the catalyst of change like poverty, unemployment, the desperation of educated young people, demographic pressure created by the young population, high cost of living and low wages, social injustice, corruption, bribery, lack of law and justice. In addition to these, the long lasting anger towards the leaders and their close environments and the bureaucracy whom were holding the economic power have triggered the popular

---

100 Alain Badiou, Tunusia, Egypt: The Universal Reach of Popular Uprisings, Revolutioary Initiative, 2011
101 Philippe C. Schmitter & Nadine Sika, Democratization in the Middle East and North Africa: a more ambidextrous process? Mediterranean politics, 22(4), 2017, pp.443-463.
102 Ömer Laçiner, (2011). Modern Türkiye'de Siyasi Düşünce, İstanbul, İletişim Yayınları, 2011'den aktaran Akbaş, Ortadoğu'da Değişim Süreci ve Türk Dış Politikası, pp.53-55.

movements.[103]

The relationship that has been established by international media between '*Syrian Civil War*' and '*Arab Spring*' had an explanatory and guiding function. The reality that is pointed out by international media through '*Arab Spring*' concept was only an external '*ideal*'. However, the reality that has come out through local/regional reports was less considering conceptualizations like '*democracy*' or '*Arab Spring*' but more related to detailed facts. Alternatively, the words like '*freedom*', '*right*' and '*justice*' that are detected from banners, videos of protest songs or in the early posts of the rebellions commenting through social media, seem to be more used in concordance with the *Syrian Civil War* on local and regional media reports. These words looked like the main symbols of the protests related to the social-cultural reality of the society and the original needs of the public.

Comparison of Global Media and Regional Media Coverage of Syrian Uprisings in 2011-2015

In this part of the study, the news reports from *international regional and local* media tools have been chosen according to the date from 2011-2015, within the concepts like '*Democracy*' and '*Arab Spring*'.

Though the findings are selected among 69.700 results regarding the Syrian Civil War on the BBC; 32.700 of them were included '*Arab spring*' and '*democracy*'. The particularly selected '8 (Eight)' BBC reports were monitored through searching those words '*freedom*', '*right*', '*justice*' then these sentences were documented on the corpus tables. Analysis of the regional reports the online newspapers which were also published in English is selected. Though they were limited to reach out within the support from Omran Center for Strategic Studies (*Syrian based research institution in Turkey*) media department's list of journals; like *Arab Weekly, Railayoum, Enab Baladi, Al Cumhuriyya, Syria Weekly* are monitored. The coverage of Syrian Civil War on local-regional media, through news reports, interviews, articles, videos or social media posts; those words seem to be used mostly forefront as follows (Arabic in Latin letters); '*hurriya*', '*karama*', '*adalet*', '*haq*' which means; '*freedom*', '*security*', '*justice*', and '*right*'.

Analysis of the words: 'Freedom', 'Justice' and 'Right' as Substitute use of 'Democracy'

According to R.H. Robins, '*new words*' are the act of expanding the vocabulary of the language by taking foreign words continuously.[104] According to Margaret J. Lifetree's definition in her doctoral thesis, 'new words' may be a new term, or a new meaning attributed to the old meaning of a used term in general language.

---

[103] SAE, (2011) Arap Dünyasında Değişim ve Türkiye, (Çevrimiçi) http://www.turksae.com/sq1_file/383.pdf.12 Ortadoğu'da Değişim Süreci ve Türk Dış Politikası.03.2012'den aktaran Akbaş, Ortadoğu'da Değişim Süreci ve Türk Dış Politikası, p.55

[104] Robert Henry Robins, General Linguistics: an Introductory Survey, London and New York: Longman, 1971, p.30

These new words could often occur in political conversations, as a brand new term, or could refer to a narrowed segment of professional's terminology as a technical term.[105]

Figure 1. The synonyms of 'word' in a flexible web of words & meanings[106]

In order to classify the words of any discourse, one needs to specify semantic classes. These semantic classes coordinate the words to be in a certain order. Yet, it's not only the matter of syntax but a matter of choice of a certain word among the enormous data. This paradigmatic choice also requires a kind of '*Discrete point analysis*' which means that no word can actually be replaced by any other. While this is the case of a certain language it becomes really very difficult to choose the right words in the same context in a different/foreign language. This point of view brings the idea of using *synonyms, antonyms, references, connotations* and *denotations* to maintain the coherence and cohesion. 'Democracy is so popular in the 21st century that the word is used by a wide range of different political systems: like '*freedom' or 'justice*,' it has become a bit of a vague catch-all for whatever political arrangements the speaker admires.'[107]

---

105 Margaret Jean Lifetree, A Study of Neologisms Found In 'Le Monde' in 1955, Royal Halloway University of London, 1967.

106 Source: wordvis.com, 15.01.2019

107 https://philosophyterms.com/democracy/ Erişim 15.05.2019

Figure2. The synonyms of 'democracy' in a flexible web of words & meanings[108]

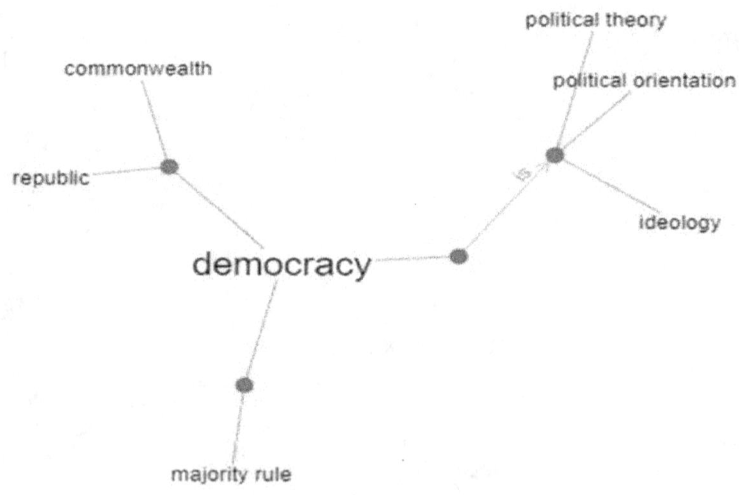

The word *democracy* which has come to mean very different things to people; wordvis.com brought the following words as synonyms of democracy; *Commonwealth, Republic, Political Theory, Political Orientation, Ideology, Majority Rule.* Considering these synonyms of 'democracy' concept, it can easily be criticized for its limitations with the political and governmental boundaries. This indication moves the core of the study into an analysis of the use of substitute words '*right', 'freedom' or 'justice*' that are used in regional media since '*democracy*' has been set as the background of '*Arab Spring'* discourse. In addition to this, back to its original course, Greek, which is a composite of *demos* and *kratos*, since *demos* can be translated as 'the people' (qua 'native adult male residents of a polis') and kratos as 'power', democracy has a root meaning of 'the power of the people'. But power in what sense? In modernity, democracy is often construed as being concerned, in the first instance, with a voting rule for determining the will of the majority. The power of the people is thus the authority to decide matters by majority rule.-However, referred to in the context of the classical (fifth and fourth centuries B.C.) terminology for regime-types '*capacity to do things*' was referred to as '*power*'. Greek criticts Raaflaub[109] and Ober[110] state that the '*Majority rule*' was an intentionally *pejorative diminution* urged by democracy. The Greek vocabulary for political regimes tended to focus in the first instance on the empowered or ruling body, which might be a single person (one), or a limited number of persons

---

[108] Source: wordvis.com, Erişim 15.5.2019

[109] Kurt A. Raaflaub, K, Democracy, Oligarchy and the Concept of the Free Citizen in the Late Fifth-Century Athens, Political Theory 11, 1983, pp.517-44

[110] Josiah Ober, The Athenian Revolution: Essays on Ancient Greek Democracy and Political Theory, Princeton: Princeton University Press, 1996.

(the few), or a large and inclusive body (the many). While the Greek vocabulary for regime-types is extensive, the three key terms of the rule of the one, few, and many are *monarchia*, *oligarchia*, and *demokratia.* Unlike, monarchia (*from the adjective monos: solitary*) and oligarchia (*from hoi oligoi: the few*), demokratia is not in the first instance concerned with '*number.*' According to J. Ober: 'Greek names of regimes divide into terms with an *–arche suffix,* and terms with *a –kratos suffix.* Aristokratia (*from hoi aristoi: the excellent*), *isokratia* (*from isos: equal*) and *anarchia* are classical regimenames that stand outside the one/few/many scheme yet fall into the *–arche/–kratos grouping.*

Table 3. Greek (and neo-Greek) terminology for regime types. Earlier (fifth-century attested) forms in bold, later (fourth-century) in plain face, post-classical/modern inventions in italic.[111]

I	II	III	IV	V
Empowered body	–kratos root	–arche root	Other regime-name terms	Related political terms: persons, abstractions
A. One	*autocracy*	**monarchia**	**tyrannia** **basileia**	**tyrannos** **basileus** (king)
B. Few	**aristokratia**	**oligarchia**	**dynasteia**	**hoi oligoi** (few)
C. Many	**demokratia** **isokratia** *ochlokratia* (mob)	*polyarchy*	**isonomia** (law) **isegoria** (speech) *isopsephia* (vote)	**hoi polloi** (many) **to plethos** (majority) **to ochlos** (mob) **isopsephos** (voter)
D. Other (exempli gratia)	timokratia (honor) gynaikokratia (women) *technocracy*	**anarchia**	**isomoiria** (shares) **eunomia** (law) politeia (mix of democracy and oligarchy: as used by Aristotle)	**dynamis** (power) **ischus** (strength) **bia** (force) **kurios** (master) **exousia** (authority. license)

Not all regime names use the *arche* or *kratos* roots; see Table: column IV. Yet (with the exception of *tyrannia* – which in the classical period had consistently negative connotations) the *–arche* and *–kratos* families tended to dominate the terminological landscape.[112]

A simple internet query with the keywords '*Arab Spring*' and '*Democracy*' relatively with '*Syrian Civil War*' as the studying case of this research identified differences in regional media through the words '*justice*', '*right*', '*freedom*' with gathering explicative series of documents. To constitute each sub-corpus as the representative of each keyword we began by using our prior knowledge of the issue, based on '*horizontal reading*' of findings to be able to focus separately on the discourse of reports that were more likely to cover on the issue. To extend the list of keywords for the query a list of sentences extracted from the reports were used. These were gathered in the first stage, then at the final part theye are read

[111] Radmedia.org: The Original Meaning of "Democracy": Capacity To Do Things Not Majority Rule
[112] Josiah Ober, The Original Meaning of Democracy, Blackwell Publishing Ltd. 2008 (Çevrimiçi) http://www.radmedia.org/leadingmatters/los_angeles/documents/OriginalMeaningDemocracy.pdf Erişim 15.5.2019

vertically by highlighting the concordances. This work is completed by defining '*extracts*' from selected reports and articles according to their sources.

The discrepancy in findings of Arab media is explained by the fact that the BBC publishes more reports whereas the reports from Arab Publishers, that were written in English, were less of numbers to reach out. Hence, to match the findings the solution was to limit the number of findings while focusing on the intensity of content on reports that are selected carefully. This query of work discipline was attentive to maintain a certain generic uniformity which included any official material published by an identified organization and the date it was published. Although these 16 reports of corpora seem quite less in terms of numbers; it seems representative as it includes the total number of flash results.

Comparison of the BBC and Regional News Report

Analysis of the BBC and Regional News Reports on Syrian Civil War

In this part of the study, 12T's approach will be applied to the findings. Regarding the Stoller & Grobe's 6T's Content Based Instruction Approach within the extension of Pembecioğlu as the 12T's approach (*Topic, Theme, Text, Thread, Task, Transfers, Transition, Thinking, Thinking, Tailoring, Taking Risks, Trend Topic-Transmedia*) is a valuable tool to analyze the data.[113] Thus, it will be used to make a comparative analysis of findings in between BBC and Regional/Local Arab media reports. According to 12T's approach; the *Topic* 'Syrian Civil War' is fictionalized through the main *Theme* 'Arab Spring' in the *Texts* news reports of BBC and Arab Media in the midst of specific *Time* 2011-2015 since the changes of events in time directly influencing the change of discourse as well.

[113] Gündüz, U. & Pembecioğlu, N. (2017). The Use And Impact Of Words On Social Media . Yeni Medya, (2) , 43-52

Table 4. The Regional and BBC News Reports of the 'Syrian Civil War'

BBC	Regional
BBC: 'Syria conflict: from peaceful protest to civil war'[114]	Al Jumhuriya: 'The Impossible Revolution: Making Sense of the Syrian Tragedy'[115]
BBC: 'Viewpoint: Why Arab Spring has not delivered real democracy'[116]	Zamaneh Media: 'Syria-Iran-Isis-and-the-Future-of-Social-Justice-in-dialogue-with-Yassin-al-Haj-Sale'[117]
BBC: Democracy or disorder? The four lessons of the Arab Spring[118]	Syria Untold: 'On the Inevitability of Militarization in the Syrian Uprising'[119]
BBC: 'Does the West want democracy in the Middle East?'[120]	Syria Untold: 'Syrian People Know Their Way'[121]
BBC: 'Arab Spring: 10 unpredicted outcomes'[122]	The Arab Weekly: 'Dashed Hopes of Arab Spring'[123]
BBC: 'Syria uprising: Assad says Aab Spring brought chaos'[124]	The Arab Weekly: 'Freedom allows youth to play active role in Tunisian civil society'[125]
BBC: 'Is the Arab Spring good or bad for terrorism?'[126]	Qunfuz: 'Introducing al-Haj Saleh's Impossible Revolution'[127]

Between the years 2011-2015; 8 news items with the title or content of '*Syrian Civil War*' and '*Arab Spring*' were selected from BBC reports. Likewise, among various Arab media news reports like *The Arab Weekly*, *Syria Untold, Al Jumhuriya, Qunfuz Zamaneh Media*; the news items were selected (that are translated in English) with the title or content of *'Syrian Civil War'* and *'Arab Spring'*, including the content about *revolution* and *uprisings era.*

As of analyzing the news reports in the revolution and uprising context; 'the language of Regional Media News' is observed to be mostly covered with the terms like freedom, justice, rights, dignity, employment and youth; whereas 'BBC

---

114 By Lina Sinjab BBC News, Damascus, Erişim15.05.2019 https://www.bbc.com/news/world-middle-east-21797661

115 By Alex Rowell, Erişim15.05.2019 https://www.aljumhuriya.net/en/academia/the-syrianization-of-the-world

116 By Gerald Butt Middle East analyst, Erişim15.05.2019 https://www.bbc.com/news/world-middle-east-27632777

117 By Frieda Afary, May 29, 2015, Erişim15.05.2019 https://en.radiozamaneh.com/24107/

118 By Roger Hardy, Middle East analyst, Erişim15.05.2019 https://www.bbc.com/news/world-middle-east-23266790

119 By Rateb Sha'bo, Syrian physician, writer, Erişim15.05.2019 https://syriauntold.com/inevitability-militarization-syrian-uprising/

120 By Owen Bennett-Jones, BBC News,19 November 2015, Erişim15.05.2019 https://www.bbc.com/news/world-middle-east-34857789

121 Features, 17 March 2014, Erişim15.05.2019 http://syriauntold.com/the-syrian-people-know-their-way/

122 Middle East,13 December 2013, Erişim 15.05.2019 https://www.bbc.com/news/world-middle-east-25212247

123 By Alaya Allani, Erişim15.05.2019 https://thearabweekly.com/dashed-hopes-arab-spring

124 Middle East, 21 September 2012, Erişim 15.05.2019 https://www.bbc.com/news/world-middle-east-19671635

125 By Roua Khlifi Friday 08/05/2015, Erişim 15.05.2019 https://thearabweekly.com/freedom-allows-youth-play-active-role-tunisian-civil-society

126 By Frank Gardner, BBC security correspondent,22 June 2011, Erişim 15.05.2019 https://www.bbc.com/news/world-middle-east-13878774

127 By Robin Yassin-Kassab, Erişim15.05.2019 https://qunfuz.com/introducing-al-haj-salehs-impossible-revolution/

News' were covered at most of the titles and contents with the highlighted concept of '*democracy*'.

Analysis of BBC Reports through 12 T's Approach Corpus 'Democracy' in BBC - Tasks and Threads

Table 5. Corpus 1. The word 'democracy' in the BBC reports in 2011-2015

1	Why Arab Spring has not delivered real	**democracy.**	
2	West's uncertain attitude towards	**democracy**	in the Arab world.
3	Iraq would become 'a beacon of	**democracy**	across the Middle East'.
4	neo-cons believed that the benefits of	**democracy**	were so self-evident that,
5	could not force a country to become a	**democracy.**	
6		**democracy**	Day takes place on Tuesday
7	A look at	**democracy**	past and present,
8	of Magna Carta - a touchstone for	**democracy**	worldwide
9	do actually represent a threat to	**democracy**	or are proof that it is
10	the Arab Spring as a springboard for	**democracy**	in a region where it was
11	able to choose its own leader as 'fake	**democracy.**	
12	populous nation itself, Western-style	**democracy**	is nowhere on the horizon -
13	the unpredictable fate of the 'old'	**democracy**	will undoubtedly be
14	West that it was not possible to	**democracy**	
15	the West actually wants	**democracy**	in the Middle East
16	Or is it, in fact, frightened of what	**democracy**	might bring?
17	What next for global	**democracy?**	
18	Europe's 'crisis of	**democracy**	is a gap between elites and
19	Intelligence Unit for the BBC's	**democracy**	Day.
20	For the reality is that Arab	**democracy**	has made little progress
21	Yet for all these displays of	**democracy**	the military and security
22	restrictions on protests hardly a basis	**democracy**	
23	Tunisian	**democracy**	faces challenges, but the
24		**democracy**	in Algeria is practiced
25	point to an opponent are pillars of	**democracy**	that are yet to be
26	At present, Arab countries are	**democracy**	in different ways
27		**democracy**	or disorder? The four lesson
28	appeared to be the harbinger of	**democracy**	has brought nothing but
29	intolerance that they are incapable of	**democracy**	
30	-anxious to encourage fledgling	**democracies**	but not to alienate old
31	forces could be an instrument of	**democracy**	was always suspect.
32	Syria or elsewhere, may decide that	**democracy**	leads nowhere, and that only
33	Does the West want	**democracy**	in the Middle East?
34	the face of it, one might conclude that	**democracy**	is thriving in the Arab world
35	the West's endless rhetoric about	**democracy**	is hollow.
36	unable to transform the yearning for	**democracy**	freedom and
37	inherent in arguing for	**democracy**	but fearing its results.
38	in Tunisia suggest that	**democracy**	can be trusted to work.
39	demonstrators demanding more	**democracy**	and an end to
40	the Middle East's most developed	**democracy**	but what would happen
41	demonstrators demanding more	**democracy**	and an end to
42	the interest of freedom	**democracy**	or ending social injustice
43	country is finding the path to	**democracy**	trouble-free
44	and especially because it denied	**democracy**	and even more
45	West has made in the past	**democracy**	when it eventually
46	Make sure that it was followed by	**democracy**	or even stability

According to results, in '8' BBC reports; the word of democracy is used '46' times as the main theme. It also seems to be used in concordance with the following words; *Western Style, promoting, practicing, incapable, harbinger* as the Western way of democracy applications and Western way of imposing of democracy as well. BBC seems to be in the position of authoritarianism onto the movements by social emancipation or democratization under the *Arab Spring* concept.

Regarding the *Threads* approach which means 'including other factors'; the use of the word 'democracy' in BBC appears to be embedded in *Arab Spring* concept. The texts also ushering certain *Tasks* like *'peacebuilding', 'history making'* within Western historical references like 'Magna Carta', 'Berlin Wall'.

Corpus 'Freedom' in BBC – Transmedia and Trend Topic

Table 6. Corpus 2. The word 'freedom' in BBC reports in 2011-2015

1	squares to the sound of	**freedom**	songs made popular by
2	balls with the word	**freedom**	written on them to bounce
3	started as a peaceful call for	**freedom**	soon turned into violence
4	the yearning for democracy,	**freedom**	and security in the
5	demanding personal	**freedoms**	alongside the political rights
6	shouting out loud calling for	**freedom**	and change
7	as protests calling for more	**freedom**	and dignity
8	Shouting out loud calling for	**freedom**	and change

Among the findings of '8' results of freedom '7' of the results were directly from one article which is titled as: *'Syria conflict: from peaceful protest to civil war'*. The article was related with the earlier Syrian conflict including the activities and comments stated by Syrians. According to 'Transmedia approach' which means 'Enrichment & Mobility of the news'; the global media seem to create the *'field of expression'* that can transcend the slipperiness of the ground by *'transmedia'* to *'represent'* the ones whom are the most influenced by the reality.

In addition to that, the word *'freedom'* seems to be used as the bottom lines of new media technology's outcomes as *trend topics* through transmedia. An access to information by new technological opportunities are created by certain concepts; like *keywords, collocation*, *Google AdWords, hashtags* and *commentators,* which are occupied with the *'instantaneous response'* as the creative output of the receivers' activation. This accumulation of active information may cause tricky effects. For instance, any *'periphrasis'* or *'connotation'* can easily be turned into a solid *'verbalism'* of single reality on online world.

Corpus 'Right' in BBC – Transmedia and Trend Topic

Table 7. Corpus 3. The word 'right' in the BBC reports in 2011-2015

1	tolerant, pluralistic, committed to	**rights**	were never likely to emerge,
2	After all, they ask, don't the human	**rights**	abusing Saudi royals get
3	freedoms alongside the political	**rights**	which were the focus of
4	badly for gender violence, reproductive	**rights**	treatment of women in
5	regimes that had scant regard for	**rights?**	

In the light of this fact, the way of use of the word *'right'* in global media come front as the *'trend topic'* finally becoming an *'international trend'* which especially comes up in concordance with the case *'humanity'*. The way it is being used is usually with *'catchy match-ups'* without even concerning the lack of information about the original matter of the fact.

Nevertheless, the word 'right' doesn't seem to be used in concordance with *'democracy'* aspect.

Corpus 'Justice' in BBC – Thinking

Table 8. Corpus 4, The word 'justice' in the Arab media in 2011-2015

1	The overthrow of Arab regimes, Mr. Assad said, had 'not worked in the interest of freedom, democracy or ending social	injustice	as much as it helped create chaos'.

Whereas there are *'13'* results for the word 'justice' in Arab Media, there is only '1' result among 8 reports of BBC. This word is also found in the text as the opposite of 'Justice' in the form of 'injustice' within the quote of *Assad's words* which can already be regarded as the '*Syrian discourse'*.

Whereas the word 'justice' is never found to be used in concordance with *'democracy'* aspect, the shocking result is that there is no mention of justice. Within the 'Thinking Approach' which includes the process and progress of thought on reporting; these reports seem to be in need of questioning according to the word *'justice';* if it is ever a non-political and non-professional word, or if it is just a romantic desire, or if it is just one of the most important core elements of the Syrian case?

The other face of the use of '*democracy*' seems to come up with only 8 results in Arab Media reports; on one hand it mostly refers to the *transferred reports* of BBC. On the other hand, the use of *'democracy'* in concordance with the words like *'political', 'societal', 'civil'* referring to the different perspectives of democracy practices.

The use of the word democracy through the BBC reports as a global trend gets higher hits. So, with these reports the tendency is not to maintain democracy but to transfer this theme into the developing countries. According tp 'Transitions' in 12T's approach which is described *as deliberate shift in emphasis from global trends, to trends in developing countries;* we may see the use of the word *'democracy'* in Arab media as a response to the *global population trend* by distincting the concept of democracy within addressing their own problems into it.

Regional and Local Arab Media Reports on Syrian Civil War

Corpus 'Democracy' in Arab Media – Transfers, Trends and Transitions

Table 9. Corpus 5. The word 'democracy' in the Arab media reports in 2011-2015

1	autocracies (and three	**democracies**	Who don't always vote much
2	global responsibility for the sake of	**democracy**	
3	of genuine political and societal	**democracy**	not the
4	formal	**democracies**	of the days before the 'Arab
5	who say that 'freedom and	**democracy**	were the main reasons for the
6	They promised civil	**democracies**	but worked instead on
7	They did not bring about a	**democracy**	based project
8	The 'Political Bureau' advocated	**democracy**	as well as social justice, and

Corpus 'Freedom' in Arab Media - Thinking and Tailoring

Table 10. Corpus 6. The word 'freedom' in the Arab media reports in 2011-2015

1	As hopes for	**freedom**	and prosperity are crushed,
2	Socialism	**freedom**	equality, brother-sisterhood
3	Those who say that	**freedom**	and democracy' were the
4	uprisings would lead to jobs and	**freedom**	
5	that relate to the issues of	**freedom**	civil society, women rights
6	agents in our struggle for	**freedom**	and change
7	country with the new-found	**freedom**	of expression and
8	conjuring the 'spirit' of	**freedom**	and justice in
9	But employment, dignity and	**freedom**	have remained mere slogans
10	when absolutely everybody's	**freedom**	is in question.
11	shifted from employment and	**freedom**	to restoring security and
12	that relate to the issues of	**freedom**	civil society, women rights
13		**freedom**	allows youth to play active

According to the approach, one other T, 'Thinking and Making Your Mind Up'; involves the word of 'freedom' used in Arab Media '13' times. The word 'freedom' is in need of (further) examination of the following questions that are necessarily paving the way for analyzing the findings: 1. *How do a reader comprehend this preference of the way of thinking of freedom and decides what to do with it?* 2. *Whose experimental applications are in 'reference'?*

To get these answers the indicators about the use of freedom in Arab Media are needed to be questioned from the '*reference points*' when it comes to the special cases according to the region. Comparing to BBC reports; in Arab media *'freedom'* is more settled with the '*active perspective*' as a result of use in concordance with the following words; *'spirit', 'peace', 'justice', 'struggle', 'prosperity', 'civil rights', 'civil society' 'women rights', 'civil liberties'* and 'hopes'. These words seem to be triggering to determine an aim and to keep a side by attending actively for the struggle for freedom.

On the final sentence of corpus puts it by questioning *everybody's freedom*; Arab media seems to be focusing on *freedom* at a political and social level, differently from the *'democracy'* understanding of Western understanding of freedom which is more related to *political boundaries* especially regarding migration case occurring on further news. Nevertheless, the word *'freedom'* doesn't seem to be used in concordance with *'democracy'* aspect.

Corpus 'Right' in Arab Media – Tailoring

Table 11. Corpus 7. The word 'right' in the Arab media in 2011-2015

1	calling for democratic reforms and human	**rights**	
2	worked with key activists including human	**rights**	sometimes even it
3	women, students, intellectuals, human	**rights**	activist
4	the issues of freedom, civil society, women	**rights**	
5	and each one will get their	**rights**	and put
6	support the Kurds' cultural and political	**rights**	
7	musicians, doctors, students, human	**rights**	activists, activist
8	(8-10% of Syrians) in Syria, let alone their	**rights**	
9	a socialist, feminist and human	**rights**	Activist
10	along with three other human	**rights**	activists Razan
11	human	**rights**	activism in Syria
12	Razan's work in defense of women's	**rights**	And human rights
13	and radicalized the field of human	**rights**	activism in Syria
14	what is right may give you the	**right**	to rule people the
15	Their	**right**	to criticize the Syrian
16	democratic reforms and human and civil	**right**	
17	including human	**rights**	Lawyer Razan
18	up rehashing the security discourse of the	**right**	sometimes
19	women, students, intellectuals, human	**rights**	activists
20	refugees, women, students, intellectuals, human	**rights**	activists

Compared to the use of BBC, the word *'right'* in Arab media as quadruple number of results is leading to a point that Syrian people's rights are such a critical tension in Syria which is mostly covered on the public's discourses.

According to the factor of *'Tailoring'* the use of the word *'right'* seems to be operating with the readers to attend actively into the case, depending upon their perceptions within the preferences and relativistic approach regarding what is right for whom and in what case. Through the reports, the reporters seem to be in the position of a catalyzer of the reader's actions. The volunteerism and activism can be seen as such results. As the reader gathers ideas and accumulates knowledge based on consequences of the actions that are put out in the outside world, the already developed 'concepts' or 'frameworks' will be less involved with the reader to interpret the world.

Compared to the Arab media, BBC makes use of the terms within the *'transmitter'* position by 'passivizing' the transferred one's self action. In other words, BBC reporters in the position of *'transporter'* are covering the case and spoiling the right of speech, by dominating what the tailoring actors should be doing or thinking about their rights.

Corpus 'Justice' in Arab Media - Taking Risks

Table 12. Corpus 8 The word 'justice' in the Arab media in 2011-2015

1		**Injustice**	
2	conjuring the 'spirit' of freedom and	**justice**	in 'Assad's Syria
3	His concern for social	**justice**	arose from his immediate
4	democracy as well as social	**justice**	and agitated against the
5	ISIS and the Future of Social	**Justice**	In dialogue with Yassin al-
6	had strong social and economic	**justice**	demands turned into a war
7	practical support to this social	**justice**	movement.
8	This is not to say anything about	**Justice**	
9	What kind of 'Left' leaves issues of	**justice**	out of its thinking and self
10	What can Iranian social	**justice**	activists and thinkers learn
11	can we forge ties between social	**justice**	struggles in Iran and Syria?
12	His concern for social	**justice**	arose from his immediate
13	democracy as well as social	**justice**	agitated against the regime's

'13' results of the word 'justice' in Arab media were analyzed with the *'Taking Risks'* category as being the mostly used ones in concordance with the words *'social, 'peace'* and *'freedom'* which can easily be described as the response of the reality. The original activists' explanations as a matter of the subject seem to handle the case as a 'Task' which is defined as to gain and maintain *'justice'*.

The texts put their tasks as to improvise, activate, motivate people as well rebellions. These texts also put forward the idea of justice as a main task to be followed by people according to Arab media. However, there seems to be not clear tasks for BBC reports even if the reports associate the word democracy with peace building and history making.

Findings and Interpretations

Analysis of Corpus Based Reports

Throughout the table; comparing the BBC reports to regional reports, it seems to be a must that the international media must strive for diversity in the media coverage of the Syrian Civil War considering the fact that '8' of the results of the word democracy were used in Arab media, whereas '46' results of the word democracy could be seen through the BBC reportings.

The regional media come up with the '13' results of justice, while BBC reports usage of justice is just '1', and that is the word *'injustice'* actually. '5' rights on BBC 'in concordance with political and women rights, compared to '20' results of rights in Arab media. And finally considering the proximity of the results 'freedom' appears to 10 times in BBC results and '13' times in Arab media reports. It can be seen that the 7 of the results of *'freedom'* appearing in BBC reports were directly from one article which is related with the earlier Syrian conflict including the activities and comments shared by Syrians.

Table 13. The numbers of findings

LIST OF WORDS					
TYPE OF DOCUMENT	**Total Number of Reports**	**Democracy**	**Freedom**	**Justice**	**Right**
Global Media (BBC Reports)	8	46	13	1	5
Arab Media (Regional and Local Reports)	8	8	8	13	20
TOTAL NUMBER OF WORDS	16	56	25	10	27

Considering, the comparative analysis of results; the substitute keywords: *'justice', 'right', 'freedom'* seem to be set relatively with 'Syrian Civil War' applied as the alternative communicative discourses of the original events from Arab media perspective. Those words which seem to be the real climate of the Syrian Uprisings could be interpreted as the real climate of Arab Spring as well. However, within 46 results on BBC the 'democracy' concept seem to be coming to the forefront in global media reports, yet within only *'8'* results on regional/local media Arab reporters seem to be less willing to use this concept. In addition to that, Arab media also makes use of the words like *'spirit', 'dignity', 'employment'* in concordance with the keywords 'justice', 'freedom' and 'right'.

As a result, in each corpus a contrastive-comparative analysis enabled the findings to single out the relation of the key words. These key words were represented as close synonyms of Syrian Civil War in contracts to the discourses of *'Arab Spring'* and *'Democracy'* as the relevant language of international news in BBC. These concepts are revealed as the transferred *'political fiction'* of the West, since the number of the word *'democracy'* only appears extremely in BBC results whereas very limited number of occurrences appear in Arab Media.

The consequences also prevail that the use of words like 'freedom', 'justice' and 'right' do not necessarily yield what 'democracy' or 'Arab Spring' refer in international media. Instead these words occur frequently as the solitary indicators of Syrian case between the years of 2011-2015.

Conclusion

The first era of Syrian Uprisings came across with the Arab Spring movement around the region. Yet at the end, the Syrian Uprisings which started at 15 March 2011 totally differed from all other regions' events by turning into an international war which still continuing in 2019; whereas every country in the MENA region had also their own specific improvements throughout the time. This fact has shown the the reality of the whole idea of Arab Spring concept on the international media as a fictional and supplemental approach. This study mainly concentrated on how BBC and regional Arab Media make use of the certain words related to Syrian Civil War on an international basis.

The political terminology that is brought by International Media like*'Arab Spring'* and *'Democracy'* do not reflect *domestic actors'* policy preferences (*justice, freedom, right)* since this terminology was intentionally created to guarantee the pursuit of particular international policies. Furthermore, this terminology that are brought by International Media observed to be used in global thinking as a professional obligation.

Nevertheless, the international media effects the receivers' decision making process by helping them in structuring their agendas towards news reports. On one hand this actively-involving process being representation of certain interests of some groups, on the other hand this is causing misrepresentations for the actual people of the Syrian case. On other words; globalization of the Syrian Civil War on international media with the *'Arab Spring'* concept; have some other independent effects; like creating rules for decision making, determining the agendas of activists and offer advantages to certain groups while disadvantaging others. Over time, strong institutions may even direct actors' policy references according to these reports.

According to Pembecioğlu; 'With the impact of the media the real meaning beneath the concepts disappeared in the last decade and minimized into the reflections of the first sight.'[128] The global catchphrases like 'demand of democracy', 'war on terror', acquired an international paradigm status by the virtue of its use by multiple actors in the media sphere of Syria. This led to the loss of the primitive perspective onto the actual events in Syria.

According to the analysis of the results through 12T's Approach; the linguistic relativity, that are set on these reports by certain concepts appeared as *common mechanisms* of international communication like *internationalization of 'Domestic Politics'* which seems to be practiced at the top of the coverage of Syrian Civil War.

According to Hamid Mowlana, the production of journalists is not an individual but a social commodity. Thus, the journalist is not only responsible for the media but also for the public. Journalism should be a way for public awareness and information. The journalist must be aware of universal values, cultural differences, and adhere to the concepts of peace, democracy, human rights, social progress and national freedom. The right of every individual and community to choose and develop their own political, economic, social and global system must be respected. As a benchmark politic advisor Hamid Mowlana and Professor of Journalism Kaarle Nordenstreng's discourse on The Global Media Debate; whereas Nordenstreng emphasizes democracy, Mowlana

[128] Gündüz, U., & Pembecioğlu, N. (2017). The Use And Impact Of Words On Social Media. Yeni Medya, (2), 43-52.

stands for the respect for cultural and traditional values.[129] In the case of freedom, Nordenstreng emphasizes the concept of national freedom, while Mowlana's personal rights such as the Settlement Family and Property are not undermined.[130]

Table 14. The Analysis of Findings_Regarding to 12T's Approach

Theme & Topic General Umbrella Term	In fact at the beginning the theme seems to be 'Arab Spring', and the topic seems to be 'Syrian Civil War'. Yet, in time, these two important terms switch with each other so that the Syrian Civil War becomes a more general umbrella term covering all the other factors.
Text: Age, Level, Interest, Language	In all these text, this study concentrates on the Language factor. Language is taken into consideration through a more contrastive perspective as to compare English and Arabic news terminology.
Thread: What Other Factors	In the texts, involving the searched terms, the use of the Word 'democracy' in BBC is embedded in Arab Spring concept. Or, the Word 'right' is associated with the words such as women, students, intellectuals, civil society, cultural, political, musicians, doctors, etc.
Task: What Duties	The texts put their tasks as to improvise, activate, motivate people as well rebellions. These texts also put forward the idea of justice as a main task to be followed by people according to Arab media. However, there seems to be not clear tasks for BBC reports even if the reports associate the Word democracy with peace building and history making.
Trends & Transfers What Tendencies	The use of the Word democracy through the BBC reports as a global trend gets higher hits. So, with these reports the tendency is not to maintain democracy but to transfer this theme into the developing countries.
Transition: What Changes	In comparison to BBC reporting's the Arab regional media concentrates on transitions of democracy as political, civil and societal.
Thinking: Process – Progress	The text of BBC do not yield so much about the thinking process of the readers. Whereas the word justice is never found with the democracy aspect, the Arab Regional media 'freedom' is more settled with the 'active perspective' as a result of use in concordance with other concepts.
Tailoring: What Kind of Details	'spirit', 'peace', 'justice', 'struggle', 'prosperity', 'civil rights', 'civil society' 'women rights', 'civil liberties' and 'hopes'.
Taking Risks What Kind of Threats	The reports of both types do not ever take risks of being misunderstood. The basic threats seem to be terrorism, ISIS, Iran, social peace and freedom. The main risk in journalism regarding such hot issues, is the misconceptions of provoking people. Thus, every word seems to be involving certain direct and indirect references, associations, dichotomies, connotations, etc.
Technology & Transmedia Enrichment & Mobility	Even if the media literacy rates are not high in middle east countries, the journalist reports could transcend to the communities. An access to information by new technological opportunities are created by certain concepts; like keywords, collocation, Google AdWords, hashtags and commentators, which are occupied with the 'instantaneous response' as the creative output of the receivers' activation

Scholars has recently begun to explore how domestic-level structures and processes affect compliance on international norms. This literature has identified

[129] Mowlana, Hamid. "The myths and realities of the "information age": A conceptual framework for theory and policy." *Telematics and Informatics* 1.4 (1984): 427-438.
[130] Gerbner, G., Mowlana, H., & Nordenstreng, K. (Eds.). (1993). *The global media debate: Its rise, fall and renewal.* ABC-CLIO.

the domestic legitimacy of an international norm as an important variable in accounting for the effects of norms on state behavior. But scholars have devoted insufficient attention to measuring the legitimacy or salience of international norms in the domestic arena and to identifying the pathways that lead to domestic salience.

Deep insights could lead to more systematic studies of the domestic impact of international norms; by identifying which '*pathways*', by which 'international norm' can enter into the national arena and 'one factor' that conditions its impact on domestic political processes.

According to anti – globalizers, global communication is mostly connected with notions such as cultural imperialism and media imperialism; they see global communication as a vehicle aiming at controlling, invading or undermining other cultures. The transmitted cultural or ideological pattern has often been seen as an invasion of Western values, particularly those of American's (McQuail, 2000).

While some people criticize Western media exports as predatory, others support it as an expression of the free market and regard the imbalance of flow as a characteristic of the wider media market, which has benefit for all.[131] Free-flow theorists tend to assume that global media has little predatory effect because the audience is voluntary, claiming that global media content is culturally neutral and ideologically innocent.[132]

However, receiving countries have often complained of media imperialism, arguing that global mass media is having negative effects on the culture and traditional values of their citizens. The idea is that cultural autonomy is undermined by imbalance in the flow of mass media content and, therefore, its national identity in an age of globalism is in danger of being subverted. McQuail points out, '*The unequal relationship in the flow of news increases the relative global power of large and wealthy news-producing countries and hinders the growth of an appropriate national identity and self-image*'.[133]

Giddens points out the tensions that exist between globalization and localization. According to Giddens, globalization is 'the intensification of world-wide social relations which link distant locations in such a way that local happenings are shaped by events occurring many miles away and vice versa'.[134]

Discourses of cultural imperialism speak to major current controversies,

---

[131] Noam, E., (1991). Television in Europe. New York: Oxford University Press.

[132] Biltereyst, D., (1995). Qualitative audience research and transnational media effects: a new paradigm? European Journal of Communications, 10(2), 245-270.

[133] McQuail, D., (2000). McQuail's mass communication theory (4th ed). London, Thousand Oaks & New Delhi: Sage Publications, pp.222 cited in Wang, Dawei, (2008). Globalization of the Media: Does It Undermine National Cultures? Intercultural Communication Studies, 17(2), 203-211.

[134] Giddens, A. 1990. The Consequences of Modernity. CA: Stanford University Press. (Stanford) cited in Wang, Dawei, (2008). Globalization of the Media: Does It Undermine National Cultures? Intercultural Communication Studies, 17(2), 203-211.

including: cultural suppression and genocide; ideas of 'globalization'; influential economic models of 'capitalism' and 'neoliberalism'; ideologies that are embedded in the global spread of concepts such as 'modern', *'progressive', 'growth', 'development', 'consumerism', 'free market', 'freedom', 'democracy', 'social Darwinism' and 'soft power'; cultural specificity of criteria and procedures for establishing 'truth'*; instrumentalization for the purposes of cultural conquest of academic disciplines such as psychoanalysis, economics, social anthropology, or marketing, or environmental crises, especially as linked to western ideologies that underwrite humanity's 'right' to dominate nature.[135]

However, cultural imperialism on the media is not limited to ethnic identities; it also seems to overlook the perception that a particular political, social, cultural terminology and its application fields which may have different understandings and activities. Since usually the people deal with others' words and representations by the means of media and advertising; and have become so accustomed to their messages, they often have trouble seeing things in its own natural way.

As known, while learning a foreign language; going to foreign countries and trying to make a living there is a specific way of separating reality from language courses. Today's international media studies which already travel all around the world through their reporters, the news coverage, requires to be highly focused on *translation science.* Becoming professional on language issues is getting important as being global and reporting events from anywhere to all around the world and carrying those reports to other countries as well. Because, when the dominant culture's language has an effect of on other languages, it is possible to see the transfer of its linguistic relativity, its fiction of reality, the imposed meanings to the other languages as well as exporting many words. In the globalization process, this effect has reached to a more decisive position.

For the final words; during the International Media Studies courses, in the lecture named *'Transnational Media'* it's been mentioned that as much being united and oriented on international level, it is important that the different nations should be supporting each other's *'local cultures'.* Because the specifics of local / locality itself is related to the nature of the international society as well. Supporting the indigenous factors of the communities, by considering their effect on the language and carrying this harmony into international level seem to be the core of successful media reporting. Such harmony will inevitably lead to the feeling that we are able to speak freely to the world, from where we are and as we are.

---

135 Boyd-Barrett, Oliver, (2018) Cultural Imperialism and Communication, Jun 2018 DOI: 10.1093/acrefore/9780190228613.013.678(Çevrimiçi) http://oxfordre.com/communication/view/10.1093/acrefore/9780190228613.001.0001/acrefore-9780190228613-e-678

Appendix: Interviews

Yaser Al- Akkad, Totino Media, Photographer, Media Editor (29 years old)

'The uprisings in Syria wasn't involved with the guns through 9 months in some areas and 6 months in other areas; we were carrying red flowers, banners and we were wanting just the government to fix the situation. But what Assad think was only we were rebellions. So we've been trapped and attacked.

Democracy defined as the public leading themselves; freedom is to act or say anything but in our country is in return of your life, we wanted to act and say freely. After all, as media people in Syria, we felt like; we must give our voice to be heard in West. Syrian media writers are writing for Western newspapers we give them what they want to hear or understand. If they care about women rights we give them women rights, if they want to hear democracy we give them democracy, to get the support we needed.'

Omar Akil, Syrian Forum, Business Director (43 years old)

'There is a saying that Arabic culture doesn't fit with democracy as long as carrying Islam, Democracy in Arabic is 'hukm ash sha'b' *(the dominion of public)* and the public is comprised %80 per cent of Sunnis yet the power is at the %10 of Alawis, who are determining what is our rights and limitations. If must say, we got the freedom of praying as we like to do in Turkey. I think this is also must be regarded as some kind of freedom which we didn't have in our country.'

Dr Sinan Hatahet, Omran Strategic Research Center, Strategy Development Authority (42 years old)

'The most important thing about this tragedy is; it is more than humanitarian crisis. It's a humanitarian crisis that is result of a political one. The regime that has been ruling country for more than 47 years now; only 2 president ruled the country, a father and Assad, and they already call it a republic and a democratic country. This is why the Syrian people were on the streets. In order to find freedom, in order to gain their dignity back. We called it in Syria: The Revolution of Dignity. We haven't called it 'The Revolution of Bread' or anything else like that. It's a 'Revolution of Dignity' to find ourselves back.

Hadia Al Kuwaji, Syrian Locul Councils Community Director, Lawyer (33 years old)

'For example hijab concept is always been related to liberalism; but liberalism concept always depends on the political situation and whoever is at the authority. As we see in Tunisia in 1950s El Habib Burgiba who is the father of liberalism was against hijab, while Zeyn Abdin bin Ali, who took the power from him, was against Islam was not against hijab.'

CHAPTER 19

A THOUGH LIFE: THE PORTRAYAL OF REFUGEES IN (TRANSNATIONAL) FILMS*

Burak Buğra Komlu[1] and Hasan Gürkan[2]

Introduction

The use of the concept of transnational cinema, which has become an established field in film studies in recent years, first begins with the nation-state debates under the influence of globalization. The main factors of this national to global change are the spread of neoliberalism, the political disintegration of the Soviet Union and the Eastern European communist bloc, the collapse of the Berlin wall and the unification of the two different Germany, and the developments that accelerate globalization by bringing the bipolar world to an end. Culturally, new social movements such as women's movements and gender politics, ethnic and religious identity discussions, the development of telecommunication technologies such as television and internet, and the development of transportation networks increase the effects of globalization on today's world with the increase of international migration. Such developments affecting the world undoubtedly affect cinema, which is a cultural production field as well.[3]

The concept of transnational cinema is used to define the formations that can be evaluated on a global ground instead of a national ground at the aesthetic, technical and representation level, as well as the global mobility of people and the production, distribution and display possibilities, with the global dynamism of capital and information[4]. Transnational cinema is the cinema that allows us to understand the global world we live in and the changing cinematic methods, while at the same time introducing them systematically. Transnational films, expressed through the interactions of people from different countries, are not only an absolute necessity, but are also seen as the result of the economic cooperation of filmmakers from different countries[5].

---

[1] Burak Buğra Komlu, Marmara University, Radio, Television and Cinema Department, Ph.D. Student, Türkiye. E-mail: burakomlu@gmail.com

[2] Hasan Gürkan, Assoc Prof. Dr., Istiye University, Communication Faculty and Maria Zambrano Fellow at Girona University, Türkiye. E-mail: gur.hasan@gmail.com

[3] Nejat Ulusay, **Melez İmgeler: Sinema ve Ulusötesi Oluşumlar**, Ankara, Dost Kitapevi Yayınları, 2008, p. 15-16

[4] Muzaffer Musab Yılmaz, **Abderrahmane Sissako Sinemasının Ulusötesi Sinema Bağlamında İncelenmesi,** (Master Thesis), İstanbul, İstanbul Üniversitesi, 2018, p. 6.

[5] Hasan Gürkan, "Kadın ve Göç: Ulusötesi Filmlerde Türkiyeli Müslüman Kadın Tasviri" **Kültürötesi**

While it is clear that transnational connections in cinema are not new, the paradigm change in social sciences causes questions such as why transnational cinema and why now. In a multicultural and a centred world where this transition towards the transnational, where academicians working in the fields of social sciences such as sociology, postcolonial theory and cultural studies, production and consumption become more interconnected with globalization, the representation of individual and collective identities has no national counterpart.[6]

There are generally three main approaches in film studies to theorize the concept of transnational. The first approach, made by Higson, focuses on the relationship with cultural and economic formations within national boundaries and it focuses on the fact that transnational constitutes an alternative to non-national areas, has a tendency to focus on production, distribution and display relations. The second approach focuses on film cultures that are shaped by a common cultural heritage or common geopolitical borders. The third and final approach is to focus on filmmakers who have made exile, diaspora and postcolonial migrations, who have been heavily influenced by cultural studies, postcolonial theory and globalization studies, and the power relations between the host culture and the guest culture, the European-centred, western nation and national cultural structure, narrative and aesthetic consisting of studies that systematically analyse the representation of cultural identity and formations. According to this approach, transnational cinema takes place around or outside of national film cultures[7].

As mentioned above, there are many different approaches to cinematic transnationalism. It is included not only in terms of the concept but also in different genres within transnational cinema. Cinematic transnationalism can support various values economically, artistically, culturally, socially and politically. The fact that transnational formations are motivated by economic values, for example, by co-productions, may lead to ignoring its other overarching goals. It is one of the aims of transnational to promote values such as common social heritage, cultural values, solidarity and belonging of societies that are outside the economy. In addition, at least two qualities of the more valuable forms of transnational cinema come to the fore: being visible to the invisible in the mainstream, in other words, a resistance to globalization as cultural homogenization, and a commitment to not overshadow the pursuit of aesthetic, artistic, social and political value for economic reasons. As a result, it is inevitable to accept that transnational cinema is a phenomenon that includes various types of values, but also has the potential to develop in many different

---

İmgeler: Ulusötesi Avrupa Sinemasında Göç, Sürgün ve Aksan Tartışmaları, Yıldız D. Birincioğlu, Uğur Baloğlu (Ed.), İstanbul, Doruk Yayımcılık, 2020, p. 453.

[6] Will Higbee, Song H. Lim, Concepts of Transnational Cinema: Towards a Critical Transnationalism in Film Studies. **Transnational Cinemas**. Vol.1 No. 1, 2010 p. 8.

[7] Will Higbee, Song H. Lim, ibid, p. 9-10.

types, open to understanding and raising awareness of today's world.[8]

In the next sections of this study, discussions on migration films are mentioned and the film *Toivon Tuolla Puolen* (*Another Face of the Hope*, 2017), directed by the Finnish director Aki Kaurismäki, and *Welcome* (2019) directed by Philippe Lioret are examined. In particular, the reason why these films are discussed in this text is to reveal how Kaurismäki and Lioret, as a director based in a western identity, have dealt with the immigrant/refugee problem in film narratives, as well as being quite popular in the last few years.

The Terms on Transnational Cinema: Immigrant Cinema, Accented Cinema, Exile Cinema, Postcolonial Ethnic and Identity Cinema

Although migration is not a new phenomenon, it is a new topic of the world as a part of the global integration that is accelerating with globalization. Global migration movements are seen as a result of rapidly changing economic, political and cultural ties between countries. Increasing migration movements cause the globalizing world to be described as the 'age of migration'[9]. As a data supporting this argument, the number of international immigrants has reached 273 million, constituting 3.5% of the world population according to the World Migration Report (2020) of the International Organization for Migration (IOM) as of today.[10]

Migration movements, which cross political boundaries play an important role in the production, distribution and exhibition of films. Unable to produce their films in their own countries, exile, oppression, economic inconvenience, ethnic, religious, it is possible to name many directors who emigrate for various reasons. As a result of the migration of these directors from various parts of the world to the central countries, the relationship between immigration and cinema makes the existence of the immigrant cinema category day by day. When immigrant cinema is discussed, the first thing is about immigrants and their host society, homeland, exile, being on the road, including the films made by immigrants or the films on immigrants, including situations related to immigration[11]. Representatives of immigrant cinema are spread over the world.

The vast majority of immigrant cinema products are citizens of the third world countries and post-colonial independence countries. This includes movements from geographies to central countries and especially to the west.

---

[8] Kathleen Newman, "Notes on Transnational Film Theory: Decentered Subjectivity, Decentered Capitalism", **World Cinemas, Transnational Perspectives**, Natasa Ďurovičová, Kathleen Newman (Ed.), Abingdon, Routledge, 2010, p.3-11

[9] Anthony Giddens, **Sosyoloji**, translated by Şebnem P. Güzel, İstanbul, Kırmızı Yayınları, 2012, p.569.

[10] https://www.umhd.org.tr/2020/06/basin-aciklamasi-dunya-multeciler-gunu/ (Accessed Date: 26.11.2020)

[11] Özgür Yaren, **Altyazılı Rüyalar: Avrupa Göçmen Sineması**, Ankara, De ki Basım Yayım, 2008, s.10-11.

Names such as Ella Shohat, Robert Stam, Hamid Naficy emphasize the third world identity of immigrant cinema representatives. It is possible to describe this mobility of immigrant cinema representatives as a 'third world fantasy'.[12]

Ella Shohat and Robert Stam consider immigrant cinema in the third cinema categorization. According to them, commercial/Hollywood cinema is the first cinema, the independent art cinema, which forms its own production and distribution network, can be categorized in the second cinema, and the third cinema which emerges as a movement against the commercial dominant cinema, aiming the active participation of the audience. In addition, they divide the third cinema into three categories. The films made by third world directors, the second category supported by the first and second world people, and the third category films consisting of diasporic and hybrid films are defined as 'postcolonial hybrid films'.[13]

Hamid Naficy explains immigrant cinema using the concept of 'independent transnational' films and developing this concept and using the concept of 'accented cinema'. According to Naficy, such films eliminate the defined geographical, national, cultural and cinematic borders.[14] Independent transnational films not only express the common themes produced by the directors who have to leave their homeland, but also include similar forms and genre features that are common in production, distribution and screening relationships.[15]

Naficy divides the immigrant cinema representatives, which he defines as accented cinema, into two groups in general. These two groups are the results of postcolonial displacements and late modernism or postmodern scattering. The first group refers to those who move from the late 1950s to the mid-1970s as a result of the aforementioned reasons, while the second group refers to the failure of nationalism, socialism and communism in the 1980s and 1990s as a result of global economies, the increase in religious and ethnic wars, immigration. It refers to the group formed as a result of developments supporting non-western migration as a result of changes in policies, unprecedented innovations in communication and media. These developments are important building blocks in the formation of immigrant cinema.[16]

After his distinction, Naficy divides immigrant cinema into three genres, which share similar narratives, identity issues, production styles and themes

---

[12] Özgür Yaren, ibid, p. 47-48.

[13] Yelda Özkoçak, "Göçmen ve Sinema: Avrupa Göçmen Sineması ve Türk Asıllı Yönetmenler", **Stratejik ve Sosyal Araştırmalar Dergisi,** Cilt 3, Sayı 3, 2019, p. 435.

[14] Gizem Parlayandemir, Deniz Oğuzcan, "Bir Can Yeleği Olarak Tony Gatlif Sineması ve Aman Doktor", **Kültürötesi İmgeler: Ulusötesi Avrupa Sinemasında Göç, Sürgün ve Aksan Tartışmaları,** Yıldız D. Birincioğlu, Uğur Baloğlu (Ed.), İstanbul, Doruk Yayımcılık, 2020, s.

[15] Neslihan Kültür, "Aksanlı Sinema ve Fatih Akın", **Maltepe Üniversitesi İletişim Fakültesi Dergisi,** Cilt.4, Sayı.2, 2017, s. 5.

[16] Hamid Naficy, **An Accident Cinema: Exilic and Diasporic Filmmaking,** New Jersey, Princeton University Press, 2001, p.10.

within accented cinema. These are exile, diasporic and ethnic filmmakers. Although such films are generally distinct from each other, there are also films, which share common features that are intertwined.[17] Based on the work of Hamid Naficy, Özgür Yaren proposes an original classification in *Altyazılı Rüyalar: Avrupa Göçmen Sineması* and examines immigrant filmmakers under the headings of 'diaspora and exiles', 'post-colonial immigrants' and 'labor immigrants'.[18]

Elsaesser uses the term 'passport-free movies' for immigrant cinema in his study of European and Hollywood cinemas. According to him, these films refer to stateless films that help the audience build identity, open new areas of solidarity, and question the idea of nation in the political and historical arena. These films, which transcend national boundaries, serve to create a collective consciousness by aiming to arouse a sense of moral compassion in the audience and anger them against injustice. From this point of view, Malik uses the term 'cinema of duty', which expresses the immigrant cinema to present the social drama of disadvantaged groups and individuals, to be in a critical position against the dominant and hegemonic ideologies, and from the perspective of immigrant and diasporic cultures.[19]

The New European structure shaped by migrations consists of subjects that have been covered in cinema since the 1960s. First generation immigrants make independent films with limited resources. These films mostly consist of documentary or documentary-style realistic films. However, in the mid-1980s, second-generation immigrant and diasporic filmmakers have certain film production opportunities. After this date, there is a quantitative increase in immigrant films. Especially films on immigration to Germany depict characters subject to gender inequality, cultural differences, loss between two cultures, prejudice and exclusion. The films of this period have become a task cinema that makes immigrants victims while explaining the problems of immigrants as the first examples of encounters with immigrants.[20] Among these: *Angst essen seele auf* (*Fear gnaws the spirit*, Rainer W. Fassbinder, 1974), *Otobüs* (*Bus*, Tunç Okan, 1974), *40m² Almanya* (*40 m2 Germany*, Teyfik Başer, 1986), *Yasemin* (Hark Bohm, 1988), *Shirins Hochzeit* (*Şirin's Wedding*, Helma Sanders-Brahms, 1976), *Drachenfutter* (*Dragon Dinner*, Jan Schütte, 1987). These filmmakers, who have film production opportunities, simultaneously appear in France, England and Germany, having been in close contact with immigration in Europe for many years.[21]In France, it is referred to as 'Beur Cinema', which is formed by immigrants from North Africa, mainly Algeria, the former colony of France.[22] 1960 in Germany and after

---

[17] Hamid Naficy, ibid, p. 11.
[18] Özgür Yaren, ibid, p. 54.
[19] Issolina Ballesteros, **Immigration Cinema in the New Europe**, Bristol, Intellect, 2015, p.13
[20] Özgür Yaren, ibid, p. 124.
[21] Nilgün Bayraktar, Mobility and Migration in Film and Moving-Image Art: Cinema Beyond Europe, New York, Routledge, 2016, p. 6.
[22] Oya Ş. Aydın, "Afrika'da Sinema Serüveni ve Cinema Beur Akımı", **Galatasaray Üniversitesi İletişim Dergisi,** 2005, cilt. 1, Sayı. 2, p.98.

that labor migration occurs as a result of the agreement between Turkey and settled here as refugees created by the children of Turkish-German cinema, as film-making practices shaped by prominent migration and diaspora experience emerges.

The increase in the number of films experienced in this period continues in the 90s. However, immigrants, who were generally in front of the camera until this period, now have more access to film production opportunities and the opportunity to tell their own stories[23].

European-born or having European citizenship filmmakers constitute one of the most important parts of immigrant cinema. These autobiographical films focus on the difficulties of living between the two cultures and often arise in the diaspora communities. It can be said that the immigrants show a tension of revolt against their adherence to their cultural and religious traditions and the oppression, which comes with assimilation. Yaren[24] defines these films as a back quarter ethos, mostly take place in the ghetto or suburbs. Against the victim stereotypes of the first period, this period leaves its place to criminal immigrant stereotypes.

Filmmakers with immigrant identity begin to be seen in auteur cinema during this period. The most important of these are Turkish-German director Fatih Akın and Tunisian-French director Abdellatif Kechiche. In this period when personal differences are felt more, it leaves the place of staying between the two cultures, which was in a dominant position in previous periods, to different dimensions related to immigration. Immigration takes place as a trope, not a theme. The reversal of the old representation stereotypes is followed by the fact that immigration lost its importance in this period, leaving it to mainstream, auteur cinema or more marginal areas. Increasing diversity in immigrant cinema brings about categorization efforts. However, categorization is open to the danger of reductionism. Because although the films show certain similarities periodically, the existence of the same themes in different periods is too much to underestimate[25].

Immigrant cinema in Europe offers a broad socio-political field that deals with the concepts of European identity and national belonging. Immigrant cinema initiates the investigation of new exclusionary attitudes such as new racism, violence, and otherness that affect the individual, social and Europe as a whole, of globalization, colonial legacy and new forms of colonialism. Immigrant cinema is reflected in movies that diversify as a reflection of the multicultural and multi-ethnic structure of New Europe. In this case, immigrant cinema presents a complex and eclectic mix of genres and forms stemming from non-western

[23] Özgür Yaren, ibid, p. 124.
[24] Özgür Yaren, ibid, p. 118-123.
[25] Özgür Yaren, ibid, p. 124-138.

traditions.[26]

Besides transnational and migration cinema, it is crucial to mention exile cinema films. The exiles experienced after the restrictions, censorship, impossibilities and fights with the regime in totalitarian countries are reflected in cinema as a field of a struggle. The exiled filmmakers cannot continue their struggle in their homeland and consequently prefer to work under exile. For this reason, the starting point of film in exile cinema is in many cases due to political reasons. Filmmakers who take over the freedom of political speech after exile face another disadvantage at this point and Gaytari Spivak's famous question is 'can the subaltern speak? can be discussed. Filmmakers who have gained freedom of expression in their new home are prone to disappear again among the cacophony of other voices who have experienced the same situation and are struggling to make their voices heard in the market.

For people living in exile, their relationships with their homeland and host society are constantly tested. This situation means neither being in the bonds of the old nor being a member of the new society for those living in exile. Thus, 'intermediate spaces', which are the distinctive production form of accented cinema as displaced persons, correspond to the intermediate spaces for these people in both societies. While this situation allows for the formation of hybrid identities, it also expresses the coexistence, fragmentation and fragmentation in a situation.

Not every exile is exiled under the same conditions and with similar forms; although there are great differences between each of them, the situation that provides the condition of exile in transnational migrations, whether voluntary or involuntary, is the underlying necessity of migration. The emotional states experienced after the exile are reflected in the films, especially being detached from their roots and homeland. The directors displaced as a result of necessity tend to use chronotopes that represent their homeland and their hopes of return through images, music and sounds, and use them in movies, especially in their first films. In this case, the most prominent features that can be said for exiled directors are political expression and the desire to return.

Another cinema similar to the aforementioned cinema concepts is diaspora cinema. The origin of the word diaspora comes from the Greek words *dia* and *sporos*. With this definition, diaspora means seed scattered to the left and right.[27] Today, it refers to the distribution of people to certain parts of the world. The first use of the definition diaspora was used to describe the Jews who dispersed to various places after the Babylonian exile. In time, the concept of diaspora, which refers to Jews, Armenians and Greeks, started to be used to describe the

---

[26] Sandra Ponzanesi, "Europe in Motion: Migrant Cinema and The Politics Of Encounter", **Social identities**, Vol. 17, No. 1, 2011, p.74.

[27] Fırat Yaldız, "Diaspora Kavramı: Tarihçe, Gelişme ve Tartışmalar", **Hacettepe Üniversitesi Türkiyat Araştırmaları Dergisi**, Cilt. 18, Sayı. 18, 2013, p. 290.

situation of all immigrant communities of different ethnic origins with the effect of globalization.[28]

Although it shows similar features with the concept of exile, exile is often an individual situation, while the diaspora is always collective. In the case of exile, homesickness and longing are at the forefront, while in the diaspora, real or imaginary communities that are maintained through communication forms such as shared cultures, networks between citizens, a sense of kinship, trade, travel, language, religion and rituals are at the forefront. While return is an important motif for some communities in the diaspora, with the expansion of this definition since the 1960s, return is no longer a necessary part of this concept. While the common values shared in the diaspora give information about the preservation of cultures to a certain extent and that they will continue to exist as the product of a common mixture, the diaspora at the same time gives us a clue that they are not organically connected between peoples and homeland.[29]

The basis of diaspora identities is a collectively idealized homeland consciousness. Diaspora communities maintain a long-term awareness of ethnic identity, which reinforces the discrimination of homeland and host communities against them. While maintaining a primary and vertical relationship with the motherland in exiles, the diaspora includes not only the homeland but also citizens from all over the world in a multi-directional and horizontal relationship, and thus plurality, multiplicity and hybridity come to the fore in the diaspora.[30]

In parallel with all these, diaspora cinema exists by differentiating from the view of exile cinema towards homeland. It does not have a tight relationship with a single homeland in diaspora cinema and does not claim to represent the people of the homeland. Looking to the past, loss and absence find less space in movies.[31]

In addition to these filmic terms, Postcolonial Ethnic and Identity Cinema can be also mentioned in film studies. The concept of post-colonial filmmakers expresses not only the tension between the first and third world, but also the struggle to defend immigrant and hybrid identities brought about by immigration. The filmmakers in this group have both ethnic and diasporic features. What distinguishes ethnic and identity cinema from others is that it always focuses on the new homeland and now. The change and transformation brought about by identity performance and the necessity of living in the place of residence are among the prominent narrative elements of ethnic and identity

[28] Gordon Marshall, **Sosyoloji Sözlüğü**, translated by. Osman Akınhay, Derya Kömürcü, Ankara, Bilim ve Sanat Yayınları, 1999, p. 151.
[29] John D. Peters, "Exile, Nomadism, and Diaspora: The Stakes of Mobility in The Western Canon", **Home, Exile, Homeland: Film, Media, and The Politics of Place**, Hamid Naficy (Ed.), New York & London, Routledge, 1999, p. 20-38.
[30] Hamid Naficy, ibid, p. 14-15.
[31] Hamid Naficy, ibid, p. 14-15.

cinema.

'Hyphen' expressions are the main problematic of ethnic identity cinema. While the hyphenated identities such as Tunisian-French, African-American, Indian-British express a stance against the homogenizing and hegemonic ideology in the country of residence, they are also determinants of another problem. This problem implies that hyphenated identities will not be seen as complete citizens to individuals without hyphens, an 'equal but not exactly' approach.[32]

The most distinctive feature of post-colonial immigrant filmmakers is that they produce films in realistic and documentary style that highlight the political agenda and social sensitivity. After the 1980s, post-colonial new generation filmmakers deal with themes such as cultural activism, anti-racism, identity crises in the combination of different cultures. This clearly shows that the inequality between the center country and third world citizens.[33]

As the last term on transnational cinema, it is a refugee (asylum seeker) cinema and it ought to be also discussed. In the 2000s, the illegal immigrant figure and its narratives began to be used in immigrant cinema to start a new subgenre. Yaren, in his work *Göçmen Sinemasını Yeniden Düşünmek*, underlines that there are two important developments in immigrant cinema during this period. The first of these is the axial shift of directors such as Fatih Akın and Gurinder Chadha, who start their careers with immigrant films and later abandone the immigrant identity struggle and adopt a broader cinema approach. Another second development is that films about illegal immigrants trying to reach Europe, which are started by Xavier Koller in 1990 with the movie *Reise der Hoffnung (Journey to Hope)*, start to proliferate.[34]

Since the 1950s, the European dream has begun to develop as a sign of a new supranational and democratic identity based on the free and safe movement of people, goods and services. The attempts to improve the quality of life, cultural diversity, emphasis on individual and social rights, called as the European dream, make Europe, the continent of democracy and welfare, a dream land and a target to be reached, with the economic, social and legal imbalances in the globalizing world.

The abolition of internal borders and free movement practices, which start with the Schengen Agreement in 1985, begin to place Europe on a wide and single plane with the participation of more member countries. On the other hand, Europe, which reaches a single external border with the removal of internal borders, begins to establish a strict control mechanism at the point of border controls with difficult acceptance situations applied for legal immigration,

---

[32] Hamid Naficy, ibid, p. 15-16.

[33] Özgür Yaren, ibid, p. 94-111.

[34] Özgür Yaren, "Göçmen Sinemasını Yeniden Düşünmek", **Moment Dergi: Hacettepe Üniversitesi İletişim Fakültesi Kültürel Çalışmalar Dergisi**, Cilt. 2, Sayı. 1, 2015, p. 212.

changing demographic structure, panoptic surveillance.[35] However, the tight control of the borders and the difficulty of immigration take the issue of immigration to a new dimension. Immigrants trying to cross borders are increasing, taking many difficulties to achieve their goals at all costs. The Arab Spring riots that spread to North Africa and the Middle East, which start with the burning of a peddler himself, cause the instability of the region and the phenomenon of illegal immigration to become unavoidable. The illegal immigration, asylum seeker and refugee crisis are not only the crisis of Europe or immigrants but also one of the most important problems of the global world on its own. In this case, it begins to deal with the issue of illegal immigration in cinema, which is a reflection of social events, however, it is a little slow.

The factors driving individuals to illegal immigration, as theorized by Michael J. Fischer, are based on three main reasons: those fleeing civil war, those who flee from natural disasters, and those seeking economic well-being. Although these three driving forces form separate categories from each other, most of the time two or three are effective simultaneously[36]. Regardless of the reasons that trigger immigration, it is associated with being on the road and seeking a safe goal to reach.

Films dealing with the issue of illegal immigration contain themes and motifs similar to the concept of accented cinema, such as travelling, border crossings, multilingualism, imprisonment, exile, longing for the past, quest, cultural encounters and claustrophobic spaces. However, permanent spaces such as congregation, ghetto and suburbs that appeared in the accented cinema leave their place in the illegal immigration films to Marc Augé's 'non-lieux' (out of place) spaces, as Ponzanesi states in his work The Non-Places of Migrant Cinema in Europe[37]. It is the concept created by the late capitalism such as hotels, motels, recreational facilities, highways, where people take place as passengers or customers, have no history, people do not have organic relationships, and refer to instant and temporary spaces. These locations include centers for illegal immigration films, immigrants who do not have full access to the new society, or refugees and asylum seekers just before they are rejected. People and relationships in these places attract attention with their singular identities and similarities to each other.[38] As Yaren states, immigrants who are forced to wait and passivity in these places remind of 'duty cinema' with the sacrifice of passive characters that are frequently used in the early stages of immigrant cinema.[39]

As mentioned above in films on illegal immigration, suspicion and hostility

---

[35] Fabrice Schurmans, "The Representation of the Illegal Migrant in Contemporary Cinema: Border Scenarios and Effects" **RCCS Annual Review**, Vol. 7, No. 7, 2015, p. 136.

[36] Stefanie V. D. Peer, "Seascapes of Solidarity: Refugee Cinema and the Representation of the Mediterranean", **Alphaville: Journal of Film and Screen Media**, Vol. 18, No. 4, 2019, p.40-41.

[37] Özgür Yaren, ibid, p. 214.

[38] Sandra Ponzanesi, "The Non-Places of Migrant Cinema in Europe", **Third Text**, Vol. 26, No.6, 2012, p.676-677.

[39] Özgür Yaren, ibid, p. 215.

towards foreigners, European skepticism after the economic recession in the last two dec,ades are perceived as intruders that will take away the jobs of immigrants and hence prevent prosperity. According to Bauman, the stranger has two faces: one is mysterious, promising pleasure, and the second is ominous, threatening and frightening[40]. It is possible to talk about situations that can set an example for both situations in illegal immigration films, however, the second case continues the dominant tradition of immigrant cinema. In addition, directors such as the Danish Susanne Bier, the French Philippe Lioret, the Belgian brothers Jean Pierre and Luc Dardenne, who reinterpret the traditional foreign archetype in post-colonial Europe and depict the suspicion of European values in their films, see immigrants not only as intruders, but also as a part of European prosperity. They bring harsh criticism to the European dream with their films.[41]

For immigrants, the European continent is the first piece of land to set foot after crossing the sea, and the seas are the most life-threatening part of the journey. The seas constitute the shortest but the most dangerous routes for illegal immigration. The importance of the sea for illegal immigrants is directly involved in fictional and documentary films and becomes one of the frequently used narrative motifs.

When we look at the topics covered in illegal immigration movies, being on the road as well as crossing the seas are the subjects of the movies. *In This World* (Michael Winterbottom, 2002), *Mediterranea* (Jonas Carpignano, 2015), *Eden à l'ouest* (*In the West*, Costa-Gavras, Paradise, 2009) are films that focus on travel. In addition, the difficulties of life after illegal immigration are discussed in films such as *It's a Free World* (KenLoach, 2007), *Biutiful* (A. G. Innaritu, 2010), *Terraferma* (Emanuele Crialese, 2011), *Ayka* (Sergey Dvortsevoy, 2018). Another trend seen in illegal immigration movies is that for illegal border crossings, illegal immigrants focus on the relationship they establish with criminal gangs. The tensions that emerge in these films are the transformation of honest and innocent immigrants into a commodity, subject to the inhumane practices of criminal organizations and human traffickers. Examples of these films are *Dirty Pretty Things* (Stephen Frears, 2002), *Daha* (*More*, Onur Saylak, 2017), *Riverbanks* (Panos Karkanevatos, 2015).

In films on illegal immigrants, it is possible to talk about prejudices, doubts and crime, as well as films based on hospitality and benevolence from a European perspective. *Welcome* (Philippe Lioret, 2009) *Le havre* (2009) and *Toivon Tuolla Puolen* (Aki Kaurismäki, 2017) are charitable host citizens who focus on their relationship with undocumented immigrants at the expense of confronting the law and society in all three films.

Illegal immigrant characters often find representation in order to identify with

[40] Issolina Ballesteros, ibid, p. 17.

[41] Sánchez E. García-Rico, "The Crisis of the European Dream: Home and Exodus in the Recent Cinema on Migrants and Refugees (2005-2018)" **Revista de Comunicación**, Vol. 18, No. 2, 2019, p. 280-281.

the audience with ethical and ideological correctness. Although the methods they prefer are different, they aim to raise awareness in order to make the injustice and inequality in the society as well as the increasing crisis of refugees, refugees and illegal immigrants visible and try to arouse sympathy by destroying the traditional ideological thought of the audience. In this case, it is possible to use the definition of political cinema, which is used for immigrant cinema or accented cinema in illegal immigration cinema.

Discussions on the Films

In this part of this chapter, *Toivon Tuolla Puolen* (*Another Face of the Hope*) directed by Aki Kaurismäki and *Welcome* directed by Philippe Lioret are discussed by using refugees and illegal immigrants as base.

The film *The Other Face of Hope* focuses on the encounter between two Finnish and Syrian characters and the host-guest relationship between them. Halid having reached Finland in hiding on a coal ship and Wikström leaving his wife and his home. Both of them leave everything behind and start a new life. Halid has managed to come illegally from Aleppo to Finland, lost his family and fiancee in the war and knows that only his brother is alive. Halid, who loses his brother during the journey, wants to search for his brother after he applies for asylum in Finland. Halid, who is taken to a center after his application for asylum, is asked to be sent back to his country as a result of his interviews with the migration center, considering that he does not meet the procedures that would require his refugee status, but he escapes from the center with the help of an officer at an asylum center. Halid, who startes to stay on the streets, crosses his way with Wickström, who decides to leave with his wife and switches business and startes a restaurant. Halid obtains a legal residence permit in Finland; his only thought is to find his brother. Kind landlords help his brother to enter Finland illegally, and he applies for asylum by going through the same legal procedures as Halid.

Halid explains the route he follows until he arrives in Finland at the immigration office. Kaurismaki draws a map of illegal immigration from Halid's mouth. The route he describes is partly known to everyone, but invisible, the most intense of illegal immigration. Virtually around Europe as illegal, from Syria to Turkey, and from there by boat to Greece and Central Europe right path loses his sister in a mixed border, while Hungary. Immigrants trying to cross from Serbia to Hungary in 2015 resulted in the harsh intervention of the Hungarian police and has been an indicator of increasing racism in Europe. [42] Following the Greece-Serbia routes from Turkey against refugees who reach Hungary face harsh intervention and treatment of refugees and bring European values by the EU countries criticized for human rights. The harshest criticism against Hungary come from France as 'it is not acceptable to build walls even for animals', but

[42] Gökçen Çıvaş, "Aki Kaurismäki Limanında Yersiz Yurtsuz Umutlar", **Kültürötesi İmgeler: Ulusötesi Avrupa Sinemasında Göç, Sürgün ve Aksan Tartışmaları,** Yıldız D. Birincioğlu, Uğur Baloğlu (Ed.), İstanbul, Doruk Yayımcılık, 2020, p. 103-104.

France expelles Romanian citizen novels from their country by paying money in 2010, and in 2015 the refugees who come to France via Italy.[43] The statement made by France is seen as a confession and has been a whole European criticism by Kaurismäki.

While being dragged from country to country, Halid finds himself in Finland, in the port of Helsinki. When he reaches Finland, Europe's stronghold of economy and democracy, all painted in black in coal, he goes to a place where he can take a shower after giving money to a street musician. The blackness sliding down from his feet gives the impression that all the evil he leaves behind will end here, and he will cleanly begin his new life. Halid gives money to the street musician and this is an example of optimism and solidarity. According to Gökçen Çıvaş,[44] blackness draining from his body indicates the change in the wave of immigration.

In order to apply for asylum, Halid askes a black officer for the location of the police station, who probably has experienced Halid's situation before and he asks 'Are you sure?'. Halid is not sure, but still wants to try his luck legally. Saying that he wants to apply for asylum at the police station, Halid confronts the audience with an inside criticism that an undesirable procedure is in operation, that the presence of a foreigner as other in this democratic country is not desired. The police officer says, 'It's okay to ask, you are not the first' and then they say 'follow me' and go to carry out the necessary procedures. The positioning of the characters in this scene contains comedy elements, but it also gives the impression that Halid is superior in terms of shooting angles.

The refuge center where they place Halid is like a clean and quiet hostel. This refugee center is an ideal example of non-location spaces that Ponzanesi uses to describe locations in asylum/refugee films. They are completely different from each other but their common point is a space and the same state of waiting.

Certain motifs of immigrant cinema are also featured in this film. There are small portable items that migrants bring with them to remind them of their homeland and past. When Halid's asylum application is rejected, he steals the tie of another asylum seeker. The emphasis on context is important because asylum seekers aiming to start a new country, a new culture, in short, a new and completely different life, have left their family, homeland, language and identity behind. However, his music, which is a universal language with the local instrument of the place where he was born and raised, is always with him as a trigger element for memory. The address or phone number written on a piece of paper, which is one of the motifs of the accented cinema, as stated Naficy, is always in Halid's pocket. Again, as Naficy states, the phone holds an important place for Halid. He constantly uses Mazdak's phone, whom he meets at the

[43] Enes Bayraklı, Kazım Keskin, "Avrupa'nın Mülteci Krizi", **Akademik İncelemeler Dergisi (Journal of Academic Inquiries)**, Cilt. 12, Sayı. 12, 2017, p. 127-128.
[44] Gökçen Çıvaş, ibid, p.100-101.

asylum center, to reach his brother.

Halid's story seems to have been constructed with a neutral perspective on the refugee crisis. Halid's interview at the immigration center is quite interesting. This scene presents to the audience that the governmental hypocrisy of the west, the center of democracy, and the borders of the 'Fortress of Europe', which they see as impassable, are completely a perception.

The current refugee crisis is based on a dichotomy. Slow-paced procedures in other areas that determine who will stay and who should go are quickly settled in the refugee situation. '*You cannot send them all home, but not all of them can stay here.*' For Halid, the other side of the hope is quickly resolved and his asylum application is rejected.

While Halid is about to be sent back, then becomes an anonymous immigrant who has lost his right to asylum. He tries to survive in a restaurant dump. It happens in this dump where he meets the restaurant owner, Wickström. Although Wickström tells him to leave this place right away, it is now Halid's bedroom. He fights for this garbage dump, which is the only place he nurtures belonging. This fight pleases Wickström, giving him work and accommodation. Refusing to fight to survive, Halid gets a result when he shows violence for the first time for where he lives. From this point on, the film gets into a melodramatic atmosphere and it proceeds with a benevolent host's risk of being illegal to keep the immigrant alive. The host characters help his sister come to Finland. The truck driver who brings him to the country does not receive transportation money because his truck is full. But the idea of hiring cheap workers in return for this kindness also lies. The restaurant is also run much cheaper than others. He does not forget to take the rental fee and commission from the small warehouse.

Right-wing tendency, anti-immigrant policies and discourses rising in Europe and Finland find their place in the film as well. The Real Finns Party (*Perussuomalaiset*), which has become the second party in Finland in recent years, has increased its votes with its nationalist rhetoric, wants to leave the European Union economically and politically and claim that their own culture may be corrupted by immigrants.[45] The statement that immigrants increase unemployment and burden the economy has found its counterpart in Finland and appears in three different scenes in this film.

Another film included in this study is *Welcome* directed by Philippe Lioret based in France. The film tells a story of Bilal, an Iraqi. Bilal, an Iraqi Kurd asylum seeker, tries to reach his girlfriend in England via France. Other reasons that pushed Bilal to immigrate to France after a three-month journey are the civil war

---

[45] https://www.bbc.com/turkce/haberler/2011/04/110419_nationalism_europe (Accessed Date: 27.11.220).

in Iraq and the ability to provide financial aid to his family by finding a job. Caught trying to reach England in a truck trailer, Bilal's attempt fails and he searches for a new route in the refugee camps in Calais. Bilal, who sets his mind to swim across the English Channel to reunite with his lover, begins to take swimming lessons in the municipality's swimming pool. Simon, swimming teacher, whose life goes wrong, is a character separated from his wife and lonely. The relationship between the two establishes the truths that Simon does not realize in his life, and helps the young lover go to England at all costs.

The film consists many motifs of immigrant cinema. English, French, Kurdish and Turkish languages make up the multilingual structure of the film. Characters with an immigrant background are presented in this movie as in every immigrant movie. The address of Bilal's girlfriend and a torn photo that Bilal carries in his pocket are among the reminders of Naficy. Bilal and other asylum seekers do not have a mobile phone, only one and receive money per call. The phone has an important place in the movie. Every time Bilal gets a chance, he calls his girlfriend's house in England. Other refugees line up behind a telephone booth.

The film starts in a center in Calais where meals are distributed for refugees. It is a gathering area where people from many Middle Eastern, Turkish, Kurdish, African, Asian nations meet the interpretation of 'no place' spaces discussed by Ponzanesi. Asylum seekers here use it as a transit stop to reach their destination. Although it is a temporary stop, when Bilal meets his Iraqi friend Zoran, he tells him that he has been here for two and a half months and another asylum seeker for three months.

Calais, where the film tells about, is an area that is used as a transit by refugees/asylum seekers, which we frequently encounter on the agenda of France and the world, causing constant tension between England and France.

The conversation on the routes to the UK between Bilal and Zoran shows that the illegal methods used for immigration are entirely in the hands of human smugglers, with strict security measures. Boats, trains, channel tunnel roads are all under strict supervision of security forces and these roads cannot be crossed without smugglers. It has now become an illegal sector after the border controls of illegal immigration. Although Bilal does not accept the idea of giving money to the smugglers, he later tries this way as persuasion. A group of refugees, including Bilal, who has made a deal with the smugglers, try to cross the border on the trailer of the truck.

Bilal is caught at the border crossing and he is arrested. As a criminal, fingerprints are taken, the number 812 is written with a pen they numbered the refugees and their belongings are checked. The photo of his girlfriend coming out of Bilal's wallet goes back to the words abused by the officials.

Due to European Union values and human rights, the French government cannot directly send innocent people back to their countries, but also prevents them from integrating into society through different legal methods. The judge's response is clear when the voluntary lawyer of the asylum seekers suggested that he is admitted to public school, as he is not of the age of majority and is not involved in crime; 'You know that it is not possible' is a question and answer to the formality that passes by this law.

Asylum seekers are exposed to discrimination and racism in many scenes in the film. In an incident when Simon meets his ex-wife at a supermarket, a black security guard prevents migrants trying to get inside to buy food and soap. Meanwhile, Simon's ex-wife, Marion, gets involved in this. The security guard just says he's doing his job. The mall is a space reserved for French citizens that separates 'us' and 'them'. It is an area closed to the foreigner. The black security officer undertaking this task is important in terms of distinguishing the other. Bauman's argument[46] that the most important feature of foreigners is 'familiar' to a great extent constitutes the structure of this scene. According to him, to regard a person as a foreigner requires the uninvited involvement of 'us' in his life and to know something about him. In another scene, the guest argues with Bilal in his house. As Bilal leaves the house, there is a noise in the apartment and his neighbour sees Bilal, and the dialogues that pass afterwards make the dimensions of racism even more visible.

'Neighbour: did you bring this kid back again?

Simon: If I did, I brought it to my own apartment.

Neighbour: but forbidden! We just want our peace here.

Simon: what's wrong? He is a 17-year-old boy.

Neighbour: It is illegal for you to bring him here. Look at that. They are dirty and sick ... They also steal. I am telling you I am going to call the authorities. I do not know what you have, but I have doubts.'

After the discussion, the neighbour reports to the police. The police, who arrive early in the morning, cannot find anyone at home. As the policemen go out of the house and close the door, they see the neighbour's mat with the text 'welcome'. The fact that the welcome letter that gives the movie its title is in front of the house of an anti-immigrant whistleblower who is racist and discriminatory is a good example of the dilemma that the director poses. For the director, who criticizes the 'Welcome' article, European values that are seen as indestructible from the outside are not as transparent as they seem.

The fact that Simon opens his house to Bilal and Zoran does not mean that he trusts them. The three of them stay at home, and hearing noise in the night, then Simon immediately goes to check. Simon, who gets angry when he sees Bilal

[46] Issolina Ballesteros, ibid, p. 27.

in the bathroom trying to get used to the bag by putting a bag on his head at that time, reproaches 'this is what it means'. The gold medal of Simon is stolen by Zoran at that night. Simon realizes later that the gold medal is out of place. This time, only Simon and Bilal are at home. He asks where his medal is and this time reacts harder in return for the favour he has done. After saying 'I help you and you are robbing me', he takes a bag and forcibly puts it on Bilal's head. Even though the relationship between the oppressed asylum seeker and the benevolent host is interrupted in this scene, the unconditional trust that will allow Simon to fully identify with Bilal and the glorification that turns into hero becomes its purest form. So much so that he gives Bilal a diamond and sapphire antique ring, which belongs to his ex-wife, to take to his girlfriend. Bilal tries to cross the English Channel twice; in the first, he is found by fishermen and he is brought back to France, in the other, he has crossed the English Channel, but 800 meters before the shores of England, the dead body and a ring are found, but this time he is sent back to France in a plastic bag.

Conclusion

The number of problematic characters in migration-themed films made by European directors is high. However, in the narrative of these films, the solidarity and benevolence between the marginal members of the society constitutes the structure that contradicts the reality understanding of other immigrant films. For example, Kaurismäki's aim to create a humanist awareness with a different perspective on the current crisis by placing characters willing to share their homes and jobs with strangers without prejudice. He wants to realize a realistic miracle in film by creating an alternative universe, not the current state of European society, but the structure that should be.

Kaurismaki prefers to create such an atmosphere in his movie. The furniture, cars he uses are selected in a retro style. Although the subject of the movie is up-to-date, the film's world seems to belong to the 1960s. In short, Kaurismäki bypasses the specific time frame in which the film takes place, creating a universal and timeless aesthetic.

With the film *Welcome*, Philippe Lioret shows a critique of France's harsh measures in combating illegal immigration. At the same time, aid to illegal immigrants, which is the main story of the film, is a serious crime under French law. After the release of the film, there are discussions between the director and the immigration minister, a proposal is made to change the existing law, but this proposal is rejected by the parliament.

Films of European directors based on migration-themed differ greatly from that of directors with an immigrant background. While the directors of immigrant origin often deal with themes such as alienation, belonging, loneliness and adaptation to the new cultural arena, European directors, on the other hand, critically describe the idea of 'helping' refugees and 'European dreams'.

CHAPTER 20

THE PERCEPTION OF MULTICULTURALITY BY EMPLOYEES IN INTERNATIONAL BUSINESSES AGAINST MIGRANTS

Gözde Mert[1]

Introduction

Migration is an old sociological phenomenon that affects individuals and society in all aspects. Generally speaking, people; individual or non-individual, voluntary or compulsory, temporary or permanent displacement due to various compelling reasons. As migrating individuals or groups carry their own cultural values, life, customs and traditions to the place they go, they cause change in the place of migration, as well as open the way for their own changes by being influenced by the values of the society in the place of migration.

The great migrations that occurred in the 20th century mostly resulted from wars and civil wars between the two countries. Asylum seekers and refugees experienced as a result of forced migration differ from migration due to economic reasons. Asylum seekers and refugees who have to leave their countries tend to take refuge in neighboring countries. The reason they leave their country is to feel safer rather than hoping for a good life[2].

We can see that the end of the 20th century and the first quarter of the 21st century witnessed two important developments in cultural terms. The first of these is the phenomenon of 'globalization', in which almost all communities begin to resemble a single pattern of cultural values with the effect of globalization; the second is the phenomenon that we call multiculturalism and its name, which exhibits an opposite cultural understanding in places, complementary to the first phenomenon. Although the phenomenon of multiculturalism has existed since the early ages of humanity, its socio-political existence emerged with modernization. Especially the nation-state systems created by modernization, the policies of creating a single type of human-single culture have brought along the policies of assimilation or dissolution of 'other' cultures over time. However, in the last 50 years, such policies have been discussed and the criticisms made as a result of this have started to be taken into consideration by the ruling powers. In this way, the administrations have entered

[1] Asst. Prof. Dr. Nişantaşı Universtiy, Faculty of Economics, Administrative and Social Sciences, Head of Bussiness Administration, Türkiye.

[2] Ayşe Tunç, "Mülteci Davranışı ve Toplumsal Etkileri: Türkiye'deki Suriyelilere İlişkin Bir Değerlendirme", **TESAM Akademi 2** (2015): 29-63, p. 32-33.

into regulations in many fields, including social, cultural and economic, in accordance with the nation-state structure in order to protect the multicultural structure. Countries with a high level of economic welfare, especially those who defend democracy and human rights, have achieved a certain success in multicultural policies. EU member providing progress in the field of democracy and human rights in the way of being in this sense, Turkey EU member Turkey, which is the path of democracy and progress in the human rights field have achieved success in this sense is allowing progress towards becoming an EU member in the field of democracy and human rights in Turkey it is said to have made significant improvements in recent years in this regard. Although it is seen that some of these developments are made in the field of management of businesses, it is controversial whether this is sufficient for international businesses with multicultural structures.

For many years, a country of emigration for economic reasons Turkey, especially the wars and conflicts taking place in neighboring countries, starting with the 1990 result came to migration, a country with and was forced to open its doors to immigrants. The majority of Syrians who emigrated from Syria, which began in April 2011 civil war the country was forced to take refuge in Turkey. Therefore, the origin of this wave of immigration Turkey has become the country with the largest immigrant population[3].

Today, more than 3.5 million refugees under international and temporary protection in Turkey, there are refugees and irregular migrants. Therefore, it can be said that asylum seekers and refugees create various negative consequences in terms of economic policies. Because problems such as insufficiency of economic resources and high unemployment rates increase the negative attitude towards immigrants and cause them to be seen as rivals by the citizens of the country. With the effect of prejudices, immigrants are seen as the cause of many problems and they are marginalized. It is known that immigrants create various negative consequences in terms of economic policies. Especially, the competition of communities for scarce economic resources constitutes the core of the problem in the attitude towards refugees and their marginalization[4]. It can also be said that prejudices, sensations and media play an important role in seeing immigrants as a problem rather than life experiences. Due to the negative perceptions in the society towards immigrants, immigrants living under difficult conditions and conditions make it more difficult to adapt to the society and they are marginalized by the society. Undoubtedly, among the reasons underlying the attitudes of individuals towards immigrants, their attitudes towards people from different cultures have a share. In this respect, it may be possible for individuals to adopt intercultural differences and to respect different cultures and to develop a positive attitude towards immigrants. Because intercultural sensitivity brings

[3] İlktürk, S. E. (2017). **Suriyeli Göçmenlerin Türkiye ve Avrupa İlişkilerine Etkileri**. (Unpublished Master's Thesis), Kocaeli University, Kocaeli.

[4] Bruce Clark, İki Kere Yabancı: Kitlesel İnsan İhracı Modern Türkiye'yi ve Yunanistan'ı Nasıl Biçimlendirdi? İstanbul: Bilgi Üniversitesi Yayınları, 2008.

along being sensitive to cultural differences and the perspectives of people from different cultures[5].

Keeping different ethnic and cultural structures in the same structure requires meeting different expectations and needs. Multiculturalism causes differences in employees' future plans, motivation factors or performance status. Although those who work in multicultural international businesses cause some problems, the institution can turn this situation into an advantage. International businesses can develop different strategic approaches to problems in such a structure and turn into a learning organization structure. This situation enables the institution to transform into a more innovative and creative structure[6].

The Concept of Culture and Multiculturality

It is said that the word culture is of Latin origin and is a combination of agriculture, agriculture, development and crops that express human activities[7]. It is a member of one or more groups with a culture determined by its own factors such as nationality Culture is a concept that expresses the lifestyle of a group and includes various elements such as shared and transmitted nutrition, language, clothing, rituals[8]. Culture is a concept that gives people feelings and thoughts about who they are, where they belong, how they should behave and what they should do. It also affects human behavior, attitude, work, productivity and actions[9].

Today, the demographic changes caused by migration, the opening of the compass between the developed and underdeveloped regions, the uncontrolled unbalanced population growth and the differentiation in the individual and the fields in the changing world affect many areas of interest of life. The values of people who live and produce together are also affected by this process and change the collective consciousness. A collective identity is built on the basis of a tradition laden with symbols, memories, works of art, customs, habits, values, beliefs and knowledge, the legacy of the past, in short, from the collective memory[10].

Although societies living together today generally have the same cultural characteristics, it is inevitable that the groups within the societies are decorated

---

[5] Dharm Bhawuk and Richard Brislin, "The Measurement of Intercultural Sensitivity Using the Concepts of Individualism and Collectivism". **International Journal of Intercultural Relations**. 1992 (16): 413-436.

[6] Gözde Mert, "Uluslararası İşletmelerde Etnik Köken ve Kültürel Çeşitliliklerin Kuşaklar Bağlamında İncelenmesi", **Journal of Administrative Sciences**, Cilt:18, Sayı:36, 2020, pp.339-371, p. 340.

[7] Terry Eagleton, **Kültür Yorumları**. İstanbul: Ayrıntı Yayınları, 2005.

[8] Mahmut Tezcan, **Eğitim Sosyolojisi**. Ankara: Zirve Yayıncılık, 2014.

[9] Robert Moran, Philip Harris and Sarah Moran, **Managing Cultural Differences**. 2007. http://www.google.com.tr/books?hl=tr&lr=&id=I9U_O1ZQJ9cC&oi=fnd&pg=PR3&dq=cultura+differences&ots=nst6UoXQ8K&sig=r6tikLJcsJMHjmUdI6rQ45GDi3A&redir_esc=y#v=onepage&q=cultural%20differences&f=false (Access: 11.10.2020).

[10] Nuri Bilgin, **Sosyal Bilimlerin Kavşağında Kimlik Sorunu**, İzmir: Ege Yayıncılık, 1994.

with their own cultural values. Within the framework of this understanding, it is expected that people with different beliefs and lifestyles living in the same geography advocate different values and be in polyphonic thinking. Pluralism not only creates different cultural values, but also ensures that common life is embellished with different cultural values. While cultural values create the common heritage of societies living together, they also incorporate different perspectives. Determining the superiority values of these values with respect to each other prepares the ground for social conflict and negatively affects social peace. In this direction, it is of great importance to perceive the diversity created by unity as a value and to approach all cultural elements with a valuing understanding in the construction of social peace. As a matter of fact, each piece of the mosaic, which is part of the common heritage, enriched the concept of culture and gave birth to the concept of multiculturalism[11].

Multiculturalism has emerged as an alternative to the assimilation approach that was common in the past[12]. The first use of the word 'multicultural' as a theory is seen to have emerged in the 1960s by being formulated as' multicultural society. Although they lived together in Canada during this period, language conflicts were formulated in the sense that it brought a solution between the French and the British[13]. When many social structures in the past are examined, It will be seen that the concept of multiculturalism as a phenomenon is not a concept that emerges today[14].

They are opposed to the assimilation of different cultures and attempting to uniformize the cultures within a society[15]. Cultural characteristics that are absorbed and assimilated within a society can survive thanks to the perception of multiculturalism. This perception is integrated with the concept of cultural diversity. According to Kymlikca (1998), The source of cultural diversity is the coexistence of multiple nations within a state. While they are defined as notions such as age, race, sexual orientation, social class, ethnic origin, religion-sect and language, Banks et al. (2001), cultural characteristics are associated with each other as in the figure 1 below[16]:

---

[11] Alper Başbay and Yelda Bektaş, "Çokkültürlülük Bağlamında Öğretim Ortamı ve Öğretmen Yeterlikleri", **Eğitim ve Bilim**, 34, 30-43, 2009.

[12] Hasan Aydın, "Multicultural Education Curriculum Development in Turkey", **Mediterranean Journal of Social Sciences,** 3 (3), 277-286, 2012.

[13] Nicolas Journet, Çokkültürlülük. (Çev. Yümni Sezen), **Evrenselden Özele Kültür**. İstanbul: İz Yayıncılık, 2009, p. 257.

[14] Mehmet Anık, **Kimlik ve Çokkültürcülük Sosyolojisi**. İstanbul: Açılık Kitap, 2012, p. 79.

[15] Hans Vermeulen and Boris Slijper, "Multiculturalisme in Canada, Australie En De Verenigde Staten, Ideologie En Beleid 1950-2000", Amsterdam: Aksant, 2003.

[16] Fadime Damgacı and Hasan Aydın, "Akademisyenlerin Çokkültürlü Eğitime İlişkin Tutumları", **Elektronic Journal of Social Sciences**, 2013, Cilt:12, Sayı:45, pp. 325-341, p. 328.

Figure 1. Diversity Variables[17]

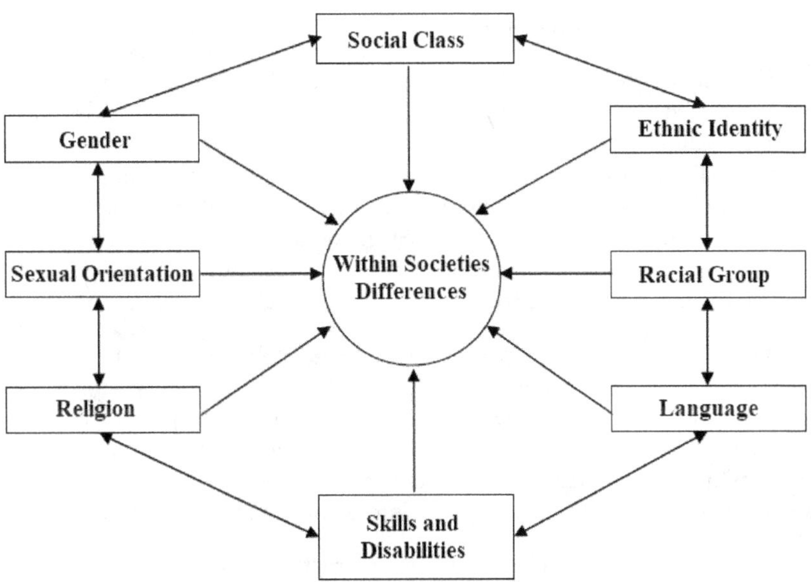

Multiculturalism in sociological studies means the coexistence of many cultures in the same country, and according to Marshall[18] (1999) for societies characterized by cultural pluralism although societies generally have the same cultural characteristics, it is inevitable that the groups within them are embellished with their own cultural patterns. These differences form the basis of multiculturalism. It includes awareness of disability, social class, education, religious orientation and other cultural dimensions[19]. Multiculturalism and cultural difference should not be perceived in a similar way. While cultural differences are based on the diversity of different cultural elements, in multiculturalism, cultural diversity of only one culture is not in question. Within the concept of multiculturalism, it includes different features from the common cultural elements in society, different religion and different identity. Multiculturalism encompasses all these cultural differences, and cultural differences are only one aspect of multiculturalism. The purpose of multiculturalism is to contain all cultures, races and religions together, to prevent conflict and confusion that may arise between them. All efforts are aimed at living together and ensuring the peace in society of individuals with equal rights

[17] James Banks, "Cultural Diversity and Education: Foundations, Curriculum and Teaching" (4th ed.) Boston: Allyn and Bacon, 2001, p. 76.

[18] Alper Başbay and Yelda Kağnıcı, "Çokkültürlü Yeterlik Algıları Ölçeği: Bir Ölçek Geliştirme Çalışması", **Eğitim ve Bilim**, 2011, Cilt:36, Sayı:161, p. 201-202.

[19] APA. Guidelines on Multicultural Education, Training, Research, Practice, and Organizational Change for Psychologists. 2002. http://www.apa.org/pi/multiculturalguidelines/homepage.html (Access 10.10.2020)

living in peace together[20].

Problems caused by Multiculturality

The understanding of multiculturalism brings along many uncertainties and problems. The most important one; This understanding, which is designed as the recognition of different cultures, is thought to include activities that are 'unicultural'. In this sense, the biggest obstacle in front of multiculturalism is; It is known to be the modern culture itself. Likewise, another major obstacle to multiculturalism is the legal structure. Since modern law is singular in principle and at the same time the pluralist legal structure does not obey this principle, it has been seen as impossible to implement[21].

If multiculturalism is not managed well, disagreements and conflicts may arise between employees within the business. Conflicts arising from these characteristics in multicultural businesses, combined with job stress, lead to conflicts. In particular, the inability to manage these conflicts will weaken the bond of individuals with the institution and create a situation of not seeing themselves as a part of that group, leading to low organizational commitment[22].

Having a multicultural structure in international enterprises can make it difficult to achieve the goals of the enterprise. In order to overcome these difficulties, common feelings and ideas among employees are otherwise, the failures to be experienced will cause problems far beyond the problems experienced by a local-scale enterprise[23].

Perception of the Society and Individuals against Migrants

It is known that the discrimination perceived by migrants who are at a disadvantage in the society on the basis of group membership has a negative impact on their psychological well-being (self-esteem, depression, somatic problems, etc.)[24,25]. What they have, race, gender, sexual orientation, etc. Individuals who think that they are excluded by the society on the basis of their characteristics show relatively insufficient psychological well-being. One of the ways disadvantaged migrants resort to coping with the negative impact of perceived discrimination is to increase the identification established with the

---

[20] Alper Başbay and Yelda Kağnıcı, op.cit, p. 202.

[21] Mustafa Aydın, **Güncel Kültürde Temel Kavramlar**. İstanbul: Açılım Kitap, 2011, p. 91-92.

[22] Kyre Luijters, Karen I. Van der Zee and Sabine Otten, Cultural Diversity in Organizations: Enhancing Identification by Valuing Differences. **International Journal of Intercultural Relations**, 2008, 32(2), 154–163, p. 154.

[23] Beliz Dereli, Çokuluslu İşletmelerde İnsan Kaynakları Yönetimi, **İstanbul Ticaret Üniversitesi Sosyal Bilimler Dergisi**, Sayı: 7, 2005, Bahar. p. 64.

[24] Michael Thomas Schmitt, Nyla R. Branscombe, Tom Postmes and Amber Garcia, The Consequences of Perceived Discrimination for Psychological Well-Being: A Meta-Analytic Review. **Psy-chological Bulletin**, 2014, 140 (4), 921.

[25] Elizabeth Pascoe and Laura Smart Richman, Perceived Discrimination and Health: A Meta-Analytic Review. **Psychological Bulletin**, 2009, 135 (4), 531.

ingroup[26]. As the identification with the inner group or the sense of belonging and belonging to the inner group increases, psychological well-being may increase[27].

Today, due to the effect of globalization, there is a significant migration wave. In order to escape from situations that affect people both materially and spiritually, such as death and destruction, people leave their wealth and migrate. The population structure and access to education and health services in the target country are of great importance. As a result of migration, an increase in local unemployment, differentiation in the form of employment and change in the social structure occur. With migration, the living space changes and new relations and problems such as cultural fusion or conflict arise[28].

The migration of immigrants from their home country to other countries due to the civil war and their transformation into a permanent situation in these countries day by day, and an adaptation problem with social, political and economic dimensions gradually turned into a security issue[29]. Undoubtedly, both common and different needs, problems and expectations come to the fore in every province where immigrants are settled. In this context, the lives of immigrants in the provinces where they are settled should be taken into consideration, from the language problem to the accommodation problem, from health to education, from employment to legal procedures.

In multiculturalism, transition between cultures is not easy because more than one culture is effective at the same time. Because the transition phase also requires change. At the beginning of this process, the individual cuts off his / her social role and status, and therefore enters a period of separation from his past. Then it goes through the process of adaptation to adapt to new roles and change takes place. In the last stage, the individual is integrated with his new role and status and cultural adaptation is achieved[30].

On the other hand, especially in the first encounter stages of acculturation, minority group members tend to compare their own situation or the situation of the culture group they belong to with the situation of other group or group members and generally make negative judgments[31]. Which of the acculturation strategies is adopted is extremely important in dealing with such intergroup

---

[26] Miguel Ramos, Clare Cassidy, Stephan Reicher and Alexander Haslam, A Longitudinal Investigation of the Rejection–Identification Hypothesis. **British Journal of Social Psychology**, 2012, 51 (4), 642-660.

[27] Katharina Schmid and Orla Muldoon, Perceived Threat, Social Identification, and Psychological Well-Being: The Effects of Political Conflict Exposure. **Political Psychology**, 2015, 36 (1), 75-92.

[28] Muazzez Harunoğulları, Suriyeli Sığınmacı Çocuk İşçiler ve Sorunları: Kilis Örneği, **Göç Dergisi**, 2016, 3 (1), 29-63.

[29] Abdullah Topçuoğlu, Ertan Özensel, and Ahmet Koyuncu, Konya'daki Suriyeli Misafirlerin Ekonomik Potansiyelleri ve İşbirliği İmkânlarının Belirlenmesi Araştırması. Konya: **MÜSİAD Konya**, 2015.

[30] Anne Montreuil and Richard Bourhis, Majority Acculturation Orientations Toward "Valued" and "Devalued" Immigrants. **Journal of Cross-Cultural Psychology**, 2001, 32(6), 698-719.

[31] Ramin Aliyev and Selahiddin Öğülmüş, S. Yabancı Uyruklu Öğrencilerin Kültürlenme Düzeylerinin İncelenmesi. **Muş Alparslan Üniversitesi Sosyal Bilimler Dergisi**, 2016, 4(1), 89-124.

negativities. The development of relations between groups has been scientifically defined under the heading of strategies called multiculturalism, melting pot, separation and exclusion. When the strategy of separation from these strategies supports segregation, exclusion if the marginalization of immigrant groups is imposed by the dominant group, and if cultural diversity is supported, the strategies and results that are called multiculturalism emerge[32].

Although parallel to the strategies of integration, separation and assimilation, the last two strategies are considered a differentiated form of marginalization. While the dominant society's strategies of integration and individualism against immigrants accept immigrants positively, assimilation, discriminatory and exclusionary strategies ignore or deny immigrants[33]. This situation is closely related to how the minority group is perceived primarily by individuals of culture and the current political power. In the studies carried out with immigrant groups on this issue, it is seen that the integration strategy is more preferred and at the same time it is the acculturation strategy that facilitates adaptation at the highest level; it has been demonstrated that this is followed by the separation strategy. Marginalization was observed to be the least preferred strategy. It is not sufficient to consider the acculturation process only in conjunction with immigrant experiences. Because there is a mutual exchange process as a result of the interaction of the two groups[34]. If the cultural characteristics that the individual acquires in the society of origin do not match, the cultural distance increases and affects the individual negatively in the acculturation process. Whether the acculturation strategy preferred by the individual or the group is accepted by the dominant group is important in terms of the acculturation process[35].

One of the most important problems in the acculturation process is the emergence of acculturation stress arising from intercultural conflict[36]. The stress of acculturation has different advocates such as socio-demographic characteristics, pre-migration experiences, social context of the dominant society, experience of acculturation after migration and acculturation gains. In different studies, it has been observed that low socioeconomic status, the dominant society's approach to multiculturalism, age, gender, education level, language proficiency, cognitive styles and intercultural experiences also affect the stress of acculturation[37]. In addition, a society that is not bound by physical boundaries is formed in nation-states together with immigrants and this society continues its

---

[32] John Berry, Immigration, Acculturation, and Adaptation. **Applied Psychology: An International Review**, 1997, 46(1), 5-68., p. 10

[33] Jan Pieter Van Oudenhoven, Colleen Ward and Anne-Marie Masgoret, Patterns of Relations Between İmmigrants and Host Societies. **International Journal of Intercultural Relations**, 2006, 30(6), 637-651.

[34] Dilara Şeker, İbrahim Sirkeci and Murat Yüceşahin, **Göç ve Uyum**, London: Transnational Press London, 2015, p. 16.

[35] Ramin Aliyev and Selahiddin Öğülmüş, (2016). Op.cit.

[36] Andrea Romero and Robert Roberts, Stress Within a Bicultural Context for Adolescents of Mexican Descent. **Cultural Diversity and Ethnic Minority Psychology**, 2003, 9(2), 171–184, p. 173.

[37] Dilara Şeker, İbrahim Sirkeci and Murat Yüceşahin, 2015, op.cit.

migrant circulation in various forms by creating its own networks within the global structure and does not break its ties with the source country[38]. This situation makes it difficult for Turkey, which hosts more than 3.5 million Syrian refugees, to produce serious policies towards refugees. Especially in certain provinces and areas such as Istanbul, Gaziantep, Hatay, Kilis and Şanlıurfa, the Syrian refugees' escaping their origin culture makes it difficult for the local people and those working in the businesses to absorb this culture.

Conclusion

Immigrants can feel themselves as foreigners in their country of immigration. Because the living environment and conditions in which the immigrant is accustomed to climate, environment, culture, language, and in this case, it functions as an element of alienation. In the process of adaptation, migrant individuals try to adapt to the lifestyle and culture in the new place on the one hand, and on the other hand, they try to protect and maintain their self and the lifestyle and culture of the place of origin. These contradictions and confusion are the basis for the formation of various emotional problems in the individual. This foreignness, which is very concrete in the person's outer world, can be reflected internally. In this way, a person can experience the feeling of not belonging to something and a place intensely by alienating his own inner state from his world and his world. From this point of view, it seems inevitable that immigrants experience many problems such as loneliness, emptiness, longing, feeling worthless, rootlessness, inferiority, guilt and skepticism in the country they migrated to[39].

When issues such as multiculturalism, diversity, and sensitivity to differences are in question in international businesses, there are differences between attitude behaviors of individuals. It is observed that some people are more sensitive to differences, while others are more insensitive and some do not tolerate differences. It is investigated where the differences arise and which variables create the difference. For example; Simith, Moallem Sherrill[40] (1997) found that living with individuals from different cultural backgrounds, education, travel, and an experience of discrimination in childhood or adulthood are the effective changes in their research, which examines the variables that affect teachers' levels of multicultural awareness. However, it has been one of the underlined focus that there are differences even among people who show similarities in terms of

[38] Maggie O'Neill, Re-imagining Diaspora Through Ethno-mimesis: Humiliation, Human Dignity and Belonging. 2013 O. G. Bailey, M. Georgiou, & R. Harindranath, **Transnational Lives and The Media: Re-Imagining Diaspora** (s. 72-81). New York: Palgrave Macmillan, p. 75.

[39] Murat Erol and Oya Ersever, Göç Krizi ve Göç Krizine Müdahale. **KHO Bilim Dergisi**, 2014, 24(1), 47-69.

[40] Robert Smith, Mahnaz Moallem and Deborah Sherrill, How Preservice Teachers Think About Cultural Diversity: A Closer Look at Factors Which İnfluence Their Beliefs Towards Equality. **Educationa/ Foundntions**, 1997, 11(2), 41-61.

these variables. Gorman[41] (1998), at this point, he stated that personality is an important variable, and based on the personality definition of Ones, Viswesvaran, and Dilchert[42] (2005), it is thought that personality would be one of the important changes in issues such as diversity and sensitivity to differences. As a matter of fact, there are studies in the literature that support this relationship. Garmon[43] (2004), who suggested that personality is an important variable, found that personality trait has an important role in the attitudes and behaviors of employees regarding diversity issues. Similarly, Unruh and McCord's[44] (2010) study found a significant relationship between diversity beliefs and personality.

International businesses are a multicultural environment where individuals from different socioeconomic levels, different political and religious views, and different traditions and customs live together. By starting to work in international business, the individual starts to acquire a new business environment. In such an environment, the individual can have the chance to improve himself in time, both intellectually and socially. This happens by communicating with new groups and can break some of the prejudices they have in the process.

It is important for the employees in international businesses to learn and be aware of the different aspects of the local or cultural groups around them as well as knowing common / national values. This will enable employees to respect other cultures, to work in harmony, to strengthen communication, to increase corporate loyalty, to create teamwork, and thus to increase productivity and performance.

[41] Arthur Garmon, Changing Preservice Teachers' Attitudes/Beliefs about Diversity: What are the Critical Factors? **Journal of Teacher Education**, 2004, 55, 201-213.

[42] Deniz Ones, Personality at Work: Raising Awareness and Correcting Misconceptions. **Human Performance**, 2005, 18(4), 389-404.

[43] Garmon, M.A. (2004). op.cit.

[44] Lori Unruh and David McCord, Personality Traits and Beliefs about Diversity in Pre-Service Teachers. **Individual Differences Research**, 2010, 8, 1-7.

CHAPTER 21

THE MAINTAINING (NON-MAINTAINING) OF CULTURAL AND SYMBOLIC CODES BY WOMEN THAT HAVE MIGRATED TO EUROPE FROM TURKEY: THE AUSTRIA (VIENNA) EXAMPLE

Nebahat Akgün Çomak,[1] Elgiz Yılmaz Altuntaş[2] and Eda Nur Akgün[3]

Introduction

This study encompasses the migrant women that live in Austria (Vienna), which is one of the countries with the highest number of migrants from Turkey. The study aims to determine as to what degree the women maintain their cultural and symbolic codes and practice their cultural rituals. Thus, rather than query as to whether the use of cultural and symbolic codes in daily life is useful, the presentation of how certain cultural and symbolic codes are reproduced for certain purposes and rituals has been envisaged. The findings of the study are important in terms of highlighting the use and reproduction elements of the cultural and symbolic codes of women that have migrated to the aforementioned country since the 60s for economic reasons and have lived there for many years.

In human history, migration plays an important role in terms of intercultural encounters and intercultural communication. The 20th century, where the 1st and the 2nd World War took place, has witnessed important migration processes. The migrants' efforts to fit in to the new country and culture and their anxiety in regards of maintaining and continuing their own cultural heritage were experienced hand in hand. As of the 60s, women migrated to European countries, especially Austria, from Turkey. This study encompasses the migrant women that live in Austria (Vienna), which is one of the countries with the highest number of migrants from Turkey. The study aims to determine as to what degree the women maintain their cultural and symbolic codes and practice their cultural rituals. Thus, rather than query as to whether the use of cultural and symbolic codes in daily life is useful, the question of how certain cultural and symbolic codes are reproduced for certain purposes and rituals has gained significance.

[1] Assc. Prof., Galatasaray University, Faculty of Communication, Türkiye.
[2] Assc. Prof., Galatasaray University, Faculty of Communication, Türkiye.
[3] Student, Freie Universitat Berlin, Germany.

In the study, the styles and elements of the use and reproduction of cultural and symbolic codes, the cultural and symbolic codes for marriage, the cultural and symbolic codes for birth, the cultural and symbolic codes for death, and the cultural and symbolic codes for social life of women that have migrated to the aforementioned country since the 60s for economic reasons and have lived there for many years have attempted to be determined by studying them.

The fact that the women that migrated to European countries maintain and reproduce their cultural and symbolic codes, to a degree, points to their bond with Turkey and their culture. Thus, due to the fact that the non-use of cultural and symbolic codes and the forgetting of rituals could point to a weakening of ties to Turkey, this has been considered to be problematic in terms of culture.

Women migrants that have lived in European countries for many years can experience the dilemma of not being able to maintain their own culture and of becoming estranged from it while discovering and trying to adapt to a new culture.

The Scope and Method of the Study 'In-depth Face-to-Face Interviews'

In the scope of the study, it was decided to conduct interviews with women over the age of 18 that had migrated to Austria from Turkey. The total number of women that were suggested to interview was 50. The participants were informed that variables like names, addresses, religion, language, ethnic roots, ideologies, sexual preferences were not included in the scope of the study and thus, thirty-one of the women that participated in the interviews agreed to answer the questions. The seventeen women that did not agree to the in-depth interviews consisted of feminists (4 women), lesbians (3 women), activists (2 women), NGO members (4 women), those fighting the patriarchal order (1 woman), those trying to solve gender inequality (1 woman), those against marriage (1 woman), those defending the superiority of women (1 woman), and those fighting against class struggle and racism (1 woman). These women also stated that this was also the reason for not participating in the interviews. In Vienna, an in-depth interview was conducted with Eda Nur Akgün, a student of The St. George Austrian High School. In the study, the in-depth face-to-face Interview method was applied. The data gathered from the In-depth Interview will be presented by being arranged with the cultural and symbolic interpretations of the researchers.

Table 1. Reasons for not participating in the study

Number of women not participated in the study	Reasons
4	being feminist
3	being lesbians
2	being activists
4	NGO members
1	fighting the patriarchal order
1	trying to solve gender inequality
1	defending the superiority of women
1	fighting against class struggle and racism
TOTAL: 17	

In the in-depth interviews, the cultural and symbolic structures directed at the women in the study, were separated into four levels: Marriage, Birth, Death, and Social Life. The four levels were also categorized within themselves according to the variables below:

1.Mariage: 1.1. Marriage age. 1.2. Looking for a wife for your son, being in-laws. 1.3. The boy's parents asking the girl's parents for permission for their son to marry the daughter. 1.4. Betrothal and the drinking of sherbet. 1.5. Engagement. 1.6. Trousseau 1.7. Exhibiting the trousseau. 1.8. Henna night. 1.9. Picking up the bride. 1.10. Sprinkling the bride's head. 1.11. The Wedding.1.12. The Wedding Dinner. 1.13. The Red-Ribbon. 1.14. The Veil. 1.15. Fancy sayings about marriage. 1.16. The Wedding convoy

2.Birth: 2.1. The pre-natal period of the mother. 2.2. The pregnancy period of the mother. 2.3. The birth of the child. 2.4. Naming the child. 2.5. The child's umbilical cord. 2.6. Passing the 40 days after birth. 2.7. The first steps of the child. 2.8. The child's first teeth. 2.9. Protecting the child from the evil eye (bad luck). 2.10. Child Mawlid (gathering where words from the Quran are read 2.11. Mother's milk. 2.12.The circumcision 2.13. Fancy sayings about birth.

3.Death: 3.1 The Funeral Home. 3.2. Mourning. 3.3. Death Mawlid.3.4. The 7th,40th,and 52nd day of the passing.3.5.The Anniversary of the passing. 3.6. Food served at the funeral home (Halwa-Lokum-Rice). 3.7. Distributing the departed's belongings. 3.8. Words of condolences about death.

4.Social Life: 4.1. Hıdırellez. 4.2. Nowruz 4.3. Celebrating the New Year. 4.4. Mawlud. 4.5. The evil eye-The evil eye talisman. 4.6. Pouring lead (to repel the evil eye). 4.7. Knocking on wood. 4.8. Burning incense. 4.9. Offerings and Animal sacrifice. 4.10. Good luck charm (with a prayer inside). 4.11. Ramadan. 4.12. Eid. 4.13. Tying strips of cloth. 4.14. The Hand of Fatima. 4.15. Leaping over a fire. 4.16. Regional foods. 4.17. Holy nights. 4.18. Ashure (Noah's pudding). 4.19. The sanctity of numbers. 4.20. The sanctity of colors. 4.21. The sanctity of stones. 4.22. The sanctity of plants. 4.23. The sanctity of animals. 4.24. Proverbs-Sayings. 4.25. Words used towards women. 4.26. Words women use for their children. 4.27. Accessories worn by women. 4.28. Words women use for men. 4.29. Prayers. 4.30. Curses. 4.31. Good luck. 4.32. Bad luck. 4.33.

Hosting guests. 4.34. The use of regional kilims-carpets. 4.35. Nicknames.

Findings

In the findings collected in this research that covered women that had migrated to Austria from Turkey, cultural and symbolic structures have been categorized on four levels as 'Marriage-Birth-Death-Social Life' and have been presented below.

3.1- Marriage:

Pre-marriage and post-marriage rituals play an important role in the lives of women that have migrated from Turkey.

3.1.1. The marriage age:

It can be seen that the age of marriage for the first wave of women that migrated to Austria from Turkey was 17 or 18. The age of marriage of the second, third, and fourth generations gradually increases. Thus, it is considered to be above 21. The age of the women that participated in the interviews was between 18 and 69. It was determined that a few of the educated women had not married and did not even think of marrying. Two of the women that participated had married a foreigner. When one takes a look at world history, we see 'Adam-Eve' as an example of the first marriage[4].

3.1.2. Looking for a wife for your son, being in-laws:

The women that participated in the interviews stated that the practice of looking for a wife for a son continued and that they had experienced it in their own marriage process. This tradition has not lost its significance.

3.1.3. The Boy's Parents Asking the Girl's Parents for Permission for their son to marry the daughter:

For all the women that participated in the interview, the case of going to the girl's house and asking the girl's father or family elder for permission took place. This is a very old tradition but still continues in modern life. The most important symbol in asking for permission is Turkish coffee being served to the guests. The making and serving of the coffee also requires a special ritual.

3.1.4. Betrothal and the Drinking of Sherbet:

The women that participated in the interviews stated that prior to the wedding, a betrothal took place and that sherbet was drunk or something sweet was eaten. They also stated that lately the betrothal and engagement occurred at

---

[4] **Encyclopedie Des Symboles**, Ed. Michel Cazenave, München, Le Livre de Poche, 1989, p. 5-7.

the same time if desired.

3.1.5. The Engagement:

All of the women that participated in the interviews wanted an engagement ceremony. The women stated that having the engagement ceremony in ballrooms rather than in homes had become popular.

3.1.6. The Trousseau :

All the women that participated in the interviews said that they looked warmly on trousseaus and that they had received a lot of trousseaus from their families.

3.1.7. Exhibiting the Trousseau:

Exhibiting the trousseau is the placement of the girl's possessions into the new house before the wedding. All the women that participated in the interviews stated that they had exhibited their trousseaus.

3.1.8. Henna Night:

All the women that participated in the interviews stated that the henna night celebration was a nice tradition. It is a tradition dating back to ancient cultures and in today's world is celebrated in homes or in halls.

3.1.9. Picking up the bride:

It is the picking up of the bride from her parents' house and taking her to where the ceremony will be held. All of the women within the study stated that the same was done to them.

3.1.10. Sprinkling the bride's head:

It is the sprinkling of coins, rice, sugar, wheat etc. over the bride's head as she leaves the house. It is done for a prosperous marriage. This continues today and all the women viewed this as a nice tradition. The sprinkling dates back to Shaman traditions.

3.1.11. The Wedding:

In all cultures, 'marriage' and 'birth' form the focal points of life. In Turkish Mythology, the marriage of 'earth' and 'sky' was the first sacred marriage[5] (Eliade, 2003:243). Therefore, the women that participated in the interviews stated that wedding ceremonies were important for them and that a wedding day was the most important day in a woman's life.

---

[5] Mircea Eliade, **Dinler Tarihine Giriş**, çev. Lale Arslan, İstanbul, Kabalcı Yayınları, 2003, p. 243.

3.1.12. The Wedding Dinner:

All the women that participated in the interviews stated that in today's world the dinner was held in wedding halls or hotel ballrooms and that it was magnificent.

3.1.13. The Red-Ribbon:

The red-ribbon is a ribbon that is tied around the bride's waist by her father or older brother as she leaves the house. The red-ribbon is a symbol of virginity. It also carries the meaning of protecting the bride from evil spirits. A red-ribbon is also tied around the head of a woman giving birth. This is also a protection from evil spirits. It is a tradition dating back to pagan culture and is a symbol that continues in modern life. The women that participated in the interviews believed that this practice is also done for the woman's sake and that it is a nice and thoughtful symbol.

3.1.14. The Veil:

A white veil is a universal symbol. The women that participated in the interviews preferred the color 'red' for their henna night celebration in accordance with their traditions. During the ceremony they opted for the color 'white' for their dress and veil.

3.1.15. Beautiful sayings about marriage: 'May Allah make you happy. I wish you all the happiness. Grow old on one pillow.'

3.1.16. The Wedding Convoy:

The women that participated in the interviews stated that a wedding convoy is unable to take place as the traffic laws abroad are very strict. The women stated that according to news in the media, 'In February 2017, a Turkish wedding convoy on the motorway was taken to court in Belgium.' The eighteen Turks who were carrying out a wedding convoy on the motorway were banned from driving and fined two-thousand Euros. The prosecutor asked, 'Is entering traffic during a wedding a tradition?' Furthermore, the prosecutor also added that there were Turks driving around sounding their horns and that there was no place for this in their culture[6].

3.2. Birth:

Throughout the scope of the study, pre-natal and post-natal rituals were taken into account. Rituals conducted by the migrant women can be stated as:

[6] http://www.euronews.com (Access: 11.12.2018).

3.2.1. The Pre-natal Period of the Mother:

In Turkish culture, as with all cultures, marriage and children are of importance. In old Turkish culture, when a child was desired, a prayer was said to God, an offering was made, and bloodless sacrifices were made. Three of the women that participated in the interviews had been unable to bear a child for two to three years. They visited holy places and made offerings, made sacrifices, and left food. One of the women stated that she had had a test-tube baby as she was unable to have a child. This tradition can be found in Turkish Epics. In the Epic of Manas, marriage and children form the focal point of the epic. The primary hero of the epic, Jakyp Khan, had been unable to have a child for seven years, so he told his wife that they should go to the 'apple tree' and pray to God[7].

3.2.2. The Pregnancy Period of the Mother:

A woman craves for various foods during her pregnancy. Among the foods that the women, who participated in the interviews, craved were plums, pickles, sweet and exotic fruits etc. There is a belief that if a woman does not eat what she craves while pregnant, there will be a birthmark on the child. This belief dates back to pagan culture. In Greek Mythology, there strange birthmarks on Zeus' son Deimos. Deimos was named 'the Marked Warrior.'

3.2.3. The Birth of the Child:

The birth of a child being depicted as the 'birth-death-birth' narrative cycle is the most beautiful explanation of continuity[8]. All of the women that participated in the interviews stated that birth was a miracle.

3.2.4. Naming the Child:

Naming a child has been an important since ancient cultures. The women that participated in the interviews stated that they had determined the name of their child before giving birth. After the child is born, the eldest in the family says a prayer and whispers the child's name into his/her right ear three times. This tradition is an important symbol that continues from the past to today. The tradition of naming the child can also be encountered in the 'Dede Korkut Stories' and epics[9].

3.2.5. The Child's Umbilical Cord:

The child's umbilical cord is a ritual dating back to ancient cultures. The umbilical cord is not discarded, it is buried in the gardens of important buildings

[7] Nebahat A.Çomak, Elgiz Yilmaz, "Manas Destanı" II.Congress Of International Social Scientists. October 22-24, Bishkek-Kyrgyzstan, 2005.

[8] Joseph Campbell, **Doğu Mitolojisi-Tanrının Maskeleri**, çev. Kudret Emiroğlu, Ankara, İmge Kitabevi. 2003, p. 11.

[9] Muharrem Ergin, **Dede Korkut Kitabı I-Giriş-Metin**, Ankara, Türk Dil Kurumu Yayınları, 1994.

(schools, mosques, churches, governmental buildings or places of art). The women that participated in the interviews said that they had buried their children's umbilical cord in the gardens of Europe's important universities.

3.2.6. Passing the 40 days after birth:

It is taking the child outside forty days after being born. The women that participated in the interviews stated that births no longer took place in homes but at hospitals and that this ritual is up to the families. This ritual is about the child being bathed with a special ceremony. Coins, rings, gold, silver, forty stones, forty different flowers etc. are placed in the water the child is bathed in. After the child is bathed, he/she is taken outside for wander about. This tradition dates back to pagan culture.

3.2.7. The Child's First Steps:

A child's first steps are always sacred and are defined as the child's standing up. The women that participated in the study stated that when a child started to walk, dinner and cake were eaten at home or in restaurants.

3.2.8. The Child's First Teeth:

The child's first teeth is a ritual dating back to ancient cultures. When a child's first teeth come out, dinner is provided as a celebration. There is a special dish made from wheat especially. A person who sees the child's first teeth gives the child a gift. The women that participated in the study said that this tradition continued and that they all prepared the 'wheat' meal and handed it out to people. Furthermore, some of the women stated that they celebrated by organizing a party.

3.2.9. Protecting the Child from the Evil Eye:

Protecting the child from the evil eye also dates back to Shaman traditions. The women that participated in the study stated that they had placed a 'gold' or 'silver' piece of jewelry on the collars of their children and that they saw these as objects that protected the children from the evil eye.

3.2.10. Child Mawlid:

It is a prayer-ritual conducted to bless the child. During a child mawlid, sweet food and drink is provided. All the women that participated in the interview stated that they had had a mawlid.

3.2.11. Mother's Milk:

After birth, in order for the mother's milk to increase, it is important that food and drink be given to the mother. Since ancient cultures, the importance of mother's milk has been emphasized. The women that participated in the interviews stated that they had given their children milk for at least two years. In Turkish epics giving milk to the child is important as can be seen in the sentence: 'the child came to the mother's breast and sucked her milk'[10].

3.2.12. Circumcisions:

Circumcisions also date back to the past and still continue today. The women that participated and that had male children stated that they had organized a circumcision ceremony. They added that nowadays circumcision ceremonies were held in halls and dinner was provided. Thus, nowadays circumcision ceremonies are organized like a wedding.

3.2.13. Beautiful Sayings about Birth:

Among the sayings about birth, the woman who participated said that the most common were: 'May Allah let them grow up with a mother and father, Maşallah.'

3.3. Death:

It can be observed that the women that migrated from Turkey mostly remained loyal to the rituals about death.

3.3.1. The Funeral Home:

All the women that participated in the interviews stated that they knew all the rituals about death and that they did everything that needed to be done. They said that they went to the funeral home and offered support.

3.3.2. Mourning:

The interviews carried out with the migrant women revealed that the mourning rituals were different. They stated that during the first week of the funeral no television was watched, and no music was listened to. Some women also stated that the mourning process could last up to one year. The women stated that on the day of the funeral and following it black clothes were worn. In Eastern cultures the color of mourning is white whereas in the West it is black.

3.3.3. Death Mawlid:

All the women that participated in the interviews stated that they knew the death mawlid and that they applied it.

---

[10] B. Ögel, **Türk Mitolojisi**, Ankara, Atatürk Kültür, Dil ve Tarih Yüksek Kurumu Yayınları:102, 1989, p. 115.

3.3.4. The 7th, 40th, and 52nd day of the passing:

The women that participated in the interview said that on the 7th, 40th, and 52nd night of the death of the person they either read Mawlid or prayers.

3.3.5. The Anniversary of the Death:

The women that participated in the interviews stated that on the anniversary of the death as well they read Mawlid or prayers and provided food.

3.3.6. Food Served at the Funeral Home: (Halwa, Lokma, Rice)

The women that participated in the interviews stated that food was provided at the funeral home. The food was prepared by neighbors and brought to the funeral home. This tradition, which dates back to ancient cultures, while once was halwa and lokma is nowadays rice with meat, dolma, pastries, various sweets, and various regional dishes.

3.3.7. Distributing the Dead Person's Belongings:

All the women that participated in the interviews stated that the dead person's belongings were handed out.

3.3.8. Sayings about Death-Words of Condolence:

'May your wound heal quickly, May Allah grant peace' 'May they rest in Heaven' 'May they rest in heavenly light' 'May Allah grant you patience.'

3.4. Social Life:

Migrant women that migrated from Turkey to Germany, Austria, and the UK continuate rituals that date back hundreds of years. It is possible to present these rituals as:

3.4.1. Hıdrellez:

Hıdrellez holds an important place in Turkish folk culture. It symbolizes two mystical heroes called Hızır and Ilyas, the arrival of Spring, and immortality. It is possible to find the origins of this belief in holy books. In the Bible and the Talmud there is a mystical hero called Ilya. In the Quran, Ilyas is a prophet[11]. The Hızır culture and symbol was first mentioned in 'The Epic of Gilgamesh.' In the story, Gilgamesh learns about the existence of a 'herb' that will resurrect his friend Enkidu from 'Utnapishtim'[12]. We come across this legend in ancient Greek and Syriac texts. Thus, 'Alexander' searched for the water of eternal life. Alexander's cook 'Andreas' found the water and alexander wanted to take the

[11] Ali Faik Demir, Nebahat Akgün Çomak, **Şaman ve Türk Dünyası**, İstanbul, Bağlam Yayınları, 2015, p.167.

[12] Gilgamiş Destanı, çev. Sait Maden, İstanbul, Türkiye İş Bankası Yayınları, 2015, p.107.

water from Andreas but he transforms into a water sprite. In these texts, Alexander was given the nickname two-horned. In Jewish legends however, 'Elijah' (Ilyas), who is shown as a prophet, goes looking for the water of life with companion Rabbi Joshua Ben Levi[13] . There is a connection between Hızır and Aya Yorgi. Aya Yorgi is another name for Saint Georges. According to Sumerian legends, it is the wedding day of the goddess of fertility 'Inanna' (in Akkadian: Ishtar, Roman: Venus, Greek: Aphrodite)[14] and the shepherd Dumuzid (Tammuz in Akkadian). On this day everywhere becomes fertile and the lands turn green[15]. Women are the most important carriers of culture. All the women that participated in the interviews stated that they knew this tradition and that they continued it.

3.4.2. Nowruz:

Among Turkish people, Nowruz is the celebration of entering Spring or Summer. The arrival of Spring is the awakening of nature. The Nowruz celebrations can be found in the Gokturk epics, Göç and Türeyiş. The Kirghiz view Nowruz as a beginning of Spring festival[16]. On Nowruz, day and night become the same length. Light defeats darkness and good overcomes evil. According to an old Iranian calendar, Nowruz is the first day of the year and of Spring. According to the Gregorian calendar it is the 21st and 22nd of March. Nowruz represents the first day of Spring. It is believed that on Nowruz day the 'Forty Pieces' are picked up, thus, it is also known as the Forties Festival. Names like the Sultan of Nowruz and March the 9th are also given. Among the Nowruz rituals are 'handing out food and milk, cleaning the house, organizing feasts, making peace with people etc.' All the women that participated in the interviews stated that they knew the Nowruz celebrations and that they celebrated it.

3.4.3. Celebrating the New Year:

All the women that participated in the interviews celebrate New Year's Eve. They cook turkey especially on this night. And as a dessert they cook pumpkin. The women also go shopping for the new year and buy each other presents. They stated that they usually celebrated the new year at home with family or close friends. They watch Turkish television programs on this night especially. Three women said that they preferred to celebrate outside of the house. The New Year celebrations can be found in all cultures. The symbols of Santa Claus or St. Nicholas are very important.

Santa Claus or St. Nicholas is an important mystical hero who is believed to

---

13 Ahmet Yaşar Ocak, **İslam Türk İnançlarında Hızır yahut Hızır-İlyas Kültü**, İstanbul, Kabalcı Yayınevi, 2007, pp. 52-56.

14 Azra Erhat, **Mitoloji Sözlüğü**, İstanbul, Remzi Kitabevi, 2010, p. 290.

15 Reverent Canon J.R. Porter, **"Le Proche-Orient" Mythologies du Monde**, der: Roy Willis, Köln, Evergreen, 2006, p.171.

16 M. Öcal Oğuz, **"Kırgız'ların Kutladığı Bayramlar ve Nevruz Pratikleri"**. Nevruz ve Renkler. Türk Dünyasında Nevruz. İkinci Bilgi Şöleni Bildirileri. (19-21 Mart), Ankara, 1996, p. 304.

hand out gifts to children in December and he is considered to be an important saint. Thus, St. Nicholas appears mainly as Santa Claus. The transformation of St. Nicholas into a legend and a beloved of children occurred in the 12th century. In a compilation published in 1582 about Christmas and Santa Claus, the bond between Santa Claus and children is evident. Thus, Santa Claus has become the protector of children[17].

3.4.4. Mawlid:

The Mawlid tradition dates back to Shaman culture. A Shaman would say a prayer in a dead person's home and conduct the ritual along with music. While conducting the ritual, the Shaman would always have a 'drum', 'tambourine', and 'lute' on him. In Turkish culture, Mawlids are the poetic texts that are read with music and that describe the birth and life of the prophet Mohammed. Mawlids are read along with prayers on nights of a person's passing and holy nights. The women that participated in the interviews stated that they knew Mawlids and participated in the reading of them.

3.4.5. The Evil Eye-The Evil Eye Talisman:

The Evil Eye (Nazar) is an old Turkish belief. In Shaman belief, they believed that when under the influence of an evil spirit, a blue colored stone had a protective effect. It is the most important symbol in Turkish culture. The Evil Eye talisman is the color 'blue' and is in the shape of an eye. The eye is a person's window that opens to the world. Nowadays, apart from belief, it is also used for decorative purposes. The women that participated in the interviews continue this tradition and also use it in accessories.

3.4.6. Pouring Lead:

The tradition of pouring lead also dates back to ancient cultures. The ritual of pouring liquid lead is to be cleansed and protected from evil. It is a tradition that still exists today. The women that participated in the interviews said that they knew the tradition and that they tried to get it done whenever possible. This tradition dates back to shaman culture. Pouring lead takes place as a ceremony. It is believed that the 'Shaman' pouring the lead had special abilities.

3.4.7. Knocking on Wood:

The tradition of knocking on wood dates back to 'Shaman' culture. Wood is knocked on three times in order to keep bad news or events at bay. The women that participated in the interviews stated that they did this frequently. Because the origin of wood is the 'tree', trees are sacred in all cultures and mythologies,

---

[17] J. Benoit, **Le Chamanisme**, Paris, Berg International, 2007, p. 10.

especially, the 'Tree of Knowledge.'

3.4.8. Burning Incense and Lighting Candles:

The Tradition of burning incense dates back to ancient cultures and in today's world is seen in many cultures. It is a ritual conducted to get rid of evil. Juniper or hawthorn is used in incense sticks. In the Epic of Manas, it mentions that female Shamans lit a fire using 'Juniper'[18]. The tradition of lighting candles also dates back to ancient cultures. The tradition of lighting candles to graves, saints, and holy stones stems from the culture of fire. The ancient Greeks and the Romans used to light candles on headstones. This pagan tradition also found its way into Christianity[19]. The tradition of lighting candles to saints is continued today. The women that participated in the interviews stated that they burned incense and lit candles on Kandil nights especially.

3.4.9. Offerings and Animal Sacrifice:

Offerings and animal sacrifice date back to old traditions. In Shaman belief, tying different colors of cloth to the Shaman's drum was an offering. Releasing horses into the wilderness is also a sacrificial ritual. This kind of sacrifice is called a bloodless sacrifice. An animal is donated to the gods and that animal, especially horses, cannot be ridden again[20]. In today's world also there is the tradition of tying different colors of cloth to trees in many cultures. Feeding birds or releasing them from their cages are also among some of the important offerings. The women that participated in the interviews stated that they knew this tradition and tried to carry it out as much as possible under their circumstances. Feeding birds especially is a symbol that is widespread in today's world. The feeding of birds in the important squares in European cities continues still.

3.4.10. Muska (Triangle Shaped Talisman):

A muska is an enchanted object that people believe protects from evil. Within muskas are talismanic writings or prayers. The shape of a muska is different too. It is shaped like a triangle and is made of seven layers of fabric or leather. Eight of the women stated that they carried a muska and the others said that they knew what it was and believed in it but did not carry one on them. Nowadays, muskas are also placed in silver and worn as an accessory.

3.4.11. Ramadan:

The women that participated in the interviews stated that they knew all the rituals of the month of Ramadan and most of them fast during it.

---

[18] Demir, Çomak, op.cit., p.183.

[19] Ibid., p.180.

[20] A. İnan. **Şamanizm-Materyaller ve Araştırmalar**. Ankara, Türk Tarih Kurumu Basımevi, 1995, p.167.

3.4.12. Eid:

The women that participated in the interviews stated that they knew the rituals of Eid and that they celebrated it. Because they live in Europe, they carry out the ritual of sacrifice when they go to Turkey.

3.4.13. Tying a Strip of Cloth:

The tradition of tying a strip of cloth is the most important symbol dating back to 'Shaman' tradition. Tying a strip of cloth is a ritual carried out especially during 'Nowruz' and 'Hidrellez' in order to make an offering. The women that participated in the interviews stated that they tied strips of cloth or red ribbons.

3.4.14. The Hand of Fatima:

The Hand of Fatima is a symbol dating back to ancient cultures. It is used as a talisman against evil. In the entrance to the courthouse of the Alhambra Palace in Andalusia, the 'stone hand' is a talisman. The women that participated in the interviews stated that they knew 'The Hand of Fatima' and that wore it as an accessory because they believed in it.

3.4.15. Leaping over a Fire:

The tradition of leaping over a fire occurs during the 'Nowruz' and 'Hidrellez' celebrations. The symbol of leaping over a fire is protection from evil and illness. The women that participated in the interviews stated that they knew this tradition and did it if circumstances permitted it.

3.4.16. Regional Food and Dishes:

All the women that participated in the interviews stated that they preferred to prepare regional dishes and that they made them at least three days a week. In the making of the dishes they use ingredients like 'dried yoghurt, pickles, dumplings, noodles, bulgur, phyllo dough, tomato paste, pomegranate syrup, jams, honey, molasses, dried fruit, dried vegetables, regional spices, rice, olives, fruit pulp, regional sweets, halwa, baclava, kataifi, and Turkish delight. All of which are brought over from Turkey.

3.4.17. Kandil Nights:

Kandil nights are holy nights. On these nights food (fried pastry, halwa) is handed out to neighbors. Mawlid is read on these nights. The women that participated in the interviews stated that they listened to Mawlid on Turkish television channels.

3.4.18. Ashure (Noah's Pudding):

Aşure is an important cultural symbol. According to the Islamic calendar, Asure is the tenth day of the Muharram. It originates from the Flood. The day of Aşure is the day Noah's ark landed on dry land. Noah and those with him cooked a meal by mixing whatever they had with them. Thus, this dish is called Aşure. Wheat, beans, chickpeas, sugar, sultanas, dried apricots, dried figs, hazel nuts, almonds, pomegranates, walnuts, cloves, orange peel, rose water etc. are used to make it. Due to the sugar in it, it is considered a sweet dish. The women that participated in the interviews stated that they knew what it was and except for five of them, the rest loved it. Eleven of them said that they made it every year.

3.4.19. The Sanctity of Numbers:

The women that participated in the interviews said that the numbers '1' '2' '3' '5' '7' '19' '21' '40' '41' '99' were lucky numbers.

3.4.20. The Sanctity of Colors:

The women that participated in the interviews said that 'White', 'Red', 'Blue', 'Purple', 'Green', 'Yellow', 'Lilac', 'Brown', and 'Pink' were their lucky colors.

3.4.21. The Sanctity of Stones:

The women that participated in the interviews had natural stones that they considered lucky. They also stated that the lucky stones were according to star signs. The famous brand 'Swarovski' can also be found in Vienna. If we take a look at the qualities, benefits, and star signs of the precious or semi-precious stones and crystals in terms of Swarovski, we see that stones have been used as talismans, good luck, prosperity, peace, symbols of energy and healing, and protection from evil throughout human history. Some of the stones mentioned by the women were: Moonstones, Onyx, Aquamarines, Pink Quartz, Bloodstones, Garnets, Amber, Amethyst, Lapis Lazuli, Citrines, Coral, Turquoise, Pearls, Jadestones etc.

3.4.22. The Sanctity of Flowers:

The women that participated in the interviews stated that they felt an intense sensitivity towards plants and flowers. 'Roses' and 'Orchids' were at the top of their list. The women preferred flowers on special occasions like 'engagements, weddings, birthdays, Valentine's Day etc.' and found them more precious on those occasions.

3.4.23. The Sanctity of Animals:

The women that participated in the interviews stated 'cats-dogs-fish' to be the preferred animals. The younger women preferred dogs.

3.4.24. Proverbs-Sayings:

While the women that participated in the interviews were chatting among themselves proverbs and sayings are used. Thus, they continue their own culture. When we asked them about proverbs and sayings that glorified women, we received replies like: 'Heaven is beneath the feet of mothers. There can be no home without a woman. A woman is a home's sun. If anyone cries it will be my mother, the rest will be crocodile tears. A mother never gives up on their child. The heart of a woman is the source of mercy. Next to every successful man is a successful woman. The girl in your arms, the trousseau in the chest.

3.4.25. Words Used for Women:

Words used for women by men close to the women that participated in the interviews: 'my wife, my love, my dear, sultan, mother, mother-in-law, my life, my sister, my bride, my beautiful daughter, my one and only, world's dearest, my beautiful bride, my aunt, sister-in-law, aunt, grandmother etc.

3.4.26. Words of Endearment Used by Women for their Children:

Among the words used by the women that participated in the interviews were: 'my little one, my lamb, little lamb, my love, my baby, my child, my dear, my pasha, my princess, my cotton ball, my lion etc.' In Yusuf Balasaguni's famous work, 'Kutadgu Bilig', in the words Aytoldı uses to give advice to his son 'Öğdilmiş', we come across the word of affection 'my lamb'[21].

3.4.27. Accessories Worn by Women: (Gold-Diamonds-Silver):

The women that participated in the interviews preferred 'gold' and 'diamonds' forrings. And for bracelets they tended to go for gold-diamond-precious stones-silver.

3.4.28. Words Used by Women for Men:

Among the words used by the women for men were: 'my husband, my love, my dear, my mister, mister, gentleman, our mister, uncle, father-in-law, father, nephew, brother-in-law, grandfather, big brother, the cornerstone of my home, the father of my children etc.'

3.4.29. Prayers:

These are the prayers known by the women that participated in the interviews

---

[21] R.R. Arat, **Kutadgu Bilig "Yusuf Has Hacib"** Metin-Çeviri-İndex. Atatürk Kültür Dil ve Tarih Yüksek Kurumu. Ankara, Türk Tarih Kurumu Basımevi, 1985, p. 104.

and heard from others close to them. Thus, we can see them as good-will wishes. Some of them were: May everything be as you desire. I wish you a good day. May Allah be pleased. May Allah turn everything you touch into gold. May there be those to help you too. Thank you. May Allah grant you health. May Allah give you a good appetite. Good luck with it. Bon appetite. May your luck be a lot. May it go to the spirits of the dead. May you see the good days of your child. Get well soon. May your conversation last forever. May Hızır (prophet) be your companion. May Allah grant your patience. Bon Voyage. Go in peace and return in peace. Happy Henna. Break a leg. May you live long. May chances be many. May you always exist. Bless you. May you never see poverty. Be sacred like water. May Allah never divert you.

3.4.30. Curses:

These are the curses known by the women that participated in the interviews and heard from others close to them. May your name be forgotten. Allah damn it. May your mouth and tongue dry out. May owls live in your house. Don't see the good of your children. May the earth fill your greed. I hope it does not work out. May poison be your bread. May your hearth go cold. May you go blind. May a fig tree grow in your hearth. May you never be able to make ends meet. May the weight of me fall on you in stones.

3.4.31. Good Luck:

Spotting a stork in the sky is good luck. Storks are the signs of children and also, 'Spotting a stork in the sky' means there will be a lot of travel that year. Ladybugs are lucky. A four-leafed clover is considered lucky. It is believed that elephants bring prosperity. The women stated that they usually carried loose change in their purses. Carrying a key is also considered good luck. However, the luckiest item for them is the evil-eye talisman.

3.4.32. Bad Luck:

This is the bad luck known by the women that participated in the interviews and heard from others close to them. Among the things they found to be bad luck were: Seeing an owl, the number 13, seeing a black cat, the caw of a crow, a 'solar' or 'lunar' eclipse, walking under a ladder, and breaking a mirror.

3.4.33. Hosting Guests: The women that participated in the interviews stated guests were very important for them.

3.4.34. The Use of Regional Kilims-Carpets: All the women like using regional objects as do the younger ones.

3.4.35. Nicknames: The use of nicknames is based on the hometown in Turkey.

Conclusion

The findings of this study, which covers the interviews conducted with women that had migrated to Austria from Turkey, highlight the fact that the women who migrated to these countries have maintained the cultural and symbolic codes that date back hundreds of years. Thus, these findings show that the women have not severed ties with their countries' culture and that in important events like marriage-birth-death-social life by applying cultural rituals, they reproduce them. The findings of the study are meaningful in terms of highlighting the use and reproduction elements of the cultural and symbolic codes of women that have migrated to the aforementioned country since the 60s for economic reasons and have lived there for many years. It is also interesting to see that not only do the older generations practice these rituals but also the younger generations. Thus, it shows that these women did not stray from their own culture while exploring a new one but reproduced it by maintaining it.

The cultural codes about marriage, birth, death, and social life that have been studied within the scope of the study are the common cultural units of society. They are also agreements shared by members of society. Since ancient cultures, women have been the carriers of culture to new generations. Thus, women play an important role in the conveyance of intercultural communication. They redefine the culture, symbols, and communication between both the elements of culture but also between women. By forming the focal point of this culture, they reshape culture and symbols. The study carried out with the women shows that the women conveyed culture and symbols without putting variables like language, religion, race, class, gender, nationality, ideology, and ethnic origin into the equation. The women interpret, maintain, and pass on their culture to new generations. They were successful in producing common meaning. Furthermore, they have maintained their culture in their cultural memory. Therefore, they have enabled the cultural bond between the past and present to strengthen and have maintained it. And this shows us that cultural continuity is very important.

The findings highlight that to achieve intercultural communication and achieve a peaceful common existence based on mutual acceptance, being able to synthesize the new culture with their own is important. The women that migrated to Austria from Turkey were able to balance the two cultures' gains by synthesizing the cultural differences and this becomes a meaningful condition in order for global neighborliness to emerge.

CHAPTER 22

THE MAINTAINING (NON-MAINTAINING) OF CULTURAL AND SYMBOLIC CODES BY WOMEN THAT HAVE MIGRATED TO EUROPE FROM TURKEY: THE CASE OF FRANCE (PARIS)

Elgiz Yılmaz Altuntaş[1] and Nebahat Akgün Çomak[2]

Introduction

In human history, migration plays an important role in terms of intercultural encounters and intercultural communication. The 20th century, where the 1st and the 2nd World War took place, has witnessed important migration processes. The migrants' efforts to fit in to the new country and culture and their anxiety in regards of maintaining and continuing their own cultural heritage were experienced hand in hand. As of the 60s, women migrated to European countries, especially France, from Turkey. This study encompasses the migrant women that live in France (Paris), which is one of the countries with the highest number of migrants from Turkey. The study aims to determine as to what degree the women maintain their cultural and symbolic codes and practice their cultural rituals. Thus, rather than query as to whether the use of cultural and symbolic codes in daily life is useful, the question of how certain cultural and symbolic codes are reproduced for certain purposes and rituals has gained significance.

In the study, the styles and elements of the use and reproduction of cultural and symbolic codes, the cultural and symbolic codes for marriage, the cultural and symbolic codes for birth, the cultural and symbolic codes for death, and the cultural and symbolic codes for social life of women that have migrated to the aforementioned country since the 60s for economic reasons and have lived there for many years have attempted to be determined by studying them.

The fact that the women that migrated to European countries maintain and reproduce their cultural and symbolic codes, to a degree, points to their bond with Turkey and their culture. Thus, due to the fact that the non-use of cultural and symbolic codes and the forgetting of rituals could point to a weakening of ties to Turkey, this has been considered to be problematic in terms of culture.

Women who agreed to participate in our research came to France for different reasons as follows: Those who immigrated to France for economic

[1] Assoc. Prof. Galatasaray University, Faculty of Communication, Türkiye.
[2] Assoc. Prof. Galatasaray University, Faculty of Communication, Türkiye.

reasons, immigrants and those who arrived in France at an early age or were born in France.

Women migrants that have lived in European countries for many years can experience the dilemma of not being able to maintain their own culture and of becoming estranged from it while discovering and trying to adapt to a new culture.

The Scope and Method of the Study 'In-depth Face-to-Face Interviews'

In the scope of the study, it was decided to conduct interviews with women over the age of 18 that had migrated to France from Turkey. The total number of women that were suggested to interview was 80. The participants were informed that variables like names, addresses, religion, language, ethnic roots, ideologies, sexual preferences were not included in the scope of the study and thus, 64 of the women that participated in the interviews agreed to answer the questions. The 16 women that did not agree to the in-depth interviews consisted of feminists (3 women), lesbians (2 women), activists (2 women), NGO members (3 women), those fighting the patriarchal order (1 woman), those trying to solve gender inequality (2 women), those defending the superiority of women (1 woman), and those fighting against class struggle and racism (2 women). These women also stated that this was also the reason for not participating in the interviews. In Paris, an in-depth interview was conducted with Elgiz Yılmaz and analyzed with Excel files by Özgür Altuntaş. In the study, the in-depth face-to-face interview method was applied. The data gathered from the in-depth interview will be presented by being arranged with the cultural and symbolic interpretations of the researchers.

Table 1. Reasons for not participating in the study

Number of women not participated in the study	**Reasons**
3	being feminist
2	being lesbians
2	being activists
3	NGO members
1	fighting the patriarchal order
2	trying to solve gender inequality
1	defending the superiority of women
2	fighting against class struggle and racism
TOTAL: 16	

In the in-depth interviews, the cultural and symbolic structures directed at the women in the study, were separated into four levels: marriage, birth, death, and social life. The four levels were also categorized within themselves according to the variables below:

1. Mariage: 1.1. Marriage age. 1.2. Looking for a wife for your son, being in-laws.1.3. The boy's parents asking the girl's parents for permission for their son to marry the daughter. 1.4. Betrothal and the drinking of sherbet. 1.5. Engagement. 1.6. Trousseau 1.7. Exhibiting the trousseau. 1.8. Henna night. 1.9. Picking up the bride. 1.10. Sprinkling the bride's head. 1.11. The Wedding.1.12. The Wedding Dinner. 1.13. The Red-Ribbon. 1.14. The Veil. 1.15. Fancy sayings about marriage. 1.16. The Wedding convoy

2. Birth: 2.1. The pre-natal period of the mother. 2.2. The pregnancy period of the mother. 2.3. The birth of the child. 2.4. Naming the child. 2.5. The child's umbilical cord.2.6. Passing the 40 days after birth. 2.7. The first steps of the child. 2.8. The child's first teeth. 2.9. Protecting the child from the evil eye (bad luck). 2.10. Child Mawlid (gathering where words from the Quran are read 2.11. Mother's milk. 2.12. The circumcision 2.13. Fancy sayings about birth.

3. Death: 3.1 The Funeral Home. 3.2. Mourning. 3.3. Death Mawlid. 3.4. The 7th,40th and 52nd day of the passing. 3.5. The Anniversary of the passing. 3.6. Food served at the funeral home (Halwa-Lokum-Rice). 3.7. Distributing the departed's belongings. 3.8. Words of condolences about death.

4. Social Life: 4.1. Hıdırellez. 4.2. Nowruz 4.3. Celebrating the New Year. 4.4. Mawlud. 4.5. The evil eye-The evil eye talisman. 4.6. Pouring lead (to repel the evil eye). 4.7. Knocking on wood. 4.8. Burning incense. 4.9. Offerings and Animal sacrifice. 4.10. Good luck charm (with a prayer inside). 4.11. Ramadan. 4.12. Eid. 4.13. Tying strips of cloth. 4.14. The Hand of Fatima. 4.15. Leaping over a fire. 4.16. Regional foods. 4.17. Holy nights. 4.18. Ashure (Noah's pudding). 4.19. The sanctity of numbers. 4.20. The sanctity of colors. 4.21. The sanctity of stones. 4.22. The sanctity of plants. 4.23. The sanctity of animals. 4.24. Proverbs-Sayings. 4.25. Words used towards women. 4.26. Words women use for their children. 4.27. Accessories worn by women. 4.28. Words women use for men. 4.29. Prayers. 4.30. Curses. 4.31. Good luck. 4.32. Bad luck. 4.33. Hosting guests. 4.34. The use of regional kilims-carpets. 4.35. Nicknames.

Findings

In the findings collected in this research that covered women that had migrated to France from Turkey, cultural and symbolic structures have been categorized on four levels as 'Marriage-Birth-Death-Social Life' and have been presented below.

Marriage:

Pre-marriage and post-marriage rituals play an important role in the lives of women that have migrated from Turkey.

The marriage age: It can be seen that the age of marriage for the first wave of women that migrated to France from Turkey was 17 or 18. The age of marriage of the second, third, and fourth generations gradually increases. Thus, it is considered to be above 21. The age of the women that participated in the interviews was between 18 and 69. It was determined that a few of the educated women had not married and did not even think of marrying. Two of the women that participated had married a foreigner. When one takes a look at world history, we see 'Adam-Eve' as an example of the first marriage[3].

*Looking for a wife for your son, being in-laws:*The women that participated in the interviews stated that the practice of looking for a wife for a son continued and that they had experienced it in their own marriage process. This tradition has not lost its significance.

The Boy's Parents Asking the Girl's Parents for Permission for their son to marry the daughter: For all the women that participated in the interview, the case of going to the girl's house and asking the girl's father or family elder for permission took place. This is a very old tradition but still continues in modern life. The most important symbol in asking for permission is Turkish coffee being served to the guests. The making and serving of the coffee also requires a special ritual.

Betrothal and the Drinking of Sherbet: The women that participated in the interviews stated that prior to the wedding, a betrothal took place and that sherbet was drunk or something sweet was eaten. They also stated that lately the betrothal and engagement occurred at the same time if desired.

The Engagement: All of the women that participated in the interviews wanted an engagement ceremony. The women stated that having the engagement ceremony in ballrooms rather than in homes had become popular.

The Trousseau: All the women that participated in the interviews said that they looked warmly on exhibiting the Trousseau.

Exhibiting the Trousseau: Exhibiting the trousseau is the placement of the girl's possessions into the new house before the wedding. All the women that participated in the interviews stated that they had exhibited their trousseaus.

Henna Night: All the women that participated in the interviews stated that the henna night celebration was a nice tradition. It is a tradition dating back to ancient cultures and in today's world is celebrated in homes or in halls.

Picking up the bride: It is the picking up of the bride from her parents' house and taking her to where the ceremony will be held. All of the women within the study stated that the same was done to them.

Sprinkling the bride's head: It is the sprinkling of coins, rice, sugar, wheat etc. over the bride's head as she leaves the house. It is done for a prosperous

[3] **Encyclopedie Des Symboles**, Ed. Michel Cazenave, München, Le Livre de Poche, 1989, p. 5-7.

marriage. This continues today and all the women viewed this as a nice tradition. The sprinkling dates back to Shaman traditions.

The Wedding: In all cultures, 'marriage' and 'birth' form the focal points of life. In Turkish Mythology, the marriage of 'earth' and 'sky' was the first sacred marriage[4] (Eliade, 2003:243). Therefore, the women that participated in the interviews stated that wedding ceremonies were important for them and that a wedding day was the most important day in a woman's life.

The Wedding Dinner: All the women that participated in the interviews stated that in today's world the dinner was held in wedding halls or hotel ballrooms and that it was magnificent.

The Red-Ribbon: The red-ribbon is a ribbon that is tied around the bride's waist by her father or older brother as she leaves the house. The red-ribbon is a symbol of virginity. It also carries the meaning of protecting the bride from evil spirits. A red-ribbon is also tied around the head of a woman giving birth. This is also a protection from evil spirits. It is a tradition dating back to pagan culture and is a symbol that continues in modern life. The women that participated in the interviews believed that this practice is also done for the woman's sake and that it is a nice and thoughtful symbol.

The Veil: A white veil is a universal symbol. The women that participated in the interviews preferred the color 'red' for their henna night celebration in accordance with their traditions. During the ceremony they opted for the color 'white' for their dress and veil.

Beautiful sayings about marriage: 'May Allah make you happy. I wish you all the happiness. Grow old on one pillow.'

The Wedding Convoy: The women that participated in the interviews stated that a wedding convoy is unable to take place as the traffic laws abroad are very strict. The women stated that according to news in the media, 'In February 2017, a Turkish wedding convoy on the motorway was taken to court in Belgium.' The eighteen Turks who were carrying out a wedding convoy on the motorway were banned from driving and fined two-thousand Euros. The prosecutor asked, 'Is entering traffic during a wedding a tradition?' Furthermore, the prosecutor also added that there were Turks driving around sounding their horns and that there was no place for this in their culture[5].

Birth

Throughout the scope of the study, pre-natal and post-natal rituals were taken

---

[4] Mircea Eliade, **Dinler Tarihine Giriş**, çev. Lale Arslan, İstanbul, Kabalcı Yayınları, 2003, p. 243.

[5] http://www.euronews.com (Access: 11.12.2018).

into account. Rituals conducted by the migrant women can be stated as:

The Pre-natal Period of the Mother: In Turkish culture, as with all cultures, marriage and children are of importance. In old Turkish culture, when a child was desired, a prayer was said to God, an offering was made, and bloodless sacrifices were made. Three of the women that participated in the interviews had been unable to bear a child for two to three years. They visited holy places and made offerings, made sacrifices, and left food. One of the women stated that she had had a test-tube baby as she was unable to have a child. This tradition can be found in Turkish Epics. In the Epic of Manas, marriage and children form the focal point of the epic. The primary hero of the epic, Jakyp Khan, had been unable to have a child for seven years, so he told his wife that they should go to the 'apple tree' and pray to God[6].

The Pregnancy Period of the Mother: A woman craves for various foods during her pregnancy. Among the foods that the women, who participated in the interviews, craved were plums, pickles, sweet and exotic fruits etc. There is a belief that if a woman does not eat what she craves while pregnant, there will be a birthmark on the child. This belief dates back to pagan culture. In Greek Mythology, there strange birthmarks on Zeus' son Deimos. Deimos was named 'the Marked Warrior.'

The Birth of the Child: The birth of a child being depicted as the 'birth-death-birth' narrative cycle is the most beautiful explanation of continuity[7]. All of the women that participated in the interviews stated that birth was a miracle.

Naming the Child: Naming a child has been an important since ancient cultures. The women that participated in the interviews stated that they had determined the name of their child before giving birth. After the child is born, the eldest in the family says a prayer and whispers the child's name into his/her right ear three times. This tradition is an important symbol that continues from the past to today. The tradition of naming the child can also be encountered in the 'Dede Korkut Stories' and epics[8].

The Child's Umbilical Cord: The child's umbilical cord is a ritual dating back to ancient cultures. The umbilical cord is not discarded, it is buried in the gardens of important buildings (schools, mosques, churches, governmental buildings or places of art). The women that participated in the interviews said that they had buried their children's umbilical cord in the gardens of Europe's important universities.

---

[6] Nebahat A. Çomak, Elgiz Yilmaz, **"Manas Destanı"**, II.Congress Of International Social Scientists. October 22-24, Bishkek-Kyrgyzstan, 2005.

[7] Joseph Campbell, **Doğu Mitolojisi-Tanrının Maskeleri**, çev. Kudret Emiroğlu, Ankara, İmge Kitabevi. 2003, p. 11.

[8] Muharrem Ergin, **Dede Korkut Kitabı I-Giriş-Metin**, Ankara, Türk Dil Kurumu Yayınları, 1994.

Passing the 40 days after birth: It is taking the child outside forty days after being born. The women that participated in the interviews stated that births no longer took place in homes but at hospitals and that this ritual is up to the families. This ritual is about the child being bathed with a special ceremony. Coins, rings, gold, silver, forty stones, forty different flowers etc. are placed in the water the child is bathed in. After the child is bathed, he/she is taken outside for wander about. This tradition dates back to pagan culture.

The Child's First Steps: A child's first steps are always sacred and are defined as the child's standing up. The women that participated in the study stated that when a child started to walk, dinner and cake were eaten at home or in restaurants.

The Child's First Teeth: The child's first teeth is a ritual dating back to ancient cultures. When a child's first teeth come out, dinner is provided as a celebration. There is a special dish made from wheat especially. A person who sees the child's first teeth gives the child a gift. The women that participated in the study said that this tradition continued and that they all prepared the 'wheat' meal and handed it out to people. Furthermore, some of the women stated that they celebrated by organizing a party.

Protecting the Child from the Evil Eye: Protecting the child from the evil eye also dates back to Shaman traditions. The women that participated in the study stated that they had placed a 'gold' or 'silver' piece of jewelry on the collars of their children and that they saw these as objects that protected the children from the evil eye.

Child Mawlid: It is a prayer-ritual conducted to bless the child. During a child mawlid, sweet food and drink is provided. All the women that participated in the interview stated that they had had a mawlid.

Mother's Milk: After birth, in order for the mother's milk to increase, it is important that food and drink be given to the mother. Since ancient cultures, the importance of mother's milk has been emphasized. The women that participated in the interviews stated that they had given their children milk for at least two years. In Turkish epics giving milk to the child is important as can be seen in the sentence: 'the child came to the mother's breast and sucked her milk'[9].

Circumcisions: Circumcisions also date back to the past and still continue today. The women that participated and that had male children stated that they had organized a circumcision ceremony. They added that nowadays circumcision ceremonies were held in halls and dinner was provided. Thus, nowadays circumcision ceremonies are organized like a wedding.

[9] B. Ögel, **Türk Mitolojisi**, Ankara, Atatürk Kültür, Dil ve Tarih Yüksek Kurumu Yayınları:102, 1989, p. 115.

Beautiful Sayings about Birth: Among the sayings about birth, the woman who participated said that the most common were: 'May Allah let them grow up with a mother and father, Maşallah.'

Death

It can be observed that the women that migrated from Turkey mostly remained loyal to the rituals about death.

The Funeral Home: All the women that participated in the interviews stated that they knew all the rituals about death and that they did everything that needed to be done. They said that they went to the funeral home and offered support.

Mourning: The interviews carried out with the migrant women revealed that the mourning rituals were different. They stated that during the first week of the funeral no television was watched, and no music was listened to. Some women also stated that the mourning process could last up to one year. The women stated that on the day of the funeral and following it black clothes were worn. In Eastern cultures the color of mourning is white whereas in the West it is black.

Death Mawlid: All the women that participated in the interviews stated that they knew the death mawlid and that they applied it.

The 7th, 40th, and 52nd day of the passing: The women that participated in the interview said that on the 7th, 40th, and 52nd night of the death of the person they either read Mawlid or prayers.

The Anniversary of the Death: The women that participated in the interviews stated that on the anniversary of the death as well they read Mawlid or prayers and provided food.

Food Served at the Funeral Home (Halwa, Lokma, Rice): The women that participated in the interviews stated that food was provided at the funeral home. The food was prepared by neighbors and brought to the funeral home. This tradition, which dates back to ancient cultures, while once was halwa and lokma is nowadays rice with meat, dolma, pastries, various sweets, and various regional dishes.

Distributing the Dead Person's Belongings: All the women that participated in the interviews stated that the dead person's belongings were handed out.

Sayings about Death-Words of Condolence: 'May your wound heal quickly, May Allah grant peace' 'May they rest in Heaven' 'May they rest in heavenly light' 'May Allah grant you patience.'

Social Life

Migrant women that migrated from Turkey to France, Germany, Austria, and the UK continuate rituals that date back hundreds of years. It is possible to present these rituals as:

Hıdrellez: Hıdrellez holds an important place in Turkish folk culture. It symbolizes two mystical heroes called Hızır and Ilyas, the arrival of Spring, and immortality. It is possible to find the origins of this belief in holy books. In the Bible and the Talmud there is a mystical hero called Ilya. In the Quran, Ilyas is a prophet[10]. The Hızır culture and symbol was first mentioned in 'The Epic of Gilgamesh.' In the story, Gilgamesh learns about the existence of a 'herb' that will resurrect his friend Enkidu from 'Utnapishtim'[11]. We come across this legend in ancient Greek and Syriac texts. Thus, 'Alexander' searched for the water of eternal life. Alexander's cook 'Andreas' found the water and alexander wanted to take the water from Andreas but he transforms into a water sprite. In these texts, Alexander was given the nickname two-horned. In Jewish legends however, 'Elijah' (Ilyas), who is shown as a prophet, goes looking for the water of life with companion Rabbi Joshua Ben Levi[12]. There is a connection between Hızır and Aya Yorgi. Aya Yorgi is another name for Saint Georges. According to Sumerian legends, it is the wedding day of the goddess of fertility 'Inanna' (in Akkadian: Ishtar, Roman: Venus, Greek: Aphrodite)[13] and the shepherd Dumuzid (Tammuz in Akkadian). On this day everywhere becomes fertile and the lands turn green[14]. Women are the most important carriers of culture. All the women that participated in the interviews stated that they knew this tradition and that they continued it.

Nowruz: Among Turkish people, Nowruz is the celebration of entering Spring or Summer. The arrival of Spring is the awakening of nature. The Nowruz celebrations can be found in the Gokturk epics, Göç and Türeyiş. The Kirghiz view Nowruz as a beginning of Spring festival[15]. On Nowruz, day and night become the same length. Light defeats darkness and good overcomes evil. According to an old Iranian calendar, Nowruz is the first day of the year and of Spring. According to the Gregorian calendar it is the 21st and 22nd of March. Nowruz represents the first day of Spring. It is believed that on Nowruz day the 'Forty Pieces' are picked up, thus, it is also known as the Forties Festival. Names like the Sultan of Nowruz and March the 9th are also given. Among the Nowruz rituals are 'handing out food and milk, cleaning the house, organizing feasts, making peace with people etc.' All the women that participated in the interviews

[10] Ali Faik Demir, Nebahat Akgün Çomak, **Şaman ve Türk Dünyası**, İstanbul, Bağlam Yayınları, 2015, p.167.

[11] Gilgamiş Destanı, çev. Sait Maden, İstanbul, Türkiye İş Bankası Yayınları, 2015, p.107.

[12], Ahmet Yaşar Ocak, **İslam Türk İnançlarında Hızır yahut Hızır-İlyas Kültü**, İstanbul, Kabalcı Yayınevi, 2007, pp. 52-56.

[13] Azra Erhat, **Mitoloji Sözlüğü**, İstanbul, Remzi Kitabevi, 2010, p. 290.

[14] Reverent Canon J.R. Porter, **"Le Proche-Orient" Mythologies du Monde**, der: Roy Willis, Köln, Evergreen, 2006, p.171.

[15] M. Öcal Oğuz, **"Kırgız'ların Kutladığı Bayramlar ve Nevruz Pratikleri"**. Nevruz ve Renkler. Türk Dünyasında Nevruz. İkinci Bilgi Şöleni Bildirileri. (19-21 Mart), Ankara, 1996, p. 304.

stated that they knew the Nowruz celebrations and that they celebrated it.

Celebrating the New Year: All the women that participated in the interviews celebrate New Year's Eve. They cook turkey especially on this night. And as a dessert they cook pumpkin. The women also go shopping for the new year and buy each other presents. They stated that they usually celebrated the new year at home with family or close friends. They watch Turkish television programs on this night especially. Three women said that they preferred to celebrate outside of the house. The New Year celebrations can be found in all cultures. The symbols of Santa Claus or St. Nicholas are very important.

Santa Claus or St. Nicholas is an important mystical hero who is believed to hand out gifts to children in December and he is considered to be an important saint. Thus, St. Nicholas appears mainly as Santa Claus. The transformation of St. Nicholas into a legend and a beloved of children occurred in the 12th century. In a compilation published in 1582 about Christmas and Santa Claus, the bond between Santa Claus and children is evident. Thus, Santa Claus has become the protector of children[16].

Mawlid: The Mawlid tradition dates back to Shaman culture. A Shaman would say a prayer in a dead person's home and conduct the ritual along with music. While conducting the ritual, the Shaman would always have a 'drum', 'tambourine', and 'lute' on him. In Turkish culture, Mawlids are the poetic texts that are read with music and that describe the birth and life of the prophet Mohammed. Mawlids are read along with prayers on nights of a person's passing and holy nights. The women that participated in the interviews stated that they knew Mawlids and participated in the reading of them.

The Evil Eye-The Evil Eye Talisman: The Evil Eye (Nazar) is an old Turkish belief. In Shaman belief, they believed that when under the influence of an evil spirit, a blue colored stone had a protective effect. It is the most important symbol in Turkish culture. The Evil Eye talisman is the color 'blue' and is in the shape of an eye. The eye is a person's window that opens to the world. Nowadays, apart from belief, it is also used for decorative purposes. The women that participated in the interviews continue this tradition and also use it in accessories.

Pouring Lead: The tradition of pouring lead also dates back to ancient cultures. The ritual of pouring liquid lead is to be cleansed and protected from evil. It is a tradition that still exists today. The women that participated in the interviews said that they knew the tradition and that they tried to get it done whenever possible. This tradition dates back to shaman culture. Pouring lead takes place as a ceremony. It is believed that the 'Shaman' pouring the lead had special abilities.

---

[16] J. Benoit, **Le Chamanisme**, Paris, Berg International, 2007, p. 10.

Knocking on Wood: The tradition of knocking on wood dates back to 'Shaman' culture. Wood is knocked on three times in order to keep bad news or events at bay. The women that participated in the interviews stated that they did this frequently. Because the origin of wood is the 'tree', trees are sacred in all cultures and mythologies, especially, the 'Tree of Knowledge.'

Burning Incense and Lighting Candles: The Tradition of burning incense dates back to ancient cultures and in today's world is seen in many cultures. It is a ritual conducted to get rid of evil. Juniper or hawthorn is used in incense sticks. In the Epic of Manas, it mentions that female Shamans lit a fire using 'Juniper'[17]. The tradition of lighting candles also dates back to ancient cultures. The tradition of lighting candles to graves, saints, and holy stones stems from the culture of fire. The ancient Greeks and the Romans used to light candles on headstones. This pagan tradition also found its way into Christianity[18]. The tradition of lighting candles to saints is continued today. The women that participated in the interviews stated that they burned incense and lit candles on Kandil nights especially.

Offerings and Animal Sacrifice: Offerings and animal sacrifice date back to old traditions. In Shaman belief, tying different colors of cloth to the Shaman's drum was an offering. Releasing horses into the wilderness is also a sacrificial ritual. This kind of sacrifice is called a bloodless sacrifice. An animal is donated to the gods and that animal, especially horses, cannot be ridden again[19]. In today's world also there is the tradition of tying different colors of cloth to trees in many cultures. Feeding birds or releasing them from their cages are also among some of the important offerings. The women that participated in the interviews stated that they knew this tradition and tried to carry it out as much as possible under their circumstances. Feeding birds especially is a symbol that is widespread in today's world. The feeding of birds in the important squares in European cities continues still.

Muska (Triangle Shaped Talisman): A muska is an enchanted object that people believe protects from evil. Within muskas are talismanic writings or prayers. The shape of a muska is different too. It is shaped like a triangle and is made of seven layers of fabric or leather. Eight of the women stated that they carried a muska and the others said that they knew what it was and believed in it but did not carry one on them. Nowadays, muskas are also placed in silver and worn as an accessory.

Ramadan: The women that participated in the interviews stated that they knew all the rituals of the month of Ramadan and most of them fast during it.

---

[17] Ali Faik Demir, Nebahat Akgün Çomak, op.cit., p.183.
[18] Ali Faik Demir, Nebahat Akgün Çomak, op.cit., p.180.
[19] A. İnan. **Şamanizm-Materyaller ve Araştırmalar**. Ankara, Türk Tarih Kurumu Basımevi, 1995, p.167.

Eid: The women that participated in the interviews stated that they knew the rituals of Eid and that they celebrated it. Because they live in Europe, they carry out the ritual of sacrifice when they go to Turkey.

Tying a Strip of Cloth: The tradition of tying a strip of cloth is the most important symbol dating back to 'Shaman' tradition. Tying a strip of cloth is a ritual carried out especially during 'Nowruz' and 'Hidrellez' in order to make an offering. The women that participated in the interviews stated that they tied strips of cloth or red ribbons.

The Hand of Fatima: The Hand of Fatima is a symbol dating back to ancient cultures. It is used as a talisman against evil. In the entrance to the courthouse of the Alhambra Palace in Andalusia, the 'stone hand' is a talisman. The women that participated in the interviews stated that they knew 'The Hand of Fatima' and that wore it as an accessory because they believed in it.

Leaping over a Fire: The tradition of leaping over a fire occurs during the 'Nowruz' and 'Hidrellez' celebrations. The symbol of leaping over a fire is protection from evil and illness. The women that participated in the interviews stated that they knew this tradition and did it if circumstances permitted it.

Regional Food and Dishes: All the women that participated in the interviews stated that they preferred to prepare regional dishes and that they made them at least three days a week. In the making of the dishes they use ingredients like 'dried yoghurt, pickles, dumplings, noodles, bulgur, phyllo dough, tomato paste, pomegranate syrup, jams, honey, molasses, dried fruit, dried vegetables, regional spices, rice, olives, fruit pulp, regional sweets, halwa, baclava, kataifi, and Turkish delight. All of which are brought over from Turkey.

Kandil Nights: Kandil nights are holy nights. On these nights food (fried pastry, halwa) is handed out to neighbors. Mawlid is read on these nights. The women that participated in the interviews stated that they listened to Mawlid on Turkish television channels.

Ashure (Noah's Pudding): Aşure is an important cultural symbol. According to the Islamic calendar, Aşure is the tenth day of the Muharram. It originates from the Flood. The day of Aşure is the day Noah's ark landed on dry land. Noah and those with him cooked a meal by mixing whatever they had with them. Thus, this dish is called Aşure. Wheat, beans, chickpeas, sugar, sultanas, dried apricots, dried figs, hazel nuts, almonds, pomegranates, walnuts, cloves, orange peel, rose water etc. are used to make it. Due to the sugar in it, it is considered a sweet dish. The women that participated in the interviews stated that they knew what it was and except for five of them, the rest loved it. Eleven of them said that they made it every year.

The Sanctity of Numbers: The women that participated in the interviews said that the numbers '1' '2' '3' '5' '7' '19' '21' '40' '41' '99' were lucky numbers.

The Sanctity of Colors: The women that participated in the interviews said that 'White', 'Red', 'Blue', 'Purple', 'Green', 'Yellow', 'Lilac', 'Brown', and 'Pink' were their lucky colors.

The Sanctity of Stones: The women that participated in the interviews had natural stones that they considered lucky. They also stated that the lucky stones were according to star signs. The famous brand 'Cartier' and 'Chopard' can also be found in Paris. If we take a look at the qualities, benefits, and star signs of the precious stones and diamond in terms of Cartier and Chopard, we see that stones have been used as talismans, good luck, prosperity, peace, symbols of energy and healing, and protection from evil throughout human history. Some of the stones mentioned by the women were: Moonstones, Onyx, Aquamarines, Pink Quartz, Bloodstones, Garnets, Amber, Amethyst, Lapis Lazuli, Citrines, Coral, Turquoise, Pearls, Jadestones etc.

The Sanctity of Flowers: The women that participated in the interviews stated that they felt an intense sensitivity towards plants and flowers. 'Roses' and 'Orchids' were at the top of their list. The women preferred flowers on special occasions like 'engagements, weddings, birthdays, Valentine's Day etc.' and found them more precious on those occasions.

The Sanctity of Animals: The women that participated in the interviews stated 'cats-dogs-fish' to be the preferred animals. The younger women preferred dogs.

Proverbs-Sayings: While the women that participated in the interviews were chatting among themselves proverbs and sayings are used. Thus, they continue their own culture. When we asked them about proverbs and sayings that glorified women, we received replies like: 'Heaven is beneath the feet of mothers. There can be no home without a woman. A woman is a home's sun. If anyone cries it will be my mother, the rest will be crocodile tears. A mother never gives up on their child. The heart of a woman is the source of mercy. Next to every successful man is a successful woman. The girl in your arms, the trousseau in the chest.

Words Used for Women: Words used for women by men close to the women that participated in the interviews: 'my wife, my love, my dear, sultan, mother, mother-in-law, my life, my sister, my bride, my beautiful daughter, my one and only, world's dearest, my beautiful bride, my aunt, sister-in-law, aunt, grandmother etc.

Words of Endearment Used by Women for their Children: Among the words used by the women that participated in the interviews were: 'my little one, my lamb, little lamb, my love, my baby, my child, my dear, my pasha, my princess, my cotton ball, my lion etc.' In Yusuf Balasaguni's famous work, 'Kutadgu Bilig', in the words Aytoldı uses to give advice to his son 'Öğdilmiş', we come across the word of affection 'my lamb'[20].

Accessories Worn by Women (Gold-Diamonds-Silver): The women that participated in the interviews preferred 'gold' and 'diamonds' for rings. And for bracelets they tended to go for gold-diamond-precious stones-silver.

Words Used by Women for Men: Among the words used by the women for men were: 'my husband, my love, my dear, my mister, mister, gentleman, our mister, uncle, father-in-law, father, nephew, brother-in-law, grandfather, big brother, the cornerstone of my home, the father of my children etc.'

Prayers: These are the prayers known by the women that participated in the interviews and heard from others close to them. Thus, we can see them as good-will wishes. Some of them were: May everything be as you desire. I wish you a good day. May Allah be pleased. May Allah turn everything you touch into gold. May there be those to help you too. Thank you. May Allah grant you health. May Allah give you a good appetite. Good luck with it. Bon appetite. May your luck be a lot. May it go to the spirits of the dead. May you see the good days of your child. Get well soon. May your conversation last forever. May Hızır (prophet) be your companion. May Allah grant your patience. Bon Voyage. Go in peace and return in peace. Happy Henna. Break a leg. May you live long. May chances be many. May you always exist. Bless you. May you never see poverty. Be sacred like water. May Allah never divert you.

Curses: These are the curses known by the women that participated in the interviews and heard from others close to them. May your name be forgotten. Allah damn it. May your mouth and tongue dry out. May owls live in your house. Don't see the good of your children. May the earth fill your greed. I hope it does not work out. May poison be your bread. May your hearth go cold. May you go blind. May a fig tree grow in your hearth. May you never be able to make ends meet. May the weight of me fall on you in stones.

Good Luck: Spotting a stork in the sky is good luck. Storks are the signs of children and also, 'Spotting a stork in the sky' means there will be a lot of travel that year. Ladybugs are lucky. A four-leafed clover is considered lucky. It is believed that elephants bring prosperity. The women stated that they usually carried loose change in their purses. Carrying a key is also considered good luck. However, the luckiest item for them is the evil-eye talisman.

Bad Luck: This is the bad luck known by the women that participated in the interviews and heard from others close to them. Among the things they found to be bad luck were: Seeing an owl, the number 13, seeing a black cat, the caw of a crow, a 'solar' or 'lunar' eclipse, walking under a ladder, and breaking a mirror.

---

[20] R.R. Arat, **Kutadgu Bilig "Yusuf Has Hacib"** Metin-Çeviri-İndex. Atatürk Kültür Dil ve Tarih Yüksek Kurumu. Ankara, Türk Tarih Kurumu Basımevi, 1985, p. 104.

Hosting Guests: The women that participated in the interviews stated guests were very important for them.

The Use of Regional Kilims-Carpets: All the women like using regional objects as do the younger ones.

Nicknames: The use of nicknames is based on the hometown in Turkey.

Conclusion

The findings of this study, which covers the interviews conducted with women that had migrated to France from Turkey, highlight the fact that the women who migrated to these countries have maintained the cultural and symbolic codes that date back hundreds of years. Thus, these findings show that the women have not severed ties with their countries' culture and that in important events like marriage-birth-death-social life by applying cultural rituals, they reproduce them. The findings of the study are meaningful in terms of highlighting the use and reproduction elements of the cultural and symbolic codes of women that have migrated to the aforementioned country since the 60s for economic reasons and have lived there for many years. It is also interesting to see that not only do the older generations practice these rituals but also the younger generations. Thus, it shows that these women did not stray from their own culture while exploring a new one but reproduced it by maintaining it.

The cultural codes about marriage, birth, death, and social life that have been studied within the scope of the study are the common cultural units of society. They are also agreements shared by members of society. Since ancient cultures, women have been the carriers of culture to new generations. Thus, women play an important role in the conveyance of intercultural communication. They redefine the culture, symbols, and communication between both the elements of culture but also between women. By forming the focal point of this culture, they reshape culture and symbols. The study carried out with the women shows that the women conveyed culture and symbols without putting variables like language, religion, race, class, gender, nationality, ideology, and ethnic origin into the equation. The women interpret, maintain, and pass on their culture to new generations. They were successful in producing common meaning. Furthermore, they have maintained their culture in their cultural memory. Therefore, they have enabled the cultural bond between the past and present to strengthen and have maintained it. And this shows us that cultural continuity is very important.

The findings highlight that to achieve intercultural communication and achieve a peaceful common existence based on mutual acceptance, being able to synthesize the new culture with their own is important. The women that migrated to France from Turkey were able to balance the two cultures' gains by synthesizing the cultural differences and this becomes a meaningful condition in order for global neighborliness to emerge.

Acknowledgment

This study was supported by Scientific Research Projects Coordination Unit of Galatasaray University-Project number 17.300.009- 'Culture, Mythology and Cultural Communication'.

CHAPTER 23

REFUGEE POLICIES AND INTERNATIONAL LEGAL FRAMEWORK: REFLECTIONS FROM TURKEY

Mustafa Oktay Alniak[1], Aylin Çelik Turan[2], Begüm Doğrusöz[3], Ece Barutçu[4], Aybüke Binay[5], Ecem Tuncer[6]

"The refugee issue should be presented to all states and people as a test of their commitment to human rights."

Sadako Ogata, United Nations High Commissioner for Refugees

Introduction

The study aims to provide information about the United Nations organization and examine the outlines of migrant and refugee problems in the international status. In this chapter, various United Nations resolutions on refugees and the basic principles of human rights were taken into account, and the principles and sanctions set out by the United Nations Organization on the flow of refugees and migrants were explained.

Here, various views of the refugee problem were examined within the scope of the legal structure of each country. Although, in principle, it is argued that countries act according to human rights principles, in reality, it has been observed that the influx of refugees in developed countries is often sanctioned in violation of human rights. In this chapter, legal practices and social problems in the context of health, education, security, right to work, right to life, and children's rights are explored with reference to different countries.

The inflow of refugees moving toward European countries has reached a large volume in recent years. European countries had a hard time countering these migrations. Among the refugees from central Asia to the Middle East and from North Africa to Europe, 4 million Syrians and one million from other countries have found shelter in Turkey.

In this chapter, sanctions by the United Nations are discussed and in order to prevent war in Turkey's neighborhood and to achieve peace, the United Nations' perception of refugees and migration is examined to be more sensitive

[1] Prof. Dr., Piri Reis Üniversitesi, Türkiye.
[2] Dr. Öğr. Üyesi, Çanakkale Onsekiz Mart Üniversitesi, Türkiye.
[3] Lisans Öğrencisi, Piri Reis Üniversitesi, Türkiye.
[4] Lisans Öğrencisi, Piri Reis Üniversitesi, Türkiye.
[5] Lisans Öğrencisi, Piri Reis Üniversitesi, Türkiye.
[6] Lisans Öğrencisi, Piri Reis Üniversitesi, Türkiye.

and realistic.

The United Nations Role

The United Nations was founded on October 24, 1945, with the signing of the "Charter of the United Nations" by 51 countries in order to achieve universal peace following World War II.[7] The United Nations deals with challenges such as peace and security, climate change, sustainable development, human rights, disarmament, terrorism, humanitarian and health emergencies, gender equality, governance, and food production. In the General Assembly, Security Council, Economic and Social Council, and other bodies and committees, the UN provide a place for its members to voice their opinions.[8]

There are six official languages in the United Nations. Arabic, Chinese, English, French, Russian, and Spanish are the languages involved. Multilingualism also provides for more engagement in the organisation's activities by all member nations, as well as increased effectiveness, better outcomes, and involvement.[9]

From a legal perspective, there is distinction between refugees and migrants. Refugees are people who are outside of their home nations and, as a result, seeking "international protection" in circumstances of torture, violence, assassination or other conditions that threaten society's peace. Their situation is frequently so perilous that they have crossed national boundaries in search of refugees in neighbouring countries. Under international law, refugees are defined and protected.[10]

Immigrants opt to improve their life by finding a job or, in some circumstances, education, family reunion, or other reasons, as opposed to fleeing due to explicit risk of persecution or death. "Refugees" are persons who cross an international boundary to avoid war or persecution, whereas " migrants" are people who cross for reasons that do not fall within the legal definition of a refugee.[11]

The Universal Declaration of Human Rights, in its fourteenth article, states: "In the face of persecution, everyone has the right to seek refugee in another country. This privilege cannot be invoked in the case of prosecution for crimes

---

[7] United Nations, "Overview", Erişim: 14 Eylül 2020, https://www.un.org/en/sections/about-un/overview/index.html

[8] Vikipedi, "Birleşmiş Milletler", Erişim: 14 Eylül 2020, https://tr.wikipedia.org/wiki/Birle%C5%9Fmi%C5%9F_Milletler

[9] United Nations, "Official Languages", Erişim: 14 Eylül 2020, https://www.un.org/en/sections/about-un/official-languages/index.html

[10] The UN Refugee Agency, "UNHCR Viewpoint: 'Refugee' or 'Migrant' – Which is right? https://www.unhcr.org/news/latest/2016/7/55df0e556/unhcr-viewpoint-refugee-migrant-right.html

[11] UNHCR, "Mülteci ve Göçmen? - Sözcük Seçimleri Önemlidir.", Erişim Tarihi: 14 Eylül 2020, https://www.unhcr.org/cy/wp-content/uploads/sites/41/2018/02/UNHCR_Refugee_or_Migrant_TR.pdf

that are not legitimate political or activities that are adverse to the United Nations' goals and objectives."

The "United Nations Convention on the Status of Refugees", drafted by the United Nations Human Rights Commission and signed in 1951, established the minimal requirements of processes to be followed while dealing with refugees. It also governed refugees' rights to work and welfare, as well as their capacity to get ID cards and travel permits, as well as the tax burden's application and the capacity to transfer their assets to another nation where they were allowed for resettlement. Deportation or forcible repatriation of refugees were likewise forbidden by the pact. Courts, education, social security, housing, and freedom of movement are among the other requirements of the UN accord on the status of refugees.[12]

In terms of the acknowledgement of refugees and refugee status, there are a lot of disparities across nations. Turkey, in particular, has attempted to close the legislative gap with a law originally legislated in 1994.

Turkey's first internal legal regulations on asylum, "or a residence permit in Turkey who defected to Turkey on individual asylum in another country for the purpose of requesting asylum to aliens who come collectively with foreigners and possible population movements for the regulation" to be applied to Turkish borders, have been prepared. It was drafted in accordance with the 1951 Geneva Convention, to which Turkey is a signatory, in order to specify the processes for obtaining asylum and moving asylum seekers individually or collectively.

Regulation on the procedures and principles to be applied to individual foreigners seeking asylum in Turkey or requesting a residence permit from Turkey to seek asylum in another country, as well as foreigners who have gathered at our borders in search of asylum and population movements that may occur (1994: clause 3).[13]

The sole distinction between refugee and asylum seeker status, according to the rule, is where the individual comes from. If the person is from one of the European nations, he is classified as a refugee, and if he is from another country, he is classified as an asylum seeker. Other than the destination, all other requirements are accepted in the same way.

Due to the geographical limitations designated by the Geneva Convention, Turkey only grants refugee status to the citizens from countries in Europe. To alleviate this restriction, the new legislation, the YUKK, has defined a conditional refugee as someone who enters Turkey from places such as Asia, Africa, and the Middle East, regions from which Turkey does not accept refugees (YUKK, 2013:

---

[12] 'Birleşmiş Milletler Mülteciler Yüksek Komiserliği Türkiye Tesilciliği', Erişim Tarihi:10.08.2020, http://www.multeci.org.tr/wp-content/uploads/2016/12/1951-Cenevre-Sozlesmesi-1.pdf

[13] 'Uluslararası Yönetim İktisat ve İşletme Dergisi, https://dergipark.org.tr/tr/download/article-file/1123572, Cilt 15, Sayı 4, 2019

clause 62)[14].

Housing Rights

Foreigners in Turkey are obliged to obtain a residence permit(YUKK, 2013: clause 19).[15] Unaccompanied children, the elderly, pregnant women, single mothers and fathers with children, and special needs people who have been tortured, sexually assaulted, or exposed to other forms of extreme psychological, physical, or sexual abuse may be eligible for specific housing options (YUKK, 2013: clause 95). In Turkey, asylum seekers are usually allowed to stay in satellite cities designated by the Ministry of Interior. These are provinces where security and public order are generally not a problem. If a foreigner is granted a work permit, they do not need to apply for a residence permit because they are allowed to stay in Turkey for the duration of their work permit (YUKK, 2013: clause 27).[16]

Right to Nutrition and Labour

Freedom of work is regulated in Article forty-eighth of Turkey's constitution of 1982, which is the highest legal norm in the country. It is regulated in many international documents, including Article twenty-three of the Universal Declaration of Human Rights, Article four of the European Convention on Human Rights, and Articles seventeenth, eighteenth, and twenty-fourth of the Geneva Convention of 1951.[17]

The YUKK has unique restrictions for the hiring of immigrants and asylum seekers. Internationally protected refugees and anyone with secondary protected status can work as dependents or independently from the moment they gain status, according to this statute. It has been agreed that these people's identification documents would also be considered work permit paperwork. However, in other situations, these people's access to the job market may be limited in terms of location, time, and industry. This limitation does not apply to refugees and anyone with secondary protection status who have lived in Turkey for three years, are married to a Turkish citizen, or have Turkish citizen children. International protection applicants and conditional refugees have six months from the date of their protection application to apply for a work permit (YUKK,

---

[14] Resmi Gazete, 13.08.2020 https://www.resmigazete.gov.tr/eskiler/2013/04/20130412.htm#:~:text=MADDE%2062%20%E2%80%93%20(1)%20Avrupa,yararlanamayan%2C%20ya%20da%20s%C3%B6z%20konusu

15 İkamet izninden muaf olanlar için bakınız: YUKK madde 20

[16] Uluslararası Yönetim İktisat ve İşletme Dergisi, Erişim Tarihi: 11.08.2020, https://dergipark.org.tr/tr/download/article-file/1123572, Cilt15, Sayı 4, 2019

[17] 1982 Anayasası Madde 48: Herkes, dilediği alanda çalışma ve sözleşme hürriyetlerine sahiptir. Özel teşebbüsler kurmak serbesttir. Madde detayı için bknz. T.C. Anayasası, https://www.mevzuat.gov.tr/MevzuatMetin/1.5.2709. pdf Erişim Tarihi:16.07.2019.

2013: clause 89).[18]

The Temporary Protection Regulation governs the employment rights of persons having temporary protection status in general. Those with this status must get approval from the Ministry of Family, Labor, and Social Services in order to work. Furthermore, these individuals are unable to get jobs that are prohibited to foreigners.[19]

The condition of getting preliminary permission has been added to the work permits of health and education professions. Before applying for a work visa, anyone interested in working in these fields must first receive a preliminary permit from the Ministry of Health or the Ministry of Education (Higher Education Institution for universities) (GKSYÇİDY, 2016: clause 6). The application of employment quotas to work permits issued in this context is a significant problem. Work permits issued under temporary protection are restricted to ten percent of the total number of Turkish citizens employed at the location.[20]

Right To Health

For a variety of reasons, asylum seekers and refugees are among the most vulnerable populations in terms of health. They face challenging living conditions, housing issues, nutrition issues, access to health and social services, violence, and so on.

It is also important to avoid international migrants with diseases as described in the literature, i.e., employ preventive and therapeutic health services so as not to endanger the residents of the host country. In this context, there are various international regulations on the use of health services by immigrants, and the right to health is mentioned in the first paragraph of Article twenty-fifth of the Universal Declaration of Human Rights discussed above as the basis for ensuring the right to health.[21]

Right To Protection

States have the main responsibility for the protection of refugees. All signatories to the 1951 Convention are required to safeguard refugees within their borders and treat them in conformity with international norms. As a result, UNHCR's mission is to support States and, in this context, contribute to refugee

---

[18] Resmi Gazete, Erişim Tarihi:02.08.2020, https://www.resmigazete.gov.tr/eskiler/2013/04/20130411-2.html

[19] Yabancılara yasak olan meslekler ve yasal dayanakları için bakınız: https://www.egm.gov.tr/yabanciyim-ikametgahve-seyahat-haklarimla-ilgili-bilgi-almak-istiyorum Erişim Tarihi: 22.04.2019

[20] 'Uluslararası Yönetim İktisat ve İşletme Dergisi, Erişim Tarihi: 03.07.2020, Cilt 15, Sayı 4, 2019, https://dergipark.org.tr/tr/download/article-file/1123572

[21] Nurdoğan, A. K., Dur, A.İ.B., Öztürk, M. , Türkiye'nin Mülteci Sorunu ve Suriye Krizinin Mülteci Sorununa Etkileri, dergipark.org.tr/tr/download/article-file/299579

protection by completing the following tasks:

- Ensure that refugees are treated in accordance with internationally accepted legal standards;
- Ensure that refugees are granted asylum and are not forcibly sent to countries where their lives and freedoms will be jeopardised;
- Encourage the use of appropriate procedures to determine whether individuals are refugees.[22]

Right To Education

Problems that arise as a result of migration have far-reaching consequences for the migrating community, as well as for families and children, and social isolation might ensue. As a result, the hosting migration administrations must take a strategic approach and design an action plan for managing disparities.

The major purpose of numerous international accords attempting to defend the right to education, which is the engine of economic, social, and political advancement, is to achieve a standard of living worthy of human dignity. Some standards and norms have been put in place to help with this. Important ones from these protocols are as follows;

- Universal Declaration of Human Rights
- American Convention on the Prevention of Violence Against Women
- Convention Against Discrimination in Education
- General Comment No. 13 of the United Nations Committee on Economic, Social and Cultural Rights: The Right to Education
- Declaration on the Prevention of Discrimination Against Women
- European Social Charter
- Additional African Protocol on Women's Rights to the African Charter on the Rights of People
- Framework Convention on the Protection of Minorities
- Helsinki Final Ticker
- European Convention on the Protection of Human Rights and Fundamental Freedoms and Additional Protocols
- Paris Charter for a New Europe
- Copenhagen Certificate
- Maastricht Treaty

[22] UNHCR, BMMYK Kıbrıs Ofisi, Aralık 2017, Erişim Tarihi: 16.09.2020, https://www.unhcr.org/cy/wp-content/uploads/sites/41/2018/05/UNHCR_Brochure_TR.pdf

The Universal Declaration of Human Rights

"The United Nations General Assembly resolution 217 A(III) of 10 December 1948, which declared the Universal Declaration of Human Rights, has been used as a means of education, dissemination, and teaching of all human rights, and has decided to teach and interpret these rights in schools and other educational institutions." The Universal Declaration of Human Rights (UDHR) was adopted by the United Nations General Assembly on December 10, 1948. The 26th article declared that all individuals, regardless of ethnicity, language, or religion, must work for the peace and tranquility of all people via education and that all people have the right to education.

Convention on The Rights of The Child

Although the right to education is not addressed alone, the Convention on the Rights of the Child emphasises that it is a right for all people, immigrants, refugees, conditional refugees, and anyone with temporary protection status. Every child is supported and safeguarded for education, according to Article 28 of the Convention on the Rights of the Child. Primary education is a right and a must for all children, regardless of their financial circumstances or prejudice.

European Convention on Human Rights

The right to education is governed under Protocol No. 1's second article (P1-2) (Annex to the European Convention on Human Rights). The following is the wording of the article: "No one should be denied the right to education." The state respects parents' rights to guarantee that their children's education and training are carried out in line with their religious and philosophical convictions in order to satisfy their educational and training obligations.

European Social Charter

The European Social Charter emphasised the importance of educating immigrant children in their native language. According to Article 1.9 of the European Social Charter: "It governs the entitlement to protection and aid for working immigrants and their families. Encourage and facilitate the teaching of the national language of the state that accepts them, or one of them if there are multiple national languages, to those who work as immigrants and their families; Due to Article 1.9, mother tongue education of the children of the person working as an immigrant should be encouraged.[23] Refugees and asylum seekers encounter several problems in achieving their basic requirements and assimilating into the country they have just entered.[23]

Children who are refugees or seeking asylum must put in far more effort to adjust to the traumatic migration process they are going through, as well as the

[23] UNICEF, Köklerinden Koparılan Çocuklar: Mülteci Ve Göçmen Çocukların Maruz Kaldığı Giderek Büyüyen Kriz, 2016.

fact that they have different cultural qualities and ethnicities than the society they have just joined, and the inability to communicate in a common language.

The Role and Support of The United Nations in Education

Technical Assistance to Governments

UNICEF and UNHCR have provided guidance and technical assistance to the national authorities for refugee children education, as well as guidance and technical assistance to integrate public schools in Bulgaria, Greece, Serbia, and North Macedonia.

Non-Formal Education and After-School Support

UNICEF, UNHCR, and the International Organization for Migration (IOM) aided their integration in 2018 by supporting the provision of non-formal education, such as homework assistance and psychosocial support, to over 16,200 children enrolled in public schools in Greece, Italy, Serbia, Bulgaria, and Bosnia and Herzegovina. Extracurricular activities for national and refugee students were funded by the IOM in Greece and Northern Macedonia in order to enrich the formal learning process, encourage personal development, and faster integration into the local society.

Capacity Building for Education Professionals

UNICEF and UNHCR funded capacity development initiatives for roughly 4,400 formal and non-formal education experts in Bulgaria, Greece, and Serbia in 2017 and 2018. In Germany, early childhood education and development has been a key component of UNICEF training on minimum protection requirements for around 2,800 managers, conservationists, and general staff in 100 centres.

Raising Awareness and Sensitising Local Communities

UNHCR, UNICEF, IOM, and NGOs have worked to raise awareness of the need for education for refugee and immigrant children in Cyprus, Germany, Greece, and Serbia.

Materials for Education

UNHCR, UNICEF, and IOM supplied educational materials and supplies to refugee and immigrant children in Greece and Serbia. UNHCR has supplied furniture and equipment to four schools in Serbia, which serve both local and refugee/immigrant students.

Transportation

IOM and UNHCR sponsored school transportation for children from housing facilities in Bosnia and Herzegovina, Greece, and Serbia to public schools in 2017 and 2018. School transportation was provided by the Bulgarian governmental agency for refugees and for children from three receiving centres in Sofia, Bulgaria.

The Rights of the Child

With UNICEF assistance, the Children's Rights Network on the Move in Greece, directed by the Greek Ombudsman for Children's Rights, monitors access to education for refugee and migrant children on a regular basis. UNICEF has also provided practical information and resources to refugee receiving centres in Germany to help them boost their monitoring systems (including access to schooling and educational results).[24]

Framework Convention for The Protection of National Minorities

The contract in question is one that ensures minorities' right to an education. In the 2nd session of the conference, the definition of the word "resident foreigners" was made in the article. People who are not citizens of that state but are lawfully residing on its territory are referred to as "resident aliens" under the treaty. Since it is under the protection of the nation-state, the right of child immigrants to education, which is growing every year, has been the topic of discussion as to how many years an individual will be recognised as a child.

Turkey's standing in reference to refugees

Despite the fact that Turkey is an immigration country, a report from the European Union Centre for Migrant Integration Policies claims that it falls behind other nations in terms of developing policies for migrant education. In later lines, it is clarified that the situation is not as it appears.

Between April 26 and September 26, 2013, the Ministry of Education released circulars and conducted numerous actions to address the issue of Syrian refugees' education in Turkey. Syrians now have access to health, education, and social welfare services because of the Temporary Protection Regulation, which went into effect in October 2014. The Ministry of Education, which works closely with the Ministry of the Interior to guarantee that children's rights to education are protected, has worked to guarantee that asylum-seeking children receive a primary school certificate. The Ministry of Labour and Social Security, as well as the Department of Financial Aid of the European Union's Employability, collaborated in 2016 to support people with refugee status through a competitive grant program for the development of social integration of disadvantaged people in immigrant communities. In addition, the Child Protection Agency helps

---

[24] UNHCR, "ACCESS TO EDUCATION FOR REFUGEE AND MIGRANT CHILDREN IN EUROPE" Erişim: 6 Ekim 2020, https://www.unhcr.org/neu/wp-content/uploads/sites/15/2019/09/Access-to-education-europe-19.pdf

refugees with their schooling.

With this circular entitled "Educational Services for Foreigners" no.2014/21 on September 23, 2014, the Ministry of National Education set the working conditions of the Ministry and provincial commissions to be constituted on how to offer educational services to Syrian children. Furthermore, the foreign 'students' information operating system (YBIS) is used to enter data for Syrian students and teachers who do not have a foreign identity number but do have a foreign identity certificate. Students' attendance, course grade information, report cards, certification, and certificate operations are all handled by the YBIS system, which works in a variety of languages.[25]

Refugee Education Policies and Research in Turkey

UNICEF Solutions to the Education Problem of Refugee Children in Turkey

It assists teachers in receiving training that improves their abilities and competencies in providing inclusive education for all disadvantaged groups through the Mone collaboration. It offers "conditional educational assistance for the education of Syrian and other refugee children" to children who are enrolled in school with the help of the European Union Civil Protection and Humanitarian Organizations (ECHO).

It establishes "Child-Friendly Spaces" in and out of camps, in collaboration with the Ministry of Family, Labour, and Social Services, to give psychosocial help to children who have been exposed to combat.

It prepares adolescents and young people to play constructive roles in their communities and organises events that bring together peer adolescents and young people with the purpose of fostering social cohesion. It assists parents in dealing with their children's issues. It provides basic necessities, including vaccinations, food, school materials, and clothes.[26]

Statistical Data of Child Refugees in Education around the World

Refugee children are five times more likely than their non-refugee classmates to attend school. Only about half of the total school-age refugees were enrolled in elementary or secondary schools in 2018.

---

[25] Dr. Selminaz Adıgüzel, "Immigrant Children"s Right of Education", Beykent Üniversitesi Hukuk Fakültesi Dergisi 2017 Haziran Sayısı,
ttps://www.researchgate.net/publication/330225368_Gocmen_Cocugun_Egitim_Hakki,
(Erişim 03.08.2020)

[26] Unicef Türkiye Milli Komitesi, "Türkiyedeki Suriyeli Çocuklar", Erişim: 6 Ekim 2020, https://www.unicefturk.org/yazi/acil-durum-turkiyedeki-suriyeli-cocuklar

Primary, Secondary and Higher Education

76 per cent of refugee teenagers did not complete high school. In low-income nations, 61 per cent of refugee children attend elementary education, but fewer than half of refugee children attend secondary school. Only 84 per cent of teenagers in the world attend secondary school, whereas 91 per cent of children attend elementary school. Only around 3% of refugees attend college or university. This rate is 37 per cent among native populations worldwide.[27]

Regional Perspectives on Refugee Education

Every area in the world has a distinctive perspective on child migration and displacement. Refugee migrations, on the other hand, are more precisely defined within regions than general migration.

Africa

Around 86 per cent of African migrants are seeking asylum in neighbouring African nations. About half of African refugees are children; nearly 3 million children have been forcibly removed from their homes and are now living in some of the worst conditions on the planet. One-third of all African immigrants are children.

Americas

In the Americas, four out of every five child immigrants live in three countries: the United States, Mexico, and Canada. The Americas are home to 6.3 million child migrants, or 21% of all child migrants worldwide. In the Americas, one out of every ten immigrants is a child. However, this average conceals two important facts: children make up a minor percentage of immigrants in North America, South America, and the Caribbean, while children make up 43 percent of all immigrants in Central America.

Asia

Asia is home to around 12 million international child migrants. While this number represents 39 percent of all migrant children, it is a small proportion given Asia's 56 percent share of the world's children population. Asia is home to the world's top five refugee-hosting countries.

Europe

By the end of 2015, Europe has taken in one out of every nine refugees on the planet, totalling 1.8 million individuals. The 5.4 million juvenile migrants in Europe account for only 7% of all migrants in the continent. Europe has the lowest proportion of children among all areas in terms of the overall migrant population. Europe is home to one-sixth of the world's child migrants.[27]

Syrian Immigrants in Turkey

For the last 100 years, these people have been repressed in their home nation and wherever else they travel. They have abandoned their motherland in dread of death in the previous decade and sought sanctuary in other nations. In Turkey, there are over five million refugees.

Is there any appreciation among the Syrian migrants claimed by Turkey for the Turkish people? Is there a feeling of gratitude? Is there anything further that can be done? Do they witness people who start begging and collecting rubbish at a young age in major cities and beyond, and do they then look around and feel embarrassed, or do they see people who admire them? Politically, in accordance with social goals, and despite demographic issues, the public has accepted the concept that the migrant population would be cared for until the conflict in Syria is ended. Sending this community, which has lost its home in Syria, into the same conflict without providing adequate circumstances there appears to be against human rights, and it is no longer conceivable. These asylum seekers who have adjusted to life in Turkey found work and contributed to society will be allowed to stay. The exploitation of conditions in political favour by political forces, as well as the inclusion of these asylum seekers in the first political elections by granting them the right to citizenship, is a significant element that will shift the political balance. In regional migrations, a scenario has evolved that is consistent with Turkey's idea of house ownership. It is expected that society would accept the condition over time, giving political parties an advantage.

These people are humiliated when they are picking up trash. How might citizens and asylum seekers expect to feel about cultural life in these circumstances? Are asylum seekers instilled with a good feeling of appreciation for the host society, or do they harbour animosity for the community in which they live? They have infiltrated Turkey's calm neighbourhoods. They settled in western Anatolia, particularly in the Marmara region. It is important to underline that inhabitants of the host country, Turkey, are behaving politely in their responses to asylum seekers who will be partners in their future bread.

What's the point of all of this? Will this major issue spawn a cascade of other issues? "What should we do as a United Nations, as a state, and as individuals?" It is impossible to say! It appears that there will be more issues than anticipated. Citizens who now split their food with tolerance will object to this arrangement in the future when they suffer. Other issues might arise as a result of differences in attire, clothes, life, and culture. As the country's government, you must finish the electoral process and concentrate on resolving the major issues.

---

[27] UNICEF, "Köklerinden Koparılanlar", Erişim:6 Ekim 2020, https://www.unicef.org/turkey/media/2291/file/TURmedia_Uprooted-ES-Turkish.pdf%20.pdf

The presidential contenders in the Istanbul mayoral election said there are 500,000 refugees in Istanbul during the election discussion on the night of June 16, 2019. The list illustrates that careful effort has been made on this matter, according to the refugee Association's May 2019 statistics. According to the Syrian voter survey, there were 21,783 Syrians over the age of 75. Total number of Syrian refugees was 3,606,737. Between the ages of 0 and 4, there were 513,050 refugees, 494,403 between the ages of 5 and 9, 544,106 between the ages of 19 and 24, and 293,828 refugees between the ages of 30 and 34.[29]

As the UN has stated, this inequitable condition resulting from conflicts of interest among industrialised nations in the area must be rectified. Political instability in the region created by the US and coalition troops, as well as new maps of the political region planned to be formed as a result of these policies, has driven nearly four million people from the region to seek asylum in Turkey. The challenges that this forced migration has produced in Turkey's government in terms of health, education, human rights, and long-term peace should be considered. From a human standpoint, it is clear that this enterprise has significant societal issues. Those who were born in Turkey and were found to be eligible became Turkish citizens.

This situation cannot be remedied even if ten refugee towns with a population of 500,000 people were built in Turkey, each with its own governors and prefects! The issue isn't only one of management. For strategic reasons, Turkey's political balances are difficult to maintain. Turkey's economic troubles are beginning to fade. In recent years, the planned progress has not been realised due to weaknesses in education, health, earthquakes, and infrastructure. How will the concerns of asylum-seekers be handled in a climate of the political division generated by insoluble challenges? It would be beneficial for the United Nations, the world's industrialised countries, and sensitive individuals to consider this topic.

What can be done from now on? The answer is contingent on the establishment of a just peace in Syria. Turkey does not have the power to solve this situation. The topic encompasses a wide range of social, economic, and cultural factors. The refugee and asylum-seeker crisis is rapidly worsening. Peace in Syria must be accomplished as quickly as possible in order to tackle this situation, and foreign forces in the region must return to their nation. At the Potsdam Conference at the end of World War II in 1945, the United Nations Organization was established; for the first time, the gift of a life in peace and in accordance with human rights for the world was considered between the United States, Britain, and the Soviet Union.[32] Unfortunately, 75 years have gone... Maybe the refugee crisis in the area will be resolved after these forces leave

Syria.[28]

Conclusion

People are fleeing insecurities and rushing to more civilised places. Nations attracting to refugees may provide economic support to the countries of origin. People desire to bring their children up in a better up places. The UN's assistance is essential in developing nations for health, education, security, and industrialisation. People desire a compassionate living environment in which to live. Developing countries' living conditions must be improved, and their welfare systems must be improved. Maintaining a system in which the wealthy get richer appears to be unjust.

It is important to look at how far the UN has progressed in terms of its organisational aims in regard to refugees. It transpires that should people have better working and living conditions, they would not flee their homelands.

If the United Nations' sanctions are stronger and influential to foster development of and security in developing nations, migration pressures would diminish. The United Nations should enhance financing for workers' rights, children's rights, and human rights, as well as for governments of developing nations to offer education, health, industrialisation, and modern farming on an economic, cultural, and educational basis.

The United Nations may offer scholarships to young children in developing countries. It is critical to prevent the exploitation of developing nations' mines, subterranean resources, and aboveground resources for the advantage of industrialised nations.

The United Nations should also establish education and development programs to help developing nations alleviate poverty, corruption, and poor governance.

Regional conflicts of interest in emerging nations should be reduced, and efficient measures to avoid launched wars should be devised by the United Nations. Mass deportations and migrant movements owing to differences in language, religion, and so on must be avoided by preventing conflicts.

Plans for the development of education quotas by wealthy nations should be created by the United Nations, and scholarships offered to develop nations across the globe should be dispersed equally.

Improving the binding nature of UN decisions, enacting penalties, and bringing continuing conflicts to a peaceful conclusion will reduce immigration

---

[28] Prof. Dr. Mustafa Oktay ALNIAK,"Asker ve Akademisyen", Liman Yayınları Sf. 193-194, 484-485, 2020, Ankara

[29] Prof. Dr. Mustafa Oktay ALNIAK,"Türkiye ve Batıda İnsan Hakları" Pelikan Yayınları, 2006, Ankara

and refugee pressures.

Conflicts and disagreements in South America, the Middle East, South Asia, and North Africa should be resolved by binding UN decisions to enable life in peace and prosperity.[28]